Entrepreneurial Urbanism in India

Kanekanti Chandrashekar Smitha
Editor

Entrepreneurial Urbanism in India

The Politics of Spatial Restructuring and Local Contestation

Springer

Editor
Kanekanti Chandrashekar Smitha
Centre for Research in Urban Affairs
Institute for Social and Economic Change
Bengaluru, Karnataka
India

ISBN 978-981-10-9569-6 ISBN 978-981-10-2236-4 (eBook)
DOI 10.1007/978-981-10-2236-4

Printed on acid-free paper

This Springer imprint is published by Springer Nature
The registered company is Springer Science+Business Media Singapore Pte Ltd.

To my beloved parents and sweet sister

Foreword

When Smitha approached me in 2014 for a possible chapter for her book on entrepreneurial urbanism, I had gently refused, given I didn't have the time or the aptitude for a book of this nature. Now, looking at the way in which this manuscript has evolved, I wish I had contributed. The reason is that Smitha has launched upon a very ambitious, but quite timely and highly policy relevant area for the research.

In 1989, Peter Eisinger published a book on the rise of the entrepreneurial state (Madison: University of Wisconsin Press), taking the case of state and local economic development policy in the USA, which highlighted the evolution of state and local government initiatives in that country to influence the market/private sector as it related to those policies. This 'rise' marked a sea change from governments' conventionally small role in the affairs of private industry that had characterized the first half of the twentieth century, at least as far as the USA was concerned. In his book, Eisinger also showed that certain state governments in the USA, rather than depending solely on supply-side strategies such as tax breaks and other incentives to encourage firm relocation, actually promoted an innovation ecosystem and created new business approaches.

Entrepreneurial states became very visible in India in the 1990s, following economic liberalization. The 1990s was characterized by intense competition among Indian states and cities for firms and jobs. A well-quoted example is the set of choices which was considered by Microsoft between Karnataka (Bengaluru) and then undivided Andhra Pradesh (Hyderabad), for locating its software development facility. The two south Indian states competed with each other quite fiercely in terms of incentives to attract the multinational, which eventually set up office in Hyderabad in 1998.

This edited book looks at three aspects of urban governance and 'entrepreneurial urbanism'—institutions, the political economy of urbanization itself, and issues pertaining to inclusion/exclusion. This book does not look at 'entrepreneurial' aspects of public–private partnership in promoting investments, but rather looks at urban entrepreneurialism in governance, which, as some authors acknowledge, is explicitly 'economic'.

The institutional part of the urban entrepreneuralist framework necessarily focuses on programmes to spur urban growth and the role of entrepreneurial governance in the context of resilient Bengaluru. It is positive to note the presence of local and civic actors in the mapping of entrepreneurial urbanism, as seen in the politics of the vision group by elitist corporate and non-governmental organizations, at the local level. The section on urban inclusion/exclusion is very interesting as it focuses on the role of entrepreneurial urbanism in the context of minorities, slum dwellers and the urban poor generally, taking the cases of Mumbai and Bengaluru.

A welcome aspect of this volume is that it discusses either side of entrepreneurial urbanism—the positive and negative aspects—given that it includes cases where governance is considered 'frail'. This should encourage us to learn lessons in cases where urban entrepreneurialism is weak, and strengthen positive elements.

Kala Seetharam Sridhar
Centre for Research in Urban Affairs
Institute for Social and Economic Change
Bengaluru

Acknowledgement

Urban transformation is no magic wand expressed in differing sociopolitical, economic, and spatial settings and governance. The idea for this volume emerged from the discourse on how Indian cities are repositioning themselves by donning new competitive roles in the globalizing economy. So far, entrepreneurial narratives from the global north and Western Europe have captured the changing economic contours intervened with speculative projects. In sharp contrast, new forms of urban governance with exclusionary entrepreneurial practices in Indian cities are generating new struggles and noticeable socio-spatial inequalities. Thus, the aim here is to provide an interdisciplinary perspective in discussing the contradictions and complex contestations in Indian cities—over divergent political and institutional landscapes—which can be described as explicitly 'entrepreneurial', while engaging with 'subaltern' discourses in urban studies.

Personally, this journey of publication has been a chance to enrich my acumen on the broader processes of evolving urban governance in India and here, foremost, my thanks and deepest appreciation to the contributors who readily accepted to be part of this project and stood by me through this journey. I am greatly indebted to Dr. Kala S. Sridhar, Centre for Research in Urban Affairs, Institute for Social and Economic Change (ISEC), Bangalore, for her constant and unconditional support and Dr. Barun Dev Pal, ISEC, for his generosity. I would like to acknowledge with gratitude, the support and encouragement I received from Dr. Marie-Héléne Zérah. I cannot forget the keen interest she evinced on the topic and wanted me to pursue it. I would like to extend my special thanks to Ms. Shinjini Chatterjee, Senior Editor, and Ms. Shruti Raj Srivastava, Editorial Assistant, Springer, at New Delhi, for their help and support and patience in the process of preparing this manuscript.

Finally, I owe a lot to my parents and my sweetest sister K.C. Muktha, who stand by me firmly and takes pride in all my work and achievements.

Contents

Editor and Contributors

About the Editor

Kanekanti Chandrashekar Smitha is a research scientist at the Centre for Research in Urban Affairs (CRUA), Institute for Social and Economic Change, Bengaluru, India. Her research focuses mainly on urban governance, service delivery, urban poverty, urban informality, urban political economy and urban political ecology. She has a Ph.D. in political science and public administration from the Institute for Social and Economic Change (through the University of Mysore). Her doctoral research examined urban governance and service delivery of water supply and sanitation in Bengaluru, assessing the impact of neoliberal urban sector reforms on service delivery and equity. Over the past several years, she has been actively engaged in varied urban research projects such as structure of Indian metropolises, rural–urban migration, urban deprivation, urban infrastructure, urban poor and urban land governance from interdisciplinary perspective. She has published several book chapters and articles in the peer-reviewed journals.

Contributors

Vinay Baindur is an urban governance researcher and activist based in Bangalore. He currently works on issues of water policy and urban commons. He works with national and international groups of researchers, activists and academics from various countries. He has worked earlier on the issues of local governments, infrastructure policy and urban legislation. He has studied the role of IFI conditions and urban governance policy and also wrote a brief commentary on the Jawaharlal Nehru National Urban Renewal Mission (JNNURM) project for the book Participolis in 2011. He is also an advisor for various NGOs, as well as information and research collectives, in different parts of India.

Qudsiya Contractor is an assistant professor at the Tata Institute of Social Sciences (TISS), Mumbai. She completed her Ph.D. as a Max Planck Institute Doctoral Fellow at the School of Development Studies, TISS. She has previously worked in the development sector on issues of displacement, human rights and urbanization. Her research interests include the anthropology of cities and development, social identities and communal politics. Her work has been published in the peer-reviewed journals and a volume edited by Laurent Gayer and Christophe Jaffrelot (2012) titled 'Muslims in Indian cities—Trajectories of marginalisation', published by Hurst & Co.

Swetha Rao Dhananka is a fellow at the University College London's Development Planning Unit and at the Indian Institute of Human Settlements, India. With a background in social work, political science and human geography, she has taught several courses at the University of Lausanne in Switzerland. Her research interests articulate around urbanization in the Global South in terms of its social effects, institutional responses and political claim-making in urban contexts. In her doctoral dissertation, she analysed a particular housing policy and the political opportunities it gave for differently resourced civil society organizations to engage with governmental actors and investigated how informality skews these opportunities. Currently, she is focusing on the 'politics of the anticipation of urban development' in peri-urban areas of Bangalore.

Sudhir Krishna is the former Secretary (Urban Development), Government of India. Currently, he is Chairman of the 5th Delhi Finance Commission, and Chairman, Committee on Standards for Smart Cities, Bureau of Indian Standards. He holds a Ph.D. in federal studies from Jamia Hamdard, Delhi, a master's degree in public management from Carnegie Mellon University, USA, and Master of Science degree in physics from Benaras Hindu University, India. His interests and publications relate to public policy, management and urban and regional development.

Debolina Kundu is an associate professor at the National Institute of Urban Affairs, New Delhi, India, and has over 20 years of professional experience in the field of development studies. She has a Ph.D. degree from Jawaharlal Nehru University, New Delhi. She has been a doctoral fellow with the ICSSR and post-doctoral fellow at the Local Government Initiative, Hungary. She has previously been engaged as a consultant with several national and international organizations. At present, she is in charge of the Data Centre and HUDCO Chair activities at NIUA. She is the editor of the journal Environment and Urbanisation, Asia. She has a large number of articles published in books and journals of international and national repute with SAGE, Oxford University Press and other leading academic publishers.

Anjali Karol Mohan is an urban and regional planner by profession with a Ph.D. in urban e-governance from the International Institute of Information Technology, Bangalore. Her broad areas of practice and research include development, urbanization and urban management, public policy and information and communication technologies and development (ICTD). Over the last two decades, Dr. Mohan has successfully completed several assignments in her individual capacity and as part of multidisciplinary teams. She has engaged with various urban planning and management exercises, both as a team leader and a team member, evolving planning tools and evaluating plans to enable inputs into policies and effective planning exercises. In particular, her experience has been in governance, public policy, institutional and organizational frameworks and training and building capacities. In addition, Dr. Mohan has designed and delivered several training and capacity building programmes, both for the state and for the non-state actors.

Raman Bhuvaneswari is an associate professor at the School of Government and Public Policy, Jindal Global University, India. She is trained in architecture–urban planning and social sciences and has a Ph.D. from the London School of Economics, UK. Her research interests are in the domains of urban governance, e-governance, urban land and economic development, gender and urban poverty. She has been consulted by international development institutions and academic institutions in India and abroad.

Xuefei Ren is a comparative urbanist, writer and critic. She is the author of two award-winning books: *Building Globalization: Transnational Architecture Production in Urban China* (2011, University of Chicago Press) and *Urban China* (2013, Polity Press). She has written on a variety of topics concerning urban social change in contemporary China, including historical preservation, mega-projects and mega-events, residential displacement, housing rights movements and environmental activism. Questioning the assumption of many specialists that the Chinese urban experience is unique, she has expanded her work in comparative domains and currently is examining the integration of informal settlements, land acquisitions and environmental activism throughout six urban regions in China, India and Brazil. She received her M.A. in urban planning from Tokyo Metropolitan University and Ph.D. in sociology from the University of Chicago. Currently, she is an associate professor of global urban studies and sociology at Michigan State University, USA.

H.S. Sudhira has a Ph.D. from the Indian Institute of Science, Bangalore. His research interest centres on how towns and cities evolve. His research has been primarily on land-use and land cover change studies exploring their consequences on environmental sustainability and understanding their interrelationships with resources and transportation. His broader area of research addresses the evolution and growth of towns and cities invoking complexity sciences, understanding planning practices and studying the effect of governance. He was a faculty member at the Indian Institute for Human Settlements (IIHS, Bangalore). Earlier, he had a stint with the Directorate of Urban Land Transport, Government of Karnataka, as a land-use and transportation specialist. He is a birdwatcher and volunteers for the India Literacy Project (ILP). Currently, he is the director of Gubbi Labs.

List of Figures

List of Tables

Chapter 1
Entrepreneurial Urbanism in India: A Framework

K.C. Smitha

Introduction

The emergence of a new global order post-1980s coincided with the post-Fordist regime, dismantling of the Keynesian welfare state and breakdown of the Bretton Woods system (MacLeod 2002; Banerjee-Guha 2010). Concomitantly, an unrelenting pace of urbanization and uncompromising and highly uneven processes of neo-liberalization in the 1990s has spurred political and economic shifts in the state's role in urban development and growth. The pursuance of a neoliberal project at multiple geographical scales and its every day political practices generated widespread contradictions, resulting in a socio-spatial polarization and an uneven urban development (Brenner and Theodore 2002b). As a result, cities have emerged as laboratories of 'geographical and institutional' reconfiguration and reproduction of urban neoliberal policy experiments such as place-marketing, enterprise, public–private partnership (PPP) and local boosterism projects producing new forms of 'urban entrepreneurialism', already evident in the cities of North America and Western European countries (ibid.). Similarly, extensive research has drawn our attention to how the economic and spatial landscape of cities in the advanced capitalist world are refashioned, contextualizing different city forms such as 'informational city' (Castells 1989), 'entrepreneurial city' (Harvey 1989; Hall and Hubbard 1996; Jessop and Sum 2000a), 'transnational city' (Smith 1999), 'world city' (Friedmann and Wolff 1982; Friedmann 1986, 1995), and 'global city' (Sassen 1991), reflecting dynamic interface between globalization and local processes (Genis 2007). Particularly the cities of global south have emerged as centres of management and service, essentially a process to integrate into the world economy/global circuits (Sassen 2002; Harris 2003). One such recent experiment envisioned for India is

K.C. Smitha (✉)
Centre for Research in Urban Affairs (CRUA), Institute for Social and Economic Change, Bangalore 560072, India
e-mail: smitha.kanekanti@gmail.com; smitha@isec.ac.in

K.C. Smitha (ed.), *Entrepreneurial Urbanism in India*,
DOI 10.1007/978-981-10-2236-4_1

building 100 'Smart Cities'[1] (2014), an intersection of 'Competitiveness, Capital and Sustainability'. These emerging urban forms are, therefore, multifaceted and at broader complex geographical scales articulated through the global systems of production, finance, technology/telecommunication, culture, politics and networking cities.

Based on the above logic, cities in the global south have been undergoing a drastic transformation in the form and governance to function as incubators of neoliberal strategies, intensifying an interspatial competition on the one hand and, on the other, accumulating economic and social tensions (Jessop 2002; Brenner and Theodore 2002a; Banerjee-Guha 2010). Cities are simply plugged into a global economy, prioritizing economic rejuvenation to stimulate national economic growth and to strengthen local revenue capacities. An interaction between the political and economic restructuring is linked to service delivery, creating a demand for local public entrepreneurs. So, such a restructuring process is essentially concerned with new forms of production process for capital accumulation (Harvey 1985, 1989) and 'place-marketing' (Brenner and Theodore 2002b). The city, therefore, has emerged as a site for 'new claims' influences by global capital and involving contestation (Sassen 1999). This process often represents 'demand-side' urbanization exacerbated by inequality and deprivation (Harvey 1985, 1989).

It is argued that the political economy of a neoliberal restructuring process is premised upon 'production of space' producing new forms of 'agglomeration economies, infrastructure configuration, transportation and communication networks, spatial division of labour and so on'. Similarly, various strategies of territorial redevelopment and place-promotion are channelized towards promoting the economic viability of space. Under these circumstances, realigned institutional practices and regulatory regimes with diverse actors, alliances and organizations are encouraged with competing hegemonic visions and developmental models (Harvey 1989; Jessop 2002; Brenner and Theodore 2002a). Therefore, city as a place is plugged into a global network not only as a place of production but also as junction of people, commodities, finance, ideas and corporate capitalism[2] with power. Logistically, urban centres have emerged as global manufacturing chains, service supply, financial chains, centre of exports of services and economic activities such as finance, health, education, culture and sports. These ambiguities arguably lie with the policy experiments in support of 'place-making processes' under contemporary global capitalism (Jessop 2000b) leading to polarization and not necessarily 'homogenization' (Banerjee-Guha 2010). These global networks through information and communication, finance and infrastructure essentially form the potential basis for capital accumulation and circulation (Harvey 1985).

[1]Please refer more on Indian Smart Cities from the following links (http://indiansmartcities.in/site/index.aspx) (http://indiansmartcities.in/downloads/CONCEPT_NOTE_-3.12.2014__REVISED_AND_LATEST_.pdf).

[2]For Instance, the Bangalore Agenda Task Force (BATF) and ABIDe in Bangalore.

As mentioned, the contemporary urban processes, to sustain and consolidate a neoliberal project, often characterize (i) cities as engines of economic growth, innovation and competition; (ii) offer market-based solutions such as replace welfare to work, informality, encourage incentives to learn or prepare for a new job and promote neo-communitarian values to tackle social exclusion and conflicts; (iii) promote principles of subsidiarity and solidarity; (iv) emphasis on the alliances, partnership and networks to improve infrastructure and to foster local entrepreneurial competitiveness (Jessop 2002; Harvey 2005) and (v) decisions are increasingly driven by cost-benefit rather than service, equity and social welfare (Brenner and Theodore 2002a). The neoliberal city is, therefore, conceptualized first as 'entrepreneurial' for achieving economic competition and innovation. In short, to secure neoliberal project, urban management was enunciated in different forms at diverse spatial scales gradually transitioning towards 'urban entrepreneurialism'. Taking a step in this direction, next section comprises two parts: first part elaborates on the conceptualization of 'urban entrepreneurialism' as a politically constructed project, politico-institutionally produced and spatially specific with deep roots in local politics. The second part sheds light on empirical reviews on the wider process of neo-liberalization and its impact at the local level in shaping and realizing 'entrepreneurial urban governance' in India. The final section discusses the contextualization of entrepreneurial urbanism in India.

The Project of 'Entrepreneurialism Urbanism'

The theoretical debates on 'Entrepreneurial Urban Governance' was highlighted and developed by (Marxist) Harvey (1989) followed by Bob Jessop's analysis which was centred around the contemporary modes of entrepreneurial discourses and narratives from Schumpeterian framework (Jessop and Sum 2000a). Harvey's body of work on urban entrepreneurialism is related to the broader neoliberal policy transformations within the framework of 'capital accumulation' and production of 'place' rather than 'territory'. Harvey (1985) categorically situates 'entrepreneurialism' within a broader framework of 'logic of capital'. While Jessop's and Sum (2000a)'s work describes cities as 'strategic actors with entrepreneurial ambitions', Harvey (1989) presents contextual representation of the three tenets of 'Urban Entrepreneurialism' which includes (i) urban governments during post-Fordist regime are strongly influenced by business elites through PPP mode; (ii) local governments implement highly speculative 'flagship projects' to enhance the 'image of the city' and (iii) urban entrepreneurialism is driven by the political economy of 'place' rather than 'territory'. However, Jessop's work emphasizes narrative strategies that cities employ for 'place-making' or 'image-making' entrepreneurial initiatives.

In the context of rapidly transforming urban governance under the influence of global economy, the new urban strategies are typically understood to involve two sets of interrelated processes at the local level. They are, foremost, prioritizing pro-growth fostering local economic development through inward investments and (ii) creating necessary conditions for attracting mobile capital (Harvey 1989; Hall and Hubbard 1996). So, urban governments are no longer concerned with the welfare and services, but rather implement thepolitical projects promoting competitive strategies and attract new forms of mobile capital for improving the local embeddedness of firms (Jessop 1998), subsequently changing the 'image of the city' (Genis 2007). The urban structuralist literature portrays such an image-making project as to make the city attractive to capital (Harvey 1989; Jessop 2000b; Brenner 2003). Secondly, organizational shifts in local governance such as increasing the role of the private sector through public–private partnership (PPP) in financing and regulating pro-growth policies are most noticeable which Harvey identifies as a shift from urban managerialism to 'entrepreneurial governance' (Harvey 1989; Jessop 1997, 1998). Finally, many recent empirical works on 'entrepreneurial urbanism' in Europe and USA have captured the changing political geographies of the state in performing and regulating urban development projects (MacLeod 2002). These explicit policy changes as well as new organizational shifts at the local level are indicative of the dominant responses to urban problems.

Meanwhile, a vast empirical literature on the discourse and narratives of 'Entrepreneurial Urbanism' have focused on the cities of North America, British as well as some of the Scandinavian and Asian cities (Boyle and Hughes 1994; Hubbard 1996; Hall and Hubbard 1996; Jessop 1997, 1998; Jessop and Sum 2000a; Chapin 2002; MacLeod 2002; Brenner 2003; Shin 2007). In other words, urban entrepreneurialism was discussed as a narrative, while examining and illustrating the defining features and explicit policy strategies of local governance. To position the city as 'competitive and innovative', various explicit institutional structures and strategies were promoted in support of acquisition of command and control functions in finance, information systems, the expansion of local tax-base and attracting investments. Such entrepreneurial activities were encouraged in the form of small firm growth, supporting virtual economy such as IT, installation of cybernetic infrastructure, promotion of scale and agglomeration economies, creating new forms of labour market relations, new cityscapes (Hall and Hubbard 1996; Jessop and Sum 2000a; Hall et al. 2014), thereby redefining urban hierarchy. Finally, an entrepreneurial city concentrates more on an orchestrated production of spectacular projects towards the creation of attractive 'urban imagery' such as flagship development projects in US cities such as restored waterfronts, sport arenas or consumption attractions, tourism as a panacea for ailing urban economies (Harvey 1989; Jessop and Sum 2000a). Certainly, these conditions are reflective of mobilizing diverse sociopolitical structures and organizational capacities for common entrepreneurial projects.

It is noteworthy to observe that the scope for urban entrepreneurialism has expanded and articulated at diverse spatial scales in the form of an ensemble of actors, dense institutional and social networks such as public–private partnership (PPP), intellectual property regimes, production and management and so on for the purpose of promoting local growth or market their space. For instance, to realize international competitiveness, dramatic transformations of urban landscape are captured in the cities of USA—Baltimore, Boston, Chicago, Cincinnati, New York

(Harvey 1989; Roberts and Schein 1993; Boyle and Hughes 1994; Gillen 2009), implementing flagship projects brokered through public–private partnership (PPP) mode. Such was the case of cities such as New York, London and Tokyo (Sassen 2002), demonstrating a changing economic character with their global role in production, finance and management systems. Similarly, Hong Kong has emerged as thriving centre for its increasingly internationalized financial and producer services sectors with a similar project undertaken in Singapore, Kuala Lumpur and Beijing (Jessop and Sum 2000a; Shin 2009) which eventually is linked to the modern imaginaries of 'competitiveness' and 'innovation'. The studies by Wu (2000) and Zheng (2011) highlighted the transformation of the city of Shanghai as a world city with skyscrapers and creative industrial clusters. Local policies were thus, remodelled to suit international standards on how a city's image must look and function. Empirical evidence clearly illustrates how the tenets of 'entrepreneurialism' such as attractiveness and 'innovation' were embedded within the local policies for promoting image building strategies and 'global' standards. Such a territorial logic of neoliberal project was identified even with 'Revanchist city' (Smith 1996), Spatial Dispossession (Harvey 2005), rescaling of state-spaces (Brenner 2004) and 'market-driven strategies of spatial fragmentation' (Ong 2006, in Roy 2011). Urban governance is, therefore, reoriented towards attracting 'capital' and promoting a lucrative business climate. Beyond these image building exercises of the cities in different ways, focus must also be directed to the effects and far reaching implications of these changes through institutions and urban built environment (Harvey 1989; Jessop and Sum 2000a; Chapin 2002; MacLeod 2002; Brenner 2003), i.e., on how the project of 'urban entrepreneurialism' explicitly produces new forms of socio-spatial exclusion.

In this context, with the policies under the construct of neo-liberalization, cities are experiencing a new forms of socio-spatial fragmentation characterized by the dismantling of local forms of communities, neighbourhood, social organizations and the subsequent economic and political exclusion of a large section of the urban population (Jessop 2002; Harvey 2005; Brenner and Theodore 2002a; Brenner et al. 2010). Therefore, there is a general increase in problems like the spatial dispersal of employment opportunities and encouragement of 'informal sector' consequently contributing to the increased disparities in wealth and income, thereby accentuating urban poverty and impoverishment noticed in all the global cities both in the north and south[3] (Roy and Ong 2011). Yet, literature on 'urban entrepreneurialism' does not provide grounded analysis precisely on how do urban disadvantaged communities such as the urban poor reel under the ongoing institutional and structural constraints, eventually struggling to survive and thrive in the context of such exclusionary entrepreneurial practices? How is the institutional and structural shift from government to governance articulated within an entrepreneurial narrative? How is the governance performed or narrated? What are the policy priorities of the local government? Who conceptualizes a vision for the city? What are the politics

[3]Such as New York, London, Tokyo, Hong Kong, Mumbai, New Delhi.

of spatial restructuring and the influence of global capital at the local level? What is the identity of city within the discourse of global modernism/capitalism? How is the realm 'urban' reconfigured influencing citizenship rights, service delivery and access to resources? Based on the theoretical observations, the next section presents empirical reviews on how neoliberalism has been localized post-1990s as a political project offering panacea for an economic crisis-ridden urban economy.

Anchoring 'Entrepreneurial Urbanism' in India

Building on a vast theoretical literature, empirical studies clearly demonstrates how local governments and their developmental policies have embraced transition from managerialism to 'entrepreneurial' forms of urban governance in the USA, Europe and South-east Asia (Harvey 1989; Sbragia 1996; Hall and Hubbard 1996; Jessop and Sum 2000a; Brenner 2003). This section seeks to engage with essentially empirical reviews on the political context of transitional urban management (both institutional and structural) in the last two decades bearing a strong imprint of 'entrepreneurial urbanism' in their strategies, mechanisms and actions in India.

Following liberalization, cities in the global south deserve an appellation of 'neoliberalized', subsequently impacting service delivery and urban poor. During the past decade, Indian cities have grown to 50 with 91 million added (Nijman 2015). As per the Census 2011, India's total urban population constitutes 31 %, contributing 61 % of GDP. As projected, urban India would contribute 75 % of the national GDP in the next 15 years. Although the pace of Indian urbanization[4] is slower as compared to other countries, yet the urban population[5] has grown from 286 million during 2001 Census to 377 million (30 % of urban population) in 2011, which is 2.76 % growth during 2001–2011[6] (HPEC 2011; Planning Commission 2012; Shaw 2012a). City governance often grappled for being costly, overburdened, inefficient and incapable of eliminating poverty. Simultaneously, post-1990s, state urban development policies categorically embraced liberalization, deregulation and privatization, introduction of 'new public management strategies' and competitive contracting of municipal services by introducing new network forms of governance that suit the market-driven global economy. A major consequence of an explicit neoliberal shift has been from state-led development to *laissez-faire* strategies

---

[4]For the 12th Five-Year Plan document on Urbanisation in India, http://12thplan.gov.in/12fyp_docs/17.pdf.

[5]By 2030, out of a total population of 1.4 billion, over 600 million people may be living in urban areas. Urban cities and towns have also increased from 5161 in 2001 to 7935 in 2011. One million plus cities have increased from 35 during 2001 to 53 in 2011 (Planning Commission 2011).

[6]The level of urbanization in India has increased from 27.7 % during 2001 to 31.1 % in 2011, i.e. an increase of 3.3 % during 2001–2011 as compared to an increase of 2.1 % during the 1991–2011 Census. It is estimated that India will have more than 87 metropolitan areas by 2031 and urban population will soar up to 600 million (HPEC 2011).

(Harris 2003; Banerjee-Guha 2002, 2009, 2010; Benjamin 2008a, 2008b; Sivaramakrishnan 2011a, b; Shaw 2012a, 2012b). Subsequently, the 'urban' was reconstituted, branding cities as 'engines of economic growth enabling neoliberal policies and programmes to materialize across the urban landscape. There is a shift in the focus of institutions, structures and actors underlying urban governance, unveiling a range of measures which include the abandonment of welfare by planning agencies, deindustrialization,[7] deregulation, flexible labour markets, chronic absence of the state from social provisioning, increase in government subsidies for the private sector, and the promotion of international organizations vision models idealizing the private sector (Banerjee-Guha 2002; Benjamin 2008a; Harris 2003; Nair 2006; Sivaramakrishnan 2011a, b; Shaw 2012a, 2012b) as an alternative path to deal with the economic crisis. Concomitantly, 73rd and 74th Constitutional Amendment Act, 1992, anchored a variety of institutional and structural experiments and strategies through which 'welfare' was restructured, redesigned and highly marketized in the form of public–private partnerships (PPP) in service delivery, withdrawal of the state from urban development, corporate influence in urban planning and policy and incorporating e-governance[8] measures. Urban development policies rolled out contextually specific form of neoliberal practices indicating the withdrawal of state making way for a more market-driven and *laissez-faire* model of 'development' (Shaw 1999, 2013). Thus, the manifestation of 'entrepreneurial' political ambitions which began at the national level from the 1990s gradually permeated the local political agendas.

In support of an urban, pro-growth model, principles of commodification and commercialization were manifested in a series of urban policy circuits such as the Megacity Programme 1993 for Infrastructure Development in the Ninth Plan and the Urban Reform Incentive Fund (URIF) in the Tenth Plan, precipitating major structural changes in Indian cities. Subsequently, urban sector reforms were rolled out, proposed and funded by international funding and donor agencies with conditionalities, for instance, the JNNURM[9] (2005–06). Urban Infrastructure

[7]Closure of public sector industries such as textile industries in Mumbai, and others in Bengaluru.

[8]Essentially, to promote an efficient city management by introducing e-governance measures such as fund-based accounting system, self-assessment of property tax system, Bhoomi programme and Urban Property Ownership Records (UPOR) in Karnataka for the management of land governance.

[9]The Indian government's flagship programme, Jawaharlal Nehru National Urban Renewal Mission (JNNURM), was launched in 2005–2006 consists of four components: (i) Urban Infrastructure and Governance (UIG) for 65 mega-cities and 28 cities with a population of 1 mm+, 17 state capitals, and 13 cities of religious and tourist centres; (ii) Urban Infrastructure Development Scheme for Small and Medium Towns (UIDSSMT) for 640 towns; (iii) Basic Services for Urban Poor (BSUP) for 65 towns; and (iv) the Integrated Housing and Slum Development Programme (IHSDP). The total project cost was Rs 1000 billion, of which 50 % was to be provided as central assistance (Sivaramakrishnan 2011a, b). Amongst the major metropolitan cities, Bengaluru received 40 projects worth Rs 27.98 billion followed by Chennai (39 projects), Kolkata (34), Ahmedabad (25), Surat (25), Greater Mumbai (24) and Hyderabad (22) (Sivaramakrishnan 2011a, b; Shaw 2012a).

Development Scheme for Small and Medium Towns (UIDSSMT), Integrated Housing and Slum Development Programme (IHSDP) and e-governance measures were introduced for promoting local accountability and transparency by streamlining the property tax system in cities, enhancing customer service and creating city governance (Sivaramakrishnan 2011a, b; Shaw 2012a). For promoting 'Good Land Governance', major e-governance initiatives were introduced in Karnataka such as Bhoomi programme and Urban Property Ownership Records (UPOR) computerizing land records for both rural and urban areas (Manasi and Smitha 2013). This apart, Nirmala Nagara—the largest municipal e-governance redressal system in Karnataka, reflects an increasing influence of international agencies to implement urban sector reforms (Ranganathan 2012). As a corollary to JNNURM, Rajiv Awas Yojana (RAY),[10] a housing scheme was introduced for promoting the rhetoric of 'Slum free India' targeting 250 cities with an estimated population of 32.10 million in slums. Urban reforms gained further an impetus with regressive legislations formalizing regulatory changes governing land ownership and land acquisition, private sector investment in urban land boosting large-scale infrastructure projects and real estate development in cities. The most significant of them include: (i) Repealing Urban Land Ceiling Regulation Act, 1999, eventually pushing the land market into the hands of private property sector; (ii) secondly, promulgation of Special Economic Zone (SEZ) Act, 2005, for acquiring agriculture lands from rural farmers to be sold to private developers constituting export-processing zones and legislation of the Right to Fair Compensation and Transparency in Land Acquisition, Rehabilitation and Resettlement Act, 2013 (LARR)[11] for governing land and easing barriers for the appropriation of rural agricultural land for private developmental purpose and (iii) finally, facilitating foreign direct investment (FDI) in construction, housing and infrastructure (Weinstein et al. 2013). These legislations as a precursor to neoliberal principles marked a swift transition towards 'realizing entrepreneurial mission of governance'.

---

[10]The central government would fund 50, 75 and 80 % of the project cost for towns, cities and urban agglomerations, respectively, with a population of more than 500,000, less than 500,000 for those in the north-eastern region in India (Jadhav 2013). See The Hindu (2011). The slum-free India scheme was to be taken up as a national mission, August 2011. http://www.thehindu.com/news/national/slumfree-india-scheme-to-be-taken-up-as-national-mission/article2358818.ece.

[11]This bill came into force from 1 January 2014 under Congress I governance. On 30 May 2014, President of India promulgated the amendment ordinance and notified the Right to Fair Compensation and Transparency in Land Acquisition, Rehabilitation and Resettlement (Social Impact Assessment and Consent) Rules, 2014. Later, under Narendra Modi led National Democratic Alliance (NDA) introduced Land Acquisition Amendment Bill 2015 in the Lok Sabha on 10 March 2015. The Bill amends the Right to Fair Compensation and Transparency in Land Acquisition, Rehabilitation and Resettlement Act, 2013 (LARR Act 2013) and replaces the Right to Fair Compensation and Transparency in Land Acquisition, Rehabilitation and Resettlement (Amendment) Ordinance, 2014.

As a part of an urban revamping programme, the Government of India (GoI)[12] announced an outlay of Rs 1000 billion for building 100 Smart Cities[13] over the span of 5 years. Further, JNNURM was to be replaced by Atal Mission for Rejuvenation and Urban Transformation (AMRUT) for rejuvenating 500[14] more cities with outlays of Rs 480 billion and Rs 500 billion, respectively.[15] Ushering in such a new urban paradigm with respect to modern municipal management, the technocratic and professional municipal cadre are expected to replace existing municipal official pattern Gandhi (2015). Chapter 2 by Debolina Kundu and SudhirKrishna, while reviewing the recent programmatic interventions in urban India such as JNNURM, Smart City programmes and AMRUT, argues that urban local governments have become visibly 'entrepreneurial' in three different but interrelated ways. These contemporary narratives of Indian urban management ventures can be argued as blatantly 'entrepreneurial' anchoring 'core neoliberal policies and programmes' into multi-layered institutions and practices at diverse urban spatial scales.

Furthermore, a multitude of actors has emerged as agents of change influencing city systems, institutions and local or municipal politics. It is evident that the city governments are increasingly networking with urban elites such as corporate, land developers and private investors to develop public spaces in which daily interactions and practices are carefully planned to bolster urban image by fostering business and consumption activities that shape local capital investments. The emergence of BATF and ABIDe in Bangalore is one such example of corporate led urban governance (Heitzman 2004; Ghosh 2005, 2006; Benjamin 2008a, 2010; Gopalan 2013; Banerjee-Guha 2010; Coelho et al. 2011). Most recently, the Bengaluru Blue Print Action Group (BBPAG)[16] (May 2016) was constituted by the Siddaramaiah government. As the government order forming the BBPAG, the Action Group will finalize a Bengaluru Blue Print and strive for its implementation (Aditya Bharadwaj 2016). Such coalitions between public–private and corporate were proclaimed to be absolutely necessary for Bengaluru's economic recouping. But these exaltations eventually led to overriding, manipulating and destabilizing urban governments and planning instruments. Progressive and alternative vision for the city was conceived and forced upon—through Master plans or City

[12]The new government in India was formed by the majority party Bharatiya Janata Party (BJP) in May 2014.

[13]A list of 98 cities which were selected for 'Smart Cities' project was released in August, 2015.

[14]With population more than 100,000 and above to receive Rs 5 billion in three instalments.

[15]The Cabinet approved the implementation of 100 'Smart City' Programme. Each state in India will get at least one Smart City (The Hindu 2015), also http://indiansmartcities.in/downloads/CONCEPT_NOTE_-3.12.2014__REVISED_AND_LATEST_.pdf.

[16]But the BBPAG has received widespread criticism from civic activists and NGOs, who view this arrangement as 'extra-constitutional' and 'undemocratic', as bypassing the constitutional mandate of the Metropolitan Planning Committee (MPC) (Mahesh 2016), and as possibly having 'elitist vision' (Aditya Bharadwaj 2016).

Development Plans (CDPs),or Vision Documents. Yet, the literature on urban politics in India ignored the implications of non-political/non-elective agents for urban governance. While examining one such ideological and institutional experimentation, Chap. 6 by Vinay Baindur in this volume clearly presents how 'entrepreneurial vision group politics', comprising corporate echelons and influential elites like NGOs, have been wielding their collective power and lobbying for changes in various mega-developmental local projects in Bengaluru. While illustrating the cases of urban development projects, the study demonstrates how these non-political entities influence the local political governance. Clearly, a transition towards 'entrepreneurial urbanism' signifies a scenario of 'less government' and 'more corporate' who advocate that cities must be 'run in a more business-like manner' (Hall and Hubbard 1996).

In tandem with decentralized governance, parastatals and development agencies such as Bangalore Development Agency (BDA), Karnataka Urban Infrastructure Development and Finance Corporation (KUIDFC), Kolkata Metropolitan Development Authority (KMDA), Chennai Metropolitan Development Authority (CMDA) and other financial institutions are mostly contesting over to gain control over the land that have increasingly shaped the decisions of urban development (Benjamin and Bhuvaneswari 2006; Weinstein et al. 2013). Exploring such urban dynamics, the chapter by Anjali Karol Mohan (Chap. 4) reveals how the state, amidst the processes of contemporary globalization, is increasingly pursuing 'good governance' through network forms of governance referred to as 'heterarchies'. Taking the case of the Municipal Reforms Programme (MRP), an e-governance intervention by the Government of Karnataka (GoK), India, the study examines how network forms of governance provide an opportunity for the state to move beyond the neoliberal policy framework of 'entrepreneurial governance' arrangements like PPP for achieving larger public value, while capitalizing on the strength of both private and civil society actors. Evidence also suggests that a combination of 'porous bureaucracy' and 'politics of stealth' is often used by local groups[17] to influence and bargain with different levels of political agents to address land issues and establish fragile claims on land in both Bangalore and New Delhi (Benjamin and Bhuvaneswari 2001; Benjamin 2004) for facilitating 'pro-poor' politics. For better understanding of the evolution of 'urban' in Karnataka, the contribution by Sudhira in this volume (Chap. 3) illustrates the emergence of 'political and bureaucratic entrepreneurship' through the evolution of a unique entrepreneurial governance mechanism affecting urban governance, as against strengthening the urban local bodies, in the city of Bengaluru.

Indeed, as Anjaria and Ulka (2013) describe, 'civic activism seems to epitomize the 'entrepreneurial' ideal of new liberalism' in Indian cities, these new political agents and deliberative horizontal governance structures by middle-class and elite groups like Residential Welfare Associations (RWAs) or Area Local Management Groups (ALMs), are pro-active citizenry donning urban social life in New Delhi,

[17]Such poorer groups of slums, pavement dwellers, street sleepers.

Mumbai, Bangalore and Chennai which have led to the 'depoliticization' and subversion of municipal politics (Heitzman 2004; Zerah 2007; Harris 2005, 2007; Baud and Dhanalakshmi 2008; Coelho and Venkat 2009; Kamath and Vijayabaskar 2009; Benjamin 2010). Such participation was often referred to as 'elite capture' of urban governance (Zerah 2009; Kundu 2011) has eventually institutionalized urban disparities. It is apparent that these elite groups are camouflaged under the ethic of a new civic activism or urban localism (Smitha 2010) which is more aligned with neoliberal urban sector reforms. In fact, the modernist vision of the city was carried forward by the new middle class exercising their agency by embracing 'participative entrepreneurialism' in favour of global capital formation. Such mobilization gave a boost to the state-led entrepreneurialism for the implementation of large-scale developmental projects and for attracting investments (Weinstein et al. 2013). Studies have dwelt into reconfigured urban citizenship within the specific urban processes in different Indian cities, and Desai (2012: 32) shows how urban citizenship and urbanism are constructed, negotiated and renegotiated 'through reshaping, regulation and governance of space and resources and contestation'. Here, a transforming urban citizenship is interrogated in the context of restructuring of governance and urban space from the perspective of an emerging 'urban entrepreneurialism'.

Further, urban centres are increasingly fostering command and control functions by implementing 'world-class' infrastructure and material projects such as expressways, urban metros,[18] flyovers, airports, urban corridors,[19] special economic zones (SEZs)[20] for minimizing transaction time and the cost of expanding global production networks. The emphasis is on the 'gentrification'[21] of space for elitist consumption such as malls, commercial centres, and gated communities, which are deeply inscribed into the city's image repertoires, essentially to manage the interface between local economy and global capital. Clearly, the new urban spectacle and image-making projects created an illusion of 'homogeneous' vision for the city which coalesced into the local entrepreneurial political agenda. The emergence of urban agglomeration[22] has precipitated land use changes in peri-urban region

[18]At the time of writing, 10 metro-rail projects had been undertaken in Indian cities such as New Delhi, Gurgaon, Bengaluru, Jaipur, Mumbai, Mumbai Monorail, Kolkata, Chennai, Kochi, Hyderabad. Recently, Tier II cities have been considered for the metro project, which include Lucknow, Kanpur, Patna, Ahmedabad, Pune, Surat, Indore, Nagpur, Coimbatore and Kozhikode.

[19]Some of Bengaluru's corridors include the Mumbai–Bengaluru Economic Corridors, Bengaluru–Tumkuru, Bengaluru–Mysuru Infrastructure Corridor (BMIC).

[20]For example, International TechPark, Manyata Embassy Business Park, WIPRO limited, Infosys Technologies.

[21]Although the term 'gentrification' is conceptualized for private property regimes of Western cities yet, in the context of developing countries like India, it has become synonymous with the contemporary forms of slum demolitions, evictions and displacement in Indian cities post-liberalization of 1990s.

[22]Urban agglomeration with the population of more than 1 million is referred as 'metropolitan city'. Census Provisional Data of 2011 indicated an increase in number of metropolitan cities to 53 constituting 42 % of Indian population (Shaw 2012b).

'*linking such social and political circuits to the material manifestation of neoliberal reforms*' (Benjamin 2008a). Local political structures are mobilized to intensify land use changes in favour of the private and corporate sectors. Such a regressive neoliberal articulation of urban governance and spatial restructuring has generated new struggles and contestations within the urban–rural and interurban scales, exacerbating sizeable socio-spatial inequalities.

Examining the dialogical relationship between urban citizens and urban policy makers within the mode of 'entrepreneurial urban governance' as contested terrain in India, Desai (2012: 32) shows 'how entrepreneurial strategies of city image making and place-marketing emerged following a brutal state supported anti-Muslim programme in Ahmedabad and the rest of Gujarat during 2002'. Certainly, such strategies, she argues, created a discursive shift away from the city and region as violent and unsafe city to region as a 'culturally dynamic and developmental space'. Further, those narratives were categorically used in promoting a 'politics of forgetting' or 'politics of erasure and denial' of marginalized groups, thereby reproducing patterns of material and symbolic exclusion inscribed in 'Hindutva politics' (Desai 2012). The study certainly unravels the practices of an exclusive urban citizenship based on the class and religion, produced within entrepreneurial governance.

Inevitable economic and respatialization of local governance was very much evident from the cities of New Delhi, Mumbai, Kolkata and Chennai (Baviskar 2002; Banerjee-Guha 2002, 2009; Benjamin 2006, 2008a, 2008b; Shaw 2012b). Drawing on Harvey (1989) thesis on 'urban entrepreneurialism', the chapter by Bhuvaneswari Raman (Chap. 5) succinctly illustrates how shifts in urban governance accompanying PPP and urban renewal projects are mobilized for transferring urban commons and lands under private tenure forms to speculative, urban real estate projects for facilitating large private players. In such initiatives, the author argues, the risks are disproportionately redistributed to the poor- and middle-income households in the cities of New Delhi, Mumbai and Chennai. Such rapid urban transformation, Banerjee-Guha (2002: 122), views as being 'facilitated by explicit state intervention promoting interrelationship of space and production of accumulation'. Therefore, valorization of local entrepreneurial ambitions was promoted by the state by actively participating in the promotion of city 'boosterism' projects, along with private investors, to attract capital and to compete vigorously with each other. This stance resonates with research on urban transition in India. For instance, Baviskar (2002) views that the bourgeois vision of New Delhi was achieved by razing thousands of working homes in the name of construction, road-widening and other 'public purposes'. While narrating the account of transformation of New Delhi's urban imaginary as a 'world-class city' on the eve of a spectacular event in the making, like 2010 Commonwealth Games, Baviskar (2011) reveals a reorientation of social and economic policies in pursuit of 'place competition' as a strategy for attracting mobile capital and people. In pursuit of such place competition, she argues, there is an inbuilt nexus between local politicians and private builders to promote such spectacular events and a business-friendly environment. Similarly, to cater to the rapidly growing global economy, many cities in southern India have emerged as the 'hub of transport' (such as Mumbai) (Harris 2003), international financial centre (Mumbai) (Banerjee-Guha 2002, 2009), and 'IT/BT hubs' or 'hi-tech information systems', 'silicon plateau' such as Bengaluru, Hyderabad, Chennai, Mumbai, New Delhi (Heitzman[23] 1999, 2003, 2004; Nair 2000, 2006; Aranya 2008), practically suggesting that these cities have become destinations for footloose global investments and a measure to integrate into the global economy. Further, the information technology (IT) clusters have provided the infrastructural stimulus for global city making.

In the context of providing global city status to Mumbai, studies by Banerjee-Guha (2002, 2009) point to the collusion between local politicians and urban managers with business and commercial interests in implementing various anti-people projects, there by legitimizing a dualistic conception of urban planning. Within the broader context of such an urban restructuring process, illicit or informal governance practices in Mumbai through OCGs with respect to property and land development have drastically redefined and altered urban governance and regulatory regime by shaping land use practices and development paradigm (Weinstein 2008). In another account of Mumbai, while recasting the form of urban governance to bolster a global competitive frame, Weinstein (2011) points to an explicit 'entrepreneurial strategies' which were employed in collusion with 'consultocracy'—planners and external consultants. In response to a state reconfiguration deeply swayed by the neoliberal globalization and competitive urbanism, the study by Weinstein (2014) narrates how during the implementation of the Dharavi Redevelopment Project, envisioning a 'slum-free city' as part of the state's mission of globalizing 'Mumbai', attention was drawn to the emergence of 'political entrepreneurship', i.e. the state's coalition with other private actors (political networks and civil society).

In contrast, the city of Bengaluru[24] in the south has emerged as an 'IT hub', 'science city', and a busy industrial and trade centre (Heitzman 1999, 2003, 2004; Benjamin 2006; Nair 2000, 2006; Aranya 2008; Sudhira 2008; Nisbett 2009). Technology in collusion with the private and corporate sectors played a significant role in bringing about an ideological shift towards promoting a new identity for the city, thereby rationalizing the liberal economic agenda (Heitzman 2004). Studies by Benjamin (2008a, b, 2010) clearly indicate that a deeply entrenched 'global capital' has led to the subversion of local politics (citing Bengaluru) in favour of political elites and corporate lobbies vigorously pursuing 'neoliberal urban sector reforms', eventually leading to 'control chaos'. While proposing to transform Bengaluru into a model of 'world city' making, the study by Goldman (2010) provides evidence of 'speculative governance', in collusion with new actors such as international financial institutions, influencing and implementing new urban projects such as the

[23]Heitzman (2003) views that the city of Bangalore (Bengaluru) 'has reached the milieu of innovation, would demonstrate "synergetic" features of organizational structure that place information systems at the heart of planning'.

[24]Bangalore suburbs have attracted numerous investments.

'Singapore' model or the 'Shanghai' model of infrastructure development. Under speculative governance, land encroachment and active dispossession of low-income groups, rural communities and the urban poor from peripheries has become very common. The study points out that 'most of these speculative activities are linked to the tangible and highly remunerative challenge of transforming the rural economies into urban real estate' (Goldman 2010: 572). For promoting developmental initiatives, a great deal of synergy is visible amongst urban development strategies, i.e. local state and private developers for 'world city making' in Chennai (Ellis 2012). Thus, urban governance in India has begun to redefine its form and practices in partnership with private and corporate sectors in order to promote urban economic speculative projects. Such collaboration precisely reflects global economic and social forces shaping and reshaping urban governance in India. These aggressive place-marketing strategies, unproblematically located within the state's purview, exemplify 'branding cities' purely from a neo-liberalization perspective; yet, there is hardly sufficient literature to capture a wider sense of urban tension and contestations in everyday practices.

An ensemble of urbanization and economic rejuvenation process has produced locally specific, contradictory spatial and scalar expressions in the form of (i) foremost, gentrification,[25] or a gradual acquisition of land for the use of upper-middle and higher income enclaves; and (ii) secondly, urban informalization—a space for employment opportunities for urban poor and middle class without protective legislation (Shaw 2012b), escalating urban inequalities. These new models of urban governance have been embraced by the state in response to opportunities and constraints fostered by the emerging influence of global actors in the urban political economy (Shatkin 2008: 388). In other words, Banerjee-Guha (2011), while enumerating 'development' contradictions in India states, views that '[a] typical neoliberal construction of space, place and scale is taking place in India that is reconstructing a new geography of centrality and marginality, making the issues of production and capitalization of space extremely crucial'.

Certainly, these aforesaid institutional practices and policies can be clearly characterized as one of the variants of neoliberalism, i.e. 'entrepreneurial' approach.

Mission of Urban Exclusion

One of the entrenched features of the political economy of India's urbanization process has been the unplanned and haphazard growth of slums[26] and informal settlements, heralding urban dualism. One of the startling implications of

[25]Gentrification has been used to refer to as a process associated with the cities of USA, to illustrate displacement of poor communities by rich outsiders (Shaw 2012b).

[26]The city of Bengaluru accounts for more than 30 % of slums, while Mumbai for 43 %, Kolkata for 36 % and Delhi for 22 % (Shaw 2012b).

'entrepreneurial' endeavours of the contemporary cities in India is urban unrest, contestation, disenfranchisement, dispossession, deprivation and marginalization of the urban poor. In essence, as the city engages in entrepreneurial ambitions by creating a climate conducive for business/investment opportunities, which inevitably has a detrimental effect in the form of thriving inequities affecting the socio-economic livelihoods of vulnerable communities. As per Census 2011, there are 37,000 urban slums in India, with an increase of 65 million when compared to 52 million during 2001 census (Nijman 2015). While urban population grew by 31 % as against 25 % growth of India's slum population[27] alone (ibid.). Considering that slums are categorized as a permanent structural feature of India's urbanization process, Nijman (2015: 420) points out that 'slums in India are usually regarded as either a nuisance or irrelevance'. A host of empirical literature confirms that under the contemporary urban redevelopment politics, a carefully manufactured 'image' building exercise[28] has inevitably rendered slums, street vendors and squatters marginalized, further deepening class inequalities (Fernandes 2004) in Indian cities.

Under the rhetoric of promoting a world-class, or global, city in Mumbai, marginalized sections such as street hawkers and the urban poor represent 'an undeserved claim on the city's public space', yet, they represent a 'nuisance', 'menace' or 'eyesore', causing the city's notorious congestion (Anjaria 2006: 2142). Modernist ideas of city-spectacular projects supported by bourgeois class of NGOs and elites determine who must own the city space and who will not (Anjaria 2006). Anjaria argues that the disjuncture between 'enterprise culture' of a thriving middle-class activism perpetuating neoliberalism and the 'entrepreneurial' city' does not recognize the political demands of 'entrepreneurial hawkers' but are rather refracted by the 'particularities of the city's spatial politics' (Anjaria and Ulka 2013). As literature sufficiently suggests, under the present urban political climate, local governments are increasingly orientated towards the implementation of anti-poor policies and redevelopment programmes. Ghertner (2011: 25), in his study, reveals that as part of resculpting New Delhi's image, 'nuisance' has become a new legal term since 2000 for demolishing slums, thus reconstituting the 'public interest'. He argues that such a nuisance discourse 'reorients the terrain of citizenship, social justice and access to the city—categories that would typically fall in the domain of Article 21' (i.e. right to citizenship)'. The discourse further reveals that the distinction between 'public' and 'private' nuisance is blurred, 're-imposing a distinctly bourgeoisie sense of social order over public space' (Ghertner 2011: 25). Thus, slums are objectified to be managed and disposed of, not as citizens with rights. Reiterating the emergence of 'new politics' in Chennai (in South India), the study by Harris (2007) reveals that new politics is exclusionary in nature and

[27]According to High Power Expert Committee (2011) estimates, approximately 24 % of India's urban population reside in slums (Planning Commission 2012).

[28]Fernandes (2004) refers to these as 'political discursive processes' rendering marginalized groups invisible and forgotten. The process constitutes a part of spatial restructuring of urban in India.

endorses public–private partnership, reflecting the existence of dualism between 'citizens' and 'denizens'. Although associational activities are extended to the upper echelons and elites, these are hardly extended to the urban poor.

In fact, Nijman (2008) argues that slum rehabilitation policies are articulated within the 'neoliberal' construct of an excessive reliance on market (donor or International Financial Agencies) or local 'self-help' agencies (including civil society like NGOs) eventually forging a political culture of promoting 'urban growth' strategy with an intense competition for land acquisition particularly in Mumbai city. Inevitably, urban governments are treading the path by increasingly engaging in an 'entrepreneurial mode of operation'. Citing the successful case of a rehabilitated Ganeshnagar D, he argues that it was both 'self-help' and intervention of NGO (The Slum Rehabilitation Society) that Ganeshnagar D was successfully rehabilitated in the neoliberal Mumbai city. But this is an exceptional case and the situation may not be the same for all the redevelopment and rehabilitation policies (Nijman 2008).

As part of a paradigm shift in urban politics in India, slum evictions are mediated through judicial decisions, perpetuated by the economic transition and the state blatantly embracing 'neoliberal ideology and market participation' (Ramanathan 2006; Bhan 2009). While implementing the urban renewal mission, explicit institutional guidelines are prepared to promote a 'slum-free city', forcing evictions and demolitions of urban slums (GoI 2010). For instance, in a frantic effort to project the image of New Delhi during the 10th Commonwealth Games (CWG) in 2010, contentious policies were enacted forcing evictions, demolitions and dispossession of the urban poor. According to the HLRN fact-finding report (2011), since 2004, 2,000,009 people in Delhi have been forcibly evicted due to the CWG. The study by Dupont (2011) clearly enumerates the fact that an explicit political strategy was embraced to building Delhi's global 'image/competitiveness' as 'world-class city' and in the process, erase or cleanse socially unwanted spaces such as slums, further exacerbating the socio-spatial polarization. The economic emphasis of the 'competition' has led 'even unclaimed spaces on which the poor squatted became prime land, 'ripe for development' (Baviskar 2006, cited in Dupont 2011). In a vivid account of exclusionary practices under 'entrepreneurial ethos of urban planning' in New Delhi, the study by Gidwani and Bharati (2011) cites how informal recyclers have been consistently disenfranchised by a variety of formal and informal manoeuvring tactics, whose lives and labour a redevalued under the global circuits of capital and their political claims suppressed in favour of bourgeois middle-class environmentalism. Even as global forces shape the local strategies within the discourse of 'roll back of the state', an equally compelling narrative is provided by Ranganathan (2011) by revealing how the state, by embracing privatization of water as a paradigm shift through 'cost recovery' and 'efficiency', has in fact legitimized the middle-class claims to city and access to state institutions.

In the latest façade for urban rejuvenation mega-projects and for attracting mobile capital promoting global city making, illuminating literature presents on how a transitional governance in support of 'elite-driven' makeover projects 'disenfranchise and disposes' the vulnerable groups such as slums in Indian cities. The work by Weinstein (2012) succinctly captures how the Dharavi Redevelopment Project (DRP), a mega-infrastructure project designed to transform Mumbai's largest slum into a multi-use and mixed-income township, did in fact facilitated cooption between the local communities and the state between 2004 and 2008. Such democratic urban citizenship practices, she argues, are not based on 'high liberal ideals but largely influenced by material considerations'. Further arguing that citizenship is inherently uneven and open to those groups within Dharavi with 'symbolic power and the political resources'—crucially linked to class, caste and historical claims on space which is required to oppose any negative publicity.

The rise of a 'new middle class' is equally held responsible for driving 'New Delhi' into a bourgeois 'world-class city' through the political mechanisms, citing the implementation of 'Bhagidari' programme.[29] The work by Ghertner (2014: 205) critiques the Bhagidari programme 'as representing an "invited space" consolidating the normative stance of private property owners into urban governance for reinforcing the vision of "world city"'. Thus, Bhagidari has led to the gentrification of political participation. The study by Bjokman (2014), citing the case of Mumbai, critiques both 'global city making' and 'post-colonial' formulations as articulations of action and law, encapsulating the transformation of Shivajinagar-Bainganwadi slum 'from planned municipal colony into illegal slum', facilitated by the politically mediated deterioration and criminalization of its water infrastructure. He further argues that in the context of liberalization-era, policy shifts have subsequently produced 'informality/illegality' as discursive effect'. Such measures categorically disrupt and jeopardize the opportunities for income and livelihood of the urban poor. On the other hand, 'subaltern urbanism', as an agent of change and distinctive political identity, 'slums' such as Dharavi, symbolizes 'economies of entrepreneurialism' and 'political agency'. But such economies are prone to be transformed into 'neoliberal populism'—through commodification of community economies (Roy 2011). The study by Nijman (2015) citing Dharavi's thriving self-organizing economic activities, reveals that the state has completely failed to provide a secure livelihood. In the mission to implement McKinsey report for transforming Mumbai into a 'world-class city, the Maharashtra State Housing Policy in its recent proposal (dated 7 April 2015) aims at a stricter implementation of 'Slum-free Maharashtra by 2022'.[30] Further, intense global and international investments at local level, booming mall culture and consumerist ethic are precipitating urban violence against young women,[31] thus rapidly transforming the urban landscape of India.

On the other hand, studies dwelling into 'subaltern urbanism' recognize a vibrant 'entrepreneurial space' and political agency in slum and describe a slum as a

[29]A programme launched by the government to increase "citizen–government" interface through residential welfare associations (RWAs) (Ghertner 2014: 171).

[30]See Shalini Nair, http://indianexpress.com/profile/author/shalini-nair/, Mumbai, Published on 15 April 2015.

[31]By 2014, India recorded highest number of rape incidents in the world (Bhowmick 2013).

'terrain of habitation, livelihood and politics' (Roy 2011). In other words, how a new urban cultural identity is perceived to undertake 'entrepreneurial activities' for enhancing competitiveness by engaging with governance mechanisms such as PPPs and networks (Jessop 1997). Similarly, McFarlane (2012), while documenting Mumbai slums, argues that shared 'social, economic and political practices exceeding borders of entrepreneurial models view poverty as a socio-economic potential and poor as 'entrepreneurial subjects'.

Empirically testing such diverse vulnerabilities and contestations, the chapter by Qudsiya Contractor (Chap. 7) argues how a discursive shift from managerial urbanism to entrepreneurial urbanism has spawned new inclusion and collaboration for the urban poor by illustrating the efforts of Muslim slum dwellers towards remaking the *mohalla*, or Muslim locality, in Mumbai. Similarly, the chapter by Xuefei Ren (Chap. 8) critically examines how entrepreneurial forms of urban governance in India have manifested in the form of redevelopment schemes and programmes, citing the case of slums near Chhatrapati Shivaji International Airport in Mumbai. In quest for adequate housing in an entrepreneurial city like Bengaluru, the contribution by Swetha explores how divergent interventions, especially through policies and community mobilization, have inevitably led to differing outcomes. Finally, the chapter by Smitha (Chap. 10) in this volume exposes how the onslaught of urban spatial restructuring process influenced by global capital interacts with localities and subsequently influence the livelihood and mobility of the urban poor in the Bengaluru metropolis. Therefore, much less attention has been paid, on the bottom-up multiple and complex contestation, despair, urban unrest and conflicts within the cities for its explicit 'entrepreneurial' urban redevelopment policies. This volume certainly fills this gap by presenting empirically grounded analysis and by examining how neoliberalism is articulated in terms of political and economic projects, spatial imaginaries and practices of contestations in Indian cities (with an emphasis on Bengaluru, Chennai, New Delhi and Mumbai).

Discussion: Contextualizing 'Entrepreneurial Urbanism' in India

Based on the reviews, the main arguments in support of 'Entrepreneurial Urbanism in India' are as follows: (i) foremost, there is a clear evidence of transition from 'government' to 'governance' through state-sponsored neoliberal policies and programmes, perpetuating political and spatial restructuring process which is inherently 'entrepreneurial'; (ii) secondly, state retreat, i.e., Keynesian sense of 'welfare state' is replaced by state as a 'facilitator' or 'steering' networks dedicated to the state's mission of superfluous 'image building', 'neoliberal interurban competitiveness' and 'innovation' in collusion with private, corporate, donor, and international financial organizations, while severely compromising on service delivery, equity and social welfare; (iii) thirdly, the emergence of 'new urban space' of partnerships and coalitions is replacing the formal decision-making circuits of local governments as a part of redesigning the form and function of urban governance; (iv) finally, urban citizenship has been reconstituted which is closely articulated within 'neoliberal' framework.

Such structural and institutional transformative processes and practices of several Indian cities clearly demonstrate a transition from managerialism to an affirmative 'entrepreneurial' style of urban planning and urban governance that constitutes the core of neoliberalism (Harvey 1989: 4; Jessop and Sum 2000a; Aranya 2003: 13), almost symbolizing the marginalization of local planning and elected local bodies in the spatial decision-making process of the city. The current political and economic restructuring model in Indian metros has a striking resemblance to similar restructuring projects and shifts being pursued in many world cities as a part of the globalization agenda through the 1980s (Harvey 1989; Jessop 2002; Chapin 2002; MacLeod 2002; Brenner 2003; Aranya 2008; Genis 2007). Post-1990s, studies have dealt with the dynamics of urbanization and processes from diverse perspectives, such as studies by Shaw (2007) and Banerjee-Guha (2010), examining transitional cities and their impact from the perspective of globalization and economic liberalization. One such urban transformation was captured in the work by Anjaria and MacFarlane (2011) based on grounded research on politics of urban space in South Asia, i.e. Indian, Pakistan, Nepal and Sri Lanka. The work by Desai and Romola (2012) explores Indian cities through the analytical lens of 'urban citizenship'. The most recent research on the political economy of Indian cities is by Shatkin (2013) examining the changing dynamics of political power and its implications on spatial and social development in Indian cities. Despite such rich illuminating literature on the changing urban contours in India (by Annapurna Shaw, Isa Baud, Renu Desai, Gavin Shatkin, K.C. Sivaramakrishnan and so on), yet there is a shortcoming in understanding how the state continues be part of 'entrepreneurialism urbanism' which has been explicitly mediated through local sociopolitical and socio-spatial trajectories, shaping and reshaping urban systems in South Asia, particularly in India.

The emphasis of this volume, therefore, is to contextualize the urban entrepreneurial initiatives and projects produced within the local context defined by interplay of institutional frameworks, policy regimes, regulatory practices and political struggles across broad spectrum of spatial scales in Indian cities. This volume provides diverse empirical evidence from cities of India (especially from New Delhi, Mumbai, Bangalore, Chennai), on how national and local political economic restructuring processes produce new forms of governance that are is ostensibly 'entrepreneurial' by firstly, exploring the specific institutional and organizational reorientation and spatial landscape during the neoliberal regime at the local level; secondly, how the local governments regulate urban development projects and assess the concomitant effects and implications of a rather passive relationship between urban government and citizens within the mode of 'entrepreneurial governance' i.e. social exclusion, urban inequality and sociopolitical contestation; thirdly, the purpose is to generate analytical lens by exploring several social contradictions and complex contestations expressed in everyday life operating through divergent political and institutional landscapes which can be described blatantly as 'entrepreneurial'. By doing so, the analysis in this volume contributes to examining twin processes: to explore how the state is 'less' involved (i.e. roll back of the state) in the local urban development projects in terms of deploying seemingly 'entrepreneurial' in differentiated ways (in collusion with private, corporate, RWAs or NGOs etc.) and, secondly, this book highlights other contemporary processes parallel to neo-liberalization impacting upon urban citizenry. This volume presents substantive analysis on how urban governance and local responses within a specific sociopolitical and spatial context forming distinctively 'entrepreneurial' thrive in the cities of South Asia, particularly in India.

The volume, therefore, contributes richly by documenting the theoretical context, competing discourses, narratives, organizational approaches, and the forces that reshape urban governance. Diverse perspectives—different in terms of social and geographical location of researchers and case studies, as well as differing theoretical and political leanings—enrich this volume by exploring 'entrepreneurial' narratives in Indian context. The focus is on how state-sponsored urban planning, redevelopment and actors are adjusting to the changes brought forward by entrepreneurial urban governance with inherent contradictions of inclusion and exclusion. In this context, this volume is organized into three sections: the first section focuses on how urban governance and institutions (rules, regulations, norms and policies) articulate the 'urban'. This sets the context for the second section focusing on the political economy of urbanization. The third section presents discussions on urban inclusion and exclusion (urban poverty).

Urban Governance and Institutions

The Harvey (1989) model of 'transitional urban governance' argues that 'urban entrepreneurialism' is most often mediated and consolidated through local policies and programmes for creating competitive and business-friendly cities. Urban entrepreneurialism is, therefore, the framework to examine urban policy agendas and programmes of both public and private institutions and actors influencing political economy of urbanization in India. In this regard, two chapters are presented under this subtheme. The chapter by Debolina Kundu and Sudhir Krishna (Chap. 2) argues that urban local governments have become 'entrepreneurial' in three different, interrelated ways. Foremost, the focus of the city agenda has shifted from social policies to economic plans (Harvey 1989). As a consequence, the function of city governments has also changed from delivering social welfare to promoting economic development. Second, different formats of public–private partnership working along with city governments have become popular ways of boosting local economies. Third, practices and discourses initiated by these public–private partnerships are proactive, innovative, and business-friendly. City marketing, land use design, image making, and competition with other cities are all cases in point. To substantiate the argument, the chapter presents the review of programmatic interventions such as JNNURM, Smart City mission and AMRUT to illustrate how cities are made more attractive for global and domestic capital.

The chapter by Sudhira (Chap. 3) is about the emergence of political and bureaucratic entrepreneurship in city governance. The author argues that as citizens and numerous private enterprises contribute to a city's 'growth', institutional structures responsible for planning, management and administration of the city have eventually transformed the notion of the 'entrepreneurial', particularly in matters of governance. Political entrepreneurship, he notes, is reflected in terms of the creation of extra-constitutional bodies to 'manage'/'advise' on city affairs apart from effecting certain amendments to legislations, thereby facilitating greater a role for the state instead of urban local bodies. Similarly, bureaucratic entrepreneurship is evident from the numerous 'parastatals' that have been spun by the bureaucracy, dwelling into the functions of urban local bodies. Based on the above analyses, the author argues that both the political and bureaucratic systems at times work in tandem towards evolving a unique entrepreneurial governance mechanism in the city of Bengaluru. Therefore, the chapter highlights and challenges the city governance as affected by the 'entrepreneurialism'.

Political Economy of Urbanization

The reorientation of urban governance transcending towards 'urban entrepreneurialism' has been clearly identified with the ongoing process of deepening the neo-liberalization of urban politics and forces of economic globalization. Urban political economy clearly demonstrates an accelerated reconfiguring of urban hierarchies and networks. These strategies demonstrate explicit 'entrepreneurial' revealing important insights into the ever expanding global linkages as well as the role of local actors in shaping the urban dynamics and contesting boundaries in the cities of India. Three chapters are presented in this volume exploring such urban dynamics. The chapter by Anjali Karol Mohan (Chap. 4) clearly demonstrates how, in the context of contemporary globalization (ICT-driven) and localization processes, the state is forging network forms of governance which are distinct from hierarchical and market (including PPPs) modes of governance. Labelled as 'post-corporatist' or anti-corporatist, network forms of governance, also referred to as heterarchies, are being posited not just as alternatives to state and markets, but also are capable of addressing the wicked problems of development. Based on the premise that no single actor (private or public) but has the capacity to tackle problems unilaterally, heterarchies are collaboration between the public, private and civil society, each of which constitutes a node in the heterarchy. Heterarchies are based on a reflexive rationality and use negotiation, dialogue and knowledge sharing as their operating code and the state is one node amongst many in the heterarchy, it is a central one and is responsible for 'meta-governance'.

The author examines the municipal Reforms Programme (MRP), an e-governance intervention of the Government of Karnataka (GoK), India, whose organizational and institutional arrangements resemble 'heterarchies', to demonstrate the varying manifestations of the state's centrality. In doing so, the author points to the potentials and pitfalls of heterarchies. The author strongly argues for forging network forms of governance which provide an opportunity for the state to move beyond the neoliberal policy framework of entrepreneurial governance arrangements like PPPs, to achieve the larger public value, while capitalizing on the strengths of the private and civil society actors.

The chapter by Bhuvaneswari Raman (Chap. 5) critically illustrates the manner in which PPP projects are mobilized for transferring urban commons and the land under private tenure forms for speculative urban real estate projects and the risks of which are disproportionately redistributed to the poor- and middle-income households. Further, the chapter throws light on the shifts in urban governance accompanying these projects. The study points out that PPP projects take on different forms including the urban renewal of squatter settlements in the established localities of a city and land development for luxury housing and special economic zones (SEZs) in the periphery. This aspect is further explored with the help of case studies of public–private partnership (PPP), urban renewal and urban infrastructure projects implemented in the cities of New Delhi, Mumbai and Chennai. The first two cases examine the urban renewal projects for land share and redevelopment of squatter settlements under PPP in the centre city neighbourhoods of Mumbai and Delhi. These cases clearly illustrate the use of new planning instruments such as the transfer of development rights (TDRs) with respect to such projects and crafting of laws to neutralize the dissent from below. Further, drawing on the evidence from the corridor development projects on the city's outskirts in Chennai metropolis, the third case examines the promotion of PPP projects for developing for luxury housing and the development of economic corridors. Based on these three cases, the study throws light on the shifting practices of urban governance with respect to the roles of, and relationship between the state and the non-state actors. In this light, this chapter traces the emerging new institutional arrangements and laws (including the real estate developers' bill under review) in facilitating the entry of large private players.

In a similar context, the chapter by Vinay Baindur (Chap. 6) explores how corporate/private entrepreneurs try to move beyond generating profits and provide employment opportunities in terms of creating a more enhanced role for themselves influencing the decision-making processes of the local self-government. Simultaneously, politicians and bureaucrats have recognized that the corporate/private sector can have an increased role in urban policy formulation and planning for promoting brand 'Bengaluru'. In Bengaluru, now actively supported by the elite NGOs, they wield a collective might, lobbying for policy changes in various speculative mega-developmental local projects. Such planned interventions in investment and urban renewal projects are conceived by national and state level task forces, vision group networks and consultants redefining Bengaluru's urban entrepreneurialism and its form of 'competitiveness'.

The author critically questions as follows: (i) What and how have the governance changes been introduced by these groups under a democratically elected local government?; (ii) How does the local government deal with or counter this entrepreneurial approach?; (iii) How does a globalized partnership between the state level politicians and the elite private sector interests (through entrepreneurial planning projects) counter democratic governance?; (iv) Are these partnerships detrimental to local democracy in Bengaluru and do they cause an erosion of local government sovereignty (even before it is fully expressed)? The chapter seeks to illustrate how the democratic processes have been violated for implementing such entrepreneurial development projects such as TenderSURE roads project, the JNNURM funded flyovers on the Outer Ring Road, the elevated road from Silk Board to Electronic City in Bengaluru.

Urban Inclusion and Exclusion

In pursuance of entrepreneurial strategies, global cities have eventually emerged as highly polarized places. The politics of the city is caught between mediating the growing discrepancy between the needs of global capital and the demands of transnational elites impinging upon demographic, socio-economic and spatial dynamics associated with the day-to-day demands of urban residents. Empirical studies on Indian metros clearly demonstrate the failure of governance at the cost of 'glurbanization'[32] strategies on less privileged and less powerful groups. In fact, studies have done to date little to clarify the forms of agency, mobilization and community resistance[33] to explicit 'entrepreneurial' endeavours of governance and planning. Four chapters are presented under the subtheme on urban inclusion and exclusion.

While examining the landscape of Mumbai, as the commercial capital of the country which is influenced by national as well as global capital flows, the chapter by Qudsiya Contractor (Chap. 7) explores how the city's socio-spatial peripheries are transformed or reproduced through active engagement amongst local residents, the state and civil society groups. Through an ethnographic fieldwork in a predominantly Muslim *basti*, the study describes the efforts of Muslim *basti*-dwellers towards remaking the *mohalla* or Muslim locality into a life space far from its stereotypical image as an undesirable, dilapidated, poverty-ridden, criminalized and denationalized urban space. The vast literature on urban entrepreneurialism has raised several theoretical concerns, significant of which is the role of the state and private capital in the disenfranchisement of the urban poor. Others, however, have argued that the discursive shift from managerial urbanism to entrepreneurial urbanism has spawned new sites of inclusion and collaboration for the urban poor.

---

[32]Term coined by Bob Jessop on urban 'entrepreneurial' strategies (Jessop and Sum 2000a).

[33]A framework to understand twenty-first-century metropolises (Roy 2009) of the global south.

However, the author argues that so far the literature has mostly failed (with a few exceptions) to highlight the bottom-up approaches at creating new technologies of governance by finding basic urban infrastructure solutions.

The chapter presents two initiatives as an illustration—the reconstruction of a local mosque in collaboration with a city-based NGO and a redevelopment proposal for a local municipal market through direct negotiations with a private builder. The analysis describes how the efforts of Muslim *basti*-dwellers are transforming a segregated and peripheral yet culturally vibrant life space by engaging with state actors through 'slum' redevelopment programmes as well as collaborating with civil society groups. The study provides a unique perspective on the processes of urban transformation shaped by global flows of capital, ideas and technologies in creating environments where claims to and ownership of the city's material (land, property) as well as sociocultural resources are (re)configured by local Muslim residents. As urban citizens and entrepreneurial subjects, they not only re-imagine the *mohalla* reunited with the city's socio-spatial landscape but also actively engage in remaking it.

The chapter by Xuefei Ren (Chap. 8) critically examines entrepreneurial forms of urban governance in India of the new millennium based on a case study of the redevelopment of the slums near the international airport in Mumbai. The chapter illustrates how such a redevelopment plan of the slums surrounding the international airport, however, has met with a strong resistance from residents, community organizations and NGOs. Several attempts of surveying the area by state agencies—in order to verify eligibility for rehabilitation—were blocked by residents and eventually, the plan has been put on hold since 2011. Based on new fieldwork conducted in 2014, this chapter narrates the messy politics of redevelopment in Mumbai and argues that the blockage of global city projects such as redevelopment of the airport slums has to be explained by both the strength of the civil society and the fragmentation of local state power, as well as the mediation of the two through electoral politics.

The chapter by Swetha Rao Dhananka (Chap. 9) compares two communities of the urban poor in the entrepreneurial city of Bengaluru in their quest for accessing adequate housing. The tactics reflect the agency of disadvantaged communities in the city. Civil society organizations (CSOs) intervened to help both the communities. One community accessed housing allotted under a public scheme called 'Basic Services to the Urban Poor' (BSUP) and the other relied on the means of mobilization and negotiation that assured land tenure to plan their own-built environment. The study reveals how the encounter between claim-making communities and political opportunities (Kriesi et al. 1995) is articulated on the one hand through bureaucracy and, on the other, through a political nexus that sustains entrepreneurial governance being challenged by the mobilization of the urban poor. This study reveals that innovation is applied in novel ways to navigate policy, political actors and to stand out of the competition amongst the urban poor. The cases in this study further show how social skill (Fligstein and McAdam 2011) of the community and brokerage by CSOs foster confidence, build strategic alliances and enable to constantly come up with innovative strategies to face entrenched politico-institutional structures. Thus, the author recommends that social skill of the community is the key to overcome the exclusionary practices of the entrepreneurial city and assert sustainable housing on their own terms.

The concluding chapter by Smitha Kanekanthi Chandrasekhar (Chap. 10) explores how the onslaught of urban spatial restructuring process influenced by global capital interacts with localities and subsequently influence livelihood and mobility of urbanites by illustrating the case of relocated slum dwellers in the Bengaluru metropolis. The study is based on two slums (namely, Jai Bheemanagar and Basaveswara) that were rehabilitated while implementing the Metro project Phase II by BMRCL. The study captures the changes occurred based on before and after the rehabilitation framework about their socio-economic conditions, livelihood activities, income and mobility. The study critically examines the role and importance of various factors influencing the decisions of slum dwellers particularly as 'passive recipients' while considering a relocation offer. The chapter particularly draws on the experiences of employed slum households in relation to the larger process of urbanization (informality, mobility, and opportunities of empowerment) and entrepreneurial urban policies and planning (resulting in displacement and rehabilitation). The question is of how rehabilitated slum dwellers renegotiate with city spaces as well as the space of their employment opportunities, which offer insights into the spatial reproduction of urban poverty.

Conclusion

The purpose of this volume is to contextualize the entrepreneurial urban initiatives and projects produced within local context and defined by the interplay of institutional frameworks, policy regimes, regulatory practices and local struggles at a broad range of geographical scales. The chapters in this volume provide diverse empirical evidence on how national and local political economic restructuring processes produce new forms of governance that are ostensibly 'entrepreneurial' by exploring (i) the specific institutional and organizational and spatial landscape influenced by the neoliberal reforms; and (ii) concomitantly capture the implications in terms of social exclusion and sociopolitical contestation and local resistance emerging from the implementation of neoliberal projects.

The contributions to this volume is at least at two different levels: first, to document the manifold ways in which urban governance has reconfigured especially the processes involving interplay of actors/stakeholders and organizations, which the literature of entrepreneurialism has ignored; and second, to analyse highly contradictory implications of ongoing spatial practices at the local level in the context of entrepreneurial urban governance in India.

References

Aditya Bharadwaj, K. V. (2016, May 10). New action group has bigwigs, but lacks heft. *The Hindu*. http://www.thehindu.com/news/cities/bangalore/new-action-group-has-bigwigs-but-lacks-heft-in-bengaluru/article8576819.ece. Accessed May 12, 2016.

Anjaria, J. S. (2006). Street hawkers and public space in Mumbai. *Economic and Political Weekly, XLI*(21), 2140–2146.

Anjaria, J. S., & McFarlane, C. (2011). *Urban navigations: Politics, space and the city in South Asia*. London and New Delhi: Routledge.

Anjaria, J. S., & Ulka, A. (2013). The fractured spaces of entrepreneurialism in post-liberalization India. In N. Gooptu (Ed.), *Enterprise culture in neoliberal India: Studies in youth, class, work and media* (pp. 190–205). New York: Routledge.

Aranya, R. (2003). Globalisation and urban restructuring of Bangalore India: Growth of the IT industry, its spatial dynamics and local planning responses. Accessed May 25, 2015. www.isocarp.net/Data/case_studies/255.pdf

Aranya, R. (2008). Location theory in reverse? Location for global production in the IT industry of Bangalore. *Environment and Plan, A 40*, 446–463.

Banerjee-Guha, S. (2002). Shifting cities: Urban restructuring in Mumbai. *Economic and Political Weekly, 37*(2), 121–128.

Banerjee-Guha, S. (2009). Neoliberalising the ‘Urban’: New geographies of power and injustice in Indian cities. *Economic and Political Weekly*, *xliv*(22), 95–107.

Banerjee-Guha, S. (2010). Introduction: Transformative cities in the new global order. In S. Banerjee-Guha (Ed.), *Accumulation by dispossession: Transformative cities in new global order* (pp. 1–16). New Delhi: Sage Publications.

Banerjee-Guha, S. (2011). *Contradictions of ‘development’ in contemporary India*. https://www.opendemocracy.net/openindia/swapna-banerjee-guha/contradictions-of-%E2%80%98development%E2%80%99-in-contemporary-india. Accessed April 9, 2015.

Baud, I., & Dhanalakshmi, R. (2008). ”Negotiated spaces” for representation in Mumbai: Ward committees, advanced locality management and the politics of middle-class activism. *Environment and Urbanisation, 20*, 483–499.

Baviskar, A. (2002). The politics of the city. *Seminar*, *516*, 40–42. At: www.india-seminar.com/2002/516/516%20amita%20baviskar.htm. Accessed January 5, 2016.

Baviskar, A. (2006, September). Demolishing Delhi: World class city in the making. *Mute Magazine*, *5*. http://www.metamute.org. Accessed April 20, 2015.

Baviskar, A. (2011). Spectacular events, city spaces and citizenship: The commonwealth games in Delhi. In J. S. Anjaria & C. McFarlane (Eds.), *Urban navigations: Politics, space and the city in South Asia* (pp. 138–161). New York & London: Routledge.

Benjamin, S. (2004). Urban land transformation for pro-poor economies. *Geoforum, 35*(2), 177–187.

Benjamin, S. (2006). *From income to urban contest in global settings: Chronic poverty in Bangalore*. http://www.chronicpoverty.org/pdfs/India%20Book%202006/chap-4.pdf. Accessed April 6, 2015.

Benjamin, S. (2008a). *Presentation two in contesting spatialities: Do everyday institutional contestations erode the neo-liberal urban reforms agenda?* http://igs.cla.umn.edu/pdf/BenjaminPaper.pdf. Accessed May 30, 2015.

Benjamin, S. (2008b). Occupancy urbanism: Radicalizing politics and economy beyond policy and programs. *International Journal of Urban and Regional Research*, *32*(3), 719–729.

Benjamin, S. (2010). Manufacturing neoliberalism: Lifestyling Indian urbanity. In S. Banerjee-Guha (Ed.), *Accumulation by dispossession: Transformative cities in the new global order* (pp. 92–124). New Delhi: Sage Publications.

Benjamin, S., & Bhuvaneswari, R. (2001). *Democracy, inclusive governance, and poverty in Bangalore* (Working Paper No. 26). International Development Department, School of Public Policy, University of Birmingham, UK. http://www.idd.bham.ac.uk/research/urban-governance/case_studies/wp%2026%20bangalore.pdf. Accessed April 20, 2015.

Benjamin, S., & Bhuvaneswari, R. (2006). Urban futures of poor groups in Chennai and Bangalore: How these are shaped by the relationships between parastatals and local bodies. In N. G. Jayal, A. Prakash, & P. K. Sharma (Eds.), *Local governance in India: Decentralization and beyond* (pp. 221–267). New Delhi: Oxford University Press.

Bhan, G. (2009). "*This is no longer the city I once knew*". Evictions, the urban poor and the right to the city in millennial Delhi. *Environment and Urbanisation, 21*(1), 127–142.

Bhowmick, N. (2013). *Why rape seems worse in India than everywhere else (but actually isn't).* http://world.time.com/2013/11/08/why-rape-seems-worse-in-india-than-everywhere-else-but-actually-isnt/.). Accessed April 6, 2015.

Bjokman, L. (2014). Becoming a slum: From municipal colony to illegal settlement in liberalisation era Mumbai. *International Journal of Urban and Regional Research, 38*(1), 36–59.

Boyle, M., & Hughes, G. (1994). The politics of urban entrepreneurialism in Glasgow. *Geoforum, 25*(4), 453–470.

Brenner, N. (2003). 'Glocalization' as a state spatial strategy: Urban entrepreneurialism and the new politics of uneven development in Western Europe. In J. Peck & H. Yeung (Ed.), *Remaking the global economy: Economic-geographical perspectives* (pp. 197–216). London: Sage Publications. doi:10.4135/9781446216767.n12

Brenner, N. (2004). *New state spaces: Urban governance and the rescaling of statehood.* New York: Oxford University Press.

Brenner, N., Peck, N. J., & Theodore, N. (2010). After liberalization? *Global, 7*(3), 327–345.

Brenner, N., & Theodore, N. (2002a). Cities and the geographies of "Actually Existing Neoliberalism". *Antipode, 34*(3), 349–379.

Brenner, N., & Theodore, N. (2002b). Preface: From the "New Localism" to the spaces of neo-liberalism. *Antipode, 3*(34), 341–347.

Castells, M. (1989). *The informational city.* Oxford: Basil Blackwell.

Chapin, T. (2002). Beyond the entrepreneurial city: Municipal capitalism in San Diego. *Journal of Urban Affairs, 24*(5), 565–581.

Coelho, K., Lalitha, K., & Vijaybaskar, M. (2011). *Infrastructures of consent: Interrogating citizen participation mandates in Indian urban governance* (Working Paper 362). Institute for Development Studies, University of Sussex, Brighton, UK.

Coelho, K., & Venkat, T. (2009). The politics of civil society: Neighbourhood associationism in Chennai. *Economic and Political Weekly, xliv*(26), 358–367.

Desai, R. (2012). Entrepreneurial urbanism in the time of Hindutva: City imagineering, place marketing and citizenship in Ahmedabad. In R. Desai & R. Sanyal (Eds.), *Urbanizing citizenship: Contested spaces in Indian cities* (pp. 31–57). New Delhi: Sage Publications.

Desai, R., & Romola, S. (2012). *Urbanizing citizenship contested spaces in Indian cities.* New Delhi: Sage Publications.

Dupont, V. D. N. (2011). The dream of Delhi as a global city. *International Journal of Urban and Regional Research, 35*, 533–554. doi: 10.1111/j.1468-2427.2010.01027.x.

Ellis, R. (2012). "A World Class City of Your Own!": Civic governmentality in Chennai, India. *Antipode, 44*(4), 1143–1160.

Fligstein, N., & McAdam, D. (2011). Toward a general theory of strategic action fields. *Sociological Theory, 29*(1), 1–26.

Fernandes, J. (2004). The politics of forgetting: Class politics, state power and the restructuring of urban space in India. *Urban Studies, 41*, 2415–2430.

Friedmann, J. (1986). The world city hypothesis, *Development and Change, 17*(1), 69–83.

Friedmann, J. (1995). Where we stand: a decade of world city research. In P. Knox & P. Taylor (Eds.), *World cities in a World System* (pp. 21–47). New York: Cambridge University Press.

Friedmann, J., & Wolff, G. (1982). World city formation: An agenda for research and action. *International Journal of Urban and Regional Research, 6*(3), 309–344.

Gandhi, J. (2015). 100 cities to turn smart, The Hindu. http://www.thehindu.com/news/national/cabinet-nod-for-smart-city-project-atal-rejuvenation-mission/article7154217.ece. Accessed April 30, 2015.

Genis, S. (2007). Globalization of cities: Towards conceptualizing a new politics of place-making in a transnational era. *University of Gaziantep Journal of Social Sciences, 6*(1), 59–77.
Ghertner, A. D. (2011). The nuisance of slums: Environmental law and the production of slum illegality in India. In J. S. Anjaria & C. Mcfarlane (Eds.), *Urban navigations: Politics, space and the city in South Asia* (pp. 23–49). New York & London: Routledge.
Ghertner, A. D. (2014). Gentrifying the state: Governance, participation, and the rise of middle-class power in Delhi. In G. Shatkin (Ed.), *Contesting the Indian City: Global visions and the politics of the local* (pp. 169–207). Oxford: Wiley-Blackwell.
Ghosh, A. (2005). Public-private or a private public? *Economic and Political Weekly, 40*(47), 19–25.
Ghosh, A. (2006). Banking on Bangalore's dream. *Economic and Political Weekly, 41*(8), 1–4.
Gidwani, V., & Bharati, C. (2011). Poverty as geography: Motility, stoppage, and circuits of waste in Delhi. In J. S. Anjaria & C. Mcfarlane (Eds.), *Urban navigations: Politics, space and the city in South Asia* (pp. 50–78). New York & London: Routledge.
Gillen, J. (2009). The co-production of narrative an entrepreneurial city: An analysis of Cincinnati, Ohio in Turmoil, Series B. *Human Geography, 91*(2), 107–122.
Goldman, M. (2010). Speculative urbanism and the making of the next world city. *International Journal of Urban and Regional Research, 35*(3), 555–581.
Gopalan, K. (2013). *Torn in two: Conflicting discourses of globalization and localization*. Germany: LAMBERT Academic Publishing.
Government of India. (2010). *Rajiv Awas Yojana guidelines for slum-free city planning, ministry of housing & urban poverty alleviation*. New Delhi: Government of India.
Hall, T., & Hubbard, P. (1996). The entrepreneurial city: New urban politics, new urban geographies? *Progress in Human Geography, 20*(2), 153–174.
Hall, S., Massey D., & Rustin, M. (2014). After neoliberalism: Analysing the present. In S. Hall, D. Massey, & M. Rustin (Eds.), *After neoliberalism? The kilburn manifesto* (pp. 3–19). Lawrence & Wishart, Independent Radical Publishing.
Harris, J. (2005). *Middle-class activism and poor people's politics: An exploration of civil society in Chennai* (Working Paper Series No. 05–72). Development Studies Institute, London School of Economics and Political Science, London.
Harris, J. (2007). Antinomies of empowerment: Observations on civil society, politics and urban governance in India. *Economic and Political Weekly, XLII*(26), 2716–2724.
Harris, N. (2003). Globalisation and management of Indian cities. *Economic and Political Weekly, 38*(25), 2535–2543.
Harvey, D. (1985). *The urbanisation of capital*. Baltimore: Johns Hopkins University Press.
Harvey, D. (1989). From managerialism to entrepreneurialism: Transformation in urban governance in late capitalism. *Geografiska Annaler. Series B, Human Geography, 71 B*(1), 3–17.
Harvey, D. (2005). *A brief history of neoliberalism*. Oxford: Oxford University Press.
Heitzman, J. (1999). Corporate strategy and planning in the science city: Bangalore as 'Silicon Valley'. *Economic and Political Weekly, XXXIV*(05), PE2–PE11.
Heitzman, J. (2003). Geographic information systems in India's 'Silicon Valley': The impact of technology on planning Bangalore. *Contemporary South Asia, 12*(1), 57–83.
Heitzman, J. (2004). *Network city: Planning the information society in Bangalore*. New Delhi: Oxford University Press.
HLRN. (2011). *Planned dispossession: Forced evictions and the 2010 commonwealth games: Fact finding mission report 14*. Report by housing and land rights network and habitat international coalition. New Delhi: Housing and Land Right Network.
HPEC. (2011). *High power executive committee report*. New Delhi: Planning Commission.
Hubbard, P. (1996). Urban design and city regeneration: Social representation of entrepreneurial landscapes. *Urban Studies, 33*(8), 1441–1461.
Jadhav, R. (2013, September 12). Government to launch slum-free India mission. *The Times of India*. http://timesofindia.indiatimes.com/india/Government-to-launch-slum-free-India-mission/articleshow/22516182.cms. Accessed April 6, 2015.

Jessop, B. (1997). The entrepreneurial city: Re-imaging localities, re-designing economic governance, or re-structuring capital? In N. Jewson & S. MacGregor (Eds.), *Realising cities: New spatial divisions and social transformation* (pp. 28–41). London: Routledge.

Jessop, B. (1998). The enterprise of narrative and the narrative of enterprise: Place marketing and the entrepreneurial city. In T. Hall & P. Hubbard (Eds.), *The entrepreneurial city* (pp. 77–99). Chichester: Wiley.

Jessop, B. (2002). Liberalism, neoliberalism and urban governance: A state-theoretical perspective. *Antipode, 34*(3), 452–472.

Jessop, B., & Sum, N. (2000a). An entrepreneurial city in action: Hong Kong's emerging strategies in and for (inter) urban competition. *Urban Studies, 37*(12), 2290–2315.

Jessop, R. D. (2000b). Globalisation, entrepreneurial cities, and the social economy. In P. Hamel, M. Lustiger-Thaler, & M. Mayer (Eds.), *Urban movements in a global environment* (pp. 81–100). London: Routledge.

Kamath, L., & Vijayabaskar, M. (2009). Limits and possibilities of middle class associations as urban collective actors. *Economic and Political Weekly*, *xliv*(26, 27), 368–376.

Kriesi, H., Koopmans, R., Wilhelm Duyvendak, J., & Giugni, M. G. (1995). *New social movements in Western Europe. A comparative analysis. Comparative and general pharmacology.* London: University of Minnesota Press.

Kundu, D. (2011). Elite capture in participatory urban governance. *Economic and Political Weekly, 46*(10), 23–25.

MacLeod, G. (2002). From urban entrepreneurialism to a 'Revanchist City' on the spatial injustices of Glasgow's Renaissance. *Antipode, 34*(3), 602–624.

Mahesh, A. (2016, May 10). Dear Bangalore Blue Print Action Group, this is not the way to plan the city. *Citizen Matters*. http://bangalore.citizenmatters.in/blogs/ideas-at-work/blog_posts/bangalore-blue-print-action-group-city-planning-bangalore-masterplan. Accessed May 12, 2016.

Manasi, S., & Smitha, K. C. (2013). Urban property ownership records (UPOR) in Karnataka: Computerized land registration system for urban properties. *Urban India, 33*(2), 79–105.

McFarlane, C. (2012). The entrepreneurial slum: Civil society, mobility and the co-production of urban development. *Urban Studies, 49*(13), 2795–2816.

Nair, J. (2000). Singapore is not Bangalore's Destiny. *Economic and Political Weekly, 35*(18), 1512–1514.

Nair, J. (2006). Social municipalism and the New Metropolis. In M. E. John, P. K. Jha, & S. S. Jodhka (Eds.), *Contested transformation: Changing economies* (pp. 125–146). New Delhi: Tulika Books.

Nijman, J. B. F. (2008). Against the odds: Slum rehabilitation in neoliberal Mumbai. *Cities: The International Journal of Urban Policy and Planning*, 25, 75–87

Nijman, J. (2015). India's urban future: Views from the slum. *American Behavioral Scientist, 59* (3), 406–423.

Nisbett, N. (2009). *Growing up in the knowledge society: Living the IT dream in Bangalore*. New Delhi: Routledge.

Ong, A. (2006). *Neoliberalism as exception: Mutations in citizenship and sovereignty*. Durham: Duke University Press.

Planning Commission. (2011). Challenges to urbanisation. In Faster, sustainable and more inclusive growth, an approach to the twelfth five year plan (2012–17), Chapter 12 (pp. 108–114). New Delhi: Planning Commission.

Planning Commission. (2012). *Report of the steering committee on urbanisation: Twelfth five year plan (2012–2017)*. New Delhi: Planning Commission.

Ramanathan, U. (2006). Illegality and the urban poor. *Economic and Political Weekly, 41*(29), 3193–3197.

Ranganathan, M. (2011). The embeddedness of cost recovery: Water reforms and associationism at Bangalore's Fringes. In J. S. Anjaria & C. Mcfarlane (Eds.), *Urban navigations: Politics, space and the city in South Asia* (pp. 165–190). New York & London: Routledge.

Ranganathan, M. (2012). Re-engineering citizenship: Municipal reforms and the politics of 'e-Grievance Redressal' in Karnataka's Cities. In R. Desai & R. Sanyal (Eds.), *Urbanizing citizenship: Contested spaces in Indian cities* (pp. 109–132). New Delhi: Sage Publications.
Roberts, S. M., & Schein, R. H. (1993). The entrepreneurial city: Fabricating urban development in Syracuse, New York. *The Professional Geographer, 45*(1), 21–33.
Roy, A. (2009). The 21st-century metropolis: New geographies of theory. *Regional Studies, 43*(6), 819–830.
Roy, A. (2011). Slumdog cities: Rethinking subaltern urbanism. *International Journal of Urban and Regional Research, 35*(2), 223–238.
Roy, A., & Ong, R. (2011). *Worlding cities: Asian experiments and the art of being global*. London: Wiley-Blackwell.
Sassen, S. (1991). *The global city: New York, London, Tokyo*. Princeton: Princeton University Press.
Sassen, S. (1999). Globalisation and the formation of new claims. In R. A. Beauregard & S. Body-Gendrot (Eds.), *The urban movement* (pp. 99–110). Thousand Oaks: Sage.
Sassen, S. (2002). Locating cities on global circuits. *Environment and Urbanisation, 14*(1), 13–30.
Sbragia, A. (1996). *Debt wish: Entrepreneurial cities, U.S. federalism, and economic development*. Pittsburgh: University of Pittsburgh Press.
Shatkin, G. (2008). The city and the bottom line: Urban megaprojects and the privatization of planning in Southeast Asia, *Environment and Planning A*, 40, 383–401.
Shatkin, G. (2013). Introduction. In G. Shatkin (Ed.), *Contesting the Indian City: Global visions and the politics of the local* (pp. 1–38). Oxford: Wiley Blackwell.
Shaw, A. (1999). Emerging patterns of urban growth in India. *Economic and Political Weekly, 31* (4), 969–978.
Shaw, A. (2007). *Indian cities in transition*, Hyderabad: Orient Longman.
Shaw, A. (2012a). Metropolitan city growth and management in post-liberalized India. *Eurasia Geography and Economics, 53*(1), 44–62.
Shaw, A. (2012b). *Indian cities*. Oxford India Short Introductions, New Delhi: Oxford University Press.
Shaw, A. (2013). Emerging perspectives on small cities and towns. In R. N. Sharma & R. S. Sandhu (Eds.), *Small cities and towns in global era* (pp. 36–58). New Delhi: Rawat Publications.
Shin, H. B. (2007). *'Entrepreneurial' local state: The implications of Beijing's shifting emphasis on urban redevelopment policies*. Asian Research Centre (Working Paper 22). London School of Economics, Asian Research Centre, London.
Shin, H. B. (2009). Residential redevelopment and the entrepreneurial local state: The implications of Beijing's shifting emphasis on urban redevelopment policies. *Urban Studies, 46*, 2815–2839.
Sivaramakrishnan, K. C. (2011a). *Re-visioning Indian cities: The urban renewal mission*. New Delhi: Sage Publications.
Sivaramakrishnan, K. C. (2011b). Urban development and metro governance. *Economic and Political Weekly*, *46*(31), 49-55.
Smith, M. P. (1999). Transnationalism and the city. In R. Beauregar & S. Body-Gendrot (Eds.), *The urban movement* (pp. 119–139). London: Sage Publications.
Smith, N. (1996). *The new urban frontier: Gentrification and revanchist city*. New York: Routledge.
Smitha, K. C. (2010). New forms of urban localism: Service delivery in Bangalore. *Economic and Political Weekly*, *xlv*(8), 73–77.
Sudhira, H. S. (2008). The emergence of world city: Bangalore. In S. Abedin, C. Johnson, R. Hu, & M. Cramer (Eds.), *Connecting cities: India* (pp. 114–137). Sydney, Australia: Metropolis Congress 2008.
The Hindu (2011). Slum-free India scheme to be taken up as national mission. http://www.thehindu.com/news/national/slumfree-india-scheme-to-be-taken-up-as-national-mission/article2358818.ece. Accessed August 15, 2015.

Weinstein, L. (2008). Mumbai's development mafias: Globalization, organized crime and land development. *International Journal of Urban and Regional Research, 32*(1), 22–39.
Weinstein, L. (2011). 'Slum-Free Mumbai' and other entrepreneurial strategies in the making of Mumbai's global downtown. In G. W. McDonogh & M. Peterson (Eds.), *Global downtowns* (pp. 234–252). Pennsylvania: University of Pennsylvania Press.
Weinstein, L. (2012). Democratic urban citizenship and mega-project development in globalizing Mumbai. In R. Desai & R. Sanyal (Eds.), *Urbanizing citizenship: Contested spaces in Indian cities* (pp. 58–81). New Delhi: Sage Publications.
Weinstein, L. (2014). One-man handled': Fragmented power and political entrepreneurship in globalizing Mumbai. *International Journal of Urban and Regional Research, 38*(1), 14–35.
Weinstein, L., Neha, S., & Gavin, S. (2013). Contested developments: Enduring legacies and emergent political actors in contemporary urban India. In G. Shatkin (Ed.), *Contesting the Indian city: Global visions and the politics of the local* (pp. 39–64). Oxford: Wiley-Blackwell.
Wu, L. (2000). The global and local dimensions of place-making: Remaking Shanghai as a world city. *Urban Studies, 37*(8), 1359–1377.
Zerah, M. H. (2007). Middle class neighbourhood associations as political players in Mumbai. *Economic and Political Weekly, XLII*(47), 61–68.
Zerah, M. H. (2009). Participatory governance in urban management and the shifting geometry of power in Mumbai. *Development and Change, 40*(5), 853–877.
Zheng, J. (2011). Creative industry clusters' and the 'Entrepreneurial City' of Shanghai. *Urban Studies, 48*, 3561–3582.

Part I
Urban Governance and Institutions

Chapter 2
Introducing Urban Entrepreneurialism in India: An Analysis of Programmatic Interventions

Debolina Kundu and Sudhir Krishna

Introduction

The pace of Indian urbanization has been slow. According to Census, India's share of urban population in 2011 was 31.16 % which substantiates that India is being described as a 'reluctant urbanizer'. Nonetheless, researchers, international agencies, and policy makers are optimistic that in the next decade or so, the rate of urbanization will increase significantly in the country. This is, in part, because urbanization is a necessary condition for economic growth perceptible in the nation's economic growth. Much of this growth is attributed to the robust urban sector performance, which contributes to over 60 % of the national GDP. On the other hand, infrastructure development in urban India has, however, not kept pace with the growth with the rest of the economy, thereby posing a constraint for sustainable growth process.

It is important to note that most of the urban local bodies (ULBs) in India and especially the smaller ones are weak both in terms of capacity to raise resources and financial autonomy. Their precarious state of finances as well as their complex institutional and fiscal framework does not allow them to make investments in capital works. Hence to empower ULBs to undertake self-resource mobilization activity, delegation of powers enacted 74th Constitutional Amendment Act (CAA), 1992 become necessary. Despite the empowerment and delegation of powers envisioned in the 74th CAA over past three decades ago, most of the ULBs in India are still plagued by serious resource constraints restraining funding even for their routine activities. The ad hoc measures of structural adjustment programmes (SAPs)

D. Kundu (✉)
National Institute of Urban Affairs, New Delhi, India
e-mail: dkundu@niua.org

S. Krishna
Bureau of Indian Standards Committee on Smart City Standards, New Delhi, India

K.C. Smitha (ed.), *Entrepreneurial Urbanism in India*,
DOI 10.1007/978-981-10-2236-4_2

initiated since the late eighties and the economic reforms and liberalization launched in the early nineties opened up the Indian economy. Such open economy policy had significant impact on the capacity to raise resource of the ULBs as well. Further, the Financial Institutions and Reforms Expansion (Debt) component of the USAID launched in the nineties tried to improve local governance in the country by bringing about financial discipline among the ULBs. However, these piecemeal efforts failed to bring about the desired changes in the urban governance structure in India.

Urban local governments transformed entrepreneurial in three different but interrelated ways. First, the focus of the city agenda has shifted from social policies to economic plans. As a consequence, the functions of city governments also change from delivering social welfare to promoting economic development. Secondly, different formats of public–private partnership introduced by city governments have become popular ways of boosting local economies. Third, practices and discourses initiated by these public–private partnerships are proactive, innovative, and business friendly. City marketing, land-use design, image making, and competition with other cities are all cases in point by Jessop and Sum (2000), Ashworth and Woogd (1990). Indian cities, of late, are undergoing a sea change in terms of urban governance and financing policies, increasingly involving the private sector in financing and management of centrally sponsored schemes.

To make cities more attractive for global and domestic capital and bring about infrastructural development, the Jawaharlal Nehru National Urban Renewal Mission (JNNURM) was designed as a reform-linked investment mission. The Mission tried to ensure financially sustainable development of the cities through efficient governance, better infrastructure, and improved service delivery. The Planning Commission's Eleventh and Twelfth Plan document further adds that the strategy must also include sector-specific policies to ensure that the structure of growth and the institutional environment in which it occurs, achieves the objective of inclusiveness in all its dimensions. The thrust of this mission-mode programme, i.e. JNNURM, was to ensure improvement in urban governance so that the ULBs become financially sound with enhanced credit rating and ability to access capital market for undertaking new projects.

The Government of India (GoI) has embarked on the ambitious Make in India (2015) initiative to create jobs. Also, attracting investment means that the environment for business must be made investor friendly. The initiative is expected to make cities investor friendly, and the responsibility lies with all levels of the government, the central government laying down the policy guidelines and the state and local governments being responsible for the implementation. According to the World Bank's Enterprise Survey (2014), businesses in India rank corruption as the number one constraint to growth, ahead of factors such as lack of access to electricity, finance, and land. Corruption arises due to the lack of a transparent and effective regulatory framework; this is highlighted in a wide range of global analytics World Bank, KPMG (2015). India ranks 142 out of 189 economies in the World Bank's Doing Business (2015) report, the second worst performing economy in South Asia. The World Economic Forum's Global Competitiveness Report ranks India as 71 out of 144 economies. India is ranked at 93rd on irregular payments and bribes, 59th on burden of government regulation, and 57th on the efficiency of the legal framework in settling disputes.

Given this background, Section "JNNURM: An Overview", analyses the present urban development policies and programmatic interventions in urban India in a bid to make cities more attractive for global and domestic capital. The analysis has been done for the recently completed JNNURM and the newly launched Missions, viz. Smart Cities Mission and AMRUT. The final section presents the overview of the government initiatives for easing constraints and doing business in Indian cities. The last section summarizes the lessons learnt and attempts to delineate a policy perspective for inclusive urban development across the country.

JNNURM: An Overview

JNNURM was a mission-mode programme which aimed at creating 'economically productive, efficient, equitable and responsive Cities' by a strategy of upgrading the social and economic infrastructure in cities. Under the JNNURM, provision of Basic Services to Urban Poor (BSUP) and wide range of urban sector reforms were introduced to strengthen municipal governance in accordance with the 74th Constitutional Amendment Act, 1992. Urban renewal was one of the thrust areas in the National Common Minimum Programme, 2004 of GoI and accordingly the Jawaharlal Nehru National Urban Renewal Mission (JNNURM) was launched on 3 December 2005 with an investment of Rs 50,000 crore in the mission period of seven years beginning from 2005/06.[1] The mission was the single largest initiative of the Government of India for planned urban development that integrated two pressing needs of urban India: massive investments required for infrastructure development and reforms those required to sustain investments. Since inception, the JNNURM mission focused on sectors such as water supply, sewerage, drainage and urban transport under the component of Urban Infrastructure Governance (UIG). The JNNURM had two submissions for the mission cities,[2] viz. (1) Urban Infrastructure and Governance (UIG) and (2) Basic Services to the Urban Poor (BSUP). Projects such as construction of roads, improving public transport, trunk network of water supply, sanitation, solid waste management and storm water drains, construction of multilevel parking lots and city beautification, etc., have been taken up under the UIG component. The JNNURM, besides attempting infrastructure development (ID) and reform in governance in 65 select cities through its ID component, was expected to provide the poor in selected cities access to basic services and land with tenurial security through its submission BSUP.

[1]The Mission was extended for 2 more years for the completion of the stipulated reforms and projects.

[2]The select 65 cities for UIG component are called mission cities.

Further, the JNNURM was expected to cater to the non-mission cities under the two components, namely (1) UIG of the Urban Infrastructure Development Scheme for Small and Medium Towns (UIDSSMT) and the Integrated Housing and Slum Development Programme (IHSDP). The programme was expected to cover all other municipal towns under the UIDSSMT. The existing programme of Infrastructure Development Scheme for Small and Medium Towns (IDSMT) and Accelerated Urban Water Supply Programme (AUWSP) has been subsumed under UIDSSMT. Like-wise, the existing Valmiki Ambedkar Awas Yojana (VAMBAY) and the discontinued National Slum Development Programme (NSDP) have been subsumed with IHSDP. Interestingly, the indicative allocation of JNNURM is biased against the non-mission cities/towns as the share of UIDSSMT and IHSDP works out to be 16 and 14 %, respectively. The remaining share of about 70 % funds is directed towards the selected 65 mission cities (JNNURM 2014).

Implementation of the JNNURM gave further impetus to urban sector reforms with renewed focus on urban renewal. The programme has been successful in enabling ULBs to execute projects on a larger scale which they never attempted earlier, resulting in improved project planning, implementation and capacity building. The programme has also led to many good practices and innovations which helped states and ULBs to maintain the momentum of urban transformation. However, these efforts have been limited to the developed states and big cities therein, thereby increasing the interstate and intercity disparities at all levels of urban development (Kundu and Samanta 2011).

Effectiveness of Reforms

The JNNURM was a landmark initiative placing India's urban agenda at a centre stage for the first time in its development history. It provided resources to the states with conditionality for the implementation of reforms and preparation of viable detailed project reports (DPRs). This necessitated the states and the ULBs to initiate reforms in accordance with 74th CAA and adhere to the guidelines set by JNNURM as well as commitments made by them as per the memorandum of agreement (MoA) at the beginning of the mission period.

A detailed review of the status of reform implementation at the end of mission period reveals that states which are economically advanced have taken reform initiatives ahead of others while the rest are at different stages of implementation (see Table 2.1). Many reasons could be attributed for delay in the implementation of reforms. Foremost, during the launch of the mission, there was lack of clarity in the nature of the reforms and inadequate specification of the processes involved. While there was some delay on the part of the Ministry of Urban Development in clarifying the content of reforms at the same time most of the state governments did not take serious initiative to understand, implement and sustain the reforms. As per the guidelines, states were expected to design reforms in collaboration with cities, but the exercise often became one of satisfying the technicalities' of reform and

Table 2.1 Status of achievement of reforms till Jan 2014

State	*Reform achievement (%)
Tamil Nadu	96.20
Karnataka	95.40
Andhra Pradesh	93.30
Gujarat	92.00
Himachal Pradesh	91.70
Kerala	91.30
Maharashtra	90.80
Chhattisgarh	89.70
Uttar Pradesh	88.70
Rajasthan	86.50
Delhi	86.30
Madhya Pradesh	86.00
Punjab	85.90
West Bengal	83.90
Jammu & Kashmir	81.70
Puducherry	81.30
Goa	78.20
Orissa	76.80
Tripura	74.30
Uttarakhand	73.90
Assam	72.30
Mizoram	72.20
Bihar	71.70
Haryana	70.50
Chandigarh	70.00
Meghalaya	69.00
Jharkand	65.10
Arunachal Pradesh	50.40
Manipur	48.90
Sikkim	48.70
Nagaland	43.30

Source www.jnnurm.nic.in
*Only for UIG Cities

drawing funds from the Government of India (GoI). For instance, introduction of the property title reform is one such reform where the state and the respective ULB were to initiate. However, given the complexity involved in the implementation of this reform, not much progress was achieved. However, the government eventually eased the method of appraisal and grants tied to reform compliance were released. Similarly, the reform on re-use of recycled water makes it mandatory for the respective ULBs to revise building by-laws to reflect re-use of recycled water and dissemination on their website. Further, the state governments took initiatives to revise the building—by-laws without assessing the capacities of ULBs to implement it. For instance, in Himachal Pradesh, the ULBs have revised the building byelaws but because of the unsuitable physical terrain, recycling and re-use was not deemed a feasible option.

Table 2.1 shows that until Jan 2014 only 7 states have been able to implement 90 % of the reforms. The north-eastern states (except Meghalaya, Mizoram and Tripura) have shown slow progress (less than 50 %.). Table 2.2 shows the achievement of state-level mandatory reforms against the set milestone. At present the score of the reform is calibrated on a standardized set of checklist. The cities are at the various stages of compliance. The score[3] of the reform needs to be calibrated on the basis of size of the city and reform compliance. JNNURM has achieved by providing a fresh momentum to the 74th Constitutional Amendment. ULBs which were inactive for decades have put in place the institutional structure by conducting municipal elections and constituting ward committees. However, even now, only 11 states have been able to transfer the function of the 12th Schedule to ULBs. In fact, many ULBs are not in a position to take over all the functions mentioned under the 12th Schedule of the 74th Constitutional Amendment, as they do not have the capacity to delivery services, such as fire services, roads and bridges, water supply, sewerage and urban forestry.

As many as 18 states have rationalized stamp duty by reducing it to 5 % (see Table 2.2). However, many of the states while reducing the stamp duty to 5 %, have also increased the surcharge to 2 or 3 % for the ULBs, thereby, increasing the total duty. So far 20 states have made desired amendments in the Rent Control Act. Though community participation law has been enacted in majority of the states, yet the pace of implementation has been slow. The 'Area Sabha'—i.e. the third tier body is the representation of people at the level of polling booth. However, creation of third tier body does not hold true for all the cities considering different population ranges of the cities. Most of the states have enacted a Public Disclosure Law but have not implemented them fully.

As per the JNNURM guidelines, the ULBs have to implement thirteen reforms which enable the ULBs to function efficiently, bring about simplification and transparency in the system of local governance and ensure that service delivery is equitable, dependable, cost-effective and sustainable.

So far ULBs have made necessary amendments in the municipal acts to incorporate most of the reforms. The implementation of e-governance in ULBs aimed at improving the system of local governance through use of information technology

[3]In September 2012, it was decided to include calibration of scores for each of the 23 reforms. Equal score of 10 was assigned to each of the reforms, irrespective of whether the reform was simple or complex, so that the total added up to 230. This was based on assigning predetermined marks/scores to each of the reform milestones in a disaggregated manner. Thus, if a state and a mission city have complied with all the reforms, it gets a score of 100 %.

Table 2.2 Status of state-level mandatory reforms

State-level reforms	Milestones	Number of states	States
Transfer of schedule 12th functions	States that have transferred all functions	11	Chhattisgarh, Gujarat, Himachal Pradesh, Jammu and Kashmir, Jharkhand, Kerala, Madhya Pradesh, Maharashtra, Orissa, Punjab, Puducherry
Constitution of MPCs	States that have constituted MPCs	7	Chandigarh, Karnataka, Maharashtra, Punjab, Rajasthan, Tamil Nadu, West Bengal
Reform in Rent Control Acts	States that have amended the Rent Control Act	20	Andhra Pradesh, Chandigarh, Chhattisgarh, Delhi, Goa, Himachal Pradesh, Jammu and Kashmir, Jharkhand, Karnataka, Madhya Pradesh, Mizoram, Nagaland, Punjab, Puducherry, Rajasthan, Sikkim, Tamil Nadu, Tripura, Uttar Pradesh, West Bengal
Reduction of stamp duties	States that have reduced stamp duty to 5 %	18	Andhra Pradesh, Assam, Chandigarh, Chhattisgarh, Delhi, Goa, Gujarat, Himachal Pradesh, Jharkhand, Karnataka, Maharashtra, Orissa, Punjab, Puducherry, Rajasthan, Tamil Nadu, Uttar Pradesh, Uttarakhand
Enactment of community participation law (CPL)	States that have passed CPL or incorporated relevant, provisions into the existing laws	13	Andhra Pradesh, Assam, Gujarat, Himachal Pradesh, Jammu and Kashmir, Karnataka, Kerala, Maharashtra, Mizoram, Tamil Nadu, Tripura, Uttar Pradesh, West Bengal
Enactment of public disclosure law (PDL)	States that have passed Public Disclosure Acts	27	Andhra Pradesh, Assam, Bihar (Bodhgaya), Chandigarh, Chhattisgarh, Goa, Gujarat, Haryana, Himachal Pradesh, Jammu and Kashmir, Jharkhand, Karnataka, Kerala, Madhya Pradesh, Maharashtra, Meghalaya, Mizoram, Nagaland, Orissa, Punjab, Puducherry, Rajasthan, Tamil Nadu, Tripura, Uttar Pradesh, Uttarakhand, West Bengal

1. 74th CAA is not applicable in Meghalaya Constitution of MPC is not applicable in Arunachal Pradesh, Assam, Chhattisgarh, Himachal Pradesh, J&K, Manipur, Meghalaya, Mizoram, Nagaland, Orissa, Sikkim, Tripura, Uttarakhand, and Puducherry
2. Repeal of ULCRA is not applicable in H.P, Manipur, Nagaland, and Kerala
3. Rent control reform is not applicable in Orissa, Manipur, and Nagaland

Source www.jnnurm.nic.in

(IT). There were eight modules[4] to be implemented by the ULBs. Among these, registration of birth and death and redress of grievances through e-governance have been implemented by the majority of the cities. However, only 29 cities have been able to implement all the eight modules. Also, most of the larger municipalities have shifted to the accrual accounting system based on double-entry bookkeeping.

Property tax is the principal source of revenue for the ULBs in India. However, over the past few decades, the system of assessment in most of the ULBs was based on annual rental value, which was non-transparent. To strengthen the resource base of local bodies, a transparent and non-discretionary property tax reforms were introduced to encourage voluntary compliance of citizens through the adoption of area-based system of property taxation. This was an important measure for improving the tax base and to strengthen the local economic development. But introduction of this reform showed mixed results. Though GIS-based property taxation has not been introduced completely in many of the ULBs, property tax coverage in most of the cities has improved through this reform. After implementation of property tax reform, 41 cities have been able to bring more than 85 % of the properties under the coverage of property tax net and the tax collection of 28 cities has been more than 90 % of the total demand (see Table 2.3).

In addition, cities have started levying water charges to recover part of the O&M cost but not to the extent of 100 % as stipulated for implementation of urban sector reforms. So far, only 7 cities have been able to do so. In most of the cities user charges related to solid waste management (SWM) is collected as a percentage of property tax or as conservancy tax. However, cities such as Bengaluru and Mumbai collect separate charges for SWM. Since property tax collection is not a buoyant source of revenue, a percentage of SWM collection only meets the operating cost. The objective of promoting services to be self-sustainable has been partially achieved and 100 % of the O&M cost could be achieved only if the initiatives by the ULBs are sustained.

In a span of seven years, implementation of all the 23 reforms was a challenge for most of the states. In order to access the funds, most of the states and cities were in a hurry to pass legislations and office orders without having much know-how as regards the reform per se or their long-term consequences. Many ULBs were not in a position to implement several reforms due to lack of financial assistance for the implementation of the reforms, for instance, the accounting reforms and the GIS-based property taxation. The process of reform implementation was slow for reforms such as introduction of property title certification, simplification of legal and procedural framework for the conversion of agricultural land for non-agricultural purposes due to the presence of multiple agencies and the fact that amending different Acts related to different agencies falls beyond the purview of the urban development department of the state.

---

[4]Eight modules include property tax, accounting, water supply and other utilities, birth and death certificate, citizen grievance monitoring, personnel management system, building plan approval, and health programmes.

Table 2.3 Status of ULB-level mandatory reforms (as on Jan 2014)

ULB-level reform	Milestones	No of cities which have achieved the reform	Name of cities
Property tax	85 % coverage	41	Hyderabad, Vijayawada, Viskhapatnam, Guwahati, Bodhgaya, Chandigarh, Raipur, Panaji, Ahmedabad, Surat, Vadodara, Rajkot, Porbandar, Faridabad, Bangalore, Mysore, Kochi, Tiruvananthapuram, Bhopal, Indore, Jabalpur, Nagpur, Nanded, Nashik, Pune, Greater Mumbai, Shillong, Puri, Amritsar, Puducherry, Chennai, Coimbatore, Lucknow, Kanpur, Allahabad, Varanasi, Agra, Mathura, Meerut, Nainital, Kolkata
	90 % tax collection	28	Vijayawada, Visakhapatnam, Tirupati, Chandigarh, Raipur, Ahmedabad, Surat, Vadodara, Rajkot, Bangalore, Kochi, Tiruvananthapuram, Bhopal, Indore, Nagpur, Nanded, Nashik, Pune, Greater Mumbai, Shillong, Chennai, Lucknow, Kanpur, Allahabad, Varanasi, Agra, Mathura, Meerut
User charges	100 % cost recovery in water supply and SWM	7	Hyderabad, Delhi Jal Board (DJB) (Water Supply), Surat, Nanded, Nashik, Pune, Greater Mumbai
Double-entry accounting system	Cities which have migrated to double-entry accrued based accounting system	37	Hyderabad, Viskhapatnam, Tirupati, Patna, Bodhgaya, MCD, NDMC, DJB, Ahmedabad, Surat, Vadodara, Shimla, Jammu, Srinagar, Ranchi, Bangalore, Mysore, Kochi, Tiruvananthapuram, Bhopal, Indore, Jabalpur, Ujjain, Nagpur, Nashik, Pune, Greater Mumbai, Bhubaneswar, Jaipur, Ajmer, Chennai, Madurai, Coimbatore, Agartala, Dehradun, Kolkata, Asansol

(continued)

Table 2.3 (continued)

ULB-level reform	Milestones	No of cities which have achieved the reform	Name of cities
e-governance	Cities that have implemented all the 8 modules	29	Hyderabad, Viskhapatnam, Tirupati, MCD, NDMC, DJB, Ahmedabad, Surat, Rajkot, Bangalore, Mysore, Kochi, Tiruvananthapuram, Bhopal, Indore, Jabalpur, Nagpur, Nanded, Nashik, Pune, Greater Mumbai, Ludhiana, Jaipur, Ajmer, Chennai, Madurai, Coimbatore, Lucknow, Kanpur
Internal earmarking of funds for services to urban poor	Which services?	49	Hyderabad, Vijayawada, Viskhapatnam, Tirupati, Raipur, MCD, NDMC, DJB, Ahmedabad, Surat, Rajkot, Vadodara, Faridabad, Shimla, Jammu, Srinagar, Bangalore, Mysore, Kochi, Tiruvananthapuram, Bhopal, Indore, Jabalpur, Ujjain, Nagpur, Nanded, Nashik, Pune, Greater Mumbai, Shillong, Amritsar, Ludhiana, Puducherry, Jaipur, Ajmer, Pushkar, Chennai, Madurai, Coimbatore, Agartala, Lucknow, Kanpur, Allahabad, Varanasi, Agra, Mathura, Meerut, Kolkata, Asansol
Provision of basic services to urban poor (BSUP)	Services done so far under BSUP?	46	Hyderabad, Viskhapatnam, Tirupati, Guwahati, Patna, Bodhgaya, Chandigarh, Raipur, DJB (WS), Panaji, Ahmedabad, Surat, Vadodara, Rajkot, Shimla, Jammu, Srinagar, Ranchi, Bangalore, Mysore, Kochi, Tiruvananthapuram, Bhopal, Indore, Jabalpur, Ujjain, Nagpur, Nanded, Nashik, Pune, Greater Mumbai, Ludhiana, Puducherry, Chennai, Madurai, Coimbatore, Agartala, Lucknow, Kanpur, Allahabad, Varanasi, Agra, Mathura, Meerut, Kolkata, Asansol

Source www.jnnurm.nic.in

An analysis of the funds released till September 2009 shows that only 58 % of the urban population had been covered during the initial four years (Kundu 2009) and this share is unlikely to have increased substantially. On an average 70 % of the total funds had been released till January 2014 in the mission cities. Only 13 states had received more than three-fourths of the total funds committed. On the other hand, only 40 % of the projects had been completed in spite of the fact that the duration of the mission deadline was March 2014. The time granted for the completion of projects was approximately two years. According to the Mid-Term Review of the JNNURM Performance Audit of JNNURM (CAG 2012), there are two main reasons for the slow release of central grants: firstly, the lack of capacity of the state to develop plans, prioritize projects and raise matching funds and, secondly, the inability of state governments to meet reform conditionalities slowed down availability of fund.

Overview of the Current Missions

There has been an increasing realization that good urban policies are prerequisites for economic and social development of cities. These need to be geared up not only for revamping urban institutional structures to improve the squalor and inefficiencies of the existing urban centres but also could boost flow of both domestic and foreign funds to the cities.

Various flagship schemes have been launched aiming to change the face of urban India with expected investments around Rs 4 trillion over the next few years. Given the multiplier potential of construction industry, the schemes are expected to assist create jobs to boost the economy. The present section overviews these interventions.

The Smart City Mission (SCM) 2015

The current Missions are directed towards innovative interventions and induce private sector participation in financing urban development in India. Involvement of the private sector in the creation and maintenance of urban utilities is expected to bring more investment in the urban sector which ultimately would create investor friendly cities. The Smart Cities Mission is an outcome-oriented programme—aiming to introduce citizen-friendly governance, and cost-effective services—relying on online services to bring about accountability and transparency. The mission promotes application of smart solutions to infrastructure and services in area-based development. The mission is based on convergence of area plans with national- and state-level sectoral financial plans, for example, the Atal Mission for Rejuvenation and Urban Transformation (AMRUT), Housing for All, HRIDAY, Swachh Bharat, and Digital India.

The Smart City proposals are expected to be citizen-driven taking into account the issues, needs, and priorities of citizens. Besides, the planning and monitoring of the mission is expected to be evidence-based. A total of 98 cities (see Fig. 2.1) have been selected for the SCM on the basis of city challenge competition. In the first stage, each state and union territory gave a score to their cities on the basis of four parameters, which includes existing service levels, institutional system and capacity, self-financing, and past track records. Based on scores, states nominated the top 98 cities and the top 20 cities among them have been selected for the funding in the first phase.

Fig. 2.1 Location of smart cities in India. *Source* Author

Special Purpose Vehicle (SPV)

The implementation of mission at the city level will be done by an SPV. The SPV will plan, appraise, approve, release funds, implement, manage, operate, monitor, and evaluate the smart city development projects. Each smart city will consist of an SPV headed by a CEO and board consisting of nominees from the central government, state government, and ULB. The states/ULBs shall ensure the following: (a) a dedicated and substantial revenue stream is made available to the SPV to make it self-sustainable and evolve its own credit worthiness for raising additional resources from the market; (b) government contribution for smart city is used only to create infrastructure that has public benefit outcomes. Thus, the execution of projects may be done through joint ventures, subsidiaries, public–private partnership (PPP), turnkey contracts, etc., suitably dovetailed with revenue streams.

At the city level, the SPV will be a limited company incorporated under the Companies Act, 2013, in which the state/UT and the ULB will constitute promoters with 50:50 equity shareholding. The private sector or financial institutions could be considered for taking equity stake in the SPV, provided the shareholding pattern of 50:50 of the state/UT and the ULB is retained. Further, state/UT and the ULB together must hold majority shareholding and control of the SPV.

It is proposed to give complete flexibility to the SPV to implement and manage the smart city project, while the state/ULB will undertake measures to support. The SPV may appoint project management consultants (PMCs) for designing, developing, managing, and implementing area-based projects. SPVs are expected to take assistance from any of the empanelled consulting firms in the list prepared by the MoUD and the handholding agencies. The state/ULB financial rules will be followed for the procurement of goods and services, transparent, and fair procedures. Model frameworks as developed by the MoUD will be used for smart city projects.

The Smart City Mission encourages the state government and the ULBs to adopt the following 'best practices' to empower SPVs and as provided under the municipal act:

(1) Delegating the rights and obligations of the municipal council with respect to the smart city project to the SPV.
(2) Delegating decision-making powers available to the ULB under the municipal act/government rules to the chief executive officer of the SPV.
(3) Delegating the approval or decision-making powers available to the urban development department/local self-government department/municipal administration department to the board of directors of the SPV in which the state and ULB are represented.
(4) Delegating the matters that require the approval of the state government to the state-level High Powered Steering Committee (HPSC) for the smart cities.

The key functions and responsibilities of the SPV include, inter alia, approval and sanction of the projects including their technical appraisal; execution of the smart city proposal with complete operational freedom; taking measures to comply with the requirements of MoUD with respect to the implementation of the smart cities programme; mobilizing resources within timelines and taking measures necessary for the mobilization of resources; approval and action upon reports of a third-party review and monitoring agency; overview of capacity building activities; review of activities of the mission, including budget, implementation of projects, preparation of SCP and coordination with other missions/schemes, and activities of various ministries; monitoring and review of quality control related matters and acting upon issues arising thereof; incorporating joint ventures and subsidiaries and entering into public–private partnerships as may be required for the implementation of the smart cities programme; entering into contracts, partnerships, and service delivery arrangements as may be required for the implementation of the smart cities mission; and determining and collecting user charges as authorized by the ULB and collecting taxes, surcharges etc., as authorized by the ULB.

The key functions and responsibilities of the SPV are to incorporate joint ventures and subsidiaries and enter into public–private partnerships as may be required for the implementation of the smart cities programme. The smart city proposals are being evaluated based on the analysis of financing plan and the sources of funding. The project cost of each smart city proposal will vary depending upon the level of ambition, model, and capacity to execute and repay. It is anticipated that substantial funds will be required to implement the smart city proposal and, towards this end, government grants of both the central and state will be leveraged to attract funding from both internal and external sources.

The success of this endeavour will depend upon the robustness of SPV's revenue model and comfort provided to lenders and investors. A number of state governments have successfully set up financial intermediaries (such as Tamil Nadu, Gujarat, Odisha, Punjab, Maharashtra, Karnataka, Madhya Pradesh, and Bihar) which can be tapped for support, while other states may consider some similar set up in their respective states. Some form of guarantee by the state or such a financial intermediary could be considered as instrument of comfort. It is expected that a number of schemes in the smart city will be taken up on PPP basis and the respective SPVs have to accomplish the set agenda.

Building new smart cities and transforming the metros will need huge funds; investments of INR 98,000 crores is to be brought into the cities through the Smart Cities Mission, under which 100 smart cities would be built, and AMRUT for 500 cities over the next five years (Mathew 2015). Only about 50 % of this amount is supposed to come from the central government, and the rest has to be shared by the states and the ULBs. ULBs in most Indian cities are not in a position to shell out the entire requirements and are looking for raising funds from the private sector. In particular for the Smart Cities Mission, it is extremely crucial for the cities to find sources of funding in order to execute the plans as per the proposals. Although all the 20 proposals talk about convergence with other schemes both at the centre and the state levels, majority of the funding is dependent on the Smart City Mission funds, PPP, and multilateral/bilateral assistance.

Madhya Pradesh is leading with 3 cities followed by Maharashtra, Gujarat, Rajasthan, Andhra Pradesh, Tamil Nadu, and Karnataka with 2 each. Odisha, Kerala, Punjab, Assam, and Delhi have 1 city each. Among the 20 cities, Bhubaneswar was the top scorer during the appraisal followed by Pune and Jaipur. It is quite interesting to note that medium-sized cities such as Solapur, Davanagere, and Belagavi have made it through the first round of challenge, while many other mega cities have not been able to make it to the first list. Among these cities, Indore has the maximum proposed budget of INR 5099.60 crores followed by Bhubaneswar (INR 4537 crores) and Jabalpur (INR 3998.5 crores), and Ludhiana has the least budget of INR 1191.18 crores.

A closer look into the financial proposals of the 20 selected cities has revealed that the 20 select cities have proposed an investment of INR 50,802 crores over five years. Ten of the 20 cities have proposed to mobilize INR 8521 crores under the PPP model, while others have also indicated this option. A total area of 26,735 acres has been identified by these cities for making them smart through necessary interventions (Press Information Bureau 2016). Figure 2.2 shows the various sources of funding as proposed by the cities in their respective SCPs. As per the given template for submission of the plans, all the cities had to detail out the financial plan (part E of all the submitted proposals) in which the ULBs had to evaluate their own capacities (also the SPVs) to undertake self-funded development projects, the availability of funds from other government schemes that will converge in SCP and the finance that can be raised from the financial market. The cities

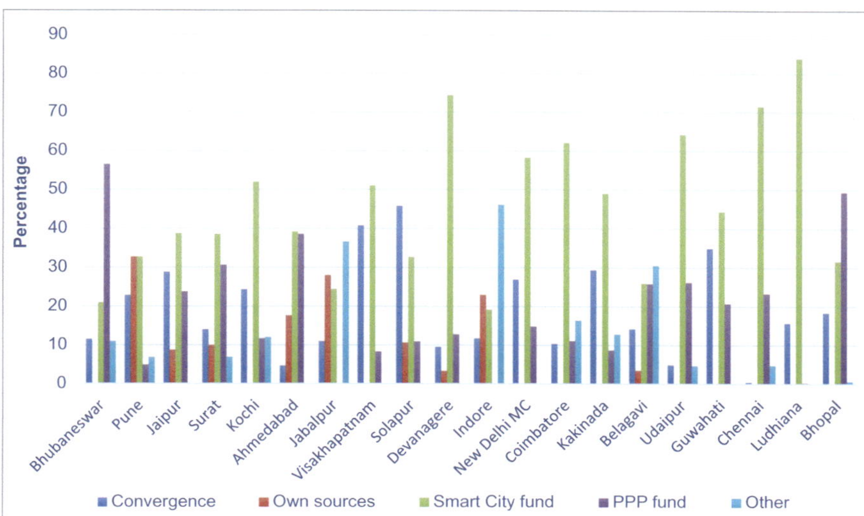

Fig. 2.2 Percentage of funding options proposed by selected smart cities. *Source*: Smart City Plans 2016 (MoUD website)

had to think about financial sources, lifetime costs of each project, and revenue and recovery of O&M. Since all the projects proposed by the cities as part of area-based development, pan-city development, and green field development are to be implemented through the SPVs, the plans also include cash flows for each financial year (annexure 3 of all submitted proposals). There has been a constant emphasis on procuring private sector funding by the cities. The central government has made it quite clear during the announcement of the mission that states and cities have to put in matching amount into the SPVs and also find avenues to bring in private funding for all the proposed projects.

Atal Mission for Rejuvenation and Urban Transformation (AMRUT)

AMRUT is expected to cover 500 cities across the country. Under AMRUT, which replaces the JNNURM, funds will be allocated based on the urban population and number of cities/towns in each state/UT. The guidelines stipulate that without availability of land and all necessary clearances, no project shall be included in the Mission. States will transfer funds to ULBs within seven days of transfer by the centre, and no diversion of funds will be allowed, failing which penal interest would be charged in addition to the action by the centre.

Under JNNURM, the MoUD used to sanction project-by-project, subject to a city preparing an integrated CDP, but under AMRUT, this has been replaced by the approval of a State Annual Action Plan by the MoUD once a year and the states have to sanction projects and provide necessary approvals at their end. In this way, the AMRUT makes states equal partners in the planning and implementation of projects, thus actualizing the spirit of cooperative federalism.

Every year, the outlay for individual city under both schemes—AMRUT and Smart City—is Rs 100 crore each. Given the significant outlays envisaged for basic infrastructure such as water and sewerage network expansion alone, even after the state and local government investments, private sector investment would be critical. Like the Smart City Mission, the AMRUT also builds on evidence, viz. available data, information, and plans on water supply and sewerage from the states/ULBs. To assess existing levels of coverage of water supply and sewerage, information will be collected from the census (2011) or based on the baseline survey done by the MoUD. No new baseline survey is envisaged, and the state/ULB should accept/endorse the earlier baseline.

Once the gap is computed, plans will be prepared to bridge the gaps. As a one-size-fits-all approach does not work, alternatives are generated in order to do more with fewer resources and see that the benefits reach the people.

Non-availability of land or delay in availability was one of the key factors that had delayed projects in the earlier mission. Another connected issue was obtaining clearances from numerous other departments. To address these issues, the policy document states that under AMRUT, projects should not be included which does not have land and work order will not be issued for new projects unless all clearances from all the concerned departments are received on time. Moreover, the cost of land purchased will be borne by the respective states/ULBs.

The basic building block for the State Annual Action Plan (SAAP) is the Service Level Improvement Plan (SLIP) prepared by the ULBs. At the state level, the SLIPs of all mission cities will be aggregated into the SAAP. Therefore, the SAAP is basically a state-level service improvement plan indicating the year-wise improvements in water supply and sewerage connections to households.

The states will decide on the inter-ULB allocation based on gap analysis and financial strength of ULBs and choose those ULBs in the first year that have higher gaps in provision of water supply and sewerage. Importantly, at the state level, the SAAP should only contain those projects where complete project cost is linked with revenue sources. This will include dovetailing with other sectoral and financial programmes of the central and state governments. A financial intermediary is proposed, also a reform in the AMRUT, in order to pool funds from all sources and release funds to ULBs on time. Such intermediaries are expected to access external sources of finance, such as debt and bonds, which small and financially distressed ULBs are unable to access. Further, through the creation of an intermediary, the potential opened by the promulgation of regulations by the Securities and Exchange Board of India (SEBI) for municipal bonds can be fully realized. During the process of developing the SAAP, the states/UTs are to explore the possibility of using public–private partnerships (PPP) as a preferred execution model. Appropriate service-level agreements (SLAs) will be induced into PPPs with strong citizen feedback eventually leading to the people–public–private–partnership (PPPP) model.

Financing is an important element of the SAAP. The maximum share will be given by the central government. The states/ULBs shall plan for the remaining resource generation at the time of preparation of the SAAP. The financial share of cities will vary across states. In some states, the ULBs may be in a position to contribute significantly to the project cost as compared to a ULB of another state. Accordingly, states shall decide during formulation of the SAAP on how the residual financing (over and above central government share) is shared between the state, ULBs, and any other source identified by the state/ULB (e.g. PPP, market borrowing). However, the state contribution to the SAAP will not be less than 20 % of the total project cost.

During the mission period, 11 reforms are to be implemented. Implementation of reforms is an important objective of the SLIP. The ULBs shall prepare a roadmap for reforms consolidated by the State Mission Director and as part of the SAAP. Some reforms may require more funds than others. For instance, assessment and collection of user charges, property tax, fee, and so on, are examples of activities which require hardly any additional funds. If funds are required to implement reforms, they can be accessed from the following: (i) the allowed components of the AMRUT; (ii) the state A&OE funds; or (iii) the Capacity Building for Urban Development (CBUD) programme funded by the World Bank.

All these are expected to form part of the SAAP; however, duplication and redundancy need to be avoided at the time of preparing the SLIP and the SAAP.

Past experience shows that projects are often delayed if release of project funds is linked to the non-completion of reforms. So, AMRUT has shifted from penalization to incentivization. Ten per cent of the annual budget allocation is to be kept apart and sanctioned to the states/UTs each year as incentive for the implementation of reforms. The mission will provide incentives for the previous year at the start of the succeeding financial year. The incentive fund is an additional fund provided by the MoUD, and no matching funds will be required to be sanctioned by the state/ULB. The State High Power Steering Committee (SHPSC) will decide the use of the incentive amount. The incentive award will be used in mission cities on admissible components of the AMRUT, including new projects. The incentive cannot be used as the state share in the project in AMRUT, but can be used by the ULBs for their project funding. Each year, unutilized funds for reform incentives will be transferred to the project fund.

Incorporation of resilience and securing projects against disasters will be done at the stage of preparation of the SLIP, particularly for the vulnerable and the poor. At the project development stage, disaster-secure engineering and structural norms would be included in the project design.

Heritage City Development and Augmentation Yojana (HRIDAY)

The objective of HRIDAY is to preserve the character and soul of a heritage city and facilitate inclusive heritage linked to urban development. The purpose is to promote adaptive urban rehabilitation by exploring various avenues involving private sector. There is a provision for private funding for management and services under HRIDAY scheme undertaken by private entities those directly or indirectly benefiting from the project. Private funding can be acquired at any stage of the scheme implementation, i.e. planning and design, implementation of works, and user fee/charges for service delivery.

Swachh Bharat Mission (SBM)

SBM aims at elimination of open defecation; eradication of manual scavenging, promote modern and scientific municipal solid waste management; effect behavioural change regarding healthy sanitation practices; generate awareness about sanitation and its linkage with public health; capacity augmentation for ULBs and create an enabling environment for private sector participation involving capex (capital expenditure) and opex (operation and maintenance).

The estimated cost of implementation of SBM (urban) based on unit and per capita cost for its various components is Rs 62,009 crore. The Government of India share as per approved funding pattern amounts to Rs 14,623 crore. In addition, a minimum additional amount equivalent to 25 % of GoI funding, amounting to Rs 4874 crore, shall be contributed by the states as state/ULB share. The balance funds is proposed to be generated through various other sources which are but not limited to private sector participation, additional resources from state government/ULBs, beneficiary share user charges, land leveraging, innovative revenue streams, Swachh Bharat Kosh, corporate social responsibility, and market borrowing and external assistance.

SBM (Urban) Component-III: Public Toilets

There will be no central government incentive support for the construction of public toilets under SBM (urban). States and ULBs are encouraged to identify land for public toilets, and leverage this land and advertise for PPP agreements to encourage the private sector to construct and manage public toilets. Additional funding support by any means other than GoI grant can be leveraged for public toilets.

SBM (Urban) Component: Solid Waste Management

ULBs are expected to prepare a DPR for solid waste management in consultation with state governments. Smaller cities can form clusters to become viable entities to attract private investment. About 100 % cost reimbursement for preparing the DPR shall be borne by the GoI as per unit cost and norms. State governments may handhold ULBs for preparing DPRs for solid waste management by empanelling/shortlisting/identifying private or government agencies.

Government Initiatives to Ease Doing Business in India

According to the reports by the World Bank's *Doing Business* (2015), India ranks poorly in terms of business environment. Restrictions plague business throughout its life cycle, making it difficult, expensive, and cumbersome to start, grow, or exit. In the liberalized regime, there is a clear need to make it easier to do business in India. Improving the business environment is likely to spur growth and generate employment for millions across the country. The Department of Industrial Policy and Promotion (DIPP) has taken up a series of measures to improve ease of doing business. The emphasis has been on simplification and rationalization of the existing rules and introduction of information technology to make governance more efficient and effective. The process of applying for an industrial licence (IL) and industrial entrepreneur memorandum (IEM) has been made online, and this service is now available to entrepreneurs on 24 × 7 bases at the eBiz website. This had led to ease of filing applications and online payment of service charges. Further, 14 services are integrated with eBiz portal which will function as a single window portal for obtaining clearances from various governments agencies.

The growth of business in India requires concerted action on several fronts—infrastructure, capital markets, trade facilitation, and skills. According to the World Bank's *Doing Business* (2015) study, a disproportionately high regulatory burden is borne by businesses today, as exemplified by India's current rank of 142 among 189 nations. India does not feature in the top 100 countries on 8 of the study's 10 indicators. On getting credit and protecting minority investors, India is ranked 7th and 32nd, respectively. On dealing with construction permits and enforcing contracts, India ranks among the bottom 10 economies in the world. It is encouraging to note that the Government of India has embarked on an ambitious reform agenda focused on improving India's performance in the World Bank's *Doing Business* rankings. These efforts, among other things, focus on implementing reforms relating to starting a business, resolving insolvency, enforcing contracts, and trading across borders. A majority of the regulatory burden imposed on business is due to the existence of a plethora of laws, rules, regulations, and procedures enforced by the states. This gives rise to a wide number of registrations, licences, and NOCs that businesses must obtain and file compliance returns on. While the World Bank Group has been working for many years with officials of the Government of India, this effort gained traction only in the last few years due to the political commitment coupled with renewed and vigorous efforts of officials of both central and state governments in India to ease doing business in the country. On 29 December 2014, Chief Secretaries of States participating in the 'Make in India' workshop finalized a 98-point action plan on 'ease of doing business', and later, it was decided that an evaluation will be conducted to assess progress by June 2015. This report captures the findings of the evaluation of this unique exercise and ranks states in terms of their implementation of the 98-point action plan based on 'competitive federalism' approach to business reform.

The results of the assessment indicate that states have embraced the challenge placed upon them to focus on further streamlining the regulatory burden on business in India. The assessment has also given rise to competition among states and UTs to undertake reforms. Most states have expressed interest to not only compete, but also to collaborate and learn from each other's experience. Many states have already embarked on ambitious reform programs or expanded their ongoing reform efforts since the announcement of the 98-point action plan. Various process streamlining and technology interventions have been undertaken in the areas of commercial taxes (time-bound VAT/CST registrations, online mechanisms for payments and returns of various taxes, etc.), labour (self-certification mechanisms for integrated returns and inspections, development of online labour, etc.), and environment (exemption of a number of green industries from approvals/consents, implementation of consent management systems, etc.), easing urban governance such as online building plan sanction.

As per the World Bank assessment, on an average, only 32 % of the proposed reforms have been implemented across the country. It is critical that these reforms be properly communicated, monitored, and evaluated, to ensure that the impact of the reforms is being felt on the ground.

Lessons Learnt and Future Perspective

It is a fact that JNNURM has been instrumental in rejuvenating the urban space in the country. Even though JNNURM provides additional central assistance to the ULBs, the discretion to exercise that option had been left to the respective state governments. Out of the 65 mission cities, the state capitals and million plus cities may not require the extent of funding under the umbrella of JNNURM as most of these cities have the capacity to generate their own resources. In fact, funding may be scaled down for them to increase the funding for smaller towns. Funding of the mission cities was decided on the basis of population based on 2001 census; the smaller states with smaller towns had some disadvantage over the large cities in the access to the funds which has resulted in disparity in the creation of infrastructure across urban centres across the country.

The nine years' experience with JNNURM has been a substantial learning experience. It has revealed weaknesses in the governance systems. Though JNNURM mandated preparation of city development plans (CDP) and detailed project reports (DPRs) before taking up any project, in many cases, the CDPs failed to link spatial planning with socio-economic planning and became a mere mandatory requisite to avail JNNURM funds. Most of the CDPs gave limited consideration to socio-economic aspects and excluded peri-urban areas. This has further limited the adequacy of CDPs and has led to haphazard growth on the cities' boundaries. The process of consultation was limited to preplan finalization stage. Further, CDP was seen as an investment plan for projects in the immediate term and not as a vision document for the city, and CDP is not a statutory document as the master plan/regional plan.

It is a fact that the JNNURM has provided for substantial central assistance to cities for infrastructure development and has indeed been effective in renewing the country's focus on the urban sector. However, the analysis exhibits a move towards polarized development and an inbuilt big-city bias. The current mission programmes, other than the Swacch Bharat Mission, are also specific to being city based. Further, all of them seek financing from the private sector and are also linked to reform. This is likely to bring in entrepreneurism in the ULBs and a competition among themselves for accessing capital from the central and state. This is the case with Smart City Challenge fund, where competition among cities is being encouraged even to access funds from the central and state. The reforms along with the ease of doing business norms are likely to bring about more of private sector participation and boost investment in the urban economy.

Acknowledgments The authors are grateful to Dr. Satpal Singh (Research Analyst) and Ms. Pragya Sharma (Research Fellow), National Institute of Urban Affairs for assistance in data analysis and development of arguments in this chapter.

References

Ashworth, G. J., & Woogd, H. (1990). *Selling the city: Marketing approaches in public sector urban planning*. London: Belhaven Comptroller and Auditor General of India, Government of India (2012): "Performance Audit of JNNURM".

Comptroller and Auditor General, Government of India. (2012). Mid-Term Review of the JNNURM Performance Audit of JNNURM.

Jessop, B., & Sum, N. L. (2000). An entrepreneurial city in action: Hong Kong's emerging strategies in and for (Inter-) urban competition. *Urban Studies, 37*, 2287–2313.

Kundu, D. (2009). "Elite Capture and Marginalisation of the Poor in Participatory Urban Governance" A Case of Resident Welfare Associations in Metro Cities in *India Urban Poverty Report 2009*, MoHUPA and UNDP, Oxford University Press.

Kundu, D., & Samanta, D. (2011). Redefining the inclusive urban agenda in India. *Economic & Political Weekly*, *xlvi*(5), 55–63.

Mathew, G. (2015, August 15). Investment challenge: Smart cities need smart funding options. *The Indian Express*.

Planning Commission. (2007). *Eleventh five year plan (2007–2012), Chapter 1* (Vol. 1). New Delhi: Planning Commission, Government of India.

Planning Commission. (2012). *Twelth five year plan (2012–2017), faster, more inclusive and sustainable Growth* (Vol. I). New Delhi: Sage Publication.

Press Information Bureau, Government of India. (2016, January 28). Government announces first batch of 20 smart cities from 11 States.

World Bank. (2015). Ease of Doing Business.

World Bank's Enterprise Survey. (2014). http://www.enterprisesurveys.org/

World Bank, KPMG. (2015). Assessment of State Implementation of Business Reforms.

Websites Consulted

http://jnnurm.nic.in

http://smartcities.gov.in/writereaddata/SmartCityGuidelines.pdf

http://amrut.gov.in/writereaddata/AMRUT%20Guidelines%20.pdf

http://hridayindia.in/wp-content/uploads/2015/01/hriday-brochure.pdf

https://swachhbharaturban.gov.in/writereaddata/SBM_Guideline.pdf

Chapter 3
Entrepreneurial Governance in a Resilient City: Bengaluru, India

H.S. Sudhira

Introduction

India is growing in full steam in terms of population, economy or vehicles. The recent provisional census data (Directorate of Census Operations 2011) for the year 2011 show that we are 1.21 billion people, nearly 17.5 % of the global population making every sixth person in the globe, an Indian. We are only next to China in total population which is contributing 19.4 % to world population with 1.341 billion people. Our population has increased over five times in the last 110 years from 0.24 billion in 1901. About 181 million people are added in the last decade with a decadal growth rate of 17.64 % and annual growth of 1.64 %.

In a rapidly urbanizing economy with fast technological changes, the need for the government is to quickly and continuously 'adapt' to these changes, ensuring a smooth and sustained workflow through interface with the people. The governance, which is the exercise of economic, political and administrative authority to manage a country's affairs at all levels, consists of the mechanisms, processes and institutions through which citizens and groups articulate their interests, exercise their legal rights, meet their obligations and mediate their differences. Poor governance generates and reinforces poverty and subverts efforts to degenerate it. Therefore, to ensure 'Good Governance' developmental schemes has to be promoted to reach all sections of the society and aid in enhancing the quality of life.

Democracy empowers citizens through decentralization of power, effective people's participation through state and non-state mechanisms, greater synergy and consolidation among various agencies and programmes of government, civil service reforms, transparency, rationalization of governmental schemes and mode of financial assistance to states, improved access to formal justice system to enforce rights, reforms and strengthening of land administration and harnessing the power

H.S. Sudhira (✉)
Gubbi Labs, 2-182, 2nd Cross, Extension, Gubbi, Karnataka 572216, India
e-mail: sudhira@gubbilabs.in; hs.sudhira@gmail.com

K.C. Smitha (ed.), *Entrepreneurial Urbanism in India*,
DOI 10.1007/978-981-10-2236-4_3

of technology for governance. In contrary, policy-making takes place at the centre (macro-level), and the actual implementations at the end-user (micro-level), by the bureaucrats/administrators, are mostly different than what was originally conceptualized or intended for, as implementation practices are embedded within colonial structures, bureaucratic autonomy and opaque systems leading to economic inefficiency, ineffectiveness and inappropriateness.

In recent times, rapid growth of the country has posed significant challenges on a host of aspects especially on cities and on planning and governance. An important aspect has been how well the city is planned, managed and administered, those activities which form the core part of an urban agenda—governance. However, enabling appropriate mechanisms through organizational structures, procedures and policies are needed. Also, apart from the formal administrative structures, the presence and involvement of civil society significantly drive the urban agenda. With the onset of economic reforms, emergence of technology-driven society (socio-technical systems) and markets, it is imperative for the governments to reinvent, realign and adapt to remain or sustain the external pressures from different stakeholders, especially with pressures of globalization. So, the need for decentralization for overall development of India's 700 million plus strong rural population cannot be ignored.

One should recognize that the urban evolution of this magnitude is a recent emergence and the nations and states have been attempting to address differently based on their respective abilities, appreciation and capacities. In no case, there is a perfect path/trajectory of evolution and so consequently, there have been both ups and downs in the process of evolution of urban (and governance). This is particularly true for a state like Karnataka in India, which like most other states has been making attempts to navigate the murky waters of defining and putting appropriate system for urban governance and planning. While there can be a set of optimal solutions, the ways to tackle them are perhaps acknowledging and appreciating the issues first.

The city of Bengaluru (earlier Bangalore) in the southern state of Karnataka, India, has been witnessing growth consistently for over a century and garnering global attention for different reasons over the time. The city has enjoyed sobriquets such as 'pensioners' paradise' and 'garden city', and lately, 'Silicon Valley of India'. Bengaluru is witnessing a strange transformation accompanied with a booming and rapidly changing economic landscape. It is now home to thousands of high-tech companies apart from numerous establishments in manufacturing, service and processing industries including textiles.

The population of Bengaluru as per the 2011 Census was 8,443,675 (2001 census: 5,686,844) while it was 163,091 in the beginning of the last century (1901). Geographically, it is located on 12.95 °N latitude and 77.57 °E longitude and it is situated at an altitude of 920 m above mean sea level. While the city was a key commercial and industrial centre of the state of Karnataka, it formally became the principal administrative centre in 1956. Nevertheless, the city has always played a key role in Karnataka's history, as well as in India, both as a model city and as an industrial centre.

While the city was 'growing' obviously, there have been many forces at play including the changing governance and political forces. In all these, the city had to embrace to different and yet varied governance practices that were 'adapted'. Before we understand the nature of governance and its evolution in Bengaluru, we will briefly review some of the key literature on public administration and governance that has influenced some of the structural changes the city has witnessed in recent times.

Governance and New Public Management

In one of the earliest reviews on public administration, Ostrom and Ostrom (1971) have analysed how public choice theory could be applicable while reviewing different aspects including the nature of decision-making entrepreneurial firms and bureaucratic organizations. A key aspect they conclude is the need for a system of public administration composed of and a variety of multi-organizational arrangements for sustaining a high level of performance for advancing public welfare.

Hood (1991) traces the early origins of a 'New Public Management' (NPM) along with the criticisms it received when it was embraced. It however survived and percolated to other countries as well with multi-lateral agencies insisting on adapting to these changes. Later Hood (1995) notes that the changes in public sector accounting in a number of OECD countries over the 1980s were central to the rise of NPM and its associated doctrines of public accountability and organizational best practice. Subsequently, Pollitt (1995) has presented evidence to support the contention that NPM has been widely adopted, with local variations, in many Western states.

However, Rhodes (1994, 1996) has noted the shortcomings of NPM as the reforms of the 1980s and 1990s deliberately fragmented service delivery systems, generating functional imperatives for inter-organizational coordination. Stating that NPM was deeply entrenched in governments, another review analyses some of the critiques of NPM and the challenges for NPM (Hood and Peters 2004).

Realizing the shortcomings in advancing the theory and purposes of public administration Osborne (2006) put forward 'New Public Governance (NPG)' as the next phase. Reviewing the notions of NPG (Osborne 2010), Villanueva (2015) notes that there are real or methodological doubts about the validity of certain approaches or concepts accounting for some social or natural realities in NPG. Nevertheless, in this case we will be analysing the evolution of governance structures in the light of the NPM paradigm.

The key challenges for administrative reforms in India particularly in the light of NPM have been reviewed by Singh (2003). Singh (2003) has analysed early attempts to reform administration in India from post-independence to recent reforms driven by globalization and influenced by information and communication technology (ICT) in administration (e-governance). Although the emergence of NPM and the need for economic efficiency in governance (through privatization) has spearheaded administrative reforms, innovations and best practices initiated by either the local administration (decentralization) or by the civic society have made these successful. Identifying the successful innovations and best practices while addressing the issues of sustainability and replicating these in different instances is difficult since most of these practices and innovations are context specific. However, in the wake of decentralization and greater autonomy at the local/grass-root level complimented by public participation can be a successful one, as evinced from the different case studies.

With this theoretical backdrop, we will briefly discuss the nature of 'urban' public administration prevailing in Bengaluru.

The Context of Bengaluru

Bruhat Bangalore Mahanagara Palike (BBMP) is the 'urban local body' (ULB), the local governmental structure representing and responsible for the city and outlying areas. Notified in January 2007, the new City Corporation replaced the erstwhile local bodies, Bangalore City Corporation (Bangalore Mahanagara Palike), 8 neighbouring councils (7 City Municipal Councils and one Town Municipal Council) and 111 outlying villages. Independent of the City Corporation, which is governed by locally elected representatives, several parastatal bodies controlled by the State government are responsible for the delivery of essential services (see Table 3.1; Fig. 3.1).

Anchoring the 'Urban'

In India, urban development has been assigned by the constitution as a state subject allowing respective states to formulate policies and legislations to govern and plan urban areas. The key organizational structure responsible and representing the citizens in urban areas are the elected local bodies. Technically for all the towns and cities in India, there exists an urban local body. In Karnataka, they are typically classified based on the size of these settlements and specifically as per the provisions of Karnataka Municipalities Act 1964 and Karnataka Municipal Corporations Act 1976.

The 74th Constitutional Amendment Act (CAA) passed in 1993 mandates the urban local bodies for administering, managing and preparing master/development plans. Instead, planning in the form of land-use planning and zoning regulations are vested with a parastatal agency created by an act of State legislature. Significant administration and decision-making powers in these areas with regard to delivery of various services rest with other parastatal organizations. Apart from the urban local bodies represented by the local elected representatives, all other organizations responsible for essential services are parastatal bodies which are controlled by the

Table 3.1 Organizations of urban development and housing in Bangalore

Organisations	Functional areas (scope of work)
Bruhat Bangalore Mahanagara Palike (BBMP)	Urban local body responsible for overall delivery of services—roads and road maintenance including asphalting, pavements and street lighting; solid waste management, education and health in all wards, storm water drains, construction of few ring roads, flyovers and grade separators
Bangalore Development Authority (BDA)	Land-use zoning, planning and regulation within Bangalore metropolitan area; construction of few ring roads, flyovers and grade separators
Bangalore Metropolitan Region Development Authority (BMRDA)	Planning, co-ordinating and supervising the proper and orderly development of the areas within the Bangalore Metropolitan Region, which comprises Bangalore urban district and parts of Bangalore rural district. BDA's boundary is a subset of BMRDA's boundary
Bangalore Water Supply and Sewerage Board (BWSSB)	Drinking water—pumping and distribution, sewerage collection, water and waste water treatment and disposal
Bangalore Metro Rail Corporation Ltd (BMRC)	Public transport system—rail-based
Karnataka Urban Infrastructure Development and Finance Corporation (KUID&FC)	Nodal agency for urban infrastructure and finance; handhold, coordinate and manage several central/multilateral projects
Karnataka Housing Board	Provisioning affordable housing
Karnataka Slum Development Board	Promote the welfare and improvement of slums

Source Author

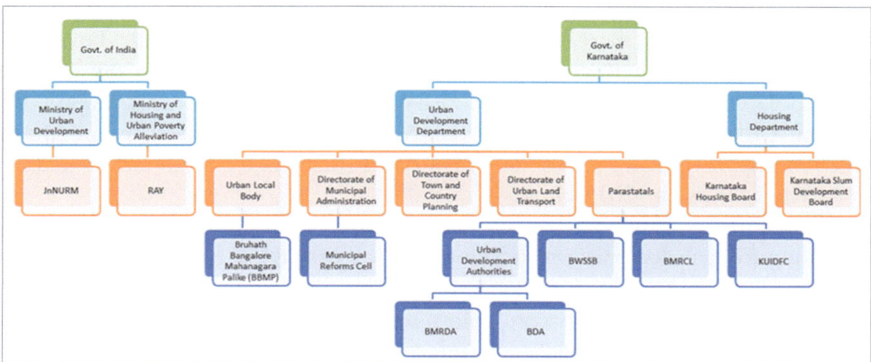

Fig. 3.1 Urban governance in Bengaluru

state government. Thus, there exist striking contrasts with respect to devolution of powers to the respective urban local bodies by the state governments much against the intent of 74th CAA of central government.

Urban Policies and Programs in India

Traditionally, policies of urban development have focused on addressing the lack of housing and delivery of basic services due to the rise in urban population. A premise while pursuing urban policies was also that the country was predominantly agrarian and largely supported by the rural economy. These are further evident from the plan outlays under the housing and urban development sector in the Five-Year Plans of the Planning Commission of India. Until recently, the positive aspect of cities as 'engines of economic growth' in the context of national economic policies was not much appreciated and, therefore, the problems of urban areas were treated more as welfare problems and as sectors of residual investment rather than as issues of national economic importance (Ministry of Urban Development 2005).

In terms of urban plans, in the initial years the focus was on land policies, which later shifted towards delivery of basic services to the urban poor, and now on urban infrastructure and governance. Ravindra (1996) has attempted to delineate the urban land policy in the country. He has examined the instruments of land policy employed by the state for interventions, broadly as: legal measures, fiscal measures and direct interventions. There have been intense debates and some large-scale initiatives to systematically tackle urbanization. The first major attempt to address the urban land problems was by the Committee on Urban Land Policy. The other initiatives were through the Task Force on Housing and Urban Development in 1985, the National Housing Policy in 1985, the National Commission on Urbanization in 1988, the Mega City Scheme during 1993–1998, the Jawaharlal Nehru National Urban Renewal Mission (JNNURM) from 2005 to present, the National Urban Transport Policy (Ministry of Urban Development, 2006), the National Urban Housing and Habitat Policy in 2007, and the most recent Model State Affordable Housing Policy for Urban Areas (draft) of September 2013 and the Smart Cities Mission (2015-current).

Evidently, the Central government has been over time formulating policies and attempting to push for uniform 'development' across states. Realizing the lack of motivation or incentives for states to pursue the overarching policies, the Government of India has initiated reforms-driven schemes and funding mechanisms. The JNNURM is one such reforms-driven mission that mandates the respective city and state governments to enter into a memorandum of agreement (MoA) to fulfil the reforms as a precondition to receive the funds or financial assistance from the Centre. To a certain extent, this has indeed pushed both the city and state government to take steps in this direction. Most of the schemes and missions that have since emerged, like the Rajiv Awas Yojana (RAY), that were meant to provide social housing for the urban poor, slums and basic public services for poor urban settlements, follow a reforms-driven agenda. This, in fact, has resulted in serious negotiations between the city, state and Central government towards arriving at a common ground and overcoming the numerous hurdles—financial, technical and even legislative.

Realizing the importance of shaping the urban areas better, the Government of Karnataka (GoK) came up with an Urban Development Policy for Karnataka in November 2009. Following the action of the Ministry of Housing and Urban Poverty Alleviation (MHUPA), and the Government of India's National Urban Housing and Habitat Policy—2007, the Government of Karnataka prepared a draft housing and habitat policy in 2009. Both the national and state policies on housing and habitat follow similar approaches and have raised concerns about inviting comments from different quarters. Notable among them is the critique of the state's policy by the Slum Janandolana (popular protest movement) and various other organizations. Notwithstanding the prevalent policies, the MHUPA has indeed prepared a 'Model State Affordable Housing Policy for Urban Areas' in September 2013. Following suit, the Department of Housing, Government of Karnataka, has notified its version of 'Affordable Housing Policy, 2013' setting clear guidelines and invite private participation in housing.

Planning in the form of land-use zoning and regulation are vested with the Bangalore Development Authority (BDA), a parastatal agency. The BDA on its part has been following the provisions of Karnataka Town and Country Planning (KTCP) Act of 1961 in the preparation and revision of the master plans. Despite the KTCP Act itself being subjected to numerous amendments and ordinances to facilitate 'urban development', debates have been raised on the efficacy of these master plans. Notable controversies on the master plan and its amendments have been with respect to the 'regularization of unauthorized construction and development' pursued by an amendment (under Section 76-FF of the KTCP Act) and the notification of its rules subsequently. Though the devolution of the planning function is one of the mandatory reforms to be fulfilled under JNNURM, the state governments skipped this by issuing a government order directing the planning agency to send the draft and final versions of the master plan 'for vetting and comments' before formal approval. However, recently the Government of Karnataka issued a draft notification for constituting a Metropolitan Planning Committee (MPC) required by one of the mandatory reforms under JNNURM and the provisions of the Constitution. On all these issues, the high handedness of the state is evident, resulting in little or no role of the local elected representatives.

Entrepreneurial Governance

In an attempt to embrace urbanization, it is the governance that is indeed bearing the brunt of fast pace of changes and expectations. As can be seen, the key laws governing the urban that were progressive came mostly during the 1960s and

1970s. Since the 1990s, there have been mostly amendments to the existing laws and even new regressive laws. The key laws governing the urban are as follows:

1. City of Bangalore Municipal Corporation Act, 1949
2. Bombay Provincial Municipal Corporations Act, 1949 (for Hubli-Dharwad and Belgaum)
3. Karnataka Town and Country Planning Act, 1961
4. Karnataka Land Revenue Act, 1964
5. Karnataka Municipalities Act, 1964
6. Karnataka Municipal Corporations Act, 1976
7. Bangalore Development Authority Act, 1976
8. Karnataka Urban Development Authorities Act, 1987
9. Karnataka Regularization of Unauthorized Construction in Urban Areas, 1991.

The state government needs to amend laws, craft policies and implement mechanisms in the process of fulfilling the requirements of the reforms agenda so as to access funds from the Centre. Local bodies with limited capacity have to assimilate and implement all of these.

Emergence of Political Entrepreneurship

There have been several attempts by the political leadership joining forces with the private sector and non-governmental organizations in addressing affairs of public administration. An experiment to promote public private partnership (PPP) and bring together citizens, NGOs, industry representatives and the erstwhile local bodies resulted in the emergence of ‘Bangalore Agenda Task Force (BATF)’ during 1999. Jalal (2005) presents the comparison of good practices in public sector reforms that have taken place in Bengaluru and Kolkata due to administrative reforms through participation of the private sector, non-governmental organizations and public. In this case, the BATF acted as an interface for synergizing the efforts undertaken by different stakeholders involving the different state-run service organizations, the public and the private enterprises. Jalal (2005) further argues that although the creation of BATF was a welcome measure in the administrative reforms, its existence and the sustainability of ‘good practices’ is in question due to the changed political scenario in the state. Although this experiment was bench-marked as one of the ‘best practices’ in urban local governance, BATF faced strong criticisms from several civil society groups for setting aside priorities favouring the urban poor and was accused of making a back door entry into policy-making (Ghosh 2005). Eventually, BATF was disbanded as soon as the government changed.

However, a new government in 2008 set up the Agenda for Bangalore Infrastructure Development (ABIDe) on similar lines as BATF. This initiative again attracted similar responses and opposition from several grass-roots advocacy groups working in the development sector. Around the same time, Janaagraha, a prominent NGO on urban governance, mooted 'Bangalore City Connect' to engage with public authorities in a public–private partnership model for advising and managing services. City Connect is comprised of industry and advisory groups apart from Janaagraha, the key non-profit entity. While ABIDe suffered from political patronage and was disbanded with the change of government, the City Connect initiative did not generate enough attraction. This history was repeated with the incumbent government creating the 'Bengaluru Blue Print Action Group (BBPAG)' in May 2016, which again drew flak from numerous civil society organizations. A concern related to the promoters of Janaagraha is Jana Urban Space Foundation that has come up with another creative project subverting the democratic process called TenderSure. Under TenderSure, specifications for urban streets are prescribed and are implemented. Though the specifications lay good emphasis for non-motorized transport, its administrative approval and procurement process has drawn flak from other citizen groups.

Evidently, the bureaucratic enterprises or the state created organizations were to manage various services such as housing, infrastructure development, water supply, law and order, and energy which resulted in 'state-capture' as against the spirit of giving power back to the people—the urban local body in Bangalore. Further the existence of many parastatal organizations, each of them acting in its own jurisdiction area, leads to the challenges in coordinating different activities. For effective planning, it is imperative that all the basic information is gathered across a common jurisdiction with the effect of creating a robust city information system. Apart from the issue of a common jurisdiction and the lack of institutional coordination, even basic information related to different sectors is extremely difficult to collect, collate and to correlate. Notwithstanding all the governance challenges, the Government of Karnataka set up an 'expert committee' for 'BBMP Restructuring' (Sept 22, 2014). The committee has since attempted to gather and consult various stakeholders, representatives and experts. In July 2015, the committee has submitted its report to the state government. The key recommendations include: (a) committee echoes and reinforces the call for setting up of a Metropolitan Planning Committee (MPC) as envisaged by the 74th CAA; (b) it supports the creation of a Greater Bangalore Authority (GBA) for the larger area of the metropolitan planning area that will have present local body divided into five smaller local bodies; and (c) the wards to be reorganized under these local bodies (Expert Committee for BBMP Restructuring 2015). Though the committee's report envisages empowering the city through a combination of legal, administrative and financial measures, it rests the key powers with the chief minister heading the state, thus defeating the purpose of devolving powers to the elected local body. Further, even the proposed Greater Bangalore Authority seems to only further the situation of 'state-capture'. Yet, the implementation of the committee's recommendation requires political will and serious commitment for furthering an efficient but liveable city with enhanced quality of life.

Emerging Bureaucratic Entrepreneurship

The 74th Constitutional Amendment Act was implemented during the early 1990s, and it coincides with the onset of an era of liberalization in India initiated by the Government of India. In yet another coincidence, the Government of Karnataka embraced some of the NPM concepts and ended up creating corporations for managing urban affairs. The Government of Karnataka, in one of its smart moves, established the Karnataka Urban Infrastructure Development and Finance Corporation (http://www.kuidfc.com/) as a public limited company in 1993. The KUIDFC works like any corporate with a board of directors, a chairperson and a managing director for day-to-day affairs.

One of the key roles of the KUIDFC is being the 'conduit' for most funds received by the state from the Centre or any multilateral agency as loans or grants. In the process, it has been spearheading and leading the effort for reforms and mechanisms, through professionally engaged project management services, for availing the grants. On the prevalence of schemes like JNNURM and RAY along with their reforms agenda, the KUIDFC has been working closely with the Urban Development Department, Government of Karnataka, in driving these reforms. In effect, it functions as a channel for all funds received externally and holds a stick through professionally engaged project management consulting services, thereby reducing or limiting the role of elected representatives. It is imperative to note that the chairperson and managing director are drawn from the powerful Indian Administrative Service (IAS) cadre that constitutes the bureaucracy in India. As a consequence, the political leadership has little or no say in matters dealt by the KUIDFC.

Over the last two decades, such bureaucratic entrepreneurship has spun-off very well in the state resulting the creation of several such 'enterprises' for key services of energy and transportation. Notable among them are as follows:

1. The Bangalore Electricity Supply Company Limited (BESCOM) created in 1999, following a spate of reforms in the energy sector. This is headed by a managing director (an IAS officer) with the Energy Minister as the chairperson.
2. The Karnataka Power Transmission Company Limited (KPTCL) also created in 1999 along with BESCOM, separating the transmission and distribution activities into two entities.
3. The Bangalore Metropolitan Transport Corporation (BMTC) created out of the Karnataka State Road Transport Corporation (KSRTC) that had inherited the erstwhile Bangalore Transport Service (BTS). The BMTC, despite charging among the highest user fares, prides itself in being a 'profit-making' enterprise.
4. The Bangalore Metropolitan Rail Corporation Limited (BMRCL) was established under a joint partnership by the Government of Karnataka and Ministry of Urban Development, Government of India.

From all these efforts, some traces of NPM are evident for the fact that the public services are now 'corporatized' or created as enterprises. However, what has not completed in the loop is to allow other private sectors to enter, thereby ensuring a

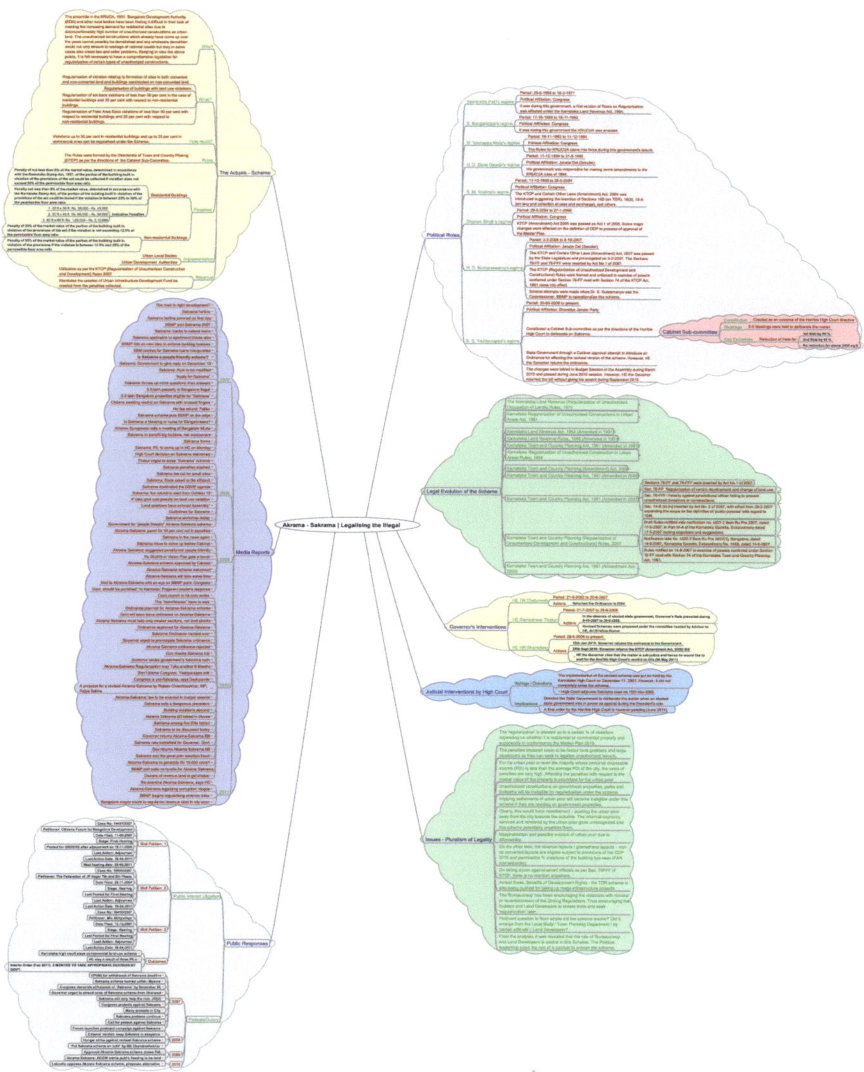

Fig. 3.2 Mind-map on *Akrama-Sakrama*

complete monopoly on the one hand and raising questions of accountability against service delivery that is paramount in public administration.

As a case in point, to drive how manifestations of the cooperation between political and bureaucratic establishment is presented by with an example of the initiative called 'Regularization of Unauthorized Development and Constructions', popularly called *Akrama-Sakrama*. Colloquially, *Akrama-Sakrama* means legalizing the illegal (see Fig. 3.2).

Further, with numerous stakeholders responsible for addressing various city functions, it is imperative that these organizations acknowledge their interdependencies formally through appropriate mechanisms. Thus, the possible way out to break the gridlock are facilitating systems and practices that ensure feedback and institutional coordination effectively. Essentially the interplay of these stakeholder/organizations involved with different city functions has to be acknowledged and bridged from short-to-medium (5–10 years) time frame planning undertaken by development authorities to near-to-short term operations undertaken by respective urban local bodies. With traces of NPM in place, and the leadership of these 'enterprises' with the bureaucracy who serve for a maximum of three years, most action plans are envisaged for their duration. In case of change in leadership, even those initiatives with longer time horizon often suffer setback due to changed priorities of the incumbent leadership. As a consequence, mostly short-term efforts rather than any long-term initiatives are realized. Thus, it is essential to link the daily operations with the planning of a 10-year period so that future chaos can be prevented. In this perspective, planning and governance have to be responsive to local and regional issues while ensuring requisite infrastructure and delivery of basic services.

The Resilient City: Civil Society Intervention

In addition to the official bodies, the civil society of Bengaluru is known for its vibrant community participation, which makes this a 'resilient' city. The spectrum of their activities ranges from literacy and green brigades to urban governance, ensuring continuous interactions with the local administration. Notable spheres of activity of these non-governmental organizations (NGOs) include: improving urban governance by Citizens Voluntary Initiative for the City (CIVIC) and *Janaagraha*; improving living conditions in slums by AWAS, APSA, Paraspara, etc.; and taking on environmental issues by the Environment Support Group, *Hasiru Usiru*, etc. Apart from the NGOs, there are numerous resident welfare associations, trade and commercial organizations, and professional organizations that have played a major role in some of the important activities of local bodies and influencing their decision-making. Civil society has contributed considerably in shaping the policies and governance structures and has always intervened whenever there has been any apathy on the part of the administration towards activities of interest to society at large that were affected by either political or bureaucratic entrepreneurship. In any case, the city has been a victim of vibrant entrepreneurial governance.

Conclusion

The overview of the nature of governance as exhibited by political and bureaucratic establishments poses grave challenges, since citizens who are at the receiving end may have to 'live' with the manifestations effected by these establishments. In the course of evolution of the city, it emerges that both political and bureaucratic establishments have deeper insights into the functioning than the citizen. As a consequence, both of these establishments know how to manoeuvre and when both of them cooperate on regressive policy and schemes; this can degenerate the system at large. However, this also suggests that when they cooperate on progressive policy, it has potential for betterment of services delivered to the citizens. It remains to be seen what mechanisms and incentives will create an ecosystem conducive for pursuing a progressive agenda in a cooperative manner.

Bengaluru is currently experiencing a remarkable transformation. It also stands out as a beacon of the globalizing world and to sustain this, it needs to systematically address the key challenges that the city is facing in terms of governance and infrastructure. A question remains, though, of who decides who decides (Frug 2014).

References

Directorate of Census Operations. (2011). *"Primary census abstract." a—Series tables: General population tables*. http://censusindia.gov.in/. May 31, 2016.

Expert Committee for BBMP Restructuring. (2015). *Government of Karnataka, Bengaluru: Way forward*, Bengaluru.

Frug, G. (2014). *Who decides who decides*. https://lsecities.net/media/objects/articles/who-decides-who-decides/en-gb/

Ghosh, A (2005). Public–Private or private public?: Promised partnership of the Bangalore Agenda Task Force. *Economic and Political Weekly* Special Articles, 19 November 2005.

Hood, C. (1991). A public management for all seasons? *Public Administration, 69*, 3–19.

Hood, C. (1995). The 'new public management' in the 1980s: Variations on a theme. *Accounting, Organizations and Society, 20*(2–3), 93–109.

Hood, C., & Peters, G. (2004). The middle ageing of new public management: Into the age of paradox? *Journal of Public Administration Research and Theory, 14*(3), 267–282.

Jalal, J. (2005). Good practices in public sector reform: A few examples from two Indian cities. *Administrative Reforms: Towards Sustainable Practices, 96*, 115.

Ministry of Urban Development. (2005). *Jawaharlal Nehru national urban renewal mission overview*.

Osborne, S. P. (2006). The new public governance? *Public Management Review, 8*(3), 377–387.

Osborne, S. P. (2010). *The new public governance: Emerging perspectives on the theory and practice of public governance*. UK: Routledge.

Ostrom, V., & Ostrom, E. (1971). Public choice: A different approach to the study of public administration. *Public Administration Review, 31*(2), 203–216.

Pollitt, C. (1995). Justification by works or by faith?: Evaluating the new public management. *Evaluation, 1*(2), 133–154.

Ravindra, A. (1996). *Urban land policy: A metropolitan perspective*. India: Concept Publishing Company.

Rhodes, R. A. W. (1994). The hollowing out of the state: The changing nature of the public service in Britain. *The Political Quarterly, 65*(2), 138–151.

Rhodes, R. A. W. (1996). The new governance: Governing without government. *Political Studies, XLIV*, 652–67.

Singh, A. (2003). *Administrative reforms: Towards sustainable practices*. India: SAGE Publications.

Villanueva, A. L. F. (2015). The new public governance? Emerging perspective on the theory and practice of public governance. *Journal of Public Governance and Policy: Latin American Review, 1*(1), 126–134.

Part II
Political Economy of Urbanisation

Chapter 4
From Hierarchy to Heterarchy: Moving Beyond Entrepreneurial Governance. Municipal Reforms Programme in Karnataka

Anjali Karol Mohan

Introduction

The state has always been an important stakeholder in the post-WW II development discourse, although its role has varied from being the primary authority 'rowing' development during the 1950s–1970s, to one that 'steers' development by allowing markets to row in this process as was the case between the 1980s and the early 1990s.[1] This changed in the 1990s when most development challenges continued to persist (Watts 1994). By the late 1990s both state and markets began to be recognized as complimentary institutions (Wolf 1993; McMillan 2002) with the argument that a choice between the two is, in effect, a choice between 'imperfect alternatives' (Wolf 1993: 64).

This recognition was accompanied by another significant transition—that in the context of development—unleashed largely by processes of ICT-enabled globalization and localization (WDR 2000).[2] On the one hand, both these have led to a context that while characterized as 'informational, global and networked' (Castells

[1]Within the development discourse, Osborne and Gaebler (1992) conceptualized the role of the state in terms of rowing and steering a boat. When the state is providing services, it is rowing the boat. However, they argued that the state should not provide services, rather should ensure these are provided. Here the role of the state is akin to that of one who is steering the boat. In conceptualizing the role of the state as steering the boat, Osborne and Gaebler distinguish a new 'entrepreneurial form of government'.

[2]The World Development Report (2000) defines globalization as the progressive integration of the world's economies which requires national and international partners to work together and manage changes relating to international trade, finance and global environmental issues. Localization is the desire of people for a say in their government. It requires national governments to decentralize political power to sub-national levels, to manage growth patterns, such as the movement of population and economic energy towards urban areas, and to provide essential public services.

A.K. Mohan (✉)
Bengaluru, India
e-mail: anjalikmohan@gmail.com

K.C. Smitha (ed.), *Entrepreneurial Urbanism in India*,
DOI 10.1007/978-981-10-2236-4_4

1998: 77), also showcases 'unstructured complexity' (Jessop 1998: 33) that is evident in social inequalities, poverty, an ever expanding informal economy coupled with housing crisis and collapse of social and physical infrastructure (Castells in Evans 2002; Sassen 2006). Termed as 'wicked' problems (Rittel and Webber 1973: 160), these have evaded solutions, whether state- or marked-led, while also demanding alternatives.[3]

On the other, these processes have rendered supra-national and sub-national state and non-state actors involved in governance, negotiation, coordination, regulation and prominent (WDR 2000). The emergence of these numerous stakeholders coupled with the demand for alternatives has paved the way for 'governance' as a means to address wicked problems of development.

Governance, while having many definitions and understood differently in different contexts, simply put, is a *process* that envisages partnerships between state and non-state actors (Stoker 1998). Conceptually, governance debates mark a shift beyond the state–market dichotomy (Stoker 1998). Empirically, these have manifested in a 'plethora of organizational configurations that failed to conform to traditional definitions of markets or hierarchies' (Podolny and Page 1998: 57). Of the many emerging organizational forms, recent years have witnessed a renewed focus on the network form, also referred to as heterarchies (Powell 1990; Ansell 2000; Jessop 1998, 2003; Castells 1998).[4]

Heterarchies are wide-ranging collaborations (and therefore different from public–private partnerships (PPPs) between public, private and civil society, each of which constitutes a node in the collaboration. Premised on the argument that 'no single actor, public or private, has the knowledge and resource capacity to tackle problems unilaterally' (Kooiman 1993b in Stoker 1998: 38), heterarchies are cited as distinct from state and markets both in the relationship between the various nodes as well as in their operating code and decision-making processes (Mayntz 1991; Rhodes 1997b; Jessop 2002 in Sørensen and Torfing 2005). It is this distinction that allows heterarchies to disseminate and interpret new information quickly, in turn, enabling these forms to cope with change (Powell 1990). This ability to cope with change is further accentuated by the rapid proliferation of ICTs which allow real-time communication and coordination amongst the various actors involved, thereby rendering these organizational forms appropriate alternatives to state and markets in addressing wicked problems.

Within heterarchies, the state is one amongst the several actors, although a central one (Ansell 2000; Fountain 2001; Jessop 1998, 2003; Rhodes 2007). Centrality

---

[3]Rittel and Webber (1973, 160) describe problems of social policy as wicked problems. These are wicked, as they are ill-defined and evade solutions—At best these can be resolved—over and over again.

[4]Heterarchies have long been used as coordination mechanisms intermediating between the state and the markets as the 'socially necessary minimum' (Jessop 1998: 32). With the rapid proliferation of ICTs, and their capacity to facilitate networking, coordination and communication across and within networks, these networks are becoming increasingly visible.

implies that the state is critical to the functioning of the heterrachy and is therefore crucial to establishing its efficacy as an alternative to states and markets. As a central node it is responsible for encouraging the nodes of the heterarchy to collaborate and work collectively. This it does so by coordinating the actions of the various nodes through dialogue and knowledge exchange. This requires the state to function differently.

In state-led development, the Weberian bureaucratic state, functioned through its hierarchies as a capacity, command and control entity (Fountain 2001), relying largely on administrative fiat and bureaucratic routine. Referred to as the traditional administration framework, this mode of functioning underwent a significant change in the market-mediated model of the 1980s and early 1990s that called for 'reinventing government' (Heeks 1999) by demanding a rolling back of the state. With this call emerged the New Public Management (NPM) framework, also referred to as the entrepreneurial governance framework whereby the state was required to adopt a pro-market working culture (Haque 2004).[5] In contrast, within heterarchies, the state's role is conceptualized differently. It is neither dogmatic as in hierarchies nor entrepreneurial as in markets (Jones and Bird 1999). Rather it is reflexive. However, scholarly work on emerging modes of governance like heterarchies is conspicuously silent on empirical evidence supporting the role of the state in operationalizing reflexive rationality. How does the state's centrality manifests empirically to operationalize reflexive rationality such that it steers the heterarchy to emerge an effective alternative to states and markets, capable of addressing development challenges is not clear. This chapter uses the Municipal Reforms Programme (hereafter MRP or the Programme), an e-governance intervention in Karnataka, India, to explore the states transition from a hierarchical capacity, command and control entity to one that can function reflexively (and therefore assuming a significantly different roles from that in entrepreneurial governance) while still being central. The MRP aims to strengthen municipalities in Karnataka through administrative reforms that are conceived, designed and implemented through organizational arrangements that resemble heterarchies. This chapter traces the evolution of the heterarchy in two phases—the pilot and scale-up—to point to how various state and non-state actors coalesce to deliver on goals of the MRP. In particular, it focuses on the role that the state plays in these two phases. In doing so, this chapter demonstrates how the state operationalizes reflexive rationality and, the implications of this reflexive mode of working on the effectiveness of network forms of governance like heterarchies.

Following this introduction, the rest of this chapter is divided into 4 sections. The next section reviews the development discourse to trace the transitioning role of the state. In particular, this section reviews literature on public–private partnerships to highlight how these differ from heterarchies. The Section "The Municipal Reforms Programmeand the State's Centrality" discusses the MRP which relies on wide-ranging collaborations between state and non-state actors to

---

[5]For detailed review of NPM, see Haque (2004), Dunleavy et al. (2006) and Stoker (2006).

design and implement e-governance reforms across municipalities in Karnataka. It particular, this section traces the evolution or structuring of the heterarchy to understand the state's role and functioning in these collaborations. In doing so, it points to how the state as a central node operationalises reflexive rationality to render heterarchies as effective alternatives to hierarchies and markets. However, it also highlights how the state can deploy the same centrality to marginalize the other nodes of the heterarchy. In, the process the state dilutes the 'diversity around purpose'—the very basis for the evolution of the heterarchy (Lipnack and Stamps 1994: 90 in McGuire 2003: 16) while also rendering the heterarchy ineffective in achieving its agenda. Drawing on the MRP, I argue that the effectiveness of the heterarchy is contingent not on the state's centrality, rather on how this centrality manifests on the ground. By merely being a central node in the heterarchy, the state does not necessarily steer the heterarchy to emerge as an effective alternative to hierarchical and market-mediated modes of governance. It is how this centrality manifests in its day-to-day functioning as is demonstrated in the MRP, which determines the effectiveness of this mode of governance. As the MRP shows, the state's centrality can also manifest such that it undermines its capacity to be reflexive, thereby, triggering a command and control behaviour. This chapter concludes with an argument that the experience of the MRP allows us neither to categorically argue for heterarchies as effective alternatives to state and market-mediated governance modes, nor does it make us reject these modes of governance as not having the capacity to deal with wicked problems. What we can argue is that, one, the success of these modes of governance is dependent on how the state's centrality manifests empirically in a given institutional and policy environment. Two, network forms of governance provide an opportunity for the state to move beyond the neoliberal framework of entrepreneurial governance arrangements like PPPs, to achieve larger public value, while capitalizing on the strengths of myriad stakeholders from the private sector and civil society actors.

From Hierarchies to Heterarchies: Reconceptualizing the Role of the State

For most part of the twentieth century, it was either the state or the markets that were considered as the main vehicles driving development. In the 1950s and 1960s, most developing countries relied on active state intervention. This transitioned in the 1980s and 1990s when there was a call for anti-interventionist market-friendly development (Escobar 2011). Despite these stands on the role of the state, most developing countries recorded dismal progress on addressing persistent development challenges.

Consequently, in the last decade of the twentieth century there was a call for alternatives to both the state-led and market-mediated modes of governance. These alternatives were sought not only to address the persistent wicked problems of development but also to manage the emerging 'informational, global and networked' (Castells 1998: 77) economy and its attendant problems. Heterarchies or network forms of governance are being acknowledged as one such alternative. This acknowledgement is also linked to the increasing visibility of numerous state and non-state actors at the supra- and sub-national level, thanks to contemporary globalization (triggered by the rapid proliferation of ICTs) and localization processes. In fact, Jessop (1998) suggests that the emergence of heterarchies is responsible for a renewed interest in the 'relatively dormant' concept of 'governance', understood as the 'negotiated interaction of a plurality of public, semi-public and private actors' (Sørensen and Torfing 2005: 195).

Heterarchies are modes of governance that comprise agencies, institutions and systems which, while being operationally autonomous are also structurally coupled by their interdependence (Jessop 1998).[6] These are argued to be distinct from markets and hierarchies (Mayntz 1991: 1; Rhodes 1997b: xii; Jessop 2002: 228ff, in Sørensen and Torfing 2005) along several dimensions, two of which I argue, are critical to understanding or re-conceptualizing the role of the state in these organizational forms. First, in a heterarchy, the relationship amongst the various nodes is pluricentric as opposed to the unicentric system of state rule and the multicentric system of market competition (Kersbergen and Waarden 2004 in Sørensen and Torfing 2005). Similarly, while heterarchies rely on reflexive rationality that deploys dialogue, negotiation and knowledge sharing as its operating code, hierarchies rely on substantive rationality that operates through administrative fiat and bureaucratic routines, while markets rely on procedural rationality that operates through contracts and legal systems (Jessop 1998, 2003). It is this pluricentric structuring relying on a reflexive rationality that allows heterarchies to disseminate and interpret new information quickly (Powell 1990), thus enabling these modes of governance to respond to wicked problems of development (Cristofoli et al. 2011).

An important point to be noted here is that heterarchies are also distinctly different from PPPs of the 1980s that were pushed by most international development agencies as a key strategy/mode of governance to deliver services (Miraftab 2004). A review of literature on PPPs shows some sort of definitional ambiguity between PPPs and heterarchies. While PPPs have diverse definitions (Bovaird 2004), there are few agreements on what exactly PPPs are (Hodge and Greve 2009). Very often, network forms of governance like heterarchies are discussed as a form of a PPP (Brinkerhoff and Brinkerhoff 2011; Börzel and Risse 2005; Lowndes and Skelcher 1998), although there are studies that distinguish these types from the 'corporatist partnerships' of the 1980s (Bovaird 2004; Jones and Bird 1999). A useful distinction by Jones and Bird (1999: 492) is as follows: partnerships of the late 1990s are 'post-corporatist or anti-corporatist' and are not limited to the integration of representatives of capital and labour into the governing process. Rather, these partnerships aim for a diverse and localized set of relationships between

[6]Heterarchies are also a form of governance. Jessop (1998) argues that many practices, including heterarchies, now understood as 'governance', have been examined under other rubrics. These include 'public–private partnerships, industrial districts, trade associations, statecraft, diplomacy, interest in 'police' (*Polizei*), policy communities and international regimes'. Since all these involve aspects of what is now termed 'governance' (Jessop 1998: 31), the concept has definite precursors.

public agencies, the private sector and hybrid organizations funded by a mixture of private and public money. In these partnerships, civil society and not-for-profit organizations are included (Jones and Bird 1999: 492). It is these partnerships that are referred to as heterarchies. These are different from the PPPs in that the latter are long-term agreements between the government and a private partner, such that the service delivery objectives of the government are aligned with the profit objectives of the private partner. This definition excludes arrangements where not-for-profit civil society groups are involved (OECD 2011). Bovaird (2004), in discussing different types of PPPs suggests that there are some that rely on traditional or 'transactional' contracts, i.e. contracts that are driven by pure economic incentives. These are different from partnerships that are based on 'relational' contracts. The latter relies on co-operation and mutual trust as well as shared problem-solving. It is these partnerships that, more recently, are being referred to as heterarchies. These partnerships, Bovaird (2004) argues, are constructed within the public governance paradigm, compared to the corporatist partnerships that follow the NPM paradigm.

Heterarchies and the State

Within heterarchies, the state is positioned very differently from its positioning in hierarchies and markets (including PPPs). While state rule is based on the undisputed centrality of the sovereign state, and market regulation is based on an infinite number of self-interested actors who are not bound by any common agenda, heterarchies involve a range of interdependent nodes which partner and negotiate to achieve a common objective (Sørensen and Torfing 2005). The state is one amongst the many nodes, although a central one (Ansell 2000; Fountain 2001; Jessop 1998, 2003; Rhodes 2007). In assuming this centrality, the state is responsible for steering (and managing) the various nodes of the heterarchy to collaborate (Burns and Stalker 1961; Powell 1990; Jessop 1998, 2003; O'Toole 1997; Börzel 1998; Podolny and Page 1998; Ansell 2000; Raab and kenis 2006; Lowndes and Skelcher 1998). It provides the framework for individual nodes within the heterarchy to pursue their aims, ensure compatibility and 'act as the primary organizer of the dialogue amongst policy communities' (Jessop 2003: 6). It is responsible for deploying and sharing information, resolving disputes, balancing power amongst various nodes, developing capacities and 'also assumes political responsibility in the event of governance failure' (Jessop 2003: 6). In other words, the state's ability to operationalize reflexive rationality is critical to the success of the heterarchy.

Yet, there is no empirical evidence demonstrating how the state operationalizes reflexive rationality in the heterarchy.[7] So far, the state's centrality remains a

[7]Jones and Bird (1999) discuss 'networking' and its relevance in setting up Education Action Zones (EAZs) in England. In doing so, they describe in detail the patterns of governance, and the relationship they involve between 'public' and 'private' partners.

theoretical construct and a hypothesis that calls for further exploration and testing, not only to establish the efficacy of heterarchies as effective alternatives to state and market modes of governance, but also to gain insights into when and how heterarchies can fail.

Like hierarchies and markets (including PPPs), heterarchies are also prone to failures (Jessop 1998, 2003; Shrank and Whitford 2011).[8] PPPs have been evaluated (for a detailed review of evaluations of PPPs, especially those in the space of long-term infrastructure contracts see Hodge and Greve 2009), although the literature on PPPs has little to say about whether and how partnerships have delivered on development (Miraftab 2004). Although delving into the failures of these modes of governance is not the intention of this chapter, understanding the manifestation of the state's centrality and the implications of there one provide insights into the potentials and pitfalls of these modes of governance.

The Municipal Reforms Programme and the State's Centrality

The MRP is an e-governance intervention of the provincial government of Karnataka [as represented by its Department of Municipal Administration (hereafter DMA)] in India. The Programme aims to strengthen municipalities by implementing technology-led administrative reforms that rely on common standards and processes. It implements five reforms that target the day-to-day functioning of municipalities.[9] These are: (i) websites for municipalities to put all information regarding their functioning in the public domain; (ii) birth and death registration and certification, which involves digitization of birth and death records, online registration of current births and deaths, and issuing computerized birth and death certificates; (iii) fund-based double entry accounting and accrual system to capture the revenue and expenditure of municipalities in real time, allowing for the timely preparation of balance sheet of income and expenditure; (iv) a public grievance and redress mechanism, or Helpline that seeks to enhance efficiency and effectiveness in service provision through citizen participation; and (v) property taxation information systems, or *Aasthi* that seeks to computerize the functions of the revenue departments of municipalities with the objective of enhancing revenue collection through effective taxation of properties (buildings and land).

---

[8]While there have been attempts to thematize (Jessop 1998) and theorize network failure (see also Shrank and Whitford 2011 for a review of literature on network failures).

[9]The main functions of municipalities include provision of basic services such as water supply, solid waste management, street lights, provision and maintenance of roads, and administration. The reforms also aim to strengthen the ULBs financially by enabling them to raise their own revenues to perform these functions.

The reforms are conceptualized, designed and implemented through multiple partnerships between state and non-state actors (see Fig. 4.1). The state actors include: (i) the DMA as the nodal agency; (ii) the Municipal Reforms Cell (hereafter Reforms Cell), as the technical cell of the DMA; (iii) the Survey of India as the technical advice support agency for mapping (GIS) and MIS; (iv) the Karnataka Urban Infrastructure Development Finance Corporation Limited as the financial agency; (v) Software Technology Parks of India, Bangalore, for operation and management of the data centre; and, last but not the least, (vi) the 213 municipalities across the province of Karnataka. Prominent amongst the many non-state actors are the (vii) eGovernments Foundation (eGov); and, (viii) the City Managers Association of Karnataka (CMAK).[10] Structured as wide-ranging partnerships between state actors, and between state and non-state actors, the Programme exemplifies heterarchies.

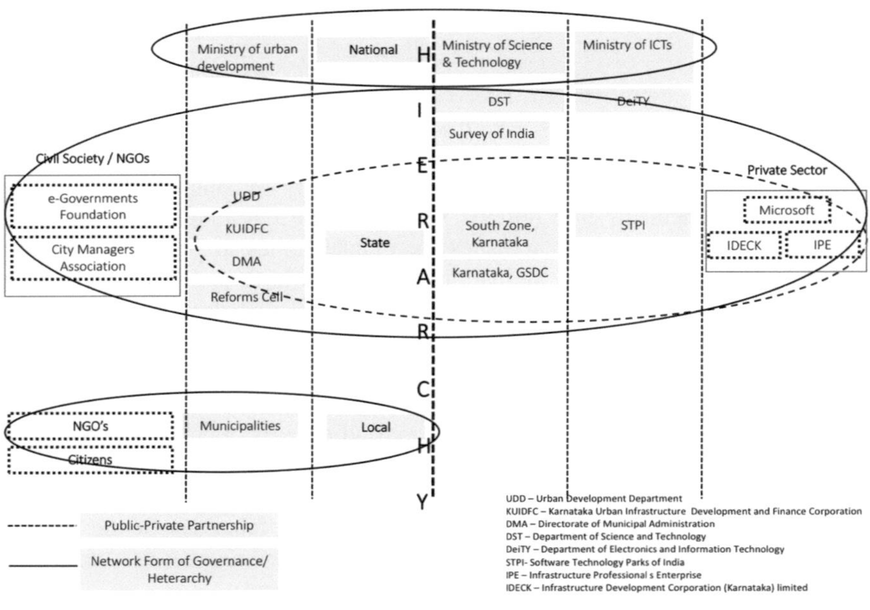

Fig. 4.1 Structuring of the municipal reforms Programme as a heterarchy

[10]In addition, the DMA, from time to time, roped in private sector organisations such as the Infrastructure Professionals Enterprise (IPE), Microsoft, and Infrastructure Development Corporation (Karnataka) Limited (iDeCK). However, these were not part of the core team that conceived and designed the MRP. Given their relatively shorter involvement, these are not a part of the collaboration, hence are not discussed.

Methods

This chapter uses the case study method observed and analysed through a 'multiple-nested research design' (Yin 1994: 286), also referred to as a 'decentred analysis' of governance, as this method allows an understanding of the broader socio-economic context within which a particular practice emerges (Bevir and Rhodes 2004: 1249). Using the Municipal Reforms Programme as the case study, this chapter draws on fieldwork carried between February 2012 and March 2013. The nested research design was deployed to understand the conception, design and implementation of the Programme through semi-structured interviews, focused group discussions and informal conversations conducted mostly at the provincial level. At the municipal level, similar methods were used to unpack how the reforms were conceived and to get an idea of how reforms were implemented and their impact on the day-to-day functioning of the municipality.

The Municipal Reforms Programme: Evolution of the Heterarchy

Initiated in 2002 as a pilot in 49 municipalities (hereafter the pilot phase), in 2006, the Programme was scaled to cover the remaining 164 municipalities (hereafter the scale-up phase). Interestingly, the municipalities chosen for the pilot cover most of the large (and relatively complex) cities in the province. To facilitate the scale-up, the DMA established a dedicated Reforms Cell in 2005, on the understanding that scaling up of reforms would require concerted effort. It was acknowledged that implementing reforms is 'like driving a car—it needs continuous pressure' (bureaucrat, Reforms Cell, 16 April 2012). Yet, initial interviews at the provincial and municipal level with the various state and non-state actors revealed that while the pilot 'progressed well', the same degree of progress was not experienced with the scale-up. Why is it that despite the establishment of a dedicated Reforms Cell the scale-up to the 164 municipalities—that are relatively smaller in size and therefore less complex—was not considered successful? The answer, I argue, lies in the role of the state in the two phases. In the rest of this section, I show how, to begin with, the state forges wide-ranging collaborations exemplifying heterarchies. Within the collaboration, in both the phases, the state maintains a centrality, although this centrality manifests varyingly in the pilot and the scale-up phase. In the pilot, the state as a central node coordinates the various nodes to work collectively by facilitating dialogue and knowledge exchange amongst them. It encouraged what Malhotra (2002) refers to as 'fluid' relations amongst the various nodes. In other words, the state steered the collaboration as a relational contract. However, in the scale-up, the state while continuing to be a central node switches to a transactional contracting mode whereby the various nodes deliver strictly as per their respective contracts. I demonstrate how this transition in the working modalities in the two phases is responsible for the unanticipated negative impacts in the scale-up. In what follows, I trace the contours of the heterarchy and within that the role of the state.

Pilot Phase (2002–2005)

The Programme was conceptualized and driven by the DMA whose main responsibility is to supervise and monitor municipalities to enable them to deliver basic services efficiently. While it was envisaged that the municipalities would eventually own and drive the reforms, the DMA, by virtue of being the main driver of reforms emerged as the central node in the collaboration. To design and implement technology-led administrative reforms, the DMA sought the help of eGov as it did not have the skills to develop or deploy technology. Since, the Programme was the first of its kind in the country, there were few experiences to learn from. Consequently, the pilot demanded preparatory ground work, primarily to understand the nuts and bolts of municipal governance and how technology can be introduced within this context. While led by the DMA, the ground work involved all the nodes as is evidenced by the following response: 'a lot of ground work was done…—preparation work to build a system. [We] interacted with the bill collectors [municipal staff], planned out the process to show what could be done. [We] built a lot of social capital with the bill collectors. A lot of learning came from the bill collectors without which this system could not have been devised. Though not IT savvy—without their knowledge it is not possible to devise or even understand the system' (team member, eGov, 26 March 2012).

Municipalities, while part of the state hierarchy, were acknowledged as critical partners in the collaboration as it was the municipal staff that was best suited to provide inputs on the functional requirements and specifications for each application supporting the reforms. Collaboration with these units of governance was forged through monthly meetings where '…representatives of municipalities were encouraged to articulate their experience with reform implementation, problems [experienced during reform implementation] and possible solutions' (senior team member eGov, 26 March 2012).

As the DMA, eGov and the municipalities immersed themselves in the preparatory work, there was a felt need for two other skill sets. First, implementation of the property tax reform, i.e. *Aasthi* required the mapping of properties on a GIS platform as well as the preparation of a detailed database describing the attributes of every property. Second, the DMA also realized the criticality of creating awareness on the utility of integrating reforms in the day-to-day functioning of the municipalities and to instil a sense of ownership amongst these units for the reforms. Given the enormity of implementing reforms in the envisaged 213 municipalities, the DMA roped in the Survey of India to map the various properties on a GIS platform and to create a database of all the properties on MIS. Similarly, to create awareness about the reforms and to ensure uptake and ownership at the local level, the DMA entered into an understanding with the CMAK to deliver on this task. The City Managers association organized peer exchange programs, information sharing between cities and various countries as well as documentation of best practices.

For instance, in 2006 'CMAK in association with the Municipal Reforms Cell organized training sessions for commissioners, engineers and personnel from Accounts Department of Nirmala Nagara towns in the Bangalore division' (CMAK 2006). Similarly, it organized a session on 'Property Tax Reforms' for top officials … to deliberate upon different issues related to property tax' (CMAK 2007). It was through such events and Programmes that CMAK facilitated knowledge exchange and experience sharing amongst municipalities. In doing so, the City Managers Association initiated learning through experiences, while also instilling a sense of ownership for reforms amongst these units of governance

Interestingly, while the MoUs between the DMA-eGov, DMA-Survey of India and DMA-CMAK formalized the relations between these nodes, in effect, the interactions were 'fluid' (Malhotra 2002: 97), i.e. the nodes did not strictly adhere to their respective roles as defined by the agreements. The DMA emerged central to this fluidity, as can be gauged from the following response:

> We [DMA] were aware that the reforms are our projects – we have given the money so therefore we need to get the work done.… As a team [at the DMA], we were encouraged to spend a day each in Survey of India and eGov and work with them.… It was like a family—we all worked together. There was a lot of information exchange and dialogue on everyday issues. There were no reporting procedures, yet, we had first-hand knowledge of what is happening in both the offices.

In fostering fluidity amongst the various nodes of the heterarchy, the DMA, in effect encouraged a relational contract between the various nodes. In the process, it ensured iterative reform implementation by steering knowledge to reframe problems in order to resolve them (Klijn 1996, in Sørensen and Torfing 2005). As a process, the DMA encouraged continuous rethinking and learning while also mobilizing the energies, wills and capacities of the other nodes, especially the municipalities to shape interdependencies, and create discursive conditions for interaction amongst the nodes (Sørensen and Torfing 2005). This, in turn, served an important function of accommodating the diverse needs of the municipalities while also seeking to instil a sense of ownership for reforms. Thus, in this phase the DMA, while a central node in the collaboration, showcased a marked transition from operating through its hierarchies to collaborating horizontally with other state and non-state actors. Even where hierarchies existed, for instance, between the DMA and the municipalities, the relationship was not one of command and control. On the contrary, the municipalities were treated as equal partners with an acknowledgement that without the active participation of the municipalities designing robust reforms and implementing these was an impossible task.

As outputs, by 2005, all municipalities in the pilot stage had adopted common standards and processes and these include the following: (i) standardized budgeting and accounting procedures; (ii) standardized system of GIS mapping of municipal jurisdictions and an MIS-based property data set; (iii) rationalization of cadre and recruitment rules to facilitate hiring of IT professionals at the provincial and municipal levels[11]; and (iv) standardized tax assessment and enhancement procedures. Adoption of these standards and processes heralded long-term systemic changes in municipal governance. In other words, the basics to reform the municipalities were in place.

In 2005–06, the DMA decided to scale-up the Programme to cover the remaining 164 municipalities in the state. To facilitate implementation, the DMA established a dedicated Reforms Cell. Despite, the experience of the pilot and, the support of a dedicated Reforms Cell, the scale-up did not happen as smoothly.

Scale-Up Phase (2006–2012)

With the expansion of the Programme to cover the remaining municipalities, the demand for updates, enhancements and improvements to the software applications increased. The DMA, in a bid to reduce its dependence on eGov (which up till the pilot phase was providing services gratis, now began to demand monetary compensation) decided to consolidate its Reforms Cell by recruiting technical staff. In 2008, a renewal contract between the DMA and eGov positioned the latter as Maintenance Support Organization, and its responsibilities (other than providing maintenance and support services to facilitate the scale-up), included enhancing capacities of the Reforms Cell staff to manage e-governance applications. Over the next two years, the Reforms Cell consolidated itself to gain a distinct identity of the technical wing of the DMA, having capacities to develop software applications. It was this consolidation which triggered a change in the role and behaviour of the DMA.

As the Reforms Cell consolidated, there emerged a greater focus on developing new applications for a host of new e-governance reforms.[12] By 2010 the Reforms Cell was rolling out applications for 24 reforms, consolidating itself as a software developer by taking over most of the functions of eGov, with the latter functioning as a Maintenance and Support Organization. Technological tools for the additional reforms were deployed at a rapid pace, leaving little or no time for dialogue with other nodes in the collaboration. By 2010, monthly meetings with the municipalities ceased which, in turn, led to a reduced involvement of the CMAK and the Survey of India as the work of both these nodes was with municipalities. Consequently, the DMA emerged as the only active node in the heterarchy. It began to centralize and broker all decisions with the other nodes contributing as per their contractual specifications. In other words, the fluidity of relations amongst the various nodes that the DMA encouraged in the pilot was missing in the scale-up.

[11] All municipalities in the state have an IT cell that is responsible for implementing e-governance reforms. The IT cell is staffed by programmers and data entry operators.

[12] The demand for new applications is attributed to a new policy thrust of the national government, advocating e-governance reforms in municipalities across the country, although the prescribed basket of reforms was much larger than those implemented as part of the Programme in Karnataka.

Consequently, on the one hand, eGov, Survey of India and city managers of Karnataka emerged as passive contributors to the reforms, while on the other, the municipalities emerged as passive recipients of reforms.

During fieldwork it was gathered that 'implementing reforms, since 2008 [scale-up], means rolling out of technology' (bureaucrat, GoK, 20 March 2012). Thus, in this phase, 'reform implementation' shifted from being understood as moulding the context for technology adoption by the municipal staff to just developing and deploying applications. The Reforms Cell distanced itself from concerns about whether the applications were being used effectively and who was using them. In the scale-up, the focus of the Programme was primarily to deploy online tools. Whether the municipalities were adopting and integrating these tools in their day-to-day functioning became a distant concern, if at all, as is evident from the following response: 'we can roll out the modules [online tools], how best they are used, is not monitored or tracked [by us] and is not our responsibility…. Taking these reforms ahead is largely dependent on the motivation and the drive of the IT engineer in the municipality' (bureaucrat, Reforms Cell, 10 December 2010). In other words, contrary to the approach in the pilot phase, in the scale-up, the state as represented by the DMA (and the Reforms Cell) distanced itself from governance concerns. By February 2013, the Reforms Cell took over most of the functions of eGov, while expanding its operations across 32 applications.

While the completion of the reforms was anticipated by 2010, the DMA sought two extensions of two years each. The Programme finally culminated in 2014. While the Reforms Cell continues to provide online e-governance solutions to municipalities across the state, as of 2014, the initial five reforms have been implemented partially and, of those implemented, not all are successful. An evaluation of the Helpline by the City Managers Association in 2006 points to the failure of this reform. CMAK (2006) observes that most complaints are not being routed through the Helpline. The telephone lines meant for receiving complaints from the citizens are often used for other office purposes, and the staff manning the Helpline was assigned the task of being receptionists in many municipalities.

A detailed review of reform implementation and working in the two municipalities of Hassan and Bidar shows that the reforms are not working well, not just in these municipalities, but across several in the province (Mohan et al. 2013). Not only are the reforms not being used by the various municipalities, there also seems to be little ownership for these reforms (Mohan et al. 2013). This was reiterated by one of the senior officials from the provincial governments who believe that 'reforms cannot be driven by the IT engineers [of the Reforms Cell. They have to be driven by those who need the reforms, i.e. the ULBs "municipalities". At the end of 7 years of its existence, MRC [Reforms Cell] should have been in great demand—municipalities should have been lining up here [at the Reforms Cell office] and seeking the services of MRC. On the contrary, many local bodies (at least the larger ones) are now requesting to be excluded from the MRC–Mysuru, Hubli Dharwad, Koppal, Tumkur, Davangere; mainly because they feel that in setting up the MRC as a software company, the objective of reforms is lost. They feel they can proceed efficiently on their own. In fact many are developing their own tools as per their requirements (bureaucrat, GoK, 15 March 2012).

My field work in the municipalities confirmed this. Several municipalities have indeed developed and deployed online tools that meet their requirements. For instance, Gulbarga municipality has developed an online tool for tax assessment and collection.[13] Conversations with the higher ups in the provincial government confirmed that Gulbarga is not an isolated case.

Conclusion

In this chapter, I set out to understand the role the state plays in network forms of governance that gained prominence in the late 1990s as a means to address development challenges. The failure of market-mediated (PPPs) and state-led development models in tackling development challenges, and the consequent recognition that addressing such challenges requires collective (private and public) resources and capacities, led to collaborations between governments, private sector and NGOs. Within these collaborations, while the state is argued to be a central node, responsible for managing and steering to heterarchy to deliver on its objectives, there is little empirical evidence demonstrating how the state's centrality manifests to do so.

I use the Municipal Reforms Programme in Karnataka, India, whose organizational arrangements resemble the description of heterarchies to point to how the state's centrality manifests such that it operationalizes reflexive rationality to manage and steer the heterarchy effectively. In doing so, I provide the much needed empirical evidence supporting the state's ability to render these modes of governance as effective alternatives to state- and market-led modes of governance like PPPs, while also arguing that these alternatives provide the state the opportunity to move beyond entrepreneurial governance models.

This chapter traces the role of the state across two phases of the Programme—pilot and the scale-up. In the pilot phase, it was observed that the state makes a clear departure from its hierarchical mode of functioning, while actively engaging itself in what appears to be a heterarchical mode of operation. In this phase, most nodes were operating on a relational contract that was facilitated by the state (DMA) by encouraging dialogue, knowledge exchange and mutual trust. Yet, this was not the case in the scale-up when the state as a central node begins to centralize and broker most decisions in the collaboration while demanding the involvement of the other

[13]In January 2013, the Reforms Cell was yet to deploy *Aasthi* in Gulbarga, claiming that the ULB had not digitized the back-end data. Yet, a visit to Gulbarga revealed that the IT cell in the ULB had procured a rudimentary tool locally. Data of all properties filing their taxes with the ULB were being digitized with this tool. Consequently, the property database with Gulbarga was an updated version of the database of the Reforms Cell which was based on the GIS survey done in 2007–2008.

nodes as per contractual agreements, i.e. the involvement of the nodes was as per the transactional contracts that were signed between the various nodes. The fluidity of relations that existed in the pilot was absent in the scale-up. It was these differences in the implementation modalities of the two phases that led to a relative success of the pilot when compared to the scale-up.

While the MRP is not demonstrative of a stable heterarchy, it does point to the state's ability to steer a collaboration to function effectively to achieve its agenda—strengthening municipalities through administrative reforms—although for a short while. This mixed experience neither allows an argument for, not against heterarchies as effective alternatives to states and markets. What can be concluded is that the success of these modes of governance is dependent on the manifestation of the state's centrality in a given institutional and policy environment. Additionally, the success of the Programme, albeit for a short span does allow us to conclude that these modes of governance open up opportunities for the state to move beyond the neoliberal framework of entrepreneurial governance arrangements.

References

Ansell, C. (2000). The networked polity: Regional development in Western Europe. *Governance, 13*(2), 279–291.

Bevir, M., & Rhodes, R. A. W. (2004). Interpreting British Governance. *British Journal of Politics and International Relations, 6*, 130–136.

Börzel, T. A. (1998). Organizing Babylon—On the different conceptions of policy networks. *Public Administration, 76*(2), 253–273.

Börzel, T. A., & Risse, T. (2005). Public-private partnerships: Effective and legitimate tools of international governance. In E. Grande & L. W. Pauly (Eds.), *Complex sovereignty: Reconstructing political authority in the twenty first century* (pp. 195–216). Accessed May 12, 2012. http://userpage.fuberlin.de/atasp/texte/021015_ppp_risse_boerzel.pdf

Bovaird, T. (2004). Public–private partnerships: From contested concepts to prevalent practice. *International Review of Administrative Sciences, 70*(2), 199–215.

Brinkerhoff, D. W., & Brinkerhoff, J. M. (2011). Public–private partnerships: Perspectives on purposes, publicness, and good governance. *Public Administration and Development, 31*(1), 2–14.

Burns, T. E., & Stalker, G. M. (1961). The management of innovation. *University of Illinois at Urbana-Champaign's Academy for Entrepreneurial Leadership Historical Research Reference in Entrepreneurship.*

Castells, M. (1998). End of millennium. The information age: Economy, society and culture vol. III. Cambridge & Oxford: Blackwell.

Castells, M. Preface in Evans, P. B. (Ed.). (2002). *Livable cities? Urban struggles for livelihood and sustainability*. Berkeley, CA: University of California Press.

City Managers Association, Karnataka. (2006). "City Manager", 10 (1). Accessed May 12, 2012. http://www.cmak.com/docs/Newsletter/vol10.pdf

City Managers Association, Karnataka. (2007). City Manager 10 (2). Accessed May 12 2012. http://www.cmakarnataka.com/docs/Newsletter/vol10.pdf.

Cristofoli, D., Mandell, M., & Meneguzzo, M. (2011). "Public networks" say Americans, "public networks" reply Europeans, but are they talking about the same issue? In *Paper for the Public Management Research Association Conference*.

Dunleavy, P., Margetts, H., Bastow, S., & Tinkler, J. (2006). New public management is dead—Long live digital-era governance. *Journal of Public Administration Research and Theory, 16* (3), 467–494.
Escobar, A. (2011). *Encountering development: The making and unmaking of the Third World.* Princeton, NJ: Princeton University Press.
Fountain, J. E. (2001). Building the virtual state: Information technology and institutional change. Brookings Institution Press.
Haque, M. S. (2004). New public management: Origins, dimensions, and critical implications. *Public Administration and Public Policy, 1*, 126.
Heeks, R. (1999). *Reinventing Government in the information age—International practice in the IT-enabled public sector reform*. London: Routledge.
Hodge, G. A., & Greve, C. (2009). PPPs: The passage of time permits a sober reflection. *Economic Affairs, 29*(1), 33–39.
Jessop, B. (1998). The rise of governance and the risks of failure: The case of economic development. *International Social Science Journal, 50*(155), 29–45.
Jessop, B. (2003). Governance and meta-governance: On reflexivity, requisite variety and requisite irony. *Governance as social and political communication* (pp. 101–16). Manchester: Manchester University Press.
Jones, K., & Bird, K. (1999). Partnership as strategy: Public–private relations in education action zones. *British Educational Research Journal, 26*(4), 491–506.
Lowndes, V., & Skelcher, C. (1998). The dynamics of multi-organizational partnerships: An analysis of changing modes of governance. *Public Administration, 76*(2), 313–333.
Malhotra, P. (2002). *From Hyderabad to "Cyeberabad": Technological visions and the everyday bureaucracy*. Unpublished Bachelor of Arts Thesis, Harvard College.
McGuire, M. (2003). Is it really so strange? A critical look at the "network management is different from hierarchical management" perspective. In *Public Management Research Association Conference, Washington, DC* (pp. 9–11). Accessed January 13, 2015. http://pmranet.org/conferences/georgetownpapers/McGuire.pdf
McMillan, J. (2002). *Reinventing the Bazaar: A natural history of markets*. New York: W.W Norton and Company, Inc.
Miraftab, F. (2004). Public-private partnerships the Trojan Horse of neoliberal development? *Journal of Planning Education and Research, 24*(1), 89–101.
Mohan, A. K., Cutrell, E., & Parthasarathy, B. (2013, December). Instituting credibility, accountability and transparency in local service delivery?: Helpline and Aasthi in Karnataka, India. In *Proceedings of the Sixth International Conference on Information and Communication Technologies and Development: Full Papers-Volume 1* (pp. 238–247). ACM.
Osborne, D., & Gaebler, T. (1992). Reinventing government: How the entrepreneurial spirit is transforming government. Reading Mass. Adison Wesley Public Comp.
O'Toole, L. J, Jr. (1997). Treating networks seriously: Practical and research-based agendas in public administration. *Public Administration Review, 57*(1), 47–52.
OECD Handout. (2011). From lessons to principles for the use of public-private partnerships. Accessed June 19, 2013. http://www.oecd.org/gov/budgeting/48144872.pdf
Podolny, J. M., & Page, K. M. (1998). Network forms of organization. *Annual Review of Sociology, 24*, 57–76.
Powell, W. W. (1990). Neither market nor hierarchy. Network forms of organization. *Research in Organizational Behavior, 12*, 295–336.
Raab, J. and Kenis, P. (2006) Taking Stock of Policy networks - Do they Matter?. In F. Fischer, G. J. Miller & M. Sidney (Eds.), *Handbook of public policy analysis: Theory, politics, and methods* (pp. 187–200), New York: CRC Press, Taylor & Francis Group.
Rhodes, R. (2007). Understanding governance: Ten years on. *Organisation Studies, 28*, 1243–1264.
Rittel, H. W., & Webber, M. M. (1973). Dilemmas in a general theory of planning. *Policy Sciences, 4*(2), 155–169.

Sassen, S. (2006). *Territory, authority, rights: From medieval to global assemblages* (Vol. 7). Princeton, NJ: Princeton University Press.

Shrank, A., & Whitford, J. (2011). *The anatomy of network failure sociological theory, 29*(3), 151–177.

Sørensen, E., & Torfing, J. (2005). The democratic anchorage of governance networks. *Scandinavian Political Studies, 28*(3), 195–218.

Stoker, G. (1998). Governance as theory: Five propositions. *International Social Science Journal, 50*(155), 17–28.

Stoker, G. (2006). Public value management a new narrative for networked governance? *The American Review of Public Administration, 36*(1), 41–57.

The World Bank. (2000). *World development report reshaping economic geography*, Washington D.C.

Watts, M. (1994). Progress in human geography—Development II: The privatisation of everything? *Progress Human Geography, 18*, 371–384.

Wolf, C. (1993). *Markets or Governments*. Cambridge, MA: MIT Press.

Yin, R. (1994). Discovering the future of the case study method. *Evaluation Practice, 15*(3), 283–290.

Chapter 5
'Speculative Spaces': The Material Practices of Urban Entrepreneurialism

Raman Bhuvaneswari

Introduction

This chapter explores the land development policies and practices of two urban development authorities' in the Extended National Capital Region (ECNR). These included the Haryana Urban Development Authority (HUDA) and the Delhi Development Authority (DDA). Since 1995, the policies of the two urban development authorities have prioritized private sector participation and, in particular, public–private partnerships for the provision of housing for middle and lower income groups. This chapter illustrates the manner in which the practices of the urban development authorities prioritize the financial interests of a specific group of developers and the state, and perpetuate speculative practices in several ways. Their models for promoting private sector partnerships are premised on real estate value gains. The state agencies act as a broker for assembling land for large development projects of private actors. The land laws and the new planning instruments are mobilized to transfer the land to developers' promoting mega-development projects in the form of townships, gated housing, and malls. Although on the one hand the production of housing units increased on paper, in reality, the vulnerability of large sections of population to hold on to their land or access housing has increased. However, large development projects do not follow a similar trajectory. The landowners/landholders counter state interventions, using the provisions in law and resorting to protest actions.

Several scholars have drawn attention to the ascendancy of real estate-led urban development strategies in India and other countries (Denis 2011; Searle 2010; Raman 2015, 2016; Anand and Rademacher 2011). This has implications for urban governance. In an influential paper, Harvey (1989) notes that real estate-led

R. Bhuvaneswari (✉)
Jindal School of Government and Public Policy, Centre for the Study of Urban Transformation, O.P. Jindal Global University, Sonipat, Haryana, India
e-mail: braman@jgu.edu.in

K.C. Smitha (ed.), *Entrepreneurial Urbanism in India*,
DOI 10.1007/978-981-10-2236-4_5

development is a feature of a wider shift in local governance practices from a focus on welfare functions towards entrepreneurial urbanism. Entrepreneurial urbanism is characterized by local governments' focus on local economic development and speculative place construction under public–private partnerships. The local governments bear the risks associated with speculative development projects. The governance shift, Harvey notes, is influenced by the macroeconomic conditions. Analysing the patterns of urban transformation in Bengaluru, Goldman (2011a, b) argued that speculative logic drives the actions of the state agencies. His thesis on speculative urbanism shows that the state actively transfers public resources to private actors and that land speculation and dispossession of rural communities have become the main business of the government.

This chapter engages with the thesis on entrepreneurial urbanism and speculative urbanism. It suggests that the turn towards real estate development and the PPP marks an intensification of the earlier entrepreneurial models adopted by the urban development authorities rather than a new turn. The development authorities promoted a model of land development promoted by urban development authorities' prior to mid-1990s is premised on tapping the land value gains and redistributing the gains across income groups (Ravindra 1996). However, in reality, the housing layouts (plots and built units) formed by urban development authorities were captured by higher income and middle income households. The shift towards private developer-dominated and real estate-led development further extends the speculative practices of the development authorities. As opposed to the earlier models, where there was a semblance of redistributing the real estate value gains, the development authorities now facilitate the transfer of valuable land to developers. The authorities, as the two case studies illustrated in this chapter, act as brokers and assemblers of land for the land-intensive projects promoted by large developers.

Findings presented in this chapter extend the thesis of Harvey (1989) and Goldman (2011a, b) in the following ways. First, this chapter sheds light on the practices of urban development authorities and their relationship with different social groups about which there is little documentation, particularly in the context of Haryana. It analyses the experience of a public–private partnership project for slum redevelopment in Delhi and the land and housing development practices in the small towns of Haryana. Harvey's account on entrepreneurial urbanism emphasizes the changes in the local government. Unlike in the context studied by Harvey, land development in the form of mega-projects is promoted by the different parastatal agencies, namely the urban development authorities, special purpose vehicles for infrastructure provision, and the industrial development corporation. Second, as argued by Goldman (2011a, b), policies and projects promoted by the urban development authorities in the two contexts are land intensive and rely on land-based incentives to attract private developers. Unlike the linear trajectory suggested by Goldman (2011a, b), the speculative projects promoted by state agencies have been mired by conflicts and have not materialized in practice (Shatkin 2011). Third, the case studies shed light on urban development practices in small towns as well as in a metro city. Scholarship on urban transformation and governance is largely metro-centric. Further, the dynamics of transformation in small towns of Haryana has not been documented. In addition, with the exception of Searle (2010, 2014), not much is known about the characteristics of developers or their engagement with the parastatal agencies. This chapter is an attempt to contribute towards such empirical and conceptual gaps.

The rest of the chapter is organized into three sections. It explores two types of PPP projects. Dhar (n.d.) lists five models of PPP projects which are as follows: (1) state–developer joint development, (2) developer–landowner partnership, (3) private developers' project on acquired land, (4) private developers' project on government land, and (5) PPP for slum redevelopment. The first case study analyses the partnership arrangements between a parastatal agency, landowners, and developers, which is described in Section "Partnerships in Land Development: The Case of Haryana's Small Towns". The second case study, described in Section "Practices of Public-Private Partnerships for Slum Redevelopment", explores a slum redevelopment project in the capital city of New Delhi. In an earlier work (Raman 2014, 2015), I had argued that the PPP is used as a mechanism for facilitating the transfer of land to private developers. I build on this argument to illustrate how the community–NGO relation can affect the dynamics of the PPP projects. The final section concludes with a discussion on the implications of the shifts in governance of land for social and spatial justice.

Partnerships in Land Development: The Case of Haryana's Small Towns

This section traces the practices of land development at the outskirts of three towns in Sonepat district. The three towns are situated along the Grand Trunk Road, a major roadway that connects the capital city of Delhi with the border towns of Punjab. The GT Road is a historic trading route that runs from Chittagong in Bangladesh to Lahore in Pakistan and Kabul in Afghanistan. The region between Delhi and Haryana is considered to be a hotbed of real estate investment, and one of the towns along this stretch, viz. 'Sonepat[1] town, was once described as 'the next Gurgaon' (*The Times of India*, 15 June 2012). In anticipation of unbridled growth, real estate developers from Delhi and small towns of Haryana announced projects for building integrated townships, gated housing complexes, malls, and residential apartments. They invested in the region from 2000, and their investments peaked in 2005. The hype of real estate growth has since slowed down. Despite so, government interventions have promoted large developers, as we showed in the last section. Following a brief introduction to the three towns, the characteristics of developers and their practices of assembling land for their projects are described in this section.

[1]http://articles.economictimes.indiatimes.com/2012-02-11/news/31050062_1_property-prices-tdi-infrastructure-region.

Drivers of Urbanization: Real Estate-Led Development

The three towns, Sonepat, Ganour, and Karnal, are within a radius of 150kms from the metropolitan city of New Delhi. Two of the three towns—Karnal and Sonepat—are said to have existed as early as the seventh century BCE (Grewal 2009). Ganour was declared as a town in the late sixties. Both Sonepat and Ganour Karnal were renowned urban centres in the Mughal regime. The two towns developed around the wholesale markets for agricultural produce and retail trade.

Post-independence, all three towns registered a steady increase in urban population (Census 2011). The Karnal town, one of the large towns in the district, registered a steady increase in urban population of more than four lakh according to 2011 census. The town's population has grown from 59,790 in 1951 to 176,131 in 1991. The towns developed around an old core built during the Mughal period. Post-independence, resettlement colonies and residential layouts developed by private actors and planned residential and industrial layouts formed by the HUDA and the HSIIDC, developed outside the old core.

The present-day economy of the towns is constituted of trade, manufacturing, and real estate. Post the partition of India, the towns experienced growth with the influx of refugees from Pakistan. The refugees invested in small trade. Alongside trade, the refugee entrepreneurs established industries for manufacturing bicycles and tyres. The famous Atlas Cycle is located in Sonepat and the Bharat Steel Tubes and, subsequently, Apollo Tyres thrived in Ganour. Between 1960 and 1980, the towns also benefited by the prosperity in the surrounding villages due to the Green and White revolutions. The Green Revolution catalysed the evolution of private agro-processing units, small industries for manufacturing agricultural implements, and public sector research institutions at Karnal town, and agricultural *mandi*s (or markets), at Sonepat and Ganour. Since the mid-1990s, the town entrepreneurs invested in setting up schools to cater to the children from the surrounding rural areas. This trend intensified in the mid-2000s, when the Government of Haryana announced a policy for developing the state as an educational hub. Entrepreneurs from Delhi and other Indian states set up universities for law, engineering, management, and public policy, to attract students from India and abroad.

Urbanization accelerated in the region post-2000, predominantly driven by the lure of high returns from real estate. The conversion of agricultural land started in the early years of the 2000s, and reached its peak in 2005, slowing down since 2010. The Government of Haryana rolled out several projects to set up an educational city and an international horticulture/fruit wholesale trading centre; and, to form the Karnal–Manesar–Palwal highway. Several of these projects are land intensive. For example, around 2000 acres were earmarked to set up the Rajiv Gandhi Educational City and another, 2000 acres for an international horticultural and wholesale fruit market. Land prices rose with the announcement of these projects. In addition, the Government of Haryana announced a policy-promoting public–private partnership. Leading developers from Delhi announced their projects for building townships, malls, and luxury housing complexes. Their projects are located on land parcels along the highway. According to newspaper accounts, large developers control nearly 2000 acres of land in the villages abutting GT Road, and in the towns of Kundli, Sonepat, and Ganour. Besides, private companies, such as the Bharat Steel Tubes, hold vast tracts of land in the region.

Our interviews with the development authorities and land developers in the region show that the sale price of agricultural land in the villages around GT Road increased from 80 Rs/ft^2 before 2000, to 450–500 Rs/ft^2 by 2015.[2] Our survey of the sale price of developed plots in the townships in 2014–2015 show the price of developed plots range between 2800 Rs/sq.ft and 4500–5000 Rs/ft^2. Land prices have gone up to Rs 200,000/yd^2 or Rs 20,000/ft^2 in villages where private developers have built integrated townships or universities. Although the land prices quoted remain as high as Rs 10–40 million per acre in the villages around Sonepat and Karnal, the actual transactions have come down due to delay in the completion of township projects.

The interventions by the state and private developers are discussed in the following sections.

State Agencies Interventions in Land

Land development for urban use, in Haryana, is regulated by different parastatal agencies, two of which are the Haryana Urban Development Authority and the Haryana Industrial Development Corporation. Both institutions prioritize policies to promote for private sector-led development, public–private partnership, and real estate-driven growth. Unlike in other Indian states, the turn towards PPP and real estate-led development is not a new phenomenon in Haryana, but the two authorities, especially the HUDA, scaled up the strategy, since 2005, following the success of Gurgaon.

The Haryana Urban Development Authority (HUDA) was created in 1975, under the Haryana Urban Development Authority Act to undertake large-scale acquisition of land. The authority acquired land for the first time in 1977. Previously, the Haryana Urban Real Estate Department acquired land, and much of the acquired land was allotted for the construction of resettlement colonies for refugees. Besides, the HUDA and the District Town Planning Department (DTP) are authorized to notify land for acquisition. The DTP decides on the area of land to be acquired in accordance with the provisions in the master plan and notify the Estate Department, which acquires the land and transfer it to HUDA for development. The acquired land is then transferred to the HUDA for development.

The Government of Haryana has been promoting land development in partnership with the private developers since 1975. The Haryana Development and

[2]Interviews with the HUDA Chief Planner, dated 23 October 2015, land broker in Rathdhana dated 6 May 2015, and land developers in Sonepat dated 14 June 2015.

Regulation of Urban Areas Act (HDRUA) provides for private developers to negotiate with agricultural landowners and assemble land for development. The DTP provides licences to developers who are able to assemble 0.45 km^2 of contiguous land. Licences are issued initially for two years and renewed subsequently. What has changed, however, is the nature of partnership with private developers. The policies, since 2005, favour large scale development projects such as integrated townships, malls, and commercial complexes.

Until 2000, HUDA's interventions was limited to selected location, often on the outskirts of the town. The authority's approach, similar to development authorities in other states, is to acquire land and develop it as plots for sale to different income groups. In addition, departing from the practices in other Indian States, private developers with licences from the DTP, also formed residential colonies. The buyers were mainly government employees and businessmen from Delhi. In 2005, HUDA projected the Gurgaon model of urban development as a way forward for building new housing and commercial complexes. Land was developed predominantly by one large real estate development company, namely the DLF. The DLF incrementally purchased land directly from farmers, since the eighties, and assembled large tract of land for building townships and luxury apartments (Bedi 2014). Several amendments were made to the Land Acquisition Act during the 1990s and 2000s, to facilitate the transfer of agricultural land to large developers (Bedi 2014). The land acquisition act was amended again in 2013, to further make it easier for claiming land for large scale development projects of private developers as well as government agencies. Further provisions in the Gurgaon model is now viewed as a blueprint for urban development in the country (Chatterjee 2013). In the context of Haryana, the regional government, especially the then chief minister, actively promoted real estate-led development and the involvement of private developers in urban development. His role was critical in facilitating the negotiations between real estate developers and farmers. He also lobbied the political party then in power to reform land acquisition act in order that agricultural land can be transferred easily for large speculative township projects and malls.

Besides HUDA, Haryana State Industrial Development Corporation (HSIDC) is involved in developing land for industrial development in Haryana State. In 2011, HUDA and HSIDC announced public-private partnership for land development as a priority policy area. Of the five models listed by Dhar (n.d.), the HUDA and HSIIDC promoted two dominant forms of partnership—joint development by a private developer and a landowner and development by a private developer on land acquired by a government agency. Under the PPP model, land is acquired and allotted to builders or licences provided to builders for the land they have purchased in the market. Once a licence is issued, the HUDA does not interfere with the developer's project. Further, the Government of Haryana introduced a single-window process for issuing licences to developers via the HUDA. These licences are issued for large-scale development under the special development project area designated by HUDA.

The projects facilitated by the two institutions are not only land intensive, but have also served as a vehicle for transferring land to a handful of large developers. By 2005, large real estate development companies held nearly 2000 hectares of land, which they have purchased from farmers (*The Times of India*, 2014). Between 2008 and 2014, HUDA and DTP issued licences to private developers for developing 84.99 km^2 of land either on their own or in collaboration with the farmers; the dominant pattern is for developers to secure licences in collaboration with the landowners.[3] Of the 84.99 km^2 of land, HUDA acquired 5.68 km^2 of land on low rates, allegedly for serving 'public interest' and sold the land to licensed developers. For example, HSIIDC and the HUDA are involved in the acquisition of land of nearly 6400 acres from three villages for setting up an education city and an international horticulture and fruit market (*mandi*). The education city, named the Rajiv Gandhi Education City, a project pushed by the then chief minister Hooda, is designed over an area of 2000 acres. The city was planned to be built in two phases and was conceptualized by a private consulting group —the Operations Research Group (ORG). HUDA sold the land acquired from three villages to private developers. According to the information provided by HUDA officials, land was acquired from farmers for around Rs 160,000 per acre since 2006 and transferred to developers at the rate of Rs 20–30 mn per acre. Although 2000 acre of land has been acquired so far and another 1000+ acres is notified for acquisition, only three universities have located in the city, with seven others listed on paper.

The announcement of the projects such as the Rajiv Gandhi educational city in 2006, led to an increase of land prices in the market by a three and a half fold from 13.60 lakh per acre to 47.15 lakh the same year. Similarly, the plan to form Kundli Manesar Palwal (KMP) highway, which is a 135-km-long peripheral expressway connecting villages and small towns lying between Kundli in North Delhi with Palwal in Haryana pushed up the land prices. Despite the fact that a substantial proportion of the middle and lower income groups are priced out of the market, the government agencies have been promoting large developers' projects for luxury housing and malls. Several projects are either incomplete or constructed units lie vacant. The land acquired by different government agencies for mega projects too lay unused due to delays and bottlenecks in the implementation.

The PPP is justified as the only way out to increase the production of housing in the region. However, as Bedi (2014) notes, although there has been an overproduction of housing units, with the high cost per unit, access to housing remains a distant dream for a large proportion of the population including the middle and lower income groups. While the real estate-led development at first promised unbridled growth, the market declined in 2010 due to various factors, including the reform of financial transactions in real estate and the financial crisis. Many constructed units in the private-developed townships and land acquired for development remain vacant, and ongoing projects have faced long delays. Unoccupied vacant units lay side by side with scarce supply of affordable housing in the state. The next section describes the characteristics of developers and their strategies.

---

[3]Interview with chief planner, HUDA, dated 13 August 2015.

Developers and the Trajectory of the Project

The entrepreneurs operating in the region are from different backgrounds. Their projects are of different scales. Based on their scale of operation, developers in the researched location may be differentiated into three groups, viz, large developers, mid-sized, and small developers. Similar to the patterns observed in other Indian cities (Raman 2016), large developers from Delhi control the development of land parcels along the GT Road. Hoardings of gated housing complexes and integrated townships along with vacant land waiting to be developed, and semi-finished malls and apartments border the two sides of the highway. The townships and housing complexes were envisaged to fulfil the housing ambition of the Delhi middle-/upper middle-class population who were unable to invest within Delhi or Gurgaon. Hidden behind the main road is the development promoted by medium and small developers. Below, we describe their characteristics and forms of land development.

Large Developers

Large developers have a pan-Indian presence. They predominantly build integrated townships covering more than 100 acres. Their projects are listed in the capital markets. The financial layout of their projects varies from a minimum of 5 billion to a maximum of 30 billion Indian Rupees. Among this group of developers are India Bulls, Ansals, TDI, Omaxe Real Estate and Builders, the Jindal Global Realty, and the Parker. All of them have an office in New Delhi, which they see as their main market.

India Bulls, headquartered in Mumbai, is the country's third largest real estate company, established in 2005. The company started in 2000, as an online securities brokerage company and subsequently diversified into different businesses, including real estate, power, and housing finance. Their main investments are in the National Capital Region (NCR) and Mumbai. According to the company's annual report, nearly 65 % of the investment is in the NCR region (India Bulls 2014). In 2011, India Bulls announced a flagship project for building an integrated township in a HUDA-controlled neighbourhood at Sonepat. The township sprawling over an area of 150 acres boats of an elite residential project, shopping mall, and recreational facilities. India Bulls is listed on the Mumbai, Luxembourg, and Singapore Stock Exchanges and is among the early generation of companies to source Foreign Direct Investment for housing development.

Ansals is one of the seven large developers in the country listed in the Bombay Stock Exchange (*Business Standard* 2015). The company was founded in the 1980s, by a school teacher—Lala Chiranji Lal Ansal. Currently, it has projects in Sonepat and Karnal. Omaxe, another large developer sourcing FDI, floated a township project sprawling over 357 acres at Sonepat. Like Ansals, Omaxe is a first-generation firm in construction and contracting business, established by two entrepreneurs—a civil engineer and a chartered accountant. The firm accelerated their real estate investment in 2001 and is listed in the National Stock Exchange since 2007. The company has projects in other northern Indian states, including Uttarakhand, Rajasthan, Delhi, and Himachal Pradesh. Besides, like other major developers, the builders have relied on FDI for financing their projects.

Unlike the earlier group, the TDI group of companies and Jindal Global Realty operate predominantly in Haryana, particularly in the second- and third-tier cities of Haryana, Uttar Pradesh, and Punjab. The TDI group has business interests in the UK. The TDI township in Kundli, Sonepat, is one of its signature projects planned on 1250 acres of land. Jindal Global Realty is floated by the Jindal group of companies, owning companies manufacturing steel, copper, power, and prefabricated concrete blocks. Its township project located in Sonepat sector 36 covers an area of 640 acres and is located at a distance of 2 km from the KMP highway. The project announced in 2011, is still in its early stages of development.

Many of these projects, though announced as early as 2011, are still in initial stages. For example, many investors in Jindal Global City are employees of Jindal Global University. The university was seen as a catalyst of real estate development in the outlying villages of Sonepat, but it did not follow a similar trajectory. The Jindal Global city project got derailed over the issue of licensing and conversion of agricultural land into urban use. Similarly, of the 1250 acres of land held by TDI group for its flagship project in Kundli, only about 1200 apartments have been constructed and 20 acres have been developed. Several of these constructed units lay vacant. According to the TDI residents' association, there are around there are 200–300 occupants. TDI developers claim that it has plans to build 7000 apartments apart from independent villas.

Medium Developers and Small Developers

The second group of developers who described themselves as mid-sized companies includes Shree Vardhman builders, Parsvnath builders, Tulip builders, and the Divine builders. These firms operate dominantly in the NCR region and particularly in the second- and third-tier towns. The scale of their projects ranges from an area of 30 acres to under 400 acres. Their projects are concentrated in different sectors in each of the three towns.

Three companies, namely, Parsvanath builders, Vardhman builders and Tulip builders, dominate the residential real estate development in four sectors of Sonepat. These builders are from a similar religious community and have extensive family ties between them and with other members of their community in building materials business. Two of them have a franchise in cement trade. Shree Vardhman builders and developers—was founded by two brothers—Sandeep and Sachit Jain. Prior to setting up the company, both of them worked as marketing managers for Parsvanath and had managed the latter's projects at Sonepat. The two entrepreneurs set up the business with the help of their extended family—Parsvanath builders who have been operating in the region since the early 2000s. All three builders belong to Sonepat and floated projects on their inherited land. Besides, they assembled land through purchasing directly from the farmers. The Vardhman brothers, with extensive contacts in HUDA supported other two builders in securing developers' licence. These firms operate predominantly in different small towns of Haryana. The Divine City's project is concentrated in one sector of Sonepat city. The company, headquartered in Delhi, was started by an entrepreneur in electronics trade. The company has business operations in Hong Kong, Singapore, and China. The entrepreneur, hailing from Sonepat diversified into real estate business after 2005, when the land market boomed along the GT Road.

The projects of small developers differ from the other group of developers described above in terms of two aspects: scale of the project and the location. They develop projects of less than an half an acre to 5 acres. Their projects are predominantly forming plots on agricultural land, and sometimes, not authorised for urban use. They also assemble land for large developers. In general, large and medium developers prefer to invest in HUDA-designated areas due to the high cost involved in converting agricultural land to non-agricultural use and subsequently planning permits from the HUDA. Small developers' projects are located in the interior land parcels, immediately outside the town boundary.

Land Access and Relationship with HUDA

Large developers acquire land in two ways—allocation by the HUDA, direct purchase, or assembly through a network of property dealers and partnership with farmers.

A dominant pattern of assembling land among large and medium developers is to either purchase land from farmers or enter into collaboration with landowners for land development. Large developers such as the TDI group, Omaxe, and Parker purchased almost all the land belonged to a village. The negotiation is done through a network of agents—connected to the village *panchayat* (local government) president, accountant, and surveyor of the revenue department. Almost, every landowner doubles up as a land broker in every village. An example is the ways by which TDI developers assembled land for their first township project in Kundli, Sonipat. The TDI township is located on land, which once belonged to residents of a village called Nangal. The villagers had in total around 1450 acres of agricultural land. They were from different caste communities: Jats, Rajputs, and Dalits, and also Muslims. The HUDA, had earmarked in the master plan for Sonipat Village agricultural land owned by residents of Nangal village along with two other villages for acquisition. The plan was to develop urban residential and commercial complex on the acquired land. The master plan was prepared in the mid-90s. HUDA issued a notification for land acquisition in Nangal. According to the villagers, they did not receive any written notification from HUDA. However, developers' middlemen started to visit the village soon after the notification appeared in leading newspapers. The brokers offered the villagers three times the compensation amount. The TDI developers also offered to develop the land collaboratively. Eventually, the TDI builder bought the land negotiating through a village resident. Although, the sale was negotiated, and advance exchanged, the builder was not able to secure all land. Some residents withdrew their offer and went to court challenging the price offered by the builder.

Another example, is the manner in which Jindal Realty assembled land for their project in a village on the outskirts of Sonepat town. Of the 3600 acres of agricultural land belonging to the village, the builder managed to rezone nearly 79 %, or roughly 2900 acres of agricultural land for urban use, using their political connection. According to the developers, a key hurdle that outsiders face in developing land in the state is the complexity of securing conversion and, subsequently, developer's licences issued by HUDA. Large developers such as Jindal Realty with political connections in the village and their power in the central party office alone invest in such unconverted land.

Many large developers started to purchase and assemble land since 2005. They purchased an acre of land for an amount of Rs 180,000–250,000 and tried to sell developed land at the rate of Rs 10,000–38,000/yd^2. Large developers such as India Bulls, TDI group, and Omaxe have substantial land in their land bank. India Bulls has a land bank of 3598 acres across the country, of which 60 % are located in the National Capital Region. Like India Bulls, Omaxe has a land bank of 4030 acres of which 74 ft^2 is under construction.

Entering into a collaboration agreement with farmers is another common practice among large and medium developers. In 2009, the Vardhman builders floated a project called Gardenia, on 14.3 acres of land. Of these, the builder owned 9.5 acres and they assembled another 3.8 acres by entering into partnership with farmers for land development. They floated a luxury housing project, costing around 650 crores. The builder used his share of land and the land purchased from farmers, as collateral to raise loan from the HDFC bank. The loan was used as a working capital from the HDFC bank. The builders enlisted the help of their family members in securing licences from the HUDA.

According to a land broker who also hold a developer licence in Sonepat town, large developers negotiate their land transactions through several intermediaries. The intermediaries perform two functions, viz. sale of built property, finance part of the construction, and assemble land. Occasionally, a broker–investor may undertake land development on a smaller scale. KS and RNK are such investors–assemblers. They buy land from farmers and sell the assembled land to large developers. Besides, they also finance small builders and retail buyers, KS started his firm after having worked as a sales and marketing manager in a renowned firm at Sonipat, owned by their relative. During his stint as a marketing person, he developed contacts with retail buyers from the villages along the GT Road and Delhi. Small developers too sometimes act as land assemblers. In his view, land assemblers consolidate a minimum area of less than 2 acres to a maximum to 30 acres. Developers such as KS make a distinction between a land developer and a developer undertaking construction projects or selling retail plots after providing on site infrastructure. According to KS and RNK, land transactions in the HUDA-developed area have declined due to several factors: slump in the real estate market as well as government assessment of land value.

The intermediaries rely on their networks with the village *panchayat* president and the *namardhar* (accountant), as the practice in many of these villages is that landowners do not resist/contest the request of the *panchayat* president. An intermediary pays around 25 % of the sale price as commission to their network members. Both developers and intermediaries prefer to transact land through their networks due to the cumbersome process of converting the land and adjudicating future conflicts with buyers.

Landowner—HUDA—Developer Relationship

The landowners' relationship with the developer was initially conflict free. However, post 2010, conflicts between farmers and developers came out in the open. One of the well-known cases is the conflict between TDI and the landowners of Nangal village. The conflict has several aspects. One group of farmers, though they had agreed to the sale, stated that the terms of transactions favoured the developer and that the developer prepared the collaboration agreement without consulting them. Another group of farmers claimed that the builder had used fake documents and hypothecated their land in the bank, without taking their consent. A third view is that though some farmers did not want to sell their land, the land was taken over by coercion. The dominant view among landowners is that in case of conflict, the HUDA acts as a broker of the developer rather than addressing farmers' concern. Several farmers in the village have gone to the court. The confrontation took a violent turn, after which a few landowners reclaimed their land. Farmers in some villages around Rai affected by the Rajiv Gandhi Educational City formed an association called the Bhoomi Adhigrahan Virodhi Sangharsh Samiti (Anti-land Acquisition Movement Group) to stall the land acquisition by the HSIIDC and the HUDA. In localities where the Jat community own land, the negotiation in such contests is done via the party channel. In such context, the conflict is adjudicated in terms of higher compensation amount.

The HUDA has selectively attempted to regulate the developers through cancelling licences.[4] Such decisions are taken only when a developer fails to pay the development fee or fails to show the financial source for completing the project. Rarely has it interfered in the conflict on behalf of landowners.

Practices of Public-Private Partnerships for Slum Redevelopment

This section explores the manner in which Public-Private Partnership (PPP) for slum redevelopment materializes in practice, drawing on the case of Kathputli squatter colony in New Delhi. Similar to the projects described above, the PPP projects for slum

[4]http://www.tribuneindia.com/news/haryana/parsvnath-loses-licence-for-sonepat-housing-project/37153.html.

redevelopment, are designed to attract private developers' through providing them with opportunities to capture the land value gains. These opportunities are created using new planning instruments such as the Transfer of Development Rights (TDRs) and the land share in locations of premium real estate value. This section builds on the earlier works (Raman 2015, 2016), which illustrated how the new planning instruments such as TDR and land share are mobilized under the PPP. Further, it explores the role of non-governmental organizations (NGOs), who are emerging as key partners in slum redevelopment projects. Discussions on the PPP arrangements have focused on the role of private developers, but have a limited focus on the role of NGOs.

The in situ development of Kathputli colony in Delhi was undertaken as part of a centrally sponsored programme under the 12th Plan—the Rajiv Awas Yojana (RAY). The Delhi Development Authority (DDA) partnered with private developers and NGOs for implementing the in situ development of squatter settlements like this colony. The colony is home to more than 3500 households and is located in a strategic location in west Delhi, abutting a main road and close to a metro station. It developed from the mid-1950s when a group of seasonal migrant artisans from Rajasthan occupied a marsh land, which was then on Delhi's fringes. At present, the colony is occupied by migrants belonging to 13 different artisan and non-artisan communities. The colony was placed on the global map in the 1970s by a well-known artist in the city, with close connections to the then ruling party. The colony was demolished for the first time on 25 May 1976,[5] when a number of other settlements in the city became subject to Indira Gandhi's emergency policies (see Tarlo 2003). In the course of this demolition, Kathputli residents were allotted plots in a resettlement colony outside Delhi, but many returned. Following this event, there were several attempts to evict the colony in 1986, 1990, 1996, and 2002, but each time the residents returned.[6]

In 2009, the then minister of urban development launched a project for the in situ redevelopment of the colony. The project was scheduled to be completed within two years, but was later extended by two more years. The DDA partnered with one of the country's largest property developers, called Raheja Developers. Besides the developer, an NGO organization actively participated in the project. The project started at Kathputli colony with the DDA awarding a contract to a professional consultancy firm in architecture and planning, Gyan Prakash and Mathur Associates (GPMA), to survey the settlement and formulate the DPR. Subsequently, the DDA awarded a contract to Raheja according to which the DDA is responsible for clearing the colony land, relocating the residents to a transit camp, and transferring the land of an area 5.22 ha along with Rs 6.11 crores to the builders in exchange for the construction of houses.[7] Further, the land would be shared on the ratio of 60:40, with the Kathputli colony residents housed in the 60 % of the land, and the developer can utilize the

[5]'Bhoole Bisre Kalakaron ke Sangharsh ki Saalgirah', *Hindustan*, 2 June 1978.

[6]Interviews with Puran, Puppeteer Dilip—Pradhan, and Bhagawati Asia Heritage Foundation, February 2014.

[7]Interview with Sahil, ex-DDA planner, dated 23 June 2014.

remaining 40 %, for developing residential and commercial projects for sale in the open market. The project also boasted of progressive policy language—community participation and partnership with the NGO to mobilize communities to participate in the project. Till date, however, the project has not progressed beyond a spiral web of surveys and spatial maps, initiated by the DDA and the NGO alternatively. The uncertainties and contestations over the terms of the project led to several conflicts among colony residents and between the colony residents, DDA and the NGO.

The conflicts between the colony residents and the DDA revolved around two aspects: the first relates to the question of who is included in the project. The inclusion/exclusion of colony residents is determined by the criteria used for selecting households. This affects the second aspect, namely the layout and housing design. The conflicts between the DDA and the colony residents brought to fore several questions about the decision-making process.

- *How was the partnership forged between the different actors?* How and why was Raheja builders chosen?
- *How were project decisions on eligible households, housing design made?*
- *How was the partnership with the NGO forged?* What was the NGO's role in the PPP?
- *How did the community respond to these decisions?*

Decisions on Partnership: The DDA, Technical Consultant, Builder, and the NGO

The two documents, i.e. the master plan and the detailed development plan, provided the framework for the implementation of the project. While the master plan is the legal document for regulating the land use and development in the city, the Detailed Project Report (DPR), as the name indicates, provides the detail of the eligible number of households, the layout design, and the design of houses.

Much before the official launch in 2009, the DDA began to formulate the project for Kathputli colony. In 2007, the DDA awarded the contract for the DPR to a private consultancy firm in architecture and planning to prepare the DPR. The process by which the firm was selected is unclear. Conversations with the director of the concerned agency suggest that the DDA approached them when the DPR had to be prepared and that they undertook this assignment as DDA is one of their important clients. And that, they were aware as early as 2008 that the construction contract would be awarded to Raheja.[8] This raises the next question as to how and why did the DDA enter into partnership with Raheja builders?

---

[8]Interview with chief architect GPMA and the team leader, GPMA November 2013. The DPR is a design document outlining the building construction norms and the plans for squatter rehousing and commercial complexes. The returns are higher for companies implementing the DPR rather

Raheja builders are among the few large developers operating across India's cities, with a record of projects such as shopping malls, IT parks, special economic zones, and high-income luxury housing. Based in Mumbai, the company specializes in implementing projects under public–private partnerships, where land for their projects is allotted by the state in exchange for housing development. The builders boasts of constructing the world's tallest building—Raheja Complex—on Kathputli colony land. They planned to build the commercial component in collaboration with Arabtec Constructions, the builders of the Burj Khalifa, the tallest building in the world located in Dubai (Ramnani 2011). The multi-storeyed apartments for housing the colony residents, originally designed in 15 storeys of 45-m-high towers, would be built behind the Raheja Phoenix Complex and would be screened off from view. According to the chairman and MD of Raheja Developers Ltd., Mr. Naveen Raheja, 'Nobody wants poor people to be their neighbour'.[9]

The process by which Raheja were selected for redeveloping Kathputli colony is murky. While the DDA claims that only Raheja submitted a tender for the redevelopment of the colony, rumour has it that the terms of the tender process were rigged to suit this company. Although eight developers enlisted by the DDA qualified in the technical bid for in situ redevelopment, only Raheja submitted the financial bid for Kathputli colony.[10] An internal audit report also criticized the DDA for the terms on which the contract had been awarded and the amount of land transferred to the developer.

Another key strategy advocated under the RAY is the partnership with a non-governmental agency for mobilizing community to participate in the project. Several non-governmental agencies were working with the colony residents to organize work cooperatives, health, and education. However, at the time of redevelopment, a new NGO—the HC—renowned for their work on housing rights in the city but new to the colony residents, represented the latter in official meetings. The colony residents claimed that the NGO came to their settlement on their own when DDA first attempted to move residents out of the colony to relocate them in the transit camp. The conflict was reported widely in newspapers. The publicity generated support from various groups outside the colony, including artists, the NGO HC, and interested citizens. The NGO on the other hand claims that they moved into the settlement because of an invitation from the colony residents. The NGO mobilized the colony residents to contest the DDA–Raheja redevelopment plan. In the following sections, we describe the manner in which the DPR, a legally binding document was produced, followed by colony residents' relationship with the NGO.

(Footnote 8 continued)

than those designing it, as construction projects for squatter rehousing and the commercial complexes are highly profitable ventures.

[9]From Slum to Skyscraper, *The Wall Street Journal*, 17 February 2012.

[10]Technical Bid, Empanelment of Developers for Development of 21 sites identified for In situ rehabilitation of JJ Clusters at different location of Delhi and Invitation for financial bid from the qualified developers for in situ development at Kathputli Colony near Shadipur, New Delhi No. F5 (21O)W D-51DDA/2008-09/2466, dated 29 January 2009.

Decision-Making Process: The DPR Document

The DPR relies on the information from demographic and spatial surveys. In an earlier work, I have described in detail the conflicts that emerged in the colony over the official surveys (Raman 2015). Right from the time the architect–consultant published the survey results, the colony residents contested the number of households listed in official survey. The DDA accommodated the residents' concerns of the first survey and ordered a second survey, which listed higher number of households in the colony. However, subsequently, the DDA hardened its position in favour of the developers' plan and kept changing the number of households eligible for housing allocation under the redevelopment project. The contestations of the survey results published by the DDA's consultant led to colony residents organising their own surveys. There were several rounds of surveys and maps—some of which were led by the non-governmental organizations and others by the DDA. Despite several rounds of surveys, a persistent dispute is over the numbers of households residing in the colony. Ignoring the opposition from the residents, the architect-planning consultant published the DPR and the builders finalized the plans for the colony. At the colony, the NGO led the colony residents to repeatedly survey the settlement and prepare plans allegedly to negotiate with the DDA.

Although the RAY project document mentions community participation, the preparation of the DPR was shrouded in secrecy. In fact, colony residents attempted to secure the document using the provisions in the Right to Information Act, 2002. Eventually, they secured the document from an architect researcher visiting their colony. Until then, they had been under the impression that the project would provide them access to land titles and housing. When they accessed the design details, they realized to their dismay that land was a going to be shared and residents were to be rehoused in multi-storeyed buildings. In my interviews with the representatives of the DDA, it was suggested that the authority did not reveal the DPR to the community as they did not have the technical knowledge to understand the document.

Raheja proposed to the DDA in 2011 to organize a tripartite agreement between the builder, the DDA, and the households of the colony. The agreement would be signed at the time of shifting the residents to the transit camp. The agreement was drafted by the builder and approved by the DDA. Interestingly, the DDA officials claimed that the community's consent for the project was secured orally in June 2011, in the presence of the ex-Chief Minister, Sheila Dikshit, and ex-union Ministers for Urban Development and External Affairs. However, many community members were unaware of these proceedings.

When the DDA and Raheja attempted to coerce the colony residents to sign, the residents took to the street. The colony leaders interviewed claimed that they came to know through a Hindi newspaper article in December 2011 about the DDA's plan to shift the colony residents to a transit camp for transferring the land to the builder. The leaders then mobilized the residents to oppose the DDA's plan, concerned by a lack of written assurance from the authority about re-allotment of a house or land in the same location. Many residents feared that once they vacated the land, there would be no guarantee that the builders would allow them to return and that they would be forced to accept resettlement. The DDA responded to their refusal to leave by organizing periodic eviction raids and initiating criminal cases against the local leaders as well as the youth in their families.

The DDA officials along with the developer managed to secure the signatures of only 574 families, of whom around 400 still remain at the transit camp. The majority of residents continue to stay in the colony till date. The stalemate between the residents and the DDA led to the legal battle that lasted for four months (Raman 2016). Despite this conflict, the DDA and the developer moved ahead with the implementation.

Throughout this conflict, the DDA acted as a broker of the developer coercing the community to accept the project on their terms. In July 2015, the then chairman of the DDA visited the area and in a public meeting ordered the community to move out of the location and that the project would take place at any cost. In a subsequent survey, the organization reduced the number of households to fit the number for which the DPR was planned. Despite the highhandedness of the DDA, the agency could not manage to force residents to vacate the colony land.

Until the election results were announced in 2015, the agency was open to negotiation with the community. This is evident by the initial stages of the DDA cancelling the consultant survey and ordering a new survey by the organization itself which reported a higher number. Further, when the legal hearing was in process, the planning authority organized a meeting at its main office on 22 February 2014 in order to settle the dispute. However, post July 2015, when the BJP government was elected to power, the DDA shifted its position and refused to negotiate any further with the community. The conflict reached a stalemate which has stalled the project till date.

NGO–Community–DDA Relationship

As mentioned earlier, an NGO, HC, offered help to the community to fight the DDA's plan and develop an alternative plan. They started their work in the colony in July 2013 and offered to help in the fight to secure land rights. The NGO and resident-led enumeration started in November 2013. Between 2013 and 2015, they mobilized the community to undertake their own surveying activities allegedly to build evidence to contest the official information. HC conducted the survey with the help of community leaders and student volunteers. The organization centralized the survey data at their office, allegedly for the ease of data analysis, but two years later, residents did not have any result of the survey finding. Arguing that the first survey could not arrive at an estimated number, the NGO organized a second survey. In the meanwhile, in February 2014, when the DDA eviction seemed imminent, the HC representatives led the community to file a case for stalling the petition at the Delhi High Court. Despite the repeated survey, HC could not ascertain the number of households in the colony. The content of the petition was rarely shared with the community members. The process was controlled by HC along with the lawyers.

The colony residents did not have direct contact with the developer until later in the conflict, and much of the interaction with the DDA was mediated by the NGO.

The Delhi High Court heard the case three times. As part of the hearing, the court instructed the colony residents to present their development plan. Since the survey results were incomplete, the NGO instructed the architect planners volunteering for the exercise to design for 3200–3400 households in the colony. Their estimates were supposedly based on a rough count of survey responses. Further, HC suggested that their estimates could be used to frame the legal proceeding against the DDA and to prepare the residents' plan sought by the court. The fact that HC rolled out new surveys without sharing the findings of earlier surveys enhanced the conflict between HC and residents, resulting in the colony residents forcing out the NGO from their settlement at a later date.

In July 2016, following the conflict, the NGO attempted to establish a people's committee. The committee formation came as a surprise to many residents as it was announced by the NGO in a public meeting and the paper document was circulated for consent. Several residents refused to sign the paper. The conflict with the NGO reached its peak towards the end of 2015. The fluid alliance between the community leaders and the HC had its ripple effect in terms of dividing the colony residents. Although the NGO representative attempted to reconcile with the colony residents, the latter severed their ties with the concerned organization.

The DDA and the NGO mobilized surveys to further their agendas—the former to justify the number of eligible households and the latter to perpetuate the myth of participatory processes. The relationship between various NGOs working at the colony was fraught with a lack of trust, competition to control various groups in the colony, and suspicion of their competitor NGOs depriving their claims to fame. The NGOs' narrative kept shifting between promising the residents of a plot, alternative maps at the time of the court hearing, and switch back to redevelopment.

Following the court judgement in April 2015, few members of the community decided to establish contact with the developer directly. These meetings did not come out in the open till December 2015, by which time the developer and their representatives attempted to elicit the support of several community members. After a period of no action till April 2016, the community members once again attempted to revive their discussion with the DDA. The community's latest position is that that their priority is location and that they have no objection to being accommodated in multi-storeyed housing.

From Land Share to TDR

In March 2015, the DDA announced that the in situ development at Kathputli Colony under the RAY programme had failed and that they plan to adopt the Mumbai model of slum rehabilitation (SR). The model, introduced in the 1990s, was designed around a mechanism called the transfer of development rights (TDRs). The SR requires the slum dwellers to form a cooperative and register with the Slum Rehabilitation Authority (SRA). The private developers are offered extra development rights (floor space ratio), which can be sold in the open market. Of the TDR, 5 % are allocated to the NGOs.[11]

Under the TDR, the state will repay the private sector for constructing housing units not in cash but with transferable development rights (Nainan 2008). The development right is defined as the permissible floor area in a particular plot, also known as the floor space index (FSI). The TDR instrument separates the land and the development rights. Therefore, it allows developers to transfer the development rights from one location to another. The Mumbai experience shows that the TDR provision allows developers to appropriate land held by squatters in neighbourhoods commanding higher value and to relocate the residents to locations of relatively low real estate value.[12] The higher value land appropriated from the squatters is then redeveloped for commercial or luxury residential apartments. After securing the consent of a certain proportion of squatters for redevelopment, a developer can request the state to acquire the land from squatters and transfer it to them for redevelopment. The practice of developers in Mumbai is to form cooperatives enrolling not necessarily squatters, but their potential clients from lower middle income or middle income households to form cooperatives and, together with the use of force, to secure the consent of squatters.

The TDR model provides an incentive based on real estate. The analysis of Kathputli Colony's project success or failure tends to remain within the project framework, especially the rhetoric of participation. Here, the NGOs are assumed to play a neutral role in representing the interests of the poor. However, the experience of both the Kathputli Colony and Mumbai's TDR raises questions on the assumptions about the role of NGOs. In an interview with the president of a slum dwellers' federation, it was revealed that large NGOs hold TDR in Mumbai worth crores of rupees. The financial incentive offered by the model, together with the difficult funding situation for NGOs, creates conditions to promote relocation of squatter settlements. The TDR is now a regularly traded commodity in Mumbai like any other asset with rates varying according the neigbourhood. Further, as an international NGO based in Mumbai commented: '… *Listing and mapping is like a gold mine ... every major project coming into the city*'. Thus, NGOs' interest in these projects is as much economic as it is about representing the interests of the community. The large international NGOs have significant power, and the connections of such NGOs in the national and the international policy arena cannot be undermined. New instruments of land development, such as land sharing, PPP for land development, and TDR together with the proliferation of surveying and mapping squatter settlements, generate incentives for all actors to push for large-scale housing projects—apart from the squatters, whose interest is in land and location as much as housing.

---

[11]Interview with deputy commissioner, Bruhat Mumbai Municipal Corporation, dated 16 January 2013.

[12]See Ninan (2008) for a discussion on the TDR experience in Mumbai.

Conclusion

This chapter is an attempt to contribute towards the empirical and conceptual gaps in knowledge on Indian cities in two ways. It explored the emerging practices and policies of land development promoted by the urban development authorities in the capital city of New Delhi and the extended national capital region. It suggested that the real estate-led development strategy promoted by the urban development authorities is an extension of earlier policies, albeit with some differences, rather than a complete departure. The agencies were set up in the country in the 1970s to facilitate access to housing to all income groups. The earlier approach of these authorities has been to acquire land and develop plots for different income groups. Their financing model relied on the sale of developed land and cross-subsidized land access to low-income groups (Ravindra 1996). The reliance of real estate profits for land development is a continuation of earlier policies, but the shift is in terms of how surplus gets redistributed among the population.

The case study on the land development practices in Haryana, discussed in Sect. 2, illustrates the scenario in small towns, on which there is dearth of research. In general, studies on small towns in India are limited. Further, there are contextual differences in terms of materialization of policies. Studies on urbanization process in Haryana have focused on Gurgaon. The HUDA, which spearheaded the model, introduced it in other parts of Haryana, anticipating a similar trajectory. Unlike Gurgaon, the dynamics of land development differed in the towns and villages around the GT Road, as shown in Sect. 2. Land development in the region is undertaken by a chain of actors with varying scales of operation. At one end are the developers with pan-Indian presence, sourcing finances in India and abroad for their township projects, and at the other end are farmer-developers converting their agricultural land on a small scale. Between the large developers and the landowners are other actors—developers who operate on a small scale, but are involved in assembly and financing land purchase, and in negotiating the rules of HUDA and the revenue department. The slump in real estate markets in 2008 further derailed real estate-led development. Though large developers announced projects and implemented them in part, the occupancy rate is often less than a third of the built area. Further, conflicts with farmers slowed down the land transfer to the developers, which also affected projects. In some cases, farmers have recovered their land. Section 2 also contributed towards filling an empirical gap on research on developers. There are very few ethnographic studies on the practices of land development with a focus on the role of developers. The social and spatial outcomes of private developer led urban development have been highlighted in some studies. For example, Benjamin (2010) explores the coalition that emerged between new economy, entrepreneurs, and the state to influence policy formulation and implementation in favour of mega-projects and local government reforms.

Section 3 exposes the materialization of a PPP for slum redevelopment. It suggests a conflictual relationship with NGOs which are taken as natural allies of the community. The discussion on PPP projects also focused on the role of developers. Both the developers and NGOs are diverse in terms of their scale of action, characteristics, and interests. Extending the Harvey and Goldman thesis, the two case studies showed the manner in which speculative practices drive the actions of the state, land developers, and non-governmental agencies. However, the trajectory of these projects is ruptured by the unpredictability in local politics and macroeconomic conditions. This unpredictability and the possibility to form flexible alliances provide political spaces, albeit narrow, for affected landowners and squatters to manoeuvre the rules and practices of urban.

The literature on public–private partnerships, predominantly supporting the official position, talks about the necessity of PPP. However, the specifics of the agents entering into partnerships with the urban development authority, their mechanisms, and conduits of engagement and the power relations have not been explored in depth, and Sect. 3 attempts to do this.

References

Anand, N., & Rademachar, A. (2011). Housing in the urban age: Inequality and aspiration in Mumbai, *Antipode, 43*(5), 1748–1772.

Bedi, J. S. (2014). *Urbanization, development and housing requirements in the national capital region*. Working Paper. Delhi: National Council of Applied Economics Research.

Benjamin, S. (2010). Manufacturing neoliberalism: Lifestyling Indian urbanity. In S. Banerjee-Guha (Ed.), *Accumulation by dispossession: Transformative cities in the new global order* (pp. 92–124). New Delhi: Sage Publications.

Chatterjee, T. (2013). The micro-politics of transformation in the context of globalization. *Journal of South Asian Studies, 36*(2), 273–287.

Denis, E. (2011). La financiarisation du foncier observée à partir des métropoles égyptiennes et indiennes. *Revue Tiers Monde, 206*(2), 139–158.

Dhar, V. R. (nd). Public private partnership in the delivery of serviced land in Delhi. Accessed June 10, 2016. http://www.amdaindia.org/pdf/arc/ppt/4/V.K.Dhar.pdf

Goldman, M. (2011a). Speculating on the next world city. In A. Roy & A. Ong (Eds.), *Worlding cities: Asian experiments and the art of being global*. Wiley-Blackwell: Sussex.

Goldman, M. (2011b). Speculative urbanism and the making of next world city. *International Journal of Urban and Regional Research, 35*(3), 555–581.

Grewal, R. S. (2009). Urban patterns in the Punjab Region since the Prehistoric Times. *JPS, 20* (1&2), 273–296.

Harvey, D. (1989). From managerialism to entrepreneurialism: The transformation in urban governance in late capitalism. *Geografiska Annaler. Series B, Human Geography*, 3–17.

Nainan, N. (2008). Building boomers and fragmentation of space in Mumbai. *Economic and Political Weekly, 43*(21), 29–34.

Nair, J. (2005). *The promise of the metropolis: Bangalore's twentieth century*. New Delhi: Oxford University Press.

Raman, B. (2015). The politics of property in land new planning instruments. *Law and Popular Groups in Delhi, Journal of South Asian Development, 10*(3), 369–395.

Raman, B. (2016). Reading into land politics: Reading into the politics of land: Real estate markets in the South-West Peri-urban Area of Chennai. *Economic and Political Weekly, 51*(17), 76–84.

Ramnani, V. (2011). Delhi set to go higher, taller. Hindustan Times, December 24. Accessed September 4, 2014. http://www.hindustantimes.com/india-news/newdelhi/delhi-set-to-go-higher-taller/article1–786375.aspx

Ravindra, A. (1996). *Urban land policy: A metropolitan perspective*. New Delhi: Concept Publishers

Searle, L. G. (2010). Making space for capital: The production of global landscapes in contemporary India. Ph.D. dissertation, University of Pennsylvania.

Searle, L. G. (2014). Contestations and conflicts conflict and commensuration: Contested market making in India's private real estate development sector. *International Journal of Urban and Regional Research, 38*(1), 60–79.

Shatkin, G. (2011). Planning privatopolis: Urban integrated megaprojects and the transformation of Asian Cities. In A. Roy & A. Ong (Eds.), *Worlding cities: Asian experiments and the art of being global*. Blackwell: Cambridge.

Tarlo, E. (2003). *Unsettling memories: Narratives of the emergency in Delhi*. Hurst, University of California Press: Permanent Black. ISBN 1850654484.

Chapter 6
The Politics of Entrepreneurial Vision Group Plans and their Impact at the Local (Government) Level, Bengaluru

Vinay Baindur

Introduction

In recent times, India's urban policy-making processes have begun to include various organized sectors such as not-for-profit organizations and corporate consultants. For example, the JNNURM secretariat hosted in the Ministry of Urban Development, New Delhi, had personnel from Pricewaterhouse Coopers (PWC) consultants during the period 2006–2011 with funding both by the Asian Development Bank (ADB), Manila and the Ministry. Similarly, the chairman of National Technical Advisory Group (NTAG) in the JNNURM[1] was Mr. Ramesh Ramanathan, co-founder, Janaagraha, a non-profit organization based in Bengaluru with 4–5 other members also being from various non-profits in India.

In certain cases, this appears to be part of a handing over process to local consultants who support urban reforms and infrastructure development in metro cities and tier-II and III towns. An example of this is the case of the ADB-financed project, North Karnataka Urban Sector Investment Program (NKUSIP), in Karnataka which was the third loan in a series of urban projects. This project created extensive opportunities for Indian firms and consortia to prepare city development plans for 20–30 smaller towns in Karnataka. It has to be noted that increasingly through such urban reforms and policies, the government, corporates and other sectors are repositioning cities as 'engines of economic growth' and as major contributors in generating the national gross domestic product (GDP). The JNNURM (2005–2014) of the Government of India (GoI) had hoped that, with massive urban sector reforms, and huge government investment, urban renewal

[1]JNNURM: The Jawaharlal Nehru National Urban Renewal Mission, Ministry of Urban Development, Government of India from Dec 2005–March 2014.

V. Baindur (✉)
Bengaluru, India
e-mail: yanivbin@yahoo.com

K.C. Smitha (ed.), *Entrepreneurial Urbanism in India*,
DOI 10.1007/978-981-10-2236-4_6

would occur in project cities. However, a study by Sivaramakrishnan (2011) showed that very few projects of urban renewal were actually implemented in the 65 mission cities. The current government[2] has also renewed this effort with a greater focus on private sector participation, by introducing a series of urban initiatives such as Pradhan Mantri Avas Yojana (PMAY), Smart Cities Mission, AMRUT and HRIDAY.[3] Some of these measures have been implemented through committees of bureaucrats at the level of state government, and a few other projects have been integrated as part of the long-term objective of implementing urban reform agenda with a consensus developed by the multilateral and bilateral development banks and agencies. These urban initiatives have been crucial in pushing towards entrepreneurial planning processes in India.

'Let the Good Times Roll' for Growth, GDP and Infrastructure

What is the imagination about these urban reforms that such missions, policies and sectors support? Both formal and informal corporate lobbies have used certain kinds of rhetoric to influence specific outcomes which are profitable to sectors such as urban housing, urban roads and urban infrastructure. The aim is to carve out a role for the corporate sector in regional and urban entrepreneurial planning. Such interventions in urban governance seem to temporarily suspend specific (Articles 13 and 21)[4] constitutional and statutory rights of citizens and render local democratically elected governments irrelevantly. A few illustrations will be discussed later in this chapter.

The process of urban development is greatly influenced by global networks interlinked with multinational corporations and international financial institutions and assembled by a 'policy community' of consultants, experts and industry associations (such as CII, ASSOCHAM and PHDCCI)[5] For instance, in the city of Bengaluru, some key forums created so far to push through urban reforms include Bangalore Agenda Task Force (BATF), ABIDe (Agenda for Bangalore Infrastructure Development), City Connect (BCCF), the Karnataka Tourism Vision Group (KTVG) and, in May 2016, the Bangalore Blue Print Action Group

[2]The present government is led by Prime Minister Narendra Modi (BJP). Elected during May 2014 Lok Sabha (House of the People) elections.

[3]Atal Mission for Rejuvenation and Urban Transformation (AMRUT) was launched in June 2015. Pradhan Mantri Avas Yojana—housing for all by 2022—is the housing mission with 2700 towns. The Ministry of Urban Development, Government of India, launched the national Heritage City Development and Augmentation Yojana (HRIDAY) scheme on 21 January 2015, with a focus on holistic development of heritage cities.

[4]Constitution of India, Article 13: Laws inconsistent with or in derogation of the Fundamental Rights, and Article 21: Right to protection of life and personal liberty.

[5]Industry associations and trade chambers CII: Confederation of Indian Industry; ASSOCHAM—Associated Chambers of Commerce of India; PHDCCI: PHD Chamber of Commerce and Industry.

(BBPAG)—the last two being active state-level committees of the current Congress government in Karnataka. According to Coelho et al. (2013: 11):

> A crucial aspect of institutional embedding and political persuasion has been a refiguring of federal relations and a new significance attached to governance structures. State governments face increasing pressure to undertake reforms and fiscal discipline through conditional grants from the centre.

JNNURM and many IFI loan-based projects are a result of such a thrust for conditional grants.

It can be observed that the present city-based projects are promoted not only to generate additional revenue streams but also to support sustainable profit mechanisms to benefit global finance capital through partnering/participating in the implementation of mega-infrastructure projects such as metrorail, high-speed rail, industrial corridors, roads and highways and expressway construction in cities.

For example, during the period 2008–2009 before the preparation process for the national 12th Five-Year (2012–2017) Plan by the union government had begun, a corporate led planning process at the city, region and state level took shape which was led by the Confederation of Indian Industry (CII) for the India@75[6] mission. The young Indian (YI) network is also a part of CII (http://www.youngindians.net) and is meant to involve youth in the same process. One of the objectives of such an exercise seems to have been to promote a middle-class majority in India by the year 2022 on the 75th anniversary year of independence.

This CII mission was to implement and 'validate' the vision of the late C K Prahlad (2004). The Boston Consulting Group (BCG), a global business strategy consultant, was the main supporter of CII and YI for this process, which set up the framework and developed the tools for this visioning and planning. Many academic institutions and consultants have partnered with and were contracted by CII in each state to realize the 'India@75 vision'. A series of stakeholder vision alignment consultations were held and endorsed by industrial leaders. The preparation and subsequent public launch of the India@75 National Vision Document[7] was accompanied by 17 state-level vision documents (which include Delhi, Karnataka and Tamil Nadu), 18 district-level development plans and city-level strategic plans including Belgaum and Mangalore in Karnataka. These plans were prepared by hired consultants. The recommendation with respect to the 'Infrastructure and Urbanization' section in the report includes a proposal for 'India to build and develop 500 well-planned world-class cities'. The fact that the AMRUT mission plans to develop 500 cities now is quite remarkable in this context. The process of preparing plans is shown in Fig. 6.1.

---

[6]http://www.indiaat75.in. In 2008–2009, Confederation of Indian Industry (CII) in collaboration with the Boston Consultancy Group (BCG) undertook a pan-India visioning exercise to validate the vision of Late Prof C.K. Prahalad. The exercise covered complete spectrum of society including students, housewives, slum dwellers, farmers, bureaucrats, academia and politicians among others; over 1000 interviews, 125 workshops with over 10,000 participants including 6 chief ministers were conducted to evolve the vision document 'India@75—The People's Agenda'.

[7]National Vision Document India at 75—CII, Young Indians and Boston Consulting Group March 2009. Accessed from: http://www.indiaat75.in/document/nvd-india@75.pdf.

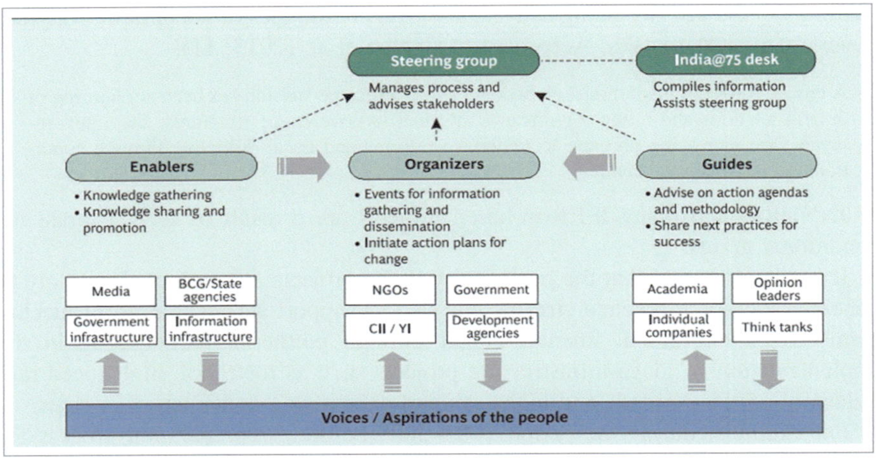

Fig. 6.1 Process and structures deployed to enable involvement and alignment from all stakeholders planned for India@75 by CII

Similarly, in a previous case from Maharashtra, Bombay First,[8] also a group of companies registered as a non-profit organisation in 1995, and McKinsey, an international consultancy, prepared the Mumbai Vision Report with the goal of 'Transforming Mumbai into a World-Class City'. This is an illustration of an entrepreneurial planning approach. The report recommended among other things:

1. Boosting metropolitan economic growth to 8–10 % per annum and making Mumbai a consumption centre;
2. Expanding mass and private transport infrastructure;
3. Dramatic increase in low-income housing (1.1 million low-income houses) and affordability and drive upgradation of housing stock;
4. Relocation and rehabilitation of slums and pavement dwellers to afford them a better quality of life and simultaneously unshackle the growth potential of city by releasing the spaces hitherto encroached upon;
5. Upgrading public safety, air pollution control, water, sanitation, education and health care;
6. Creating a dedicated 'Mumbai Infrastructure Fund' with an annual funding of Rs 1500 crore; enhance user charges;
7. Make governance more effective, efficient and responsive by institutional restructuring including corporatizing key departments and streamlining important processes such as building approvals;

[8]Bombay First, modelled on 'London First', is a civil society organization started in 1993 by prominent industrialists of Mumbai. The mission of Bombay First is 'to make the city a better place to live, work and invest in'. It wanted to serve the city with the best that private business can offer.

8. Generating momentum through more than 20 ‘quick wins’ to show visible on-the-ground impacts; and
9. Enabling implementation through committed public–private resources, led by the chief minister: create a single coordinating body, make government organizations accountable for results and encourage active corporate and NGO participation.

Then Chief Minister (CM) of Maharashtra state released the report in September 2003. Based on the recommendations of these consultants, a ‘Mumbai Task force’ was set up led by the chief minister and the chief secretary and a senior bureaucratic official—the secretary (special projects) as member secretary of the task force. Thus, a support structure was established to take forward this prescribed agenda for ‘strategic transformation’ of Mumbai through entrepreneurial planning. This prompt state government action was supported and followed by a massive grant from the World Bank and its partners such as the Cities Alliance. This technical assistance (TA) grant was approximately US$ 4.6 million. A series of loans from the World Bank also followed where 2 main projects—the Mumbai Urban Transportation Project (MUTP) and the Mumbai Urban Infrastructure Project (MUIP)[9]—were launched. Subsequently, Phase I and Phase II of this TA project for Mumbai transformation resulted in the formation of the Mumbai Transformation Support Unit (MTSU) in July 2005, which acted as a secretariat for the Chief Minister’s Task Force based in the All India Institute of Local Self-Government (AIILSG) in Mumbai, and Bombay First itself was the secretariat for the Citizens Action Group formed in July 2004. Many billion rupees of infrastructure projects were developed through the implementation of road, suburban rail and expressways. This has dislocated and uprooted hundreds of thousands of slum dwellers, urban poor and migrants who were then to be housed in multi-storeyed (ground + 9 and more floors) apartment structures sometimes without elevator lifts and bare basic amenities, with NGOs and federations of slum dwellers being the mediators. The road projects included in MUTP were the Santa Cruz–Chembur Link Road (SCLR) and the Jogeshwari–Vikhroli Link Road (JVLR). Bombay First through its Chairman and Governing Board continued to participate in conceptualizing and formulating plans and also by organizing conferences such as ‘Mumbai Megamorphosis’ in November 2009. Phase III of the Mumbai Urban Transport Project was approved in December 2011 by the Government of Maharashtra. It is estimated to cost Rs 52,000 crore. The project includes a fast suburban rail corridor from Chhatrapati Shivaji Terminus to Panvel with a connection to the proposed new Navi Mumbai International Airport, as well as extending the Harbour Line to Borivali. This project is proposed to be completed in 2031.

Clearly, this process has resulted in a huge loss to the people of Mumbai and India in terms of the fact that the process of governance mandated by the constitution was deliberately neglected, because of the overwhelming clout of the

---

[9]MUIP will boost MUTP: Chandrashekhar. Accessed from: http://timesofindia.indiatimes.com/city/mumbai/MUIP-will-boost-MUTP-Chandrashekhar/articleshow/47530010.cms.

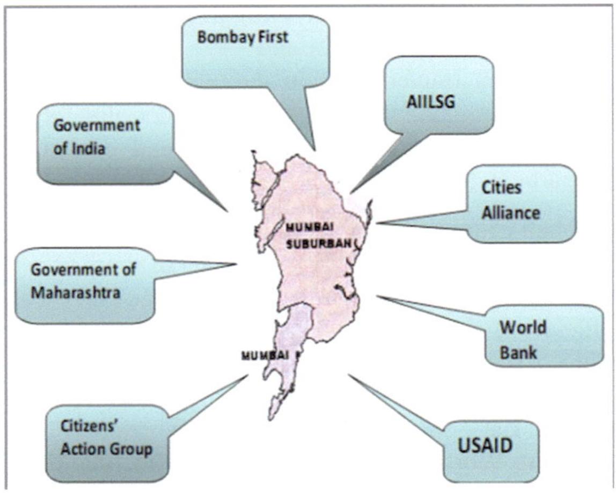

Fig. 6.2 Illustration from Bombay First presentation in the World Bank meeting, 2010

Bombay First industrialist members by ignoring the existing Metropolitan Planning Committee and being instead dependent on the techno-bureaucratic MMRDA and the MTSU for policies, concepts and project implementation. This demonstrates the role played by entrepreneurial planning and how it has far-reaching implications with concept plans for the Mumbai Metropolitan Region for 2032/2052 being initiated through consultants appointed in 2010 (see Fig. 6.2).

The investment of US$1 trillion for infrastructure proposed during the 12th Five-Year Plan (2012–2017)[10] is a culmination of this policy trend of entrepreneurial planning based on the numerous reports/initiatives of the private and corporate sectors which are by now integral to the government planning process. The private sector is in a broad multi-sector partnership with the union and state governments, and therefore, it was expected to help generate around $500 million worth of funding to achieve the target. With such a huge expected funding contribution in partnership with the government and the support of various consultants and advisors, the influence of these corporate groups with reference to the plan was multiplied many times over.

Beyond Democracy: Creating Entrepreneurial Governance and Planning Processes

The equitable allocation of resources is considered as important as the constitutional principles of equality before law and one person one vote. As local government delivers basic amenities (water supply, roads, drains and streetlights) closest to all

[10]Government plans $1 trillion spending on infrastructure. Accessed from: http://www.livemint.com/Politics/PgVi4YqgvUXMpUfST9kr7I/Government-plans-1-trillion-spending-on-infrastructure.html.

citizens in a municipal ward, diverting resources from human development and to reallocate funds to more profitable ‘infrastructure growth’ come into direct conflict with both the role of local government and constitutional norms.

In the year 2001, on the recommendation of the World Bank consultants and state government finance advisors, the Karnataka Government as part of the Karnataka Economic Restructuring Loan-I (KERL-I, 2000–01) had discontinued the accrual of a 2 % surcharge on stamp duties (land sale transaction charges) to the local government which skewed the fund allocation away from delivering basic amenities such as water supply and roads, towards funding the implementation of mega-infrastructure projects such as flyovers. At present, the same bias still continues with greater availability of resources and funds for entrepreneurial planning and expensive infrastructure projects, while the local government is unable to get funds to employ new staff for maintaining facilities and city governance.

The separation of powers and functions in government as in the case of elected representatives like the MPs/MLAs/corporators in 3 tiers of government (especially, local government) is part of the framework of principles in the Indian constitution. Similarly, the union and state governments provide funds, and the local government deliver basic amenities. Recent newer institutional forms such as government committees for infrastructure or other corporate lobbies blatantly violate the constitution. Instead, they must be allowed to debate in the democratic forums, and elected councils must take decisions regarding infrastructure projects. According to the laws of local government, committees constituted for infrastructure projects must conform to the democratic principles which act as built-in checks and balances of the working of the constitution.

As illustrated earlier, some entrepreneurial groups have tried to take over city governance and planning by claiming to represent interests of urban citizens. By doing so, the very concept of citizenship is reconstituted to exclude the urban working poor, the labour, migrants and the deprived communities. Many of these groups are closely involved in the preparation of plans, policies, primers, drafting legislation and guidelines and in the identification and implementation of contracts and projects. Some of them are funded by the corporate sector and/or their foundations. These are non-profits which operate through a consensus by aligning their objectives for city growth. They have together decided which sectors should grow and the ‘stakeholders’ who should profit from this growth at the city level. Similarly, the future investment destinations and new locations of manufacturing and services are planned by the entrepreneurial investment interests with tacit support from government and the backing from some key industry associations. The case of Belagavi city in north Karnataka is a good example. CII had selected Belagavi and prepared city-level plans, and the same city was also selected for the implementation of a series of World Bank debt-financed 24 × 7 water supply projects,[11] and in January 2016, Belagavi was selected for the first shortlist in the implementation of the union government’s new Smart City Mission. Thus, certain

[11]Karnataka Urban Water Supply Improvement Project—KUWASIP—2004–2012.

cities are repeatedly beneficiaries of such projects, while the people for whom these are planned and implemented tend to remain deprived of the results.

The policy-making process has undergone major changes with politicians and bureaucrats recognizing that the private/corporate sector should and can have an increased role in policy-making and planning. These are non-profits which are also represented on various union or state government committees regarding infrastructure, investment, public–private partnerships (PPP), urban governance, affordable housing, microfinance, banking, transport and so on. Some of them like the Jana Group from Bengaluru have a variety of family led non-profits and companies with newer ones being added. The chart below shows how this has been happening.

If the local and regional planning paradigm is framed by multilateral banks, bilateral funders and corporate funded non-profits, it is observed that such entrepreneurial plans overpower Metropolitan Planning Committees (MPCs)/District Planning Committees (DPCs) without proper deliberation, debate or discussion. The process of the ABIDe task force appointed by the Government of Karnataka in preparing the Plan Bengaluru-2020, funded by the Namma Bengaluru Foundation, also illustrates how entrepreneurial planning has influenced urban governance in Bengaluru. The question is: Why is the mandatory constitutional framework disregarded except to convert the local government into a 'rubber stamp' authority for approval of these plans?

More recently, a campaign led by the same corporate groups lobbied for a directly elected mayor for a five-year term for the city of Bengaluru. It was assumed as if one elected representative, i.e. the mayor, could miraculously take charge and solve all of the urban problems if she/he were to be empowered with executive powers without other representatives to 'hinder or stall' the democratic process. The notion of a directly elected mayor militates against the basic spirit of a democratic process of the three-tier governance suggested in the 74th Constitutional Amendment Act. This is because it is not possible to have an adequate caste rotation/reservation or representation if the term is five years for one directly elected mayor. This might result in the election of a mayor from the scheduled caste or scheduled tribe (i.e. marginalized castes and tribes) communities only after a gap of 20–25 years depending on the rotation in reservation. Therefore, the arrangement of a directly elected mayor would be a massive setback to the principles of inclusion and diversity. Similarly, considering an argument for the election of a mayor based on the Bengaluru vision planned by a set of profit-oriented entrepreneurs, commercialization and corporatization are also inconsistent with these constitutional principles.

Thus the argument against the concept of a directly elected mayor comes from the need to have a representative, democratic and decentralizing electoral process, with caste-based reservation and by upholding the principles enshrined in the Indian constitution. There is a need for representation of the historically deprived urban poor, and further, abundant safeguards need to be identified and implemented to ensure the compliance with principles in conformity with Part IX-A (74th CAA).

In the Indian context, the conflict between the processes of globalization and constitutionally mandated principles of equality and social justice implemented through the form of reservation for backward and historically deprived castes and communities (SC/ST, Women) is openly visible. Upholding constitutionally mandated principles shows how the nation can move forward and is consistent with the long-standing demands for maintaining social justice and equality. Such principles should be extended even to assess the elections to municipal and local governments, use of resources and decision-making process regarding the planning and allocation of resources for the fulfilment of basic public needs. On the other hand, based on the demand of the globalized policy terrain represented by profit-oriented corporates and MNCs, there is an attempt to place a city such as Bengaluru in the governance framework of New York or London.

Is Entrepreneurial Planning Predatory?

From the global to the regional and to the local level, many infrastructure projects have been conceptualized and implemented which has resulted in what I term as a *predatory* impact. The term predatory captures the targeted nature of such infrastructure projects that dislocates and displaces the poorer and economically vulnerable sections of the society in multiple ways. Such infrastructures exclude urban poor from not only accessing but also displacing them from commons/resources, further alienating them from the urban spaces.

The effort to restructure urban landscapes may be required sometimes, such as for the public transport project, the bus rapid transit (BRT), which can benefit even the most deprived communities. Influenced by the global capital and clandestine objectives of entrepreneurial planned projects, city planning has become highly predatory in nature by introducing changes in the governance processes and reinforcing infrastructure development (such as access controlled toll roads), and by imposing norms of oppressive corporatized governance (such as infrastructure levies and toll payments, development cess, tax burdens) on the public to support the profits of corporates. Health, education and access to public commons are relegated to secondary social welfare objectives. To fulfil two interdependent agendas, i.e. the entrepreneurial vision-based planning and infrastructure growth at the local level, local democracy has been sacrificed. Such entrepreneurial planning ideology seems to be more consistent with the vision of a city state or a Union Territory which negates the need for an elected (BBMP) municipal council.[12]

Corporate echelons in the city have consistently pushed forward entrepreneurial and investment-oriented plans for boosting economic growth. But such an entrepreneurial vision insisting on economic growth alone cannot drive a city vision and is inconsistent with democratic norms. These corporate groups insist on a new legislation for Bengaluru which does not conform to constitutional mandates and

[12]In 2004, Mr. N.R. Narayan Murthy, former chairman, Infosys, Bengaluru, demanded that Bengaluru can be converted into a Union Territory such as Chandigarh or Puducherry.

principles. For instance, the Bengaluru Region Governance Bill 2010[13] could not be introduced due to severe critical opposition from the people, *panchayat* (village elected government) representatives and MLAs. Despite such opposition, there emerged a consensus among corporate groups such as members of ABIDe and later on the Bangalore Political Action Committee (BPAC), who agreed that such a bill suited their legislative requirements of governance, planning and policy. Those corporate networks used their influence both officially and informally to push forward this entrepreneurial vision-based planning and development of the city. This was possible by misusing the institutions and mechanisms within the governments without any legal backing and openly flouting the principles of decentralization, democratization, people's participation and people's power of decision-making through elected representatives as enshrined in the Constitution of India.

City Entrepreneurial Makeover Through Globalized Governance

Pursuing the ideology of entrepreneurial planning at the local level has immensely benefited large real estate, land developers, etc., which have lobbied for increasing expenditure on massive infrastructure projects. For example, this was done through government-appointed committees such as the Committee for Commercialisation of Infrastructure, 1996, headed by Rakesh Mohan (former Deputy Governor of Reserve Bank of India), and more recently, KTVG under the co-chairperson Mr. V. Ravichandar, who was a member of multiple committees such as the former BATF and the Greater Bengaluru Municipal Corporation (BBMP) Restructuring Committee, appointed by Government of Karnataka, as well as the Bangalore Blue Print Action Group (BBPAG) a vision group appointed in May 2016 (see Annexure 1).

The question is whether implementation of infrastructure projects shall aim to improve the quality of life for all in an inclusive manner respecting the diversity in a democratic framework? Or will it deliver only a soulless and cultureless 'alien' constructed urban space based on the promoter's enslavement to predatory global finance capital?

Thus far, infrastructure projects have been promoted and marketed through entrepreneurial planning discourse with a development outcome so as to be made acceptable to both the politicians and common man. Though entrepreneurial planning is projected as a banal and neutral service provision for citizens, in many specific cases, the infrastructure projects at the local level disempowers and brutalizes the population by increasing their vulnerabilities and often chronically depriving them to access the basic needs such as health, education, water supply and dignified housing by diverting limited government budgets.

---

[13]This bill was drafted partly by lawyers and the consultants for ABIDe task force during BJP rule in Karnataka (2008–13).

Are the infrastructure advocates and companies (mentioned earlier) creating spaces which have a cultureless impact on many local users? Or are they merely generating revenue for the promoters most of whom do not belong to the site/city as residents? Does it become an excuse to negotiate or bargain away local democracy for benefitting a few at the cost of the urban majority? This results in oppression in the city, which is heightened due to the unbalanced role of the 'market' forces resulting in the eviction of street vendors and others by the repeated surveillance, use of force and usurious corruption. But while these kinds of experiences are faced regularly and almost normalized in the lifestyle of the urban poor, a culturally inconsistent streetscape, building or infrastructure could worsen the situation manifold.

There are numerous instances in some countries, where earlier infrastructure schemes or projects built in boom town eras are being deconstructed to allow for reclamation of landscapes. For instance, the demolition of flyovers (transport infrastructure supporting access control for private cars in many cases) in countries such as Germany, the UK and South Korea (see Fig. 6.3).

> Among the crowd watching was Leicester's city mayor Sir Peter Soulsby, who said watching the demolition was exciting, despite the experts decision to do the job without the use of explosives.
>
> He said: "It's still very satisfying to watch. It's been a white elephant for the city ever since it was built and people have been talking about pulling it down for a long time."
>
> "Now we can get the monster out of the way[14]".

However, in India, the city vision is still bound in terms of concrete, glass and high-rises. The insertion of built spaces (now termed as 'software glass' according to an architect) at the Information Technology Park Ltd (ITPL) is a typical example. Similarly, the construction of high-rise structures in the commons used by the landless Dalit (marginalized caste) villagers for subsistence agriculture near Whitefield on the outskirts of Bengaluru had a huge disorienting impact in terms of culture, livelihood, status, dignity and quality of life and brought immeasurable and unquantifiable loss to the villagers. In Karnataka state, the local language Kannada has a word which is commonly used to describe the lived experience of violence/oppression: '*himse*'. In this case, it implies economic violence created due to the imposition of those conditions from the urban reform agenda in combination with investment-oriented mega-infrastructure projects resulting in deeper human alienation. The lack of fund allocation further increases the imbalances with respect to access to basic amenities, along with the incalculable loss for the people in terms of participation in the local governance.

In this context, it is apparent that implementation of infrastructure projects can be located to deliberately keep the majority of people especially the poor, women and children away from being able to use or benefit from them. Global finance capital and the corporate sector deploy infrastructure to increase profit margins, while the

---

[14]http://www.leicestermercury.co.uk/Demolition-Belgrave-Flyover-begins/story-20637264-detail/story.html#ixzz3vF8GjlEl.

Fig. 6.3 Flyover Demolition, Chatham, UK. *Source* Photograph by Chris Whippet. Licensed under CC BY-SA 2.0 via Wikimedia Commons; Flyover Demolition at Chatham U.K https://commons.wikimedia.org/wiki/File:Flyover_Demolition,_Chatham_-_geograph.org.uk_-_1437084.jpg#/media/File:Flyover_Demolition,_Chatham_-_geograph.org.uk_-_1437084.jpg

local government underwrites the major financial implications and bears the risk of land acquisition/provision, materials and resource allocations. Essentially, infrastructure linked with the frameworks of capital converts the impact of such projects into 'economic violence' on the citizens. For instance, a study on the 'development' of Hebbal Lake, in Bengaluru (Baindur 2014: 20–21), indicates the exclusion of poorer sections of society to enjoy the precincts of the lake: 'The phenomenon of public space now is only about the paying public, and the non-paying public who cannot have these experiences just because they do not pay. The displacing of place occurs when public choices are replaced by the intentions of manager-stakeholders'.

'Economic violence' in the name of infrastructure projects could be an assault on the livelihood of either a street vendor family headed by a single mother, or a worker at a small and medium enterprise (SME) factory, or evict the urban poor who are forced to relocate further away from the city and their sources of livelihood. Such relocation allows for the creation of an export promotion zone or an SEZ, thus uprooting people from their everyday livelihood. Similarly, the psychological violence results in isolation and alienation with newly created urban spaces that often have little or no use for the urban poor. As poor urban residents gaze upon the opulent structures wasting resources and spilling over with multiple lights and glitz, they are left with a sense of dissatisfaction, worthlessness, a deep sorrow and resignation which is symptomatic of a society driven by neoliberal economics. In India, the urban poor face additional structural and institutionalized forms of violence such as casteism, a kind of apartheid, and economic oppression bearing violent impacts which go beyond the mere lack of access to resources.

Infrastructure Advocacy Processes: Forming Coalitions and Building Roads

Currently, corporate influence on urban governance, decision-making and projects as well as policies is most apparent in Bengaluru which manifests itself in 'hybrid governance' formed by the partnership of elected political representatives and corporate money power. Most often, urban sector reforms and policies related to infrastructure projects have been pushed through a closed and deliberately assembled network of entrepreneurs, bankers, consultants, real estate builders, developers, mall owners, architects, contractors and so on. Such powerful groups have been restructuring Bengaluru, influencing the use of its public space and urban commons such as streets, roads and parks, in support of corporate sector vision of growth. Sponsorship of museums and converting botanical gardens into theme parks and tourism destinations as opposed to the venues for a family/community picnic are some of the steps currently underway.

Through state government-funded urban renewal projects, corporates have taken advantage of institutional structures supported by the 'reforms'[15] which is anti-poor and anti-people and destroy democratic decision-making processes. An example of the changing governance forms is to plan and implement transportation and traffic infrastructure in the city of Bengaluru. For instance, the history of the urban reform agenda in Bengaluru begins with the setting up of parastatal bodies such as boards and corporations for delivery of services. The study by Chandrashekhar (2011: 69) describes these parastatal bodies as part of the government yet independent from government functioning: '… as parastatal bodies, they take care of functions which constitutionally have been devolved to local bodies, such as infrastructure, welfare of the weaker sections, women and child development and so on'.

Soon after the launch of JNNURM in December 2005, a partnership was set up, in the form of Bangalore City Connect Foundation (BCCF) funded by the CII, Southern Region (CII), through a memorandum of understanding (MoU) with the NGO Janaagraha being the secretariat in 2006 (see Annexure 2).

The background for this urban reform actually begins in August 2004, when the newly formed Congress–Janata Dal (Secular) coalition government discontinued an earlier government–corporate partnership, viz. BATF[16] (from November 1999 till

[15]The JNNURM (2005–2014), for instance, introduced 16 reforms in 2005 and later 7 reforms in 2008–2009 as part of the urban reform agenda.

[16]BATF, the Bangalore Agenda Task Force, was constituted in Bengaluru in 1999 through a government order by the Government in Karnataka headed by Chief Minister S.M. Krishna to provide a role outside the local elected government for local corporate groups. The BATF was headed by Nandan Nilekani and then at Infosys in Bengaluru.

February 2004), despite continuous efforts by the Congress party and corporate sector to re-establish BATF. The Janata Dal (Secular) a regional-level political party, as a coalition partner in the government, on the other hand resisted this and refused to allow this partnership to continue. The logic behind the rejection was that adequate official capacity existed in the government with its bureaucrats to execute/carry out all assigned activities, and there was no need for any kind of expert/vision group or task force from the corporate sector to be formed.

However, what emerged as a result of this was possibly a form of corporate revenge politics. Kamath (2007: 4, 6) in an interview with one of the key persons behind BCCF, ex-BATF member V. Ravichandar quotes:

> How I see this working in the future is City Connect will be a foundation which will function as a platform on which different stakeholders can come together to discuss and decide on a particular issue (if government does not want to give up too much power they can choose one issue, like transportation).
>
> …On a general level people thought the BATF was a page 3 phenomenon and there were lots of people- then and now- who stepped forward to be a part of it. But it was a lot of hard work. I do believe that it will come back—maybe it will be called another name.

Such a new ‘hybrid governance’ form evolved by former BATF members to tide over such ‘political risk’ to corporate government partnerships has its roots in this kind of rejection. During this period, similar efforts to form BATF in Delhi had also failed. The Hindu newspaper[17] quotes Mr. Deve Gowda—a former prime minister and the JD(S) national president in October 2005:

> Indicating his ire at being painted as the one who does not want best infrastructure for Bengaluru and taking a dig at his bête noir, the Maharashtra Governor and former Chief Minister S.M. Krishna, Mr. Deve Gowda said: “I am aware of the problems and the need for improving the transport system in Bengaluru. But should we not come up with what is best for the city? Do we not have efficient bureaucrats and officials and technical experts who can tackle this?
>
> Mr. Deve Gowda, whose dislike for the Bengaluru Agenda Task Force (BATF) is well known, reads from historian Janaki Nair’s book on “Bengaluru as a metropolis”, in which the BATF is referred to as an initiative that failed to deliver its promises on the public–private partnership.

Following this, in 2006, the Bengaluru City Connect Foundation (BCCF trust) drafted an MoU (forming the Bengaluru Traffic and Transportation Initiative—BTTI) with the Bangalore Metropolitan Land Transport Authority (BMLTA), a parastatal body, arguing that there was lack of capacity within government agencies for the implementation of urban transport infrastructure. Therefore, it is not surprising that some members of the defunct BATF moved into the non-profit sector and continued to work on policy and projects without any notion of democratic accountability to the elected representatives. One would also wonder why, despite the presence of the elected Bengaluru Mahanagara Palike (BMP), key decisions about the

[17]‘Deve Gowda unimpressed with Infosys chief's new blueprint for development’, http://www.thehindu.com/2005/10/17/stories/2005101717800100.htm.

city-level reforms were not placed before the city council. The answer may be found in a state-level reform[18] mandated by JNNURM: transferring all special agencies that deliver civic services in urban areas to ULGs over a period of five years and *creating accountability platforms for all urban civic service providers in transition.*

This reform (*about the accountability platform and transition period*) was introduced stealthily along with three other reforms into the JNNURM conditions. These were lobbied for by some former members of BATF (which had also presented itself as an accountability platform for all stakeholders, during 1999-2004) in a series of meetings in New Delhi which were held between November 2004 and February 2005 with the United Progressive Alliance (UPA) government officials as well as the opposition parties—to counteract 'political risk[19]'. This business—non-profit partnership—the 'City Connect[20]' was introduced only in Bengaluru and Chennai and in a few other cities.

Such an entrepreneurial intervention was initiated by these groups based on their perspective and consensus about both lack of infrastructure and un-governability in the city, i.e. because of the messy and what was to them 'illegible local politics'. The elite from the city demanded good governance and international standards in service delivery and infrastructure which would suit them, and they increasingly felt that the elected local government politicians were essentially unaccountable to them. Kamath and Vijaybaskar (2013: 162) state, for instance, how the RWAs (resident welfare associations) in affluent areas are more confident in their effectiveness on the discourse of urban reforms. There is an increasing reliance on credentialed 'expertise' of private sector. This resonates well with the urban reformers' emphasis on outsourcing tasks to private consultants, as local governments are deemed incapable. In Bengaluru, the elected BMP Council's 5-year term ended in November 2006, and the BCCF (as a continuation of key members from the BATF) was positioned as the default institutional arrangement to implement the JNNURM reforms. It was a corporate sector and non-profit sector partnership which was itself an accountability platform 'for all urban civic service providers in transition'. It was also meant to identify and set a vision for the city by corporates such as those from IT/BT sectors, real estate developers and transport and infrastructure contractors through new governance mechanisms and projects planned for Bengaluru. The formation of not-for-profit forums like the BCCF happened within the entrepreneurial economy.[21] Janaagraha had earlier received financial and other support from organizations such as IFC, WB, USAID and CII and later from the Omidyar Network. The agenda of these funders and supporters has resulted in

---

[18]State-level reforms, Page 15 Annexure 2 JNNURM revised Guidelines 2011 MoUD GoI. www.jnnurm.nic.in.

[19]'Lobbying for change: the story of corporate India's engagement in urban governance', Lalitha Kamath, CASUMM, Feb. 2007, www.casumm.wordpress.com.

[20]City Connect is a collaborative platform catalyzed by Business for Civil Society and Government to work together to make cities more livable. www.cityconnect.in.

[21]Jana Group, as Janaagraha and its sister organizations are now known, consists of around 6–7 NGOs targeting microfinance, microhousing, etc.

various projects including privatisation of policy-making, urban commons, public spaces and resources. The study by Urs and Whittel (2009: 76) claim ‘So while corporate agenda directs (and finances) it the brilliance of *Janaagraha’s* positioning on wide range of ‘social’ issues, it can undermine and scuttle without losing its credibility’.

A subcommittee on BTTI projects was formed by BMLTA in 2008 with members from Janaagraha, City Connect, as well as officials from BBMP and the Urban Development department. In one of the subcommittee meetings held on 8 September 2010, it was recorded that BBMP had begun the road hierarchy process and had started classifying roads as arterial and sub-arterial and the director Karnataka Road Development Corporation Limited (KRDCL) brought this to the notice of BMLTA. Yet, it was the BCCF which was appointed as the coordinator of the working group on the road hierarchy and sort of took over the entire urban road hierarchy and design process unofficially. Later, this has resulted in the Tender SURE (Specifications for Urban Road Execution) project. While working *pro bono* for this government subcommittee, the India Urban Space Foundation (IUSF)/Jana Urban Space (JUSP) was funded by different industry associations (CII, BCIC, FKCCI) and corporate funders such as Omidyar Network and MARG. The Bengaluru design group JUSP (part of the Jana Group) identified key roads in the city’s central business district and lobbied and garnered support from the state government and the engineers from BBMP. So, in 2011, due to the efforts of BCCF, the chairman of CII Karnataka, Kris Gopalakrishnan (former CEO of Infosys), Kiran Mazumdar Shaw of Biocon and BPAC and number of others lobbied with the then CM Sadanand Gowda. A government order (GO) was issued in September 2011 stating that IUSF/JUSP would prepare the design and detailed project report (DPR) for the implementation of Tender SURE project. As a result, the Government of Karnataka allocated Rs 200 crores for developing 50 roads in the city as well as in other towns of the state. Though there was an elected local government since March 2010, corporate lobbied for the implementation of Tender SURE project only with the state government and the BBMP remained unaware of this.

As a precursor pilot to Tender SURE project, during 2008–2009, the entrepreneurial efforts resulted in laying Vittal Mallya Road. Approximately Rs 4 crores was spent for laying the 430-m Vittal Mallya Road, for an elite mall ‘U. B. City’ which was constructed on the same road by demolishing the beer factory located there earlier. It was clear that the objective of upgrading Bengaluru’s Vittal Mallya Road was to showcase the ‘U.B. City’ mall. But during 2011 itself, both the electronic and print media reported and highlighted the bad flooding on this road due to lack of appropriate design for draining rainwater.

Despite the existence of the elected BBMP council since March 2010, such parallel process of entrepreneurial planning and governance process caused a huge and irreparable loss to the democratic process by functioning as an unofficial ‘vision group’ for Bengaluru. The vision for the city must be developed at the level of the municipal government for participation, planning and decision-making based on the people’s mandate.

At present, the 'Tender SURE' road project has been implemented at the central business district of Bengaluru. The number of roads covered under this project and the funds allotted have changed from time to time. But in the next phase, the local government BBMP will have to bear the high cost of implementing these very expensive road projects. For roads such as Mahatma Gandhi Road, funds were received from both JNNURM and World Bank under KMRP project for upgrading footpaths. Now, it is proposed for upgradation once again under this project, in the next phase. The selection of only certain roads under Tender SURE project demonstrates a strong bias towards the development of mainly commercial areas of the city. This would help create some places with invisible entry rules; ' world-class' ghettos, pockets of exclusion—through these expensive high-end infrastucture schemes meant for the elite.

The entrepreneurially planned road contracts like Tender SURE demand high investments from government that create an island of opulence in the middle of a city which is surrounded by areas deprived of amenities in the periphery especially in slums. Such deprived areas particularly low-income neighbourhood face chronic deficiencies in amenities such as health care, water supply and educational facilities. For instance, some areas such as Devara Jeevana Halli (DJ Halli) near the city's outskirts have a high urban poor population, particularly Muslim minorities and Dalits. At a public hearing on public health which was organized by Jan Arogya Andolana Karnataka (JAAK) in the DJ Halli area, December 2013, 'residents alleged that they are turned away without treatment, denied basic medication or forced to pay bribes'.[22] In the same area, death of a 5-year girl child was reported, as having occurred due to malnourishment.

Field visits on the Tender SURE road project show the actual issues; for instance, a major thrust of these roads is to provide space below the 4+ m wide footpath for laying cables, ducts and pipes. The design also includes space for cycling paths, but they have not actually implemented. In reality, cycle tracks are missing, which could have been useful for those working in the service sector (such as restaurants, hotels, shops and malls) as against the elite and upper middle-class users who possess sophisticated bicycles. Similarly, only those vendors who are not stationary, such as those with pushcarts, are allowed, evicting cobblers, vendors of newspaper and fruit sellers and so on.

In May 2016, the Government of Karnataka in keeping with the previous trends and patterns has once again appointed a new task force called the Bangalore Blue Print Action Group (BBPAG), but it is really a 'vision group' and implementation committee. The blueprint being referred to here is an outline framework prepared by Janaagraha. As in earlier cases explained here, the Metropolitan Planning Committee has not discussed or debated this blue print or any other a plan since it has not yet met even once, after being constituted in 2015. It must be

[22]'D.J. Halli residents say State has abandoned them', http://www.thehindu.com/news/cities/bangalore/dj-halli-residents-say-state-has-abandoned-them/article5452523.ece.

pointed out here that many of the members of this action group are from previous task forces such as BATF, e.g., V. Ravichandar, Kalpana Kar and Ramesh Ramanathan.

Thus, urban commons and public spaces of many cities and towns are being appropriated by the commercial for-profit sector and real estate. The entrepreneurial planning process of using the urban land for global capital has expanded to the urban streets affecting the commons and the common man in the city.

Conclusion

This elite capture of decision-making processes and governance structures, by members of entrepreneurial planning groups lobbying for the creation of infrastructure for the economic growth of Bengaluru, is in conflict with the human development of citizens. Some of the proposed entrepreneurial planning interventions include highly expensive and profitable signal-free corridors, underpasses, toll-based expressways, metrorail and stilt flyovers. Many of these projects are proposed to be access controlled through high toll rates and by restricting certain vehicles (such as cycles, buses, animal drawn carriages and other non-motorized transport), but on the other hand only allowing cars, SUVs, etc., in conflict with the National Urban Transport policy (NUTP-2006). This is creating further threshold barriers to accessing livelihoods and basic resources for the poverty-stricken and the urban majority.

Prioritising such infrastructure growth against basic needs, the BBMP's property taxes are diverted away from the core functions of local government such as water supply, streetlights, roads and roadside drains which directly impacts the workers, street vendors, the restaurant users and owners, the pedestrians and cyclists, taxi drivers, auto-rickshaw drivers, tea vendors, cobblers and others.

While we assess the loss and the high cost of such a process of entrepreneurial planning taking place in many cities and towns on democracy and the constitutional architecture and ideology, the urban deprived communities are facing forcible eviction. The level of rehabilitation and/or resettlement does not meet the requirements at any scale since these sites are 15–20 km away from their livelihoods, schools and hospitals. They are pushed to the peripheries where there is a lack of basic amenities as well. They are also deprived from grievance redress mechanisms which can help them solve their problems to some extent through the representative democratic structures.

With entire governance structures becoming defunct due to such an entrepreneurial planning approach, the biggest casualty has been 'social & economic justice and planning', which demonstrates that the concerns of citizens such as land, water and other common resources will be snatched away unless there is a move to introduce planning programmes that empower decision-making structures mandated by the constitution and statutes, and all efforts to disable these are thwarted.

Annexure 1

The process of task forces from 1999 – 2016 in Bangalore

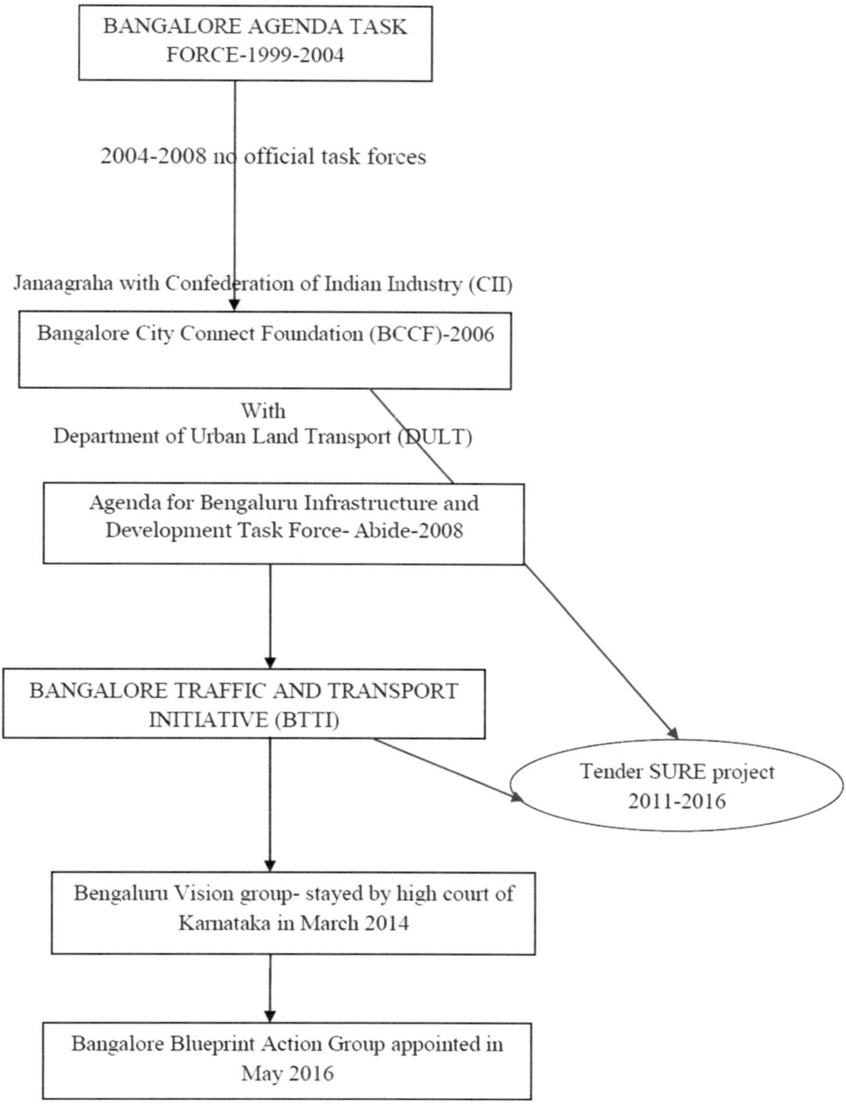

Annexure 2

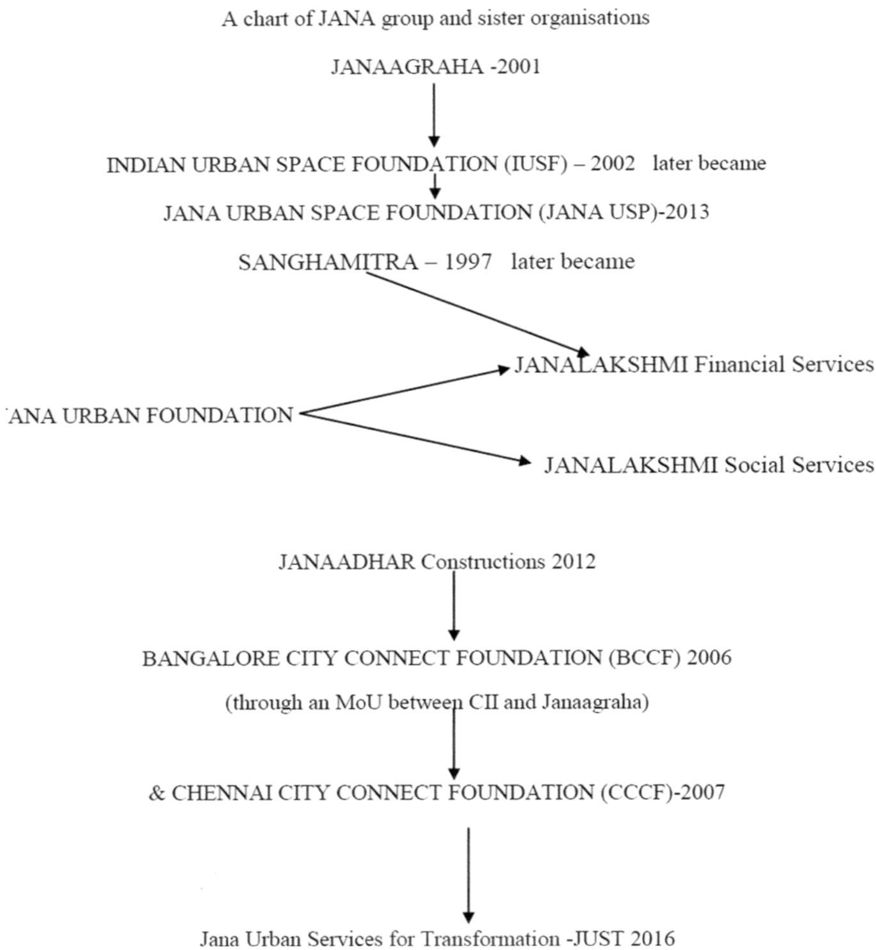

References

Baindur, M. (2014). Bengaluru lake story: Reflections on the spirit of a place. *Journal of Cultural Geography, 31*(1), 32–56. doi:10.1080/08873631.2013.873296

Chandrashekhar, L. (2011). *Undermining local democracy: Parallel governance in contemporary South India*. New Delhi: Routledge.

Coelho, K., Kamath L., & Vijayabaskar, M. (2013). Opening up or ushering in? Citizen participation as mandate and practice in urban governance. In K. Coelho, L. Kamath & M. Vijayabaskar (Eds.), *Participolis—Consent and contention in neoliberal Urban India*. New Delhi: Routledge.

Kamath, L. (2007). Lobbying for change: The story of corporate India's engagement in urban governance.

Kamath, L., & Vijayabaskar, M. (2013). Urban reforms and the middle classes: Fragmented collective action and the incomplete project of stakeholder participation. In K. Coelho, L. Kamath & M. Vijayabaskar (Eds.), *Participolis—Consent and contention in neoliberal Urban India.* New Delhi: Routledge.

Prahlad, K. C. (2004). *The fortune at the bottom of the pyramid: Eradicating poverty through profits*. Wharton: Wharton School of Publishing.

Sivaramakrishnan, K. C. (2011). *Re-visioning Indian cities: The urban renewal mission*. New Delhi: Sage Publications.

Urs, K., & Whittel, R. (2009). *Resisting reform: Water profits and democracy*. New Delhi: Sage Publications.

Part III
Urban Inclusion and Exclusion

Chapter 7
Remaking the '*mohalla*': Muslim *basti*-dwellers and Entrepreneurial Urbanism in Mumbai

Qudsiya Contractor

Introduction

Shaheed[1] is a 30-year-old housing rights activist with a national network for the housing rights of *basti*-dwellers[2] and a native of UP, who lives in Rafi Nagar since 2000, a neighbourhood in Shivaji Nagar. Shivaji Nagar is a predominantly Muslim *basti* located in an industrial suburb at the outskirts of the island city of Mumbai. It is situated on the city's oldest and largest garbage dumping ground subjecting it to the worst living conditions. Earlier, Shaheed used to make a living as a tailor and was active in taking up issues of housing and sanitation in his neighbourhood. I interviewed Shaheed over lunch at his house one day. We rode on his motorcycle up to his house in Rafi Nagar II,[3] which comprises 450 households located in close proximity to the dumping ground. It is very difficult to say where the limits of the dumping ground end and where Rafi Nagar begins. Rafi Nagar had the appearance of a refugee camp. There is garbage lying everywhere—polythene bags, scrap metal and glass, that is being sorted by bare hands and segregated into sacks and weighed. We reached a small clearing, and Shaheed stopped there. As we got off, he said, 'This is my humble abode (*gareebkhana*)'. He paused and then added, '*Samjhe* (understood)? My home. Do come in'. The floor of his house was completely broken, and there were no walls. There were just plastic sheets tied around metal poles and bamboo sticks, like a large tent. All his household items were lying

[1]Names of individuals have been replaced with pseudonyms.
[2]The word *basti* means settlement in Hindi and Marathi. I choose to use the term *basti* as opposed to slum, as this is what is colloquially used by those who reside there to describe their localities.
[3]Rafi Nagar I is considerably larger comprising 3000 households, most of which possess documents to prove their 'legal' status.

Q. Contractor (✉)
Centre for Study of Social Exclusion and Inclusive Policies, Tata Institute of Social Sciences, Mumbai 400088, India
e-mail: qudsiya.contractor@gmail.com

K.C. Smitha (ed.), *Entrepreneurial Urbanism in India*,
DOI 10.1007/978-981-10-2236-4_7

scattered around. Rafi Nagar had been recently demolished, and his house was among those broken down by the BMC.[4] In 2005, Shaheed's neighbourhood was given a notice for evacuation by the municipal authorities as it was declared 'unauthorized' since it had come up after 1995. There is also a perception that Shivaji Nagar's image as a 'Muslim' area makes it more vulnerable to frequent demolitions. Shaheed pointed out that many predominantly Hindu- and Marathi-speaking *basti* settlements that have come up much later are not targeted for demolition like the Muslim *bastis* in Shivaji Nagar. The stereotyped image of Muslim *bastis* as dangerous sites of criminality that need to be dealt with and restrained makes them more vulnerable to harsher treatment from municipal authorities. As Shaheed put it, 'whenever the names of *our* [emphasis added] areas come up they feel different. Whether it is the municipal authorities or the police they feel these areas are dangerous. Why they feel these areas are dangerous I don't know [pauses to answer a phone call]. Perhaps it shows somewhere that this is a Muslim community, these are not good people, more crime happens here, more criminal-type people stay here. This is the message they get'.

Shivaji Nagar has a population of approximately six lakhs of which Muslims constitute more than two-thirds, while the rest comprise Dalits, Christians and migrants from outside Maharashtra.[5] The city's poorest reside here, and the area lacks even the most basic civic amenities such as water supply and sanitation. Shivaji Nagar is situated in M (east) ward of Mumbai, which according to the Mumbai Human Development Report (2009) has the lowest Human Development Index at 0.05, much lower than the city's average of 0.56.[6] It came into existence in the early 1970s following the demolition of several *bastis* across the city as part of the state's 'slum'[7] clearance drives. Following the resettlement of *basti* dwellers from other parts of the city, the population of Shivaji Nagar had a large proportion of lower-caste and lower-class Muslims right from its formation. The older residents ascribe this to the large number of Muslims living in the *bastis* that were cleared. One of the first to be resettled was a locality of butchers (from the *qureshibiraderi*, a Muslim low caste) working in a municipal slaughterhouse (popularly referred to as *katalkhana*) that was relocated close to the garbage dump. The *katalkhana*, along with its predominantly *arzal* Muslim workforce (the rest were largely Dalits) that lived in close proximity to their workplace, was originally located in Bandra (a western suburb). This locality was evicted to make way for an express highway that today connects the western suburbs in the city. The

---

[4]Brihanmumbai Municipal Corporation.

[5]This is an unofficial estimate based on those of local NGOs and elected representatives in the area. Official sources do not give segregated data based on religion and language.

[6]For a detailed account on the history of Shivaji Nagar and its living conditions, see Contractor (2011).

[7]This is a term largely used by the state administration and the use of which has transcended into popular usage by the media, non-state policy actors including NGOs and INGOs. It can be argued that its usage has had a far-reaching impact on Indian urbanism through elitist connotations of nuisance tied to dominant perceptions of conduct and visual aesthetics (Ghertner 2011).

katalkhana was relocated a few kilometres away from the garbage dump, thus moving an unpleasant, dirty business to the margins of the city. The workers on the payroll of the Brihanmumbai Municipal Corporation (BMC) were allotted houses in a housing colony close to the *katalkhana*, in multi-storeyed buildings. Others, who were contract workers, were allotted plots in an open stretch of land that was being used before for garbage disposal. Therefore, garbage or filth is not just a material thing but a conceptual entity whose parameters could be extended to the undesirability of the marginalized and excluded in the city (Kaviraj 1997).

Recent work has extensively highlighted the agenda of urban planning in the city as being driven by the commercialization of land use and real estate market (Banerjee-Guha 2002; Nijman 2000; Sharma and Sita 2000; Harvey 2008). Others have noted that the state's ethno-nationalist imaginations of the city have impacted its landscape (Hansen 1996; Singh 1993; Doshi 2013; Punwani 2003). The combined influence of ethno-religious and class-based marginalization has meant that *basti* residents of predominantly Muslim areas remain among Mumbai's most undeserved and vulnerable. The role of ethnic discrimination in eviction politics is evidenced by the fact that the demolitions targeted not only 'illegal' slums settled after the 1995 cut-off date but also areas where the majority of residents' ethno-religious backgrounds have made them vulnerable to the xenophobic campaigns of the Shiv Sena (Doshi 2013). This chapter explores how the city's socio-spatial peripheries are transformed or reproduced through an active engagement between local residents, the state and civil society groups. Through ethnographic fieldwork[8] in a predominantly Muslim *basti*, it describes the efforts of Muslim *basti*-dwellers towards remaking the *mohalla* or Muslim locality into a life space far from its stereotypical image as an undesirable, dilapidated, poverty ridden, criminalized and denationalized urban space. The vast literature on urban entrepreneurialism has raised several theoretical concerns, significant of which is the role of the state and private capital in the disenfranchisement of the urban poor. Others, however, have argued that the discursive shift from managerial urbanisms to entrepreneurial urbanisms has spawned new sites of inclusion and collaboration for the urban poor. However, this literature mostly fails (with a few exceptions) to highlight bottom-up approaches at creating new technologies of governance by finding basic urban infrastructure solutions. The chapter describes two such initiatives as an illustration—the reconstruction of private homes and a local mosque in collaboration with a city-based NGO and a redevelopment proposal for a local municipal market through direct negotiations with a private builder. It describes the efforts of Muslim *basti*-dwellers at transforming a segregated and peripheral yet culturally vibrant life space by engaging with state actors through 'slum' redevelopment programmes as well as collaborating with civil society groups. The chapter argues that processes of urban transformation shaped by global flows of capital, ideas and technologies create environments where claims to and ownership of the city's material (land, property) as well as sociocultural resources are (re)configured

[8]Fieldwork was conducted in 2009–2010 and 2016.

by local Muslim residents. As urban citizens and entrepreneurial subjects, they not only reimagine the *mohalla* reunited with the city's socio-spatial landscape but also actively engage in remaking it. The changing agenda of urban (re)development influenced by global capital flows on the one hand and the influential global human rights discourse on the other hand have created new opportunities for the city's local elites as well as the disenfranchised. In the case of the city's *basti*-dwelling Muslims, these efforts highlight the urgent need to expand the ideological terrain, where newer possibilities of sociocultural transformation as well as the inclusion of diverse community needs can be realized.

Entrepreneurial Urbanism and the Urban Subaltern

Urban governance in recent years has seen a shift from managerialism that focused primarily on local provision of services, facilities and benefits to city dwellers to entrepreneurialism fostering and encouraging local development and employment growth (Harvey 1989). For Harvey, urban entrepreneurialism in the right political and economic circumstances is understood to foster progressive and socialist transition with inter-urban competition opening up a way to a zero-sum pattern of development. For scholars like Harvey, the main concern is to devise a geopolitical strategy of inter-urban linkage that mitigates inter-urban competition and shifts political horizons away from the locality and into a more generalizable challenge to capitalist uneven development. In this context, urban entrepreneurialism seems to on the one hand 'sustain and deepen capitalist relations of uneven geographical development and thereby affects the overall path of capitalist development in intriguing ways'. On the other hand, they also hold the 'potential for transformation into a progressive urban corporatism, armed with a keen geopolitical sense to mitigate if not challenge the hegemonic dynamic of capitalist accumulation to dominate the historical geography of social life' (Harvey 1989, p. 16). A distinctive feature of 'competition states' and 'entrepreneurial cities' is their self-image as being proactive in promoting the competitiveness of their respective economic spaces in the face of intensified international, inter-regional and intra-regional competition, the dynamics and effects of which vary across nations, regions and cities (Jessop 1997). Others have noted that urban entrepreneurialism though largely defined in terms of shifts in city governance encompasses far more than the transformation of the local state but involves the changing nature of economic, social and political processes operating at both the global and local levels (Hall and Hubbard 1996). In other words, new urban politics forge a new cultural politics of identity at the urban level, changing the ways in which city-dwellers see themselves and others. Hence, cities are in a constant process of being reimagined as economic, political and cultural entities that must seek to undertake entrepreneurial activities to enhance their competitiveness by the redesigning governance mechanisms such as public–private partnerships and networks (Jessop 1997). But in recent years, there has been a need to shift the focus of debates on urban entrepreneurialism to informal settlements and cities of the global south in order to broaden its horizon to include 'ordinary' spaces that demand rethinking the techniques and scope of contemporary urban entrepreneurialism (McFarlane 2012). According to McFarlane (2012), policy and civil society forms of travelling urbanism are located on a shared terrain of urban entrepreneurial development, to the point that any division between elite and ordinary urbanism is in many cases untenable. However, this is not just a shared terrain but a shared ideological resonance that holds common across multiple expression of urban entrepreneurialism, whether economic (e.g., financially disciplined and business savvy residents), social (privileging a few 'active' and 'do-it-yourself' residents over the, so the implication goes, unorganized and passive neighbourhood/city at large) or political (e.g., self-managed forms of local development that enact shifts in responsibility from the state to community-based groups). These practices while exceeding borders of entrepreneurial models are based on their view of poverty as a socio-economic potential and the poor as entrepreneurial subjects (McFarlane 2012, p. 2796).

In the Indian context, the city is a site of opportunities and possibilities for the marginalized. It offers a promise for those who choose to make a life in it, a promise of economic and social mobility, and freedom from the drudgeries of social stigma. City life also offers its residents a chance to make a fresh start by providing opportunities to make the most of one's own abilities irrespective of the privileges, and social capital one accumulates through social status. The 'slum' seems to be most prominent in the socio-spatial representations of 'subaltern urbanism' as a terrain of habitation, livelihood, self-organization and politics. Such an understanding of subaltern urban spaces is a radical yet vital challenge to dominant apocalyptic and dystopian narratives of the megacity as it resurrects the subaltern space of the slum as that of a vibrant and entrepreneurial urbanism (Roy 2011). Within this context, the acts and practices of the marginalized geared towards bringing about change in their immediate environments can be understood as aimed at redistribution of social goods and opportunities in the form of the (unlawful and direct) acquisition of collective consumption (land, shelter, piped water, electricity, roads), public space (street pavements, intersections, street parking places), opportunities (favourable business conditions, locations and labels) and other life chances essential for survival and minimal living standards (Bayat 1997, p. 59). It is through these gradual and 'molecular' changes that the urban subalterns attain cultural and political autonomy from the regulations, institutions and discipline imposed by the state, by gaining control over their working lives regulating their time and coordinating their space. By initiating gradual 'molecular' changes, the poor in the long run 'progressively modify the pre-existing composition of forces and hence become the matrix of new changes' (Bayat 1997). On a similar note, Simone (2004) provides us with another way of understanding how the urban subaltern engages in contributing to the transformation of the urban environment through acts of social collaboration. Through the notion of 'people as infrastructure', he extends the notion of infrastructure to activities of the marginalized within the city. He describes this as a specific economy of perception and collaborative practice that is constituted through the capacity of individual actors to circulate across and become familiar with a broad range of spatial, residential, economic and transactional positions. Such a reconceptualization recognizes residents' needs to generate acts and contexts of social collaboration inscribed with multiple identities rather than in overseeing and enforcing modulated transactions among discrete groups (Simone 2004). In the following sections, the chapter will situate the trajectory of Mumbai's Muslims as a marginalized urban community and describe the efforts of Muslim *basti* dwellers at finding infrastructure solutions as bottom-up approaches to urban entrepreneurialism or '*subaltern*' urban entrepreneurialism.

Trajectories of Urban Marginalization

Historically, Muslims formed a substantial minority in Mumbai city with their economic engagements ranging from being traders to constituting the mill workforce in the cotton textile industry (Hansen 2001; Chandavarkar 1994). Muslim localities in colonial Bombay represented a sociocultural diversity, and their spatial location was closely linked to their position in the city's economy. Parts of the city that had high concentrations of Muslims as early as the eighteenth century are distinctly noted as Muslim areas even today. According to the 1901 census, these areas were Chakla, Umarkhadi, Kharatalao, Nagpada, Mandvi and Dongri, which still have a significant proportion of the city's Muslim population. The 'Muslim quarter' of the city being fairly diverse had *mohallas* associated with caste-like groups or interrelated occupational groups among Muslims that were linguistically and culturally distinct (Masselos 1976; Chandavarkar 1994). This included working-class neighbourhoods housing the industrial workforce, which were segregated along religious and caste lines as a manifestation of the social organization of labour in the city. Entire *mohallas* were identified (for certain parts even within 1901 Census data) with specific, at times occupational groups—business communities such as Khojas, Memons, Bohras, Ansari weavers and Qureshi butchers. Conforming to broader trends of nationalist politics and communal mobilization, religious festivals and processions became occasions for the manifestations of political identities and the contestation and coding of social space in the city (Hansen 2001; Masselos 1976). The 1930s and 1940s saw an incipient isolation of the Muslim working class in the economy as well as spatially in the city, and the process became even more pronounced after independence (Hansen 2001).[9] Post-independence, Hindu nationalist agendas, discourse and institutions gradually penetrated everyday life and acquired a growing, though not uncontested, social respectability in contemporary Indian society (Jaffrelot 1996). Bombay was no exception to this, and the rise of Shiv Sena in the 1960s marked the beginning of the

[9]It is probably important to note that despite the communalization of city politics in the 1940s, there was no mass exodus of Muslims from Bombay to Pakistan after 1947. For a detailed discussion, see Hansen (2001).

communalization of the cultural and political environment of the city (Appadurai 2000; Lele 1995).[10] Shiv Sena offered the rhetoric of ethno-religious unity, regional cultural pride and also a solidarity that repackaged older anti-Muslim myths (Hansen 2001). The politico-cultural strategies of the Shiv Sena relied heavily on spatial tactics (Foucault 1986), which included violently rewriting urban space as sacred national and Hindu space (Appadurai 2000). The Shiv Sena took to slums and working-class neighbourhoods with its Hindu–Marathi chauvinism in the light of the growing insecurities of urban living (Appadurai 2000; Heuze 1995; Sen 2008). Nationally, it joined hands with the BJP to further its agenda of *hindutva* for a Hindu nation, which radically transformed the city's geography. Their spatial strategies widely used public spaces as sites for the display of the Hindu rights, violent political strategies and anti-Muslim rhetoric (Hansen 2001). Mhaskar (2013) notes that the feeling of *karahiyat* [Urdu: nausea, disgust, hate, etc.] combined with suspicion, in terms of terrorism and mafia, creates barriers for Muslims seeking employment and self-employment opportunities. Hence, the spatial segregation of Muslims in the city can be attributed to the growing economic, political and sociocultural alienation of Muslims as well as violence eventually transforming the spatial location of Muslims in the city.

The incidents that followed the demolition of the Babri Masjid in Ayodhya on 6 December 1992 including the bomb blasts in March 1993 have had a lasting impact on the city's landscape that saw communalization of the city's geography at its peak.[11] Many chose not to go back to their homes in mixed neighbourhoods in the city (Masselos 1995; Punwani 2003; Robinson 2005). It has been argued that it is the scarcity of housing in Mumbai that translated the explosive violence of 1992–1993 into the imaginary of cleansed space, a space without Muslim bodies (Appadurai 2000). Soon after the riots and as a consequence of the violence, one witnessed the formation of new boundaries around communal identities, defined through a process of naming at the intersection of religious identity, nationality and personal identity (Mehta and Chatterji 2001). This was the case, in particular, in Dharavi,[12] where the lines of demarcation between Hindu and Muslim dominated areas were designated as 'India–Pakistan borders'. Some have remarked that after 1992–1993 riots, religion-based segregation intensified in the working-class *chawls* of Mumbai. The Bombay Improvement Trust (BIT) chawls in Nagpada have become more rigid 'only Muslim' or 'only Hindu'; those that are located facing each other even in the same compound or street are now more resolutely aloof from each other (Khan 2011). Yet those few who continue to live in mixed neighbourhoods do so in suspended animosity owing to the betrayal of their neighbours during the violence, while they and their homes were attacked, looted and

---

[10]For a detailed account of the birth and rise of the Shiv Sena, see Gupta (1982), Heuze (1995), Lele (1995), Sen (2008) and Eckert (2003).

[11]For the worst affected areas in the city during the 1992–1993 riots, see the Srikrishna Commission report (1998) and the report of the Indian People's Human Rights Tribunal (1994).

[12]The largest slum in the city if not in Asia.

vandalized (Khan 2011). Other areas with an already sizable Muslim population saw a further influx of Muslims from other parts of the city such as in central Mumbai areas of Nagpada, Madanpura, Bhendi Bazar or Mohammed Ali Road, some parts of Wadala such as Kidwai Nagar or Byculla. In the suburbs of Jogeswari (west), KurlaGovandi and Mumbra were further concentrated with Muslims. Over the past decade, middle-class Muslim localities such as Millat Nagar, a large complex of apartments off Lokhandwala in Andheri (west) and Mira road, a distant suburb in north-west Mumbai, have become noticeable and distinct as Muslim localities (Robinson 2005). The city's Muslims remain highly concentrated in its *basti* neighbourhoods and some in its overcrowded dilapidated industrial districts. According to a recent study, a high proportion of the city's Muslim population (21 %) live in slums, while 70 % reside in low-class areas and only about 5 % are located in middle-class areas followed by 1.6 % in high-class localities of the city. In general, Sunni and Shia communities make up the Muslim population living in the city's *bastis*. This excludes affluent groups such as Memons, Khojas and Bohras (Jain and Shaban 2009).

Shiv Sena's sustained dominance in the BMC and the city's police force from the late 1960s through the 1990s has ensured the institutionalization and democratization of the spatial exclusion of Muslims in Mumbai's *bastis* (Singh 1993). A study conducted by YUVA (1996) traces the concentration of Muslims over a period of two decades in a progressively shrinking settlement now surrounded by Hindu settlements. Drawing municipal ward boundaries between the exclusive Hindu and Muslim areas has institutionalized this division. In a documentary film '*I live in Behrampada*' (1993) that captures a Muslim *basti* during the communal violence of post-Babri Masjid demolition period, an old woman reacted towards the state's move towards the clearing of slums with a predominantly Muslim population in Behrampada as part of a 'Clean Bombay' campaign after the riots, 'What new place? Where will they dump us? We're afraid. We've lived here so long, yet faced so many problems. What will happen to us elsewhere? When our homes grow old, they make us leave. Once we're settled there, they'll push us out again. Will we never have a place that is home?'

In an act to reclaim the city from its cosmopolitan image and to establish its regional affiliations, the Shiv Sena–BJP alliance renamed Bombay to Mumbai in 1995 (Hansen 2001). Placed in power, their spatial tactics through democratic processes/institutions transformed several other landmarks in the city by renaming them after Chhatrapati Shivaji, the Hindu Maratha warrior king and icon of the Shiv Sena. Today, several public spaces (including government offices, commercial establishments, lanes, streets, parks and even traffic islands) across the city are marked with the installation of grand statues of Shivaji (mounted on a horse holding a sword) decorated with forked saffron flags.

One of the central concerns of Shiv Sena's campaign before the 1997 BMC elections was pollution—physical pollution caused by an inadequate infrastructure and the constant influx of new migrants, and cultural pollution caused by 'anti-national' elements, foreign cultures (Western and Muslims) and degenerate works of art emerging from leftist and liberal milieus in Maharashtra (Hansen 2001). Most of the party's media campaigns called for a transformation of Mumbai to a beautiful and green city free of disease and dirt. The most ambitious part of this transformation of Mumbai was the Slum Rehabilitation Scheme (SRS) envisioned by Thackeray to remove the massive slum areas in the city and thus resolve 'the major problem of dirt', as Thackeray put it (Hansen 2001).[13] Before the scheme was implemented, the minister of housing, ChandrakantKhaire, stated that it was meant predominantly for Maharashtrians and that 'aliens'—Pakistanis and Bangladeshis—would never be given access to the plan (Hansen 2001). The SRS was brought in by the Shiv Sena when it came to power in 1995 to fulfil their election promise to provide free housing to the city's slum dwellers. This scheme was a modified version of what had been proposed by the previous government lead by the Congress following recommendations by the Afzalpurkar Committee constituted by the Shiv Sena. The committee comprised government officials, representatives of the housing industry, architects and prominent NGOs. Under this particular scheme, the emphasis was placed on the private sector's involvement, which seemed to substantiate the accusations against the Shiv Sena/BJP vision to serve the interests of entrepreneurs and builders. It is understood that the concern is more on the physical dimensions of the city than with the lives of the poor (Singh and Das 1995). Thus, Hindu nationalist and xenophobic regionalist imaginaries became concretely embedded in resettlement policy through the exclusionary cut-off date eligibility criterion for resettlement, which invoked a symbolic barrier to an imagined tide of invading migratory outsiders (Doshi 2013, p. 7). This eligibility criterion is determined by an 'unauthorized' or 'illegal' status defined by the Slum Rehabilitation Act (1995) as those slum settlements that have been built after January 1995. The date was extended to January 2000 by the Congress-led government in June 2009 just before the assembly elections in order to fulfil an election promise made in 2004. These xenophobic regionalist imaginaries have, however, not been limited to the Shiv Sena. Subsequent Congress and NCP governments also have taken forward the legacies of ethno-nationalist chauvinism through the slum policy discourse and practice (Doshi 2013). Hence, planning as a key government technique not only generates knowledge about realities through tools such as surveying or mapping but also actively engages in shaping spatial location of slums. As Scott (1998) argues, the point of simplifying and making legible a certain socio-economic reality is to manage and manipulate this reality towards achieving certain ends.

However, this is clearly not limited to the realm of politics or state institutions. Antagonisms against Muslims and more particularly the Muslim poor are not just commonplace but also deep-rooted. In the recent history of the Mumbai city, the 1992–1993 riots were instrumental in translating the problem of space into the imaginary of cleansed space, a space without Muslim bodies. Furthermore, in a city

[13]However, the issue of cleaning up Bombay was not limited to the slums. Clearing the footpaths and removal of beggars have been high on Shiv Sena's agenda for a long time and continue to be targetted (see Hansen 2001).

where daily sociality involves the negotiations of immense spatial stress, the much spectrality that surrounds housing can create the conditions for a violent reinscription of public space as Hindu space (Appadurai 2000). On the other hand, in a city that is increasingly becoming more intolerant to diversity in residential housing, moving to mixed neighbourhoods even for middle-class and upper-class Muslims has become a challenge (Falzon 2004; Thorat et al. 2015). The mainstream's concerns for security and the negative cultural stereotyping of Muslims are among the reasons for them to be confined to Muslim areas in the city. It is in this context that one has to understand how Muslim *basti*-dwellers engage in transforming their life space through acts of social collaboration driven by the aspirations of a dignified life as urban citizens. The next section describes the efforts of Muslim *basti*-dwellers in Shivaji Nagar at transforming a segregated and peripheral yet culturally vibrant life space by engaging with state actors through 'slum' redevelopment programmes as well as collaborating with civil society groups.

Urban Subalterns as Entrepreneurial Subjects

Landownership in Shivaji Nagar is very complex as is the case in most *bastis* across Mumbai. Those allotted plots by the municipal corporation were relocated on land owned by the state government; others occupy land of the municipal garbage dump and also old farm lands (*gaothans*). Those situated on municipal corporation land are recognized as tenants by the state who were allotted housing on the submission of documentary proof of residence in the city such as ration cards and payment of a deposit amount towards the rental agreement. At the beginning, the rent for residential dwellings was 15–25 rupees and that for commercial establishments was 55 rupees. Today, the residents pay a rent of Rs 300, and the rent for commercial establishments is Rs 400. The area has grown considerably since its formation in terms of the density of population and the area it covers. There has also been an influx of newer residents who have either purchased tenements from earlier residents or rented them. However, subletting is 'illegal' since the residents do not have ownership of the land and are tenants themselves. The rents here are as low as Rs 400–500 per month for a small single room. A large proportion of the new residents come through social or kinship ties with those resettled here, hence further increasing the concentration of Muslims. The new residents are viewed as 'encroachers' by older residents and outsiders especially by state authorities and non-local NGO workers. However, the older residents do see the cause for this influx as a need for a familiar, safe and affordable space to live in. There is also a significant difference between the resettled areas and the relatively newer settlements. The living conditions in the latter are appalling due to the proximity to the dumping ground and a complete lack of state infrastructure and amenities such as water, sanitation and electricity. The poorest of Shivaji Nagar live there.

Despite its proximity to the garbage dump and the marshy land it stands on, Shivaji Nagar has been the centre of housing and slum resettlement speculation for some years now. This is essential because the land that it occupies has become prime property in the burgeoning real estate market. In the decade of the 1990s, the floor space index (FSI)[14] of M ward was changed twice under Chief Minister Narayan Rane (who was then with the Shiv Sena) to be further liberalized. This coupled with the deindustrialization resulted in the entry of many new land plots into the market and drew builders to this otherwise 'unpleasant' area (Nainan 2008).[15] According to Nainan (2008), it is the demand for housing from the high-end segment in a particular location and the availability of relatively cheaper industrial lands in predominantly slum-dominated areas which is dictating where PAP (Project Affected People) townships such those of M ward come up. The urban periphery of the city has emerged in planning and development imaginaries as the ideal location to resettle displaced slum dwellers with ambitious redevelopment initiatives relying on severe state violence affecting many northern periphery residents deemed illegal and ineligible for resettlement (Doshi 2013).

In 2001, Shaheed (who was introduced in the beginning of the chapter) formed a cooperative housing society of local residents from his neighbourhood called the Mohammad Rafi Nagar RehvasiEktaSangh. Shaheed is the elected president of the society, and his role largely involves addressing complaints of local residents, resolving conflicts or disputes, etc., related to landownership and housing issues. The society has also been collaborating with local NGOs working on housing rights in the area to address these issues whenever they concern the entire locality. The society also extended its activities to address the educational needs of out-of-school children in the area in collaboration with these local NGOs. This started as a centre called Mahatma PhuleVarg that was built in the locality for these children to make up for lost time at school, eventually preparing them to be reintegrated into the mainstream education system. However, this centre remained functional only for two years till it was demolished along with several other houses in Rafi Nagar by the BMC authorities in 2004.

Weinstein (2012, p. 59) argues that though scholars of global urban citizenship have demonstrated that the right to challenge the actions of the growth machines that drive urban political agendas in globalizing cities represents a fundamental expression of democratic citizenship, their theorizations have not adequately revealed the barriers that prevent some groups from challenging these actions. Based on an analysis of the ongoing US$2 billion Dharavi Redevelopment Project

---

[14]Floor space index (FSI) refers to a certain permissible land to construction ratio that prescribes how much construction is permissible on a certain piece of land. This is governed under the Maharashtra Regional and Town Planning Act. An associated instrument is TDR or Transferable Development Rights of a particular piece of land which cannot be realized on the same land because the land and the development on it area protected (see Nainan 2008).

[15]According to Nainan (2008), a ward-wise analysis of where slum Transferable Development Rights (TDR) has been granted in the city shows that 64 % (21,74,478.41 m^2) of all the TDR generated in lieu of slum rehabilitation has been granted in M ward. And most of this generated TDR has been consumed in Juhu in K (west) and Santacruz in H (west) wards, both part of some of the high-end segments of the city.

designed to transform Mumbai's largest 'slum' settlement into a multi-use, mixed-income township and attract global real estate investment to India's commercial capital—she argues that by participating in the project's planning process, some residents, workers, and activists have acquired political presence and a form of democratic citizenship. Furthermore, she argues that the opportunity to engage has not been available to all disadvantaged populations equally. Hence, the form of democratic citizenship produced through the engagement of poor and working-class people in the struggles around globally oriented urban development is inherently uneven, open only to those social groups with the political resources required for participation. Similarly, Doshi (2013) offers an alternative interpretation of urban capital accumulation by investigating the differential political subjectivities of displaces in slum residents in Mumbai. Based on a study of mass slum clearances for the redevelopment in the city, she argues that Mumbai's redevelopment entails not uniform class-based dispossessions but a process of accumulation by differentiated displacement whereby uneven displacement politics is central to the social production of land markets. The 'redevelopmental subjectivities' these processes create are influenced at key junctures by market-oriented resettlement, ideologies of belonging, desired of improved housing and participation in non-governmental groups. Furthermore, this articulated assemblage of power-laden practices reflects and reworks, class, gender and ethno-religious relations, profoundly shaping evictees' experience and political engagement. Hence, eviction politics is not just a dynamic of volatile class relations represented through the city's planning agendas. Rather it exposes how ethno-nationalist xenophobic agendas of the city's ruling class push the marginalized to its fringes through violent communal spatial strategies.

As discussed earlier, the events that followed the demolition o the Babri Masjidf illustrate how political violence plays a significant role in the way urban localities are ruptured, created and transformed. In class-mixed Muslim localities or *mohallas*, the experience and memories of violence have become part of a larger collective memory linked to feelings of insecurity, influencing the construction of the Muslim *mohalla* itself. More significantly, mainstream stereotyping of Muslims based on their non-vegetarian food cultures manifested through notions of disgust and ritual pollution has marginalized them to the city's peripheries. Muslims remain vulnerable due to their marginal political patronage, which means a marginal share of basic amenities and infrastructure. Despite past experiences of state violence through evictions and forced resettlement, Muslim *basti*-dwellers as urban subalterns are constantly engaged in negotiations with state authorities to make the most of the housing market conditions and the shift in the state's slum policies that seems to be more receptive to the rights of *basti*-dwellers[16] to transform their own living environment. Many *basti* neighbourhoods within Shivaji Nagar are in the process of forming cooperative housing societies under the current SRS offered under the aegis of the SRA. The diverse interests of residents have also resulted in the

[16]For a discussion on this paradigm shift, see Anand and Rademacher (2011).

involvement of several players such as local NGOs and private builders in the speculation of resettlement and area development. The residents of Shivaji Nagar themselves engage in construction and reconstruction of homes, public spaces, gutters, roads, etc., in order to improve the living conditions and cater to the community's aspirations. These activities are almost entirely carried out by local construction contractors who employ local knowledge and indigenous methods of construction suited to the local terrain, governmental sanctions and availability of resources. The following are illustrations of the efforts of Muslim *basti* dwellers in Shivaji Nagar at finding infrastructure solutions as bottom-up approaches to urban entrepreneurialism or '*subaltern*' urban entrepreneurialism. Two such initiatives are described as an illustration—a redevelopment proposal for a local municipal market through direct negotiations with a private builder and the reconstruction of homes and a local mosque in collaboration with a city-based NGO.

Aspiring 'World-Class'

Nizam (45 years) has been living in Shivaji Nagar since 1972. He works as a meat vendor and has a rented stall since the last three decades at the municipal marketplace (*mandi*) located in Shivaji Nagar. The *mandi* has 51 licensees (that comprise Muslims, Dalits and Kolis) that include those who run general stores, sell vegetables, mutton, chicken and fish. Each licensee pays a rent of Rs 120 per month for the stall they occupy to the BMC. The condition of the stalls was appalling, and most are broken with very little or poor maintenance from the municipal corporation. There was no electricity or water supply; those working there had to carry the water they need for their businesses from home. Gradually, there has been an influx of hawkers that have set up vegetable and fruit stalls right at the entrance of the marketplace. Most of these are from neighbouring *bastis* (and largely non-Muslims) that have been encouraged by local municipal authorities and the police through the payment of *hafta* (extortion) as a fee to safeguard their businesses. This has affected the businesses of the licensee stalls inside the marketplace.

Meanwhile, Nizam along with the other licensees at the *mandi* has submitted an application for market development under the area development schemes offered by the SRA. The group formed a cooperative society and approached builders with a proposal for rebuilding and modernization of the existing marketplace structure. After a few meetings with prospective builders, they have finally signed an agreement with one of them under the SRA for converting the *mandi* into a mall. A detailed plan was then discussed, agreed upon and finalized, according to which the existing 51 licensees would be given stalls on the ground floor of the new structure complete with modernized infrastructure, maintenance and sanitation services. It would provide them a decent work environment with water and electricity to keep their business premises clean and create an ambience (*mahol*) that will attract more customers. The rest of the four floors will be opened up for other commercial establishments. However, the SRA has a set of guidelines for what can be offered as low-cost housing or commercial establishments to *basti* dwellers under the scheme. Private builders that are being roped in as part of the scheme are not just open to offering more than what has been promised as part of the scheme, they are also more accessible than the Slum Rehabilitation Authority. This has led to several direct negotiations and agreements between Shivaji Nagar residents and private builders. For Nizam, it is not just private investment but rather the state's commitment to the development of backward areas like Shivaji Nagar and safeguarding the rights of its residents to a dignified life that will take the city closer to its aspirations of becoming world-class, 'if Mumbai has to be made like Singapore, this cannot be done by builders alone, the municipality has to be supportive. If the municipality creates hurdles how will this go ahead? Right from those sitting in the ward office, right up to the commissioner have to be supportive otherwise what is the point of the builder investing so much money here?'

During a recent visit, the *mandi* was bustling with activity as usual. Three flags coloured green, blue (with a white Ashoka chakra) and saffron (with an 'Om' in black lettering) on individual poles hung limp as though exhausted in the sweltering heat. A bright hoarding a few metres from the entrance announced an upcoming public event to commemorate Hanuman Jayanti (birth anniversary) organized by a local community-based organization and sports club. Unauthorized hawkers crowed the entrance that had a brand new signboard. The interiors seemed to have been recently repaired, and many more stall owners seemed to be in business. The proposal for rebuilding and modernization of the market had been shelved since the SRA had scrapped its schemes for area development. The private builders with whom they were collaborating had been taken over by the next generation after the death of the company's owner who was more open to such projects compared to his successors who do not see this as a lucrative business opportunity anymore. Nizam, who was at his meat stall, was not very hopeful of any new opportunities with the current government. Although in this case the collaboration seems to have hit a roadblock due to the state's withdrawal from investing in area development alongside slum resettlement, it illustrates how such efforts need a greater commitment to multi-sectoral development of dilapidated neighbourhoods like Shivaji Nagar. Local Muslim politicians attribute the inability of the state to address infrastructure and housing concerns in areas like Shivaji Nagar to its predominantly Muslim demographic. As IrshadKaskar from the Republican Party of India (RPI) put it, 'like they say Mumbai *hum sabki* (Mumbai city belongs to all of us), everyone should get the facilities of the BMC. But it is very clear that where there is a high concentration of Muslims such areas remain neglected. [...] Who would want to live in dirt and garbage? People live here out of compulsions not because they like to live in these conditions. [...] Who wants to live in *jhopdis* (hutments)? These are poor people. Still they try to improve their homes by putting a plastic sheet or a tin roof'.

Remaking the mohalla

Rizwanis an entrepreneur in his early thirties engaged in the construction business. Originally from Solapur, he has spent most of his life in Shivaij Nagar. He has had no formal training in construction but has learnt the trade on the job from his peers and his father who has been in this business. In 1997, Rizwan's father through some acquaintance and meagre financial support from the late politician Pramod Mahajan and an IPS officer friend (both of whom happen to be from his hometown) landed a license for building construction with the municipal corporation. The company has grown considerably since then, with six licenses, a substantial annual turnover and key municipal projects such as the construction of police stations and health centres. Rizwan, who has taken over from his father, has now expanded the business to private construction broadening the scope of their work. Most of his private construction contracts involve the construction or reconstruction of private houses, and his clients mainly belong to low-income groups who prefer cost-effective but sturdy construction. According to Rizwan, the average expenditure on construction of a house in Shivaji Nagar is between 4 and 6 lakhs though a few even spend nearly 10–12 lakh if they can afford it. Rizwan is quite well known for his work in his locality. His business flourishes through local networks and the trust of his clients, which help him build a good reputation.

Through the construction business, Rizwan has been engaged in voluntary work such as the distribution of aid after the Mumbai floods in 2006. Since then, he has been actively engaged in social work, helping locals in procuring public documents, addressing supply issues with the local public distribution system (ration) and mobilizing financial assistance for education and marriages. Rizwan is often involved in road and gutter repairs funded by local residents or politicians when the BMC fails to attend to them. Dabbling in private construction and social work has given Rizwan the space to collaborate with new partners to innovate with local materials and construction techniques to address local needs. One such collaboration was with a city-based experimental urban research and action collective (henceforth referred to as 'the collective'). Along with two other local construction contractors, their experiments in Shivaji Nagar included upgradation of sewage systems, reconstruction of private houses and a local mosque. These projects were mainly based on the premise that residents were experts in their neighbourhoods through their everyday experiences of places they live in and work.

Among the collaborative projects was the reconstruction of a local mosque, the design of which was developed with detailed consultations with the trustees of the mosque management and designers from the collective. Located in the interiors of Shivaji Nagar, this mosque was a 10- by 15-ft temporary structure, initially used as a *madrasa* since 1986. The mosque had been registered in 1991 and is currently managed by a team of 12 members. The plan was for it to be reconstructed in its original location in a crowded neighbourhood based entirely on crowd funding. After a few meetings and discussions, it was agreed that the reconstruction plan needs to be cognizant to the constraints of space and costs yet remains true to local needs, community aesthetics and aspirations. The outcome of the consultations was an innovative design that took into account aesthetics as well as optimum use of space for multiple activities. A couple of years since, the project has undergone some major changes with insufficient funds and the inability to find architects locally to execute it. Consequently, the trustees made some modifications to the plan to suit local skills, budget and needs addressing a few main concerns—optimum utilization of a small space for prayers (*namaz*), ablution section (*wazukhana*), restroom (*istinjakhana*) and religious teaching (*deenitaleem*). The construction of the mosque is still a work in progress like many other structures in Shivaji Nagar awaiting resources (both human and financial) to see its completion. Collaborations such as these have been very satisfying for Rizwan who described the experience as simply 'superb'. His work has earned him international acclaim and mainstream media attention locally. He has even been rewarded for his innovative construction solutions by a global building materials manufacturing giant. Rizwan through his political patronage and the trust he has built based on his business and social work has been able to create solutions to address the community's housing and infrastructure needs. Though these efforts demonstrate upward mobility, they remain insufficient to address other concerns of Muslim *basti* dwellers such as spatial segregation, state negligence and discrimination in the mainstream housing market. Clearly, informality is not an essential preference of the *basti* dwelling Muslims; it serves primarily as an alternative to the constraints of formal structures. They perhaps aspire and practise integrated life, only if they can afford its social and cultural, not to mention economic, costs (Bayat 1997). Hence, the coproduction of entrepreneurialism requires attention to both the mobile models that constitute relations between different groups, from states and donors to activists and residents, and the local contexts and histories that shape, translate and differently enact entrepreneurialism (McFarlane 2012).

Conclusion

The lives of majority of *basti* dwellers in Mumbai have been shaped by troubled and ambiguous experiences of localities. These have come to be experienced, for instance, as places to which one has been forced to belong. For decades, city planning has been preoccupied with aspirations of turning Mumbai into a city of global stature. This imagination fuelled by the city's elite has essentially been translated into plans that have no room for the city's poor. Millions of people have been compelled to leave their neighbourhoods and forced to set up new lives in unfamiliar surroundings. Muslim *basti* dwellers in Mumbai, much like their non-Muslim counterparts, have been subjected to technologies of the state that have sought to confine them to spaces of relegation in its efforts to realize futuristic visions of making Mumbai a global city. The state's imaginations of an urbane future have been deeply influenced by elitist notions of what is polluting and undesirable, which include not just the poor in general but also immigrants (more specifically non-Maharashtrians), Dalits and Muslims in particular. Shivaji Nagar represents a socio-spatial periphery in the city shaped by the processes of exclusion, coercion and violence. Its formation and existence exemplify the multiple inequalities and lines of exclusion which expose the paradox and complexity of urban transformation in contemporary Mumbai. Processes of urban transformation shaped by global flows of capital, ideas and technologies create environments where claims to and ownership of the city's material (land, property) as well as sociocultural resources are (re)-configured by local Muslim residents. As urban citizens and entrepreneurial subjects, they not only reimagine the *mohalla* reunited with the city's socio-spatial landscape but also actively engage in remaking it. The changing agenda of urban (re)development influenced by global capital flows on the one hand and the influential global human rights discourse on the other hand have created new opportunities for the city's local elites as well as the disenfranchised. In the case of the city's *basti*-dwelling Muslims, these efforts highlight the urgent need to expand the ideological terrain, where newer possibilities of sociocultural transformation as well as the inclusion of diverse community needs can be realized.

Acknowledgments I would like to thank Shadab Arab for his assistance in fieldwork.

References

Anand, N., & Rademacher, A. (2011). Housing in the urban age: Inequality and aspiration in Mumbai. *Antipode, 43*(5), 1748–1772.

Appadurai, A. (2000). Spectral housing and urban cleansing: Notes on millennial Mumbai. *Public Culture, 12*(3), 627–651.

Banerjee-Guha, S. (2002, January). Shifting cities: Urban restructuring in Mumbai. *Economic and Political Weekly*, *37*, 121–128.

Bayat, A. (1997). Un-civil society: The politics of the 'informal people'. *Third World Quarterly, 18*(1), 53–72.

Chandavarkar, R. (1994). The origins of industrial capitalism in India. Cambridge: Cambridge University Press.

Contractor, Q. (2011). "Unwanted in my city"—The making of a "Muslim slum" in Mumbai. In L. Gayer & C. Jaffrelot (Eds.), *Muslims in Indian cities—Trajectories of marginalisation* (pp. 23–42). London: Columbia University Press.

Doshi, S. (2013). The politics of the evicted: Redevelopment, subjectivity, and difference in Mumbai's slum frontier. *Antipode, 45*(4), 844–865.

Dutta, M. (1993). *I live in Behrampada*. Produced by Majlis.

Eckert, J. (2003). *The charisma of direct action: Power, politics and the Shiv Sena*. New Delhi: Oxford University Press.

Falzon, M. A. (2004). Paragons of lifestyle: Gated communities and the politics of space in Bombay. *City & Society, 16*(2), 145–167.

Foucault, M. (1986). Of other spaces. *Diatrics, 16*(1), 22–27.

Ghertner, A. (2011). The nuisance of slums: Environmental law and the production of slum illegality in India. In J. S. Anjari & C. McFarlane (Eds.), *Urban navigations: Politics, space and the city in South Asia* (pp. 23–49). New Delhi: Routledge.

Gupta, D. (1982). *Nativism in a metropolis: The Shiv Sena in Bombay*. Delhi: Manohar Publishers.

Hall, T., & Hubbard, P. (1996). The entrepreneurial city: New politics, new urban geographies? *Progress in Human Geography, 20*(2), 153–174.
Hansen, T. B. (1996). Globalisation and nationalist imaginations: Hindutva's promise of equality through difference. *Economic and Political Weekly, 31*(10), 603–605 + 607–616.
Hansen, T. B. (2001). *Violence in urban India—Identity politics, Mumbai and the post-colonial city*. New Delhi: Permanent Black.
Harvey, D. (1989). From managerialism to entrepreneurialism: The transformation in urban governance in late capitalism. *Geografiska Annaler: Series B Human Geography, 71*(1), 3–17.
Harvey, D. (2008). The right to the city. *New Left Review, 53*, 23–40.
Heuze, G. (1995). Cultural populism: The appeal of the Shiv Sena. In A. Thorner & S. Patel (Eds.), *Bombay: Metaphor for Modern India*. Delhi: Oxford University Press.
Indian People's Human Rights Tribunal. (1994). *The people's verdict: An enquiry into the December 92 and January 93 riots in Bombay*. Bombay: Indian People's Human Rights Commission.
Jaffrelot, C. (1996). The Hindu nationalist movement and Indian politics 1925 to the 1990s. London: Hurst.
Jain, R., & Shaban, A. (2009). *Socio-economic and educational status of Muslims in Mumbai and its suburbs*. Mumbai: Maharashtra State Minorities Commission, Government of Maharashtra.
Jessop, B. (1997). The entrepreneurial city: Re-imagining localities, redesigning economic governance, or restructuring capital? In N. Jewson & S. MacGregor (Eds.), *Realising cities: New spatial divisions and social transformation* (pp. 28–41). London: Routledge.
Kaviraj, S. (1997). Filth and the public sphere: Concepts and practices about space in Calcutta. *Public Culture, 10*(1), 83–113.
Khan, S. (2011). After violence: How the Mumbai riots changed life for Muslims in chawls. In N. Adarkar (Ed.), *The chawls of Mumbai: Galleries of life* (pp. 103–110). Delhi: ImprintOne.
Lele, J. (1995). Saffronisation of Shiv Sena: Political economy of city, state and nation. *Economic and Political Weekly, 30*(25), 1520–1528.
McFarlane, C. (2012). The entrepreneurial slum: Civil society, mobility and the co-production of urban development. *Urban Studies, 49*(13), 2795–2816.
Masselos, J. (1976). Power in the Bombay 'mohalla', 1904–15: An initial exploration into the world of the Indian urban Muslim. *South Asia, 6*(1), 75–95.
Masselos, J. (1995). Postmodern Bombay: Fractured discourses. In S. Watson and K. Gibson (Eds.), *Postmodern cities and spaces*. Oxford: Blackwell.
Mehta, D., & Chatterji, R. (2001). Boundaries, names, alterities: A case study of a "communal riot" in Dharavi, Bombay. In V. Das, M. L. A. Kleinman, M. Ramphele, & P. Reynolds (Eds.), *Remaking a world: Violence, social suffering and recovery*. 201–249. New Delhi: Oxford University Press.
Mhaskar, S. (2013). *Indian Muslims in a global city: Socio-political effects on economic preferences in contemporary Mumbai*. MMG Working Paper 13-04. Gottingen: Max Planck Institute for the study of Religious and ethnic diversity. www.mmg.mpg.de/workingpapers.
Nainan, N. (2008). Building boomers and fragmentation of space in Mumbai. *Economic and Political Weekly, 43*, 29–34.
Nijman, J. (2000). Mumbai's real estate in 1990s: De-regulation, global money and casino capitalism. *Economic and Political Weekly, 35*(7), 575–582.
Punwani, J. (2003). My area, you area': How riots changed the city. In S. Patel & J. Masselos (Eds.), *Bombay and Mumbai: A city in transition*. New Delhi: Oxford University Press.
Robinson, R. (2005). Tremors of violence: Muslim survivors of ethnic strife in Western India. New Delhi: Sage.
Roy, A. (2011). Slumdog cities: Rethinking subaltern urbanism. *International Journal of Urban and Regional Research, 35*(2), 223–238.
Scott, J. C. (1998). *Seeing like a state: How certain schemes to improve the human condition have failed*. New Haven, London: Yale University Press.
Sen, A. (2008). *Shiva Sena women—Violence and communalism in a Bombay slum*. New Delhi: Zubaan.

Sharma, R. N., & Sita, K. (2000). Cities, slums and government. *Economic and political Weekly, 35*(42), 3733–3735.
Simone, A. M. (2004). People as infrastructure: Intersecting fragments in Johannesburg. *Public Culture, 16*(3), 407–429.
Singh, G. (1993). Hindutva's low-intensity war against Bombay's riot victims. *Economic and Political Weekly, 28*(19), 908–910.
Singh, G., & Das, P. K. (1995). Building castles in the air: Housing scheme for Bombay's slum dwellers. *Economic and Political Weekly, 30*(40), 2477–2481.
Srikrishna (Justice), B. N. (1998). *Report of the Srikrishna commission: An inquiry into the riots at Mumbai during December 1992 and January 1993*. Mumbai: High Court.
Thorat, S., Anuradha, B., Vinod, M., & Firdaus, R. (2015). Urban rental housing market: Caste and religion matters in access. *Economic and Political Weekly, 50*(26 & 27), 47–53.
Weinstein, L. (2012). Democratic urban citizenship and mega-project development in globalising Mumbai. In Renu Desai & Ramola Sanyal (Eds.), *Urbanizing citizenship: Contacted spaces in Indian cities* (pp. 58–81). New Delhi: Sage Publications.
YUVA. (1996). Planned segregation: Riots, evictions and dispossesion in Jogeshwari East. Mumbai and Geneva: COHRE.

Chapter 8
Fragile Entrepreneurialism: The Mumbai Airport Slum Redevelopment Project

Xuefei Ren

Introduction

In February 2014, the new terminal of the Mumbai International Airport flung open its doors for business, and soon after, the building garnered rave reviews in architectural magazines. Designed by a renowned architecture firm headquartered in Chicago—SOM (Fig. 8.1), Mumbai's new airport building was rated by BBC as 'one of the world's most spectacular airports' and praised by another UK-based blog as 'the greatest building in the twenty-first century'.[1] None of these reviews, however, mentioned anything about the dramatic conditions on the other side of the airport fences: the spectacular sprawl of slum settlements encircling the airport that house more than 400,000 people (Fig. 8.2). Many are long-time residents who settled here half a century ago and who over time transformed the marshy land into habitable living quarters and made their home here. As part of an ambitious plan approved by the State Government of Maharashtra, they will have to be resettled elsewhere to modernize airport facilities and also to build shopping malls and luxury hotels. The striking new terminal and the slums showcase the immense polarization in the built environment in Indian cities, between global architecture and the informal city. The redevelopment of the airport slums offers a microcosm of an urban India in transition, caught between global aspirations to build world-class cities and local realities of extreme inequality.

This chapter uses the airport slum redevelopment project in Mumbai as a case study to examine the emerging forms of urban governance in Indian cities. Slum

[1]See http://www.som.com/news/the_worlds_most_spectacular_new_airports, and http://blogs.spectator.co.uk/culturehousedaily/2014/10/why-bombay-airport-is-the-greatest-21st-century-building-and-what-we-can-learn-from-it/.

X. Ren (✉)
Global Urban Studies & Sociology, Michigan State University, East Lansing, MI, USA
e-mail: renxuefe@msu.edu

K.C. Smitha (ed.), *Entrepreneurial Urbanism in India*,
DOI 10.1007/978-981-10-2236-4_8

Fig. 8.1 The international terminal of the Mumbai airport, designed by SOM. Source: Author

Fig. 8.2 The slum settlements adjacent to airport runways. Source: Author

redevelopment is well documented in the scholarship on urban India (O'Hare et al. 1998; Mukhija 2003; Das 2003; Bhide 2011; Sharma 2011). But as some have pointed out, the current literature on urban transformations in India tends to oscillate between two perspectives—the framework of neoliberalism and the post-colonial perspective (Shatkin and Vidyarthi 2014). The framework of neoliberalism focuses on entrepreneurial forms of governance, such as policies and projects sponsored by the state, private sector, and international institutions to make Indian cities more competitive for investment in the international marketplace (Banerjee-Guha 2002; Nijman 2008; Goldman 2011). The post-colonial perspective emphasizes the incompleteness of neoliberal and entrepreneurial approaches, often attributing the failure or blockage of 'world-class' city-making projects to subaltern contestations (Benjamin 2008).

The two perspectives capture some of the major trends of urban restructuring taking place in Indian cities, but much remains unexplained. The meta-narrative of neoliberalism cannot explain why some localities are more resilient to neoliberal redevelopment drives, while others are less so (Weinstein 2014). The post-colonial perspective often fails to acknowledge other factors at work—beyond subaltern contestations—that erode world-class city-making projects, such as fragmented state power prevalent throughout urban India.

Going beyond the neoliberal and post-colonial frameworks, recent scholarship has sought a third way of interpreting urban social change in India by paying attention to the graduated forms of citizenship obtained in the contestations over urban development. This third perspective takes notice of the incompleteness of neoliberal projects and incremental claims-making on the part of citizens. For example, some have documented how slum dwellers in Mumbai over the years have gained access to housing, and the redevelopment process has become more inclusive, albeit still unequal (Anand and Rademacher 2011). Others have noted the differentiated accesses to housing along gender and ethno-religious divides (Appadurai 2000; Doshi 2013; Chatterjee 2014). Recent studies have also focused on new actors in urban politics, for example, by uncovering how political entrepreneurs, real estate developers, middle-class residential associations, and elite urban task forces compete, cooperate, and form ad hoc coalitions to advance their agendas (Searle 2014; Weinstein 2014; Sami 2014; Ghertner 2014). These studies spotlight the particularities of urban India that do not fit neatly in the narrative of neoliberalism.

This chapter builds on this recent dynamic scholarship, but shifts the focus away from individual actors to the politics of coalition building among various stakeholders across state agencies, private sectors, and civil society groups. Based on fieldwork conducted in 2014 on the airport slum redevelopment in Mumbai, I examine how urban entrepreneurialism manifests itself differently in Mumbai than in post-industrial cities in the West, where the concept was initially conceived (Harvey 1989). I argue that urban governance in India is characterized by 'fragile entrepreneurialism', given the extreme fragmentation of state power at the urban scale. A new coalition of stakeholders has to be reassembled for specific projects, and prior success does not guarantee smooth alliance building in the future, even with the same stakeholders involved.

For the airport slum redevelopment case, the stakeholders formed coalitions for two pilot projects of resettling slum dwellers, to expand runways in 2000–2002, and to build an expressway connecting the airport terminal in 2008–2011. But the same stakeholders, comprised of state government authorities, the airport company, and NGOs, could not reassemble themselves again for the main phase of the project (2007–present), which involves large-scale resettlement of more than 400,000 residents from 32 slum pockets. The project has been delayed for eight years as no plans have been made regarding how to resettle the residents. The study highlights that slum redevelopment in Mumbai largely hinges upon unpredictable associational politics, and the current redevelopment model favouring private gains falls far short to solve the housing shortage in the maximum city.

Urban Entrepreneurialism Revisited

Writing more than two decades ago, David Harvey described the transition of urban governance in the West as a shift from 'managerialism' to 'entrepreneurialism' (Harvey 1989). After the collapse of the Keynesian welfare state in the 1970s, a consensus was reached among policy-makers in post-industrial cities in West Europe and North America regarding the position of local governments: instead of being merely service providers (i.e. as managers), local governments had to be much more competitive, innovative, and willing to experiment with new policies and programmes to alleviate the stressed fiscal conditions of their cities (i.e. as entrepreneurs). As for how to be innovative and entrepreneurial, Harvey discussed four alternative strategies—to create particular advantages for the production of goods and services, to promote consumption, to build command-and-control functions, and to compete for subsidies from the federal government with other localities. These strategies should cultivate a favourable climate for investment, and they will also spawn uneven development between and within cities.

What distinguishes entrepreneurial urban governance from conventional managerial modes of governance, as argued by Harvey, is a public–private partnership in which local state power combines private capital to promote projects oriented for competition and capital accumulation. Urban entrepreneurialism is also characterized by speculation in project design and execution, as well as selective targeting of specific localities, projects, and places as opposed to the metropolitan territory as a whole.

The Mumbai airport redevelopment project might be an example of Harvey's entrepreneurial strategies, a project that aimed to create advantages in production and consumption through investment in a state-of-the-art airport that would enhance the profile of Mumbai as a hub for international business, investment, and tourism. The project also had to compete with others for central government funding, as it was one of the flagship infrastructure projects approved under the central government's JNNUR (Jawaharlal Nehru National Urban Renewal Mission) programme. In addition, private–public partnership lies at the core of the project design and implementation. Back in 2006, the Airport Authority of India privatized the Mumbai International Airport, and management was entrusted to a consortium led by a private company GVK, and a private–public partnership was formed by establishing Mumbai International Airport Ltd (MIAL). The airport slum redevelopment was endorsed by the Maharashtra State development agencies. The design and execution of the project is largely speculative in nature: slum dwellers will have to be relocated, only a small portion of the vacated land will be used for the expansion of the airport, and the rest will be used for private property development. Thus, the airport slum redevelopment project seems to be no different from the profit-driven, entrepreneurial projects led by public–private partnerships in post-industrial cities in the West, as described by Harvey.

But Indian cities present a different political and institutional context from post-industrial cities in the West (Ren and Weinstein 2013). State power is highly fragmented at the local level and who is being entrepreneurial and about what is often unclear. As will be examined in the next sections, coalition building for entrepreneurial projects has proved to be especially precarious and difficult to achieve, due to the extreme forms of fragmentation of state power and high degrees of organization in slum settlements. It is rare to find an individual or institution powerful enough to ‘put a particular stamp upon the nature and direction of urban entrepreneurialism’ (Harvey 1989, 7). In the airport redevelopment case, the stakeholders managed to build a coalition for project’s pilot phase, but the fragile coalition fell apart for the main phase. Thus, in the Indian context where municipal governments have little power and autonomy, urban entrepreneurialism has taken a highly fragile and contingent form.

Dealing with Slums in the Maximum City

This section reviews slum housing policies in Mumbai and situates the airport slum redevelopment project in the historical context. From the 1950s to the present, slum housing policies in Mumbai have experienced three phases: demolition and clearance in the 1950s and 1960s; upgrading in the 1970s and 1980s; and a market-led redevelopment scheme after 1991 (O’Hare et al. 1998; Burra 2005). Demolitions and displacement have become rare as they are politically infeasible, but they do take place periodically. For example, the large-scale demolition drives in 2004 and 2005 displaced more than 400,000 people in Mumbai. Community organizations, NGOs, and residents routinely upgrade their residential quarters, sometime with and more often without help from the state and international institutions. Since the early 1990s, state support has sharply declined and slum housing policies in Mumbai shifted to a more market-led model, with the inauguration of the Slum Redevelopment Scheme (SRS) in 1991.

The current phase of slum housing policies is centred on the market-led SRS. Funding from the private sector is actively sought for redeveloping slums and resettling residents, and in return, developers are given a certain amount of developable land to recover their investment. As land and housing prices in Mumbai soared in the 1990s, redeveloping slum settlements in central locations has become a profitable business. The cost of building resettlement housing is relatively low, compared to the profit to be made by constructing market-rate commercial properties. In most redevelopment projects in Mumbai, in situ rehabilitation[2] is offered to eligible slum dwellers—those who can prove their residency by an arbitrary cut-off date of 1 January 2000. Ex situ resettlement is the norm if the project involves large infrastructure construction such as metrorails, road construction, and airport expansion. The SRS is not a top-down neoliberal policy but rather a result of compromises and struggles between mainstream development drives and housing rights movements in Mumbai (Anand and Rademacher 2011).

After more than two decades in operation, the privatized model of the SRS has had little impact on improving the housing conditions in Mumbai. According to the latest census in 2011, still nearly 55 % of the city's population lives in slum settlements and places not officially classified as slums often have slum-like conditions.[3] The market-led redevelopment policy has exacerbated housing inequalities in Mumbai: developers are awarded transferable development rights to build market-rate housing, and meanwhile, slum residents are 'rehabilitated' in poorly constructed high-rise towers, either in situ or on the cheapest land possible on the periphery without basic amenities (CEHAT 2006; Housing and Land Rights Network 2014).

In addition to the flawed design of the SRS, Mumbai's slum housing policies are further undermined by the fragmented landownership structures. Mumbai's slums have developed on land owned by the central, state, and municipal governments and also on private land. In the federalist structure, each state can frame its own policies and programmes for slum redevelopment, but these do not apply to slums built on land belonging to the central government. The airport slum is a case in point—it sits on land that belongs to the Airport Authority of India, a central government agency. The central agencies such as railway, airport, and port authorities often have large land holdings, reflecting the colonial history of urban development (Burra 2005). In Mumbai, upgrading programmes in the 1970s and 1980s did not touch the slums on the central government's land. State and municipal agencies are not allowed to provide services to these slums, and they cannot evict them because many slum dwellers have settled here before the cut-off date of 1 January 2000 (Arputham and Patel 2010). The airport slum has expanded massively and precisely because it falls in a regulatory vacuum between the central and state government.

The central government agencies are willing to cooperate with state-level and municipal authorities for slum redevelopment only when they are desperate to reclaim the land (Burra 2005). The first time in Mumbai that a central government agency agreed to rehabilitate a slum was the project relocating families living next to railway tracks: in this case, the Ministry of Railway and the State Government of

[2]'Rehabilitation' is a term commonly used in housing policy circuits in Mumbai, referring to the process of relocating residents from slums to buildings and sites with better infrastructure and living conditions, such as flats built by private developers participating in the Slum Redevelopment Scheme.

[3]http://www.indiaonlinepages.com/population/slum-population-in-india.html.

Maharashtra shared the costs, with support from powerful NGOs such as society for the promotion of area resource centers (SPARC) (Patel et al. 2002). The airport redevelopment project marks the second large-scale project involving rehabilitating slum settlers on central government land in Mumbai, and as will be examined in the next sections, its progress was not as smooth as the railway project, and the fragile alliance of the state authorities, private sector, and NGOs fell apart after two pilot projects.

Fragile Entrepreneurialism

This section examines fragile forms of entrepreneurialism that characterizes urban governance in Mumbai by delving into the details of the airport slum redevelopment project. The airport slum is one of the largest slum redevelopment projects in Mumbai, involving relocation and resettlement of almost half a million people currently residing on 125 ha of land that legally belongs to the Airport Authority of India. Many of the slums are in the low-lying areas vulnerable to flooding, so that the Airport Authority did not construct any facilities on these lands. From the 1950s, people began to settle here, filled the swamps, and made the marshy land habitable. Some live in precariously close to airport runways and have to put up with the pollution and noise from the air traffic (Fig. 8.3). International flights land

Fig. 8.3 A family living on the other side of the airport fence. Source: Author

Fig. 8.4 Residents of Jari Mari, one of the airport slums, watching flights taking off and landing. Source: Author

and take off almost every two minutes, and airplane watching has become a favourite pastime for residents in Jari Mari, whose huts dot the hills overlooking the runways (Fig. 8.4). Other slum pockets further away from the airport runways more resemble a 'normal' neighbourhood, with lively markets, shops, schools, and community organizations such as churches, mosques, and NGOs (Fig. 8.5). With a large population and a variety of businesses—from cattle raising and light manufacturing to retail and street vendors, redeveloping the airport slum presented challenges as deep and daunting as those faced in the nearby Dharavi area.

Precarious Coalitions

In a report prepared by MMRDA, the Maharashtra State development agency described the Mumbai International Airport as 'the most constrained airport in the world' (MMRDA 2012). The Mumbai airport has an operating site area of only 678 ha, about one-third of the size of Delhi and Hyderabad airports (MMRDA 2012). Because of the confined space, the two runways had to be built intersecting each other, a configuration that substantially increased the pre-take-off waiting time. Facing severe space constraints, the Airport Authority of India collaborated with

Fig. 8.5 Street life in Sahar village, one of the slums adjacent to Sahar expressway. Source: Author

state-level development agencies in 2002 for the first time, as it was desperate to evict some slum settlers to expand the runway so that aircrafts did not have to take a sharp turn before taking off. Providing funds for resettlement, the Airport Authority worked with the Slum Rehabilitation Authority (SRA) to relocate 1850 families in 2002 (Burra 2005). The SRA, in turn, worked with a state government company—SPPL (Shivshai Punarvasan Prakalp Ltd.)—to construct 27 rehabilitation buildings in a north-west suburb of Dindoshi. Jockin Arputham, a leading housing rights advocate and head of the National Slum Dwellers Federation, was invited to be the facilitator between the community and state authorities. The consent of 70 % of residents was needed for the project to proceed, and Arputham, together with SPARC—the leading housing rights NGO in Mumbai, helped to convince residents to relocate. Arputham led a survey to determine eligibility and collected and verified documents from residents. The resettlement of the 1850 families took two years—between 2000 and 2002, but the actual planning and negotiation phase took almost a decade. Delays in the negation process stemmed from the time lags in securing approvals from the Ministry of Aviation, coupled with the rapid turnover of personnel among officials in state government agencies (CEHAT 2006).

This pilot project was completed, largely because the scale of resettlement was small and the task of expanding runways so urgent so that the Airport Authority had no choice but to join hands with SRA and local NGOs. Moreover, the resettlement was carried out without much opposition from residents partly due to the weak political leadership of the community being relocated. The families were from Rafique Nagar, a predominately Muslim neighbourhood in the Jari Mari area. Without a strong leadership that could pose opposition, residents in large agreed to relocate despite being aware that their livelihood would be negatively affected, as the resettlement site in Dindoshi is far away from the airport, where most residents had jobs. Life after resettlement was harsh—the resettlement site was not connected to main roads and lacked basic amenities (CEHAT 2006).

The second pilot project took place in 2008, when the Airport Authority collaborated with MMRDA and SRA to build the Sahar Elevated Access Road (SEAR) to connect the international terminal with the Western Expressway. This project also received funding from the central government's JNNUR programme, and the Airport Authority and MMRDA split the cost of road construction and the resettlement of residents. The MMRDA was responsible for building the stretch from the Western Expressway to the Hyatt Hotel, while the privatized airport company (MIAL) built the stretch from Hyatt to the international terminal. Commissioned in 2008 under the MUIP (Mumbai Urban Infrastructure Project), the 3.3-km-long access road was finally completed in 2014, when the new international terminal opened its operation.

A slum survey conducted by MMRDA counted 1000 families to be resettled for the SEAR project. Residents resisted the surveys, and some women were arrested by the police under the charge of 'preventing public servants from carrying out their work' (CRH 2012). According to the official cut-off date of 1 January 2000, only 700 families qualified and they were resettled in a SRA housing complex in Vidyavihar. To minimize resistance, MMRDA provided temporary accommodation in Goregoan to those not eligible. About 200 families from Subhash Nagar whose houses sat on private land were given Rs 4 million per room. An NGO, Committee for Housing Rights, conducted a study on rehabilitation and found similar results with the first pilot project—that residents were resettled on the cheapest possible land without basic amenities (CRH 2012).

The airport authority thus has worked together with state-level development agencies to form a precarious coalition to carry out two infrastructure projects deemed to be the most urgent for the modernization of the Mumbai airport. They faced constant resistance (i.e. obstruction in the survey process) from those within the community, who were not eligible by the official cut-off date. But such resistance was overcome in the two pilot projects, with NGOs acting as brokers for the first project and with MMRDA using both force and concession to relocate residents for the second project. For the main phase of the redevelopment project of relocating all of the 32 slum pockets, however, neither the Airport Authority nor the state government agencies were willing to bear the cost of relocating residents. In addition to intergovernmental fragmentation between central and state-level authorities, the coalition building was further complicated with the entry of new actors—a privatized airport company and its contracted developer (Housing Development and Infrastructure Ltd., or HDIL) that were put in charge of relocating residents.

Privatization of the Airport and Legal Battles

In 2006, the Mumbai International Airport was privatized, and the privatization introduced new layers of complexity to the already murky situations of who should be responsible for resettling residents. The complications and conflicts between different stakeholders eventually ended up in the court, as the contracted developer, HDIL, could not deliver what it promised in the contract—such as relocating slum dwellers in a timely manner.

The Ministry of Aviation contracted the management and operation of the airport to GVK, a private company, and MIAL was formed with GVK holding majority shares. As part of the agreement, the land belonging to the Airport Authority of India was leased out for 30 years to MIAL, which planned to relocate the residents currently living on airport land and to devote a small portion of the reclaimed land to expand runways and airport facilities, as well as develop commercial property—i.e. building hotels, offices, and residential properties that targeted the middle class. In 2007, MIAL contracted HDIL to undertake the slum redevelopment project. HDIL was chosen from a number of competing bids because it has a 'land bank'—i.e. available land to build resettlement housing for slum dwellers. HDIL was to be responsible for clearing slums and building resettlement housing. It would not be compensated in cash, but instead awarded transferable development rights, both on the cleared airport land and elsewhere in Mumbai. After the Airport Authority of India approved the subcontracting arrangement, a 'slum rehabilitation contract' was signed between MIAL and HDIL in 2007.

MIAL then entered into a series of other agreements with state government agencies. In April 2006, the State Government of Maharashtra issued a 'State Support Agreement' to support the modernization and upgrading of the airport. In December, MMRDA signed an agreement with MIAL memorializing their cooperation. At about the same time, HDIL also obtained permission from SRA to build rehabilitation housing. Thus, the airport slum redevelopment had acquired endorsement from all major state agencies—including MMRDA, SRA, and the Government of Maharashtra.

But overhauling a slum redevelopment project of this scale would require more than the signing of agreements and the issuance of planning guidelines. The coalition of multiple stakeholders would first have to conduct a survey to determine how many people currently resided on the airport land and then determine the eligibility criteria for rehabilitation. The project, however, fell apart at the very first step, as neither the state development authority nor the private developer could manage to complete the survey. Since many residents would not qualify under the official 1 January 2000 cut-off date, they demanded that the government first release details of rehabilitation before carrying out the survey. Because of the resettlement scale—more than 400,000 people—MMRDA did not want to use force to complete the survey, such as by sending in police officers, but neither did it want to offer concessions as it previously had done in two pilot projects.

Without the assistance from the state agencies and NGOs, HDIL itself could not carry out any slum clearance work that it had promised to do in its contract with MIAL. Six years later, in 2013, MIAL terminated the contract with HDIL. HDIL, already having invested in the construction of resettlement housing, sued all other major parties involved in the project, including the Airport Authority of India, MIAL, the State Government of Maharashtra, MMRDA, and SRA. HDIL argued that it had received too little support from central and state government agencies, especially the critical nodal agencies of MMRDA and SRA. The Bombay High Court ruled that the dispute was a narrow affair between MIAL and HDIL, that state agencies were not responsible for project delays, and that HDIL was responsible for any losses incurred because it breached the contractual obligations (Bombay High Court 2013).

The Contested Slum Survey

Conducting a slum survey is often the most contested part of any slum redevelopment project, as residents who do not qualify by the official cut-off date strongly resist being surveyed. The documentation required of the so-called basic socio-economic survey is labour-intensive: every structure, family, and business must be documented, and residents must multiple documents to prove their housing tenure. The survey data becomes critical evidence to prove one's tenure status when residents negotiate with developers and state authorities over resettlement. Participation of NGOs in such surveys is often critical, because they have networks and familiarity with the local community, as compared to government surveyors. Some NGOs are willing to survey the slum population, as a strategy to intervene in the redevelopment process, as it extends some protection simply by documenting the residents.

The difficulty of conducting such surveys can be seen in other redevelopment projects. SPARC documented its experience of conducting the survey for the Dharavi Redevelopment Project in 2007–2008. Patel et al. (2009) noted that even with their extensive networks in Dharavi, the survey was interrupted multiple times because of resistance from residents. Residents, uninformed about the details of the resettlement plan, distrusted government authorities and NGOs. Also the resettlement eligibility criteria excluded many kinds of residents: renters, dwellers unable to furbish the required documents to prove their tenure, and others who bought their dwelling after the 1 January 2000 cut-off date. Opposition to the survey also came from political parties—some members of the Shiv Sena party objected to the survey.

The airport redevelopment project did not advance as much as the Dharavi project. The state development authority began the survey without any NGOs, and instead, police was sent to assist surveyors. Residents refused to corporate with the survey—some families locked their house and left when the surveyors came, and residents demanded that the details of resettlement would have to be released first before the survey. The survey was finally stopped in October 2012, when the local collector wrote to MMRDA questioning the surveying of properties on non-airport land. In an interview, Arputham commented that the state government stopped the survey, partly because the state did not want to rehabilitate too many people.[4]

If the slum survey is the contested battleground for redevelopment, then determining the eligibility of residents is the biggest battle of all. Slum dwellers are deemed eligible for a free 269 ft^2 SRA apartment only if they can prove that they were on the electoral roll on and prior to 1 January 2000. If the current cut-off date is adopted, then between 40 and 50 % of the residents in the airport slums cannot qualify. One might assume that a more recent cut-off date would be more inclusive, but Delhi's experience proved otherwise. In a short period, the cut-off date in Delhi has been updated three times, from 1 April 2002 to 31 January 2007, and to 4 June 2009. But residents must show a voter ID card for all three time points in order to qualify. The eligibility rates among slum dwellers in Delhi were lower than in Mumbai, under 50 % on average, and this reflects the difficulty of assembling the necessary documents (Sheikh and Banda 2014).

As the cut-off date is often controversial, state development authorities and private developers sometimes try to push their projects forward by extending the cut-off date to include more residents. MMRDA, the authority that determines eligibility, in the past has made concessions on several large-scale infrastructure projects by extending the cut-off date or doing without it altogether. The most celebrated case is the Mumbai Urban Transport Project (MUTP) beginning in 2007, designed to rehabilitate families living close to railway tracks. For the MUTP project, the cut-off date was based on date of the slum survey. Some developers even would lure ineligible residents by helping them to fake documentation, so that they would not stir up trouble opposing the projects. For the airport redevelopment project, MMRDA must make some sort of concession if it wants the project to proceed, but MMRDA is reluctant to decide on the terms of concession, as the land belongs to the central government, the airport has been privatized, and the project is not entirely a public infrastructure project like those it has worked on previously. Thus, the airport slum redevelopment presents a highly complex case that the loose alliance of state agencies and private companies is not simply prepared to handle.

Mumbai's NGOs and Deep Democracy

The airport slum redevelopment project has been closely watched by a number of housing rights NGOs in Mumbai. State government agencies in the past invited NGOs to facilitate resettlement processes, but for the main phase of the project, no NGOs have been invited to participate. The lack of involvement of NGOs as

[4]Interview with Jockin Arputham, 23 August 2014.

facilitators further weakened the already fragile redevelopment coalition comprised of uninterested state agencies and private companies.

In an open letter sent to the press in 2007, Arputham restated where his NGO—National Slum Dwellers' Federation—stood towards the airport slum redevelopment; that is, residents have to be involved in the design and implementation; otherwise, he warned that residents could be quickly mobilized to put a stop to the airport slum redevelopment, by blocking roads and airport runways (Patel and Arputham 2007). He insisted that the slum survey had to be conducted by an NGO—instead of by the developer (HDIL) or state government agencies, to ensure transparency and fairness. But in spite of its prior experience with surveys in the airport slum area, the state government did not officially invite Arputham to conduct the survey. In 2010, as the state government began surveying the airport communities by itself, Jockin Arputham and Sheela Patel jointly published an article raising a number of concerns, including how the cleared land will be used, the absence of any public agency to monitor the rehabilitation process, whether all residents need to be relocated, and specific terms over resettlement and eligibility (see Arputham and Patel 2010). Neither the airport company nor the state development agencies were willing to address any of these issues raised by Mumbai's two prominent NGOs. The lack of interest from the state government and the Airport Authority to work together with NGOs shows that for every project, a new coalition has to be reassembled from scratch even with the same stakeholders involved.

The Committee on Rights to Housing (CRH), another NGO closely involved in the organizing of airport slum residents, takes a more confrontational stance by stating that all residents should be resettled if redevelopment takes place. In an interview with the head of CRH, Sweta Delma, she corrected me several times that the airport land occupied by slums does not belong to the airport company, but to the people living there.[5] She knows that the airport authority legally owns the land, but she believes that families who have lived in the airport slums for generations have a right to stay. CRH was actively involved in organizing protests to prevent the state government to conduct the baseline survey, and it helped to formulate a central slogan for the protests—*Hi Jameen aamchya hakkachi, naahi GVK chya baapaachi* (this land is ours by right, it does not belong to GVK). The demands put forward by CRH are much more radical than SPARC and NSDF. For example, they demanded in situ rehabilitation instead of ex situ. Instead of following the cut-off date to divide the residents into the eligible and non-eligible, they believe that eligibility should extend to every family living in the airport slums. They demand bigger resettlement apartments than the government-mandated 269 ft^2, so that large families can be accommodated. And lastly, maintenance fees should be waived too in resettlement colonies.

NGOs have redefined urban governance in Mumbai with their ability to empower the poor by circulating knowledge about their communities, and

[5]Personal interview, 25 August 2014.

Appadurai (2002) calls these practices 'deep democracy'. There is no doubt that Mumbai's housing NGOs have made substantial progress in protecting slum dwellers' rights to housing, but NGOs cannot solve Mumbai' housing crisis. The pragmatic NGOs such as SPARC and NSDF are powerful brokers between the community and developers, and the more radical NGOs can help to obstruct slum surveys. But neither has the capacity to rehabilitate the residents in large numbers living on extremely precarious sites, such as those areas adjacent to airport runways. In other words, NGOs can deepen democratic practices and sometimes carry out small-scale slum resettlement projects, but it is ultimately the task of the state to provide housing for the large number of the poor.

Conclusion

With an in-depth case study of the airport slum redevelopment project in Mumbai, this article has examined the specificity of urban entrepreneurialism in contemporary Indian cities. The airport slum redevelopment project, designed to relocate slum settlements to make way for expanding the airport and constructing commercial real estate, is an example of urban entrepreneurial projects for world-class city-making. However, urban entrepreneurism in India takes a fragile form, and unpredictable coalition politics shape the trajectories of large-scale redevelopment projects. For the airport slum case, the stakeholders across the public, private, and NGO sectors formed an alliance for two pilot projects to expand runways and construct an expressway. The private airport company and state government authority, relying on the NGOs as brokers, used both incentives and coercion to resettle slum dwellers to clear the land. However, for the main phase of the redevelopment project, state authorities, the private sector, and NGOs could not reassemble themselves to tackle the task of conducting a slum survey, and the project has been put on hold since 2007.

This study attempts to break away from the meta-narratives of neoliberalism and post-colonialism, by focusing on coalition and alliance building processes over redevelopment. Neither of the perspectives can fully explain the twisted trajectory of the airport slum redevelopment over the past fifteen years. Neoliberal projects designed to improve Mumbai's standing as a world-class city are constantly challenged by grass-roots resistance, but the outcomes of redevelopment largely depend on project-based negotiations and alliance building. For each project, or even each phase of the same project, a new alliance has to be reassembled. The larger the scale of the redevelopment is, the more the difficult it is for any single entrepreneur—either private or public—to put together a coalition to undertake the project. In the process, slum residents gain differentiated access to resettlement depending on the extent to which the state development agencies and private sector are willing to make concessions. The official cut-off date is only a reference, and eligibility is constantly negotiated. The question of 'who' is being entrepreneurial and 'how' becomes fuzzy in the Indian context. When the tasks at hands are urgent, such as for critical infrastructure projects badly needed in the city, state development agencies often are willing to work with the private sector and solicit help from NGOs. But when the projects get more challenging, the 'entrepreneurial' spirit quickly disappears as no single actor is willing, or able to build a coalition across the state, private, and NGO sectors.

Overall in cities such as Mumbai with more than 50 % of its population living in slum settlements, the current market-led redevelopment model is no solution to the city's housing problems. The design of the SRS favours private gains, and each project has to be negotiated intensely among stakeholders. The NGO sector can provide some protection against displacement, but it does not have the capacity to improve the housing conditions for slum dwellers at a large scale. The challenge faced by Mumbai is thus whether or not the state government can recognize the vast informal city as part of the city, incorporate it in the formal planning, and open up land in the metropolitan region to build housing for the poor.

References

Anand, N., & Rademacher, A. (2011). Housing in the urban age: Inequality and aspiration in Mumbai. *Antipode, 43*(5), 1748–1772.

Appadurai, A. (2000). Spectral housing and urban cleansing: Notes on Millennial Mumbai. *Public Culture, 12*(3), 627–651.

Appadurai, A. (2002). Deep democracy: Urban governmentality and the horizon of politics. *Public Culture, 14*(1), 21–47.

Arputham, J., & Patel, S. (2010). Recent developments in plans for Dharavi and for the airport slums in Mumbai. *Environment and Urbanization, 22*(2), 501–504.

Banerjee-Guha, S. (2002). Shifting cities: Urban restructuring in Mumbai. *Economic and Political Weekly, 37*(2), 121–128.

Benjamin, S. (2008). Occupancy urbanism: Radicalizing politics and economy beyond policy and programs. *International Journal of Urban and Regional Research, 32*(3), 719–729.

Bhide, A. (2011). The slum and the development plan. In Urban Design Research Institute (UDRI) (Ed.), *Mumbai reader* (Vol. 10, pp. 203–217). Mumbai: UDRI. www.udri.org/.../MumbaiReader10/04%20Amita%20Bhide%20-%20The%20Slum%2. Accessed December 20, 2015.

Bombay High Court. (2013). HDIL versus MIAL, Airport Authority of India, the State of Maharashtra, The Collector of Mumbai, the MMRDA, and the Slum Rehabilitation Authority, Arbitration petition (L) no. 902 of 2013.

Burra, S. (2005). Towards a pro-poor framework for slum upgrading in Mumbai, India. *Environment and Urbanization, 17*(1), 67–88.

Center for Enquiry into Health and Allied Themes (CEHAT). (2006). *Uprooted homes, uprooted lives: A study of the impact of involuntary resettlement of a slum community in Mumbai*. Mumbai: CEHAT.

Chatterjee, I. (2014). Social conflict and the neoliberal city: A case of Hindu–Muslim violence in India. In G. Shatkin (Ed.), *Contesting the Indian city: Global visions and the politics of the local* (pp. 145–175). Malden, MA: Wiley Blackwell.

Committee for the Right to Housing (CRH). (2012). *Privatisation of Mumbai airport: Loot Made Legal*. Mumbai: CRH.

Das, P. K. (2003). Slums: The continuing struggle for housing. In S. Patel & J. Masselos (Eds.), *Bombay and Mumbai: The city in transition* (pp. 207–234). New Delhi: Oxford University Press.
Doshi, S. (2013). The politics of the evicted: Redevelopment, subjectivity, and difference in Mumbai's slum frontier. *Antipode, 45*(4), 844–865.
Ghertner, A. D. (2014). Gentrifying the state: Governance, participation, and the rise of middle-class power in Delhi. In G. Shatkin (Ed.), *Contesting the Indian City: Global visions and the politics of the local* (pp. 176–207). Malden, MA: Wiley Blackwell.
Goldman, M. (2011). Speculative urbanism and the making of the next world city. *International Journal of Urban and Regional Research, 35*(3), 555–581.
Harvey, D. (1989). From managerialism to entrepreneurialism: The transformation in urban governance in late capitalism. *Geografiska Annaler Series B, Human Geography, 71*(1), 3–17.
Housing and Land Rights Network. (2014). Forced to the fringes: Disasters of 'resettlement' in India. New Delhi,
Mukhija, V. (2003). *Squatters as developers?* Aldershot, UK: Ashgate.
Mumbai Metropolitan Regional Development Authority (MMRDA). (2012). Modified interim draft development plan for Chhatrapati Shivaji International Airport Notified Area (CSIANA), Mumbai 2010–2014.
Nijman, J. (2008). Against the odds: Slum rehabilitation in neoliberal Mumbai. *Cities, 25*, 73–85.
O'Hare, G., Dina, A., & Barke, M. (1998). A review of slum housing policies in Mumbai. *Cities, 15*(4), 269–283.
Patel, S., & Arputham, J. (2007). An offer of partnership or a promise of conflict in Dharavi, Mumbai? *Economic and Political Weekly, 19*(2), 501–508.
Patel, S., Arputham, J., Burra, S., & Savchuk, K. (2009). Getting the information base for Dharavi's redevelopment. *Environment and Urbanization, 21*(1), 241–251.
Patel, S., d'Cruze, C., & Burra, S. (2002). Beyond evictions in a global city: People-managed resettlement in Mumbai. *Environment and Urbanization, 14*(1), 159–172.
Ren, X., & Weinstein, L. (2013). Urban governance, mega-projects, and scalar transformations in China and India. In T. Samara, S. He, & G. Chen (Eds.), *Right to the city in the global south: Transnational urban governance and socio-spatial transformations* (pp. 107–126). New York: Routledge.
Sami, N. (2014). Power to the people? A study of Bangalore's urban task force. In G. Shatkin (Ed.), *Contesting the Indian City: Global visions and the politics of the local* (pp. 121–144). Malden, MA: Wiley Blackwell.
Searle, L. G. (2014). Conflict and commensuration: Contested market making in India's private real estate development sector. In G. Shatkin (Ed.), *Contesting the Indian City: Global visions and the politics of the local* (pp. 65–90). Malden, MA: Wiley Blackwell.
Sharma, R. N. (2011). Urban renewal and its implications to resettlement and rehabilitation. In Urban Design Research Institute (UDRI) (Ed.), *Mumbai reader* (Vol. 09, pp. 203–217). Mumbai: UDRI.
Shatkin, G., & Vidyarthi, S. (2014). Introduction: Contesting the Indian city: Global visions and the politics of the local. In G. Shatkin (Ed.), *Contesting the Indian city: Global visions and the politics of the local* (pp. 1–38). Malden, MA: Wiley Blackwell.
Sheikh, S., & Banda S. (2014). *The Delhi Urban Shelter Improvement Board (DUSIB): The challenges facing a strong, progressive agency*. A report of the Cities of Delhi project. New Delhi: Center for Policy Research.
Weinstein, L. (2014). *The Durable slum: Dharavi and the right to stay put in globalizing Mumbai*. Minneapolis: University of Minnesota Press.

Chapter 9
Planning their Homes in Entrepreneurial City: The Capacities of Urban Poor and the Constraints of Public Policy

Swetha Rao Dhananka

Introduction

This chapter compares two urban poor communities assisted by the same NGO in the entrepreneurial city of Bengaluru (earlier Bangalore, in southern India) in their quest to access adequate housing. One community was the target of housing delivered by the state, while the other mobilized to build housing on its own. The aim is on the one hand to present the different housing outcomes by identifying constraints in housing policy formulated within the framework of entrepreneurial governance and on the other hand to highlight the nurtured capacities of the poor to plan and build their neighbourhood on their own terms.

The presented argument draws from a qualitative study conducted in the city of Bengaluru between 2009 and 2010 on the sociopolitical conditions to claim adequate housing for the urban poor. This chapter deals with entrepreneurialism in two forms: first, it argues not only that the entrepreneurial city is about politico-institutionally produced economic competition and innovation, but also that these economic imperatives trigger capacities within civil society organizations (CSOs) to coshape urban transformations. They learn to veer around neoliberal priorities by developing entrepreneurial (Roy and Ong 2011) and social skill (Fligstein and McAdam 2011). These skills serve to resist and navigate policies and political networks produced within the entrepreneurial city. Entrepreneurial skill will be defined 'as the ability to initiate and nurture new endeavours and ideas in the pursuit of the right to the city', while social skill signifies the capacity of individuals or collective actors possessing a highly developed cognitive capacity for reading

S. Rao Dhananka (✉)
Development Planning Unit UCL, London, United Kingdom
e-mail: swetha.raodhananka@unil.ch

S. Rao Dhananka
Indian Institute for Human Settlements, Bangalore, India

K.C. Smitha (ed.), *Entrepreneurial Urbanism in India*,
DOI 10.1007/978-981-10-2236-4_9

people and environments and to frame lines of action for mobilizing people (Fligstein and McAdam 2011).

Second, this chapter deals with urban entrepreneurialism that finds expression in a particular public housing policy, producing forms of socio-spatial exclusion. I illustrate this by describing the tensions that arise in an entrepreneurial city of Bengaluru that prioritizes monetary profit making (almost at any cost), but that also ought to deliver public welfare to its citizens. Public housing for the urban poor represents an exemplary case to demonstrate tension as housing necessitates urban land, an asset that unequal players compete for.

Two slum-dweller communities are discussed that were assisted by the same NGO. While one community was successful in developing crucial entrepreneurial and social skills among its members to claim and plan their own neighbourhood, the other had to deal with the constraints of housing policy—having to face competition among themselves, competition over productive land, and contending the vested interests of slum leaders and government officials. The reason I argue that policy specifications represent constraints is that the current experiment which is under way in urban India is to reconcile the systems of public welfare (a constitutional provision) with imperatives of the entrepreneurial city, which displays contradicting priorities of resource allocation. The entrepreneurial city allocates resources to demanding infrastructure projects, fuelling the ambitions of a 'worlding city' (Roy and Ong 2011), whereas public welfare ought to allocate resources for the uplift of the poor (Chatterjee 2004). This contradictory engagement produces particular policies aimed at the urban poor within an entrepreneurial city. Simultaneously, these policies aim to make resource allocation to welfare financially viable for the city too. Such requirements forge a particular type of policy prescribed from top-down, i.e. centrally planned and integrating the much-fancied model of a public–private partnership (PPP). To mediate such tensions, an institutionalized role of an NGO is foreseen.

Within such contradictory imperatives in the southern Indian city of Bengaluru, this chapter presents two cases of urban poor communities that worked with an NGO called AVAS. AVAS was actively involved and assisted both communities for more than 10 years to facilitate access to housing. One community battled for adequate housing without being target or having to respond to the prevalent housing policy. The other was ear-marked for an in situ housing development project under Basic Services to the Urban Poor (BSUP), a component of the Jawaharlal Nehru National Urban Renewal Mission (JNNURM) (2005–2012) which was implemented through a PPP model. The outcome of these processes to access to housing was different. While the former was successful to create a functioning and sustainable neighbourhood, the latter is still grappling with low quality of construction and suffers from weak unity within the community.

In the next section, I describe the conceptual considerations for framing the case studies. Further, I narrate the distinct trajectories of both housing processes articulated within the policy environment for the latter community. Then, I analyse the factors that contributed to the different outcomes, and finally, I formulate a conclusion and outlook.

Means to Bridge Public Welfare with Neoliberal Imperatives

Ongoing experiments within the entrepreneurial urbanism framework are about the imbrication of neoliberal imperatives with public welfare. To understand the effects of this imbrication on the place of the poor in the city, it is important to consider the path dependency of welfare policies and the highly context-specific emergence of neoliberalism in India (Sager 2011: 149).

The Governance of Public Welfare

The post-colonial thinker Chatterjee (2004) describes the current form of public welfare in India on the basis of the way the British Empire administered population, called techniques of governmentality. These are rationally manipulable instruments to reach sections of society as target of policies, transforming the inhabitant into a 'subject' rather than a rightful citizen. The poor as targets of policies with their inherited status of subjects inherently impacts their relationship to the state as one of dependency of the benefits prescribed by the policy. But as the entitlements are exclusive and outnumbered by the numbers of poor in a populous country such as India, claiming governmental benefits becomes an issue of political negotiation. Their relation with the state is hence a political one. Such 'subjects' are members of what he refers to as '*political society*' as against right-bearing citizens, which he refers to as *civil society* (Chatterjee 2004). Belonging either to political or civil society in Chatterjee's terms consequently also means to possess differential resources, not only in terms of money and time, but also in terms of social skills to mobilize and create audiences (Boudreau 1996; Schram 2004), and the entrepreneurial skill to veer around policies and agents. The socio-historical position of the urban poor, also characterized by caste in the Indian context, influences the resources they have and experiences with the state that recursively shape values, beliefs, and ideology to perceive and access 'political opportunities' (Carmin and Basler 2002). India's public welfare schemes are mostly derived from the same logic of making the poor targets of specific policies, including some and excluding others. The housing policy presented in the next section follows this logic.

Neoliberal City-Making: PPP and Organizations in Bengaluru

During the post-economic liberalization of the 1990s, India awakened to the new millennium, re-envisioning the urban. This vision relates to urbanism that is caught between its past and the relational references to urbanism conceptualized and built elsewhere (Roy and Ong 2011). The materiality, the economic output, and the efficiency of Indian cities are referenced to cities such as Shanghai and Singapore, despite trajectories of cities being path-dependent. The leap towards the ideal-typical entrepreneurial city in the Indian context is full of challenges, contradictions, legal, and policy prescriptions, which currently do not necessarily remedy the increasing societal inequality (Banerjee-Guha 2009).

Historically, the poor have had a particular 'place' in relation to the city through caste stratification and its representation in the physical cityscape through the colonial reordering. The British introduced the distinction between the informal and the planned city as an 'orderly, hygienic, scientific, technologically superior and civilized space' (Kaviraj 1997 in Mehra 2011) and reinforced it with the implementation of rigid urban laws and standards.

Such a distinction became more visible through the planned, serviced, and orderly settlements of the British in contrast to the space inhabited by the 'native' Indians that was left to sprawl and became informalized mostly at the periphery of cities. At the same time, municipalities ensured the governance of those population leading 'informal lives'.

Within the entrepreneurial city of Bengaluru, the current policy environment is reproducing historical trends. Housing the urban poor requires land, and land in urban India 'unleashes value for which unequal players compete. Capitalization of land has become the main business of governments and corporates' (Goldman 2011) and leaves the poor to their own devices when they are displaced temporarily or permanently.

I argue that the colonially derived system of welfare governance and the imperatives of the entrepreneurial initiatives of the city of Bengaluru come together and are eventually institutionalized in policies that attempt to imbricate public welfare and neoliberal imperatives. As immediate profit making becomes a component of welfare policy, top-down planning and implementation are secured and beneficiary participation is avoided. A much-fancied PPP model serves this purpose in the delivery of housing for the urban poor. This model was derived from Mumbai, was developed in the 'Plan Vision' published in 2003—two years before the launch of the JNNURM (Jawaharlal Nehru National Urban Renewal Mission) —, and suggested various methods of capitalization of space (Banerjee-Guha 2009). The formulation of PPP within public housing delivery was conceived for Dharavi, a 'slum' housing more than 70,000 hutments. The entire slum was planned to be developed into a modern township with high-rise buildings that would be free for sale in the market with a proportionate number of housing, which would be reserved for the evicted slum-dwellers. Such PPP initiatives were heavily backed and propagated by international institutions such as the World Bank (WB), the United Nations Development Programme (UNDP), and the Asian Development Bank (ADB).

It cannot be denied that institutionalized forms of PPP are a permanent feature of urban governance of an entrepreneurial city such as Bengaluru. Urban governance consists of a process of blending and coordinating public and private interests[1] (Sager 2011). Bengaluru has been a forerunner for integrating private actors into urban governance. Earlier PPP models shaped up into specialized bodies to lobby and coordinate interests. The first such body was BATF (Bangalore Agenda Task Force) created in 1999 and included notable personalities mainly from the private sector and few from elite NGOs, who were mainly representing middle-class concerns (Ghosh 2005). It was constituted as an extra-constitutional body working with the government and was considered to be an innovative form of PPP, vastly discussed in the literature. The follow-up to BATF was ABIDe set up in 2008. Both were deemed by scholars and critiqued as ‘unconstitutional, undemocratic, and non-representative’ (Sami 2014). The same PPP logic was also integrated as a modality of policy implementation. As the domain of public housing needs considerable capital to secure land, inevitably the construction is prone to be modelled within a PPP framework, where commercial units within the buildings are made financially viable. In Karnataka, the public contribution came mainly in the form of land acquisition and subsidy, wherein the construction is delivered privately.

The next section describes the housing policy, which was implemented during 2009–2010 and also narrates the involvement of AVAS and the actions of the affected community.

Facilitating Housing: One NGO and Two Differential Outcomes

In this empirical section, I first discuss the housing policy and then introduce the case of two urban poor communities in Bengaluru. Both communities undergo a transition in the status of their habitation. There are three types of housing in Bengaluru: official public, official private, and unofficial private (Perry 1998: 90). While these three categories appear to be firm and delineated, they are strongly interlinked and interdependent. ‘Official public’ refers to the delivery of public housing by the Government of Karnataka (GoK). ‘Official private’ includes the housing built by private builders that inscribe into the formal housing market. The last category of ‘unofficial private’ subsumes all informal housing forms. The third category includes those not entitled to housing provided by public delivery and those who are not able to afford official private housing or those breaching legal norms.

The first community, the Sanyasikunte slum in the South of Bengaluru, transited from unofficial private to official public, and the second slum in Janashaktinagar

[1]It can be understood as the process through which local authorities, along with private interests, seek to enhance publicly declared collective goals. It is a process shaped by those systems of political, economic, and social values from which the urban regime derives its legitimacy (Sager 2011).

also located in the South of Bengaluru changed its status from unofficial private to official private.

Housing Policy as a Constraint

The first part of the empirical section focuses on the housing policy called Basic Services to the Urban Poor (BSUP) under which one of the case studies was a beneficiary. BSUP formed the subcomponent of the JNNURM that was launched during 2005–2012 to upgrade cities as engines of economic growth.

The overall implementation of the scheme was to be overseen by the Karnataka Urban Infrastructure Development Finance Corporation (KUIDFC),[2] a state nodal agency. The reception of central funds was conditional on fulfilling some prescribed urban governance reforms.

The JNNURM-BSUP scheme that was underway during my fieldwork was implemented either through the KSDB (Karnataka Slum Development Board) or the City Municipal Corporation, Bruhat Bengaluru Mahanagarapalike (BBMP). There were clear guidelines laid down for BSUP projects, which included an institutionalized role for NGOs to mediate between the beneficiary community and the government. Further, guidelines were to include participatory exercises relating to the design and the construction process of the dwelling units. But the fact is that government failed to adhere to all of them (Kamath 2012).

In Bengaluru city, 54 BSUP projects[3] were initiated at different phases of the implementation and a total of 11,603 dwelling units were aimed to be built (KSCB annual report 2010). But there was no transparent criteria list to show how the 54 slums were chosen. While interviewing officials of the KSDB, they failed to provide consistent responses. A unit cost was budgeted for 2735 $ for which 50 % was endorsed by Central Funds and 50 % from the GoK, which included 12 % beneficiary contribution. The criteria for eligibility were minimum proven five years of residence, possession of ration card, and voter id and a caste certificate to avail a decrease 2 % in beneficiary contribution (KSCB annual report 2010). An identified beneficiary was given a biometric card making him/her eligible for an unit. Beneficiaries were given ‘only’ possession certificates, which permitted lifelong possession without ceding ownership. The slum-dwellers clearly deplored having no say in the design or the construction of the units (Kamath 2012). Furthermore,

[2]The KUIDFC was a special purpose parastatal created to liaise between lenders (both multilateral and private) and municipalities. Its role was to assist the urban local bodies to place proposals in front of the sanctioning committees of the JNNURM, manage grants, and release funds to the urban local bodies (Ranganathan 2008: 7).

[3]Within the BSUP revised guidelines, it was explicitly stated that private sector participation in development, management, and financing was strongly encouraged and such projects would be given priority, as it was believed that it will help ‘leverage private capital and bring efficiency’ (Modified guidelines for BSUP, 2009).

full costs of maintenance, services, and amenities had not been included in the detailed project reports (DPRs), such that the affordability for continued residence was doubtful. For the housing implementation process, the policy included an institutionalized role for NGOs to broker between the beneficiary community and the government.

It was the only public housing scheme underway in the city of Bengaluru during fieldwork between 2009 and 2010. It had just entered its third and final phases. From the mandatory reform agenda, the participation bill was yet to be ratified in the State and there were other backlogs, which prevented the release of funds from the Centre, grossly delaying the construction of the units.

AVAS: Access to Housing on Behalf of the Urban Poor

AVAS (Association for Voluntary Action and Service) was an NGO registered as a trust in Bengaluru in 1980. Over the years, AVAS[4] came to define itself as a service organization. The founder was also able to complement the available resources when needed with private-funding sources.[5] When I met AVAS, they were working in various slum communities since the time of inception of the organization. At the time of fieldwork, housing for the urban poor was still a top priority area for the organization, but they were also in the process of diversifying, restructuring, and formalizing other domains (such as youth, education, and health).

AVAS came to life during the period when government measures for the urban poor were radical, exclusionary, and criminalizing (Schenk 2001). The head of the organization came from an elite background and possessed enough credibility through her work with AVAS as it functioned totally on a voluntary basis. Other staff members came from the middle classes and had graduate and post-graduate education and capacities to engage and deal with a variety of actors. AVAS' presence in slum localities was an important anchor for the communities. AVAS's staff learned about needs and capacities of the community by continuously interacting with them.

They promoted awareness on housing but also made it a point to inform the community about good practices and attitudes in the domains of health, collective saving, and accounting skills. They also promoted awareness about government programmes and schemes. They taught them administrative skills, how to face officers and bribing expectations. In doing so, they boosted the self-confidence of the community members.

---

[4]AVAS prides itself in having workers and employees who have stayed with them for more than 20 years.

[5]The main driver was the founder of AVAS, the daughter of an industrialist. AVAS was rather well endowed with regard to material resources. The founding trustee coming from an elite background assured financial stability through the renewal of donor-funding (from Germany).

Veering Through Housing Policy: A Long Journey to Housing Non-fits

This first episode of AVAS' assistance involved the residents of the Sanyasikunte slum, who were exposed to two housing policies with unsatisfactory outcomes. The trajectory of this community is one of perseverance in their housing ambition and AVAS's commitment, despite internal dissonance with the leaders and their political connections.

This community was settled on municipal land but could not get it legalized/declared as it was a low-lying land a near lake, which was frequently prone to flooding. Hence, the community could not be rehabilitated in situ. The city municipality had to allot alternative land. But the community demanded for a site, which was near to their present habitation close to their work and school location. After years of resistance against rehabilitation far away, land was finally allocated just metres away from the lake. This land was transferred to the KSDB, which was responsible for the declaration and rehabilitation of the slum-dwellers on the basis of the government order.

Within the purview of KSDB's rehabilitation initiatives, each time the state government would release funds for work, the leaders of this community along with their political connections would divert the funds against the completion of the building. Building material would often get stolen and resold by slum leaders themselves. The tendered company would build with lower quality material, as government officials and local politicians would siphon off from the allocated budget. AVAS had recognized the limits of capacity building within this community and had learnt that if people were not able to oppose their own leaders, not much room was left for positive development. This happened even after promoting awareness on how power networks worked in detriment to their quest. Valmiki Ambedkar Aawas Yojna (VAMBAY), the precursor to the BSUP scheme, was brought to the community and one part of the land had got developed. But as expected, the soil on that land was very loose and its stabilization swallowed more money, resulting in a dearth of funds, which left the community without adequate housing. Urban services such as sanitation, electricity, and water were not integrated and hence delayed the rehabilitation and AVAS had to assist the communities to claim these services from different government agencies. The outcome was that the entire exercise had resulted in an incomplete concrete slum.

A few years later, AVAS brought BSUP to the community to build the second part of the land next to the VAMBAY housing development. The plan from the KSDB was to build ground floor plus additional three floors. The ground floor had been earmarked for commercial purposes loyal to the PPP model, which made urban land viable by making space available for commercial activities. But the community fiercely resisted the inclusion of commercial space and demanded ground floor for housing.

AVAS members justified the resistance, citing the Asian Games Village that was built in the 1980s—a PPP model that had set a negative example. AVAS members considered the PPP model for urban poor housing a 'disguised land grab'. The Asian Games housing units were allotted to both urban poor and commercial entities. But the quality of the construction was 'deliberately' kept so poor that after 20 years when the area had become prime location, the site was up for destruction and the land eventually could be tendered away to builders. Yet another reason for the community's resistance to vertical housing was that there was the necessity of including an elevator, inflating the maintenance cost for slum-dwellers. Moreover, vertical buildings would not allow for incremental expansion of the living space as the family grew. After AVAS' intervention, the community finally accepted to be housed in a ground plus one floor project. According to KSDB data, 210 families were housed in these apartments. AVAS was very particular that the outcome of this second phase under BSUP had to be satisfactory, believing that they had taught the community to monitor the construction work and the materials delivered on site. As for all the other public housing projects, KSDB had published a tender for the same site and no one was interested to take up the work knowing the stronghold of the community leaders and their vested interests.

A year later, I visited the site without being accompanied by AVAS members. The construction site was a dire sight. The KSDB and government engineers executing the project had not done any participatory planning with the community, even though it was a part of BSUP guidelines. A copy–paste method of 'matchbox' apartments (the way the community called it) was constructed with lowest quality material and poor planning. There were rumours that *rangoli* powder[6] was being mixed with the concrete, making it brittle, and the planned thickness of the walls was being further reduced. Such observations scared future residents. Even though community members were working in the construction sector themselves, they were in principle not given any chance to participate in building their future homes. Frequent conflicts and tensions between the government-tendered construction workers and the community members were constantly triggered due to the use of bathrooms and the lack of construction quality. During my field visit, I could well imagine the fear of living in these blocks. The staircase handrail and the cement on the terrace were crumbling, there was no waterspout, and the apartments was not *vastu*[7] compliant. Hence, some of the future inhabitants, despite the substantial beneficiary contribution invested, further shelled out their savings to upgrade the 'slum-like' quality of construction and get the unit secured physically, as well to adhere to *vastu* principles.

---

[6]*Rangoli* is a white, shaded rock powder traditionally used for decorative purposes.

[7]*Vastu* is the traditional Hindu system of architecture, which emphasizes directional alignment.

Access to Housing on their Own Terms

AVAS came into contact with the second community of Janashaktinagar during the 1980s. This decade was known for the government's ambition for beautification through forced eviction and brutally demolishing squatter settlements (Schenk 2001). Meanwhile, AVAS was trying to gather slum-dwellers across the city for a big rally to draw attention towards the plight of the poor. When AVAS urged them to participate in the rally, they met with a lot of distrust and resistance. The poor had experienced that any external agent wanting to help ultimately would turn to be manipulative or even exploitative. Nevertheless, after some discussion, they realized that they were not alone in their plight. Consequently, women of the slum approached AVAS with a letter, enumerating all their problems. With the help of AVAS, this community over the years established a functional neighbourhood on their own terms, where incremental investments to their houses were possible. AVAS initially held meetings with the community and set up a saving scheme, which eventually prepared them to initiate action towards land entitlements. The slum was located beside an upcoming ring road. The BDA decided to form a layout in that area, and it was emerging that government was unwilling to allot land to the poor. Meanwhile, the land they occupied was promising to raise its value and attract potent investors. Nevertheless, with the assistance of AVAS, they persevered with protests and constant appearances at the government offices to assert the land. The government tried to actually incite dwellers to illegally occupy space, as this would appear as uncontrollable population growth with increasing internal conflict and such dynamics would give them enough reason to evict the growing community to 'avoid squalor and maintain public calm'. This was the government's strategic way of avoiding allotting land to urban poor. AVAS insisted on behalf of the community for allotment letters and distributed (AVAS-made) ID cards to the existing families to contain the number to 127 families. Through perseverance, BDA eventually allotted them the land and started forming an in situ layout, by crushing their existing huts without assuring any transit accommodation. With no shelter above their roof, the community's plight during the monsoon became unbearable. AVAS in the meantime could mobilize private funds from the Rotary Club, which contributed to the building of 24 houses. The community objected to the construction of houses and demanded that the amount was to be divided equally between all the families. Upon agreement with the donor, each family was instructed to lay the foundation with the amount from the Rotary Club and their savings supplemented the remaining. To continue the construction, AVAS managed to arrange for a loan from HUDCO (government-owned housing and urban development corporation) and guaranteed 100 % repayment in four years. Finally, the community was able to build their houses by themselves, learned financial management skills, paid back the loan, gained credibility for bankability, and even won the National Habitat Award for their efforts. At present, the locality has been transformed into a neighbourhood where residents have planned the houses according to their needs and lifestyles as well as accommodating incremental family growth. Nevertheless, almost 15 years after the initial negotiations with the BDA, the community members are yet to receive their property documents and they again sought the assistance of AVAS. Within this community, AVAS was able to induce considerable social and entrepreneurial skills involving finance and document management, respect from government officials, and had enough legal and institutional knowledge to face bureaucrats.

Discussion and Analysis

Both the narrations were documented and shared during fieldwork in 2010 by loyal AVAS coordinators who had a longstanding commitment to these two communities. The information gathered was triangulated in separate interviews with community members. The common factors to both the communities were that at the outset, both were informally squatting on land, had internal issues with slum leaders, and were faced with the same evolving political regime spanning from the 1980s to 2010 during which AVAS was working with them. Both communities at the outset were very similar, yet the housing outcomes turned out to be different.

In this section, I present a general critique of the urban renewal mission and the BSUP policy. Foremost, I discuss how this policy influenced the emerging built environment in Sanyasikunte slum and in contrast discuss the self-conceived and built neighbourhood in Janashaktinagar. Second, I also identify the contrasting community development processes involved in both the localities. Such an analysis brings to light the pitfalls of housing policy and demonstrates the emerging opportunities for successful housing processes driven by the community. Finally, I comment on the work of AVAS and the larger role of civil society organization in the delivery of services, particularly housings for the urban poor.

Despite the critiques of the JNNURM mission and its subcomponents (Sivaramkrishnan 2011; Kamath 2012; Rao Dhananka 2013), one must acknowledge that the grandeur of the ‘renewal’ exercise brought unprecedented awareness of the potentials and pitfalls of urbanization. At least rhetorically, it integrated the language of good governance and community participation. Unfortunately, most of the States in India during the implementation of the renewal mission did not seriously embrace the prescribed pro-participation reforms within the JNNURM and particularly the BSUP guidelines that included the participation law, public disclosure law, community participation fund, and participatory budgeting. A closer analysis of these provisions can be found elsewhere (Rao Dhananka 2013). Unfortunately, the occasion was not seized to conduct inclusive participatory social exercises to give the urban poor a voice and hence a rightful place in the city. The whole exercise was merely tick-boxed by engineers who were unable to recognize the necessity of participation, nor did they have the capacity to conduct a meaningful social exercise. It seemed that the efforts were mainly made to avail funds from the Centre.

Policy and Emerging Built Environment

Figures 9.1 and 9.2 were taken during fieldwork and give a glimpse into the built environment that emerged during the fieldwork in Sanyasikunte and in Janashaktinagar. The construction of the latter community was completed and built earlier, but at the time of fieldwork, the community was still waiting for the property documents from the BDA. The former locality was a construction site with the main structure standing and the interiors still having to be completed.

One can notice how in the policy-targeted community in Sanyasikunte the buildings and the apartments are all uniform. Incremental expansion is not possible, as the built structure and quality does not allow it. At the same time, there is hardly any empty space in the developed area. The second picture depicts a colourful neighbourhood that was incrementally built according to the needs of the habitants. Incremental development allowed for a community hall to be recently built to celebrate family events and festivals.

Indeed, one distinctive factor between both narrations was the tenure status that the housing policy provided against the status the second community managed to assert through effective community participation. As Kamath (2012) noted in her study of housing delivery through the BSUP, the beneficiaries were issued ‘only’ possession certificates, which permitted lifelong possession without ceding ownership to the next generation. So the unit received by the residents of Sanyasikunte did not represent a generational asset, which defeated the principle argument that the security of tenure accelerated the process of housing improvement, capital accumulation, and hence the upliftment of slum-dwellers from poverty. The PPP model that the community resisted was also anticipated to be unsustainable fearing that the land would be reclaimed for commercial purposes as witnessed with the buildings of the Commonwealth Games in Bengaluru. The frail construction quality of the houses raised suspicions and scared the community to move into their allotted dwellings. They had to invest from their own savings in order to actually inhabit the

Fig. 9.1 Emerging apartment buildings in Sanyasikunte. *Source* Author

Fig. 9.2 Self-planned and built neighbourhood in Janashaktinagar. *Source* Author

apartments and getting them *vastu* compliant. Even though the BSUP policy guidelines specified a participatory approach to the design and construction, none was adhered to, despite having construction workers among the community. Prototype delivery resulted in unsustainable housing in terms of quality and needs of the poor. Moving from informal into public formal housing also meant that dwellers were on the rolls and had to pay to access urban services. Usually, the poor rely on cheap housing and services to afford food, education, and health care services (Gilbert 2007). Hence, when they move into formal housing necessitating payments for urban services, they compromise on those investments that in the long run would yield most benefits and would be most sustainable.

The Janashaktinagar community battled for more than 20 years to finally get the property documents in their hands. Despite the long wait for formal documents, they could incrementally invest in their assets, improve housing, extend them to accommodate their growing families and indeed became bankable. The emerging neighborhood included space for livelihoods with small commercial entities run by community members, which also served as important meeting points. As I visited the community, they proudly showed me the newly constructed community hall built from their own savings that was complemented with funds leveraged from a political party during election time. The community in Janashaktinagar successfully built their neighbourhood by collectively gauging their financial capacities and incrementally accessing space and services as needed. Their built environment is suited to their needs and lifestyles.

Their situation confirms the findings by Gilbert (2007) who argues that 'there is a conflict between improving the physical quality of housing and improving the housing conditions of poor people'. While the aim of the JNNURM was to renew urban spaces to leap into 'world-class cities', the implementation of the BSUP only removed a few huts and put the inhabitants into 'concrete slums', as an interviewee referred to the newly constructed public housing. The case studies show that housing policy being planned centrally, prescribed top-down, accommodating imperatives of an entrepreneurial city with no community participation at any stage, leads to a built environment that is there for its own sake and less to meet the needs of its residents. In the case of Sanyasikunte, while the residents got a roof over their head at a considerable cost, the entire process seemed to have benefited the slum leaders and the bureaucrats who siphoned off materials and money for their own benefit.

Policy and Community Processes

The case studies demonstrate that the housing process had the power to either split the community or promote effective community participation. In Sanyasikunte, the nexus between local politicians, bureaucrats, and slum leaders reinforced exclusionary dynamics. The BSUP policy targeting eligible beneficiaries, equipped bureaucrats with power to interact with local slum leaders to use housing as political currency. Thus, to counter possible misappropriation was difficult, as no transit housing during the in situ redevelopment was arranged. This compelled the community to get scattered in search of cheap rental housing, thereby breaking the necessary geographical proximity to unite the community against exploitative slum leaders and to keep monitoring the work underway. In this sense, the leadership blocked the progress, controlled and captured the benefits aimed for the poor, and misused them for private (political) interests (De Wit and Berner 2009). Housing involves not only the laying of brick and mortar to form a shelter, but the housing processes holds the potential to trigger awareness about health, safety, financial, planning, and leadership skills. While a holistic approach was rhetorically suggested in the implementation guidelines, engineers executing the project were not trained to trigger such a social exercise, as only the spent budget and the building being constructed counted during monitoring of the BSUP policy (Sivaramkrishnan 2011). In other words, not only are the specifications in the housing policy guidelines important, but also the monitoring mechanisms. In sum, the opportunity was missed to engage the community holistically in the processes to promote social skills.

In contrast, with the support of AVAS, the community at Janashaktinagar was engaged in all the above-mentioned processes, which sufficiently empowered the community. Sustainability comes from cultivating skills that let the community manage their own neighbourhood, which includes interacting with the bureaucrats and lay claim to benefits and services from the state. Containing the number of families, continuous community meetings to spread awareness in diverse domains fostered community cohesion. The episode showed that unity highly depended on social skill rather than material resources.

The intervention of AVAS is a critical point to discuss. The toolkit provided by the BSUP policy suggested communities could seek the support of NGOs throughout the project process and NGOs had a critical role to play in ensuring communities to come together. Hence, it was not the local authority which ensured capacity building, but rather NGOs who were expected to cooperate in this mission and act as brokers enabling access and interface between local authorities and the communities. The role of NGOs prescribed by policy is rather ambiguous. While the government could expect through a brokering organization to avoid having to deal directly with the poor, the organization was given a role of interest aggregation from the bottom up. In other words, AVAS being in such a brokering role on the one hand, they had to comply with the terms of such a brokerage in view of housing delivery from the government. On the other hand, AVAS had to represent the interests of the poor.

AVAS took such a role in Sanyasikunte community. While AVAS stood loyal to the community despite difficulties and discontinuities, it did articulate the interests of the poor. AVAS achieved to sustain the resistance against the PPP model and ground + 3 housing, but at the same time, within the same community, AVAS was not successful in having the design and orientation of the apartments changed to be *vastu* compliant nor in curbing the influence of slum leaders with vested interests.

AVAS was not able to foster similar community dynamics, as in the Janashakti community, which produced a sustainable housing outcome. The reasons behind this failure in my view lay in the prevalence of patronage networks comprising slum leaders and government agents that could not be broken, as the housing benefit represented very important political leverage. This leverage comes with allocative power of housing units; hence, the prevalence of such dynamics circumvents the NGO and reinforces the status quo.

The engagement of AVAS in Janashaktinagar nurtured entrepreneurial capacities to veer around neoliberal priorities of the city, but had not to deal with a particular policy to which AVAS would be accountable. In this case AVAS did not have to balance their role as a brokering organization within a policy framework; they could engage in claim-making without having to concede any dues towards the government agents.

The contrasting trajectories of both communities show the role of policy and how policy can be constitutive of community and the built environment. Even though funds were released within two consecutive policy frameworks in Sanyasikunte, the entire exercise was rather a constraint. Community development could have been enhanced with more scope for community self-determination and participation. AVAS taught a political society community in Janashaktinagar social skills, unleashing entrepreneurial skills to claim their rightful place in the city.

Urban Poor as Partners

This chapter shows how a committed NGO like AVAS fostered entrepreneurial and social skills among an urban poor community and could bring about a sustainable housing solution. They assisted the community to claim tenure and services from the state and by proving bankability to private banks and donors. The NGO, having accumulated these positive experiences with one community, could not achieve similar outcomes within a public housing policy framework.

This study shows the intricacies of having to bridge systems of public welfare with imperatives of the entrepreneurial city in Bengaluru. These integrate contradicting priorities of resources allocation. When resource is accounted for only in monetary terms, then the involvement of the poor might not be evident, as they might seem resourceless. But when they are viewed as a resource themselves, they can work as equal partners with other players. Worldwide 'a billion squatters' are building the cities from scratch (Neuwirth 2006), developing the land and servicing the city. When the poor are considered as a resource, then it would 'only' take for the government to provide area-wise infrastructure and make land legally available for upgrading (Bhan 2015). Such an approach has been the success factor for organizations such as the Asian Coalition for Housing Rights.[8] In the recent past, it has achieved in upgrading slums in 230 cities into sustainable neighbourhoods across 19 countries in Asia, with only 14.5 million USD of donor funding. Flexible finance at the duty of the decisions of the communities themselves and building community architect networks[9] were the programme's chief tools to bring about change.

The aim of this study was not to unconditionally support the self-help debate that has been going on ever since de Soto's thesis on the 'mystery of capital' (2000). Rather, it explored housing outcomes for the urban poor under particular contrasting conditions of active involvement of one single NGO in the process. The insights from this case study do not confirm that favourable housing outcomes are achieved when the poor are left to their own devices (Berner and Phillips 2005). The potential of the poor has to be harnessed and the community united. Only then can they cultivate a level of self-esteem to challenge those at whose mercy they often are—the agents of the state. This requires serious and sustained effort from engaged community members and organizations involved with the community. Mere policy rhetoric does not suffice to recognize that the poor are not only equal, but probably the most important partners in urban development.

Acknowledgments An earlier version of this chapter was presented at the 2014 Swiss Human Geography Symposium in Fribourg, Switzerland. I would like to thank the participants for their useful comments. I also gratefully acknowledge the financial support of the Swiss National Science Foundation and my host institutions the Development Planning Unit at UC London and the Indian Institute for Human Settlements in Bengaluru.

---

[8]http://www.sustainablecitiescollective.com/david-thorpe/274361/upgrade-slums-230-cities-just-145-million-impossible-they-did-it.

[9]http://communityarchitectsnetwork.info/about.php.

References

Banerjee-Guha, S. (2009). Neoliberalising the "Urban": New geographies of power and injustice in Indian cities. *Economic & Political Weekly, 44*(22), 95–107.

Berner, E., & Phillips, B. (2005). Left to their own devices? Community self-help between alternative development and neo-liberalism. *Community Development Journal, 40*(1), 17–29.

Bhan, G. (2015, June 9). From slums to neighbourhoods. *The Hindu*. Bengaluru.

Boudreau, V. (1996). Northern theory, southern protest: Opportunity structure analysis in cross-national perspective. *Mobilization: An International Quarterly, 1*(2), 175–189.

Carmin, J., & Balser, D. B. (2002). Selecting repertoires of action in environmental movement organizations: An interpretive approach. *Organization & Environment, 15*(4), 365–388.

Chatterjee, P. (2004). *The politics of the governed: reflections on popular politics in most of the world*. Columbia University Press.

De Wit, J., & Berner, E. (2009). Progressive patronage? Municipalities, NGOs, community-based organizations, and the limits to slum dwellers' empowerment. *Development and Change, 40*(5), 927–947.

Fligstein, N., & McAdam, D. (2011). Toward a general theory of strategic action fields. *Sociological Theory, 29*(1), 1–26.

Ghosh, A. (2005). Public-private or a private public? Promised partnership of the Bangalore agenda task force. *Economic & Political Weekly, 40*(47), 4914–4922.

Gilbert, A. (2007). The return of the slum: Does language matter? *International Journal of Urban and Regional Research, 31*(4), 697–713.

Goldman, M. (2011). Speculative urbanism and the making of the next world city. *International Journal of Urban and Regional Research, 35*(3), 555–581.

Kamath, L. (2012). New policy paradigms and actual practices in slum housing. *Economic and Political Weekly, XLVII No. 47 & 48,* 76–86.

Kriesi, H., Koopmans, R., Wilhelm Duyvendak, J., & Giugni, M. G. (1995). *New social movements in Western Europe. A comparative analysis. Comparative and general pharmacology*. London: University of Minnesota Press.

Mehra, D. (2011). Caste and class in Indian cities: Habitation, inequality and segregation. In M.-H Zérah, V. Dupont & S. T. Lama-Rewal (Eds.), *Urban policies and the right to the city in India. Rights, responsibilities and citizenship* (pp. 39–42). New Delhi: United Nations Educational, Scientific and Cultural Organisation and Centre De Sciences Humaines.

Neuwirth, R. (2006). *Shadow cities. A billion squatters, a new urban world.* New York: Routledge.

Perry, A. (1998). Law and urban change in an Indian city. In E. Fernandes & A. Varley (Eds.), *Illegal cities. Urban change in developing countries*. New York: Zed Books.

Ranganathan, M. (2008). Beneficiary? Stakeholder? Consumer? Citizen-State dynamics in Bangalore's urban reforms. In *Cities and citizenship graduate student symposium*. UC Berkeley.

Rao Dhananka, S. (2013). *Of housing and politics: Mapping political opportunities for mobilising in Bangalore, India* (Unpublished Thesis). Switzerland: University of Lausanne.

Roy, A., & Ong, A. (2011). *Worlding cities: Asian experiments and the art of being global*. West Sussex: Wiley-Blackwell.

Sager, T. (2011). Neo-liberal urban planning policies: A literature survey 1990–2010. *Progress in Planning, 76*(4), 147–199.

Sami, N. (2014). Power to the people? A study of Bangalore's urban task forces. In G. Shatkin (Ed.), *Contesting the Indian city: Global visions and politics of the local*. Wiley-Blackwell.

Schenk, H. (2001). *Living in India's slums: A case study of Bangalore*. New Delhi: Manohar Publishers & Distributors.

Schram, S. F. (2004). The praxis of poor people's movements: Strategy and theory in dissensus politics. *Perspectives on Politics, 1*(04), 715.

Sivaramkrishnan, K. C. (2011). *Re-visioning Indian cities. The urban renewal mission*. New Delhi: Sage Publications.

Chapter 10
Spatial Reproduction of Urban Poverty in Entrepreneurial City: Bengaluru, India

K.C. Smitha

Introduction

This chapter explores the impact of 'Rehabilitation package' implemented by BMRCL 'metro project' Phase I on two slums, in Bengaluru[1] metropolis. The study presents the findings based on an analysis of 'before and after' rehabilitation framework with respect to income, livelihood and mobility. The chapter particularly draws on the experiences of employed household members in relation to a larger process of urbanization and urban planning influencing displacement, dispossession, resettlement and mobility. The question is, how do the rehabilitated/resettled slums negotiate and renegotiate with the city spaces as well as the space of their employment and income opportunities which offers critical insights into the spatial reproduction of urban poverty.

The context is an urban spatial restructuring process influenced by global capital that offers channels for engagement or disengagement highlighting the vulnerability of the urban poor. In fact, a variety of neoliberal initiatives introduced in the national context are translated into policy induced evictions, displacement and resettlement which is articulated through various redevelopment projects such as metro in the local context. As a result, new forms of polarization intensifying inequalities at different spatial scales continue to proliferate in the city. Therefore, the key driver for the study was to assess the impact of the rehabilitation package

[1]The city of Bangalore was officially renamed as 'Bengaluru' on 1 November 2014, by the Government of Karnataka. In this chapter, the usage of both Bengaluru and Bangalore implies the same city.

K.C. Smitha (✉)
Research Scientist, Centre for Research in Urban Affairs (CURA),
Institute for Social and Economic Change, Bangalore, India
e-mail: smitha.kanekanti@gmail.com; smitha@isec.ac.in

K.C. Smitha (ed.), *Entrepreneurial Urbanism in India*,
DOI 10.1007/978-981-10-2236-4_10

implemented by the BMRCL metro project, on the two slums, namely Basaveswaranagar and Jai Bheemanagar in the city.

It is acknowledged that cities in India have emerged as nodes of network and global capital for promoting innovation and competition, thus recasting the structure and organization of urban governance (Banerjee-Guha 2010). Underlying the twin process of institutional and spatial changes, are cities particularly in the global south, creating new economic spaces in the context of ascendance of information technology, global operation of firms, corporate and service sectors and in the process recasting work and labour relations (Sassen 2002; Heitzman 2004; Aranya 2008; Sudhira 2008) extolling place-based features and associated imaginaries. From the perspective of political economy of urbanization, the state sponsored urban restructuring process can be problematized in two differing and yet interrelated ways: firstly, there is an overwhelming evidence[2] of corporate and private sector influence on policy; secondly, the increasing role of PPP (public–private partnership) in urban redevelopment projects to recoup finances (which does not fully acknowledge the efforts towards demographic and social segregation) has eventually socio-economically and politically marginalized the urban poor in the city (Heitzman 1999; Ghosh 2005, 2006; Banerjee-Guha 2010; Shaw 2012a, b; Shatkin 2014). Post-liberalization, therefore, entrepreneurial governance is routed through a process of restructuring the 'urban' by introducing several renewal projects such as 'infrastructure', 'slum clearance' or 'slum-free' cities those entail eviction and relocation crystallizing uneven development (Baviskar 2002, 2011; Benjamin 2004, 2010; Weinstein 2011, 2014). Such practices of intense global or international activities at the local level have a profound impact on the urban poor in terms of job displacement, low wages, booming land prices, and continued economic and social isolation in the city. This explains the proliferation of an informal economy, clearly placing the urban poor in the lowest rung of the urban hierarchy. Theoretically, this addresses two key issues: foremost, repositioning of cities of India in the global economy and secondly, a complex articulation of global capital is generating new forms of spatial division of labour, eventually perpetuating poverty. This collection, therefore, builds upon the debates centred on the transition of urban governance towards 'urban entrepreneurialism'.

Certainly, there is a dearth of empirical studies in contextualizing how day-to-day neoliberal political practices manifest at broad range of spatial scales generating new forms of urban poverty in global cities such as Bengaluru metropolis. Further the spatial dimension of survival strategies of urban poor in metro cities such as Bengaluru needs further probe. The study by Vacquier (2010) in New Delhi and by Coelho et al. (2012) in Chennai throws considerable light on how resettled communities fall victims to the vicious cycle of 'working poverty' embedded in the spatial dispersion of economic activities.

---

[2]For instance, the BATF (Bengaluru Agenda Task Force), ABIDe, and privatization of services in Bengaluru.

Entrepreneurial City: Bengaluru's Economy and Structure

The city of Bengaluru[3] is referred to as 'million-plus' city and one of the fastest growing cities of the twenty-first century with a decadal population growth of 37.7 % (CDP 2009). The city is India's fifth largest in terms of metropolitan area and occupies one of the top 100 global city economies.[4] A cursory glimpse at the policy documents and master plans of the city clearly demonstrates that it is spearheading global competition[5] by emerging as the 4th largest hub of technological clusters[6] in the world (Aranya 2003; Rode and Chandra 2008; Nisbett 2009). In addition, there is a huge concentration of small and medium enterprises (SMEs)[7] largely located in the periphery of the city. Thus, against the backdrop of such an economic transition, the city proudly hosts more than 250 multinational companies[8] has emerged as a leading hub of information technology/biotechnology[9] industries, earning its tag as the 'Silicon Valley of India' (Heitzman 2003, 2004; Aranya 2003, 2008; Rai 2006; Dittrich 2007; Nisbett 2009; Sudhira et al. 2007; Sudhira 2008; Goldman 2010).

Therefore, the economic growth rate of Bengaluru is the highest post-liberalization, particularly, in terms employment generation,[10] hosting a vast labour force, manufacturing and service sector, business clusters,[11] real estate and ownership of dwellings and activities such as trade, hotels, signature malls and restaurants making it entrepreneurially/economically a viable destination.[12] Therefore, following the tenets of Harvey's (1989) 'urban entrepreneurialism' in North America's urban governance, I argue that the Bengaluru is an entrepreneurial city in terms of boosting huge infrastructure projects (flyovers, metro, road expansion projects, and special economic zones). Here, entrepreneurial governance is ostentatiously routed through economic well-being with concerted efforts towards

---

[3]Bengaluru is the sixth largest and third most populous city in India.

[4]UK Economic Outlook Report: 2009, PricewaterhouseCoopers, 2009.

[5]According to the GaWC Global City Ranking (2010), the city ranks 59th (The World According to GaWC; Classification of Cities 2010, 14 September, 2011).

[6]Over 130 multinational IT companies and 928 software export oriented companies are located in Bangalore. The cumulative investment in IT was to the tune of $1 billion with a turnover of about $1.59 billion from software exports between 2000 and 2001 alone (Aranya 2003).

[7]The Peenya industrial area of Bengaluru city hosts more than 4000 small and medium sized enterprises (Sudhira 2008).

[8]Bengaluru host more than 30 % of IT workforce in the country (Sudhira 2008).

[9]By 2004, Bangalore accounted for 35 % of country's software exports and has since been growing by 30 % annually (Rode and Chandra 2008).

[10]For instance, 66 % of the employment was generated by the service sector during 2004–05 in Bengaluru (Narayana 2008, 9).

[11]Bangalore–Mysore Infrastructure Corridor; Mumbai–Bengaluru Economic Corridor; IT Growth Corridor; Special Economic Zones (SEZs), etc.

[12]By 2004, the city has garnered Rs 45 billion worth of foreign investment (The Brookings Institution 2013).

promoting innovation–technology, place-bolstering strategies by engaging with public–private partnerships (PPP), and creating jobs in the high-end service sector to compete with global markets. Further, these new urban speculative infrastructure models with global-city ambitions are mediated through large finances from international financial institutions (the World Bank, Japanese International Bank Corporation, Asian Development Bank, etc.) through an entrepreneurial campaign promoting transformation of Bengaluru into a 'Singapore Model or Shanghai Model' (Nair 2000; Roy 2009; Goldman 2010; Benjamin 2010). These entrepreneurial urban planning strategies are driven to display the city's spectacular wealth and consumption with large pools of urban subaltern engaged in the informal sector.

The spiral effect of an increasing population has led to an exponential growth of the city. The conurbation area[13] of the city has increased from 365.65 km^2 in 1971 to 800 km^2 by 2009 (Narayana 2008; CDP 2009). Two specific determinants of the city's growth are attributed to the intense international activities due to the concentration of IT/BT industries concomitantly spurring the immigration[14] of both the intelligentsia and rural labour into the city. While the Bengaluru population, according to the 2011 census, stands at 8.43 million, the urban poor have drastically spiralled to 13.86 lakh out 84.25 lakhs which is approximately 16.45 %[15] of the total population. The most visible consequence of such a horizontal expansion of this city is the tremendous increase in the population density throughout the metropolitan area.[16] Thus, Bengaluru's metro, has been christened as 'Namma Metro' aimed at to promoting both comforts and contribute significantly in the reduction of traffic congestion and carbon emissions[17] in the city. But constructing such a massive infrastructure project entails the acquisition of both public and private properties affecting the local communities either directly or indirectly (Goldman 2010; Benjamin 2010). In India, such a rehabilitation package[18] involves offering highly subsidized concrete houses with security of tenure which seems to be an attractive proposition, particularly for slum dwellers (Vacquier 2010; Coelho et al. 2012). However, such acts of acquisition and relocation seriously impacts

---

[13]First zone (i) erstwhile city corporation area comprising 226 km^2; (ii) former eight Town Municipal Councils (TMCs) and 111 villages forming the peri-urban area; and (iii) villages extending up to Bengaluru Metropolitan Area limits as proposed by BDA (Sudhira 2008).

[14]According to the Census 2001, 13.4 % of the total population constitutes migrants into the city.

[15]Annual report of Karnataka Slum Clearance Board (2011–2012). But unofficial figures state that between 25 % and 35 % of the city's population constitute the urban poor.

[16]The population density rose from 9260 km^2 in 1991 to 10,710 km^2 as per 2001 census (BMRCL 2003). As per 2011 census, the density is 4378 km^2.

[17]Between 1991 and 2005, the number of registered vehicles in the city rose from 0.68 million to 202 million, constituting an increase of more than 200 % (BDA 2007, 38).

[18]Rehabilitation package consists of two categories, namely (i) in situ rehabilitation: this does not involve giving away the location advantage in exchange for housing assistance and (ii) relocation and resettlement (R&R): in this case, slum dwellers are literally evicted from their occupied land and relocated to an earmarked rehabilitated land. In the case of Bengaluru metro project, the second category of R&R has been applied.

income, livelihood and mobility of the urban poor. Particularly, those dwellers who are relocated under R&R rehabilitation package are often subjected to lots of hardships and inconvenience either due to the loss of residential premises or land in a specific location and who eventually forego their daily wages or informal jobs[19] in the vicinity. This chapter, therefore, explores the following dialectic questions: under local transformative processes (institutional, structural and spatial), how do rehabilitated slums negotiate and renegotiate with the 'urban space' in the context of externally imposed entrepreneurial urban planning instruments so as to integrate into the city? How do the different spatial locations enable or constraint opportunities of employment and income, thereby, contribute for upward or downward mobility of the rehabilitated slum dwellers? This study draws attention to the spatial dimension of the role of agency as part of critically assessing the urban poverty.

Framework for the Study

Figure 10.1 clearly describes how the 'Bengaluru Metro Rehabilitation' package affects the broader aspects of income, livelihood and mobility of the relocated slum households. Especially, the issue of land tenure is very critical as far as the city of Bengaluru metropolis is concerned (Benjamin 2004; Goldman 2010). For implementing various forms of developmental projects in the city, the state is highly informalized,[20] intensifying accumulation. Besides the issue of employment, opportunities and income are the primary factors which determine the upward or downward mobility of the poor households. Arguably, the notion of 'employment' has undergone drastic structural changes in the local context (Roychowdhury 2008). Most of the jobs are unregulated with low wages, mostly contracted out (absence of job security), outsourced, highly capital intensive or technology intensive and so on. The city of Bengaluru attracts a large scale in-migrants in search of employment opportunities. A majority of these migrants mostly settled in slums are employed in the informal[21] sector[22] drives them to settle down in the vicinity of economic centres of the city. As Lefebvre (1991) views 'urban space' as an object of political struggle, eventually the situation generates a place-specific

[19]Informal economy accounts to 60–70 % for Bengaluru city (BDA, n.d).

[20]As per Roy (2009), the definition of 'informality' or 'informalization' is an outcome of the acquisition of land for developmental projects.

[21]Roy (2009) defines informality as 'a state of deregulation, where the ownership, use and purpose cannot be fixed, mapped according to any set of regulations or the law'. Such deregulation, unmapping or practices of exceptionalism is purposive action and planning reflecting territorial practices of state power.

[22]A broader definition of an informal economy in the context of developing countries is associated with the changing dynamics of labour market, particularly the employment arrangement of the working poor (Chen et al. 2006).

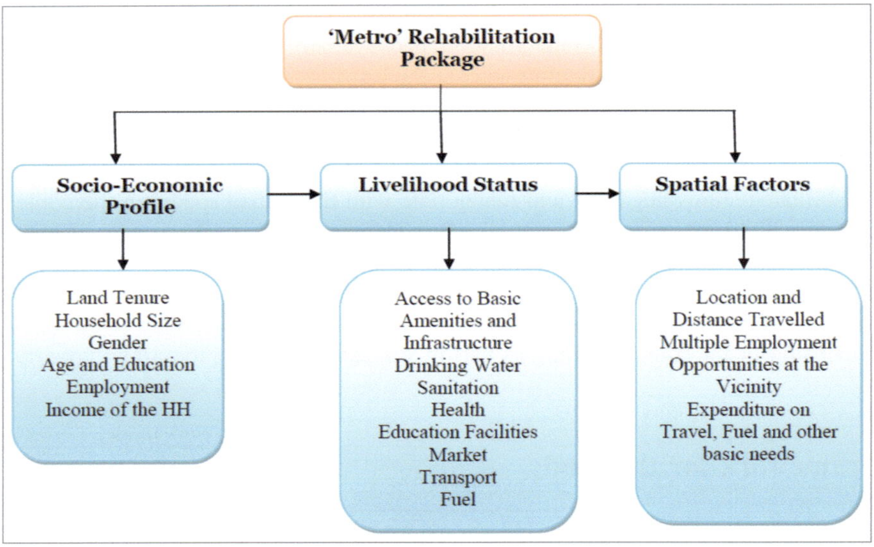

Fig. 10.1 Framework to study 'metro' rehabilitation package. *Source* Author

identity, thus treating 'urban space[23]' as a poor-man's 'agency' i.e. engaged in a range of activities promoting both physical and personal identity to contest urban degradation and stigmatized social life. Post-globalization studies have drawn our attention to the spatial dimension of dispossession of the urban poor through processes of information technology (Castells 1996), post-modernity (Harvey 1989) and so on. Spatial metaphors and terms are now permeating urban studies such as 'de-re-territorialisation' (Brenner, 1999), 'glocalization' (Swyngedow 1997), 'global–local nexus' (Peck and Tickell 1994) 'world–city' (Sassen 1991) reflective of institutional and structural reconstitution of urban space.

Thus, institutional and structural reconstitution of the city has a bearing on how a specific location or place enables or constraints employment opportunities and thereby mobility of income for the urban poor and, on the other, the right to city is expressed through security of tenure (see Fig. 10.1). Social disabilities such as illiteracy, lack of skills and the loss of strong resource networks further cause a disjuncture between the urban poor and the capacity to integrate. Particularly, the security of employment has a direct correlation with their living conditions and standards in addition to the land ownership and access to basic services. Yet, one has to bear the brunt and literally struggle for finding a secure shelter or jobs in a metropolitan city like Bengaluru.

[23]The study by Gotham and Krista (2002) rightly points out that 'space' has been viewed as an object of consumption, means of production and geographical site of social action by urban scholars such as Castells Harvey and Lefebvre.

Most often rehabilitation schemes implemented in India for urban slums, such as the one by BMRCL Metro, imply geographical relocation and, therefore, completely alter their employment status and income of the recipients. Although BMRCL has secured the land tenure and upgraded their living conditions by providing better quality of basic services, yet, the issue related to their labour and livelihood security and thereby their upward mobility continuous to unattended. Thus, spatial dimension of the survival strategies applied by the urban poor's has been largely missing from the literature on urban poverty.

Structure of the Study

As BMRCL's rehabilitation package involves the relocation of only two slums, namely (i) Basaveswaranagar and (ii) Jai Bheemanagar (see Fig. 10.2), the study focused on both the slums. These two slums have been relocated to different distinctive geographical locations i.e. while Jai Bheemanagar slum has been relocated near to Peenya IInd stage, Basaveswaranagar slum has been relocated to Srigandadakavalu, Magadi Road.

Initially, our target sample was 'eligible households' from both the slums constituting 80 households from Peenya IInd stage and 178 households from Srigandadakavalu, Magadi Road. But during the primary survey, we could interview only 50 households at Peenya and 52 households at Srigandadakavalu,

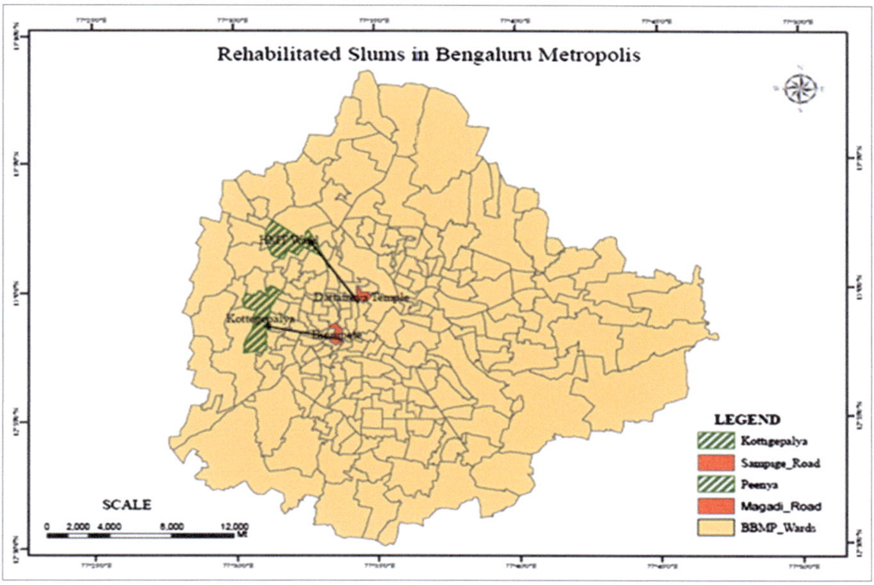

Fig. 10.2 Map of rehabilitated slums in Bengaluru metropolis. *Source* Author

Table 10.1 Profile of relocated slums in Bengaluru metropolis

Relocated slums	Relocated areas	Acquired property	Total HHs	Actual location	Date of occupation	Actual occupied HHs	No of blocks	Total land relocated dwelling (in Acres)	Principle language spoken
Basaveshwaranagar	Srigandadakavalu, Kottigepalya	2008–09	120	City railway station-Magadi road	2010	65	3	4.25	Tamil
Jai Bheema nagar	Peenya IInd stage	2008–09	103	Sampige road Malleshwaram	2009	86	3	3.70	Tamil

Magadi Road. Thus, a total of 102 relocated households were interviewed. The sample size was restricted to only those households with a proper 'eligibility proof' i.e. those occupied and possessed the ownership/registered document. A comparison of two groups of relocated households allowed us for a reliable assessment of the impact of the resettlement on the specific group of community. In addition, a qualitative discussion was conducted to understand the overall profile and background of the project and the impact of resettlement. The methodology used for the study includes qualitative, ethnographic and quantitative data collected through structured questionnaire. Semi-structured interviews and focus group discussion was held with the local community leaders and the officials of BMRCL metro project. Analysis of the primary survey is presented in the next section. Profile of the relocated slums in Bengaluru metropolis is presented in the Table 10.1 above.

Socio-economic Profile

An analysis of the socio-economic profile of the two relocated slums is presented here. Since our sample size is small, traditional methods are used to infer results to understand the initial socio-economic characteristics of the households in both the slums.

Figure 10.3 reveals that a majority of the households from both the slums (72 % from Magadi road and 65 % from Peenya) shares a common geographical origin i.e. to Karnataka. Two reasons can be attributed: (i) these two slums are old settlements aged between 30 and 40 years and so original migrants are not alive and (ii) two generations of family members are actually born in Bengaluru city. Their first generation i.e. their ancestors can be traced back to neighbouring states such as Tamil Nadu or Andhra Pradesh.

Similarly, more than 32 % (Peenya IInd stage) and 22 % of the households (Magadi road) trace their origin to Tamil Nadu, while 6 % (Magadi) and nearly 2 % (Peenya IInd stage), respectively, are from Andhra Pradesh.

While a majority of the households from both the slums speak Tamil (i.e. 54 % in Magadi road and more than 90 % in Peenya IInd Stage) i.e. their mother tongue is Tamil. Both the slum groups share a geographical homogeneity in terms of tracing their origin of first generation back to Tamil Nadu. Notwithstanding the similarities of their geographical origin of the two sets of sample groups, they display difference in two aspects i.e. the number of households who have actually accepted the offer of 'rehabilitation package' and physically relocated and actual date of occupying the relocated dwelling.

Similarly, the principle religion of the households in both the slums is Hinduism. In other words, more than 90 % of the households from both the slums belong to Hindus, while 4 % (Magadi road) and nearly 6 % (Peenya IInd stage), respectively, are Christians from Peenya. Only 2 % of the households are Muslims from Magadi road.

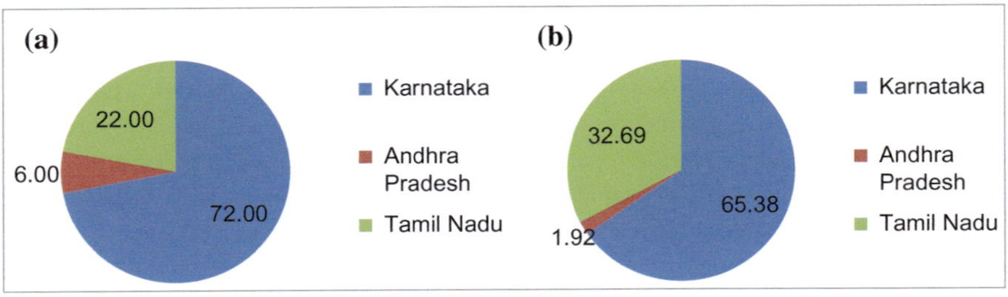

Fig. 10.3 Geographical origin of households at **a** Magadi road and **b** Peenya II stage

Distribution of Households by Caste

In both the slums, a majority of the households belong to (i.e. 78 % in Magadi road and 90 % in Peenya) Scheduled Caste (see Fig. 10.4) followed by 6 % (Magadi road) and nearly 4 % (Peenya IInd stage), respectively, belong to Scheduled Tribe. This is followed by backward caste (Only 8 % (Magadi road) and nearly 4, respectively). Only 8 % from Magadi road and nearly 2 % from Peenya IInd stage, respectively belong to unreserved category.

Gender Profile

Our pool of respondents comprises 46 % of female and 36 % of male from Magadi road (see Fig. 10.5), while at Peenya IInd stage, nearly 54 % are male and 46 % are female. But this distribution of respondents by gender does not determine their employment status at the household level as most of the household members i.e. both male and female are employed away from their dwelling and this was the reason that the survey was conducted mostly during late evening and weekends.

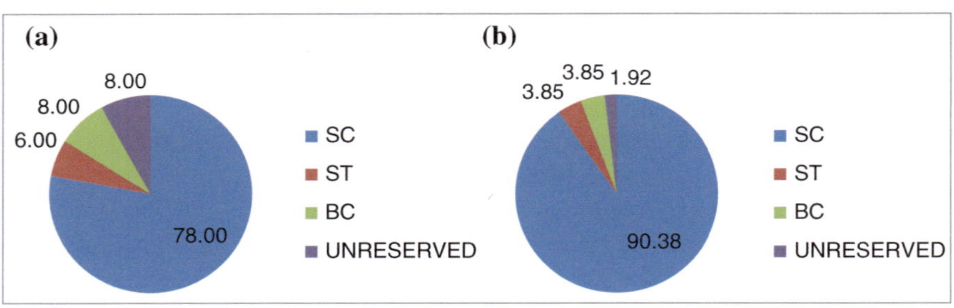

Fig. 10.4 Caste profile at **a** Magadi road and **b** Peenya II Stage

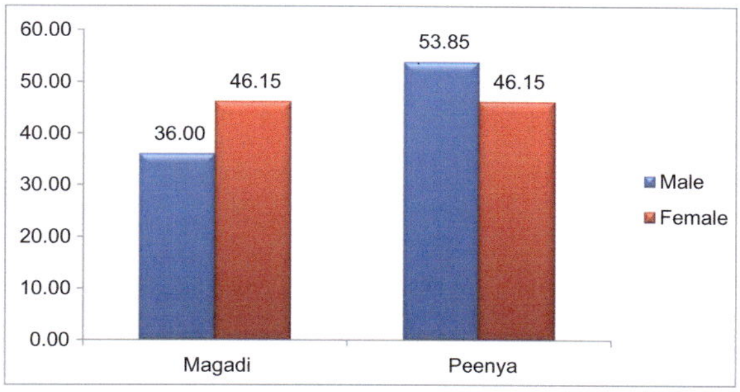

Fig. 10.5 Gender Profile

Distribution of Households by Size

At present, the family size (see Fig. 10.6) in both the slums varies between 4 and 6 (58 and 79 %, respectively). But in Magadi road, 28 % of the household size is between 7 and 9 which is considerably big (as against 7 % in Peenya), given the fact that they are located in Bengaluru metropolitan city.[24]

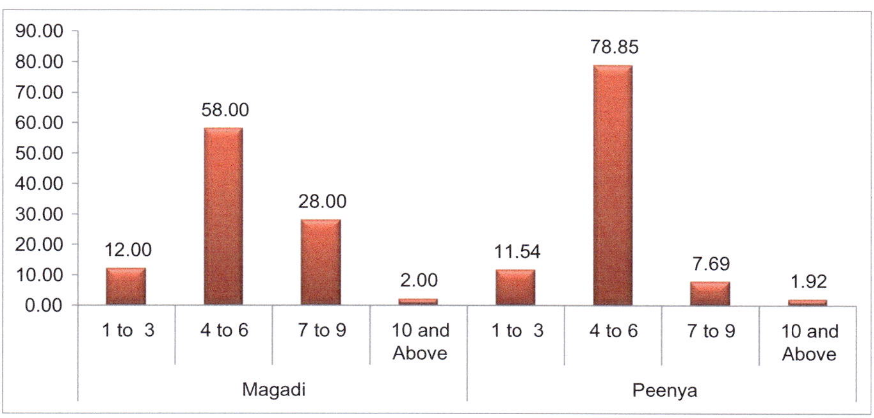

Fig. 10.6 Household size at Magadi road and Peenya II stage

[24]But unfortunately, the study could not present the sharp changes in household size before and after relocation.

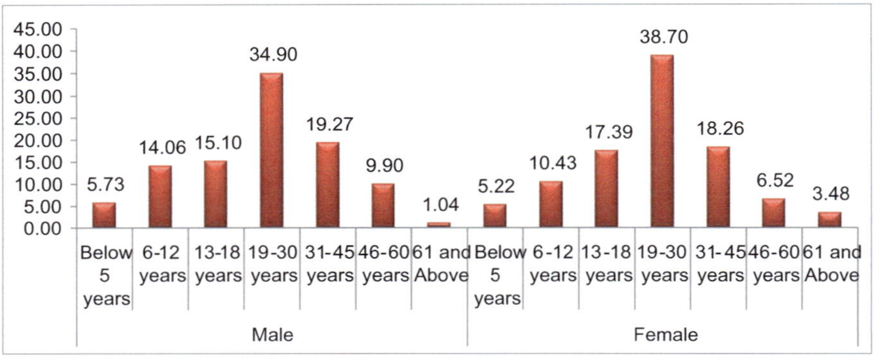

Fig. 10.7 Distribution of households by age and gender of both Magadi road and Peenya II stage

Distribution of Households by Age and Gender

Figure 10.7 clearly illustrates that a majority of household members (both male and female) belong to the age group of 19–30 years (male 34 % and female 38 %) followed by the age group of 31–45 years (male 19 % and female 18 %). The population belonging to both these age groups (i.e. between 19–30 and 31–45) has direct correlation with the employment status, particularly female. We can, thus, infer that a majority of the employed household members in the age group of 19–45 years.

Distribution of Households by Education

Education is one of the determining factors for employment opportunities and income mobilities, thereby contribute for the improved lifestyle. At Srigandadakavalu, Magadi road, the chart below (see Fig. 10.8) clearly demonstrates that a majority (nearly 23 %) of the female are illiterate as against male (only 11 %). Similarly, those who have studies up to the level of high school are slightly more among male than female (male account for 37 % and female for nearly 34 %). Those with a higher educational qualification such as graduation are slightly more among male (7 %) as against female (only 3 %). While among female, at least one is postgraduate. Those female holding diploma qualification is higher (16 %) than male (10 %).

A similar observation can be made for Peenya IInd stage (see Fig. 10.9), with female illiterates outnumbering (38 %) male (22 %). Those who have attended up to primary, middle and high school levels are more among male than female (16 per cent, 16 per cent and nearly 31 per cent, respectively, for male). But the

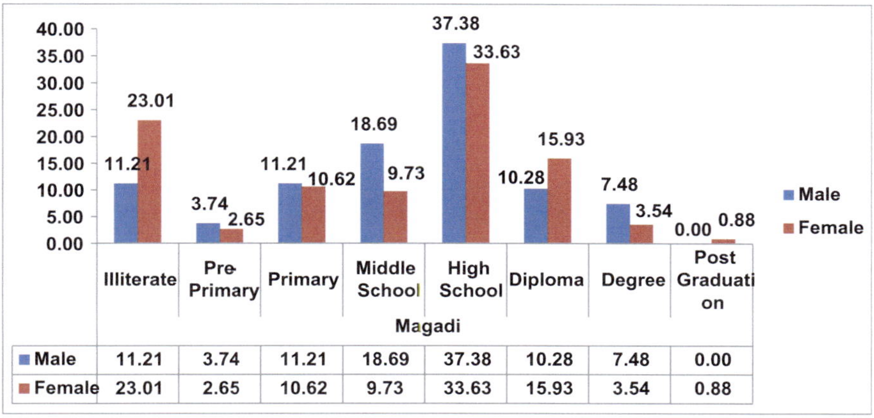

Fig. 10.8 Distribution of households by education at Magadi road

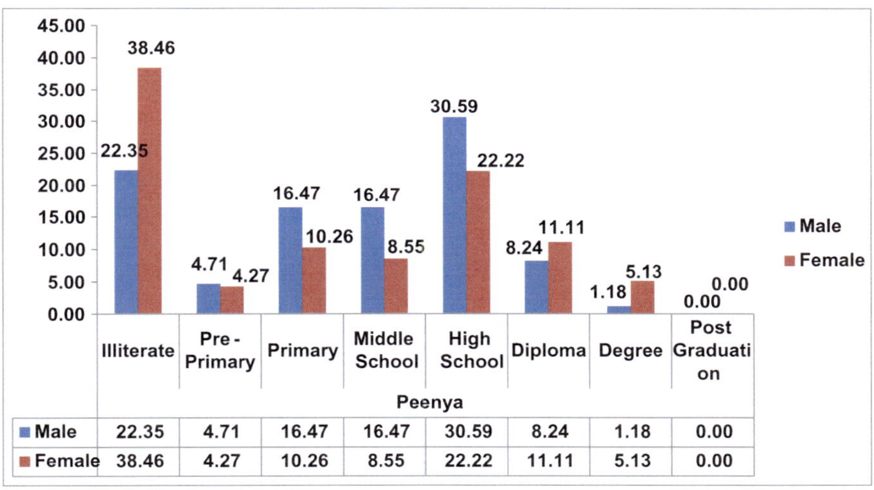

Fig. 10.9 Distribution of households by education in Peenya II stage

trend of holding a higher degree such as graduation and diploma is high among female (11 and 5 %, respectively) than male. This trend can be found particularly among the younger generation of the households aged 16–22 years who are inclined towards higher education. One of the encouraging trends is that those male and female who have attained higher and vocational degrees are exposed to better employment opportunities and thereby earn higher income.

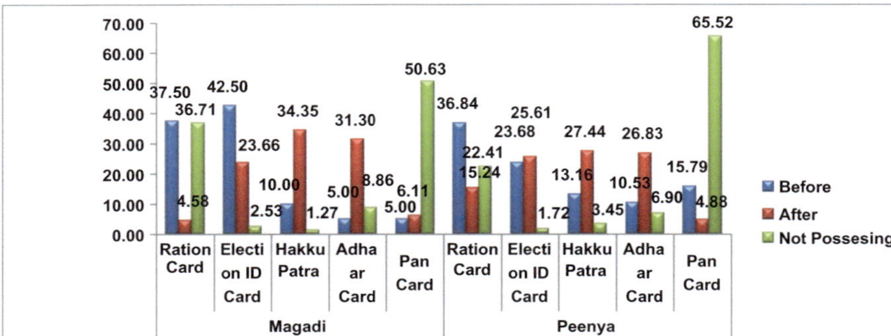

	Magadi Ration Card	Magadi Election ID Card	Magadi Hakku Patra	Magadi Adhaar Card	Magadi Pan Card	Peenya Ration Card	Peenya Election ID Card	Peenya Hakku Patra	Peenya Adhaar Card	Peenya Pan Card
Before	37.50	42.50	10.00	5.00	5.00	36.84	23.68	13.16	10.53	15.79
After	4.58	23.66	34.35	31.30	6.11	15.24	25.61	27.44	26.83	4.88
Not Possesing	36.71	2.53	1.27	8.86	50.63	22.41	1.72	3.45	6.90	65.52

Fig. 10.10 Possession of ID cards by households at Magadi road and Peenya II stage

Possession of Identity Cards (ID)

Possession of identity cards such as identification through the PDS (public distribution system) and election/voter cards, 'Hakku-Patras', Adhaar[25] and PAN (Permanent Account Number) cards are very crucial for slum dwellers to localize and integrate into the city. In fact, possession of ID cards is an acknowledgement of their physical presence in the city; while non-possession disempowers them from accruing various social benefits such as access to basic amenities such as water supply, electricity, sewerage and UGD connections. The study tried to assess the possession of ID cards before and after relocation of both the slums.

It can be clearly noticed (see Fig. 10.10) that the families with 'Hakku Patras'[26] before (only 10 % in Magadi and 13 % in Peenya) relocation are few compared to families possessing them after relocation (34 % in Magadi and 27 % in Peenya). However, the families in possession of 'PDS cards' are higher in number (37 % in Magadi and nearly 37 % in Peenya) before relocation as against those after relocation.

Possession of both 'Adhaar' and PAN cards entitles slum dwellers to various benefits such as housing and bank loans. Those families who do not possess PAN cards are high in number in both the slums (50 and 65 %). The numbers of families without 'PDS cards' is equally high in both the slums (37 % in Magadi road and 22 % in Peenya). Possession of Aadhar cards is highest (31 and 27 %) in both the relocated slums.

[25]Unique Identification (UID/Adhaar) was introduced by the Central government of India in 2009. UID is linked to bank transactions for household LPG subsidy and other governmental schemes. It consists of both demographic and biometrics details of individuals in the country.

[26]'Hakku Patras' or 'Swadhinapatra' are lease documents issued by the local authorities like Bruhat Bangalore Mahanagarapalike (BBMP), Bangalore Development Authority (BDA) or Karnataka Slum Development Board (KSDB) for a period of 20 years or more.

Security of Tenure

'Legality' or 'formality' of slum dwellers is ascertained by their security of tenure. Jai Bheemanagar slum, which was centrally located in the junction between City Railway station and Sampige road, Malleshwaram, received their 'Swadhinapatra' in 1991 from BBMP, and similarly, households in Basaveswaranagar slum originally located in between the City Railway Station and Magadi road received 'Hakku Patra' in 1991 from BBMP. Yet, these official residence documents are not registered as proof of their ownership. So, residents without formal land titles or legal documents[27] are under the risk of eviction. However, after relocation, nearly 71 households of Jai Bheemanagar slum (Peenya IInd stage) and 65 households from Basaveswaranagar slum (Srigandadakavalu, Magadi) have registered with the BDA; thus, formalizing their physical existence in the city.

Section II: Labour, Informality and Mobility

In the following section, findings are presented that offer insights into labour, livelihood and mobility i.e. jobs, income, distance travelled, mode of travel, expenditure on fuel, travel and food in determining how the urban poor cope with the transformed physical and material conditions of a specific 'spatial location' to delineate the cause and consequences of urban poverty.

Employment Profile by Gender (Before and After Resettlement)

The central issue of livelihood and mobility of slum dwellers largely depend on their employment opportunities. The study examines the changes brought about in the employment due to the relocation process. Various factors influence the employment reconfiguration of the slum households which include: (i) changes in demographic structure, (ii) education and skills and (iii) strong resource networks. For slum dwellers, finding jobs is a major challenge and a daily pursuit. These dwellers, usually without education and required skills, tend to be drawn to informal jobs which are mostly unpredictable. Such informal jobs largely depend on networks and contacts with friends, relatives and former employers. Besides, 'urban space' in the central district anchors multiple job opportunities.

Changes in the space strongly influence the evolution of urban employment profile based on access to multiple job opportunities (labour market) for those

---

[27]Most of the formal procedures involved in obtaining legally registered documents are often costly, involving corruption and extremely complex procedures.

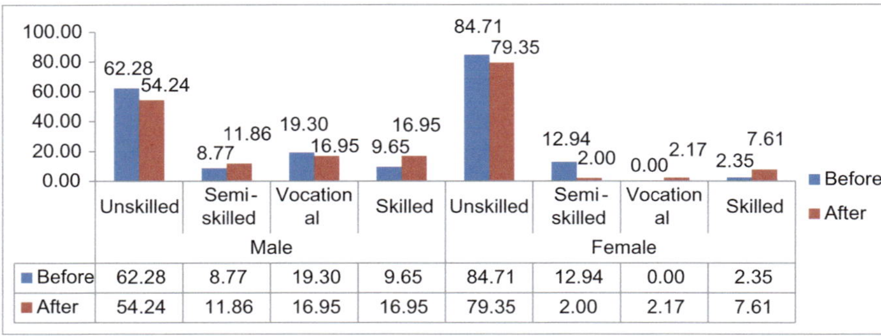

Fig. 10.11 Employment profile by gender (*before* and *after* resettlement) at Magadi road and Peenya II stage

working in the informal sector. Further, such a process has a direct correlation for income mobility and thereby improves the purchasing power of households. Here, the occupation profile of the households is expanded in order to understand the divergence in impact on gender i.e. on both male and female before and after relocation.

Our study clearly displays (see Fig. 10.11) that 'relocation' to a newer area has indeed affected the employment opportunities of the slum dwellers. The proportion of male, who are mostly employed in unskilled jobs, has declined significantly (from 62 to 54 %) after relocation in both the slums. But men employed in 'semi-skilled and skilled' jobs have significantly increased in percentage (from nearly 9 % to nearly 12 and nearly 10 % to nearly 17 %, respectively). Alternatively, the proportion of women employed in unskilled jobs has declined (from 85 to 79 %) after resettlement. Similarly, the proportion of women employed in 'skilled' jobs has increased considerably (from 2 to nearly 8 %) after relocation. The study by Mitra (2006), as mentioned in Coelho et al. (2012), refers to this trend as a 'physical segmentation of the labour market', symbolizing area-wise specialization and physical proximity in terms of distance to economic activities in the core city which determines the accessibility of certain kind of jobs to a certain population. Unemployment, in this instance, is eclipsed by spatial segregation of the community, thus perpetuating a vicious cycle of unemployment—the working poor becoming poorer.

Occupation Profile by Gender (Before and After Resettlement)

An occupational profile by gender based on various economic activities pursued by them is presented in Table 10.2.

The results presented in the table (see Table 10.2) clearly show that the relocation process has had both positive as well as negative implications on the

Table 10.2 Occupation profile by gender (before and after resettlement)

Occupation profile		Before resettlement			After resettlement		
		Male	Female	Total	Male	Female	Total
Unskilled	Domestic work	1.75	48.2	21.6	2.5	51.1	23.8
	House keeping	2.63	1.2	2.0	0.0	3.3	1.4
	Construction-coolie	32.46	20.0	27.1	25.4	14.1	20.5
	Daily wage	0.88	0.0	0.5	0.8	1.1	1.0
	Cleaner-helper	5.26	14.1	9.0	7.6	8.7	8.1
	Painting	18.42	0.0	10.6	16.9	0.0	9.5
	Security	0.88	0.0	0.5	0.8	0.0	0.5
	Self-employed	0.00	1.2	0.5	0.0	1.1	0.5
Semi-skilled	Tailoring	2.63	1.2	2.0	3.4	0.0	1.9
	Factory work	2.63	4.7	3.5	5.9	1.1	3.8
	Garment work	3.51	7.1	5.0	2.5	9.8	5.7
	Street vendor	0.00	0.0	0.0	0.0	0.0	0.0
Vocational	Mason	0.88	0.0	0.5	0.8	0.0	0.5
	Driver	12.28	0.0	7.0	11.9	1.1	7.1
	Carpenter	1.75	0.0	1.0	0.8	1.1	1.0
	Construction-mestry	1.75	0.0	1.0	1.7	0.0	1.0
	Electrician	1.75	0.0	1.0	1.7	0.0	1.0
	Plumber	0.88	0.0	0.5	0.0	0.0	0.0
Skilled	Office work	6.14	2.4	4.5	8.5	3.3	6.2
	Sale assistant	0.00	0.0	0.0	0.0	0.0	0.0
	Business	1.75	0.0	0.0	1.7	0.0	1.0
	Other salaried job	1.75	0.0	1.0	6.8	4.3	5.7
Total		100.00	100.00	100.00	100.00	100.00	100.00

employment status of slum dwellers. Those positive implications include the following:

i. First, Peenya is one of the largest industrial belts in the city of Bengaluru. Due to relocation, particularly those households from Peenya IInd stage have an advantage in terms of accessing small, medium and large scale industries where they could be employed. Especially those women with the required skill have an opportunity of being employed in semi-skilled jobs such as Tailoring in 'Garment factories' (9.8 %). Even men have diverse opportunities of being employed in small and medium scale industries such as engineering (iron-melting making), electrical or plastic goods and motors.
ii. Secondly, our findings confirm that a professional upward mobility among a few men and women, particularly the second generation of the family members, who are educated up to higher secondary and undergraduation are employed in better paid jobs such as office and administration (male 8.5 % and female 3.3 %) and other salaried/white-collar jobs (male 6.8 % and female 4.3 %).

iii. One of the interesting effects of the resettlement process seems to be that women household members are relatively freed from daily chores (fetching water, collecting fuel wood etc.) with an improvement in the access to basic infrastructure and security of tenure which considerably freed women from daily chores spiralling in the number female labour particularly among the younger generation.
iv. Those male employed in vocational jobs such as mason, driver, carpenter, construction workers, electrician and plumber during pre-resettlement have continued to retain the same jobs even post-resettlement.

Thus, the entire resettlement process i.e. a shift in location, has drastically altered the employment profile of slum dwellers, particularly those employed in informal jobs such as unskilled and semi-skilled jobs with significant negative implications. They include the following:

i. Majority of women those are undereducated/illiterate and employed in informal jobs such as domestic maid (from 48 % before and 51 % after rehabilitation) have continued in the same jobs after relocation. Because, the newer area at present is rather isolated from the city which is actually a non-residential area. But a majority of the working women have not changed their jobs, instead have chosen to travel long distances to their former jobs. Most evidently, more women have started working after relocation in order to contribute to the declining family income.
ii. One of the most visible impacts has been on the elderly women who have discontinued their previous jobs after resettlement as they could not travel long distance or could they afford the cost of travelling. These women were mostly employed as cleaners/helpers or construction coolies and factory work. After relocation, new jobs are not offered citing their old age. As a result, women contribution to the family's income has drastically reduced.
iii. But those men (reduced from 32 to 25 %) and women (reduced from 20 to 14 %) who were employed as construction coolies or daily wage labour (such as painters reduced from 18 to 17 %; for housekeeping from 2.63 % to None) could not afford to continue in their jobs for the obvious reason that there are at present located far away from the core city area which has considerably increased the commuting time concomitantly their travel cost. A few opine that most of them have lost their professional network which they were part of in the pre-resettled location.
iv. These daily wage earners mostly rely on resource and social networks for information from friends, relatives, acquaintances or present employers in seeking employment opportunities. But relocation has completely cut them off from such networks. Besides, the new area is devoid of any complementary, commercial or industrial activities in the vicinity. As a result, there has been drastic reduction in the number of male and female employed as construction coolies (from 27 to 20 % after relocation). Similarly, those male engaged as painters has slightly reduced (from 10.6 to 9.5 %). Such a change in the

employment status post-relocation has a direct correlation with the income profile of households, particularly those in low income brackets.

v. There is a clear evidence of stagnancy or downward mobility for youth aged between 17 and 21 years, mostly educated up to SSLC, who could not to afford to join jobs in the vicinity of the newly shifted areas. Otherwise, in the pre-resettled areas such as Malleshwaram and Magadi road, they were occupationally localized. As they were just 2–3 kms away from the core city of Majestic, employed as mechanics in garage, car washers, cleaners, helpers, construction coolies and so on. Some of them were employed on contract basis in small scale factories such as steel, plastic making and reliance vegetable marts. One of the advantage they had in the pre-resettled location was that they could easily engage in multiple jobs in a single day which is completely absent in the new location.

vi. Most importantly present new location completely cuts them off from public work programmes including credit assistance, accessibility to multiple job market and skill upgradation which can hasten up the process of an upward mobility of income. Therefore, state sponsored relocation programmes, especially in the Indian context may eventually produce a state of 'spatial ghettoization'. Such spatial ghettoization is through physical distance and exclusion of the newly occupied dwelling from the core city, intensifying economic marginality, thereby reinforcing 'working poverty' (Coelho et al. 2012).

Income Profile by Gender (Before and After Resettlement)

The demographic changes brought about by relocation of slums have induced alterations in the employment pattern, thereby impacting drastically on the family income. A brief comparative analysis (see Fig. 10.12) of income profile by gender is presented below (before and after resettlement).

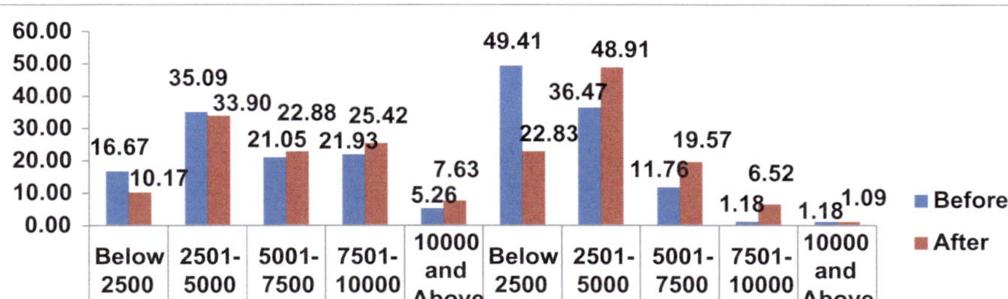

	Male					Female				
	Below 2500	2501-5000	5001-7500	7501-10000	10000 and Above	Below 2500	2501-5000	5001-7500	7501-10000	10000 and Above
Before	16.67	35.09	21.05	21.93	5.26	49.41	36.47	11.76	1.18	1.18
After	10.17	33.90	22.88	25.42	7.63	22.83	48.91	19.57	6.52	1.09

Fig. 10.12 Income profile by gender (*before* and *after* resettlement)

The average mean monthly income for male was Rs 1778 pre-resettlement as against Rs 1683 post-resettlement. Similarly, the average mean monthly income for female pre-settlement was Rs 1744 as against Rs 1575 post-resettlement.

Most importantly, post-resettlement, the average mean income of both male and female has slipped, particularly for those household members whose income is below Rs 2500. Given the fact that, the city of Bengaluru hosts urban poor between 15 and 19 % of its 10 million population, a majority of the Bengaluru's urban poor are employed in informal or tertiary sector such as construction labour, cab drivers, in hotels or eateries, helpers, cleaners, mechanics, street vendors and rag pickers. It is estimated that on an average, Rs 120 per day is required for surviving in a city such as Bengaluru which invalidates the poverty line estimate of Rs 30 per day set by Indian Planning Commission (Prashanth 2014).[28]

There is a noticeable decline of those members of the household of both male and female (from 16 to 10 % for male and nearly 49 to 23 % for female) earning to below Rs 2500 post-resettlement. We understand that such decline is supported by various reasons as follows:

i. Majority of household members who use to earn below Rs 2500 were mostly illiterates employed in low paid or informal jobs such as helpers, cleaners, mechanics, construction coolies and other daily wage jobs. In fact, the resettlement process has produced a trade-off between a better housing facility and implied employment rigidity in the new area which is far away from the core city. As a result, most of them (both male and female) are unable to engage in multiple jobs in a single day, which was possible before resettlement.
ii. Particularly, those aged members of the household have significantly dropped their previous jobs. They were unable to continue with their previous jobs for the fact that they could not bear the cost of travelling to faraway place.
iii. Youth aged between 17 and 22 remained occupationally instabilized as they could not be employed in temporary or informal jobs in the vicinity. Certainly, the resettlement process has disabled them from contributing to their family income.

There is a significant variation with respect to those male and female earning between Rs 2500 and Rs 5000. While the income of male shows a more or less similar trend, (35 and 33 %) between pre and post-resettlement, there is a noticeable increase in the number of female who are earning between Rs 2500–5000 (from 36 % to nearly 49 %) per month and those who earns Rs 5000–7500 (from 12 % to nearly 20 %) per month. Similarly, there is also a considerable increase in the number of male and female earning between Rs 7501–10,000 (21–25 % male and from 1–6 % in the case of female) per month. Certain reasons can be attributed to this increase in the number of female earning more post-resettlement.

---

[28] G.N. Prashanth "State has more urban poor than national average: Study", 21 July 2014, *Deccan Herald*, p. 7.

i. First, in many families, women from second generation, particularly those educated up to high school and upper secondary have found employment as tailors in 'garment factories' located in the vicinity at both Peenya IInd stage and Srigandadakavalu, Magadi road.
ii. Besides, some of them are employed as office workers (3.3 %) and in other salaried jobs (4.3 %) such as school teacher.

The income profile of the relocated households clearly illustrates the following facts:

i. In a global city like Bengaluru, for those members who are less educated or illiterate and are employed in the informal and daily wage jobs certainly find the entire process of resettlement as having disruptive implications for their employment opportunities and thereby the upward mobility of their income.
ii. In fact, it clearly appears that upward income mobility is mainly confined to those who are exposed to higher education and skill and, in such cases, the 'resettlement' process has a relatively less disruptive effect. This actually proves that those with stable jobs and higher income are exposed to and live in more rigid forms of housing.

Access to Basic Amenities

The security of tenure through a permanent housing facility has a direct impact on access to basic amenities and infrastructure (such as water supply, drainage, toilets, electricity connection and garbage collection) facilities. Local authorities such as Bengaluru Water Supply and Sewerage Board (BWSSB), Bruhat Bengaluru Mahanagarapalike (BBMP) and Karnataka Slum Development Board (KSDB) are responsible for providing basic amenities to the urban slums in the city. In addition, many international financial institutions such as ADB, World Bank, JIBC (Japanese International Bank Corporation) and AusAID are lending loans as a part of extending infrastructure and basic services to the urban poor residing in slums.

From the study, it is clearly understood that post-resettlement process, both the slums are well connected to water supply, toilets and electricity facility. Households are adequately connected with underground drainage as well as individual toilets. In fact, each household has access to two toilets and bathrooms. But one of the problems encountered at Srigandadakavalu, Magadi road slum is that two to four houses in each block share the same UGD, causing severe blockage, overflow and stagnation of the drains every week. As a result, most of the households incur cost of maintenance for these private amenities in the resettled site. Besides, a few households have complained that as tiles in toilets are not laid firmly, they get easily separated from the floor.

Access to Social Infrastructure (Education, Health and Transport services)

Access to social infrastructure such as education (schools and colleges) and health facilities (primary health care centres and hospitals) and transport services determine the well-being of slum dwellers. But post-resettlement, one of the most worrying aspects is a sharp deterioration in access to these social services such as education, health and transport in the vicinity of the new dwelling.

Distribution of Households by Distance

Post-resettlement, households from resettled slums faced severe problem with urban mobility i.e. particularly the transport facility. The main problem was the choice of location for resettlement complex itself and the associated distance needed to reach and access public transport services. At Peenya IInd stage, although metro network is just half a kilometre from the dwelling, people felt that public BMTC buses were not reliable. Hence people had to walk an average distance of 1 km to reach the BMTC bus stop. The situation was worse in Srigandadakavalu, Magadi road. The entire dwelling is located interior by at least a 2 km distance from the main Magadi road. As a result, households were forced to depend on multiple forms of transport services such two wheelers, autos (three wheelers) or four wheelers. After continuous struggle, at present households have managed to arrange for one BMTC transport service, which is now available for two trips a day.[29] But majority of the households at the relocated slums opt for private autos, incurring huge amounts per month on travel alone (see Table 10.3). Therefore, relocated slums are facing serious problems related to urban mobility.

- Post-resettlement, 60 % of households from Magadi road travel 7–10 km and 24 % travel 16 kms and above to reach their workplace. While 72 % travel a distance below 3 km and 24 % travel 4–6 km to access the market and, on the other hand, 66 % travel below 3 km and 20 % travel a distance of 4–6 km to access health care facilities. Similarly, 18 % travel 4–6 km and 16 % travel 11–15 km to access educational institutions.
- Similarly, at Peenya, the highest distribution of households is found for those who travel 7–10 km (44 %), followed by those who travel 11–15 km (21 %) and 16 km and above (21 %) to reach their workplace. A majority of the households travel below 3 km (67 %) followed by those who travel 4–6 km (27 %) to access market facilities. To access health care facilities, a majority of the households travel at least below 3 km (nearly 58 %), followed by those

[29]One trip in the morning and another trip in the evening.

Table 10.3 Distribution of households by distance travelled from Magadi road and Peenya II stage

Area	Distance travelled	Work place	Market	Health care	Education
Magadi	Not applicable	0.00	0.00	0.00	46.00
	Below 3 km	4.00	72.00	66.00	14.00
	4–6 km	6.00	24.00	20.00	18.00
	7–10 km	60.00	4.00	10.00	4.00
	11–15 km	6.00	0.00	4.00	16.00
	16 km and above	24.00	0.00	0.00	2.00
	Total	100.00	100.00	100.00	100.00
Peenya	Not applicable	0.00	0.00	0.00	51.92
	Below 3 km	11.54	67.31	55.77	30.77
	4–6 km	1.92	26.92	7.69	5.77
	7–10 km	44.23	3.85	25.00	5.77
	11–15 km	21.15	0.00	7.69	5.77
	16 km and above	21.15	1.92	3.85	0.00
	Total	100.00	100.00	100.00	100.00

travelling a distance 7–10 km (25 %). Those travelling to access educational facilities are split between those who travel below 3 km (31 %) and those who travel more than 3 km up to 15 km (nearly 6 %).

Distribution of Households by Mode of Transport

As mentioned earlier, after relocation to newer areas, each household from the both the slums had to commute an average distance of 2–3 km for accessing facilities such as market, health, education or work place. Different modes of transport are chosen such as bus, two/four wheelers or in combination of bus and auto, auto and bike.. The most affordable mode of travel selected was public bus services (see Table 10.4).

A majority of the households at Srigandadakavalu, Magadi road, rely on public transport bus to access their workplace, market and health care and education facilities (54, 22, 18 and 24 %, respectively). A relatively more number of households rely on a combination of services such as bus and auto (22, 18 and 16 %, respectively) for commuting. During emergencies such as health care, 40 % of the households totally rely on autos followed by 22 % who use auto to reach market. While 22 % used their own bikes to access market.

Similarly, at Peenya IInd stage, a very high number of households rely on public bus to access the workplace, markets, and health and education facilities (86, 56 and 25 %). While nearly 14 % rely on auto for accessing health facilities during emergencies and relatively good number of households i.e. 33 and 23 % walk down to access market and educational facilities.

Table 10.4 Distribution of households by mode of transport at Magadi road and Peenya II stage

Area	Mode of transport	Work place	Market	Health care	Education
Magadi	Not applicable	0.00	0.00	0.00	46.00
	Walk	4.00	12.00	8.00	8.00
	Bus	54.00	22.00	18.00	24.00
	Bike	10.00	24.00	14.00	0.00
	Auto	6.00	22.00	40.00	2.00
	Car	2.00	0.00	0.00	0.00
	Auto/bus	22.00	18.00	16.00	16.00
	Auto/bike	2.00	2.00	4.00	4.00
	Total	100	100	100	100
Peenya	Not applicable	0.00	0.00	0.00	59.62
	Walk	0.00	32.69	23.08	9.62
	Bus	86.54	55.77	55.77	25.00
	Bike	9.62	5.77	7.69	1.92
	Auto	1.92	5.77	13.46	1.92
	Car	1.92	0.00	0.00	1.92
	Auto/bus	0.00	0.00	0.00	0.00
	Auto/bike	0.00	0.00	0.00	0.00
	Total	100	100	100	100

Distribution of Households by Travel Expenses

Post-resettlement, households commuting longer distance at an average of 2–3 km to access work place, market, health care services and education facilities obviously involve incurring travel expenditure. As a result of expenditure on travel, there is a considerable fall in the real income of the households thereby curtail their purchasing power and impact standard of living (see Table 10.5).

- A majority of the households at Srigandadakavalu, Magadi road, spend at least below Rs 1000 to access markets, health care and educational facilities (82, 68 and 34 %, respectively), followed by those spending Rs 1001–3000 (74, 18, 32 and 16 %, respectively). Those probably using two or four wheelers (14 % of household) spend Rs 5001–7000 on travel/commuting for work place
- At Peenya IInd stage, 75 % of the households spend Rs 1001–3000 on commuting to the workplace, which is a considerable expenditure on travel alone, followed by those who spends Rs 5001–7000 (nearly 15 %) to reach the workplace. Households (11 %) also spent considerable amount (Rs 1001–3000) on travel to access health care and education facilities.

Table 10.5 Distribution of households by travel expenses (at Magadi road and Peenya II stage)

Area	Travel expenses	Work place	Market	Health care	Education
Magadi	Not applicable	0.00	0.00	0.00	46.00
	Below 1000	10.00	82.00	68.00	34.00
	1001–3000	74.00	18.00	32.00	16.00
	3001–5000	0.00	0.00	0.00	4.00
	5001–7000	14.00	0.00	0.00	0.00
	7001 and above	2.00	0.00	0.00	0.00
	Total	100.00	100.00	100.00	100.00
Peenya	Not applicable	0.00	0.00	0.00	59.62
	Below 1000	7.69	92.31	88.46	25.00
	1001–3000	75.00	5.77	11.54	11.54
	3001–5000	0.00	1.92	0.00	1.92
	5001–7000	15.38	0.00	0.00	0.00
	7001 and above	1.92	0.00	0.00	1.92
	Total	100.00	100.00	100.00	100.00

'Spatial Ghettoization': Urban Space as 'Agency' in Entrepreneurial City

Analytically and empirically, the study locates a dialectic relationship between the spatial context and reconstitution of identity for urban poor on the one hand, and (duality of structure) on the other, the challenges imposed by the 'entrepreneurial' planning instruments through rehabilitation. In a city like Bengaluru, though the 'rehabilitation package' has satisfied the relocated slum community in terms of providing material and infrastructure needs, tenure security and trust in the immediate area by overcoming social discrimination; yet the findings clearly demonstrate that the rhetoric employed under 'package' has, in fact, become a potential source of economic insecurity and contested space.

Further, field observation clearly indicates that the entire package has generated an opposition from the affected community severely condemning BMRCL as being insensitive and disseminating inaccurate and insensitive information about the location. Although the rehabilitation package has assisted the urban poor to escape from the distressful lifestyle, yet the newer location has counterbalanced by pushing the community with physical and spatial ghettoization as well as the absence of choice. And most of them are unsure of what the future holds them. Relocated residents are using various 'spatial metaphors' like 'what is the use of a castle without proper food and income to live' deeming that the relocation has disrupted their lifestyle in many ways. We can contend that the shift to a new location lacked a transformative impact in the sense that they had to bear the cost of travelling back to the work and incur an additional expenditure to access social amenities such as health care, education, market and transport. In other words, a mere physical and material nature of relocation of slums has been source of discontent among the urban poor residents. In fact, redevelopment projects such as 'metro' has been profoundly disruptive and disempowers by casting a shadow of uncertainty among the urban poor even as they struggle to cope with the extremely poor living conditions in Bengaluru metropolis.

References

Aranya, R. (2003). Globalisation and urban restructuring of Bangalore India: Growth of the IT industry, its spatial dynamics and local planning responses. http://www.isocarp.net/Data/case_studies/255.pdf. Accessed May 25, 2015.

Aranya, R. (2008). Location theory in reverse? Location for global production in the IT industry of Bangalore. *Environment and Plan A, 40*, 446–463.

Banerjee-Guha, S. (2011). *India'a new urban policy and contemporary urban planning: Socio-spatial injustices in Mumbai's redevelopment*. Mumbai Reader, 9, pp. 10–21. http://www.udri.org/udri/MumbaiReader09/01%20Swapna%20Banerjee%20Guha%20-20India%92s%20New%20Urban%20Policy%20&%20Contemporary%20Urban%20Planning.pdf. Accessed April 25, 2015.

Banerjee-Guha, S. (2010). Introduction: Transformative cities in the new global order. In S. Banerjee-Guha (Ed.), *Accumulation by dispossession: Transformative cities in new global order* (pp. 1–16). New Delhi: Sage Publications.

Baviskar, A. (2002). The politics of the city. In *Seminar* (Vol. 516, pp. 40–42). www.india-seminar.com/2002/516/516%20amita%20baviskar.htm. Accessed January 5, 2016.

Baviskar, A. (2011). Spectacular events, city spaces and citizenship: The Commonwealth Games in Delhi. In J. S. Anjaria & C. McFarlane (Eds.), *Urban navigations: Politics, space and the city in South Asia* (pp. 138–161). New York, London: Routledge.

BDA. (n.d). *Draft master plan-2015, an integrated planning approach towards a vibrant international city*. Bangalore: Bengaluru Development Authority. http://www.bdabangalore.org/brochure.pdf. Accessed May 1, 2015.

BDA. (2007). *Revised master plan-2015: Vision document* (Vol. 1). Bangalore: Bangalore Development Authority.

Benjamin, S. (2004). Urban land transformation for pro-poor economies. *Geoforum, 35*(2), 177–187.

Benjamin, S. (2010). Manufacturing neoliberalism: Lifestyling Indian urbanity. In S. Banerjee-Guha (Ed.), *Accumulation by dispossession: Transformative cities in the new global order* (pp. 92–124). New Delhi: Sage Publications.

BMRCL. (2003). *Bengaluru Metro (Phase I): Environmental impact assessment studies and management plans* (Vol. V). Bangalore: BMRCL.

Brenner, N. (1999). Globalization as reterritorialization: The re-scaling of urban governance in the European Union. *Urban Studies, 36*(3), 431–451.

Castells, M. (1996). *The rise of the network society*. Oxford, Cambridge, MA: Blackwell.

CDP. (2009). *Urban infrastructure and governance, Volume One, Revised City Development Plan: JNNRUM*. Bangalore: Bruhat Bangalore Mahanagarapalike.

Chen, M., Joann, V., & James, H. (2006). Informality, gender and poverty: A global picture. *Economic and Political Weekly, 41*(21), 2131–2139.

Coelho, K., Venkat, T., & Chandrika, R. (2012). Labour and livelihoods in a slum resettlement colony. *Economic and Political Weekly, xlviI*(47, 48), 53–63.

Dittrich, C. (2007). Bangalore: Globalisation and fragmentation in India's Hightech-Capital. *ASI, 103*(S), 45–58.

Ghosh, A. (2005). Public-private or private public? *Economic and Political Weekly, XL*(47), 19–25.
Ghosh, A. (2006). Banking on Bangalore's dream. *Economic and Political Weekly, XLI*(8), 1–4.
Gotham, K. F., & Krista, B. (2002). Using space: Agency and identity in a public-housing development. *City and Community, 1*(3), 267–289.
Goldman, M. (2010). Speculative urbanism and the making of the next world city. *International Journal of Urban and Regional Research, 35*(3), 555–581.
Harvey, D. (1989). *The condition of postmodernity*. New York: Free Press.
Heitzman, J. (1999). Corporate strategy and planning in the science city: Bengaluru as 'silicon valley'. *Economic and Political Weekly, XXXIV*(05), PE2–PE11.
Heitzman, J. (2003). Geographic information systems in India's 'silicon valley': The impact of technology on planning Bangalore. *Contemporary South Asia, 12*(1), 57–83.
Heitzman, J. (2004). *Network city: Planning the information society in Bangalore*. New Delhi: Oxford University Press.
Lefebvre, H. (1991). *The production of space*. Cambridge, MA: Blackwell.
Mitra, A. (2006). Labour market mobility in low income households. *Economic and Political Weekly, 41*(21), 2123–2130.
Nair, J. (2000). Singapore is not Bangalore's destiny. *Economic and Political Weekly*, *XXXV*(18), 1512–1514. http://www.epw.in/system/files/pdf/2000_35/18/Singapore_Is_Not_Bangalores_Destiny.pdf. Accessed March 20, 2015.
Narayana, M. R. (2008). Globalisation and urban growth: Evidence from Bangalore (India), Discussion Paper Series-F-544, *Centre for International Research on the Japanese Economy (CIRJE), Tokyo: University of Tokyo and Bangalore: ISEC*. http://www.e.u-tokyo.ac.jp/cirje/research/dp/2008/2008cf544.pdf. Accessed April 12, 2014.
Nisbett, N. (2009). *Growing up in the knowledge society: Living the IT dream in Bangalore*. New Delhi: Routledge.
Peck, J., & Tickell, A. (1994). Searching for a new institutional fix: The after-Fordist crisis and global-local disorder. In A. Amin (Ed.), *Post-Fordism: a reader*. Cambridge, MA: Blackwell.
Prashanth, G. N. (2014). State has more urban poor than national average: Study, 21st July, 2014, Deccan Herald. http://www.deccanherald.com/content/420879/state-has-more-urban-poor.html. Accessed on July 22, 2014.
Rai, S. (2006, March 20). Is the next silicon valley taking root in Bangalore? *The New York Times*. http://www.nytimes.com/2006/03/20/business/worldbusiness/20bangalore.html?_r=0. Accessed January 10, 2015.
Rode, P., & Chandra, R. (2008). *Urban India: Comparing Mumbai, Delhi, Kolkata and Bangalore*. London: Urban Age Program.
Roy, A. (2009). Why India cannot plan its cities: Informality, insurgence and the idiom of urbanisation. *Planning Theory, 8*(1), 76–87.
Roychowdhury, S. (2008). Class in industrial disputes: Case studies from Bangalore. *Economic and Political Weekly, XLIII*(22), 28–36.
Shatkin, G. (2014). Introduction. In G. Shatkin (Ed.), *Contesting the Indian city: Global visions and the politics of the local* (pp. 1–38). Oxford: Wiley Blackwell.
Shaw, A. (2012a). Metropolitan city growth and management in post-liberalized India. *Eurasian Geography and Economics, 53*(1), 44–62.
Shaw, A. (2012b). *Indian cities, Oxford India short introductions*. New Delhi: Oxford University Press.
Sassen, S. (1991). *The global city: New York, London, Tokyo*. Princeton: Princeton University Press.
Sassen, S. (2002). Locating cities on global circuits. *Environment and Urbanisation, 14*(1), 13–30.
Sudhira, H. S. (2008). The emergence of world city: Bangalore. In S. Abedin, C. Johnson, R. Hu, & M. Cramer (Eds.), *Connecting cities: India* (pp. 114–137). Sydney, Australia: Metropolis Congress.
Sudhira, H. S., Ramachandra, T. V., & Bala Subrahmanya, M. H. (2007). City profile: Bangalore. *Cities, 24*, 379–390.

Swyngedow, E. (1997). Neither global nor local: Globalization and the politics of scale. In K. R. Cox (Ed.), *Spaces of globalisation: Reasserting the power of the local* (pp. 137–166). New York: Guilford Press.
The Brookings Institution. (2013). The 10 traits of globally fluent metro areas: Bangalore, global cities initiative: A Joint Project of Brookings and JP Morgan Chase. http://www.brookings.edu/research/reports/2013/06/26-global-metro-traits-mcdearman-clark-parilla. Accessed April 15, 2015.
Vacquier, D. (2010). *The impact of slum resettlement on urban integration in Mumbai: The case of the Chandivli project*. Occasional Paper No. 26. New Delhi: Centre de Sciences Humaines.
Weinstein, L. (2011). Slum-free Mumbai' and other entrepreneurial strategies in the making of Mumbai's global downtown. In G. W. McDonogh & M. Peterson (Eds.), *Global downtowns* (pp. 234–252). Pennsylvania: University of Pennsylvania Press.
Weinstein, L. (2014). 'One-man handled': Fragmented power and political entrepreneurship in globalizing Mumbai. *International Journal of Urban and Regional Research, 38*(1), 14–35.

FSC www.fsc.org
MIX
Papier aus verantwortungsvollen Quellen
Paper from responsible sources
FSC® C105338

If you have any concerns about our products, you can contact us on
ProductSafety@springernature.com

In case Publisher is established outside the EU, the EU authorized representative is:
Springer Nature Customer Service Center GmbH
Europaplatz 3, 69115 Heidelberg, Germany

Printed by Libri Plureos GmbH
in Hamburg, Germany

SpringerBriefs in Applied Sciences and Technology

SpringerBriefs present concise summaries of cutting-edge research and practical applications across a wide spectrum of fields. Featuring compact volumes of 50 to 125 pages, the series covers a range of content from professional to academic.

Typical publications can be:

- A timely report of state-of-the art methods
- An introduction to or a manual for the application of mathematical or computer techniques
- A bridge between new research results, as published in journal articles
- A snapshot of a hot or emerging topic
- An in-depth case study
- A presentation of core concepts that students must understand in order to make independent contributions

SpringerBriefs are characterized by fast, global electronic dissemination, standard publishing contracts, standardized manuscript preparation and formatting guidelines, and expedited production schedules.

On the one hand, **SpringerBriefs in Applied Sciences and Technology** are devoted to the publication of fundamentals and applications within the different classical engineering disciplines as well as in interdisciplinary fields that recently emerged between these areas. On the other hand, as the boundary separating fundamental research and applied technology is more and more dissolving, this series is particularly open to trans-disciplinary topics between fundamental science and engineering.

Indexed by EI-Compendex, SCOPUS and Springerlink.

Gianluca Maracchini · Marco D'Orazio

Thermal Comfort in Emergency Architectures

Enhancing Livability in Temporary Housing Solutions

Springer

Gianluca Maracchini
Department of Civil
Environmental and Mechanical Engineering
University of Trento
Trento, Italy

Marco D'Orazio
Department of Construction
Civil Engineering, and Architecture
Polytechnic University of Marche
Ancona, Italy

ISSN 2191-530X ISSN 2191-5318 (electronic)
SpringerBriefs in Applied Sciences and Technology
ISBN 978-3-032-06794-4 ISBN 978-3-032-06795-1 (eBook)
https://doi.org/10.1007/978-3-032-06795-1

This Springer imprint is published by the registered company Springer Nature Switzerland AG
The registered company address is: Gewerbestrasse 11, 6330 Cham, Switzerland

Preface

This book provides an in-depth overview of the challenges of creating adequate, livable indoor environments in temporary housing solutions during emergencies. Ensuring comfortable indoor environments is important, considering that these structures are often designed by neglecting thermal comfort issues since they are intended for short-term occupancy, while instead being occupied for a longer time.

Through a literature review of case studies, the book highlights how indoor hygrothermal environment conditions and energy efficiency are important areas of optimization for these buildings. The effectiveness and reliability of passive and active measures for cooling and heating are explored, providing practical examples from the literature to overcome extreme indoor temperature fluctuations and offer a healthier environment for displaced populations.

The readers will find discussions on the importance of evaluating indoor hygrothermal environmental and thermal comfort through the illustration of an in-depth case study. In particular, experimental and numerical activities are carried out to evaluate the indoor hygrothermal condition of an emergency temporary construction system, and the results are showcased. The effectiveness of passive strategies such as shading, natural ventilation, cool paints, and thermal inertia increase is also investigated to improve comfort and prevent issues like moisture accumulation and mold growth, which can pose serious health risks to occupants.

Intended for architects, engineers, humanitarian professionals, and researchers, this book is a valuable resource for anyone involved in planning, designing, or implementing emergency shelters. It provides actionable insights into creating sustainable, energy-efficient, and thermally comfortable environments for displaced people.

Trento, Italy — Gianluca Maracchini
Ancona, Italy — Marco D'Orazio

Competing Interests The authors have no competing interests to declare that are relevant to the content of this manuscript.

Contents

Chapter 1
Introduction

Abstract In recent years, there has been an increase in conflicts, natural disasters, and migrant crises, necessitating the rapid deployment of temporary housing solutions. These shelters, while crucial for immediate relief, often provide poor indoor hygrothermal conditions, potentially causing health issues during prolonged occupancy. In this context, it is essential to investigating and improving their thermal environments. This book collects and presents the results of a series of experimental and numerical activities carried out by the authors to improve the livability of temporary housing solutions. The comprehensive workflow represents a guide for researchers and practitioners addressing the same issues in this field. The book is structured as follows. First, architectural characteristics and requirements of temporary housing solutions are briefly summarized and presented with a particular focus on the impact of these features on the thermal environment. Then, a scientific literature review of studies addressing thermal comfort in temporary housing is provided. Finally, the authors' experimental and numerical activities are collected and presented. The findings are discussed and compared to other temporary solutions, offering a broader perspective on addressing the challenges of thermal comfort in emergency architectures.

Keywords Emergency architecture · Temporary housing solutions · Thermal comfort · Moisture-related issues · Passive strategies

Conflicts, natural disasters, and migrant crises have become increasingly frequent in recent years, often exacerbated by climate change. These events can lead to severe urban destruction, rendering cities unusable and significantly impacting the sustainable development of urban environments and societies.

In the aftermath of such catastrophes, people often find themselves shocked, traumatized, and deeply concerned about their future due to the loss of relatives,

In this chapter: G.M.: Conceptualization, Methodology, Writing—Original Draft, Visualization, and Project Administration. M.d.O.: Writing—Review and Editing.

G. Maracchini and M. D'Orazio, *Thermal Comfort in Emergency Architectures*,
SpringerBriefs in Applied Sciences and Technology,
https://doi.org/10.1007/978-3-032-06795-1_1

friends, and possessions. Housing provision plays a crucial role in recovery, allowing displaced individuals to regain a sense of normalcy.

Adequate shelter provides the conditions for living with protection, security, comfort, and privacy while also helping to prevent the spread of diseases and reduce mortality rates. However, providing new houses or repairing damaged ones can take time in chaotic post-disaster situations.

To address immediate housing needs, it is of paramount importance to develop and provide temporary accommodations where people can be located as quickly as possible. To address emergency needs, two main forms of temporary accommodation are typically deployed:

- *Emergency shelters*, such as tents, which are intended to accommodate as many displaced individuals as quickly as possible.
- *Temporary housing units*, which offer more stable and protective living conditions than shelters, aiming to ensure basic standards of dignity, privacy, and the ability to resume daily routines.

These housing units are usually built using modular, lightweight, and prefabricated systems that enable fast assembly and are meant for short-term use. Consequently, the quality of the indoor hygrothermal environment is often overlooked during the design phase.

Considering the diverse climatic conditions in which these buildings can be placed and the possible lack of suitable environmental control systems in emergency scenarios, unacceptable indoor hygrothermal conditions often occur during the stay of displaced people. These conditions can include extremely high temperatures in summer and coldness in winter, which may cause diseases and mortality after prolonged exposure. This phenomenon is especially prevalent in countries with hot climates, where these buildings are increasingly adopted. However, it is also becoming more frequent in temperate climates, particularly considering the rise in atmospheric temperature due to global warming.

Although these structures are intended for short-term use, it is quite common for forcibly displaced populations to remain in them for extended periods—sometimes even for years or decades—effectively turning emergency camps into semi-permanent settlements. Currently, it is estimated that over 60 million people worldwide live in temporary accommodations in a state of displacement. This situation underscores the urgent need to investigate the indoor hygrothermal environment of these construction systems, enabling correct improvements to their hygrothermal performance before or during their service life.

While the indoor hygrothermal environment of conventional permanent buildings has been extensively studied in the literature, only a few recent studies have focused on the indoor thermal environment of temporary lightweight units. Considering the possible lack of suitable environmental control systems, passive cooling techniques are preferred to reduce indoor overheating in hot climates. Numerous studies focus on the effectiveness of passive strategies in traditional buildings. However, only a few recent works investigate the impact and effectiveness of these measures when applied to low-cost/emergency construction systems. Moreover, these studies generally focus on applying or optimizing a single passive strategy in a specific climate. At the same time, only a few compare different strategies, consider their effectiveness across various climatic scenarios, and consider costs or operational feasibility.

This book resumes the advancement in the literature for optimizing the thermal performance of temporary housing solutions. It presents an in-depth case study that collects authors' experimental and numerical activities to address these research gaps. The case study provides a comprehensive workflow of activities that may guide researchers and practitioners in optimizing the indoor environment of temporary construction systems.

In particular, the book is structured as follows:

- Chapter 2 presents the main characteristics and requirements of temporary housing solutions, focusing on their impact on the thermal environment.
- Chapter 3 reports a review of studies addressing the issue of thermal environment in temporary housing solutions.
- Chapters 4, 5 and6 collect and revise the experimental and numerical results of the activities carried out by the authors to improve the thermal environment of a temporary housing solution.

Through the different chapters, this book will encompass the following aspects:

- Characterization of the system in terms of in situ thermal transmittance and airtightness performance and experimental monitoring of the indoor hygrothermal environment (Chap. 4).
- Experimental evaluation of potential moisture-related issues, such as internal surface condensation and mold growth, and possible mitigation measures evaluated through numerical simulations (Chap. 5).
- Assessment of the effectiveness of various passive cooling strategies in reducing indoor overheating and thermal discomfort in different climatic locations also considering costs and operational feasibility to provide suggestions on improving the livability of these systems (Chap. 6).

This comprehensive analysis aims to contribute valuable insights into developing and improving temporary housing solutions, supporting more sustainable and comfortable living environments for displaced populations in diverse climatic conditions.

Chapter 2
Design and Requirements

Abstract Temporary housing serves as a critical bridge between immediate shelter and permanent housing, helping affected individuals regain stability and normalcy. This chapter focuses on defining and understanding temporary housing solutions (THS) in terms of minimum requirements and characteristics, providing a valuable reference for engineers and architects when developing THS. First, definitions of emergency shelters, temporary shelters, and THS are provided along with the essential criteria for developing adequate THS according to international standards, i.e., affordability, habitability, cultural acceptability, and accessibility. Then, the technical characteristics of THS are discussed, considering their possible contribution to thermal comfort, including minimum dimensions, shapes, orientation, construction systems, and envelope material characteristics. The importance of using locally sourced, sustainable materials is also discussed, as well as the need for improved thermal insulation and fire-resistant flooring to ensure comfort and safety. The chapter concludes by stressing the ongoing need for research and development to enhance the thermal performance of THS, especially in extreme climates.

Keywords Emergency architecture · Temporary housing solutions · Design requirements · Design criteria · Construction system

2.1 Definitions

Several definitions of temporary housing can be found in the literature [1]. The United Nations Disaster Relief Office [2] defined temporary housing as one of the eight typologies of post-disaster shelter provision. Similarly, Quarantelli [3] proposed a distinction between *shelter* and *housing* due to the unclear and inconsistent ways these terms are often used in previous disaster literature. Accordingly, he defined

---

In this chapter: G.M.: Conceptualization, Methodology, Validation, Investigation, Data Curation, Writing—Original Draft, Visualization, Supervision, and Project Administration. M.d.O.: Conceptualization, Methodology, Writing—Review and Editing.

G. Maracchini and M. D'Orazio, *Thermal Comfort in Emergency Architectures*,
SpringerBriefs in Applied Sciences and Technology,
https://doi.org/10.1007/978-3-032-06795-1_2

sheltering as a place where people are located in the immediate aftermath of a disaster, i.e., when daily activities are still suspended. Differently, he refers to *housing* as a place that allows people to return to their responsibilities and daily routines. Based on this distinction, he categorized four stages of housing provision, i.e.:

1. *Emergency shelter*, where people stay for a short period just after the emergency, such as a public shelter or a friend's house.
2. *Temporary shelters*, such as tents or public mass shelters, in which people stay for no more than some weeks after the disaster.
3. *Temporary housing*, used for six months or several years, where people reside until they are resettled in a permanent place [4] and that allows people to return to their daily routines and activities. They generally take the form of a prefabricated or rented house.
4. *Permanent housing*, which corresponds to the return to the rebuilt or new house to live permanently.

Temporary housing (TH) provision is central to the recovery process of people affected by a disaster. Indeed, although protected, emergency shelters do not allow people to resume their daily lives [4, 5], while temporary shelters are not designed to last longer and may rapidly decay due to external factors [6]. Since the reconstruction/repairing process of permanent housing may take time, TH solutions (THSs) allow for bridging the relevant time gap between temporary shelters and permanent housing [7]. When THSs are provided, security replaces chaos and uncertainty for the first time, helping people feel safe and have social recognition. Moreover, THSs are intended to offer a comfort level that is more consistent with the expected standard of living [4], which is determinant in promoting the return of people to normalcy and which has a primary role in reconstruction programs [8]. In the next sections, common requirements and characteristics among emergency architectures are discussed also by referring to related thermal comfort implications (Sect. 2.2). The sustainability issues of these construction systems are also highlighted (Sect. 2.3).

2.2 Requirements and Characteristics of THS

International law protects the right to access *adequate* housing, i.e., the right to live in security, peace, and dignity. This right contains the freedom of choosing a residence with the security of tenure, preserving protection principles such as protection from forced eviction. Governments must ensure this right when individuals or groups, including refugees and internally displaced people, cannot access adequate housing, especially during crises [9].

The concept of "*adequacy*" is more than having a house with four walls and a roof. It underlines the importance of including the availability of services in a shelter response, a settlement lens, and cultural identity. "*Adequate*" housing should ensure the security of tenure and should meet several critical criteria, such as

- *Affordability*, i.e., the cost should allow occupants to maintain access to other vital goods and services necessary for living with dignity.
- *Habitability*, i.e., the structure should ensure physical safety, provide sufficient living space with optimal lighting conditions, ventilation, and thermal comfort, and offer access to adequate water, sanitation, and hygiene facilities. It should also provide areas for the diverse needs of household members, such as sleeping, food preparation, eating, and storage.
- *Cultural acceptability*, i.e., the housing should align with the occupants' cultural norms and practices.
- *Accessibility*, i.e., housing should be usable by all, including those with mobility limitations.
- *Location*, i.e., the housing should be in an area with easy access to employment opportunities and crucial community services.

In an emergency, quickly providing temporary accommodation is paramount as part of life-saving responsibilities and mandate of humanitarian actors. Indeed, post-disaster accommodations are more than just bricks and mortar or a tent; they safeguard those uprooted from adverse weather conditions providing a safe and healthy living environment while offering privacy, dignity, comfort, and emotional security [10].

The following subsections briefly summarize the requirements and characteristics of emergency architecture in terms of minimum dimensions, shape and orientation, construction systems, material, and thermal properties based on Standards and existing literature. According to the aim of this book, the relationship between these characteristics and indoor thermal comfort is also discussed.

2.2.1 Dimensions

It is a human need and right of a family to have an adequate space to dwell, feel safe, and carry out essential domestic activities. A dwelling must ensure privacy and separation between sexes, different age groups, and families within a given household according to cultural and social norms. With this regard, the dimensions of an emergency architecture become highly important for people's well-being.

The United Nations High Commissioner for Refugees (UNHCR) and the Sphere Handbook 2018 provide the minimum requirements for floor space of emergency architectures needed to guarantee an adequate standard of living [9, 10], practically expressing the right to adequate housing in humanitarian contexts. In particular, a differentiation in terms of minimum requirements is considered between warm and cold climates.

In cold climates/seasons, the minimum dimensions of the living space range from 4.5 to 5.5 m^2 per person, with a minimum height of 2 m at the lowest point to minimize the internal volume that requires heating.

Concerning tropical or warm climates/seasons, the minimum covered living space per person is reduced to 3.5 m^2, since, based on cultural habits, certain activities, such as cooking, can be carried out outside. Thus, these dimensions exclude cooking facilities and kitchen spaces, while shaded external spaces adjacent to the shelter can be established for these activities. Concerning the height, a value higher than the "cold" prescriptions is considered (2.6 m) to aid circulation and ventilation.

Based on these considerations, cold minimum dimensions should be always considered when

- more time is expected to be spent inside (e.g., cooking, eating, and studying);
- the building design includes cooking spaces and bathing or sanitation facilities;
- more space is required to store belongings (such as warm clothes and blankets);
- in climates with both cold and hot seasons (e.g., arid climates).

These minimum dimensions, which mainly apply to the emergency phase including THSs, are grounded in the beliefs, principles, duties, and broader rights declared in the Humanitarian Charter. However, it should be noted that they do not consider extra spaces for belongings such as washing machines and fridges or for running home businesses (tailoring, hairdressing, etc.) that may be present when forcibly displaced people have access to income opportunities, such as in more developed countries. Moreover, these minimum dimensions should also be revised considering cultural habits and social norms (for which these dimensions cannot be acceptable), the guidance of national authorities or the humanitarian response sector, and the physical limitations of the context (e.g., confined settlements, dense urban settings, and extreme climatic conditions where shelter materials are not readily available).

2.2.2 Shapes and Orientation

When designing emergency architectures, practitioners and decision-makers must consider the relationship between building shape/orientation and the resulting thermal environment [11]. From the Standards, there are no specific prescriptions or suggestions regarding the shape of emergency architectures, although it may significantly influence the indoor thermal environment.

Gable roofs, for example, generally perform better than flat roofs regarding thermal regulation in summer [12]. Indeed, convex shapes reduce indoor heat gain by naturally creating shaded areas throughout the day based on the angle of solar radiation, while higher interior spaces regulate humidity and heat more effectively than lower ones (see Fig. 2.1). On the contrary, flat roofs can be more widely used in areas with less intense solar radiation or where thermal storage of solar energy is desired.

Concerning orientation, for hot climates, emergency architectures should be designed and oriented to enhance ventilation while reducing direct sunlight exposure. A higher ceiling can aid air circulation, and a covered outdoor area can provide shade, protect from rain, and serve as a space for food preparation and cooking. The roof should ideally have a slope for adequate rainwater drainage and include

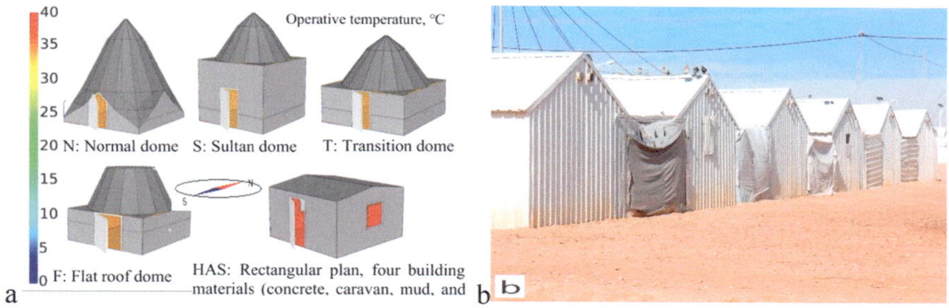

Fig. 2.1 **a** Shape comparison from [11]; **b** transitional shelter [18]

large overhangs for additional shading, except in areas prone to high winds where overhangs may need modification for stability [9].

In the literature, different shapes and sizes can be found for emergency architectures [13]. Common shapes are rectangular, ellipsoidal, and triangular [14, 15] but in some cases, dome-shaped buildings can also be found [11, 15, 16].

Traditionally, the design and layout of emergency buildings have been based on the emergency plans created by local authorities and the UNHCR [15]. As a result, the appearance and style of these buildings can be nearly identical in each refugee colony. Conversely, in areas prone to frequent disasters and experiencing an increasing refugee population, where local resources are scarce, refugees often construct their housing solution under the guidance of technicians. These structures typically incorporate traditional local design elements, with characteristics adapted to the local climate also improving thermal comfort [16, 17].

2.2.3 Construction Systems

Because of their unique architectural functions, the construction systems of THS differ substantially from those of ordinary residential structures. Indeed, temporary buildings must be delivered more quickly than permanent buildings. To this end, most temporary solutions take advantage of low-cost, prefabricated, and lightweight construction systems because of their flexibility and low cost of transportation and deployment.

These construction systems can be grouped into two main typologies, i.e., ready-made units and kit supplies [1].

Ready-made units are usually constructed off-site in the factory and then transported to the site where they will be placed. Since transportation may be complex, they can be disassembled into a few parts to be quickly assembled on-site.

The kit supplies try to solve transportation issues that may arise in areas with difficult access and the need for heavy transport systems (Fig. 2.2). Instead of producing finishing units, they provide small, lightweight, and easy-to-handle prefabricated

Fig. 2.2 "Paper Log" kit relief housing by Shigeru Ban.—Photo by Forgemind Archimedia. *Source* https://www.dwell.com/article/shigeru-ban-architecture-b8178206

elements that can be assembled to build the final unit. In these cases, local people can also participate in the construction process.

Concerning the specific construction technologies adopted, they can vary depending on the climate and type of use. Shelters intended for continuous daytime use may benefit from heavy construction systems with high thermal capacity, especially in summer and warm regions, which help maintain a stable indoor temperature. In this case, attention must be paid to structural design in seismic risk areas.

Conversely, lightweight systems with low thermal mass and good thermal insulation may be more appropriate for shelters primarily used at night, as they quickly adapt to cooler evening temperatures without retaining excessive daytime heat in summer/warm regions. In this case, a timber-based construction system can be employed [10].

Shelters in colder environments would have to withstand the weight of snow and strong winds, which increases their complexity and cost. Therefore, the design standards must account for local weather conditions to ensure structural integrity. Additionally, it is crucial to focusing on minimizing the living space and preventing cold air infiltration in cold-weather emergencies. This can be achieved by sealing rooms with plastic sheeting and sealing tape and using thermal insulation in the building envelope to block cold air and retain warmth effectively.

Finally, it is generally suggested that the design of emergency architecture allows future modifications by the occupants to suit their needs, such as internal partitioning for greater privacy and future expansion [1].

2.2.4 Envelope Materials

Emergency shelter and housing needs are best met when local and sustainable materials and construction methods are adopted. However, external materials are often used, especially when materials are not locally available in sufficient quantities. For this reason, plastic sheeting has become the most common component in many humanitarian responses due to its flexibility and compatibility with rigid materials, making it suitable for a wide range of uses in both rural and urban settings [10]. Since the selection of appropriate materials for the shelter envelope is critical to insulation against outdoor conditions and plays a significant role in improving the indoor thermal environment, in the following subsections, the main materials adopted for wall, roof, and floor elements in emergency architectures are summarized and their adequacy discussed [13].

2.2.4.1 Wall and Roof Elements

Materials adopted for walls and roofs are generally similar in emergency buildings. They can be categorized into finished products (such as expanded polystyrene, inverted box rib, and metal) and natural raw materials (like locally sourced materials and mud). The choice between them mainly depends on different aspects, such as local availability and funding.

If the local government or the humanitarian organizations have sufficient funding to purchase and transport building materials, the housing structures tend to be uniform and orderly [19, 20]. The refugee area receives finished products or raw materials from suppliers directly at the site and technicians who aim to assemble and install them. These standardized houses often lack sufficient consideration of thermal performance, while the degradation of discarded THSs materials, especially EPS, may constitute an environmental challenge [19].

If materials are not provided or political, social, or resource limitations prevent the delivery of necessities to refugees, they often resort to low-quality, inexpensive materials [14]. In such cases, refugees are forced to build homes using materials near their camps, often relying on local resources, aligning with local customs and environmental conditions. In this case, the housing solutions built to meet the varying needs of disaster victims can be quite different [21].

Common local materials include wood, bamboo, reeds, and straw [16, 19, 22–25]. These materials were seen as agricultural waste but now are recognized as key to meeting sustainability goals, contributing to achieving the "6Zs" targets for ecological refugee shelters (i.e., zero emissions, zero energy, zero waste, zero cost, zero indoor air pollutants, and zero environmental impact after demolition) [26]. Local materials significantly reduce material, transportation, and labor costs, but they can also help maintain more stable indoor temperatures throughout the year compared to standardized housing solutions [16, 27]. The use of local materials remains a low-carbon concept, and although many scholars advocate for their increased use [17, 28,

29], further research is needed to understand better how to balance cost-efficiency with high thermal performance.

Several new materials and technologies with energy-saving potential and environmentally friendly properties have been introduced to emergency architecture designs in recent years, such as phase change materials (PCM) [30] and recycled plastics [29]. PCM provides excellent thermal performance and can significantly enhance the thermal storage of lightweight systems [31]. Using PCM makes it possible to reduce the thickness of the building envelope, which decreases the weight [32], while also addressing issues related to indoor temperature fluctuations [30]. In Kuznik et al. [33], it is demonstrated that PCM can reduce maximum indoor temperatures by up to 8.5 °C, extending the hours of comfortable indoor temperatures. However, since THSs are often constructed in extreme climates, technical challenges must be resolved before PCM can be widely adopted. The high cost of PCM is the primary barrier to its application in THS [34], and the material's stability needs improvement, as its performance varies across different climate zones [35]. Even within the same region, the melting point of PCM shifts with the seasons, which can cause adverse effects during specific periods [36]. While these new materials offer great potential for improving the thermal performance and inertia of THSs, there is still considerable room for development.

2.2.4.2 Floor Elements

The floor is a fundamental component of the building envelope. Common flooring materials are included in the building construction and those added by refugees. Since standard building-floor materials, such as concrete and metal, may not provide adequate insulation for a comfortable indoor environment [37, 38], refugees have often adopted self-made solutions, such as using local materials, carpets, and mats inside their temporary accommodation to improve the thermal performance of floors. These makeshift solutions, however, may lead to a severe fire risk, also considering that many disaster victims cook directly on the floor. Therefore, high thermal resistance and fire-resistant flooring should be considered to enhance thermal performance and reduce fire hazards.

2.2.5 Thermal Properties

The most prominent area of research on emergency architecture remains focused on improving thermal insulation and inertia [19, 39–41]. Thermal resistance plays a crucial role in determining whether the indoor climate of a THS is suitable for habitation. Indeed, unlike conventional buildings with high thermal resistance primarily aimed at enhancing energy efficiency in already comfortable environments, in THS, thermal resistance may be the sole factor ensuring a livable indoor climate for refugees.

In traditional buildings, advanced envelope materials are becoming more energy-efficient, green, and sustainable. However, such advancements are more challenging to achieve in THS, where research remains focused on enhancing the thermal performance [38, 42]. Given the wide variations in outdoor temperature and solar radiation across different regions, it is essential to selecting materials with appropriate thermal resistance suited to the specific climate zone [43, 44]. As indicated in Qin et al. [13], higher thermal resistance is generally found in tropical and cold regions and lower thermal resistance in subtropical and temperate areas. This is because higher thermal resistance is more effective at mitigating the influence of extreme outdoor temperatures on the indoor environment. However, examples of low R-values, around 0 $(m^2\ K)\ W^{-1}$, can be found in all climate zones, suggesting that the thermal resistance of THSs is not always tailored to the specific environmental conditions, forcing disaster victims to endure extreme temperatures [14].

Finally, it should be noted that good insulation is advantageous in consistently cold climates or during cold nights but can prevent the release of hot indoor air during warmer seasons, leading to indoor overheating issues [38, 45].

2.3 Sustainability Issues

Temporary housing solutions may be unsustainable from the economic, environmental, and social points of view.

According to UNDRO [2], the price of a temporary house can be higher than that of a permanent one, and even three times more expensive, according to Hadafi and Fallahi [46]. First, temporary houses are often produced in a different region than where they are needed. Importing and transporting units and materials necessarily involve high costs. Then, the costs related to the construction of the whole infrastructure system needed to make the temporary settlements functional (electricity, water, roads, sewerage, etc.) must also be considered. Moreover, the lifespan of a temporary unit is generally short, making the average investment cost per year of use very high [47]. As a result of these high costs, the works on permanent construction may be delayed due to the critical consumption of resources [6].

A discussion on whether temporary housing is needed is crucial, considering the social problems that may arise if people stay in temporary units longer than planned. Indeed, temporary settlements are not designed for long periods of occupation [8]. Making temporary houses more comfortable and resistant, even considering their ephemeral condition, generally means making these buildings more durable than the short time for which they are required. Consequently, when temporary houses are no longer needed, they will still be usable, with the problem shifting to what to do with these large structures. It is not uncommon that there is no plan for that, and then the units are dismantled or deconstructed without concern about future use, which is an approach that causes resource losses [48].

Finally, it should be noted that the temporary settlement site becomes significantly polluted if all the infrastructure, foundations, debris, and garbage are not adequately removed to restore the place as it was before the occupation. The cleaning and dismantling processes represent additional costs [48].

In conclusion, temporary housing becomes unsustainable due to the massive number of resources employed to build the units, the lack of a plan for reuse of houses, and the site pollution.

References

1. D. Félix, J.M. Branco, A. Feio, Temporary housing after disasters: a state of the art survey. Habitat Int. **40**, 136–141 (2013). https://doi.org/10.1016/j.habitatint.2013.03.006
2. UNDRO, *Shelter After Disaster: Guidelines for Assistance* (1982)
3. E.L. Quarantelli, Patterns of sheltering and housing in US disasters. Disaster Prev. Manag. **4**, 43–53 (1995). https://doi.org/10.1108/09653569510088069
4. C. Johnson, Impacts of prefabricated temporary housing after disasters: 1999 earthquakes in Turkey. Habitat Int. **31**, 36–52 (2007). https://doi.org/10.1016/j.habitatint.2006.03.002
5. H. Arslan, N. Cosgun, Reuse and recycle potentials of the temporary houses after occupancy: example of Duzce, Turkey. Build. Environ. **43**, 702–709 (2008). https://doi.org/10.1016/j.buildenv.2007.01.051
6. F. Steinberg, Housing reconstruction and rehabilitation in Aceh and Nias, Indonesia-rebuilding lives. Habitat Int. **31**, 150–166 (2007). https://doi.org/10.1016/j.habitatint.2006.11.002
7. C. Johnson, G. Lizarralde, C.H. Davidson, A systems view of temporary housing projects in post-disaster reconstruction. Constr. Manag. Econ. **24**, 367–378 (2006). https://doi.org/10.1080/01446190600567977
8. C. Johnson, Strategic planning for post-disaster temporary housing. Disasters **31**, 435–458 (2007). https://doi.org/10.1111/j.1467-7717.2007.01018.x
9. SPHERE, *The Sphere Handbook 2018* (2018)
10. UNHCR, *Emergency Handbook* (UNHCR, 2019). https://emergency.unhcr.org/. Accessed 5 Nov 2020
11. S. Ibrahim, M. Ali, B. Baranyai, I. Kistelegdi, Simulation-based analysis of earthen heritage architecture as responsive refugee shelters (Case study: domes of northern Syria), *The International Archives of the Photogrammetry, Remote Sensing and Spatial Information Sciences* XLIV-M-1-2 (2020), pp. 365–372. https://doi.org/10.5194/isprs-archives-XLIV-M-1-2020-365-2020
12. Y. Lin, R. Zmeureanu, Three-dimensional thermal and airflow (3D-TAF) model of a dome-covered house in Canada. Renew. Energy **33**, 22–34 (2008). https://doi.org/10.1016/j.renene.2007.02.002
13. M. Qin, B.T. Chew, Y.H. Yau, Z. Yang, X. Han, L. Chang, Y. Liu, S. Pan, Characteristic analysis and improvement methods of the indoor thermal environment in post-disaster temporary residential buildings: a systematic review. Build. Environ. **235** (2023)
14. R. Thapa, H.B. Rijal, M. Shukuya, Field study on acceptable indoor temperature in temporary shelters built in Nepal after massive earthquake 2015. Build. Environ. **135**, 330–343 (2018). https://doi.org/10.1016/j.buildenv.2018.03.001
15. UNHCR, *Shelter Design Catalogue* (2016), pp. 21–35
16. S. Domínguez-Amarillo, Á. Rosa-García, J. Fernández-Agüera, N. Escobar-Castrillón, Architecture of the scape: thermal assessment of refugee shelter design in the extremes climates of Jordan, Afghanistan and South Sudan. J. Build. Eng. **42**, 102396 (2021). https://doi.org/10.1016/j.jobe.2021.102396
17. D. Albadra, D. Coley, J. Hart, Toward healthy housing for the displaced. J. Archit. **23**, 115–136 (2018). https://doi.org/10.1080/13602365.2018.1424227

18. D. Albadra, N. Kuchai, A. Acevedo-De-los-Ríos, D. Rondinel-Oviedo, D. Coley, C.F. da Silva, C. Rana, K. Mower, A. Dengel, D. Maskell, R.J. Ball, Measurement and analysis of air quality in temporary shelters on three continents. Build. Environ. **185**, 107259 (2020). https://doi.org/10.1016/j.buildenv.2020.107259
19. Y. Yu, E. Long, Y. Shen, H. Yang, Assessing the thermal performance of temporary shelters. Procedia Eng. **159**, 174–178 (2016). https://doi.org/10.1016/j.proeng.2016.08.152
20. F. Moran, D. Fosas, D. Coley, S. Natarajan, J. Orr, O.B. Ahmad, Improving thermal comfort in refugee shelters in desert environments. Energy Sustain. Dev. **61**, 28–45 (2021). https://doi.org/10.1016/j.esd.2020.12.008
21. A. Biswas, A. Puriya, Comparative assessment of Indian post-disaster temporary housing strategies. J. Arch. Eng. **26**, 05019009 (2020). https://doi.org/10.1061/(asce)ae.1943-5568.0000386
22. S. Yang, S. Wi, H.M. Cho, J.H. Park, B.Y. Yun, S. Kim, Developing energy-efficient temporary houses for sustainable urban regeneration: manufacturing homes with loess, pearlite, and vermiculite. Sustain. Cities Soc. **61**, 102287 (2020). https://doi.org/10.1016/j.scs.2020.102287
23. N. Shinohara, M. Tokumura, M. Kazama, Y. Yonemoto, M. Yoshioka, N. Kagi, K. Hasegawa, H. Yoshino, U. Yanagi, Indoor air quality and thermal comfort in temporary houses occupied after the Great East Japan earthquake. Indoor Air **24**, 425–437 (2014). https://doi.org/10.1111/ina.12082
24. A. Copping, N. Kuchai, L. Hattam, N. Paszkiewicz, D. Albadra, P. Shepherd, E. Sahin Burat, D. Coley, Understanding material and supplier networks in the construction of disaster-relief shelters: the feasibility of using social network analysis as a decision-making tool. J. Hum. Logist. Supply Chain Manag. **12**, 78–105 (2022). https://doi.org/10.1108/JHLSCM-01-2020-0007
25. R.M. Garay, R. Herrera, C. Mejías, Project shelter, part 2: structural verification. Revista de la Construccion **18**, 68–86 (2019). https://doi.org/10.7764/RDLC.18.1.68
26. M. Dabaieh, Design and build with straw, earth and reeds for a minus carbon and plus energy building practice, in *IOP Conference Series: Earth and Environmental Science* (Institute of Physics Publishing, 2019), p. 12063
27. M. Dabaieh, The 6 Zs refugee shelter, in *33rd PLEA International Conference—Passive and Low Energy Architecture: Design to Thrive—PLEA2017* (Edinburgh, Scotland, 2017)
28. N. Morishita, S. Haj Ismail, R. Cetin, Pre-design of transitional rural housing for Syria with recycled rubble from destroyed buildings, in *IOP Conference Series: Materials Science and Engineering* (Institute of Physics Publishing, 2017), p. 082024
29. A. Moreno-Sierra, M. Pieschacón, A. Khan, The use of recycled plastics for the design of a thermal resilient emergency shelter prototype. Int. J. Disaster Risk Reduct. **50**, 101885 (2020). https://doi.org/10.1016/j.ijdrr.2020.101885
30. S. Sonnick, L. Erlbeck, K. Schlachter, J. Strischakov, T. Mai, C. Mayer, K. Jakob, H. Nirschl, M. Rädle, Temperature stabilization using salt hydrate storage system to achieve thermal comfort in prefabricated wooden houses. Energy Build. **164**, 48–60 (2018). https://doi.org/10.1016/j.enbuild.2017.12.063
31. L. Xu, W. Zhang, W. Wang, B. Gao, M. Chen, Impact of different improvement measures on the thermal performance of ultra-thin envelopes. Energy **203**, 117802 (2020). https://doi.org/10.1016/j.energy.2020.117802
32. F. Kuznik, J. Virgone, J.J. Roux, Energetic efficiency of room wall containing PCM wallboard: a full-scale experimental investigation. Energy Build. **40**, 148–156 (2008). https://doi.org/10.1016/j.enbuild.2007.01.022
33. C. Wang, S. Deng, J. Niu, E. Long, A numerical study on optimizing the designs of applying PCMs to a disaster-relief prefabricated temporary-house (PTH) to improve its summer daytime indoor thermal environment. Energy **181**, 239–249 (2019). https://doi.org/10.1016/j.energy.2019.05.165
34. X. Wang, W. Li, Z. Luo, K. Wang, S.P. Shah, A critical review on phase change materials (PCM) for sustainable and energy efficient building: design, characteristic, performance and application. Energy Build. **260**, 111923 (2022)

35. X. Mi, R. Liu, H. Cui, S.A. Memon, F. Xing, Y. Lo, Energy and economic analysis of building integrated with PCM in different cities of China. Appl. Energy **175**, 324–336 (2016). https://doi.org/10.1016/j.apenergy.2016.05.032
36. J. Guo, G. Zhang, Investigating the performance of the PCM-integrated building envelope on a seasonal basis. J. Taiwan Inst. Chem. Eng. **124**, 91–97 (2021). https://doi.org/10.1016/j.jtice.2021.04.066
37. Y. Wang, L. Wang, E. Long, S. Deng, An experimental study on the indoor thermal environment in prefabricated houses in the subtropics. Energy Build. **127**, 529–539 (2016). https://doi.org/10.1016/j.enbuild.2016.05.061
38. C. Cornaro, D. Sapori, F. Bucci, M. Pierro, C. Giammanco, Thermal performance analysis of an emergency shelter using dynamic building simulation. Energy Build. **88**, 122–134 (2015). https://doi.org/10.1016/j.enbuild.2014.11.055
39. C. Crawford, P. Manfield, A. McRobie, Assessing the thermal performance of an emergency shelter system. Energy Build. **37**, 471–483 (2005). https://doi.org/10.1016/j.enbuild.2004.09.001
40. L. Zhang, X. Meng, F. Liu, L. Xu, E. Long, Effect of retro-reflective materials on temperature environment in tents. Case Stud. Therm. Eng. **9**, 122–127 (2017). https://doi.org/10.1016/j.csite.2017.02.001
41. X. Meng, C. Wang, W. Liang, S. Wang, P. Li, E. Long, Thermal performance improvement of prefab houses by covering retro-reflective materials. Procedia Eng. **121**, 1001–1007 (2015). https://doi.org/10.1016/j.proeng.2015.09.069
42. R.G. Zafra, J.R.M. Mayo, P.J.M. Villareal, V.M.N. De Padua, M.H.T. Castillo, M.B. Sundo, M.S. Madlangbayan, Structural and thermal performance assessment of shipping container as post-disaster housing in tropical climates. Civ. Eng. J. (Iran) **7**, 1437–1458 (2021). https://doi.org/10.28991/cej-2021-03091735
43. L.F. Cabeza, M. Chàfer, Technological options and strategies towards zero energy buildings contributing to climate change mitigation: a systematic review. Energy Build. **219**, 110009 (2020)
44. F. Ascione, N. Bianco, G. Maria Mauro, D.F. Napolitano, Building envelope design: multi-objective optimization to minimize energy consumption, global cost and thermal discomfort. Application to different Italian climatic zones. Energy **174**, 359–374 (2019). https://doi.org/10.1016/j.energy.2019.02.182
45. L. Huang, E. Long, J. Ouyang, Measurement of the thermal environment in temporary settlements with high building density after 2008 Wenchuan earthquake in China. Procedia Eng. **121**, 95–100 (2015). https://doi.org/10.1016/j.proeng.2015.08.1027
46. F. Hadafi, A. Fallahi, Temporary housing respond to disasters in developing countries—case study: Iran-Ardabil and Lorestan province earthquakes. World Acad. Sci. Eng. Technol. **42**, 1522–1528 (2010). https://doi.org/10.5281/zenodo.1074408
47. C. Johnson, Strategies for the reuse of temporary housing. Urban Transform. 323–331 (2008)
48. H. Arslan, N. Cossgun, The evaluation of temporary earthquake houses dismantling process in the context of building waste management, in *International Earthquake Symposium* (2007)

Chapter 3
Indoor Environment in Emergency Architectures

Abstract Temporary housing serves as a critical bridge between immediate shelter and permanent housing, helping affected individuals regain stability and normalcy. This chapter examines the hygrothermal environment and thermal comfort in temporary emergency shelters, especially when subject to extreme weather conditions often faced in post-disaster scenarios. The chapter also addresses passive strategies, including shading devices, cool roofs, green infrastructure, and natural ventilation, evaluated for their effectiveness in reducing discomfort and enhancing energy efficiency. The role of renewable energy systems is finally analyzed, being considered an alternative solution to active heating and cooling systems. These insights provide a basis for the improvement of the design and deployment of emergency construction systems to effectively meet the user needs of displaced populations in terms of indoor comfort.

Keywords Emergency architecture · Temporary housing solutions · Hygrothermal environment · Thermal comfort · Passive strategies · Active strategies

3.1 Introduction

The design of temporary housing solutions for emergency situations generally needs particular care to ensure the comfort and well-being of occupants. At this aim, several key factors have emerged as essential to creating livable and efficient temporary shelter solutions.

Concerning indoor hygrothermal comfort, maintaining stable temperatures within a comfort range is critical for people's well-being in emergency camps. Insulation, ventilation, and heating systems can be designed for this aim, contributing to the overall resilience of the structure under harsh conditions [1]. Similarly, hygrothermal

In this chapter: G.M.: Conceptualization, Methodology, Validation, Investigation, Data Curation, Writing—Original Draft, Visualization, Supervision, and Project Administration. M.d.O.: Conceptualization, Methodology, Writing—Review and Editing.

G. Maracchini and M. D'Orazio, *Thermal Comfort in Emergency Architectures*,
SpringerBriefs in Applied Sciences and Technology,
https://doi.org/10.1007/978-3-032-06795-1_3

optimization is fundamental to prevent mold growth and moisture accumulation, which is critical for maintaining occupant health. In this case, moisture control measures and adequate ventilation are essential for a healthy and comfortable indoor environment.

Energy efficiency also plays an important role in emergency housing design. With limited energy resources, as may happen in a post-disaster situation, achieving high energy performance through optimized envelopes can be extremely important. Again, design measures such as adequate insulation along with an optimized shelter orientation may passively reduce operational energy consumption, contributing to creating more sustainable emergency shelters [2].

Lastly, external factors such as shading play a substantial role in energy consumption and thermal regulation within lightweight temporary housing. Passive design techniques such as shading devices can reduce the energy demand for space cooling and improve thermal conditions [3].

However, creating emergency architecture that provides thermally comfortable and energy-efficient environments is challenging, due to limited resources and the need for quick deployment, requiring a multifaceted comprehension of the emergency context for selecting the best trade-off. In this chapter, the results of experimental campaigns carried out in the literature to evaluate the indoor hygrothermal conditions of emergency architectures are collected and discussed. Thence, the effectiveness of passive and active strategies used to improve indoor conditions are finally investigated.

3.2 Hygrothermal Environment

The indoor air temperature (T_i) of a THS generally depends on both external and internal conditions. External conditions include outdoor climate, solar radiation, and building materials. Internal conditions, or subjective factors, mainly involve the occupants' behavior that, in an emergency context, can include the opening and closing of doors and windows.

Data collected from various tropical areas shows that T_i is consistently above 20 °C, with peak temperatures of 53 °C [1]. In subtropical and temperate zones, where there are distinct hot and cold seasons, indoor temperatures range from 24 to 51.5 °C during hot seasons and drop below 10 °C, even below 0 °C in some cases, in cold seasons [1]. As a result, refugees often experience unbearable extreme temperatures throughout the day, challenging indoor comfort. These significant temperature fluctuations within the same zone require cooling and heating solutions for improving thermal comfort.

Indoor humidity (RH_i) is another critical factor affecting the livability of THS, though less data is available in the literature. Humidity levels vary widely, with maximum RH_i in the literature ranging from 26 to 100% and minimum RH_i ranging from 10 to 80% [1]. In Pan et al. [4], for example, refugees may experience RH_i values above 70%, which could cause discomfort due to a wet sensation. It should be noted that in emergency contexts, however, the discomfort level can be different from that observed in traditional buildings since, being highly subjective, it depends on the importance given by refugees to the impact of humidity. This notwithstanding, high humidity can lead to objective issues like condensation, mold, and structural decay, which may affect building integrity and, indirectly, occupant health [5, 6].

3.3 Thermal Comfort Assessments

Current thermal comfort models are not always accurate or suitable under specific conditions, with some even demonstrating very low accuracy [7]. This issue is also relevant to THSs, where no specific standards or models for assessing indoor thermal comfort exist. Thence, most researchers rely on existing standards such as ASHRAE 55 [8], ISO 7730 [9], EN 15251 [10], CIBSE [11], and GB 50736-2012 [12] to evaluate THS thermal comfort [1]. These are typically used to determine acceptable temperature and humidity ranges or to calculate indicators like Predicted Mean Vote (PMV) and Predicted Percentage of Dissatisfaction (PPD). Researchers have also employed questionnaires to understand refugees' subjective perceptions of comfort [13].

This raises a fundamental question, i.e., whether using these general standards for THSs and, more in general, emergency architecture is appropriate. Some researchers recognize that such approaches may be partially or entirely unsuitable and have sought ways to refine these methods. For example, the steady-state PMV model tends to overestimate summer thermal sensations in unconditioned buildings in warm climates, but this can be adjusted with an expectation factor [14, 15]. Similarly, acceptable indoor temperatures might be higher in low-humidity tropical desert climates [15]. In contrast, other studies applied standard values for simulations without adjustments or used fixed comfort limits from different guidelines (e.g., a lower temperature limit of 17 °C based on UNHCR [16], and an upper-temperature limit of 25 °C based on EN 15251 [10, 18]), which may not reflect the specific conditions in THSs [17].

Data from the literature on thermal discomfort in emergency architectures has been compiled by Qin et al. [1], covering both single-season and year-round measurements and predicted values. The results showed that thermal comfort is achieved in only 26.47% of cases, while 73.53% fall within the thermal discomfort range, indicating poor overall thermal performance in emergency architectures according to existing standards. However, this does not necessarily mean that refugees cannot endure these conditions. In Thapa et al. [19, 20], 80% of people considered themselves in a thermally comfortable condition with indoor air temperatures higher than 11 °C during winter, which contradicts the thresholds set by current standards. This can be traced back to the high resilience of displaced people that can strongly adapt to indoor conditions while prioritizing basic survival needs like food, clothing, and shelter over thermal comfort [13, 21]. This fact highlights the importance of subjective experiences and expectations in thermal comfort research. Considering the complex psychological state of displaced people, indeed, it becomes fundamental to evaluate how psychological factors influence thermal comfort studies. Several researchers show that results on thermal comfort measurements in post-disaster situations can vary depending on the timing of the measurements [1]. For instance, thermal comfort measurements carried out several years after a disaster often show improved results compared to the same measurements taken immediately after the event, when the psychological distress is generally higher [22]. This is because occupants may get accustomed to their indoor environment, increasing their tolerance to uncomfortable conditions while the time from the disaster increases. In any case, staying for a long time in poorly designed THSs with inadequate living conditions can lead to high levels of psychological distress and health issues, as noted by Morishima et al. [22]. Thus, the improvement of these spaces is strongly needed to improve the lives of the inhabitants.

3.4 Passive and Active Measures for Thermal Comfort

Disaster or emergency camp locations are typically far from energy grids, meaning refugees often face energy shortages. This makes it challenging to regulate indoor temperatures through active measures. As a result, many studies have focused on improving the building envelopes to enhance the building thermal performance through passive cooling and heating strategies [1]. Additionally, renewable energy systems, which have yet to be widely used in THSs, offer further potential for improving indoor thermal comfort. In the following subsection, the main passive cooling, active heating, and passive energy strategies adopted in the literature for improving THS thermal comfort are briefly described and discussed, to provide a useful reference on the different effectiveness level of these strategies in improving indoor thermal comfort.

3.4.1 Passive Cooling Strategies

3.4.1.1 Cool Roofs and Walls

Cool roofs (CRs) and cool walls (CWs) are an affordable and effective passive cooling solution for improving energy efficiency and building comfort. They can be applied to conventional and non-conventional buildings and are particularly useful in reducing the urban heat island effect [23]. Typically, CRs and CWs involve enhancing roof and wall surfaces, respectively, with white coatings or reflective paints, which reflect sunlight and emit infrared radiation, thereby reducing heat absorption [24–27]. In conventional buildings, they also help save energy by reducing the energy needed for cooling systems. Among them, CWs are less effective than CRs due to their higher costs and lower impact on the indoor environment [28].

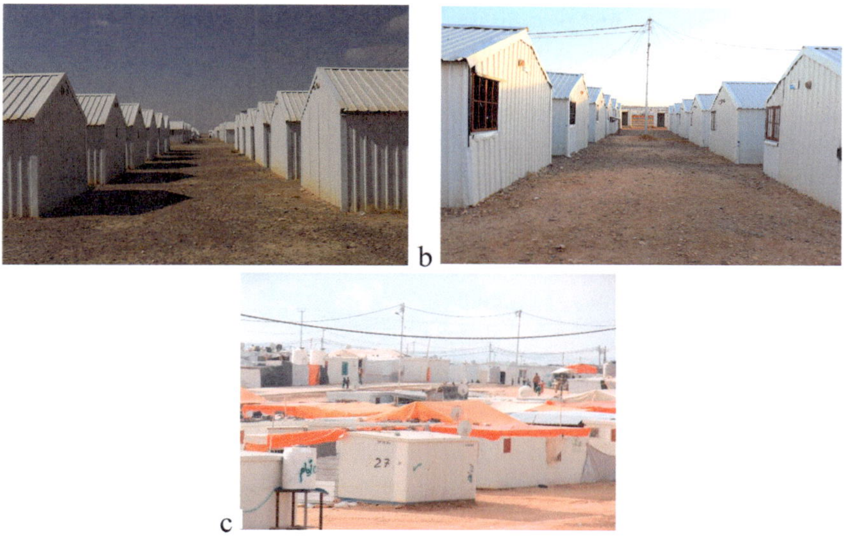

Fig. 3.1 Emergency architecture implementing white surfaces for passive cooling: **a** [15]; **b** [30]; **c** [31]

Due to their low cost with respect to other strategies, CRs are especially valuable where financial resources are limited, such as in emergency scenarios [26, 29]. Unlike other structural modifications, which may be more expensive, indeed CRs only require periodic repainting as long as the roof remains undamaged, making them sustainable over time [28].

In the emergency contexts, CRs have proven to improve thermal comfort, especially in non-air-conditioned rooms, by reducing indoor temperatures by around 3 °C [27]. This notwithstanding, CRs are not yet widely used in THSs. In many cases, THSs are already designed with white surfaces, reducing the need for additional coatings (see Fig. 3.1). Additionally, THSs built from local materials may not allow refugees to purchase cool coatings, which limits their adoption and diffusion.

3.4.1.2 Green Roofs and Walls

Integrating green vegetation with buildings aligns well with sustainable, eco-friendly principles. Whether through green cladding or perimeter greening, vegetation offers unique advantages that other methods cannot match. Greenery not only blocks and absorbs solar energy, reducing heat gain on building surfaces, but also cools the surrounding air through evapotranspiration, helping to mitigate the heat island effect and lower temperatures of the surrounding area [32]. However, the cooling effect can persist even during colder seasons when non-leafing plants contribute to unwanted heat loss.

Despite these benefits, post-disaster relief programs rarely include greenery as part of cooling strategies, with only two studies referencing its use in THSs [33, 34]. Creating dedicated green spaces within refugee colonies could provide long-term refugees with opportunities to grow plants, thereby enhancing biodiversity, addressing heat issues, and improving quality of life [33]. Additionally, placing THSs near green areas or incorporating green cladding on buildings could reduce heat. Some studies have also explored the possible use of green walls in THSs, which may offer multiple benefits, such as passive heating and air purification [35, 36], showing a more sustainable and holistic way to improve the living indoor and outdoor conditions in emergency camps.

3.4.1.3 Shading Devices

Shading devices are a practical solution for preventing direct sunlight from entering indoor spaces, contributing to reducing indoor overheating during the cooling season. Indeed, the sun irradiates the internal and external surfaces of the building envelope throughout the day, increasing their outdoor surface temperatures. High surface temperatures on external walls make heat gains entering the room, which, in lightweight constructions, may lead to higher internal temperatures (T_i) than outdoor ones. Various studies have demonstrated the effectiveness of shading devices in improving the indoor thermal environment, with reductions in T_i ranging from 0.21 to 7.1 °C [14, 15, 30, 37].

In emergencies, shading devices are generally applied to roofs, walls, and windows to reduce heat gain (Fig. 3.2). Roof shading devices reflect a large amount of solar radiation during midday, then reducing the indoor heat gain coming from the roof [17]. Wall shading works well during the day but can trap heat at night, preventing the facade from cooling down [38]. Window shading, installed either inside or outside, reduces the amount of solar radiation entering through windows, with external shading generally considered more effective, reducing the maximum T_i by 4.1 °C, followed by interlayer shading (3.8 °C) and internal shading (1.6 °C) in Samani et al. [39].

The ideal shading system would adjust seasonally, to allow the solar heat gain to pass when beneficial, such as during the heating season. However, adjustable shading devices are generally impractical for THSs due to their complexity [40].

3.4.1.4 Natural Ventilation

Natural ventilation (NV) is one of the most affordable cooling methods, just requiring a correct, strategic location of the openings within the building. Designing an effective NV system is, however, complex since factors such as the number, size, and location of the opening, as well as outdoor wind speed and temperature, generally affect NV airflow within THSs and then its effectiveness as a passive cooling solution [42]. To evaluate the NV effectiveness and optimize the placement and size of ventilation

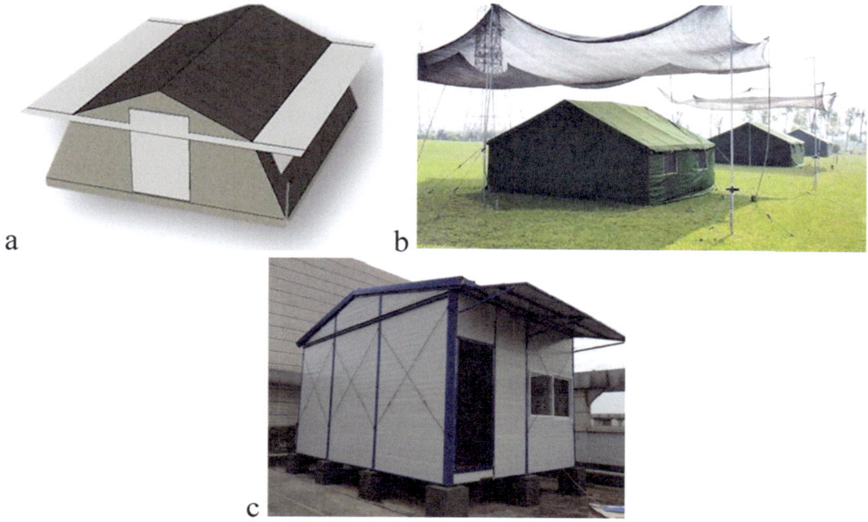

Fig. 3.2 Shading systems adopted in emergency architectures: **a** [17]; **b** [41]; **c** [38]

openings, numerical simulations are generally carried out in the literature, using tools like ANSYS [43], EnergyPlus [29], and BIM [44]. Studies have shown that when the position of window openings is optimized, indoor maximum temperatures (T_i) can be reduced by as much as 15 °C [42].

Several factors are often overlooked in NV strategies. In desertic climates, for instance, NV can be impracticable due to the possibility of sand intrusion and, then, the need to seal windows to prevent sand entry [40]. Moreover, NV can only bring T_i to equilibrium with outdoor air temperatures (T_o) and cannot lower it more than that, necessitating additional passive cooling methods in extremely hot regions [37]. Finally, while most studies focus on single THSs, refugee camps usually consist of densely packed colonies of buildings, where air circulation and ventilation vary depending on the density and location of the shelters, such as in the center or on the periphery of the colony [33]. These factors should be carefully considered for effective NV design in real-world settings.

3.4.2 Active Heating and Passive Energy Measures

During hot summer, improving indoor thermal environments in THSs is more common due to the concentration of refugees in subtropical or tropical regions like Syria, Venezuela, Afghanistan, South Sudan, and Myanmar [45]. Fewer solutions are available for colder areas, where heating is essential, but fewer refugees reside. During the colder months, maintaining a comfortable indoor temperature (15–19 °C) largely depends on the outdoor temperature, the building type, the insulation quality, the building orientation, and the heating system's capacity.

While modifying the envelope material may help, it often cannot fully address the cold conditions within THSs. Passive heating technologies are less effective in these colder regions, and active heating is usually not feasible due to limited resources [37].

Governments sometimes provide active heating equipment, but inconsistent fuel or unaffordable costs make them unreliable [46]. Refugees may resort to homemade solutions for space heating, such as cast-iron coal or wood-burning stoves. Concerning the latter, a stove with a 5–7 kW output is often sufficient to heat a 40–70 m^2 space in most cold regions (see Fig. 3.3). If the furnace is also used for cooking, it is essential to ensuring stability and a clean energy source while considering the possible fire and other risks. Indeed, these solutions generally also come with significant safety risks related to fire, gas poisoning, and asphyxiation [31, 46, 47] while inexpensive fuels, often used out of necessity, may produce low heat and harmful pollutants. To increase safety, catalytic combustion technology has been suggested as a possible solution. However, while this technology offers safer and cleaner fuel combustion, its high cost makes its applicability quite limited for THSs [48].

Off-grid THSs also lack sufficient energy, making active cooling or heating systems not so standard or a luxury [49]. On the contrary, passive energy solutions, such as renewable sources like photovoltaic (PV) systems, are gaining attention as an alternative solution for space heating in emergency scenarios [17, 50] (see Fig. 3.4). PV systems, indeed, can indirectly improve indoor comfort by supplementing energy needs for cooling, heating, and ventilation. In Borodinecs et al. [51], for example, solar panels have been used to reduce fuel consumption by up to 96% in THSs, while providing additional energy for other domestic needs. In Park et al. [52], flexible housing units powered by solar PV systems have also been developed, enhancing units' indoor comfort and energy efficiency.

a b

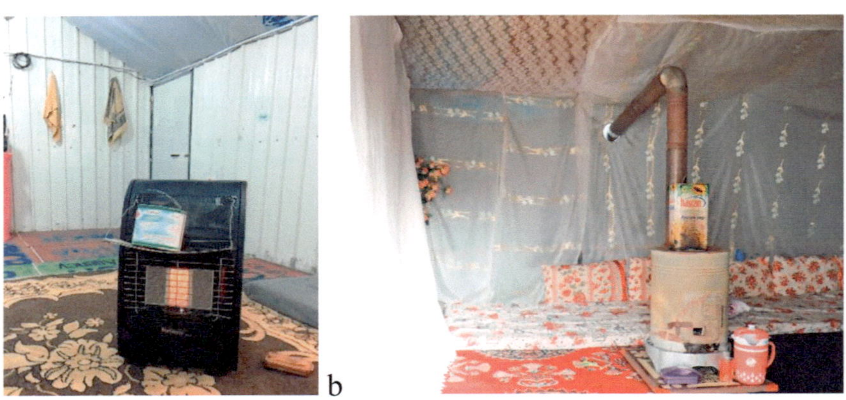

Fig. 3.3 **a** Gas heater used in winter in Azraq and Zaatari refugee camps; **b**) gas hob in self-built shelter in Adana, Turkey [31]

Fig. 3.4 **a** A tent with a PV stand-alone system [17]; **b** integration of renewable energy systems [36]; **c** flexible modular emergency architecture with renewable energy integration [52]

However, it should be said that, while renewable energy-integrated THSs are promising, several issues remain unsolved. Indeed, first of all, the energy generated by PV systems must match indoor demand, which requires careful calculation. Moreover, the high initial investment, long payback periods, and complex supply chains may hinder widespread adoption in refugee camps [53]. Finally, ongoing maintenance and repair costs for PV systems must be also taken into account as their service life increases.

In conclusion, integrating renewable energy and passive technologies into THSs can significantly improve comfort and sustainability, but cost and resource barriers remain critical challenges to implementation on a larger scale.

Acknowledgements Financial support for this activities was provided by the AC-Engineering S.p.A. through the "POR FESR Marche 2014/2020" (Research Project No. 15345).

References

1. M. Qin, B.T. Chew, Y.H. Yau, Z. Yang, X. Han, L. Chang, Y. Liu, S. Pan, Characteristic analysis and improvement methods of the indoor thermal environment in post-disaster temporary residential buildings: a systematic review. Build. Environ. **235** (2023)
2. R. Sarmento, M. Posani, P. Fernandes, A.M. Rodrigues, M.G. Gomes, Energy efficiency in modular emergency shelters: impact of envelope finishings and shadowing. J. Build. Eng. **94**, 110029 (2024). https://doi.org/10.1016/j.jobe.2024.110029
3. S. Liu, W. Ge, X. Meng, Influence of the shading nets on indoor thermal environment and air-conditioning energy consumption in light-weight buildings. Energy Rep. **11**, 4515–4521 (2024). https://doi.org/10.1016/j.egyr.2024.04.032
4. L. Pan, H. Zheng, T. Li, Effects of the indoor environment on EEG and thermal comfort assessment in males. Build. Environ. **228**, 109761 (2023). https://doi.org/10.1016/j.buildenv.2022.109761
5. S. Domínguez-Amarillo, Á. Rosa-García, J. Fernández-Agüera, N. Escobar-Castrillón, Architecture of the scape: thermal assessment of refugee shelter design in the extremes climates of Jordan, Afghanistan and South Sudan. J. Build. Eng. **42**, 102396 (2021). https://doi.org/10.1016/j.jobe.2021.102396
6. L. Bellia, F. Minichiello, A simple evaluator of building envelope moisture condensation according to an European Standard. Build. Environ. **38**, 457–468 (2003). https://doi.org/10.1016/S0360-1323(02)00060-4
7. T. Cheung, S. Schiavon, T. Parkinson, P. Li, G. Brager, Analysis of the accuracy on PMV-PPD model using the ASHRAE global thermal comfort database II. Build. Environ. **153**, 205–217 (2019). https://doi.org/10.1016/j.buildenv.2019.01.055
8. ASHRAE, ANSI/ASHRAE Standard 55. ASHRAE Standard **55**, 2013 (2020)
9. ISO, EN ISO 7730:2005 ergonomics of the thermal environment—analytical determination and interpretation of thermal comfort using calculation of the PMV and PPD indices and local thermal comfort criteria (2005)
10. EN 15251, Indoor environmental input parameters for design and assessment of energy performance of buildings—addressing indoor air quality, thermal environment, lighting and acoustics (2007)
11. CIBSE, CIBSE guide a: environmental design. Envrion. Des. **19** (2015)
12. N. Razali, Y. Wah, Design code for heating ventilation and air conditioning of civil buildings. J. Stat. Model. Anal. **2** (2012)
13. R. Thapa, H.B. Rijal, M. Shukuya, Field study on acceptable indoor temperature in temporary shelters built in Nepal after massive earthquake 2015. Build. Environ. **135**, 330–343 (2018). https://doi.org/10.1016/j.buildenv.2018.03.001
14. O.S. Asfour, Learning from the past: temporary housing criteria in conflict areas with reference to thermal comfort. Int. J. Disaster Risk Reduct. **38** (2019). https://doi.org/10.1016/j.ijdrr.2019.101206
15. F. Moran, D. Fosas, D. Coley, S. Natarajan, J. Orr, O.B. Ahmad, Improving thermal comfort in refugee shelters in desert environments. Energy Sustain. Dev. **61**, 28–45 (2021). https://doi.org/10.1016/j.esd.2020.12.008
16. R. Potangaroa, *Climate Responsive Design Tools for Emergency Shelter, Geneva* (2006)
17. C. Cornaro, D. Sapori, F. Bucci, M. Pierro, C. Giammanco, Thermal performance analysis of an emergency shelter using dynamic building simulation. Energy Build. **88**, 122–134 (2015). https://doi.org/10.1016/j.enbuild.2014.11.055
18. L. Zhu, Y. Yang, S. Chen, Y. Sun, Numerical study on the thermal performance of lightweight temporary building integrated with phase change materials. Appl. Therm. Eng. **138**, 35–47 (2018). https://doi.org/10.1016/j.applthermaleng.2018.03.103
19. R. Thapa, H.B. Rijal, M. Shukuya, H. Imagawa, Study on the wintry thermal improvement of makeshift shelters built after Nepal earthquake 2015. Energy Build. **199** (2019). https://doi.org/10.1016/j.enbuild.2019.06.031

20. R. Thapa, H. Bahadur Rijal, M. Shukuya, H. Imagawa, Study on winter indoor thermal environment of temporary shelters built in Nepal after massive earthquake 2015, in *IOP Conference Series: Earth and Environmental Science* (2019)
21. D. Albadra, M. Vellei, D. Coley, J. Hart, Thermal comfort in desert refugee camps: an interdisciplinary approach. Build. Environ. **124**, 460–477 (2017). https://doi.org/10.1016/j.buildenv.2017.08.016
22. R. Morishima, S. Usami, S. Ando, T. Kiyono, M. Morita, S. Fujikawa, T. Araki, K. Kasai, Living in temporary housing and later psychological distress after the Great East Japan earthquake of 2011: a cross-lagged panel model. SSM Popul. Health **11** (2020). https://doi.org/10.1016/j.ssmph.2020.100629
23. K.L. Uemoto, N.M.N. Sato, V.M. John, Estimating thermal performance of cool colored paints. Energy Build. **42** (2010). https://doi.org/10.1016/j.enbuild.2009.07.026
24. R. Levinson, H. Akbari, Potential benefits of cool roofs on commercial buildings: conserving energy, saving money, and reducing emission of greenhouse gases and air pollutants. Energy Effic. **3** (2010). https://doi.org/10.1007/s12053-008-9038-2
25. V. Costanzo, G. Evola, L. Marletta, Cool roofs for passive cooling: performance in different climates and for different insulation levels in Italy. Adv. Build. Energy Res. **7** (2013). https://doi.org/10.1080/17512549.2013.865556
26. S. Boixo, M. Diaz-Vicente, A. Colmenar, M.A. Castro, Potential energy savings from cool roofs in Spain and Andalusia. Energy **38** (2012). https://doi.org/10.1016/j.energy.2011.11.009
27. D. Borge-Diez, A. Colmenar-Santos, F. Mur-Pérez, M. Castro-Gil, Impact of passive techniques and clean conditioning systems on comfort and economic feasibility in low-cost shelters. Energy Build. **62**, 414–426 (2013). https://doi.org/10.1016/j.enbuild.2013.03.032
28. K. Sun, W. Zhang, Z. Zeng, R. Levinson, M. Wei, T. Hong, Passive cooling designs to improve heat resilience of homes in underserved and vulnerable communities. Energy Build. **252** (2021). https://doi.org/10.1016/j.enbuild.2021.111383
29. D. Borge-Diez, A. Colmenar-Santos, C. Pérez-Molina, M. Castro-Gil, Passive climatization using a cool roof and natural ventilation for internally displaced persons in hot climates: case study for Haiti. Build Environ. **59**, 116–126 (2013). https://doi.org/10.1016/j.buildenv.2012.08.013
30. M. de Castro, N. Kuchai, S. Natarajan, K. Adeyeye, D. Fosas, F. Moran, N. McCullen, Z. Wang, D. Coley, ShelTherm: an aid-centric thermal model for shelter design. J. Build. Eng. **44** (2021). https://doi.org/10.1016/j.jobe.2021.102579
31. D. Albadra, N. Kuchai, A. Acevedo-De-los-Ríos, D. Rondinel-Oviedo, D. Coley, C.F. da Silva, C. Rana, K. Mower, A. Dengel, D. Maskell, R.J. Ball, Measurement and analysis of air quality in temporary shelters on three continents. Build. Environ. **185**, 107259 (2020). https://doi.org/10.1016/j.buildenv.2020.107259
32. A.B. Besir, E. Cuce, Green roofs and facades: a comprehensive review. Renew. Sustain. Energy Rev. **82**, 915–939 (2018). https://doi.org/10.1016/j.rser.2017.09.106
33. L. Huang, E. Long, Architecture and planning design strategy of post-disaster temporary settlement with high building density—analysis based on the questionnaire in Dujiangyan after Wenchuan earthquake. Procedia Eng. (2015)
34. B.N. Del Castillo Velasco Martínez, J.R.G. Chávez, Y.M. Kuwabara, Analysis and evaluation of bioclimatic systems to characterize their performance in experimental modules. Energy Procedia (2017)
35. M. Dabaieh, A.A. Serageldin, Earth air heat exchanger, Trombe wall and green wall for passive heating and cooling in premium passive refugee house in Sweden. Energy Convers. Manag. **209** (2020). https://doi.org/10.1016/j.enconman.2020.112555
36. M. Dabaieh, J. Alwall, Building now and building back. Refugees at the centre of an occupant driven design and construction process. Sustain. Cities Soc. **37**, 619–627 (2018). https://doi.org/10.1016/j.scs.2017.11.002
37. Y. Wang, L. Wang, E. Long, S. Deng, An experimental study on the indoor thermal environment in prefabricated houses in the subtropics. Energy Build. **127**, 529–539 (2016). https://doi.org/10.1016/j.enbuild.2016.05.061

38. Y. Wang, E. Long, S. Deng, Applying passive cooling measures to a temporary disaster-relief prefabricated house to improve its indoor thermal environment in summer in the subtropics. Energy Build. **139**, 456–464 (2017). https://doi.org/10.1016/j.enbuild.2016.12.081
39. P. Samani, V. Leal, A. Mendes, N. Correia, Comparison of passive cooling techniques in improving thermal comfort of occupants of a pre-fabricated building. Energy Build. **120**, 30–44 (2016). https://doi.org/10.1016/j.enbuild.2016.03.055
40. D. Fosas, D. Albadra, S. Natarajan, D. Coley, Improving the thermal comfort in new shelters healthy housing for the displaced design recommendations for Azraq refugee camp (2019). https://doi.org/10.6084/M9.FIGSHARE.8977556
41. Y. Jiang, X. Chen, An experimental study on the improvement of indoor thermal environment of tents by shading in summer. J. Phys.: Conf. Ser. 042087 (2019)
42. H.H. Lin, J.H. Cheng, A study of the simulation and analysis of the flow field of natural convection for a container house. Sustainability (Switzerland) **12** (2020). https://doi.org/10.3390/su12239845
43. M. Dabaieh, Design and build with straw, earth and reeds for a minus carbon and plus energy building practice, in *IOP Conference Series: Earth and Environmental Science* (Institute of Physics Publishing, 2019), p. 12063
44. M. Akeila, C. Preece, K.K.K. Kuok, Evaluating the environmental performance of 3D printed shelters in Jordan. J. Constr. Dev. Ctries. **26** (2021). https://doi.org/10.21315/jcdc2021.26.2.6
45. UNHCR, *Refugee Data Finder—Key Indicators* (2024). https://www.unhcr.org/refugee-statistics. Accessed 9 Oct 2024
46. N. Shinohara, M. Tokumura, M. Kazama, Y. Yonemoto, M. Yoshioka, N. Kagi, K. Hasegawa, H. Yoshino, U. Yanagi, Indoor air quality and thermal comfort in temporary houses occupied after the Great East Japan earthquake. Indoor Air **24**, 425–437 (2014). https://doi.org/10.1111/ina.12082
47. D. Kimemia, A. van Niekerk, R. Govender, M. Seedat, Burns and fires in South Africa's informal settlements: have approved kerosene stoves improved safety? Burns **44**, 969–979 (2018). https://doi.org/10.1016/j.burns.2017.11.006
48. L. He, Y. Fan, J. Bellettre, J. Yue, L. Luo, A review on catalytic methane combustion at low temperatures: catalysts, mechanisms, reaction conditions and reactor designs. Renew. Sustain. Energy Rev. **119** (2020)
49. D.S. Lee, M. Iacocca, Y.K. Joshi, Energy usage modeling for heating and cooling of off-grid shelters. J. Build. Eng. **35** (2021). https://doi.org/10.1016/j.jobe.2020.102054
50. L. Xu, W. Zhang, W. Wang, B. Gao, M. Chen, Impact of different improvement measures on the thermal performance of ultra-thin envelopes. Energy **203**, 117802 (2020). https://doi.org/10.1016/j.energy.2020.117802
51. A. Borodinecs, D. Zajecs, K. Lebedeva, R. Bogdanovics, Mobile off-grid energy generation unit for temporary energy supply. Appl. Sci. (Switzerland) **12** (2022). https://doi.org/10.3390/app12020673
52. B. Park, J. Cho, Y. Jeong, Thermal performance assessment of flexible modular housing units for energy independence following disasters. Sustainability (Switzerland) **11** (2019). https://doi.org/10.3390/su11205561
53. X. Luo, H. Liu, X. Zhao, P. Mao, Managing the additional cost of passive buildings from the supply chain perspective: a case of Nanjing China. Build Environ. **222** (2022). https://doi.org/10.1016/j.buildenv.2022.109351

Chapter 4
The HOMEDONE Experience: Indoor Environmental Monitoring

Abstract Temporary shelters, though designed for short-term use with lightweight materials, are often occupied for extended periods, especially in low-income regions. Despite their provisional nature, ensuring adequate thermal comfort in such structures over time is essential, but limited research exists on this topic. This chapter addresses this gap by presenting the results of an experimental campaign aimed at characterizing and evaluating the hygrothermal indoor environment of the HOMEDONE construction system, i.e., a modular, lightweight shelter constructed from 3D-reinforced EPS panels. Following a preliminary assessment of the in situ thermal transmittance of the panel and the airtightness of a modular experimental unit, the indoor hygrothermal climate was monitored through spring and summer. Findings indicated that low thermal transmittance of the panels and strong airtightness enhance the thermal performance of the system. Still, with closed openings, the indoor temperature and humidity can reach unacceptably high levels during warmer seasons due to the low thermal and moisture buffering capacities of the building elements. Long-term occupancy in hot climates remains challenging for HOMEDONE units, underscoring the need for improvement intervention to mitigate overheating and ensure thermal comfort.

Keywords Emergency architecture · Temporary housing solutions · Experimental monitoring · Hygrothermal environment · Thermal comfort · Airtightness · In situ thermal transmittance

In this chapter: G.M.: Conceptualization, Methodology, Validation, Formal Analysis, Investigation, Data Curation, Writing—Original Draft, Visualization, Supervision, and Project Administration. M.d.O.: Conceptualization, Methodology, Writing—Review and Editing.

G. Maracchini and M. D'Orazio, *Thermal Comfort in Emergency Architectures*,
SpringerBriefs in Applied Sciences and Technology,
https://doi.org/10.1007/978-3-032-06795-1_4

4.1 Introduction

This chapter presents some of the experimental results of the activities carried out by the authors to characterize and evaluate the hygrothermal indoor environment of a lightweight, modular construction system called HOMEDONE [1]. The work can be subdivided into the following three phases:

- First, in situ thermal transmittance measurements were performed on an experimental HOMEDONE unit to expand existing data and provide input for future analytical models aimed at improving comfort and energy performance.
- Second, as dry-assembled modular systems often exhibit substantial air leakage, affecting comfort and energy use, a blower door test was conducted to assess the airtightness of the unit [2].
- Last, indoor temperature and humidity were monitored during spring and summer to identify potential comfort issues and provide benchmarks for simulation and future system enhancements.

4.2 The Case Study

4.2.1 The Construction System

Among the various prefabricated technologies available for emergency housing, systems using synthetic materials like expanded polystyrene (EPS) stand out for their cost-effectiveness and ease of deployment [3, 4]. However, detailed studies focusing on the indoor hygrothermal performance of such systems remain limited [2, 3].

The system analyzed in this chapter, the HOMEDONE system, employs prefabricated panels made of reinforced EPS, designed for rapid assembly and flexibility in emergency or low-income contexts. It has been implemented in scenarios ranging from post-earthquake shelters in Central Italy to field hospitals during the COVID-19 pandemic, as well as affordable housing initiatives in developing nations [5].

These panels consist of a dense EPS core (45–65 kg/m^3) reinforced with a galvanized steel mesh (S235JR [6]), forming a rigid 3D structure (Fig. 4.1). Their standard dimensions—about 120 cm in length and 240–340 cm in height—allow for easy handling and on-site installation without the need for cranes.

HOMEDONE modules can be delivered either as fully pre-assembled units or as flat-pack kits for on-site construction, reducing transport volume and costs [7]. A patented hooking system allows simple assembly using only an Allen key, making it feasible even in remote areas with limited access to heavy equipment or skilled labor, while silicone sealant ensures watertight and airtight joints. Internal and external finishing layers, such as plastic sheets, steel sheets, and multi-layer systems, can be applied upon request.

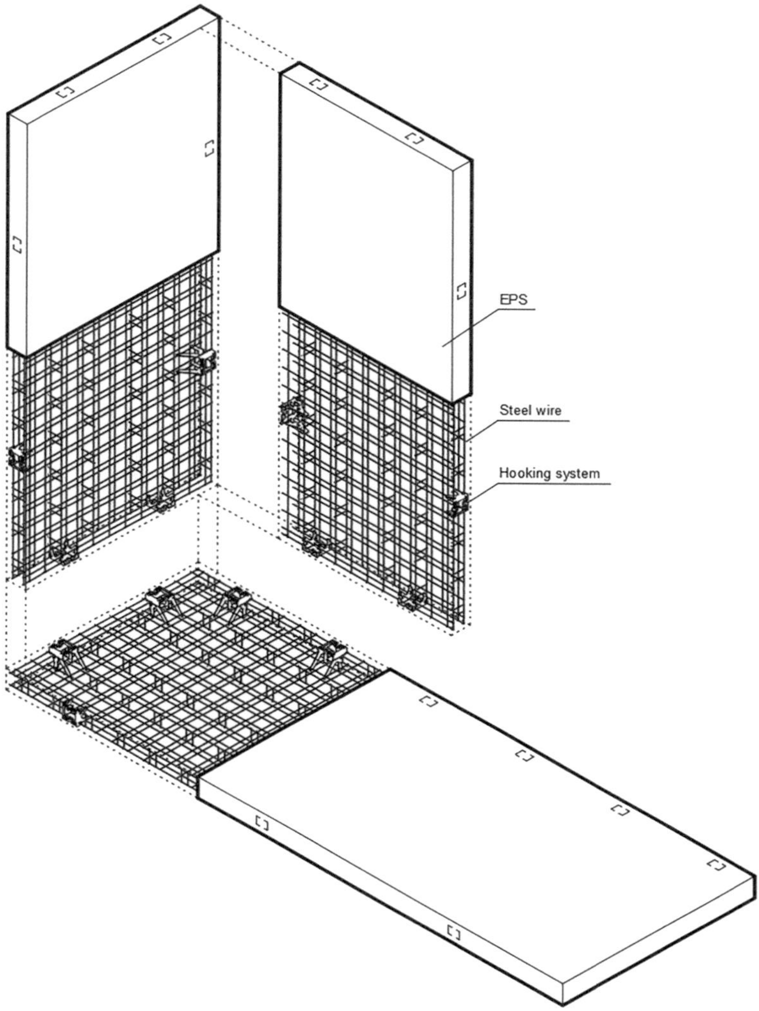

Fig. 4.1 HOMEDONE panels and assembly process

Foundations consist of steel beams and rods, allowing installation on uneven terrain and facilitating removal post use. Thanks to its modularity, the system supports reconfiguration, expansion, and reuse—making it suitable for both temporary and semi-permanent applications [8–10].

4.2.2 Experimental Mock-Up

An experimental mock-up was set up in the Mediterranean climate of Ancona, Italy [11] (Figs. 4.2 and 4.3). This unit, whose main dimensions are reported in Fig. 4.4, represents the smallest one suitable for emergency housing that can be used to build multi-unit homes. The mock-up was constructed off-site using 24 reinforced EPS panels, each measuring 1.2 m × 2.4 m × 0.12 m, except for the two end panels on the longitudinal facades, which were 1.08 m long. The construction of the unit took four hours.

Fig. 4.2 Installation site of the assembled unit

Fig. 4.3 Transportation of the assembled unit

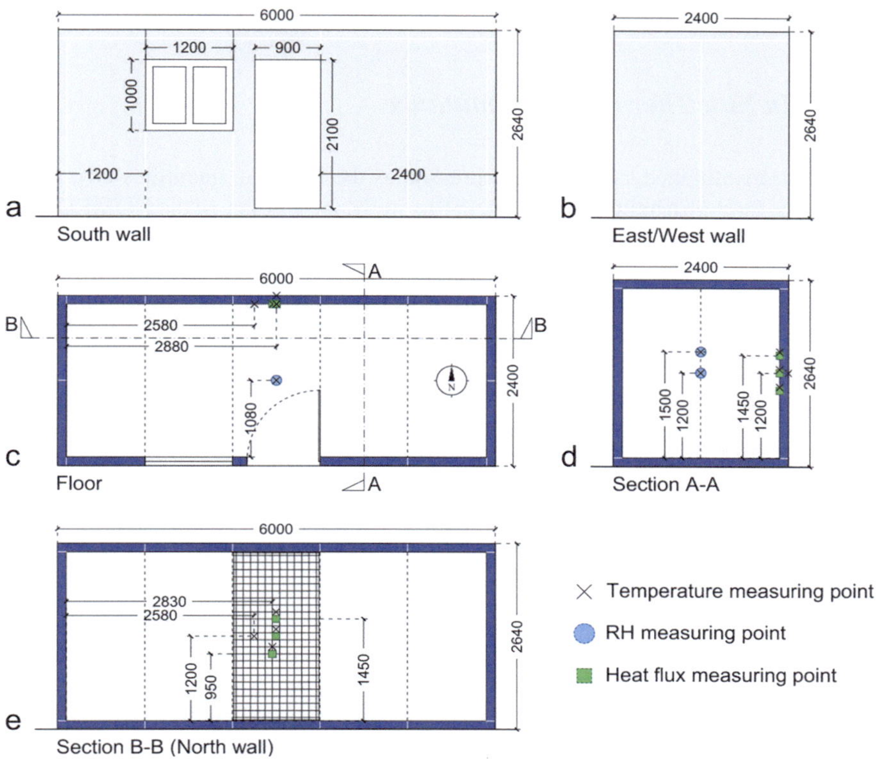

Fig. 4.4 Dimensions (in millimetres) of the experimental unit and sensors placement

One window and one door were installed, specifically both on the south side to simulate maximum solar exposure during the hot season and poor ventilation conditions, as would occur in densely populated settlements [12]. According to technical specifications, the double-glazed window has a solar transmission coefficient of 0.4 and a U-value of 1.42 W/m^{2}K. The external door, a 24 mm thick fiberglass slab with PVC layers, has a U-value of 1.31 W/m^{2}K.

The unit lacked finishing materials, electrical, plumbing, or HVAC systems to simulate worst-case usage scenarios. To ensure air and water tightness, panel junctions and steel connections were sealed with silicone glue.

The unit was then placed on two external steel beams, which provided support and allowed horizontal adjustment. As a result, the unit was raised about 30 cm above ground, preventing direct contact with the soil (Fig. 4.3).

4.3 Methods

4.3.1 In Situ Thermal Transmittance

Thermal transmittance, commonly expressed as the U-value, quantifies how much heat passes through a building element. In this study, the U-value of the HOMEDONE panel was measured directly on-site to (i) assess the actual thermal performance of the system, (ii) complement existing performance data, and (iii) provide robust input for subsequent simulations. On-site testing is especially relevant for composite panels like those in HOMEDONE, where theoretical estimates may not reflect real conditions accurately [13–17].

To determine both the air-to-air transmittance (U) and the surface-to-surface conductance (Λ), the heat flow meter method was applied, in accordance with the standard ISO 9869-1:2014 [18]. This method involves continuous monitoring of heat flux across the panel, along with the corresponding air and surface temperatures on both sides of the wall.

To improve the reliability of the data, specific precautions were adopted as prescribed by the standard:

- Measurements were taken on the north-facing wall, to avoid direct solar radiation.
- The external surface temperature sensor was positioned at the center of the panel and covered with white duct tape, chosen to match the color and reflective properties of the EPS surface and reduce external thermal interference.
- Three heat flux meters and four thermocouples were installed on the north wall, placed away from known thermal bridges. This arrangement helped verify the uniformity of thermal behavior, including any influence from internal steel reinforcements.

Figure 4.4 shows the location of the sensors. The heat flux q was measured using Hukseflux HFP01 sensors (accuracy $\pm 5\%$), installed on the inner face of the panel. Surface temperatures (T_{si} and T_{so} for indoor and outdoor surface, respectively) were monitored using PT-100 thermocouples, while air temperatures (T_i and T_o for indoor and outdoor air temperatures, respectively) were recorded using DMA 572.1 LSI Lastem thermohygrometers (uncertainty of 0.1 °C and 1.5% RH). The indoor sensor was placed at room center, 1.2 m above floor level, and the outdoor sensor was positioned on the roof, protected from weather exposure.

Data logging occurred at 1-min intervals using an LSI Lastem ELO105 data logger, storing averaged values every 10 min. The U-value was computed using the average method, as recommended by ISO 9869-1:2014, due to its ease of use and fast data processing. The method applies the following formulas:

$$U = \frac{\sum_{j=1}^{n} q_j}{\sum_{j=1}^{n} \left(T_{ij} - T_{oj}\right)} \tag{4.1}$$

$$\Lambda = \frac{\sum_{j=1}^{n} q_j}{\sum_{j=1}^{n}\left(T_{sij} - T_{soj}\right)} \tag{4.2}$$

The total monitoring period was defined based on [18], which states that measurements must extend over a minimum of three days, continuing until the values calculated over three consecutive nights differ by no more than 5%. Since the tested wall is a lightweight construction—characterized by a specific heat capacity per unit area below 20 kJ/m^{2}K—only nighttime data was considered, to eliminate the influence of solar gains and ensure stability of the thermal gradient.

To further guarantee the reliability of the results, a minimum indoor–outdoor temperature difference of 3 °C was maintained during the entire test, in line with literature recommendations [19]. To achieve this, a small electric heater was used inside the experimental unit, stabilizing the internal temperature around 24.5 °C. This setup produced a thermal gradient higher than 5 °C, which was adequate for obtaining accurate and consistent transmittance values.

4.3.2 Airtightness

Modular dry-assembly construction systems are typically more prone to air leakage than conventional masonry or cast systems [2]. To assess the airtightness performance of the HOMEDONE solution and to guide potential design improvements, a Blower Door Test (BDT) was conducted following standard protocols [20]. This test, widely used in both research and practice, relies on the principle of mass conservation, where the airflow rate introduced or extracted via a fan equals the amount lost through gaps in the building envelope.

The test was carried out using an Infiltec Blower Door E-3 220 v connected to the entrance opening of the unit (Fig. 4.5), enabling control of indoor pressure. A digital gauge (Infiltec DM4) was used simultaneously to record pressure and airflow, featuring a range of ±1250 Pa (accuracy 0.1 Pa) and 50–11,050 m^3/h (accuracy ±5%).

To simulate a conservative (worst-case) scenario, the experimental module was left without any internal or external finishes. Panel junctions were sealed with silicone only, and no electrical or HVAC systems were installed. This configuration allowed evaluation of the basic airtightness performance of the construction system under early-use or emergency conditions.

Air leakage measurements were performed with closed openings, in line with Methods 1 and 2 from [21]. Five increasing pressure differences (ΔP) were applied, with 5 Pa increments, starting from the lowest measurable flow (approximately 50 m^3/h). All measurements were corrected to account for baseline pressure drift and for air density variations between indoor and outdoor environments.

Fig. 4.5 Fan (de)pressurization test equipment

Data collected during the depressurization phase were plotted on a log–log graph of flow rate versus pressure differential. Using the least-squares method, two key parameters were extracted:

- the flow coefficient C_{env} [$m^3/(h\ Pa^n)$]
- the flow exponent n.

These values fit the following empirical model:

$$q_{env} = C_{env} \cdot \Delta P^n \tag{4.3}$$

where q_{env} represents the airflow rate through the building envelope (m^3/h).

To account for standard atmospheric conditions (20 °C, 101,325 Pa), the airflow coefficient C_{env} was converted to a normalized value C_L, as recommended by the reference standard [21]. Using this adjusted coefficient, the air leakage rate at any reference pressure ΔPr can be computed through the equation:

$$q_{pr} = C_L \cdot \Delta P_r^n \tag{4.4}$$

Once the normalized airflow coefficient C_L was obtained, the leakage rate at a reference pressure of 50 Pa (denoted as q_{50}) was computed using Eq. (4.4). From this reference value, several commonly adopted airtightness indicators can be derived such as the air change rate at 50 Pa (n_{50}):

$$n_{50} = \frac{q_{50}}{V} \tag{4.5}$$

where V represents the internal volume of the tested unit [21].

Before running the official test sessions, preliminary trials were conducted to verify that environmental and technical conditions were within acceptable limits, as outlined in ISO 9972 [21]. These prerequisites included

- ensuring that the product of the indoor–outdoor temperature difference and the building height remained below 250 m K;
- confirming that wind speed near ground level was under 3.0 m/s, or that Beaufort force remained below level 3;
- verifying that the correlation coefficient (R^2) for the regression used to derive C and n was greater than 0.98;
- ensuring the airflow exponent n fell within the 0.5–1.0 range.

Wind conditions near the ground were initially estimated visually using the Beaufort scale, then confirmed through hourly records from a nearby meteorological station positioned at a higher elevation than the test site. Since wind speed increases with altitude, compliance with the standard could reasonably be assumed when the recorded speed fell below the required threshold [20, 22].

4.3.3 Hygrothermal Measurements

To assess the hygrothermal performance of the prototype unit and support appropriate design improvement for thermal comfort, a four-month monitoring campaign was carried out, spanning from March 3 to July 4, 2017.

The indoor environment was monitored in free-running conditions, meaning the module was unoccupied and not equipped with any heating, cooling, or mechanical ventilation systems—a configuration consistent with real-world scenarios in temporary settlements or off-grid contexts.

Using the equipment described in Sect. 4.3.1, measurements included (Fig. 4.4).

- indoor and outdoor air temperature and relative humidity (RH);
- internal surface temperatures and heat flux on the north-facing wall;
- external weather variables, such as global and diffuse solar radiation and atmospheric pressure, sourced from a nearby weather station.

At the beginning of the campaign, the window remained closed, replicating conditions of poor ventilation, as often observed in crowded emergency contexts. Later in the study, a small ventilation opening of approximately 0.08 m^2 was introduced to simulate natural air exchange due to stack effect and infiltration through construction joints. The size of the opening was calculated to produce an air change rate of roughly 0.4 h^{-1}, excluding additional infiltration, in accordance with [23, 24].

This experimental setup allowed to investigate the influence of outdoor climate conditions—in particular, temperature and solar gains—on the thermal behavior of the indoor environment under realistic occupancy constraints.

4.3.4 Thermal Comfort Assessment

A preliminary evaluation of thermal comfort was carried out on a selection of representative days using the adaptive comfort model described in [23]. This approach, typically used for buildings without active cooling, has also been recently adapted for temporary shelters [25]. For each warm day, the acceptable operative temperature range (T_c) was determined based on Eq. (4.6), applying an 80% acceptability threshold, which corresponds to category II comfort (moderate expectation). As suggested in [25], the model was modified to better reflect conditions where the running mean temperature (T_{rm}) dropped below 10 °C or exceeded 30 °C—thresholds not originally covered in the EN 15251 formulation:

$$T_c = \begin{cases} 23.75 \pm 3\,^{\circ}\mathrm{C} & T_{rm} < 10\,^{\circ}\mathrm{C} \\ 20.75\,^{\circ}\mathrm{C} \div (0.33T_{rm} + 21.8\,^{\circ}\mathrm{C}) & 10\,^{\circ}\mathrm{C} < T_{rm} < 15\,^{\circ}\mathrm{C} \\ 0.33T_{rm} + 18.8 \pm 3\,^{\circ}\mathrm{C} & 15\,^{\circ}\mathrm{C} < T_{rm} < 30\,^{\circ}\mathrm{C} \\ 28.70 \pm 3\,^{\circ}\mathrm{C} & T_{rm} > 30\,^{\circ}\mathrm{C} \end{cases} \tag{4.6}$$

In this analysis, the operative temperature—used to assess compliance with the acceptable comfort range (T_c)—was approximated by the indoor air temperature (T_i). This simplification, deemed adequate for a first-level comfort assessment, is supported by preliminary simulation results. Moreover, the assumption is justified by two main factors:

i. the limited window-to-wall ratio, which minimizes the influence of solar gains on the mean radiant temperature, and
ii. the compact geometry and low thermal mass of the unit, which reduce spatial temperature differences between air and surfaces [26].

4.4 Results

4.4.1 In Situ Thermal Transmittance

Before the tests, the thermal homogeneity of the panel internal surface was assessed by comparing temperature and heat flux values at different locations. No significant variations were observed between the surface temperatures and heat flux measurements, indicating that the embedded steel bars did not significantly affect the surface temperature.

Figure 4.6 reports the indoor and outdoor surface and air temperatures (T_{si} and T_{so}, and T_i and T_o, respectively) and the heat flux (q) measured from May 13 to 17, 2017. The graph also shows the calculated conductance (Λ) and air-to-air U-value (thermal transmittance) both equal to 0.24 W/(m^{2}K). This value is significantly lower than the values typically seen in other temporary housing (0.43–0.60 W/m^{2}K, as noted by Tanyer et al. [2]) and even below the standards set by Italian regulations for new buildings in Ancona (0.34, 0.32, and 0.30 W/m^{2}K for walls, slabs, and roofs, respectively). This low U-value is attributed to the thickness of the EPS panels.

From Λ, the conductivity (λ) of the homogenized materials was calculated as 0.0288 W/(mK).

4.4.2 Airtightness

Table 4.1 reports the results of the pressurization method. Ambient parameters measured successfully met test condition requirements. The airflow exponent (n) was slightly below the upper bound equal to 1.0. Since n theoretically ranges from 0.5 (large openings with turbulent flow) to 1.0 (small openings with laminar flow), it can be inferred that most of the air leakage paths in the unit can be categorized as “small openings” [27, 28]. As a result, an infiltration rate n_{50} of 2.55 h^{-1} was obtained denoting a good airtightness improving thermal and energy efficiency during the heating season. Indeed, while general comparisons with other construction systems

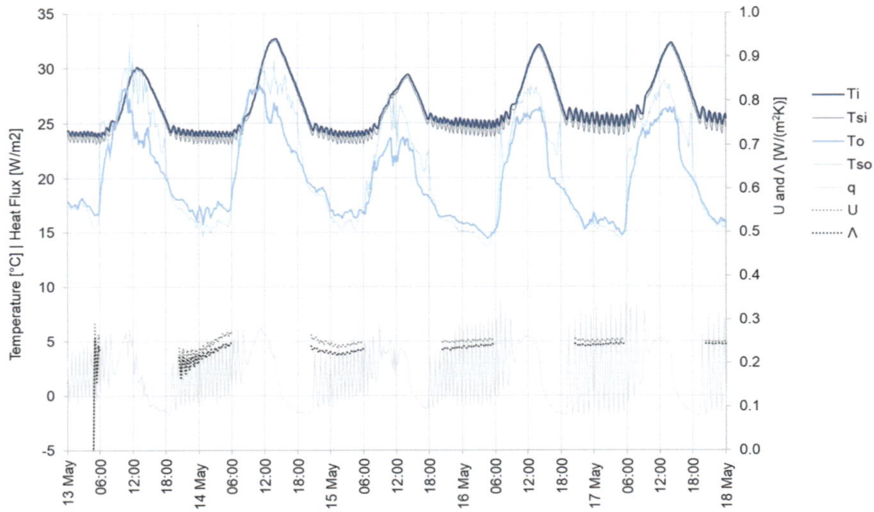

Fig. 4.6 Experimental measurements and in situ thermal transmittance (U)/conductance (Λ) calculation

Table 4.1 BDT results

C_{env}	n	R^2	C_L	q_{50} (m^3/h)	n_{50} (h^{-1})
4.294	0.737	0.993	4.264	76.05	2.55

are challenging due to the varying factors affecting n_{50} values (such as unit geometry, number and type of openings, and finishing systems), this value is lower than those typically found in temporary units like container houses, which range from 9.0 to 25.0 h^{-1} [2]. This superior airtightness is likely due to the effective sealing of the panels with silicone and the minimal number of openings. To further improve airtightness, it can be recommended to apply internal and external finishing layers, which were not used in this study to simulate the worst-case scenario.

4.4.3 Indoor Hygrothermal Environment

This section reports selected result from the indoor hygrothermal monitoring of the experimental unit. Given the large amount of data collected, only a few representative days are shown—specifically, those characterized by clear sky conditions, with closed openings (Sect. 4.4.3.1) and slightly open windows (Sect. 4.4.3.2).

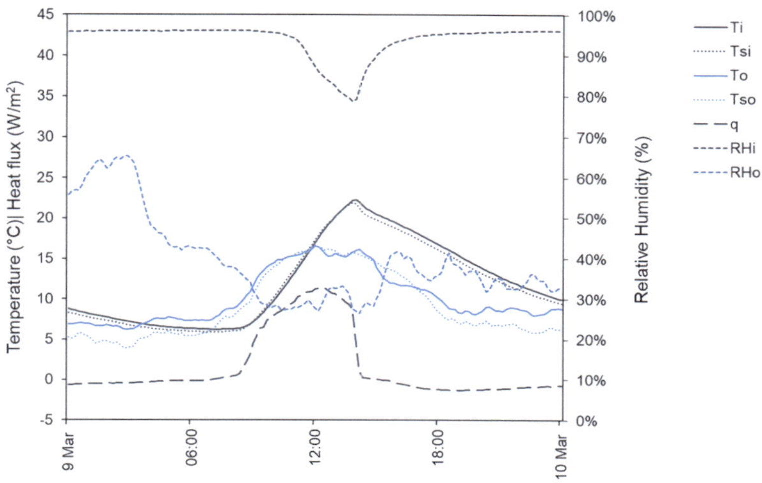

Fig. 4.7 Measurements of a representative day with window closed and clear sky

4.4.3.1 Indoor Environment with Closed Openings

Figure 4.7 shows the monitoring results for a representative clear-sky day, specifically March 9, 2017. During this day, the window remained closed to replicate critical conditions often encountered in overcrowded emergency settlements, where adjacent units may block airflow and limit ventilation [29]. Outdoor temperatures gradually rose from 7 to 16 °C, while global solar radiation peaked at 715 W/m^2, with diffuse radiation contributing about 35% of the total.

The comparison between indoor air temperature (T_i) and internal surface temperature (T_{si}) indicated negligible differences, consistent with the small volume of the unit, which limit temperature stratification (see Fig. 4.7).

Then, the indoor air behavior was analyzed over the day and two distinct thermal phases were observed over the 24-h period:

- a heating phase from approximately 07:00 to 14:00, where T_i progressively increased;
- a cooling phase from 14:00 to 07:00, characterized by a steady decrease in T_i.

Heating Period

The heating phase observed during the daytime can be divided into two distinct sub-periods:

- from 07:00 to 08:00, when the indoor air temperature (T_i) remained stable and lower than the outdoor temperature (T_o);

- from 08:00 to 14:00, where T_i began to increase progressively, eventually exceeding T_o.

In the early morning (first sub-phase), the high thermal resistance of the building envelope became apparent. Despite the outdoor temperature rising with the sun, the interior remained thermally inert, as evidenced by minimal heat flux (q) through the north wall (see Fig. 4.7). Around 08:00, when direct sunlight began entering through the south-facing window, T_i started to rise (second sub-phase), and heat transfer through the envelope increased. The heat flux peaked at approximately 10 W/m^2, indicating the onset of solar gains both through glazing and conduction.

Interestingly, T_i continued to rise even as T_o leveled off or slightly declined, reaching a maximum differential of about 6 °C. The alignment of the indoor and outdoor temperature peaks, with no significant delay, confirmed the lack of thermal inertia in the lightweight structure. Since the window and door remained closed, the absence of ventilation contributed to overheating inside the module.

It is also worth noting that, until approximately 18:00, the external surface temperature on the north wall (T_{so}) was generally higher than the ambient air temperature (T_o), with peak differences reaching 3 °C. This was likely caused by reflected solar radiation from nearby surfaces, such as the ground or adjacent units, contributing to localized warming of the façade.

Cooling Period

During the cooling period, i.e., from around 14:00 to 7:00, the mock-up position relative to nearby buildings prevented further solar radiation from entering through the south window. As a result, T_i began to decrease, following the reduction in solar heat gain (Fig. 4.7). However, T_i remained higher than T_o through time, indicating the low capacity of the system to release heat to the outdoor environment. This was further evidenced by the low negative (outward) q measured in the north wall during this period.

Concerning surface temperatures, at night, from approximately 18:00 to 7:00, T_{so} was consistently lower than T_o, with a maximum temperature difference of 3 °C. This was likely caused by the "sky-cooling" effect, where the building envelope loses heat at night due to longwave radiation exchange with the atmosphere.

Relative Humidity and Moisture Issues

Regarding relative humidity (RH), with the openings closed, the indoor RH values were consistently higher than the outdoor RH, with indoor RH staying close to 95% at night. During the daytime, indoor RH dropped as the air temperature inside the unit increased.

These high RH levels were likely caused by the evaporation of water droplets that formed overnight due to condensation on the internal surfaces of the unit. This was

Fig. 4.8 Roof interior surface condensation

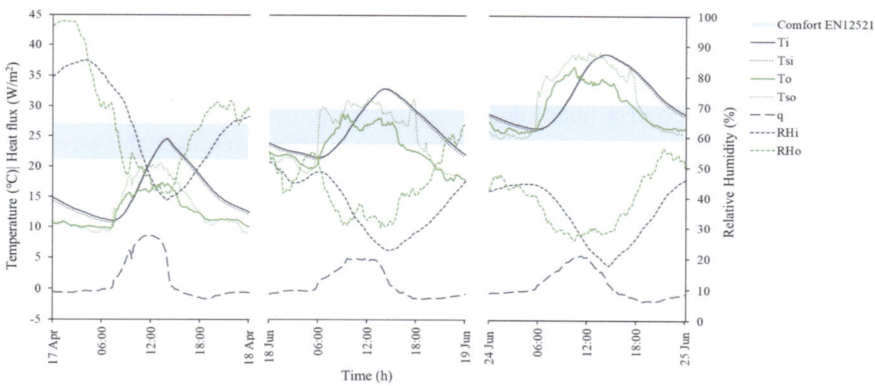

Fig. 4.9 Measurements of three representative days with the window opened and clear sky

observed mainly at the junctions of the roof panels and the north wall panels (see Fig. 4.8). The condensation issues, likely a combined result of the sky-cooling effect and thermal bridges, will be explored further through hygrothermal simulations in Chap. 5.

Indoor Environment with Natural Ventilation

To enhance moisture exchange between indoor and outdoor environments and simulate realistic use conditions [29], the window was slightly opened, creating an opening area of 0.08 m^2. Figure 4.9 shows the measurements taken on three sunny days with open windows. During these days, outdoor temperatures (T_o) peaked between 25 and 37 °C, with global solar radiation reaching 909, 960, and 899 W/m^2, and diffuse radiation accounting for approximately 40% of the total.

As expected, the open window allowed indoor relative humidity (RHi) to more closely follow outdoor levels (RHo), ranging from 20 to 50%. Additionally, no condensation caused by sky-cooling effects was observed. However, despite improved natural ventilation from the stack effect, solar radiation between 12:00 and 15:00 still led to indoor overheating, with a temperature difference of up to 7 °C between indoor (T_i) and outdoor air temperatures (T_o). The open window helped release some heat through natural ventilation but was insufficient to prevent overheating completely.

4.4.4 Thermal Comfort Assessment

Preliminary thermal comfort assessments were made by comparing the indoor operative temperature (assumed equal to air temperature) with the acceptable limits as per [23]. At night, when outdoor temperatures fell below the lower comfort threshold, achieving indoor thermal comfort was challenging, even though indoor temperatures remained higher than outdoors (as observed on April 17 and June 18 in Fig. 4.9). This suggests that occupants may experience cold at night and should keep windows closed during the coldest hours unless the indoor temperature is lower than the outdoor temperature. During the day, temperatures were more comfortable on cooler days (e.g., April 17), but overheating and discomfort were more pronounced on hotter days (e.g., April 18 and June 24). In these cases, keeping windows and doors open is recommended to reduce overheating.

4.5 Discussion

This section discusses the main experimental results obtained from the experimental activities described in the previous sections. In particular, the experimental campaign provided valuable insights into the hygrothermal behavior of the HOMEDONE unit when exposed to external environmental factors. The results showed that, without HVAC, solar shading, or natural ventilation (as could be the case in densely packed emergency camps), the indoor air temperatures in the unit were significantly higher than the outdoor ones, with a maximum difference of about 7 °C during the day and little thermal shift. This pattern aligns with findings from studies on other lightweight temporary disaster-relief housing [30–32]. The main causes are the limited thermal storage capacity of the EPS material, the low thermal transmittance of the HOMEDONE panels, and the good airtightness of the system. Unlike heavier construction systems, which benefit from higher thermal inertia, the low thermal storage capacity of the EPS panels led to a quicker thermal response to external factors, especially solar radiation entering through the window. Furthermore, the low thermal transmittance and airtightness contributed to daytime overheating by restricting outward heat transfer.

Regarding relative humidity (RH), indoor RH values reached a constant 95% during the night, primarily due to the EPS panels' low ability to absorb moisture when the window remained closed. At night, the surface temperatures at panel junctions fell below the indoor air temperature, causing condensation on internal surfaces. Because the EPS panels do not absorb liquid water on their inner side, the water droplets evaporate during the day, adding moisture to the indoor air and driving higher RH levels. The limited vapor permeability of the EPS, combined with poor natural ventilation due to the airtightness, restricts moisture exchange between indoor and outdoor environments. This results in consistently high indoor moisture levels, creating unhealthy conditions that increase the risk of mold growth [33].

However, experimental results demonstrated that indoor humidity levels quickly resemble outdoor conditions when minimal natural ventilation is introduced (for example, by slightly opening a window, as would typically occur in real usage scenarios or if the unit has more openings with reduced airtightness).

Finally, several general conclusions can be drawn from the preliminary comfort assessments:

- During the heating season, indoor overheating may improve comfort levels for occupants. However, solar heat gain is minimal on cloudy or rainy days, meaning indoor overheating rarely occurs. At night, the indoor temperatures gradually align with outdoor levels due to the low thermal storage capacity of the system, meaning additional heating equipment would be necessary to maintain adequate comfort during colder months.
- In the cooling season, daytime overheating can negatively affect comfort. Indoor temperatures potentially rise above skin temperature, leading to discomfort as the human body struggles to dissipate heat through radiation or convection, relying solely on sweating. In the absence of HVAC systems, passive cooling methods, such as shading devices, increasing internal thermal storage, and enhancing natural ventilation, could be essential to improve thermal comfort inside the unit. At night, the low thermal transmittance and airtightness of the unit help maintain indoor temperatures above outdoor levels, creating more comfortable conditions for occupants. However, without proper ventilation, RH levels can rise to uncomfortable levels due to thermal bridges at junctions and the inability of EPS material to absorb moisture. These conditions lead to condensation, with water droplets evaporating during the day and increasing humidity. In the presence of occupants, additional heat and moisture would further raise the likelihood of condensation.

In conclusion, without addressing issues related to temperature extremes and moisture during the cooling season, occupants risk heatstroke, while mold growth can lead to unhealthy indoor conditions. As a result, this construction system should not be used for long-term habitation unless appropriate measures—such as applying passive cooling techniques and improving the moisture-buffering capacity of the panels—are implemented beforehand.

References

1. M. D'Orazio, G. Maracchini, An experimental investigation on the indoor hygrothermal environment of a reinforced-EPS based temporary housing solution. Energy Build. **204**, 109500 (2019). https://doi.org/10.1016/j.enbuild.2019.109500
2. A.M. Tanyer, A. Tavukcuoglu, M. Bekboliev, Assessing the airtightness performance of container houses in relation to its effect on energy efficiency. Build. Environ. **134**, 59–73 (2018). https://doi.org/10.1016/j.buildenv.2018.02.026
3. H. Wallbaum, Y. Ostermeyer, C. Salzer, E. Zea Escamilla, Indicator based sustainability assessment tool for affordable housing construction technologies. Ecol. Indic. **18**, 353–364 (2012). https://doi.org/10.1016/j.ecolind.2011.12.005
4. N.H. Ramli Sulong, S.A.S. Mustapa, M.K. Abdul Rashid, Application of expanded polystyrene (EPS) in buildings and constructions: a review. J. Appl. Polym. Sci. 47529 (2019). https://doi.org/10.1002/app.47529
5. A.S. Sferra, Emergency: innovative prefabricated construction components for an eco-solidarity architecture. TECHNE J. Technol. Arch. Environ. 328–334 (2017). https://doi.org/10.13128/Techne-20788
6. European Committee for Standardisation (CEN), EN 10027-1: 2005 designation systems for steels—part 1: steel names. Eur. Stand. **3**, 1–25 (2005)
7. D. Félix, D. Monteiro, J.M. Branco, R. Bologna, A. Feio, The role of temporary accommodation buildings for post-disaster housing reconstruction. J. Housing Built Environ. **30**, 683–699 (2014). https://doi.org/10.1007/s10901-014-9431-4
8. IFRC, Post-disaster shelter: ten designs (2013)
9. E. Wagemann, Need for adaptation: transformation of temporary houses. Disasters **41**, 828–851 (2017). https://doi.org/10.1111/disa.12228
10. H. Arslan, Re-design, re-use and recycle of temporary houses. Build. Environ. **42**, 400–406 (2007). https://doi.org/10.1016/j.buildenv.2005.07.032
11. M. Kottek, J. Grieser, C. Beck, B. Rudolf, F. Rubel, World map of the Köppen-Geiger climate classification updated. Meteorol. Z. (2006). https://doi.org/10.1127/0941-2948/2006/0130
12. L. Huang, E. Long, J. Ouyang, Measurement of the thermal environment in temporary settlements with high building density after 2008 Wenchuan earthquake in China. Procedia Eng. **121**, 95–100 (2015). https://doi.org/10.1016/j.proeng.2015.08.1027
13. G. Desogus, S. Mura, R. Ricciu, Comparing different approaches to in situ measurement of building components thermal resistance. Energy Build. **43**, 2613–2620 (2011). https://doi.org/10.1016/j.enbuild.2011.05.025
14. G. Ficco, F. Iannetta, E. Ianniello, F. Romana, M. Dell, U-value in situ measurement for energy diagnosis of existing buildings. Energy Build. **104**, 108–121 (2015). https://doi.org/10.1016/j.enbuild.2015.06.071
15. P. Baker, U-values and traditional buildings. Historic Scotland Technical paper 10 70 (2011)
16. F. Asdrubali, F. D'Alessandro, G. Baldinelli, F. Bianchi, Evaluating in situ thermal transmittance of green buildings masonries: a case study. Case Stud. Constr. Mater. **1**, 53–59 (2014). https://doi.org/10.1016/j.cscm.2014.04.004
17. L. Evangelisti, C. Guattari, P. Gori, V.R. De Lieto, In situ thermal transmittance measurements for investigating differences between wall models and actual building performance. Sustainability (Switzerland) **7**, 10388–10398 (2015). https://doi.org/10.3390/su70810388
18. ISO 9869-1, Thermal insulation—building elements—in-situ measurement of thermal resistance and thermal transmittance heat flow meter method (2014)
19. I.A. Atsonios, I.D. Mandilaras, D.A. Kontogeorgos, M.A. Founti, A comparative assessment of the standardized methods for the in-situ measurement of the thermal resistance of building walls. Energy Build. **154**, 198–206 (2017). https://doi.org/10.1016/j.enbuild.2017.08.064
20. Y. Ji, L. Duanmu, Airtightness field tests of residential buildings in Dalian, China. Build. Environ. **119**, 20–30 (2017). https://doi.org/10.1016/j.buildenv.2017.03.043
21. EN ISO 9972:2015, Thermal performance of buildings—determination of air permeability of buildings—fan pressurization method (2015)

22. ASHRAE, *ASHRAE Handbook—Fundamentals* (2013), pp. 21.1–21.67. https://doi.org/10.1017/CBO9781107415324.004
23. EN 15251, Indoor environmental input parameters for design and assessment of energy performance of buildings—addressing indoor air quality, thermal environment, lighting and acoustics (2007)
24. M. Marocco, F. Orlandi, *Qualità del comfort ambientale. Elementi per la progettazione* (Editrice Dedalo Roma, Roma, Italy, 2000)
25. P. Samani, V. Leal, A. Mendes, N. Correia, Comparison of passive cooling techniques in improving thermal comfort of occupants of a pre-fabricated building. Energy Build. **120**, 30–44 (2016). https://doi.org/10.1016/j.enbuild.2016.03.055
26. N. Walikewitz, B. Jänicke, M. Langner, F. Meier, W. Endlicher, The difference between the mean radiant temperature and the air temperature within indoor environments: a case study during summer conditions. Build. Environ. **84**, 151–161 (2015). https://doi.org/10.1016/j.buildenv.2014.11.004
27. M.W. Liddament, *Air Infiltration Calculation Techniques—An Application Guide* (Air Infiltration and Ventilation Center, Coventry, 1986)
28. ATTMA, *Measuring Air Permeability of Building Envelopes (Dwellings): Technical Standard 1* (The Air Tightness Testing and Measurement Association (ATTMA), Northampton, UK, 2010)
29. Y. Wang, L. Wang, E. Long, S. Deng, An experimental study on the indoor thermal environment in prefabricated houses in the subtropics. Energy Build. **127**, 529–539 (2016). https://doi.org/10.1016/j.enbuild.2016.05.061
30. D. Albadra, D. Coley, J. Hart, Toward healthy housing for the displaced. J. Arch. **23**, 115–136 (2018). https://doi.org/10.1080/13602365.2018.1424227
31. X. Wang, W. Li, Z. Luo, K. Wang, S.P. Shah, A critical review on phase change materials (PCM) for sustainable and energy efficient building: design, characteristic, performance and application. Energy Build. **260**, 111923 (2022)
32. L. Huang, E. Long, Architecture and planning design strategy of post-disaster temporary settlement with high building density—analysis based on the questionnaire in Dujiangyan after Wenchuan earthquake. Procedia Eng. (2015)
33. E. Di Giuseppe, *Nearly Zero Energy Buildings and Proliferation of Microorganisms* (Springer International Publishing, Cham, 2013)

Chapter 5
The HOMEDONE Experience: Assessment and Mitigation of Moisture-Related Issues

Abstract This chapter investigates moisture-related risks in lightweight emergency buildings, focusing on the HOMEDONE modular construction system. Starting from experimental observations of surface condensation under real operating conditions, a detailed hygrothermal assessment was performed through numerical simulations. Simulations were extended across multiple climatic contexts and included the evaluation of surface condensation, mold growth risk, and the influence of material properties such as temperature-dependent thermal conductivity. Furthermore, the potential of passive mitigation strategies based on moisture-buffering (MB) internal layers—namely, cementitious render and gypsum plasterboard—was assessed. Results confirmed that both surface condensation and mold growth may represent critical issues in lightweight shelters, even in warm climates, and that appropriate MB layers can effectively reduce or eliminate these risks, with the choice of material depending on climate severity.

Keywords Surface condensation · Mold growth · Hygrothermal simulation · Moisture buffering · Lightweight construction · Emergency housing · EPS panels

5.1 Introduction

Temporary housing solutions represent a critical component in disaster recovery strategies, providing displaced individuals and communities with essential shelter following disruptive events. Due to the necessity for rapid assembly, affordability, and ease of transport, these structures are commonly built using lightweight, modular, and prefabricated construction technologies [1, 2]. While such systems are specifically designed for short-term occupancy, in practice they are frequently occupied for much longer durations, sometimes years or even decades [3]. This prolonged

In this chapter: G.M.: Conceptualization, Methodology, Validation, Formal Analysis, Investigation, Data Curation, Writing—Original Draft, Visualization, Supervision, and Project Administration. M.d.O.: Conceptualization, Methodology, Writing—Review and Editing.

G. Maracchini and M. D'Orazio, *Thermal Comfort in Emergency Architectures*, SpringerBriefs in Applied Sciences and Technology,
https://doi.org/10.1007/978-3-032-06795-1_5

use often highlights significant limitations concerning their indoor environmental quality, particularly related to moisture and thermal comfort [4, 5].

Among the available prefabricated lightweight systems, solutions based on expanded polystyrene (EPS) panels have gained popularity due to their affordability, ease of handling, and excellent insulation properties [6]. Despite these benefits, EPS-based systems can exhibit several issues related to the indoor moisture management, primarily due to their low vapor permeability and negligible moisture buffering capacity. As a result, such structures may suffer from condensation phenomena at internal surfaces and within structural junctions, potentially leading to mold growth, compromising occupant health [7].

In the HOMEDONE experience, a prefabricated lightweight housing system based on reinforced EPS panels was studied with the aim of systematically evaluating and addressing moisture-related issues identified during experimental monitoring activities. The HOMEDONE system, recently implemented as temporary housing in post-earthquake scenarios in Central Italy and also explored as an affordable housing solution in developing countries [8], provided an ideal case study for assessing the potential condensation risks associated with EPS-based modular systems. Indeed, prior experimental investigations conducted in Mediterranean climatic conditions revealed consistently high indoor relative humidity levels and the presence of condensation at internal surface junctions, even in scenarios characterized by limited occupancy and minimal internal moisture production.

Motivated by these findings, this chapter presents the results of a detailed investigation carried out by the authors of the moisture behavior of the HOMEDONE temporary housing system [9]. The section is structured in two main phases:

- First, in response to the condensation issues experimentally observed in Chap. 4—where high indoor relative humidity (RH) due to surface condensation was recorded—dynamic hygrothermal simulations were carried out to verify and quantify the occurrence of moisture-related phenomena such as condensation and mold growth during a full year of occupancy. These simulations were also extended to a broader range of climatic contexts to assess geographical variation.
- Then, to explore feasible mitigation measures, Heat and Moisture Transfer (HAMT) simulations were carried out to test the potential of adding an internal layer with moisture buffering capacity. These simulations evaluated the effectiveness of this solution across all considered climate scenarios, demonstrating its capacity to reduce indoor humidity peaks and limit condensation risk without compromising thermal comfort.

These phases constitute a structured and replicable methodology for evaluating moisture safety in prefabricated emergency housing, providing critical insights for designers, manufacturers, and humanitarian agencies involved in the rapid deployment of lightweight shelters.

5.2 Materials and Methods

5.2.1 Hygrothermal Simulations

Bidimensional dynamic hygrothermal simulations were conducted to numerically evaluate the moisture-related issues that were previously identified through experimental measurements in Chap. 4. The primary objective of these simulations was to verify and quantify the risk of surface and interstitial condensation and to assess mold growth potential during typical annual occupancy cycles. Additionally, to ensure generalizability of the results, the simulations were extended to a wider set of climatic conditions, beyond those originally observed.

The analyses were performed using the DELPHIN 6.0 software developed at the Technical University of Dresden and extensively validated in prior literature [10, 11]. DELPHIN enables simulation of coupled heat, moisture, and matter transfer in porous building materials, under both standard and real climatic boundary conditions, including temperature, relative humidity, wind, short- and long-wave radiation, and driving rain [12]. A bidimensional model was adopted to simulate the wall–roof junction, where thermal bridges are expected due to the presence of steel connections (Fig. 5.1), which were identified as critical zones during experimental monitoring.

The hygrothermal properties of materials used in the simulations are summarized in Table 5.1. Most parameters were taken from the DELPHIN material database [13].

The boundary climatic conditions included three distinct contexts: the Mediterranean climate of Ancona (Italy), the hot desert climate of Cairo (Egypt), and the humid continental climate of Oslo (Norway), as reported in Table 5.2. This selection captures a wide spectrum of environmental stresses—high- and low temperatures, variable RH levels—allowing the evaluation of the system's performance in diverse

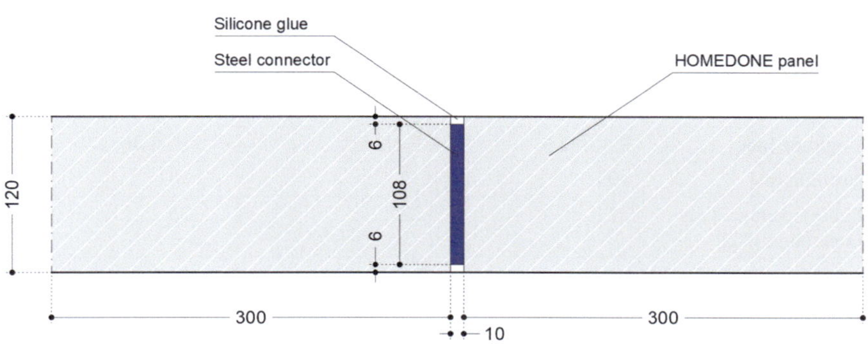

Fig. 5.1 Schematic representation of the HOMEDONE panel connection system at the junctions between the roof and walls, utilized for hygrothermal simulations in the DELPHIN software [10]. A 0.1 mm-thick air layer is employed to accurately gauge the internal surface relative humidity of the vapor-tight silicone adhesive. Dimensions are shown in millimeters

Table 5.1 Key hygric and thermal characteristics of the materials used in DELPHIN 6

Properties	EPS	Steel	Silicone glue[a]
Density ρ [kg/m^3]	45	7800	3500
Thermal conductivity λ [W/(m K)]	Temperature-dependent [14]	47.0	3.3
Thermal capacity [J/kg K]	1500	470	1000
Vapor resistance [–]	50	200,000	–
Hygroscopic sorption at RH = 80% [m^3/m^3]	6×10^{-4}	1.5×10^{-8}	–
Effective saturation (long-term) [m^3/m^3]	0.935	1.5×10^{-6}	–
Water absorption [$kg/(m^2\ s^{0.5})$]	10^{-5}	10^{-6}	–

[a] Vapor tight

global regions. Such coverage supports the definition of guidelines that remain valid for most latitudes and deployment scenarios.

Indoor climate profiles were defined in accordance with [15], assuming high-occupancy usage and applying sinusoidal temperature and RH profiles with superimposed daily and seasonal variations, as suggested in [13]. Initial temperature and moisture content for materials were set to 20 °C and 80% RH, respectively. The critical RH threshold for surface condensation was set to 95%, and simulations were

Table 5.2 Characteristics of climates utilized in the hygrothermal simulations

Location	Ancona, Italy	Oslo, Norway	Cairo, Egypt
Weather file	ASHRAE/IGDG, WMO 161910	ASHRAE/IWEC, WMO 014880	ASHRAE/IWEC, WMO 623660
Latitude [deg]	N 43.62	N 59.9	N 30.13
Longitude [deg]	E 13.52	E 10.62	E 31.40
Elevation [m]	105	17	74
Highest average daily temperature [°C]	27.3	22.4	35.2
Lowest average daily temperature [°C]	0.0	−13.2	11.4
Annual average solar global horizontal irradiance (GHI) [$kWh\ m^{-2}\ day^{-1}$]	3.25	2.41	5.26
Köppen classification	Csa (hot-summer Mediterranean climate)	Dfb (humid continental climate)	BWh (hot desert climate)

run for four consecutive years to ensure that a steady-state moisture content was reached.

5.2.2 Moisture Buffering

Moisture buffering (MB) refers to the capacity of hygroscopic materials to moderate fluctuations in indoor relative humidity by passively adsorbing and desorbing moisture at the surface level. This ability is particularly valuable in lightweight and airtight constructions—such as those based on EPS panels—where indoor humidity can otherwise rise rapidly due to limited vapor permeability and absence of natural moisture regulation mechanisms.

To investigate the potential of moisture buffering as a mitigation strategy for condensation and mold growth, the methodology already described in Sect. 5.2.1 was used to perform additional dynamic hygrothermal numerical simulations. The aim was to assess whether incorporating hygroscopic internal layers could reduce or prevent moisture-related issues.

Two alternative internal moisture buffering layers were considered at this aim:

- a 3 mm-thick cementitious finishing render (also known as basecoat), commonly used for interior surface protection, and
- a 12.5-mm thick gypsum plasterboard, directly applied to the internal face of the EPS panels.

Both materials were selected for their availability, affordability, and feasibility in emergency housing applications, as well as for their contrasting hygrothermal properties. Material properties for both layers were obtained directly from the DELPHIN 6.0 materials database.

5.2.3 Mold Growth Risk

To assess mold growth risk, simulation results at the internal surface of the junction were post-processed using the dynamic VTT mold growth model [16]. This index-based model accounts for material properties, temperature, RH, and time of exposure, providing a mold growth index (M) from 0 (no risk) to 6 (complete surface colonization). The input parameters assumed medium material sensitivity, a very sensitive surface factor, and a declination factor of 0.1, consistent with conservative modeling approaches [17, 18]. The interpretation of the mold growth index values for each climate is summarized in Table 5.3.

For the cementitious render, a particular modeling assumption was introduced in accordance with the literature: the mold growth calculation was performed only starting from the second year of simulation. This was due to the alkaline nature of freshly applied cementitious surfaces, which temporarily inhibits mold growth

Table 5.3 Mold index classifications based on [17]

Mold index (*M*)	Description
0	No growth
I	Minimal mold presence detected on the surface under microscopic examination, indicating an initial stage of localized growth
II	Several distinct colonies of mold observed on the surface via microscope
III	Visual evidence of mold on the surface showing less than 10% coverage, or up to 50% mold coverage when viewed under a microscope
IV	Visual observation reveals mold on the surface with coverage between 10 and 50%, or more than 50% when seen through a microscope
V	Abundant mold growth visible on the surface, exceeding 50% coverage
VI	Dense mold growth observed, covering nearly 100% of the surface area

through pH-driven biocidal effects [18]. As such, the first year was excluded from mold index (M) calculations when the VTT model was applied to this case.

5.3 Results and Discussion

5.3.1 Condensation Risk and Moisture Safety

The analysis of condensation risk was based on the evaluation of surface relative humidity (RH) over time. Figures 5.2 and 5.3 report the annual hourly variations of internal surface RH at the roof and north-facing wall junctions, respectively. In addition, Fig. 5.4 illustrates the percentage of annual hours during which surface RH exceeded 95%, i.e., the threshold conventionally assumed as indicative of condensation risk, for both the heating season (from October 1 to March 31) and the cooling season (from April 1 to September 30).

Results obtained for the Ancona climate were consistent with experimental findings. Specifically, surface condensation was observed not only during the heating season—as typically expected in lightweight structures—but also during summer nighttime hours, due to radiative cooling effects. This dual-season condensation behavior was especially prominent at roof junctions, where the number of critical hours with RH $\geq$95% exceeded those observed at the wall junctions (Fig. 5.4). The difference can be primarily attributed to the sky-cooling phenomenon, which is more intense at horizontal roof surfaces exposed to the night sky, as noted in prior studies [4].

Similar results were obtained for the other two simulated climates (Cairo and Oslo). As expected, colder climates resulted in a higher number of hours with surface condensation risk, due to lower outdoor temperatures and higher surface RH

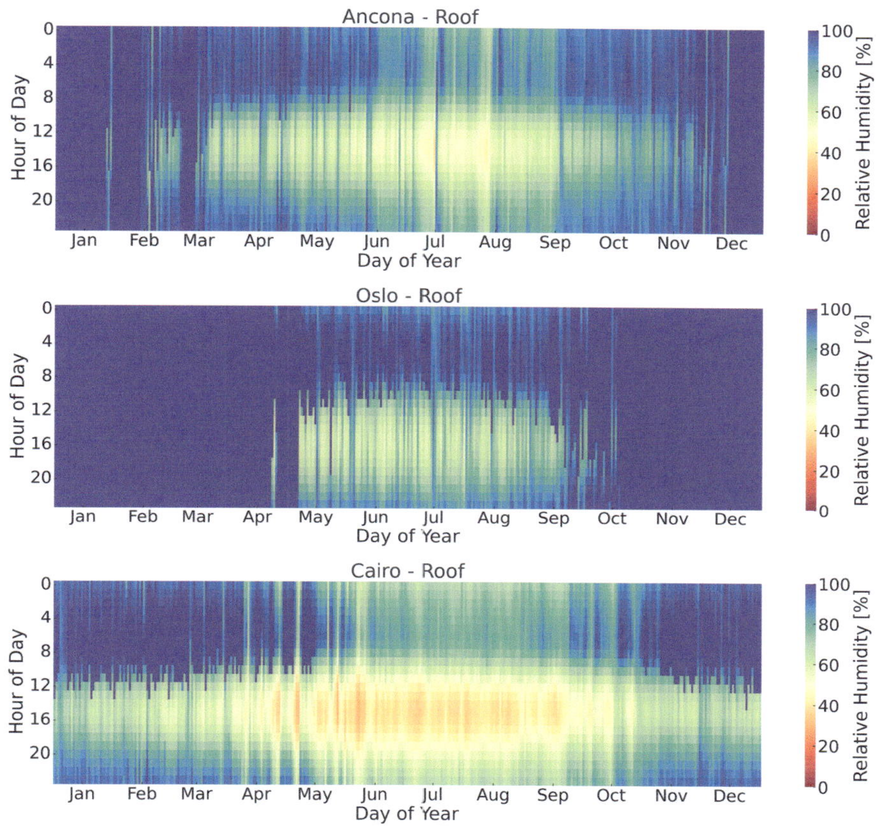

Fig. 5.2 Indoor roof surface relative humidity at the junction derived from numerical simulations across three distinct climate scenarios

gradients. These outcomes confirm that, despite the good thermal insulation performance of the EPS panels, the construction system remains vulnerable to moisture accumulation at critical junctions.

To complement the condensation analysis, the long-term risk of biological growth was also evaluated. Figure 5.5 presents the mold growth index (M) calculated for the roof junction surface—the location identified as most susceptible to prolonged high RH. In all climatic scenarios, the M value rapidly increased during the first simulation year and stabilized around a value of 3.5, indicating moderate to high mold development risk. According to the classification proposed by Ojanen et al. [17], such values correspond to visible fungal colonization, considered unacceptable in habitable environments (see Table 5.3).

The convergence of both condensation and mold growth analyses suggests that the current system configuration, in the absence of specific mitigation strategies, cannot ensure adequate moisture safety over long-term occupancy. These findings

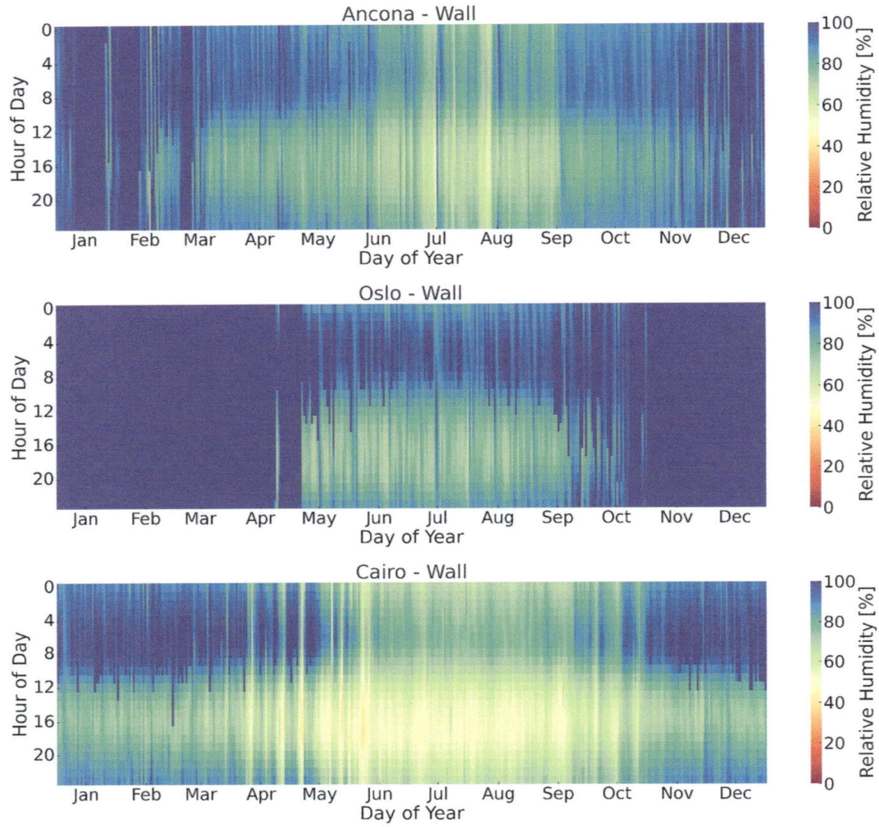

Fig. 5.3 Humidity levels at the north wall's indoor surface at junction points, as derived from numerical simulations under three varying climate scenarios

highlight the need for further improvements in moisture management, particularly at junctions and surface interfaces most affected by radiative cooling and thermal bridging effects.

5.3.2 Moisture Buffering

Figures 5.6 and 5.7 illustrate the indoor surface RH trends at the roof junction—the location previously identified as most susceptible to condensation—with different MB layers for each of the three climatic conditions: Ancona, Cairo, and Oslo. Results show that both MB layers significantly reduced surface RH levels when compared to the unprotected configuration. In particular, the cementitious basecoat maintained RH below the critical condensation threshold (95%) in both Ancona and Cairo climates

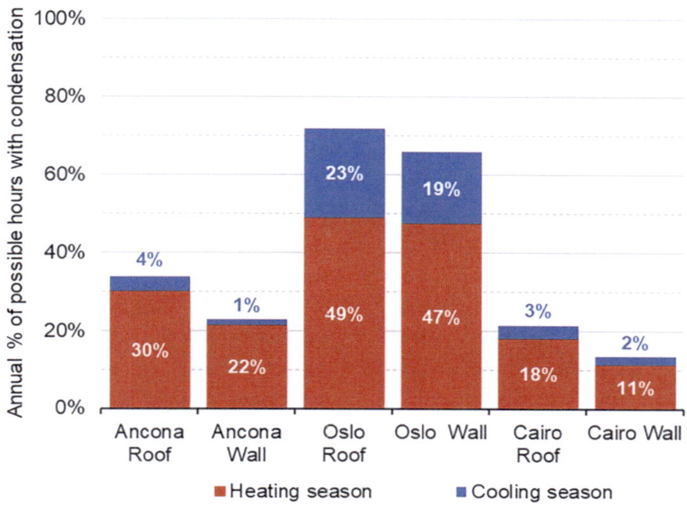

Fig. 5.4 Assessment of annual condensation risks for exterior roof and wall systems across different climatic conditions during both heating and cooling seasons

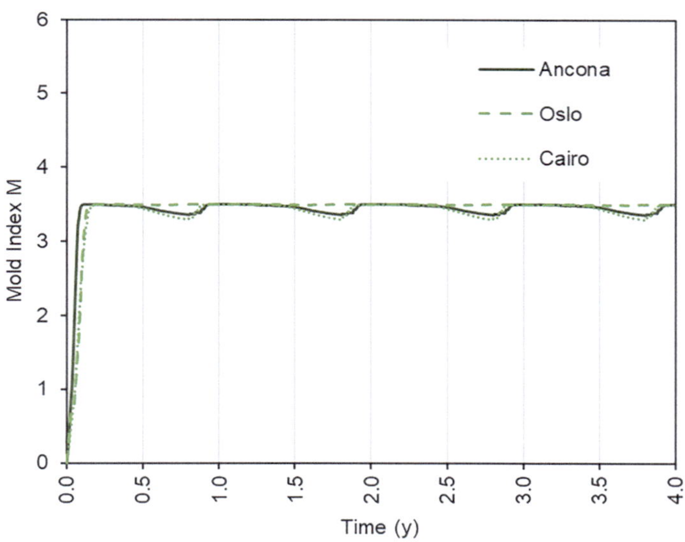

Fig. 5.5 Findings from the VTT damage assessment model indicating the mold index (M) at roof junctions

throughout the entire year. Differently, in Oslo, due to the extreme winter temperatures and reduced evaporative potential, a residual 6% of annual hours remained above the condensation threshold, indicating that this strategy alone is insufficient in cold and humid environments.

To address this limitation, simulations were also conducted for the gypsum plasterboard layer, which demonstrated superior moisture-buffering performance. In the Oslo scenario, this solution successfully maintained RH below 95% for the entire year, eliminating the residual condensation hours observed with the basecoat.

The effectiveness of the MB layers in reducing mold growth risk was also evaluated using the dynamic VTT model. Figure 5.8 reports the resulting mold growth index (M) for the roof junction in all climate scenarios. For the basecoat, M remained below the critical threshold (M = 1) in both Ancona and Cairo, indicating negligible fungal growth risk. Nevertheless, in Oslo, a measurable mold growth risk persisted, suggesting the need for improved buffering. Once again, the adoption of gypsum

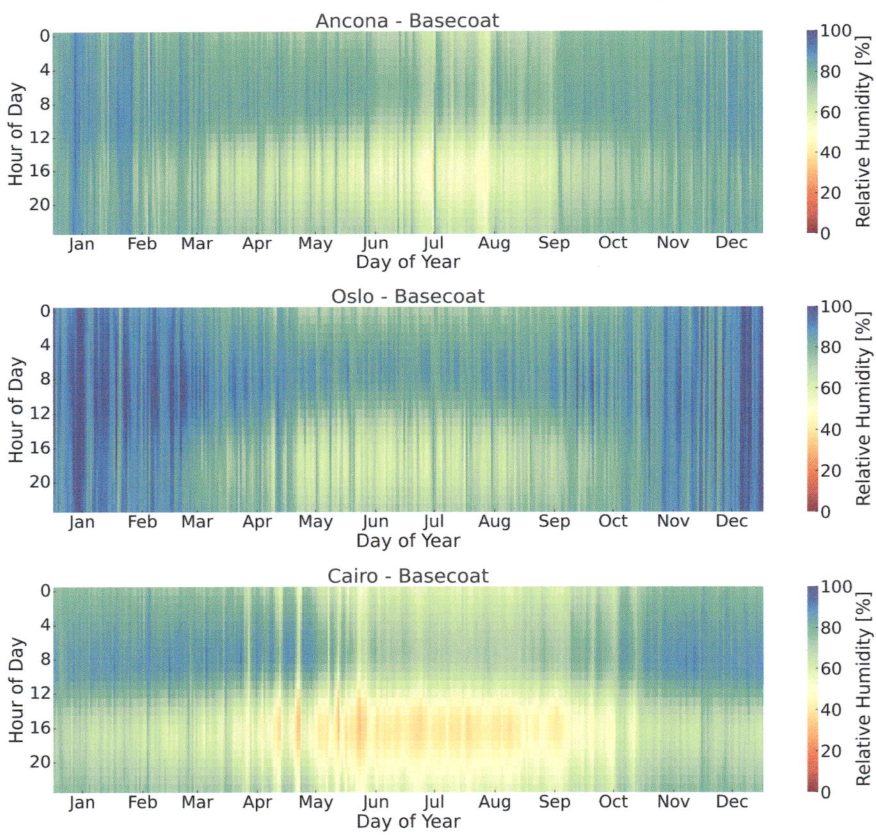

Fig. 5.6 Indoor humidity levels at junction points obtained from numerical simulations under the three climatic conditions for the basecoat

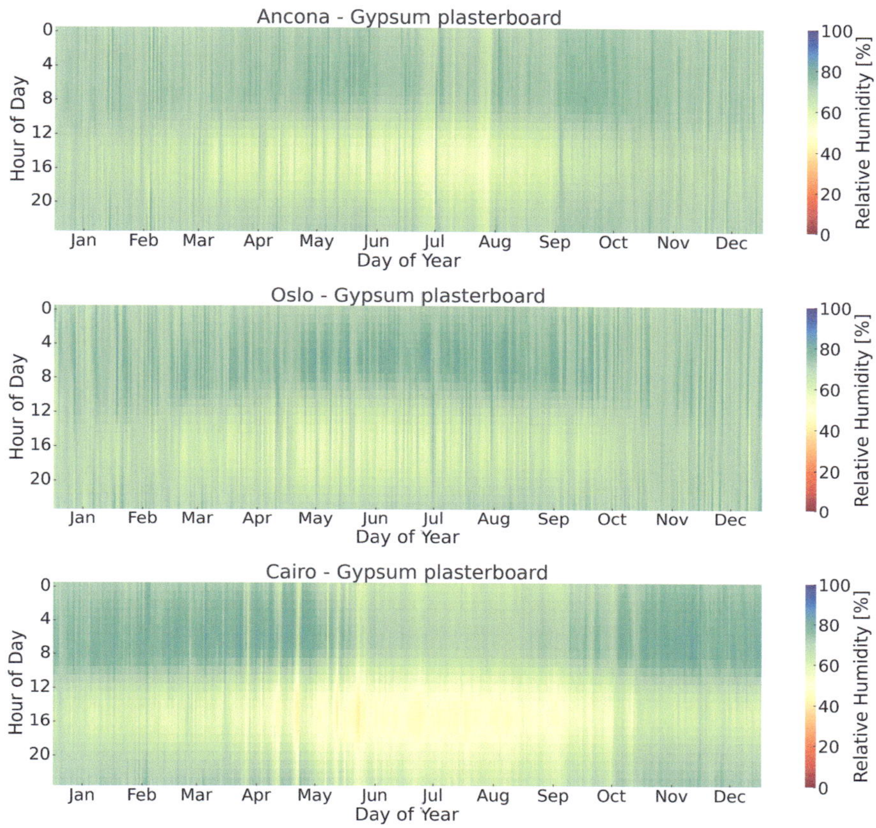

Fig. 5.7 Indoor humidity levels at junction points obtained from numerical simulations under the three climatic conditions for the gypsum plasterboard

plasterboard proved effectiveness: in this case, the M index remained at 0 across the entire simulation period, even in the harshest climate.

These findings confirm that internal MB layers represent a practical and low-cost strategy for enhancing the moisture safety of lightweight emergency constructions. A cementitious basecoat may suffice in milder climates, whereas in colder and more humid contexts, a gypsum board layer is recommended to ensure full protection against condensation and biological growth.

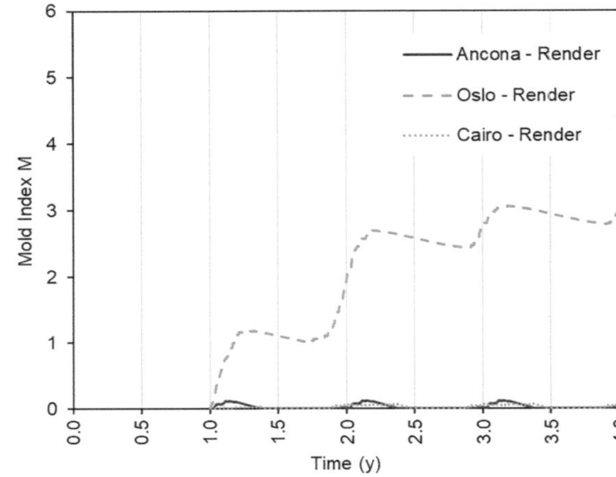

Fig. 5.8 VTT damage model results showing the mold index (M) at roof junctions following the application of a 3 mm-thick cementitious render on the interior surface of the panels

References

1. IFRC, Post-disaster shelter: ten designs (2013)
2. D. Félix, D. Monteiro, J.M. Branco, R. Bologna, A. Feio, The role of temporary accommodation buildings for post-disaster housing reconstruction. J. Housing Built Environ. **30**, 683–699 (2014). https://doi.org/10.1007/s10901-014-9431-4
3. UNRWA, Palestine refugees | UNRWA—United Nations Relief and Works Agency for Palestine refugees in the Near East (2021). https://www.unrwa.org/palestine-refugees. Accessed 5 Nov 2020
4. Y. Wang, L. Wang, E. Long, S. Deng, An experimental study on the in-door thermal environment in prefabricated houses in the subtropics. Energy Build. **127**, 529–539 (2016). https://doi.org/10.1016/j.enbuild.2016.05.061
5. D. Albadra, D. Coley, J. Hart, Toward healthy housing for the displaced. J. Arch. **23**, 115–136 (2018). https://doi.org/10.1080/13602365.2018.1424227
6. H. Wallbaum, Y. Ostermeyer, C. Salzer, E. Zea Escamilla, Indicator based sustainability assessment tool for affordable housing construction technologies. Ecol. Ind. **18**, 353–364 (2012). https://doi.org/10.1016/j.ecolind.2011.12.005
7. A.M. Tanyer, A. Tavukcuoglu, M. Bekboliev, Assessing the airtightness performance of container houses in relation to its effect on energy efficiency. Build. Environ. **134**, 59–73 (2018). https://doi.org/10.1016/j.buildenv.2018.02.026
8. A.S. Sferra, Emergency: innovative prefabricated construction components for an eco-solidarity architecture. TECHNE J. Technol. Arch. Environ. 328–334 (2017). https://doi.org/10.13128/Techne-20788
9. M. D'Orazio, G. Maracchini, An experimental investigation on the in-door hygrothermal environment of a reinforced-EPS based temporary housing solution. Energy Build. **204**, 109500 (2019). https://doi.org/10.1016/j.enbuild.2019.109500
10. J. Grunewald, *Diffusiver und konvektiver Stoff-und Energietransport* (University of Technology Dresden, Germany, 1997)
11. J.M.P.Q. Delgado, N.M.M. Ramos, E. Barreira, V.P. de Freitas, A critical review of hygrothermal models used in porous building materials. J. Porous Media **13**, 221–234 (2010). https://doi.org/10.1615/JPorMedia.v13.i3.30
12. S. Claude, S. Ginestet, M. Bonhomme, G. Escadeillas, J. Taylor, V. Marincioni, I. Korolija, H. Altamirano, Evaluating retrofit options in a historical city center: relevance of bio-based insulation and the need to consider complex urban form in decision-making. Energy Build. **182**, 196–204 (2019). https://doi.org/10.1016/j.enbuild.2018.10.026

13. P. Pihelo, T. Kalamees, The effect of thermal transmittance of building envelope and material selection of wind barrier on moisture safety of timber frame exterior wall. J. Build. Eng. **6**, 29–38 (2016). https://doi.org/10.1016/j.jobe.2016.02.002
14. M. Khoukhi, N. Fezzioui, B. Draoui, L. Salah, The impact of changes in thermal conductivity of polystyrene insulation material under different operating temperatures on the heat transfer through the building envelope. Appl. Therm. Eng. **105**, 669–674 (2016). https://doi.org/10.1016/j.applthermaleng.2016.03.065
15. EN 15026, Hygrothermal performance of building components and building elements—assessment of moisture transfer by numerical simulation. CEN (2007)
16. E. Vereecken, S. Roels, Review of mould prediction models and their influence on mould risk evaluation. Build. Environ. **51**, 296–310 (2012). https://doi.org/10.1016/j.buildenv.2011.11.003
17. T. Ojanen, H. Viitanen, R. Peuhkuri, K. Lähdesmäki, J. Vinha, K. Salminen, Mold growth modeling of building structures using sensitivity classes of materials, in *Thermal Performance of the Exterior Envelopes of Buildings XI* (2010)
18. H. Viitanen, M. Krus, T. Ojanen, V. Eitner, D. Zirkelbach, Mold risk classification based on comparative evaluation of two established growth models. Energy Procedia **78**, 1425–1430 (2015). https://doi.org/10.1016/j.egypro.2015.11.165

Chapter 6
The HOMEDONE Experience: Envelope Optimization for Thermal Comfort

Abstract This chapter explores the thermal behavior of the HOMEDONE lightweight emergency housing system, with particular attention to overheating risk in hot climates. The study combines experimental data, dynamic thermal simulations, and passive strategy modeling to assess and improve indoor thermal comfort without relying on mechanical systems. Several passive measures are investigated—cool materials, shading, natural ventilation, and internal thermal inertia—both individually and in combination, across three representative climates. Results show that natural ventilation and cool envelope strategies are the most effective, but their performance strongly depends on climate and aging conditions. A cost-effectiveness analysis further informs the selection of optimal solutions for emergency deployment. The study highlights the importance of passive design integration to ensure livability and resilience in temporary shelters.

Keywords Thermal comfort · Overheating · Passive cooling · Lightweight envelope · Natural ventilation · Cool materials · Shading devices · Thermal inertia · Cost-effectiveness · Emergency housing

6.1 Introduction

Temporary housing solutions have become increasingly critical due to frequent natural disasters, conflicts, and other emergency situations worldwide. Although originally intended for short-term use, these housing solutions are frequently occupied for much longer durations, underscoring the importance of ensuring adequate indoor thermal comfort. Nevertheless, emergency buildings often fail to provide acceptable indoor environmental conditions—particularly during hot seasons—posing risks to the health and well-being of their occupants.

In this chapter: G.M.: Conceptualization, Methodology, Validation, Formal Analysis, Investigation, Data Curation, Writing—Original Draft, Visualization, Supervision, and Project Administration. M.d.O.: Conceptualization, Methodology, Writing—Review and Editing.

G. Maracchini and M. D'Orazio, *Thermal Comfort in Emergency Architectures*,
SpringerBriefs in Applied Sciences and Technology,
https://doi.org/10.1007/978-3-032-06795-1_6

The HOMEDONE system is an innovative lightweight construction method using reinforced expanded polystyrene (EPS) panels developed to build temporary housing solutions. This system has been employed in several emergency situations, including earthquake recovery efforts and healthcare facilities during the COVID-19 pandemic [1]. Although promising in terms of rapid deployment, modularity, and affordability, the thermal comfort performance of HOMEDONE constructions has required thorough investigation to ensure occupant well-being under varying climatic conditions.

This chapter specifically addresses the optimization of the HOMEDONE envelope to enhance thermal comfort. Detailed numerical simulations were conducted, focusing on a variety of passive cooling strategies, including shading, cool finishing materials, natural ventilation, and increased internal thermal inertia [2]. The study unfolds in three main phases:

- First, the indoor temperature and other environmental variables of a full-scale prototype were used to calibrate a simulation model. This calibration process ensured the reliability of the numerical tools adopted and improved the accuracy of input parameters.
- Then, the validated model was used to analyze the summer performance of a representative reference building in free-running conditions under different climatic scenarios.
- Finally, several passive cooling strategies—selected for their low cost and ease of implementation in emergency contexts—were tested through simulations. These included natural ventilation, solar shading, increased indoor thermal mass, and the use of reflective finishes. Each solution was evaluated not only in terms of its ability to reduce overheating but also considering its impact on thermal comfort, associated costs, operational feasibility, and potential for combination with other strategies.

Through this structured workflow, the chapter provides actionable insights on improving indoor conditions, particularly by examining trade-offs between thermal comfort enhancement, cost-effectiveness, and operational feasibility [3]. These findings offer critical guidance for policymakers, architects, engineers, and humanitarian workers in selecting and implementing suitable passive strategies to ensure healthier and more comfortable indoor environments in lightweight emergency shelters.

6.2 Materials and Methods

6.2.1 Building Energy Simulation Tool

Building energy simulation was performed using the graphical interface DesignBuilder version 6.0 [4]. EnergyPlus version 8.9 [5] was employed as the core numerical engine for conducting simulations, given its robust capabilities in assessing detailed energy performance and thermal behavior of buildings.

The simulations used six time-steps per hour to ensure accurate and granular resolution of the building thermal response throughout the day. To enhance accuracy, the conduction transfer function method combined with an effective moisture penetration depth (EMPD) model was adopted [6–8]. Adaptive convection algorithms were also applied to model both internal and external convective heat transfer coefficients accurately. These algorithms dynamically adjust the coefficients based on environmental conditions, airflow patterns, and surface temperatures, providing a more realistic representation of convective heat exchanges compared to static models [9]. Finally, to represent infiltration in the numerical model, the Flow Coefficient model was employed.

6.2.2 Model Calibration

Model calibration was conducted by comparing the experimental indoor air temperature ($T_{i,\text{exp}}$) with simulated values ($T_{i,\text{num}}$). The data obtained from the experimental campaign carried out in Sect. 4.2 was used at this aim. Concerning outdoor environmental conditions, air temperature ($T_{o,\text{exp}}$) and relative humidity were used along with additional meteorological data such as horizontal global solar radiation, horizontal diffuse radiation, and atmospheric pressure provided by a nearby weather station. To evaluate model performance, three statistical metrics were calculated, i.e., the Root Mean Square Error (RMSE), the Mean Bias Error (MBE), and the Coefficient of Variation of the RMSE (CVRMSE). These metrics were then compared with established benchmark ranges from the literature focusing on the calibration of temporary shelters and naturally ventilated buildings [10–13].

6.2.3 Thermal Comfort Assessment

The evaluation of thermal comfort conditions within the HOMEDONE units was based on the adaptive thermal comfort model specified in EN 16798-1:2019 [14]. This model is broadly adopted for naturally ventilated buildings and has been proven effective in previous studies involving temporary housing scenarios (see, e.g., [2, 15]).

The model defines comfort ranges as a function of the running mean of the outdoor air dry-bulb temperature (T_{rm}), typically calculated over the previous 7 days. However, since the original formulation of the standard excludes days with T_{rm} values below 10 °C or above 30 °C, a modified approach was implemented to extend the applicability to more extreme weather conditions [2, 15]. This ensures that thermal comfort assessments also consider edge-season and particularly warm summer periods, where discomfort risks are more pronounced. The revised mathematical formulation adopted in this study is detailed in Eq. (6.1):

$$T_c = \begin{cases} (21.6 \pm 3.5)^{\circ}C & T_{rm} < 10^{\circ}C \\ (0.33T_{rm} + 18.3 \pm 3.5)^{\circ}C & 10^{\circ}C < T_{rm} < 30^{\circ}C \\ (28.2 \pm 3.5)^{\circ}C & T_{rm} > 30^{\circ}C \end{cases} \quad (6.1)$$

Long-term thermal comfort evaluation was conducted using the "percentage outside the range" method from EN ISO 7730:2005 [16], which quantifies the percentage of time in which indoor temperatures fall outside of the adaptive comfort range. This method has been employed effectively in previous research efforts focused on naturally ventilated and low-energy buildings [3]. For the scope of this study, the criteria for thermal discomfort were aligned with CIBSE Guide A [3], which stipulates that overheating should not exceed 3% of occupied hours from May to September, equivalent to 1.25% of the entire year. This threshold is considered a conservative benchmark, especially relevant in the context of vulnerable occupants or emergency housing contexts where thermal adaptation opportunities may be limited.

This dual-level methodology—short-term adaptive comfort assessment and long-term overheating evaluation—ensures a comprehensive analysis of the thermal performance of the HOMEDONE unit under a range of environmental conditions.

6.2.4 Passive Cooling Measures Modeling

A range of passive cooling strategies can be employed to mitigate indoor overheating and enhance thermal comfort in hot climates, particularly in low-resource or emergency contexts. These strategies are conventionally categorized into three main groups: heat dissipation, heat modulation, and heat protection techniques [17]. Within the domain of temporary emergency housing, the applicability of such techniques is subject to constraints such as cost, material availability, ease of installation, and minimal alteration to the building's overall structure.

In line with these constraints, the present study focused on a set of passive measures that are both low-cost and easy to implement. These solutions were selected to ensure feasibility for large-scale deployment and ease of application even by non-specialized labor forces. The selected strategies include natural ventilation and the application of high-reflectance surface treatments (classified as heat dissipation techniques), external shading systems such as overhangs and slatted blinds (heat protection techniques), and the addition of internal thermal mass through gypsum boards (a heat modulation technique).

These passive measures were individually modeled and simulated to assess their impact on the thermal performance of the HOMEDONE unit. In particular:

- Natural ventilation was implemented through different window operation schedules;
- Cooling finishing materials were simulated by altering surface albedo and emissivity;
- Shading systems were modeled in multiple geometrical configurations to evaluate their effectiveness against direct solar gains;
- Internal thermal mass was increased by simulating the addition of internal gypsum board linings on walls and ceilings.

A detailed description of the modeling methodology for each of these passive strategies is presented in the following subsections (from Sects. 6.2.4.1 to 6.2.4.4). The quantitative performance of each intervention was then evaluated and compared using the performance metrics discussed in Sect. 6.2.5.

6.2.4.1 Cooling Materials

Within the broader family of cooling technologies—including cool tiles, metal roofs, elastomeric membranes, and asphalt shingles—this study focused on white surface coatings incorporating micro- and nanotechnological additives. These coatings have been demonstrated to effectively mitigate overheating while maintaining low costs and easy applicability without the need for specialized labor.

Cooling materials are characterized by two key surface properties: high solar reflectance (SR), generally equal to or greater than 0.70, and high thermal emittance (ε), typically equal to or greater than 0.75 [18]. These properties enable such materials to significantly limit solar heat gains during the day and to dissipate accumulated heat rapidly during the night via infrared radiation [17, 19, 20].

To assess their influence on building performance, two implementation configurations were considered. The first involved the application of the reflective coating solely on the roof surface (Cool Roof, CR), while the second extended the treatment to both roof and external vertical walls (Cool Roof and Walls, CRW).

The influence of cooling materials on indoor thermal conditions was simulated by modifying the SR value of the building envelope from a baseline of 0.40—representing standard construction practices—to 0.90, which corresponds to the upper range of values reported in the literature (e.g., [12, 21]).

It should be noted that losses in reflectance and emittance can be induced by chemical degradation, surface weathering, accumulation of organic and inorganic particulates, and biological fouling. These phenomena can be especially pronounced in urban or polluted environments and may occur within a few months of installation

[22–26]. Thence, it is essential to consider for the degradation in performance of reflective coatings over time and to plan effective maintenance activities.

6.2.4.2 Shading

Two distinct shading strategies were evaluated in this study and applied to windows facing the south, east, and west orientations, i.e.:

- external overhangs with lateral fins, each with a horizontal projection depth of 0.5 m (see Fig. 6.1);
- external slatted blinds, currently available as part of the commercial HOMEDONE construction system.

These solutions are designed for direct integration with the window frames and do not require specialized labor for installation—an important advantage in emergency scenarios where construction teams may lack technical expertise.

The slatted blinds were modeled with horizontal orientation for south-facing windows and vertical orientation for east- and west-facing ones to maximize solar control based on the solar path and façade exposure. The slats were designed with a 45° inclination and spaced at 0.018 m. Each slat had a width of 0.025 m and was positioned 0.05 m away from the window glazing. A standard thickness of 0.01 m and a thermal conductivity value of 0.1 W m^{-1} K^{-1} were adopted for all shading elements.

A preliminary simulation set was conducted to determine the optimal activation temperature setpoint for deploying the shading systems. These simulations indicated

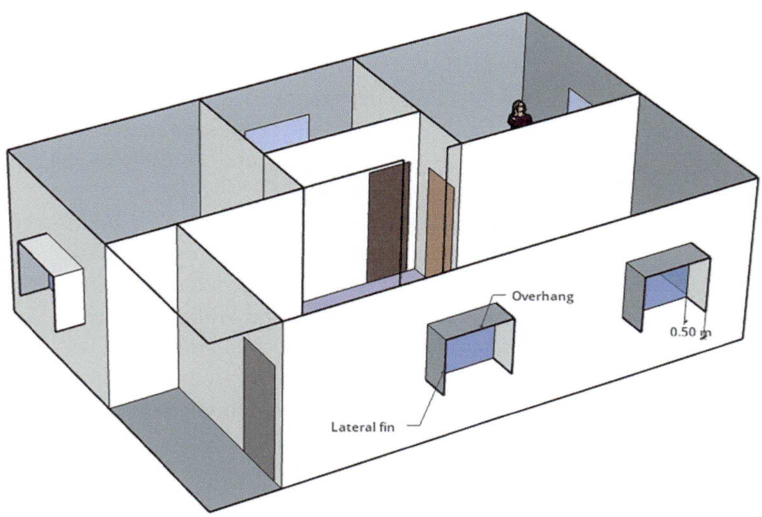

Fig. 6.1 A model schematic showing external overhangs and lateral fins

that using a setpoint lower than 26 °C yielded negligible benefits in mitigating overheating and, conversely, negatively affected indoor conditions during colder periods by reducing desirable solar gains. As a result, a conservative setpoint of 26 °C was selected for shading activation, providing a balanced performance across seasonal variations and climatic contexts. This threshold was applied consistently across all shading scenarios analyzed.

6.2.4.3 Natural Ventilation

A passive natural ventilation strategy (NV) was modeled to simulate the manual operation of windows by occupants in response to indoor thermal conditions. The logic for window activation was defined through a set of operational rules, which allowed openings only when all the following conditions were simultaneously satisfied: (1) indoor air temperature (T_{inum}) exceeded 26 °C; (2) indoor temperature was higher than outdoor air temperature (T_{oexp}); and (3) wind speed was below 10 m/s. This multi-criteria approach aimed to maximize the cooling potential while avoiding discomfort due to excessive wind exposure or the ingress of hot outdoor air. The choice of the 26 °C threshold aligns with previous findings indicating its effectiveness as an overheating setpoint in naturally ventilated buildings [2, 27].

In line with the ASHRAE Handbook of Fundamentals [28], airflow due to both wind pressure (QW) and stack effect (QS) should be considered for accurate natural ventilation modeling. However, in this specific case—where the midpoints of the inlet and outlet window openings are located at the same height—the stack effect was considered negligible due to the absence of vertical pressure gradients [2, 27]. As a result, only wind-driven ventilation was considered in the airflow model.

The airflow rate generated by wind (QW) was calculated using the standard formula provided by ASHRAE [28, 29]:

$$Q_W = C_W A_0 V \tag{6.2}$$

where

- A0 represents the effective opening area of the window. For the purposes of this simulation, A0 was conservatively set to 5% of the total window area (i.e., 0.06 m^2 per window), accounting for partial obstructions common in densely populated emergency camps [30].
- V denotes the outdoor wind speed.
- CW is the effectiveness coefficient of the opening, determined as a function of the angle between the wind direction and the window's orientation [28, 29, 31].

This simplified but robust modeling framework allowed the analysis to focus on realistic occupant behaviors and architectural constraints typical of emergency shelter scenarios, while preserving the essential physics of wind-driven ventilation.

6.2.4.4 Internal Thermal Inertia

In this study, the enhancement of indoor thermal stability was addressed by adding a continuous internal layer of gypsum board to all major envelope components, specifically the internal surfaces of walls and the underside of the roof. Multiple gypsum board thicknesses were analyzed, ranging from 5 to 25 mm, the latter representing the upper limit typically feasible in this building typology [6, 15]. To reflect practical installation scenarios, 50 and 100 mm air gaps were modeled between the gypsum boards and the EPS structural panels on the walls and roof, respectively. These cavities not only facilitate mounting but also serve as technical voids for routing electrical cables or other service lines.

The thermal and physical properties of the gypsum board were set as follows: thermal conductivity $\lambda = 0.32\ \mathrm{W\ m^{-1}\ K^{-1}}$, specific heat capacity $\varsigma = 1100\ \mathrm{J\ kg^{-1}\ K^{-1}}$, and density $\rho = 1150\ \mathrm{kg\ m^{-3}}$. Moisture-related properties, which influence the transient thermal response of the material under varying humidity conditions, were extracted directly from the material database embedded in DesignBuilder version 6.0 [4].

6.2.5 Performance Indicators

The effectiveness of each passive cooling strategy was evaluated using a set of quantitative performance indicators aimed at capturing both overheating risk and overall thermal comfort. These included the average of the top 5% of indoor temperatures ($T_{\max,\,5\%}$), and the percentage of time during which occupants were exposed to thermal discomfort due to excessive heat throughout an entire year of simulation [2]. Given that certain strategies—particularly those increasing thermal mass or employing fixed shading—might also influence thermal conditions during colder months, a complementary set of indicators was calculated. These consisted of the average of the lowest 5% of indoor air temperatures ($T_{\min,\,5\%}$) and the percentage of hours experiencing discomfort due to cold exposure. This dual focus enabled a more comprehensive understanding of each strategy's impact across seasonal variations.

6.2.6 Cost–Benefit Analysis

In addition to thermal comfort outcomes, financial implications were also analyzed, recognizing their importance in emergency scenarios where cost-effective solutions must be prioritized. Actual implementation costs—including materials and labor—were collected for each passive measure and are reported in Table 6.1. These figures reflect the incremental cost added to the HOMEDONE unit's base construction price as a direct consequence of implementing the strategy.

Table 6.1 Additional costs incurred by the manufacturer for implementing passive solutions in the reference building

	S	CR (SR = 0.9)	CRW (SR = 0.9)	G (25mm)
Cost [€]	900	600	2200	6100
Cost [€ m^{-2}]	16	10.5	38.1	106

S: Shading; CR: Cool Roof; CRW: Cool Roof and Walls; G: Gypsum board

Among the analyzed interventions, the increase of internal thermal inertia through gypsum board application showed the highest capital investment, with a total cost increase estimated in the range 10–15% of the baseline unit cost. This was attributed to multiple factors: the greater quantity of materials required, the need for specialized labor to perform a multi-phase installation, and the improvement in housing quality obtained post installation, including enhanced utility of the technical voids for routing electrical and service equipment.

Operational or running costs were excluded from the analysis, as the building configuration assumed no HVAC system—a plausible scenario for many temporary shelters, particularly in hot climates. Maintenance costs were also not considered in the present study.

6.2.7 Reference Building

To evaluate the influence of various passive cooling strategies under realistic usage scenarios, a numerical model of a reference building was developed. This building corresponds to a temporary housing unit recently implemented in emergency camps and also adopted in several developing countries for affordable residential purposes [1]. The geometric configuration of the reference building is presented in Fig. 6.2.

The building envelope—including all external and internal partitions, the roof, and the floor—was constructed using reinforced EPS panels. The hygrothermal characteristics of these components were defined based on the outcomes of the calibration process performed on the experimental single-room unit (Sect. 6.2.2). Windows and external doors shared the same thermal performance as those modeled in the experimental unit, whereas internal doors were simulated as 35 mm-thick wooden panels with a thermal conductivity (λ) of 0.099 W m^{-1} K^{-1}.

The floor system was modeled as being in direct contact with a structural concrete foundation. Internally, it was finished with an 80 mm-thick cast-in-place lightweight concrete slab ($\lambda = 0.38$ W m^{-1} K^{-1}, specific heat $\varsigma = 1000$ J kg^{-1} K^{-1}, and density $\rho = 1200$ kg m^{-3}), topped by a 10 mm-thick layer of ceramic stoneware tiles ($\lambda =$ 1.3 W m^{-1} K^{-1}, $\varsigma = 1000$ J kg^{-1} K^{-1}, $\rho = 2200$ kg m^{-3}). These configurations reflect the actual finishing details adopted by the system manufacturer.

In the baseline model—i.e., the version without any passive cooling enhancements—a continuous thin rendering layer was applied to both the internal and external

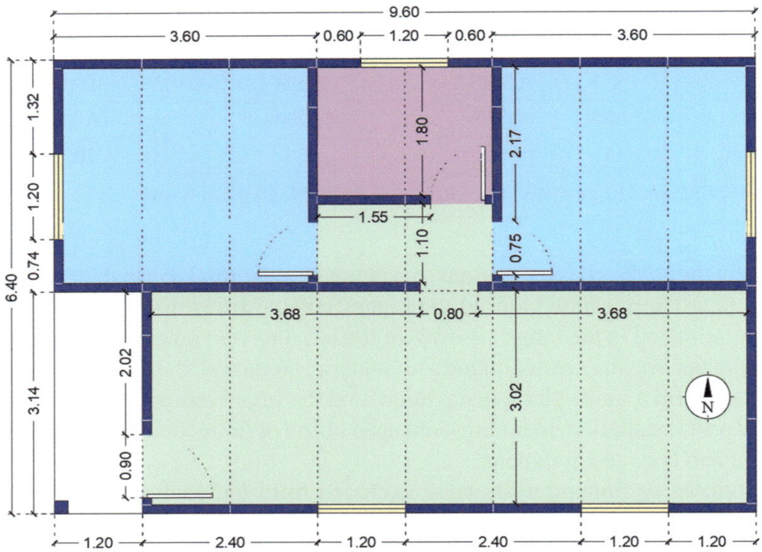

Fig. 6.2 Layout of the reference building considered for numerical simulations. Dimensions are in meters

surfaces of the walls and to the internal side of the roof. The rendering thickness was 4 mm on the exterior and 3 mm on the interior. The thermal and solar absorptances of the render were set at 0.9 and 0.6, respectively.

Recognizing the significant variability in internal activities across emergency contexts, this study adopted standardized assumptions for internal gains based on EN 16798-1 [32]. A constant internal gain density of 6.15 W m^{-2} was assigned uniformly across all rooms. Each room was defined as a separate thermal zone, as illustrated in Fig. 6.2. A uniform infiltration rate of 0.6 air changes per hour (ACH) was adopted, consistent with both the standard and prior modeling approaches in similar research [6, 21]. This infiltration rate is notably higher than that used for the single-room experimental unit, accounting for increased air leakage expected in multi-room layouts due to additional openings, construction joints, and potential penetrations from appliances and lighting fixtures [33].

Finally, no mechanical HVAC systems were considered in the model, aligning with common configurations in emergency settlements or low-income regions where such systems are often absent due to economic limitations. This assumption enabled the study to focus exclusively on the influence of passive strategies on thermal comfort performance.

6.2.8 Climatic Locations

Three different climatic contexts were selected for the simulation analyses, each representing distinct regions where HOMEDONE housing units might realistically be deployed. The selection was guided primarily by differences in annual average global horizontal irradiance (GHI), which is a critical determinant of thermal loads in buildings without HVAC systems. In particular, we select

- Ancona, Italy, corresponding to a hot-summer Mediterranean climate (Csa, Köppen classification) and serving as the reference for model calibration. It is characterized by a GHI of 3.25 kWh m^{-2} day^{-1}. Ancona was chosen also because it was directly affected by the 2016 Central Italy earthquake, which generated significant demand for temporary housing [1].
- São Paulo, Brazil, representing a hot-humid subtropical climate and recording a GHI of 4.77 kWh m^{-2} day^{-1}, which was selected due to its substantial and ongoing need for affordable housing solutions, particularly in informal settlements and urban peripheries. The climatic challenges in such regions necessitate effective passive cooling solutions.
- New Delhi, India, as an exemplar of very hot-dry climates, located in a region that regularly experiences intense heatwaves. With a GHI of 5.23 kWh m^{-2} day^{-1}, it represents one of the most thermally demanding contexts. Furthermore, the city has faced high rates of internal displacement driven by climate-related disasters such as floods and extreme heat events, with a record number of displacements in the first half of 2019 [34].

A detailed overview of the climatic characteristics of each location is provided in Figs. 6.3 and 6.4. Figure 6.3 illustrates the annual air temperature variations across the three sites, offering a comparative view of their thermal profiles. Then, given the importance of wind dynamics in natural ventilation strategies, Fig. 6.4 reports an additional analysis focused on wind velocity, frequency, and predominant directions during the summer months.

6.3 Results and Discussion

6.3.1 Model Calibration

The results of the model calibration are presented in Fig. 6.5, which compares experimental observations and numerical simulations of indoor air temperature ($T_{i,\,\mathrm{exp}}$ vs. $T_{i,\,\mathrm{num}}$). The agreement between simulated and measured data was strong, with only minor deviations observed, particularly in the peak temperature values. Key statistical indicators (RMSE, CVRMSE, and MBE) were calculated to evaluate model accuracy. For indoor air temperature, these metrics yielded values of 0.56 °C, 4.98%, and −2.39%, respectively. These values are in line with, or even better than, those

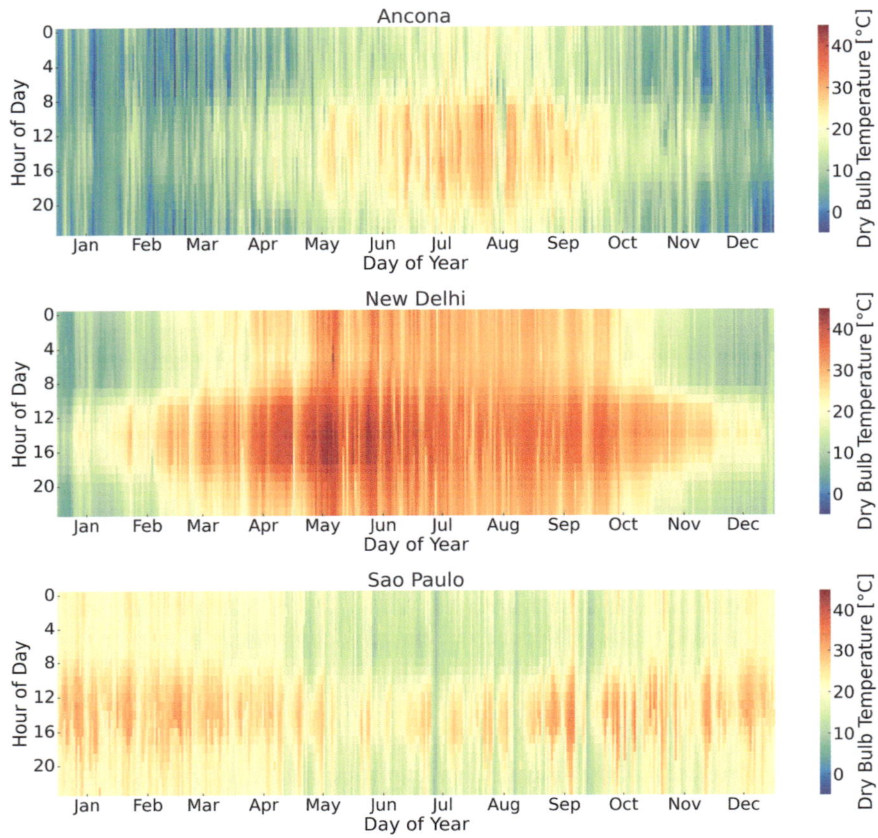

Fig. 6.3 Hourly dry-bulb air temperatures for the three distinct climates throughout the year

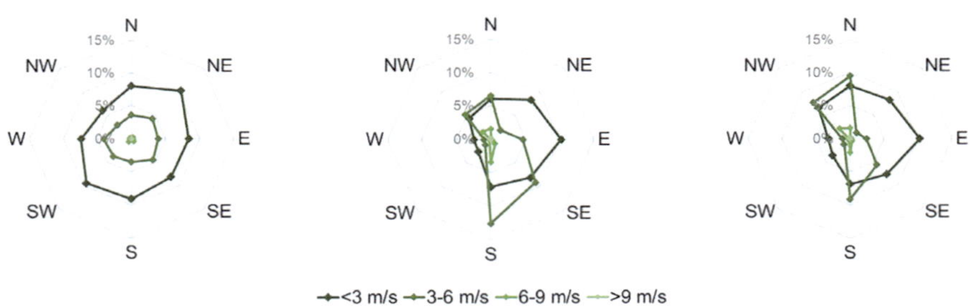

Fig. 6.4 Wind direction, speed, and frequency throughout the year in the specific locations during the summer season

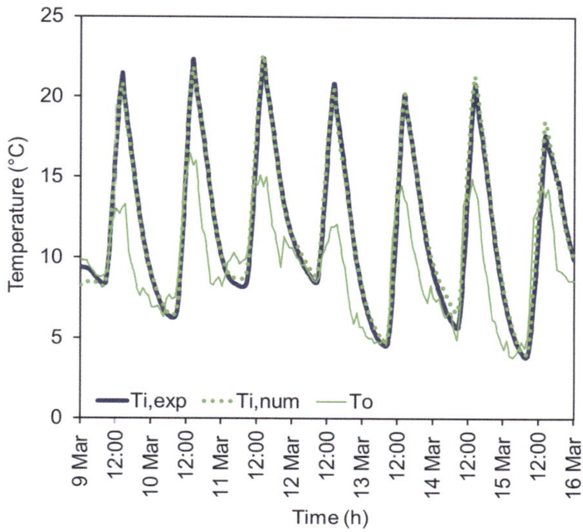

Fig. 6.5 Comparison of experimental (exp) and numerical (num) indoor air temperatures of the experimental unit

reported in existing literature for the calibration of naturally ventilated and temporary buildings. Specifically, prior studies indicate RMSE values between 0.9 and 2.9 °C (maximum absolute errors up to 21.9 °C), MBE from −5.9 to 1.9%, and CVRMSE from 1.7 to 20.3% [11–13].

Notably, the calibration process required minimal tuning of input parameters. The only adjustment made was to the solar absorptance value, which was reduced from 0.4 to 0.1. This change aligns with values reported in the literature for highly reflective white surfaces [35], and underscores the reflective properties of the materials used in the HOMEDONE system.

The overall consistency between the numerical and experimental results supports the validity of the simulation assumptions, including the exclusion of thermal bridges at panel junctions. Consequently, the calibrated model can be considered sufficiently accurate for further simulations involving passive strategies, as also supported by similar validations in prior works [36, 37].

6.3.2 Thermal Performance in the Initial State

6.3.2.1 Indoor Air Temperatures

Figure 6.6 illustrates the simulated indoor air temperatures for each thermal zone (room) of the reference building on the hottest days of the year in Ancona. The results clearly show a significant overheating of the indoor environment, with peak indoor air temperatures exceeding outdoor values by 5–10 °C. When comparing the thermal behavior of the individual rooms, all zones exhibited similar overall profiles. Slight

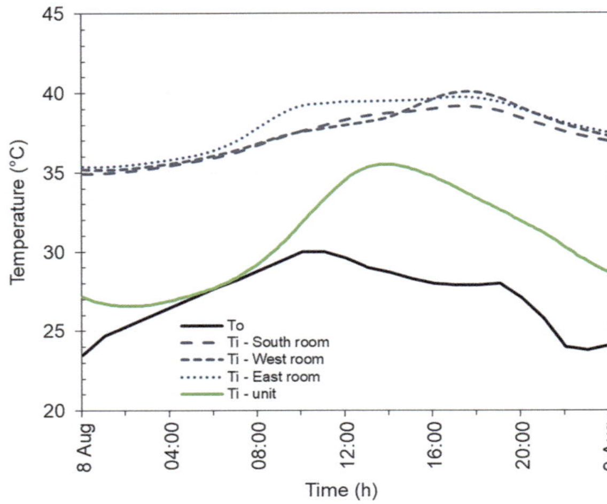

Fig. 6.6 Indoor air temperatures of reference buildings in Ancona, Italy, on the hottest days

differences emerged in the summer due to varying window orientations, which caused temporal shifts in peak indoor temperatures throughout the day. Among the rooms, the west-facing room consistently exhibited marginally higher peak temperatures. This is likely due to the cumulative heat gain dynamics: as solar radiation begins to enter the west-facing window in the late afternoon, the indoor air temperature has already increased significantly due to heat transfer from adjacent zones earlier in the day. These findings from Ancona are consistent with trends observed across the other two climatic contexts and during different times of the year. Therefore, for clarity and conciseness, only the results from the west-facing room are reported and analyzed in subsequent sections.

Figure 6.7 presents a comparison of indoor and outdoor air temperatures for the west room under each of the three climate scenarios. Interestingly, the lowest thermal gradient between indoor and outdoor air was recorded in São Paulo, despite it being the second hottest climate among the three. This outcome can be primarily attributed to its relatively lower direct solar irradiance during the hottest months (average of 3.38 kWh m^{-2} day^{-1}), which limits the solar radiation penetrating through the windows, thereby mitigating indoor heat gain.

6.3.2.2 Indoor Thermal Comfort

In Fig. 6.7, indoor operative temperatures and corresponding comfort limits—as defined by the adaptive thermal comfort model described in Sect. 6.2.3—are presented alongside outdoor air temperatures for each of the three climate scenarios. Considerably higher discomfort periods were observed across all climates due to indoor overheating effects. São Paulo demonstrated the lowest percentage of indoor discomfort hours related to heat (11.2%), a result consistent with the moderate and constant outdoor conditions. In contrast, Ancona recorded 29.5% of discomfort hours

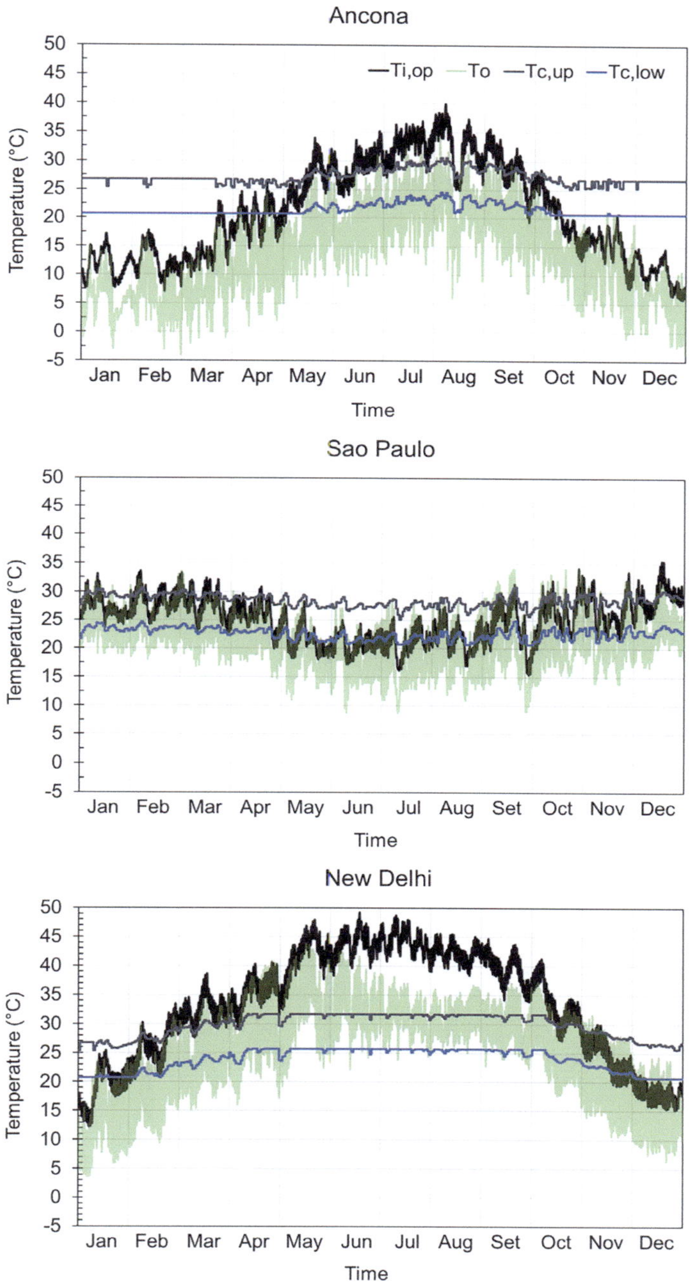

Fig. 6.7 For each climate, indoor temperatures of the west room in reference buildings ($T_{i,\,\mathrm{op}}$), outdoor air temperatures ($T_{o,\,\exp}$), and comfort limits ($T_{c,\,\mathrm{up}}$ and $T_{c,\,\mathrm{low}}$)

due to overheating, and New Delhi experienced a striking 68.3%—more than two-thirds of the year—indicating severe overheating within the shelter. All three cases substantially exceeded the 3% discomfort threshold defined by CIBSE Guide A [38] for overheating prevention between May and September. This finding underlines the inadequacy of the baseline configuration to ensure thermal comfort and confirms the necessity of implementing passive cooling strategies to mitigate indoor overheating, even in temperate and subtropical settings.

6.3.2.3 Summer Heat Gain Characteristics

Given the demonstrated need for improving indoor thermal comfort across all examined climates, Fig. 6.8 presents a breakdown of summer heat gains for the reference building under each location-specific scenario. This analysis serves as a foundational reference for identifying which passive cooling strategies are most suitable for deployment.

As expected, internal gains—arising from occupant-related activities—accounted for the largest portion of total heat gain in all climate scenarios, ranging from 59 to 63% followed by solar gains through windows (25–28%). These figures underscore the dominant role of windows in facilitating solar heat gain in summer, a trend also observed in lightweight temporary structures evaluated in previous studies [12]. As such, window-related interventions should be prioritized when developing passive cooling strategies.

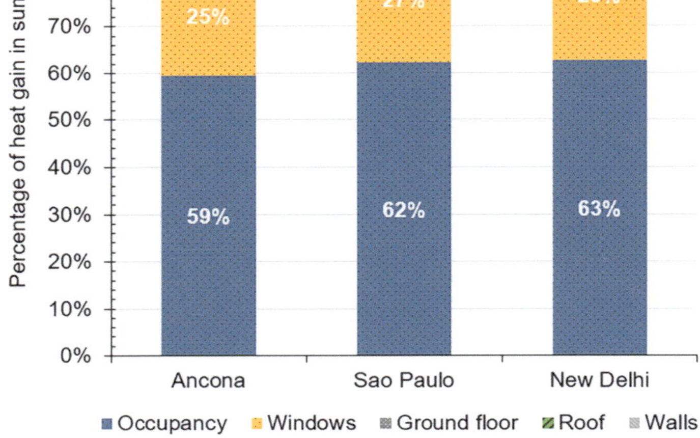

Fig. 6.8 The detailed breakdown of the reference building heat gain during a summer month in Ancona (August), Sao Paulo (December), and New Delhi (June)

Ground floor heat gains were more important in climates where nighttime indoor temperatures fell below ground temperature, as observed in Ancona and São Paulo. Roof-related heat gains were found to be positively correlated with local global horizontal irradiance (GHI), implying a greater need for roof-specific improvements in high-GHI climates such as New Delhi. In contrast, heat gains through opaque wall elements accounted for only 1% of the total summer heat input.

6.3.3 *Passive Cooling Techniques*

6.3.3.1 Cooling Materials

Figure 6.9 presents the performance impact of the cooling materials strategy. Both CR and CRW configurations led to a consistent and nearly linear reduction in indoor temperature metrics as the solar absorptance of the building envelope decreased. The reduction of solar heat gain due to reflective coatings on exterior surfaces resulted in a downward shift of peak and average high temperatures, confirming the effectiveness of surface albedo enhancement in mitigating overheating.

As expected, the CRW strategy—extending the reflective treatment from the roof to the walls—achieved greater thermal performance improvements compared to CR alone. This suggests that when feasible, full-envelope reflective strategies may offer greater benefits in climates with high solar exposure.

6.3.3.2 Shading

The impact of shading strategies on indoor thermal performance was assessed for both types of devices examined in this study: external slatted blinds and overhangs with lateral fins. Figure 6.10 reports their influence on the average of the top 5% of maximum indoor temperatures ($T_{max, 5\%}$) across the three climatic contexts. The results demonstrate that both shading systems deliver comparable reductions in $T_{max, 5\%}$, indicating a consistent capacity to mitigate peak overheating regardless of location. However, slatted blinds were found to perform marginally better in all scenarios. This enhanced performance is attributed to their superior ability to block solar radiation from penetrating east- and west-facing windows—façades that are particularly vulnerable during summer mornings and afternoons due to their orientation relative to the sun's path.

It is also important to note that neither shading system had any measurable impact on the building's thermal performance during the coldest periods. This seasonal neutrality enhances their appeal as passive strategies, offering significant summer benefits without compromising winter conditions.

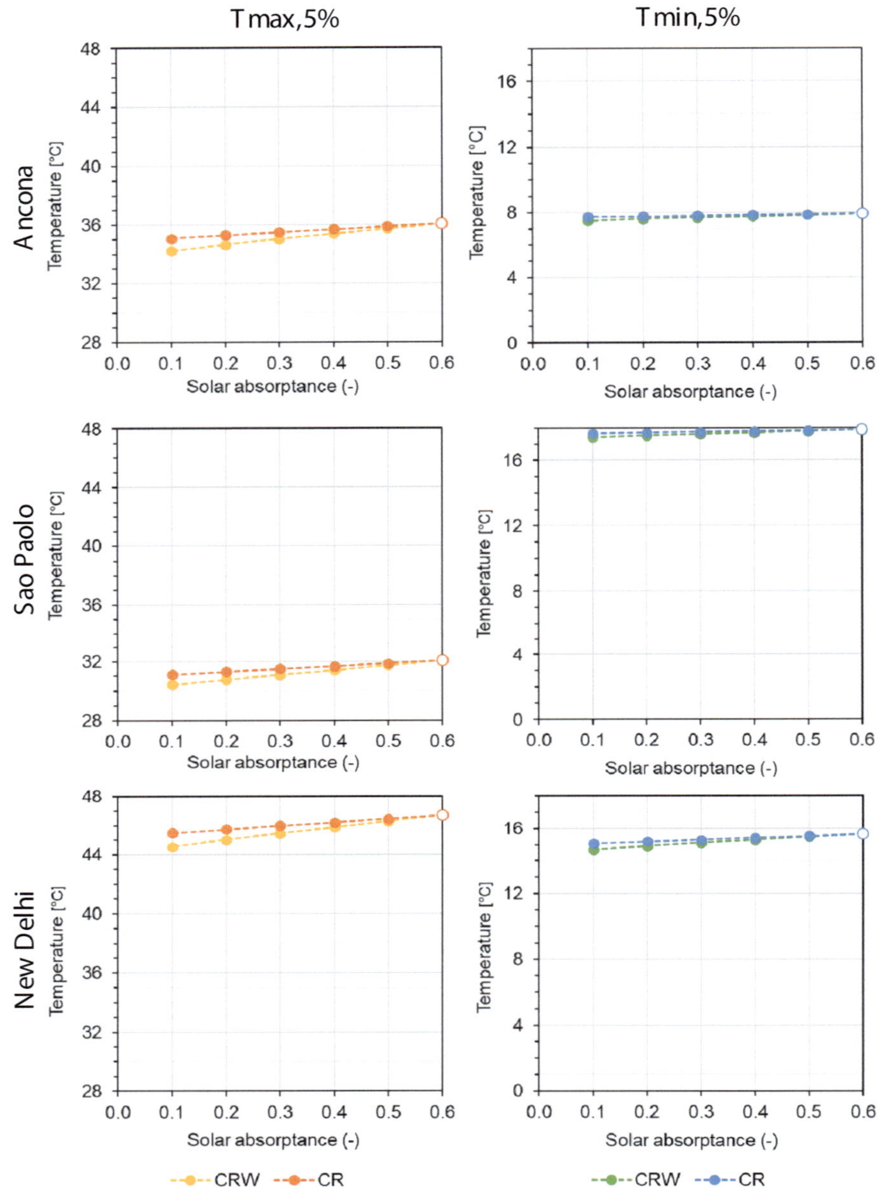

Fig. 6.9 Impact of solar absorptance on living room indoor temperature across three climates. CR: Cool roof; CRW: Cool roof and walls

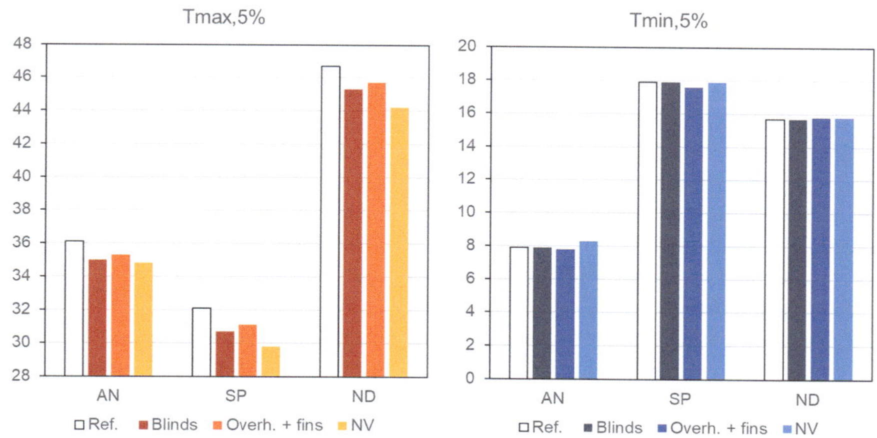

Fig. 6.10 Indicators of performance for natural ventilation and shading techniques across various climate zones (AN: Ancona; SP: Sao Paulo; ND: New Delhi) in the western room

6.3.3.3 Natural Ventilation

The performance of the natural ventilation (NV) strategy was evaluated and summarized in Fig. 6.10. The data confirm the effectiveness of NV in mitigating overheating during the hottest months across all considered climates. Among the analyzed locations, the greatest reduction in $T_{max, 5\%}$ was observed in New Delhi, followed by São Paulo and then Ancona. These differences can be directly linked to local climatic conditions—specifically, wind speed and the thermal gradient between indoor and outdoor air. A higher thermal gradient typically results in more effective heat removal when cooler outdoor air is introduced into an overheated indoor environment. Similarly, greater wind speeds increase the volume of fresh air entering the space, thereby enhancing cooling through convection.

In New Delhi, the pronounced thermal gradient during summer was the primary driver of NV effectiveness. Although the average wind speed was relatively low (1.43 m/s), the extreme indoor–outdoor temperature differential amplified the cooling potential. In contrast, São Paulo exhibited a more moderate thermal gradient but had the highest average summer wind speed (2.84 m/s), which compensated for the smaller temperature differential. Ancona, on the other hand, demonstrated the least effective NV performance, owing to its combination of relatively low wind speed (1.64 m/s) and a modest thermal gradient.

These findings underscore the strong dependence of natural ventilation performance on site-specific climatic factors. The variability in outcome highlights the importance of tailoring NV strategies to local meteorological conditions when designing passive cooling interventions for temporary or emergency buildings.

6.3.3.4 Internal Thermal Inertia Increasing

Figure 6.11 presents the results obtained by enhancing the thermal storage capacity of the HOMEDONE unit through the application of interior gypsum boards of varying thicknesses (G strategy). As anticipated, increasing the thickness of these internal linings led to a progressive reduction in maximum summer temperatures ($T_{max, 5\%}$) and a corresponding increase in minimum winter temperatures ($TT_{min, 5\%}$). This demonstrates the dual seasonal benefit of internal thermal inertia: mitigating summer overheating and reducing cold stress during winter.

Among the three climates, São Paulo exhibited the most pronounced reduction in $T_{max, 5\%}$ when thermal inertia was increased. This finding can be attributed to the lower baseline overheating intensity in São Paulo, which allows the gypsum boards to interact more effectively with the indoor air, storing cool nighttime energy and releasing it during warmer daytime hours. In contrast, the higher overheating levels in New Delhi may reduce the effectiveness of this dynamic thermal exchange.

An added benefit of this strategy is its capacity to elevate indoor temperatures during colder periods—a positive side effect in emergency shelters lacking active heating. By enhancing nighttime heat retention, gypsum board linings contribute to greater year-round thermal comfort, reinforcing their utility as a passive solution for diverse climate contexts.

6.3.4 Comparison, Combinations and Trade-Offs

6.3.4.1 Thermal Comfort

In this section, the performance of the different passive strategies is compared, taking into account both their individual and combined effects. For all the passive strategies, only the best-performing configurations—based on their ability to reduce the upper 5% of peak indoor air temperatures ($T_{max, 5\%}$)—were considered, e.g., slatted blinds for shading (B), and 25 mm-thick gypsum boards for thermal inertia enhancement (G).

Overall, the most effective strategies in terms of reducing $T_{max, 5\%}$ (see Table 6.2) and minimizing hours of thermal discomfort due to overheating (see Figs. 6.12 and 6.13) were the two heat dissipation approaches: natural ventilation (NV) and the cool roof and walls configuration (CRW). These were followed by the heat protection strategy (B) and the thermal inertia strategy (G). NV consistently outperformed all other measures in nearly all climates, with the exception of Ancona, where its performance was limited by lower summer wind speeds and a milder overheating profile compared to New Delhi. In that specific context, CRW yielded marginally better results. Nevertheless, considering the potential drawbacks of reflective materials in winter and their likely degradation in polluted urban contexts within a year of installation, NV can still be considered the most robust and universally effective strategy across all locations.

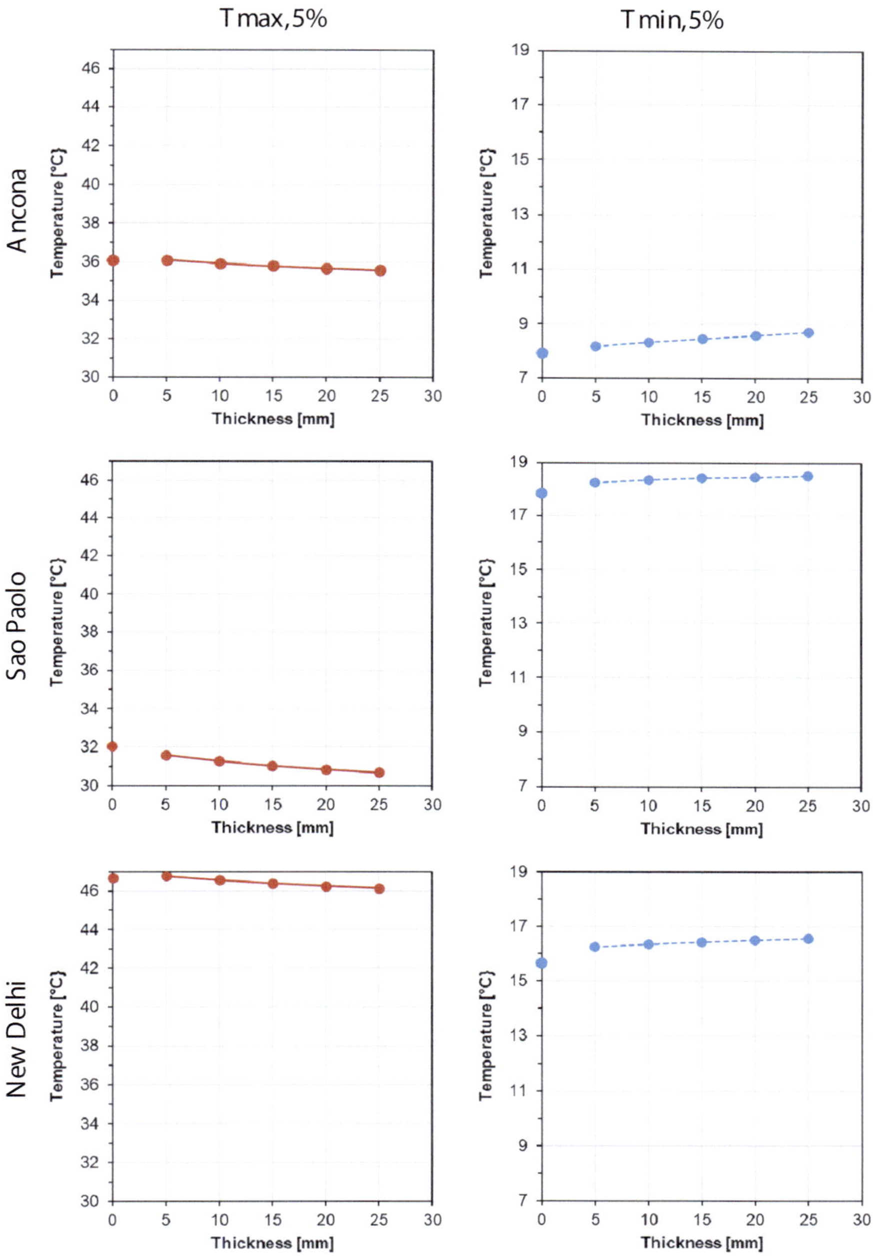

Fig. 6.11 The effect of the interior gypsum layer on the indoor air temperature within living rooms across three distinct climate zones

Table 6.2 A comparison of various techniques based on $T_{max, 5\%}$ and $T_{min, 5\%}$ variations, along with a ranking of solutions according to their effectiveness in lowering $T_{max, 5\%}$ (indicated in parentheses)

	$T_{max, 5\%}$ [°C]			$T_{min, 5\%}$ [°C]		
	AN	SP	ND	AN	SP	ND
Ref.	36.1	32.1	46.7	7.9	17.9	15.7
NV	−1.2 (2)	−2.2 (1)	−2.5 (1)	0.3	0.0	0.1
B	−1.1 (3)	−1.4 (3)	−1.4 (3)	0.0	0.0	0.0
G	−0.5 (5)	−1.4 (4)	−0.6 (5)	0.8	0.7	0.9
CR	−1.0 (4)	−0.9 (5)	−1.2 (4)	7.7	17.7	15.1
CRW	−1.8 (1)	−1.6 (2)	−2.2 (2)	−0.4	−0.5	−1.0
NV + B	−1.2 (2)	−2.6 (3)	−3.0 (2)	0.3	0.0	0.1
NV + G	−1.0 (4)	−3.1 (1)	−1.4 (4)	1.3	0.6	2.5
NV + CR	−1.2 (3)	−2.5 (4)	−3.0 (3)	0.2	−0.2	−0.4
NV + CRW	−1.8 (1)	−2.8 (2)	−3.3 (1)	−0.1	−0.5	−0.9
NV + B + CRW	−2.1 (1)	−3.1 (2)	−3.7 (1)	−0.1	−0.5	−0.9
All	−1.5 (2)	−3.8 (1)	−2.5 (2)	0.9	0.2	0.1

"All" refers to the combination of all strategies

At the opposite end, the G strategy was the least effective in Ancona and New Delhi. Notably, the application of gypsum boards (G) in these two climates led to an actual increase in the total hours of thermal discomfort due to overheating (Figs. 6.12 and 6.13). This phenomenon can be attributed to the fact that average indoor summer temperatures in these cases already exceeded the upper comfort threshold. Thus, although increased thermal inertia helped reduce temperature fluctuations, it did not bring peak values below the threshold. At the same time, minimum indoor temperatures, which were originally within the comfort band, were raised beyond the upper limit due to the heat retention effect—ultimately reducing the total number of comfort hours. In São Paulo, on the other hand, the baseline indoor temperature profile during summer remained closer to the comfort zone. Hence, the dampening effect from the thermal inertia measure proved effective in both lowering maximum and raising minimum temperatures within acceptable comfort limits.

Table 6.2, Figs. 6.12, and 6.13 also report the results of combining NV with each of the other passive strategies: NV + B, NV + G, NV + CR, and NV + CRW. As expected, the most favorable outcome was achieved by combining the two top-performing strategies—NV and CRW—across most climates. An exception was observed in São Paulo, where the combination NV + G outperformed others due to the specific efficacy of the G strategy in that climatic context.

The results from the comprehensive combination of all passive strategies—both with and without the inclusion of the G strategy—are also shown in Table 6.2 and Figs. 6.12 and 6.13. Interestingly, deploying every strategy simultaneously did not necessarily yield the best outcome. In both Ancona and New Delhi, the combination

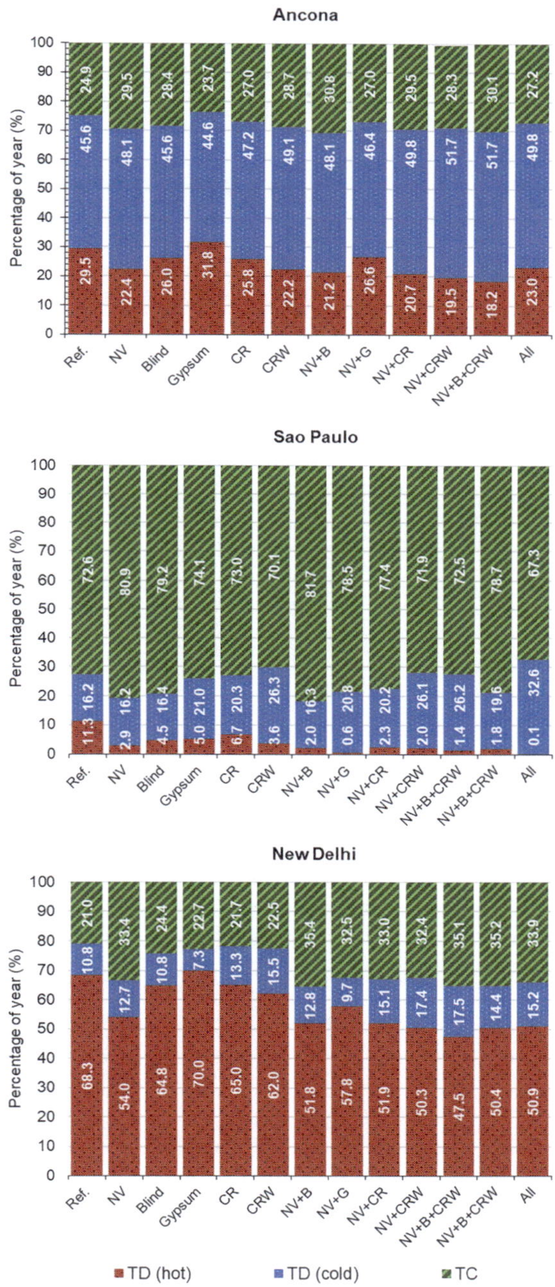

Fig. 6.12 Thermal comfort and discomfort for occupants evaluated according to EN 16798-1 [14], considering both individual and combined passive cooling strategies across various locations

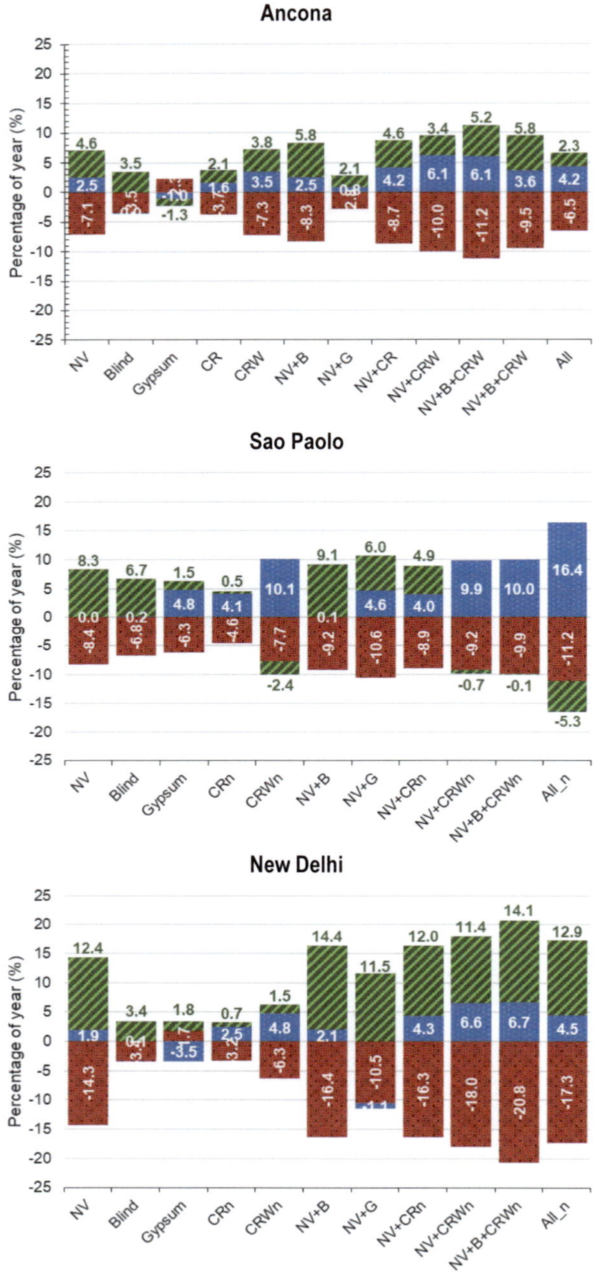

Fig. 6.13 Percentage differences in the duration of thermal comfort/discomfort between the reference building and the building post implementation of the various measures

of NV + B + CRW outperformed the full-strategy approach. This suggests that selective implementation, rather than maximizing the number of interventions, can optimize performance while avoiding unnecessary costs. In São Paulo, by contrast, the complete set of combined strategies achieved the best thermal comfort results, due to the favorable contribution of the G measure in that setting.

Importantly, only in São Paulo was it possible to stay below the critical 1.25% annual threshold for overheating discomfort defined by CIBSE Guide A [38], particularly when implementing the NV + G and full-combination strategies.

Finally, a more global perspective on thermal comfort can be drawn by evaluating the total increase in comfort hours—i.e., hours no longer characterized by discomfort due to either hot or cold conditions. Under this metric, the NV + B combination emerged as the best overall strategy in all three climates, leading to comfort hour gains equivalent to 5.8%, 9.1%, and 14.4% of the total annual hours in Ancona, São Paulo, and New Delhi, respectively.

6.3.4.2 Cost-Effectiveness and Operational Feasibility

Given the central role of financial constraints in emergency housing scenarios, a comparative analysis of the proposed passive strategies was conducted in terms of both cost and cooling effectiveness. Figure 6.14 illustrates this dual comparison, presenting results in terms of maximum temperature reduction ($T_{max,5\%}$; Fig. 6.14a) and the percentage of thermal discomfort hours due to overheating (Fig. 6.14b). Costs refer to the additional manufacturing expenditures required for each strategy prior to unit delivery.

As is common in multi-criteria decision-making, the goals of minimizing cost and maximizing cooling performance are inherently conflicting. Consequently, a single universally optimal solution does not exist. Instead, the analysis relies on the concept of Pareto optimality: a strategy is considered Pareto optimal when no other solution performs better in both cost and effectiveness simultaneously. The set of such non-dominated strategies defines the so-called Pareto front, which is plotted for each climate in Fig. 6.14a, b. In all climate contexts and aging conditions, the Pareto front is composed exclusively of strategies involving natural ventilation (NV), either alone or in combination with other measures. The strategies NV, NV + CR, NV + B, NV + CRW, and NV + B + CRW consistently form the Pareto front across all climates. Only in the São Paulo case do the more expensive NV + G and "All combined" strategies also qualify as Pareto-optimal solutions. While identifying a single "best" solution among Pareto-optimal alternatives remains inherently subjective and context-dependent, several general insights can be drawn.

First, the NV strategy emerges as the most cost-effective option in all climates due to its zero implementation cost. As such, it represents an immediate improvement over the no-intervention baseline scenario and is the first logical step toward enhanced thermal comfort in emergency contexts.

At the other end of the spectrum, strategies incorporating gypsum boards (G)—namely NV + G and the All Combined strategy—represent the most expensive

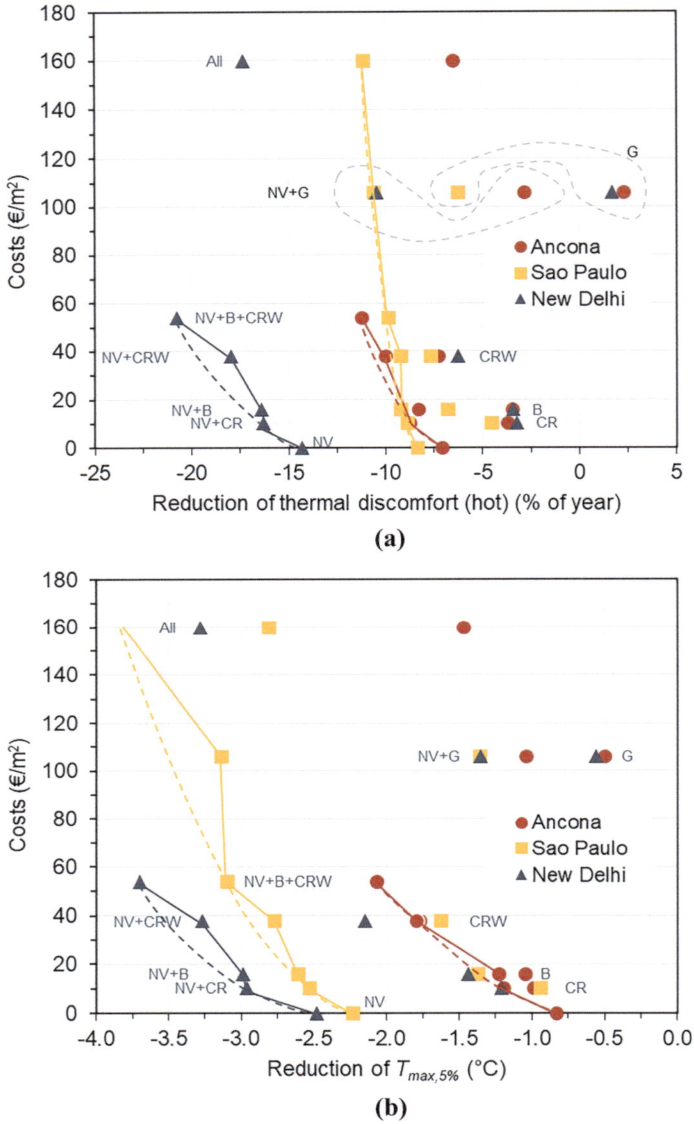

Fig. 6.14 Analysis of various passive strategies regarding **a** costs and the decrease in $T_{\max, 5\%}$; **b** costs and the mitigation of thermal discomfort caused by overheating. Dashed and solid lines indicate theoretical and actual Pareto fronts, respectively, displaying optimal solutions for each climatic region

options. As shown in Fig. 6.14, these higher costs are not matched by proportionally higher cooling benefits, even in the São Paulo case. For this reason, and given that G-based solutions do not belong to the Pareto front in Ancona or New Delhi, the increase in thermal inertia cannot be recommended for lightweight emergency housing in these climates unless the cost of implementation is substantially reduced. Moreover, the G strategy poses significant feasibility challenges: it requires skilled labor, may face logistical complications due to the added weight and volume of materials, and reduces usable interior space—constraints that are particularly problematic in emergency deployment contexts.

Among the remaining strategies, NV + CR and NV + B consistently emerge as the lowest cost combinations across all climate scenarios. NV + CR offers the best performance in terms of cost-effectiveness—calculated as the ratio between investment cost and thermal performance. This relationship is visually represented in Fig. 6.14 by the slope of the line connecting the NV marker (representing zero-cost baseline optimization) to each strategy marker: the flatter the slope, the greater the cost-effectiveness.

Additionally, in certain contexts where winter discomfort due to cold is a significant concern—such as in Ancona—NV + B may be preferred over NV + CR. This is because its slightly higher cost is compensated by a negligible increase in cold-related discomfort hours (see, e.g., Fig. 6.12), a factor that further strengthens its year-round appeal.

In summary:

- NV + CR may be considered the optimal trade-off in hot climates, provided that its performance is not expected to deteriorate significantly over time due to surface aging. In polluted contexts, its adoption should be contingent upon the feasibility of periodic cleaning and maintenance by occupants.
- NV + B, on the other hand, is the most robust and reliable strategy across diverse conditions—hot or temperate—and offers the best compromise between thermal comfort, economic viability, and operational feasibility.

Therefore, NV + B should be prioritized as the first-line solution for improving indoor environmental quality in lightweight temporary housing units, particularly where long-term durability, ease of implementation, and occupant independence are essential.

Acknowledgements Financial support for these activities was provided by the AC-Engineering S.p.A through the "POR FESR Marche 2014/2020" (Research Project No. 15345).

References

1. A.S. Sferra, Emergency: innovative prefabricated construction components for an eco-solidarity architecture. TECHNE J. Technol. Arch. Environ. 328–334 (2017). https://doi.org/10.13128/Techne-20788

2. P. Samani, V. Leal, A. Mendes, N. Correia, Comparison of passive cooling techniques in improving thermal comfort of occupants of a pre-fabricated building. Energy Build. **120**, 30–44 (2016). https://doi.org/10.1016/j.enbuild.2016.03.055
3. F. Harkouss, F. Fardoun, P.H. Biwole, Passive design optimization of low energy buildings in different climates. Energy **165**, 591–613 (2018). https://doi.org/10.1016/j.energy.2018.09.019
4. D. Cockcroft, DesignBuilder building simulation (2021). www.designbuilder.co.uk
5. DOE, EnergyPlus (U.S. Department of Energy's, 2017)
6. P. Samani, A. Mendes, V. Leal, N. Correia, Pre-fabricated, environmentally friendly and energy self-sufficient single-family house in Kenya. J. Clean. Prod. **142**, 2100–2113 (2017). https://doi.org/10.1016/j.jclepro.2016.11.073
7. J. Woods, J. Winkler, Effective moisture penetration depth model for residential buildings: sensitivity analysis and guidance on model inputs. Energy Build. **165**, 216–232 (2018). https://doi.org/10.1016/j.enbuild.2018.01.040
8. J. Woods, J. Winkler, D. Christensen, *Evaluation of the Effective Moisture Penetration Depth Model for Estimating Moisture Buffering in Buildings* (Contract, 2013)
9. V. Costanzo, G. Evola, L. Marletta, A. Gagliano, Proper evaluation of the external convective heat transfer for the thermal analysis of cool roofs. Energy Build. **77**, 467–477 (2014). https://doi.org/10.1016/j.enbuild.2014.03.064
10. E. Fabrizio, V. Monetti, Methodologies and advancements in the calibration of building energy models. Energies (Basel) **8**, 2548–2574 (2015). https://doi.org/10.3390/en8042548
11. A. O' Donovan, P.D. O' Sullivan, M.D. Murphy, Predicting air temperatures in a naturally ventilated nearly zero energy building: calibration, validation, analysis and approaches. Appl. Energy **250**, 991–1010 (2019). https://doi.org/10.1016/j.apenergy.2019.04.082
12. Y. Wang, E. Long, S. Deng, Applying passive cooling measures to a temporary disaster-relief prefabricated house to improve its indoor thermal environment in summer in the subtropics. Energy Build. **139**, 456–464 (2017). https://doi.org/10.1016/j.enbuild.2016.12.081
13. C. Wang, S. Deng, J. Niu, E. Long, A numerical study on optimizing the designs of applying PCMs to a disaster-relief prefabricated temporary-house (PTH) to improve its summer daytime indoor thermal environment. Energy **181**, 239–249 (2019). https://doi.org/10.1016/j.energy.2019.05.165
14. EN, EN 16798-1:2019 Energy performance of buildings—Ventilation for buildings—Part 1: Indoor environmental input parameters for design and assessment of energy performance of buildings addressing in-door air quality. Therm Environ Light Acoust (2019)
15. M. D'Orazio, G. Maracchini, An experimental investigation on the indoor hygrothermal environment of a reinforced-EPS based temporary housing solution. Energy Build. **204**, 109500 (2019). https://doi.org/10.1016/j.enbuild.2019.109500
16. ISO, EN ISO 7730:2005 Ergonomics of the thermal environment—analytical determination and interpretation of thermal comfort using calculation of the PMV and PPD indices and local thermal comfort criteria (2005)
17. D.K. Bhamare, M.K. Rathod, J. Banerjee, Passive cooling techniques for building and their applicability in different climatic zones—the state of art. Energy Build. **198**, 467–490 (2019). https://doi.org/10.1016/j.enbuild.2019.06.023
18. H. Akbari, R. Levinson, Evolution of cool-roof standards in the US. Adv. Build. Energy Res. (2008). https://doi.org/10.3763/aber.2008.0201
19. J.P. de Brito Filho, J.R. Henriquez, J.C.C. Dutra, Effects of coefficients of solar reflectivity and infrared emissivity on the temperature and heat flux of horizontal flat roofs of artificially conditioned nonresidential buildings. Energy Build. **43**, 440–445 (2011). https://doi.org/10.1016/j.enbuild.2010.10.007
20. M. Zinzi, S. Agnoli, Cool and green roofs. An energy and comfort comparison between passive cooling and mitigation urban heat island techniques for residential buildings in the Mediterranean region. Energy Build. **55**, 66–76 (2012). https://doi.org/10.1016/j.enbuild.2011.09.024
21. D. Borge-Diez, A. Colmenar-Santos, C. Pérez-Molina, M. Castro-Gil, Passive climatization using a cool roof and natural ventilation for internally displaced persons in hot climates: case

study for Haiti. Build Environ **59**, 116–126 (2013). https://doi.org/10.1016/j.buildenv.2012.08.013
22. M.-D. Cheng, W. Miller, J. New, P. Berdahl, Understanding the long-term effects of environmental exposure on roof reflectance in California. Constr. Build. Mater. **26**, 516–526 (2012). https://doi.org/10.1016/j.conbuildmat.2011.06.052
23. R. Paolini, A. Zani, T. Poli et al., Natural aging of cool walls: impact on solar reflectance, sensitivity to thermal shocks and building energy needs. Energy Build. **153**, 287–296 (2017). https://doi.org/10.1016/j.enbuild.2017.08.017
24. M. Sleiman, G. Ban-Weiss, H.E. Gilbert et al., Soiling of building envelope surfaces and its effect on solar reflectance—part I: analysis of roofing product databases. Sol. Energy Mater. Sol. Cells **95**, 3385–3399 (2011). https://doi.org/10.1016/j.solmat.2011.08.002
25. R. Paolini, G. Terraneo, C. Ferrari et al., Effects of soiling and weathering on the albedo of building envelope materials: lessons learned from natural exposure in two European cities and tuning of a laboratory simulation practice. Sol. Energy Mater. Sol. Cells **205**, 110264 (2020). https://doi.org/10.1016/j.solmat.2019.110264
26. R. Levinson, P. Berdahl, A. Asefaw Berhe, H. Akbari, Effects of soiling and cleaning on the reflectance and solar heat gain of a light-colored roofing membrane. Atmos. Environ. **39**, 7807–7824 (2005). https://doi.org/10.1016/j.atmosenv.2005.08.037
27. UNI/PdR 13.1:2019, ITACA—Istituto per l'innovazione e trasparenza degli appalti e la compatibilità ambientale—Environmental sustainability of construction works—Operational tools for sustainability assessment—Residential buildings (2019) (in Italian)
28. ASHRAE 55, *Ashrae Handbook Fundamentals* (2017)
29. DOE, Engineering reference, in *EnergyPlus Version 8.9 Documentation* (U.S. Department of Energy (DOE), 2019)
30. K. Menberg, Y. Heo, R. Choudhary, Sensitivity analysis methods for building energy models: comparing computational costs and extractable information. Energy Build. **133**, 433–445 (2016). https://doi.org/10.1016/j.enbuild.2016.10.005
31. P. Heiselberg, K. Svidt, P.V. Nielsen, Characteristics of airflow from open windows. Build. Environ. (2001). https://doi.org/10.1016/S0360-1323(01)00012-9
32. UNI (2019) UNI/TS 11300-1—Prestazioni energetiche degli edifice—Parte 1: Determinazione del fabbisogno di energia termica dell'edificio per la climatizzazione estiva ed invernale (in Italian)
33. ASHRAE, *ASHRAE Handbook-Fundamentals* (2013), pp. 21.1–21.67. https://doi.org/10.1017/CBO9781107415324.004
34. IDMC, Mid-Year Figures 2019 | Internal Displacement Monitoring Centre (IDMC) (2019). http://www.internal-displacement.org/mid-year-figures. Accessed 5 Nov 2020
35. M. Taleghani, D.J. Sailor, M. Tenpierik, D.A. Van Den, Thermal assessment of heat mitigation strategies: the case of Portland State University, Oregon, USA. Build. Environ. **73**, 138–150 (2014). https://doi.org/10.1016/j.buildenv.2013.12.006
36. D. Coakley, P. Raftery, M. Keane, A review of methods to match building energy simulation models to measured data. Renew. Sustain. Energy Rev. **37**, 123–141 (2014). https://doi.org/10.1016/j.rser.2014.05.007
37. S. Martínez, P. Eguía, E. Granada et al., A performance comparison of multi-objective optimization-based approaches for calibrating white-box building energy models. Energy Build. **216**, 109942 (2020). https://doi.org/10.1016/j.enbuild.2020.109942
38. CIBSE, The limits of thermal comfort : avoiding overheating in European buildings. CIBSE Tm52 1–25 (2013)

Chapter 7
Conclusions

Abstract This concluding chapter synthesizes the key findings of the book, summarizing the significance of thermal comfort and indoor hygrothermal conditions in emergency and temporary housing. The main insights derived from experimental monitoring and numerical simulations are discussed, highlighting the most effective passive cooling and moisture management strategies. Natural ventilation, reflective materials, and moisture-buffering layers emerged as critical solutions, balancing performance, cost-effectiveness, and operational feasibility. The chapter emphasizes the importance of context-specific approaches and calls for further research on adaptable guidelines and occupant-focused strategies in emergency architectural practices.

Keywords Thermal comfort · Overheating · Passive cooling · Lightweight envelope · Natural ventilation · Cool materials · Shading devices · Thermal inertia · Cost-effectiveness · Emergency housing

This book addresses the critical issue of thermal comfort in temporary housing solutions, highlighting the significance of ensuring adequate indoor hygrothermal conditions in emergency architectures. Temporary housing, while initially intended as short-term shelters, often becomes long-term accommodations. Underestimating thermal comfort in these structures can lead to severe health risks and reduced livability, especially considering the diverse climatic conditions and absence of suitable environmental control systems.

A structured approach combining literature review, experimental analyses, and numerical simulations has been employed throughout this work to comprehensively assess and optimize indoor comfort conditions. The investigation presented herein addressed three main objectives: to characterize the typical architectural requirements influencing thermal comfort, to systematically evaluate indoor environmental quality

In this chapter: G.M.: Conceptualization, Writing—Original Draft, Supervision, and Project Administration. M.d.O.: Conceptualization, Writing—Review and Editing.

G. Maracchini and M. D'Orazio, *Thermal Comfort in Emergency Architectures*, SpringerBriefs in Applied Sciences and Technology,
https://doi.org/10.1007/978-3-032-06795-1_7

and moisture-related issues, and to propose practical and cost-effective passive strategies for thermal comfort improvement.

In Chap. 2, a detailed overview of design and construction requirements of temporary housing solutions was presented, emphasizing the impact of architectural characteristics—such as dimensions, orientation, materials, and construction techniques—on thermal comfort. The analysis demonstrated that appropriate building orientation, compact design, and the strategic selection of materials are foundational in achieving comfortable indoor environments, especially where active conditioning systems are not feasible.

The literature review discussed in Chap. 3 highlighted the prevalence of inadequate thermal conditions in existing emergency shelters globally. It revealed gaps in current thermal comfort models, suggesting a critical need to refine these models by incorporating occupants' adaptability and psychological resilience factors, often heightened in post-disaster scenarios. Passive cooling strategies emerged as essential tools, with natural ventilation, reflective surfaces, and shading systems showing particular promise due to their effectiveness, ease of deployment, and low cost.

Experimental monitoring carried out within the HOMEDONE experience (Chaps. 4 and 5) reinforced the importance of accurate, real-world characterization of temporary structures. Measurements indicated significant overheating and moisture accumulation issues, especially at thermal bridges and junction points. Numerical simulations further quantified condensation risks and mold growth potential across diverse climatic contexts, confirming that moisture-related concerns can significantly compromise indoor environmental quality. The introduction of moisture-buffering internal layers, such as cementitious renders and gypsum plasterboards, proved effective in mitigating these problems, highlighting the importance of considering hygric properties in material selection.

The optimization strategies evaluated in Chap. 6 through comprehensive numerical simulations offered actionable insights into the effectiveness of passive interventions. Among various strategies, natural ventilation and cool roofs stood out as consistently effective solutions for mitigating overheating, particularly when combined strategically. Conversely, increasing internal thermal inertia through gypsum boards, although beneficial in some contexts, posed significant financial and operational challenges, reducing its feasibility for broad emergency application.

In conclusion, achieving thermal comfort in emergency architecture demands a balanced integration of passive cooling and moisture management strategies, informed by careful consideration of climatic context, operational feasibility, and cost-effectiveness. The findings presented here demonstrate that even modest interventions—such as promoting natural ventilation and applying reflective coatings—can significantly enhance thermal comfort and livability in temporary structures.

Ultimately, the insights gained through this study provide valuable guidance to practitioners, policymakers, humanitarian agencies, and researchers involved in the design and implementation of emergency housing. Further research should continue to address context-specific optimization of passive strategies, consider occupant behavior more explicitly, and develop adaptable guidelines capable of informing real-world humanitarian interventions.

MIX
Papier aus verantwortungsvollen Quellen
Paper from responsible sources
FSC® C105338

If you have any concerns about our products,
you can contact us on
ProductSafety@springernature.com

In case Publisher is established outside the EU,
the EU authorized representative is:
Springer Nature Customer Service Center GmbH
Europaplatz 3, 69115 Heidelberg, Germany

Printed by Libri Plureos GmbH
in Hamburg, Germany

Optimisation of ZnO Thin Films

Saurabh Nagar · Subhananda Chakrabarti

Optimisation of ZnO Thin Films

Implants, Properties, and Device Fabrication

Springer

Saurabh Nagar
Department of Electrical Engineering
Indian Institute of Technology Bombay
Mumbai, Maharashtra
India

Subhananda Chakrabarti
Department of Electrical Engineering
Indian Institute of Technology Bombay
Mumbai, Maharashtra
India

ISBN 978-981-10-9257-2 ISBN 978-981-10-0809-2 (eBook)
DOI 10.1007/978-981-10-0809-2

Softcover reprint of the hardcover 1st edition 2017

Printed on acid-free paper

This Springer imprint is published by Springer Nature
The registered company is Springer Nature Singapore Pte Ltd.
The registered company address is: 152 Beach Road, #21-01/04 Gateway East, Singapore 189721, Singapore

Preface

Extensive research is currently carried out on ZnO as a potential material for the fabrication of optoelectronic devices such as laser diodes (LDs) and light-emitting diodes (LEDs) in the ultraviolet (UV) region because of its wide bandgap (3.437 eV at 2 K) and a large excitonic binding energy of 60 meV at room temperature. However, the bottleneck in ZnO-based devices is the creation of reliable and reproducible p-type films, because ZnO is an intrinsically n-type material due to defects such as oxygen vacancies and zinc interstitials. The low solubility of dopants and self-compensating process on doping further aggravate the problem. This monograph describes the different implantation mechanisms which can be used to achieve strong, reliable and stable p-type ZnO thin films which would result in revelations in the optoelectronics field in the UV region. This monograph will be very useful for new doctorant students who want to work on doping and implantation of ZnO thin films and subsequently fabricating optoelectronic devices. Chapter 1 of the monograph emphasises the importance of ZnO in the field of optoelectronics for ultraviolet (UV) region and also discusses the material, electronic and optical properties of ZnO. Chapter 2 discusses the optimisation of the pulsed laser-deposited (PLD) ZnO thin films in order to make successful p-type films and in order to achieve the high optical output required for higher efficiency devices. It also discusses a hydrogen implantation study on the optimised films to confirm whether the implantation leads to improvement in the optimised results. Chapter 3 gives details about the various implantation studies performed on ZnO thin films in order to achieve successful and reliable p-type ZnO films. Conventional ion implantation (CII) was used to implant lithium and phosphorus ions, while plasma immersion ion implantation (PIII) was used to implant phosphorus and nitrogen ions. Once the p-type ZnO was achieved, the fabrication and characterisation of the different ZnO-based optoelectronic devices were carried out which have been discussed in Chap. 4. The successful fabrication of heterojunction devices such as p-ZnO/n-Si diode and p-ZnO/p-Si detectors is demonstrated. Fabrication of p-ZnO/n-ZnO homojunction LED is also demonstrated. The last chapter summarises the various results of the experiments presented and provides an insight into potential further studies in this field.

We would like to thank Prof. David C. Look of Wright State University for sharing his knowledge, which has helped us in better understanding of the subject. We would also like to thank Dr. Suhas Jejurikar, Dr. Nilanjan Halder and Dr. Bhavesh Sinha for their fruitful discussions when they were in IIT Bombay. We are thankful to Dr. S.K. Gupta, Mr. Arindam Basu and Mr. B.V. Subhramanyam for helping me out in performing the LEAF experiments. We are also thankful to the SPM facility at IIT Bombay for performing the AFM measurements. We are thankful to all our present and past group members Dr. Arjun Mandal, Dr. Saumya Sengupta, Dr. Sourav Adhikary, Sandeep Kala, M. Kulasekaran, Aijaz Ahmed, Saikalash Shetty, Hemant Ghadi, Goma KC and Akshay Balgarkashi. We would like to thank all the laboratory members and facility staff of IITBNF. We are grateful to our funding agencies namely Department of Science and Technology, Govt of India, and MCIT through IIBNF.

Keywords—II–VI semiconductors, ZnO, LEDs, Detectors, Pulsed laser deposition, Sputtering, Low-Energy Accelerator Facility, Plasma immersion ion implantation, X-ray diffraction, Atomic force microscopy, Scanning electron microscopy, Van der Pauw Hall, Photoluminescence, Thermally stimulated current, Electroluminescence, Spectral response.

Mumbai, India

Saurabh Nagar
Subhananda Chakrabarti

Contents

About the Authors

Saurabh Nagar received his Bachelor of Technology in electronics and communication engineering from the Bengal College of Engineering and Technology, West Bengal University of Technology, India, and completed his Ph.D. from the Department of Electrical Engineering, Indian Institute of Technology Bombay, Mumbai, India, in 2013. He worked as a Research Associate at the Indian Institute of Technology Bombay for 9 months followed by a Postdoctoral Fellow at Institut des Nanotechnologie de Lyon (INL), Ecole Centrale de Lyon, for 18 months. Presently, he is a scientific employee at the Institute Functional Oxides for Energy Efficient Information Technologies at Helmholtz-Zentrum Berlin. His research interest includes ZnO-based optoelectronics devices and oxide-based materials for memristor applications.

Subhananda Chakrabarti received his M.Sc. and Ph.D. degrees from the Department of Electronic Science, University of Calcutta, Kolkata, India, in 1993 and 2000, respectively. He was a Lecturer in the Department of Physics, St. Xavier's College, Kolkata. He has been a Senior Research Fellow with the University of Michigan, Ann Arbor, from 2001 to 2005; a Senior Researcher with Dublin City University, Dublin City, Ireland, from 2005 to 2006; and a Senior Researcher (RA2) with the University of Glasgow, Glasgow, UK, from 2006 to 2007. He joined as an Assistant Professor in the Department of Electrical Engineering, IIT Bombay, Mumbai, India, in 2007. Presently, he is a Professor in the same department. He is a Fellow of the Institution of Electrical and Telecommunication Engineers (IETE), India, and also a Member of the IEEE, MRS (USA), SPIE (USA), etc. He is the 2016 medal recipient of the Materials Research Society of India and was also awarded the 2016 NASI-Reliance Industries Platinum Jubilee Award for application-oriented innovations in physical sciences. He serves as an Editor of the IEEE Journal of Electron Device Society. He has authored more than 250 papers in international journals and conferences. He has also co-authored a couple of book chapters on intersubband quantum dot detectors.

Dr. S. Chakrabarti serves as reviewer for a number of international journals of repute such as Applied Physics Letters, Nature Scientific Reports, IEEE Photonics Technology Letters, IEEE Journal of Quantum Electronics, Journal of Alloys and Compound and Material Research Bulletin. His research interests lie in compound (III–V and II–VI) semiconductor-based optoelectronic materials and devices.

Abbreviations

ABE/A°X	Acceptor-bound-exciton
AFM	Atomic force microscope
Al	Aluminium
ALD	Atomic layer deposition
Au	Gold
CII	Conventional ion implantation
CVD	Chemical vapour deposition
DAP	Donor-to-acceptor pair
DBE/D°X	Donor-bound exciton
EL	Electroluminescence
FA	Free electron-to-acceptor
FWHM	Full width at half maximum
FX	Free exciton
GaN	Gallium nitride
IPA	Isopropyl alcohol
ITO	Indium tin oxide
k/k_B	Boltzmann constant
KrF	Krypton Fluoride
LD	Laser diode
LEAF	Low-Energy Accelerator Facility
LED	Light-Emitting Diode
LO	Longitudinal optical
MBE	Molecular beam epitaxy
NBE	Near-band-edge emission
Ni	Nickel
NiO	Nickel oxide
PIII	Plasma immersion ion implantation
PL	Photoluminescence
PLD	Pulsed laser deposition
RF	Radio frequency

rms	Root mean square
RTEL	Room temperature electroluminescence
SEM	Scanning electron microscope
SIMS	Secondary ion mass spectroscopy
TCE	Trichloroethylene
Ti	Titanium
TSC	Thermally stimulated current
UV	Ultraviolet
V_O	Oxygen vacancy
XRD	X-ray diffraction
Zn_i	Zinc interstitials
ZnMgO	Zinc magnesium oxide
ZnO	Zinc oxide

List of Figures

List of Tables

Chapter 1
Introduction

Abstract Extensive research is currently carried out on ZnO as a potential material for the fabrication of optoelectronic devices such as photodiodes, laser diodes (LDs) and light-emitting diodes (LEDs) in the ultraviolet region because of its wide bandgap (3.437 eV at 2 K) and a large excitonic binding energy of 60 meV at room temperature. However, because of intrinsic defects such as oxygen vacancies and zinc interstitials, ZnO is intrinsically deposited as an n-type material. Being a II–VI semiconductor compound, group I and group V elements are considered suitable p-type dopants for ZnO. In this monograph, authors concentrate mostly on the different methods undertaken to achieve strong, reliable and stable p-type ZnO films. Ion implantation, being a suitable technique to achieve selective and localised doping, was used to dope ZnO with different group I and group V elements. Lithium and phosphorus ions were implanted using the conventional ion implantation technique, while plasma immersion ion implantation was used to implant phosphorus and nitrogen ions in the ZnO thin films. Such studies would bring interesting revelations in the optoelectronics field for the ultraviolet range and help to produce devices for the commercial market at a much cheaper cost.

Keywords II–VI semiconductor · ZnO · LED's · Detectors

In recent years, researchers across the globe have shown great interest in zinc oxide (ZnO) as a semiconductor material, primarily due to its interesting prospects in the field of optoelectronics applications owing to its wide and direct bandgap (~3.437 eV at 8 K) [1]. In fact, ZnO has become a strong competitor of gallium nitride (GaN), another wide bandgap semiconductor (~3.4 eV at 300 K), as they share most common properties. However, due to its large exciton-binding energy of 60 meV (GaN: 21–25 meV), the devices fabricated from ZnO have a much greater probability of surviving at higher temperature. Moreover, ZnO is highly resistant to radiation damage required for space applications. Finally, in terms of suitability for wet etching, the availability of high-quality ZnO bulk crystals and the potentially lower cost for ZnO-based devices, ZnO ranks higher than GaN as well as other

S. Nagar and S. Chakrabarti, *Optimisation of ZnO Thin Films*,
DOI 10.1007/978-981-10-0809-2_1

transparent conductors like indium tin oxide (ITO). Therefore, ZnO is capable of replacing its competitors in the near future [2, 3].

ZnO growth is possible with most known processes, including chemical vapour deposition (CVD), molecular beam epitaxy (MBE), RF sputtering and pulsed laser deposition (PLD), among others. Due to its large exciton-binding energy, it can also be used for near-band edge emission (NBE) at room temperature and higher temperatures. ZnO has also been a suitable candidate for space applications due to its high resistance to radiation damage. Recently, ZnO has also found applications in transparent thin film transistors [1].

1.1 Material Properties

Most of the II–VI binary compound semiconductors crystallise as either zinc blende or hexagonal wurtzite structure where each anion is surrounded by four cations or vice versa. The crystal structure of ZnO is wurtzite (B4), zinc blende (B3) and rock salt (B1), as shown in Fig. 1.1. Of these, wurtzite structure is the thermodynamically stable phase in ambient conditions. The zinc blende structure is stabilised only by growth on cubic structures, while rock salt structure can be obtained at high pressures [1].

The wurtzite structure has a hexagonal unit cell with lattice parameters, a and c. Figure 1.2 shows the wurtzite structure of ZnO [4]. The structure is composed of two hexagonal-close-packed sub-lattices, each of which consists of one type of atom displaced with respect to each along the c-axis [1].

As mentioned earlier, ZnO has many important properties that make it a deserving candidate for primacy in the semiconductor industry. Some of its properties are wide bandgap, large exciton-binding energy and high resistance to radiation damage, among others. ZnO has a melting point of 1975 °C and is insoluble in water and alcohol, but can be dissolved in dilute acids. Some of the other properties of ZnO are given in Table 1.1 [5].

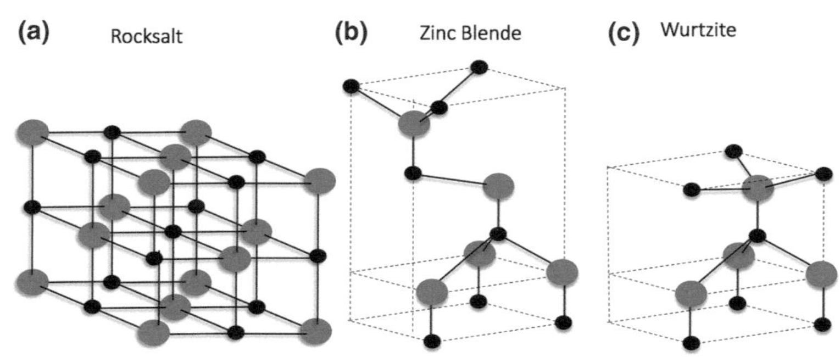

Fig. 1.1 Representation of ZnO crystal structures: **a** rocksalt, **b** cubic zinc blende and **c** wurtzite. The gray and black spheres denote Zn and O atoms respectively

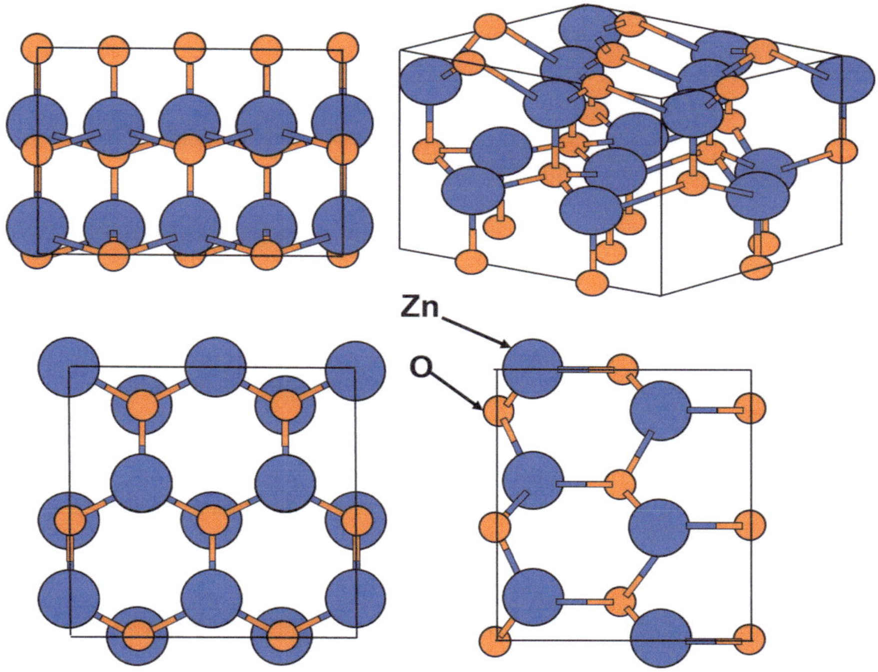

Fig. 1.2 Crystalline forms of ZnO in the wurtzite structure

Table 1.1 Properties of ZnO

Properties	Specifications	Comments
Structure	Wurtzite	Same as hexagonal
Bandgap	3.3 eV	Wide bandgap semiconductor
Exciton-binding energy	60 meV	Higher than GaN (21–25 meV)
Piezoelectricity	1.2 cm^{-2}	Highest among all semiconductors
Hardness	$\sim$5 Ω	For single crystal
Toxicity	Very low	Same as other compound semiconductors

1.2 Electronics Properties

ZnO is intrinsically an n-type semiconductor material due to the existence of native defects such as zinc interstitials (Zn_i) and oxygen vacancies (V_O), as well as the presence of impurities in the form of hydrogen, which act as donor states in ZnO [6, 7]. A vacancy is an unoccupied lattice site, which results in an unsatisfied bond within lattice. A vacancy is created when species leave lattice sites and move to the surface. Interstitial defects are present if species do not occupy the lattice site but remain in crystal and disturb the ideal structure of the crystal. Figure 1.3 shows the various defects present in a crystal [8]. The bulk electron mobility is in the range of 200–400 cm^2/Vs, which is limited by the acoustic and phonon scattering. However, in the case of thin films, the electron mobility is typically in the range of 1–100 cm^2/Vs due to the interface roughness and grain boundary scattering [3]. A major obstacle in fabricating ZnO-based bipolar devices is the difficulty of achieving high-quality, reliable and reproducible p-type ZnO. Thus, there are not much data on the hole transport in p-type ZnO due to the problems associated with obtaining p-type ZnO. This lack of data explains why the commercial usage of ZnO-based bipolar devices has not yet been realised in the research community, although it has so many advantages over other materials.

The introduction and activation of p-type dopants are technically quite challenging. The self-compensating process of the dopants tends to transform the p-type films back to n-type over time [9, 10]. Moreover, the dopants have a low solubility in ZnO. Thus, forming shallow acceptor levels is difficult, which aggravates the problem of p-doping [11, 12].

Because ZnO is a II–VI semiconductor material, group I and group V elements are supposed to be the p-type dopants for ZnO and form shallow acceptor levels, required for p-type conduction. However, most of these elements form deep acceptor levels and hence do not contribute to p-type conduction. p-type doping in ZnO is possible by substitution of Zn sites with group I elements or oxygen sites with group V elements. Park et al. [13] showed that group I elements are better p-type dopants than group V elements, in terms of forming shallow acceptor levels. However, they tend to occupy interstitial sites rather than substitutional sites and thus act like donors [14]. Nevertheless, researchers around the world have reported p-type ZnO films by doping group I elements such as lithium (Li), sodium (Na) and potassium (K) [15–22]. Due to the large size of the group V elements, the theory

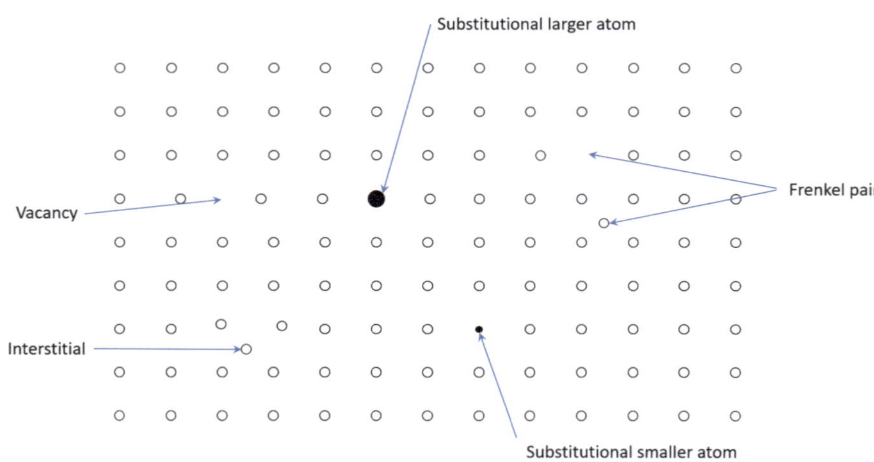

Fig. 1.3 Defects in crystals

suggests that it is difficult to achieve shallow acceptor levels [13]. Among the group V elements, nitrogen (N) is best suited to form p-type ZnO thin films because of its similar atomic size compared to oxygen. Substituting oxygen atoms by nitrogen doping, the acceptor activation energy is predicted to be around 100 meV, which is among the smallest. However, Li et al. [23] revealed that stability using nitrogen doping is an issue due to compensation of acceptor states by hydrogen. Nonetheless, successful p-type ZnO has been reported by various researchers across the world [24–34]. p-type ZnO has also been reported by other group V elements such as phosphorus (P) [35–42], arsenic (As) [9, 43–50] and antimony (Sb) [46, 51–59]. As these elements have very large atomic size compared to oxygen, substitution by these atoms tends to form deep acceptor levels at around 200 meV. Limpijumnong et al. [46] have reported the formation of a defect complex with the dopant atom and the Zn site, e.g. As_{Zn}–$2V_{Zn}$, which forms shallow acceptor levels and contributes to p-type doping. Apart from these dopants, p-type ZnO has also been reported by co-doping methods. In this method, a donor–acceptor (group I and group III, or group III and group V) elements are co-doped together [60–67].

Most of these reported results of p-type ZnO films have been achieved using non-localised mechanisms, which is not desirable for device fabrication. Ion implantation is a suitable technique for attaining selective and localised doping. Although researchers have successfully demonstrated p-type ZnO films using ion implantation technique, the existing reports are minimal [68–71]. In this report, implantation technique has been applied in order to achieve high-quality, reliable and reproducible p-type ZnO films.

1.3 Optical Properties

Intrinsic and extrinsic effects strongly affect the optical properties of a semiconductor. Intrinsic transitions take place between electrons in conduction band and holes in valence band. These also include excitonic transition due to Coulomb interaction. Extrinsic transitions relate to defects and dopants, which create discrete electronic states in the bandgap. The electronic states of bound excitons depend upon the type of semiconductor. Thus, excitons can be bound to neutral or charged donors or acceptors. Hence, there are mainly three types of transitions, i.e. shallow neutral-donor-bound exciton (DBE/D°X), shallow neutral-acceptor-bound-exciton (ABE/A°X) and defect-related transitions like free-to-bound (electron-acceptor) or bound-to-bound (donor–acceptor) [72].

The conduction band of wurtzite ZnO is mainly constructed from s-like state, whereas the valence band is created from p-like states, which are split into three sub-bands (A, B and C) due to the influence of crystal fields and spin-orbit coupling [1]. The free exciton (FX) transitions are related to transitions from conduction band to a valence band, or vice versa, and Teke et al. [72] observed this peak around 3.3771 eV. In any direct bandgap semiconductor, DBE/D°X and ABE/A°X are the most important extrinsic transitions. The neutral shallow DBE dominates in

ZnO because of the presence of donors, due to unintended impurities such as Zn_i and V_O. ABE peaks are observed when acceptors are included in the sample. The D °X peaks for the A excitons are positioned at 3.3598, 3.3605, 3.3618, 3.3650 and 3.3664 eV. Higher D°X peaks are accredited to excited-state transitions. The A°X peaks are found to be present at 3.3564, 3.3530 and 3.3481 eV [72]. Other than these important transitions, transitions like electron-acceptor (FA) peak are observed in the range 3.3–3.33 eV, whereas donor–acceptor peaks are found at 3.21–3.23 eV. Yellow/green luminescence is also observed in samples having very high defect density. These peaks correspond to deep-level transitions of the sample due to its defects [72].

1.4 Light Emitters

The wide bandgap and large exciton-binding energy of ZnO make it a very promising candidate for fabrication of light emitters, which requires that the junction devices provide high electron and hole concentration in the active region. While electron concentration is easier to achieve, the requirements of achieving high hole concentration make the device fabrication difficult. Hence, different materials having high hole concentration are used as other materials to fabricate heterojunction devices [73–75]. However, some researchers also report fabrication of homojunction light emitters [48, 76, 77].

1.4.1 Heterojunction Light-Emitting Diodes

To fabricate a heterojunction device, two issues need to be considered: (1) band offsets at the heterojunction (Fig. 1.4) and (2) defects at the heterojunction interface. The band offsets are given by [3]:

$$\Delta E_c = E_c(\text{n-ZnO}) - E_c(\text{p-emitter}) \tag{1.1}$$

and

$$\Delta E_v = E_v(\text{p-emitter}) - E_v(\text{n-ZnO}) \tag{1.2}$$

In the case of ZnO junction light emitters, the valence band offset is the limiting factor because of the presence of large energy barriers to hole injection. For this to take place, the hole concentration should be larger than the electron concentration and ΔE_c should be larger than ΔE_v. The defects at the interface occur due to

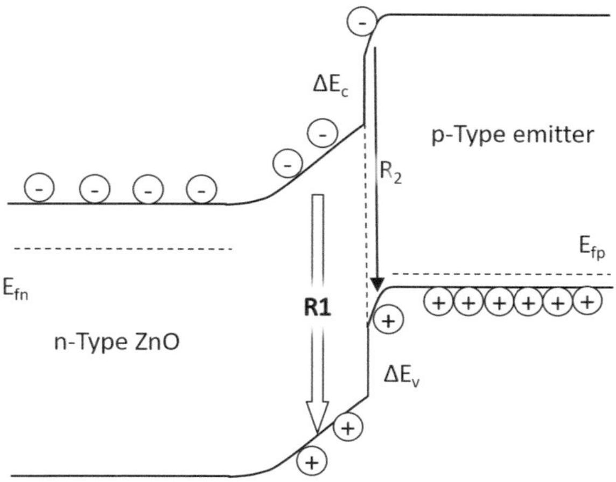

Fig. 1.4 Band diagram of a ZnO junction diode illustrating carrier recombination processes with electrical injection

differences in crystal structure and chemical bonding. To reduce these differences, a high crystal quality at the active region is required.

Among the p-emitters, GaN is the most widely used material, because the crystal structure and electronic properties of GaN and ZnO are very similar. Moreover, high-quality p-type GaN can easily be made. Alivov et al. [78] successfully fabricated p-GaN/n-ZnO heterojunction LED where they observed an electroluminescence (EL) peak around 430 nm, which matched the cathodoluminescence spectrum of GaN:Mg, suggesting that the active region is in the GaN region. To shift the active region to ZnO, they further modified the structure by fabricating a n-ZnO/p-$Al_{0.12}Ga_{0.88}N$ heterojunction [79]. Other researchers have also fabricated heterojunction devices based on GaN [80–82]. Researchers have also successfully demonstrated the use of heterojunction devices by using other p-type materials such as Si, SiC and other oxides such as NiO and $SrCr_2O_2$ [73–75, 83–86].

1.4.2 Homojunction Light-Emitting Diodes

Several reports have been published regarding the achievement of p-type ZnO films, but realisation of room-temperature electroluminescence (RTEL) based on ZnO p–n homojunction diode is quite limited. Tsukazaki et al. [76] successfully demonstrated a RTEL of a ZnO homojunction LED structure. The EL demonstrated a peak at 440 nm corresponding to donor-to-acceptor peak. However, the emission of green band near 2.2 eV is larger than the blue band, which Tsukazaki et al. [87] eliminated by optimising the growth parameters. Liu et al. [48, 88] and Lim et al. [77] also demonstrated RTEL dominated by deep-level emission. Lim et al. further improved the device structure to achieve UV emission.

1.5 Light Detectors

Spectroscopic instruments, used for chemical and biological analysis as well as solar blind imaging, require UV light sources and detectors for its efficient functioning [3]. Although light detection is possible using semiconductors having bandgap less than the targeted photons, for efficient UV detection, it is preferable to detect only the desired UV photons rather than other shorter wavelengths. Hence, UV detectors are generally fabricated from wide and direct bandgap semiconductors corresponding to the UV spectral region. Researchers use ZnO to fabricate UV detectors because of its useful electronic and optical properties in the UV region. Photoconductors are the simplest types of detectors in which the conductivity of the material changes when photo-generated current is added [89]. Due to its simplicity, ZnO-based photoconductors are the most widely studied device [90–95]. Schottky or ohmic contacts are deposited on ZnO thin films to complete the device. Another type of detector is the junction detector or a photodiode, which is typically a p–n junction (heterojunction or homojunction) device. This device has the advantage of having lower dark current as opposed to photoconductors. The device works in the reverse bias mode: under illumination, the photo-generated carriers are quickly swept out of the depletion region, due to the electric field resulting in an increased reverse bias current [89]. Difficulty in p-doping of ZnO has restricted the fabrication of homojunction photodiodes, although Ryu et al. [96] did demonstrate one of the homojunction photodiodes. However, demonstration of several heterojunction photodiodes has been reported using Si, NiO and ZnTe [3, 97–101].

Although p-type ZnO thin films were reported before this monograph was started, the reliability of the obtained p-type ZnO thin films had not been investigated. Hence, this work was undertaken in order to produce reliable and reproducible p-type ZnO over a long period of time, which would further support the fabrication of stable ZnO-based devices required for commercial production. For successful commercialisation of these devices, optical efficiency should be as high as possible. Thus, methods to improve the optical efficiency of the ZnO thin films were also studied herein.

Chapter 2
Optimisation of PLD Parameters

Abstract Progress in the fabrication of ZnO-based optoelectronic devices lies in producing reproducible, reliable and stable p-type ZnO films, because of the intrinsic n-type nature of the deposited ZnO films. Hence, for successful conversion of its carriers from n-type to p-type, it is desirable that the deposited ZnO film has as low an electron concentration as possible. Moreover, for the fabrication of optoelectronic devices, the films should have very high optical quality. The growth of highly oriented films with the least strain will offer an added advantage in fabricating these devices. Hence, the deposition parameters of temperature and pressure using pulsed laser deposition (PLD) were optimised keeping these things in mind. A substrate temperature of 650 °C and oxygen pressure of 40 mTorr were found to be optimised growth parameters as it had the lowest carrier concentration of 1.01×10^{17} cm^{-3} a reasonably high Hall mobility of 16.1 cm^2 V^{-1} s^{-1} and also had the highest optical quality. Once the PLD parameters were optimised, hydrogen implantation was carried out to see whether it further enhanced the electrical and optical properties of the thin film. While the Van der Pauw Hall measurements did not reveal any significant changes in the electrical characteristics of the thin films, the optical quality of the implanted films was found to increase by two orders of magnitude when compared to the as-deposited sample. Such an enhancement in the optical luminescence of the ZnO thin films may be helpful in fabricating highly efficient ZnO-based devices.

Keywords PLD · X-ray diffraction · Atomic force microscopy · Scanning electron microscopy · Van der Pauw Hall · Photoluminescence · Hydrogen implantation · Thermally stimulated current

---

Part of the chapter has been reprinted from [S. Nagar et al. "Increased photoluminescence of hydrogen-implanted ZnO thin films deposited using pulsed laser deposition technique", Journal of Luminescence, Vol. 15, Pg 307–311, 2014 (with permission from Elsevier)]

S. Nagar and S. Chakrabarti, *Optimisation of ZnO Thin Films*,
DOI 10.1007/978-981-10-0809-2_2

2.1 Introduction

Progress in the fabrication of ZnO-based optoelectronic devices lies in producing reproducible, reliable and stable p-type ZnO films, because of the intrinsic n-type nature of the deposited ZnO films. Hence, for successful conversion of its carriers from n-type to p-type, it is desirable that the deposited ZnO film has as low an electron concentration as possible. Moreover, for the fabrication of optoelectronic devices, the films should have very high optical quality. The growth of highly oriented films with the least strain will offer an added advantage in fabricating these devices.

Deposition of ZnO thin films was carried out using PLD over ⟨001⟩ sapphire substrates. A very low lattice mismatch between ZnO and sapphire substrates explains the use of the substrate. In this study, we optimise (i) the substrate temperature and (ii) the oxygen pressure, keeping in mind the above-mentioned requirements for fabrication of devices.

The deposited films were characterised in order to observe the structural, electrical and optical properties of the films with an intention to obtain films with the least strain, defects and carrier concentration and the highest optical efficiency. The structural properties were characterised using XRD and SEM, while the electrical and optical properties were measured with the Van der Pauw Hall technique and PL, respectively.

2.2 Temperature Optimisation

2.2.1 Experimental Details

ZnO thin films were deposited over ⟨001⟩ sapphire substrates using PLD technique. The 99.999% pure ZnO target was ablated using a KrF excimer laser (248 nm with a 20-ns pulse) for the deposition. The energy density and the target-to-substrate distance were maintained at 1.94 J cm^{-2} and 5 cm, respectively. To attain uniform deposition and avoid pit formation, the target was rotated at a frequency of 10 Hz, the same as the laser frequency. Prior to deposition, a high vacuum of 3×10^{-5} mTorr was kept in the chamber, and the substrate was degreased by treatment with trichloroethylene (TCE), acetone and isopropyl alcohol (IPA) for 2 min each. The deposition was performed in a high vacuum chamber under a background oxygen pressure of 0.1 mTorr for 25 min by varying the temperature from 400 to 800 °C.

2.2.2 Results and Discussion

2.2.2.1 Structural Properties

The X-ray diffraction pattern for the film deposited at 650 °C is as shown in Fig. 2.1. Peaks at 34° and 72° could be clearly seen which corresponds to the ⟨002⟩ and ⟨004⟩ ZnO peaks which suggest that ZnO films grow with a highly c-axis

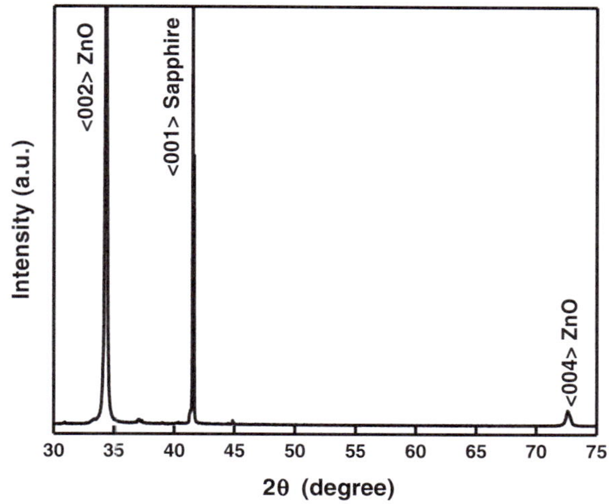

Fig. 2.1 X-Ray Diffraction spectrum of sample deposited at 650 °C, showing the ⟨002⟩ and ⟨004⟩ ZnO peaks

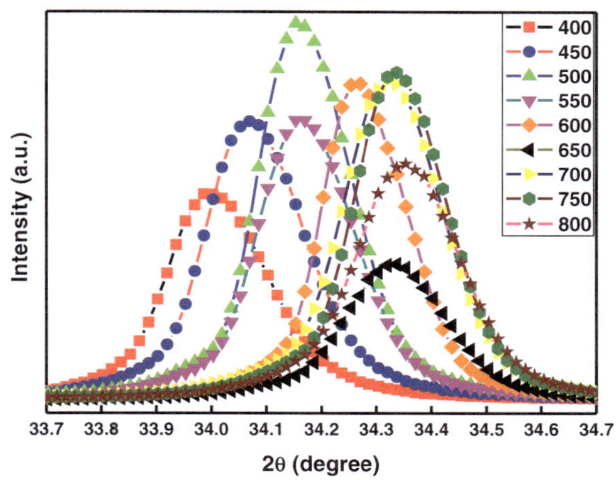

Fig. 2.2 ⟨002⟩ peak positions for different samples

orientation. Absence of other ZnO peaks indicates high crystalline quality of the deposited films which is not the case for films deposited by other techniques like spray pyrolysis or Atomic Layer Deposition (ALD) [102, 103]. It is to be noted that similar spectra was observed for samples deposited at other temperatures. However, a closer examination of the ⟨002⟩ peak positions for different samples (Fig. 2.2) displays that the peaks were at different 2Θ angles for different samples. This was due to the lattice strain, calculated by the following equation, caused by the mismatch between the lattice constants of ZnO and sapphire.

Table 2.1 FWHM values of the ⟨002⟩ peak position for samples deposited at different temperatures

Deposition temperature (°C)	FWHM values (°) (correct up to 2 decimal places)
800	0.22
750	0.19
700	0.20
650	0.20
600	0.18
550	0.19
500	0.19
450	0.20
400	0.22

$$\text{Strain} = (d_{\text{subs}} - d_{\text{film}})/d_{\text{subs}} \tag{2.1}$$

where d_{subs} and d_{film} are the *d*-spacing of the substrate and the film, respectively. Further, the FWHM values of the ZnO peaks was found to decrease with an increase in substrate temperature until 650 °Cm then increase slightly, followed by further decrease at 700 °C (Table 2.1). From the table, it can be seen that the FWHM value for sample deposited at 650 °C is not the lowest, but this sample has the least strain and thus serves as a better candidate for device applications.

The surface morphology of the ZnO thin films was studied using SEM. Epitaxial film growth for all the samples was confirmed as no grain formation was observed in the samples. However, due to the lattice strain in the films, cracks were observed in the samples. The cracks seemed to reduce with increase in deposition temperature.

2.2.2.2 Electrical Properties

Temperature-dependent (80–300 K) Van der Pauw Hall measurements were performed to study the effect of deposition temperature on the electrical properties of the films (Figs. 2.3 and 2.4). The electron concentration was found to decrease from 3.1×10^{18} cm^{-3} at 800 °C to 1.49×10^{18} cm^{-3} at 650 °C followed by further increase to 4.23×10^{18} cm^{-3} at 400 °C at 400 °C at 300 K (Table 2.2). The corresponding Hall mobility was calculated to be 15.7, 24 and 8.69 cm^2 V^{-1} s^{-1}, respectively. Although no major changes in the electron concentration values was found for any of the samples with increase in temperature, a slight increase in the Hall mobility values was identified. As there was no grain formation in the films due to the epitaxial growth of the films, the grain boundary scattering, which is generally affected by temperature, was negligible, thus explaining the increase in mobility values. The measurements revealed that all the films have n-type characteristics.

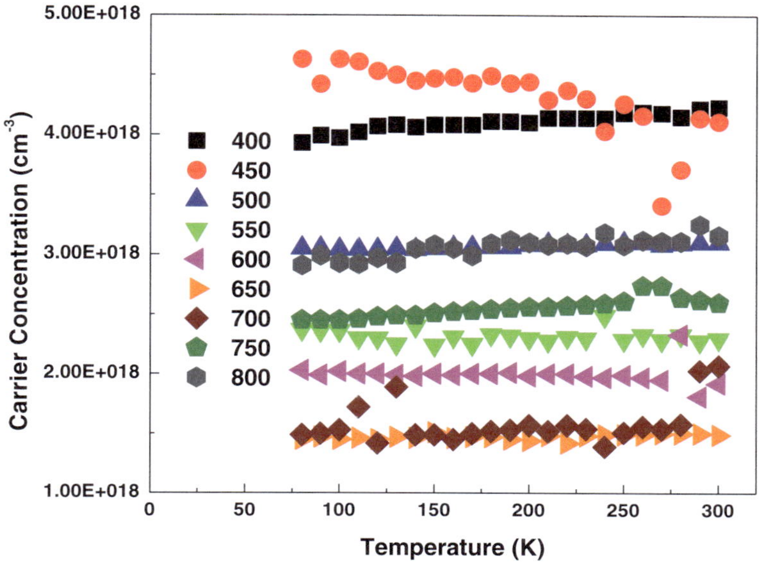

Fig. 2.3 Variation of electron carrier concentration with temperature from 80 K to 300 K

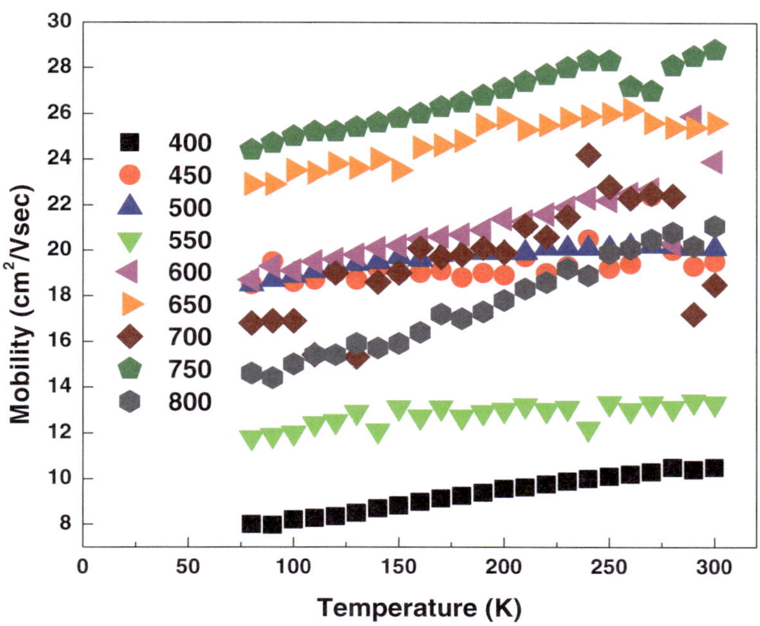

Fig. 2.4 Variation of electron Hall mobility with temperature from 80 to 300 K

Table 2.2 Electron carrier concentration and Hall mobility values for the obtained samples taken at 300 K

Substrate temperature (°C)	Electron carrier concentration (cm^{-3})	Hall mobility ($cm^2\ V^{-1}\ s^{-1}$)
	300 K	300 K
800	3.16×10^{18}	21.1
750	2.6×10^{18}	28.8
700	2.07×10^{18}	18.5
650	1.49×10^{18}	25.6
600	1.92×10^{18}	23.9
550	2.3×10^{18}	13.3
500	3.1×10^{18}	20.1
450	4.11×10^{18}	19.5
400	4.23×10^{18}	10.5

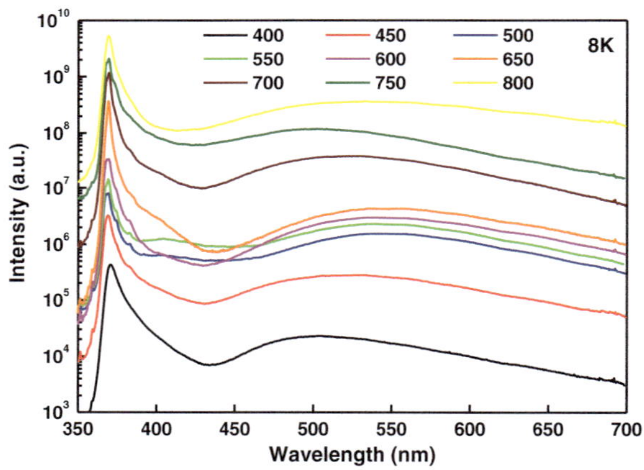

Fig. 2.5 Low temperature PL spectra (8 K) of the samples showing NBE and deep-level emissions

2.2.2.3 Optical Properties

The effect of substrate temperature on the optical properties of the thin films was measured by performing PL measurements. The low-temperature (8 K) PL spectrum of the different samples is shown in Fig. 2.5. A dominant D°X emission around 3.36 eV was obtained for all the samples in the NBE region [72, 104]. Other peaks around 3.37, 3.33 and 3.25 eV corresponding to FX, peak due to extended defects and second replica of the LO phonon, respectively, were also observed from the spectrum [72, 105]. Figure 2.6 shows the integrated PL peak intensity of different samples for the D°X peak. The PL intensity is first found to decrease at lower temperatures until 550 °C, followed by an increase to reach a maximum at 650 °C. Further increase in the deposition temperature leads to a decrease in the PL intensity. Along with the NBE peaks, deep-level defect peaks centred around 2.4 eV, leading to yellow and green emissions are also detected. These defect peaks

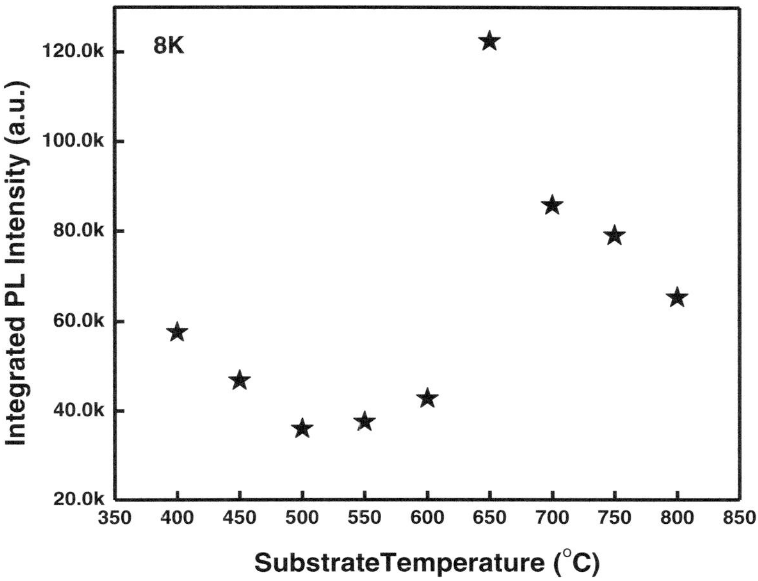

Fig. 2.6 Integrated PL peak intensity for the D°X peak of all samples taken at 8 K

arise due to intrinsic defects such as Zn_i (yellow emission) and V_O (green emission). A closer look at these peaks suggest that the green emission occurs at higher temperatures (>650 °C), while the yellow emission is seen at low and intermediate substrate temperatures. However, the intensity of these defect peaks is much lower when compared to the NBE peaks because of the growth of stoichiometric thin films from PLD which is not the case for films grown by other methods [106, 107].

Figure 2.7 shows the temperature-dependent spectrum for a sample deposited at 650 °C. A dominant D°X and a FX shoulder peak are observed at lower temperatures, as mentioned above. At higher temperatures, the FX peak starts to dominate the D°X peak. The peak intensities of FX and D°X with temperature are shown in Fig. 2.8. While the D°X peak diminishes with temperature and vanishes above 150 K, the FX peak intensity first increase and then starts to decrease. The thermal dissociation of bound excitons into free excitons at higher temperatures leads to such an observation [108]. Decrease of the FX peak with temperature >150 K is due to the increase in the number of defects with temperature. The evolution of the PL peak energies for the FX and D°X with temperature is shown in the inset of Fig. 2.8. The band gap shrinkage of ZnO is calculated by fitting the temperature dependence of FX peak with temperature using Varshni's equation:

$$E_g(T) = E_g(0) - \alpha T^2/(T + \beta) \tag{2.2}$$

where $E_g(0)$ is the band gap of ZnO at $T = 0$ K, and α and β are the fitting parameters calculated to be 7×10^{-4} eV K^{-1} and 515 K, respectively. The band

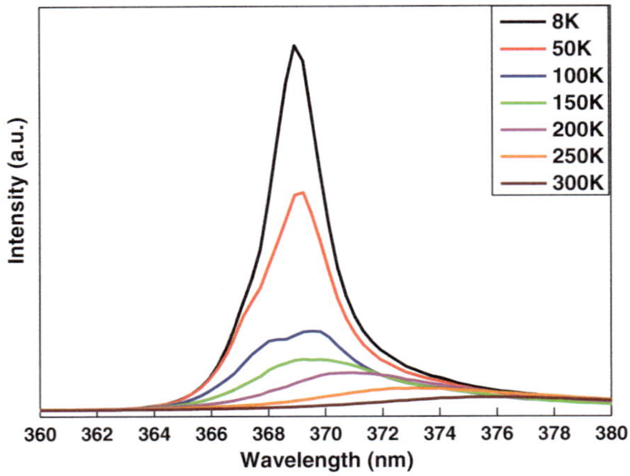

Fig. 2.7 Temperature-dependent Photoluminescence spectrum for the sample deposited at 650 °C

Fig. 2.8 PL peak intensity variation with temperature for the FX and D°X peaks deposited at 650 °C. *Inset* temperature dependence using Varshni's law

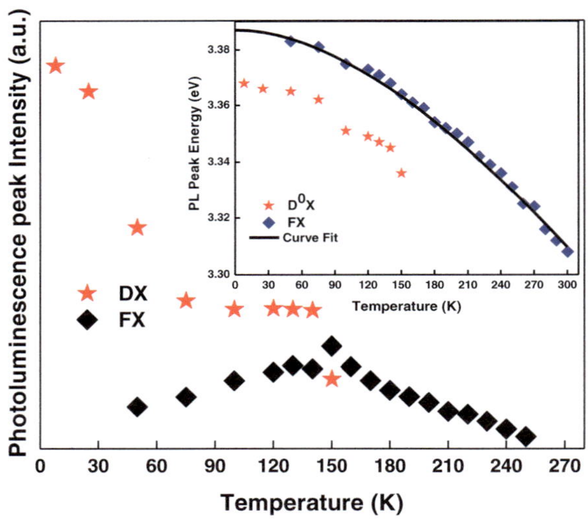

gap of the ZnO film is found to be 3.387 eV, which is in agreement with previously reported values [72, 109].

2.2.3 Conclusion

To summarise, PLD technique was used to deposit ZnO thin films over ⟨001⟩ sapphire substrates by varying the substrate temperature from 400 to 800 °C. XRD and SEM results confirmed deposition of highly c-axis-oriented ⟨002⟩ epitaxial ZnO films for all the samples. Temperature-dependent Van der Pauw Hall measurements were carried out in order to achieve the optimised sample having the lowest electron carrier concentration and high mobility values for obtaining better p-type films in future. The sample deposited at 650 °C was found to give the lowest carrier concentration of 1.49×10^{18} cm^{-3} and a high Hall mobility value of 24 cm^2 V^{-1} s^{-1}. Temperature-dependent PL measurements were carried out to study the optical properties of the thin films and also to attain a film with highest optical quality. Sample deposited at 650 °C was found to be the optimum sample as it had the lowest strain, carrier concentration, a reasonably high Hall mobility value and the best optical quality. As the substrate temperature increases, the ZnO atoms get sufficient energy to diffuse across the substrate, thus resulting in much uniform and high-quality film. However, increasing the substrate temperature too high results in out-diffusion of the ZnO atoms from the surface of the substrate which again degrades the quality of the film. It can be noticed from the various structural, electrical and optical properties that at 650 °C, the ZnO atoms get sufficient energy to diffuse across the substrate uniformly without out diffusing form the surface, thus resulting in the optimised parameters.

2.3 Pressure Optimisation

Once the temperature of deposition was optimised, it was required that the oxygen pressure is also optimised so that the carrier concentration becomes minimal along with increased optical luminescence observed from PL spectra. For this purpose, ZnO thin films were deposited over ⟨001⟩ sapphire substrates using the same energy density, target-to-substrate distance and deposition time as mentioned in Sect. 2.2.1. The optimised substrate temperature of 650 °C was used for deposition. The oxygen pressure in this case was varied from 0.1 to 60 mTorr.

2.3.1 Results and Discussion

2.3.1.1 Structural Properties

XRD results verify the deposition of (002) ZnO thin films with peaks around 2θ angle of 34° and 72° corresponding to the ⟨002⟩ and ⟨004⟩ ZnO peaks (Fig. 2.9). The (002) peak shows a shift in position for the various samples, which may be due to the strain developed in the films. The strain in the films has been calculated using Eq. 2.1 and has been plotted for different samples (Fig. 2.10). It is observed that the strain first increases with oxygen pressure up to 10 mTorr, followed by a decrease to attain a minimum value at 40 mTorr. Upon further increasing the oxygen pressure, the strain is found to increase.

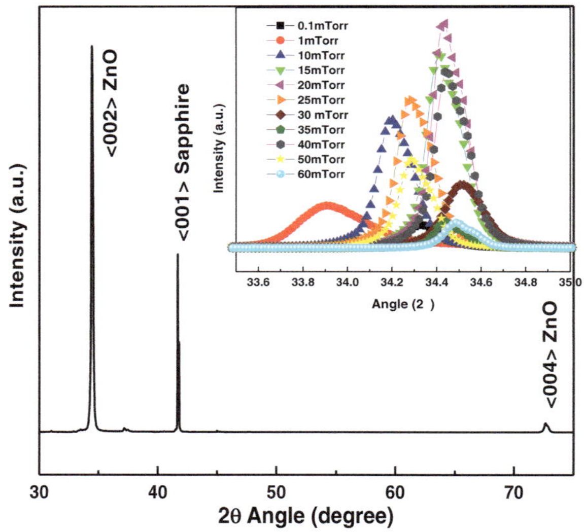

Fig. 2.9 XRD image of the sample deposited at 40 mTorr showing the ⟨002⟩ and ⟨004⟩ ZnO peaks. *Inset* shows the ⟨002⟩ peak positions of all the samples

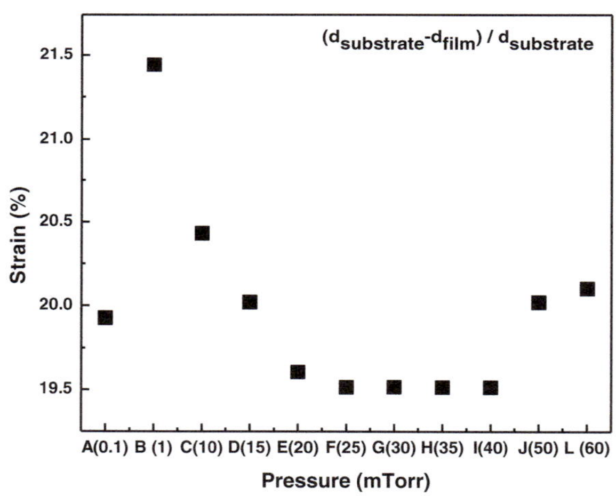

Fig. 2.10 Variation of lattice strain of ZnO thin films with oxygen pressure

SEM images of the ZnO surface are shown in Fig. 2.11. As the oxygen pressure is increased, grain formation starts to take place. Moreover, the grains are not continuous at lower oxygen pressure (up to 15 mTorr). When the pressure is further increased, the grains grow denser continuously, corresponding to the high quality of the films. However, increasing the pressure beyond 40 mTorr again leads to less dense films and discontinuous grains. A possible reason might be the collisions of the atoms at high pressure during deposition.

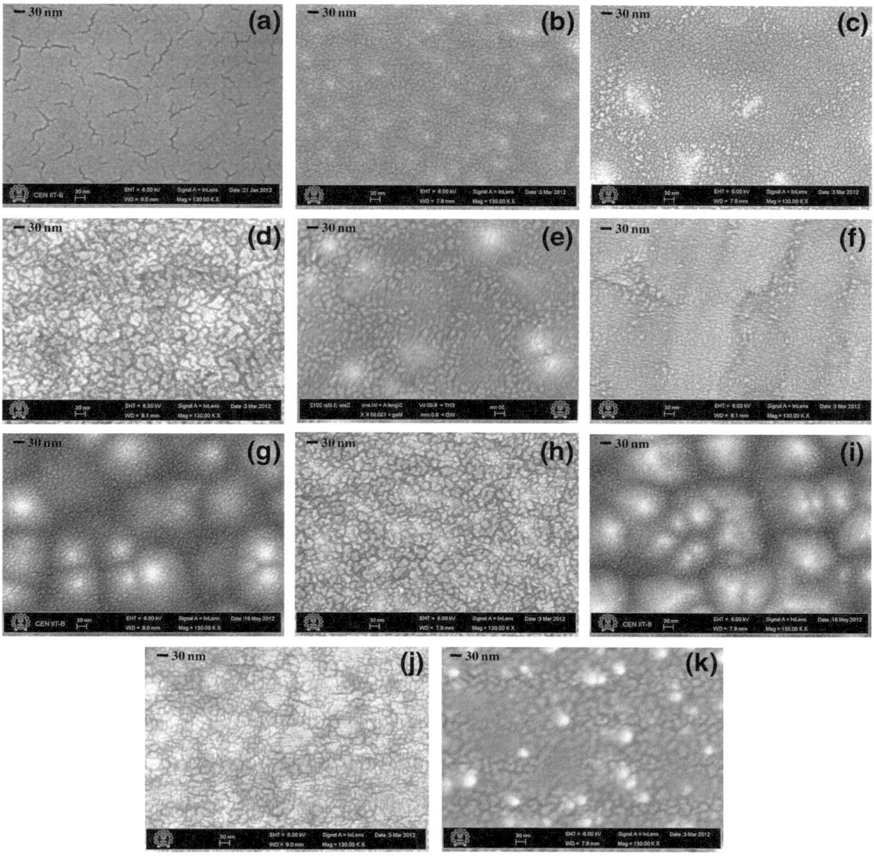

Fig. 2.11 Scanning electron microscopy (*SEM*) images of different samples: **a** 0.1, **b** 1, **c** 10, **d** 15, **e** 20, **f** 25, **g** 30, **h** 35, **i** 40, **j** 50 and **k** 60 mTorr, respectively

2.3.1.2 Electrical Properties

Temperature-dependent (80–300 K) Van der Pauw Hall measurements were performed to study the electrical properties of the ZnO thin films (Figs. 2.12 and 2.13). Table 2.3 shows the carrier concentration and Hall mobility values at 80 and 300 K. The electron carrier concentration decreases with increase in oxygen pressure, because the amount of V_O reduces as the pressure increases. However, at higher oxygen pressures (>40 mTorr), the value again increases by an order of magnitude. This may be because less energy is transferred to the substrate due to increased collision among atoms. The Hall mobility values also decrease with pressure until 25 mTorr, after which it starts increasing to gain a sufficiently high value of 16.1 cm^2/V s. The high mobility value at 0.1 mTorr may be due to the lack of grain formation in the sample, leading to negligible grain boundary scattering. In

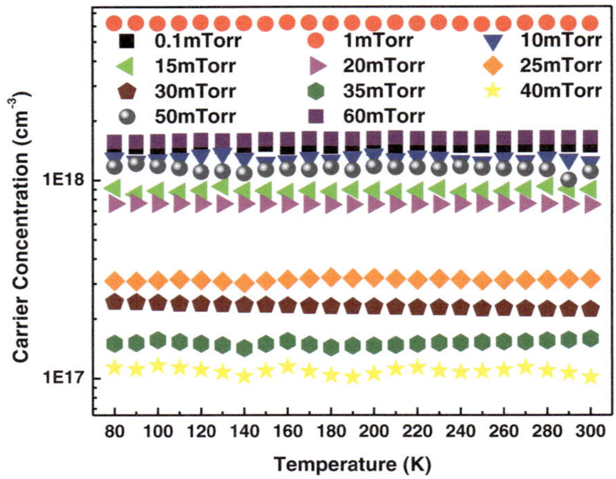

Fig. 2.12 Variation of carrier concentration with temperature for various samples

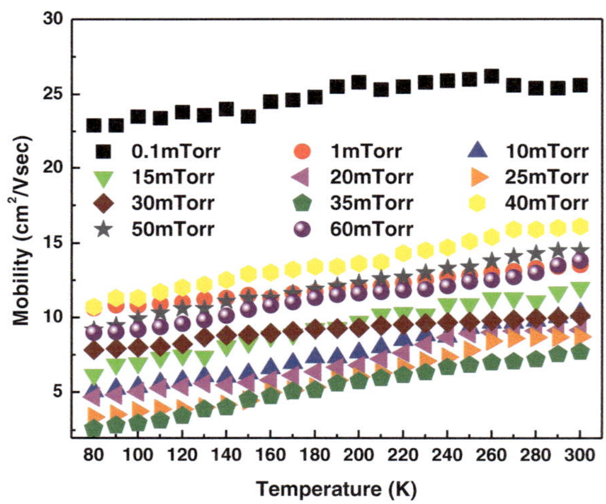

Fig. 2.13 Variation of Hall mobility with temperature for different samples

this case, too, the variation of carrier concentration with temperature is not observed. However, the Hall mobility tends to show an increase in value with temperature.

2.3.1.3 Optical Properties

Figure 2.14 shows the PL spectra of different samples taken at 8 K of the NBE region. A dominant D°X peak is visible for all the samples around 3.36 eV, along with FX peak at 3.37 eV. The other peaks at 3.33 and 3.25 eV are due to extended defects and LO-phonon replica [72, 104, 105]. Deep-level defect peaks around

Table 2.3 Carrier concentration and Hall mobility values for the obtained samples at 80 and 300 K

Pressure (mTorr)	Carrier concentration (cm^{-3})		Hall mobility (cm^2/V s)	
	80 K	300 K	80 K	300 K
0.1	1.45×10^{18}	1.49×10^{18}	24	25.6
1	6.2×10^{18}	6.14×10^{18}	10.6	13.5
10	1.3×10^{18}	1.23×10^{18}	5.05	10.3
15	9.12×10^{17}	8.92×10^{17}	6.14	12
20	7.72×10^{17}	7.5×10^{17}	4.67	9.15
25	3.1×10^{17}	3.16×10^{17}	3.36	8.71
30	2.43×10^{17}	2.2×10^{17}	7.83	10.2
35	1.5×10^{17}	1.58×10^{17}	2.61	7.7
40	1.13×10^{17}	1.01×10^{17}	10.7	16.1
50	1.17×10^{18}	1.1×10^{18}	9.15	14.5
60	1.57×10^{18}	1.64×10^{18}	8.97	13.8

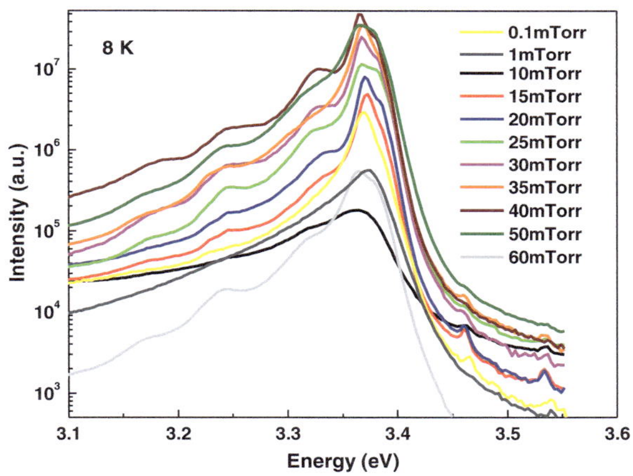

Fig. 2.14 PL spectra of the samples taken at 8 K showing NBE transition

2.5 eV are also observed in the samples, although the intensity of the peak is quite low when compared to the NBE peak. This suggests that the ZnO films thus grown are of high quality. The integrated PL peak intensity for D°X peak of different samples is shown in Fig. 2.15. The intensity first decreases with pressure until 40 mTorr, followed by an increase, to attain a highest value at 40 mTorr oxygen pressure. The increased oxygen available during deposition causes fewer defects related to V_O, causing the film to be of higher quality. However, increasing the oxygen pressure further leads to increased collision among atoms, thus reducing the peak intensity.

The temperature-dependent spectra for a sample grown at a pressure of 40 mTorr are shown in Fig. 2.16. A dominant D°X peak is observed at lower

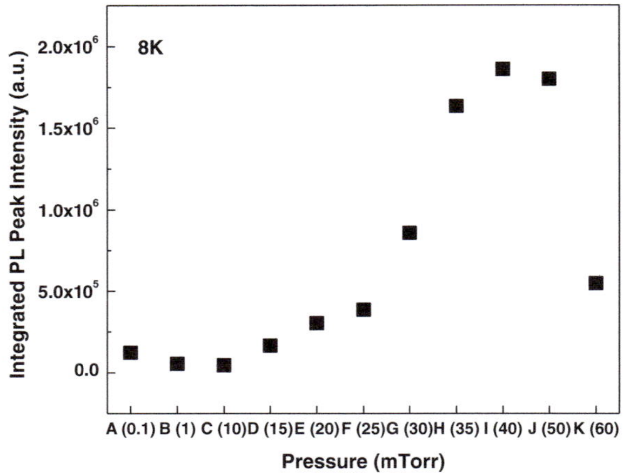

Fig. 2.15 Integrated PL peak intensity at 8 K for the D°X peak of all samples

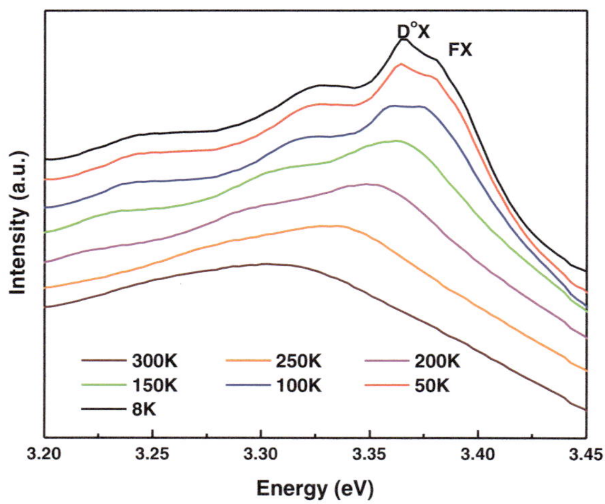

Fig. 2.16 Temperature-dependent PL spectra for the sample grown at 40 mTorr

temperatures with an FX shoulder. Enhanced thermal dissociation of bound exciton to FX leads to domination of FX peak over D°X peak with temperature [108]. Figure 2.17 shows the FX and D°X PL peak intensities with temperature. A rapid decrease in the D°X peak is observed, which vanishes entirely beyond 150 K. The FX peak, on the other hand, first increases up to 50 K, after which it starts to decrease. Inset of Fig. 2.17 shows the evolution of the PL peak energy with temperature for the D°X and FX peaks, which can be fitted using Eq. 2.2.

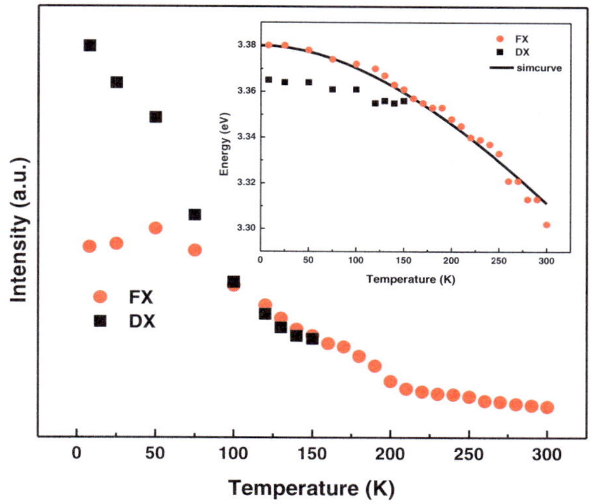

Fig. 2.17 Variation of PL peak intensities with temperature for the FX and D°X peaks for sample deposited at 40 mTorr. *Inset* temperature dependence using Varshni's law

2.3.2 *Conclusion*

ZnO films were deposited over ⟨001⟩ sapphire substrates at an optimised temperature of 650 °C in different oxygen pressure. Highly c-axis-oriented ⟨002⟩ epitaxial films were obtained for all the samples. The sample deposited at a pressure of 40 mTorr was found to have the lowest strain and very high grain density, as observed from SEM. Temperature-dependent Van der Pauw Hall measurements within a range of 80–300 K were obtained to achieve an optimal sample with low carrier concentration and high mobility values. The lowest concentration of 1.01×10^{17} cm^{-3} at 300 K was obtained with a corresponding Hall mobility of 16.1 cm^2 V^{-1} s^{-1} for a sample deposited at an oxygen pressure of 40 mTorr. Temperature-dependent PL spectra were also examined to study the optical behaviour of the films and to obtain a sample with high optical quality. The oxygen pressure of 40 mTorr yielded an optimal sample with the least strain and carrier concentration, along with a high Hall mobility value and the best optical quality. It is a well-known fact that an increase in the pressure of a chamber reduces the mean free path of the particle. Hence, at low pressures, the mean free path is more which corresponds to the atoms in the plume travelling more distance, and thus, the plume does not converge at the substrate leading to non-uniformity and degraded film quality. Similarly, too high a pressure causes to plume to converge well before the substrate, and hence, most of the atoms are unable to get deposited on the film again leading to poor film quality and non-uniformity. From the results obtained through the various characterisation techniques, it is believed that at an oxygen pressure of 40 mTorr, the plume converges at the substrate leading to high-quality films.

2.4 Hydrogen Ion Implantation

Once the temperature and oxygen pressure was optimised, hydrogen ion implantation was carried out to see whether it further enhanced the electrical and optical properties of the thin film. An approach similar to the one described in Sect. 2.2.1 was applied to deposit ZnO thin films over ⟨001⟩ sapphire substrate. However, here, the optimised values of temperature and oxygen pressure (650 °C and 40 mTorr, respectively) were used during the deposition time to obtain Sample A.

The films thus deposited were subjected to hydrogen ion implantation using Low-Energy Accelerator Facility (LEAF) at Bhabha Atomic Research Centre (BARC), Mumbai, India. Energy of 50 keV with a dose of 5×10^{12} ions/cm^2 was used for implantation. Thus, Sample H1 was obtained. As implantation leads to defects in the films, Sample H1 was subsequently rapid thermal annealed at 750, 800, 850 and 900 °C in oxygen ambient for 30 s to produce Samples H2–H5, respectively. RTP was performed on Sample A at the same temperatures and using the same annealing parameters (samples B to E) to compare them with the implanted samples.

2.4.1 *Results and Discussion*

2.4.1.1 Structural Properties

XRD was performed on the obtained samples to study the effect of hydrogen implantation and subsequent annealing on the structural properties of the thin films (Fig. 2.18). The results confirm the deposition of highly c-axis-oriented ⟨002⟩ ZnO films for all the samples. No other peaks have been found in the XRD peaks, which suggest that ZnO preferentially grow in the ⟨001⟩ direction due to its lowest surface free energy. A closer look at the ⟨002⟩ peak for the different samples shows that the Samples H1–H5 are at a higher 2θ angle as compared to Sample A. The strain developed due to the hydrogen implantation and subsequent annealing causes this effect (Fig. 2.19). The strain was found to increase for Sample H1, which is due to the implantation-related defects. The reduction of defects on annealing leads to lower strain in these samples, although the strain is still higher when compared to Sample A.

2.4.1.2 Electrical Properties

Room temperature Van der Pauw Hall measurements were taken in order to visualise the effect of implantation on the electrical properties on the thin films (Table 2.4). A decrease in the carrier concentration and Hall mobility is observed for Sample H1 as compared to Sample A. The heating caused by hydrogen

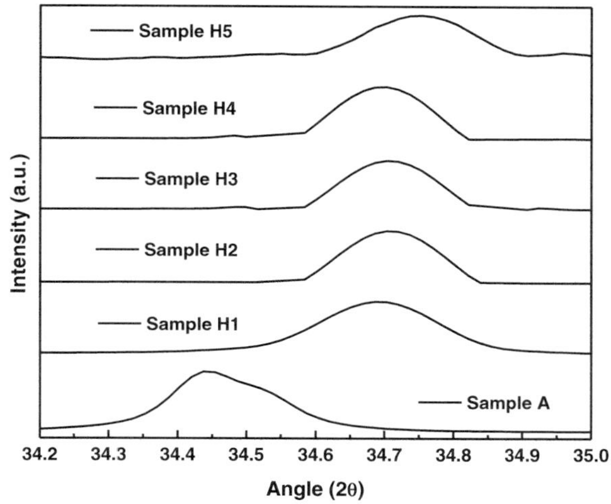

Fig. 2.18 XRD spectra of the different samples showing the ⟨002⟩ ZnO peak. The peak shifts for the implanted samples are clearly visible

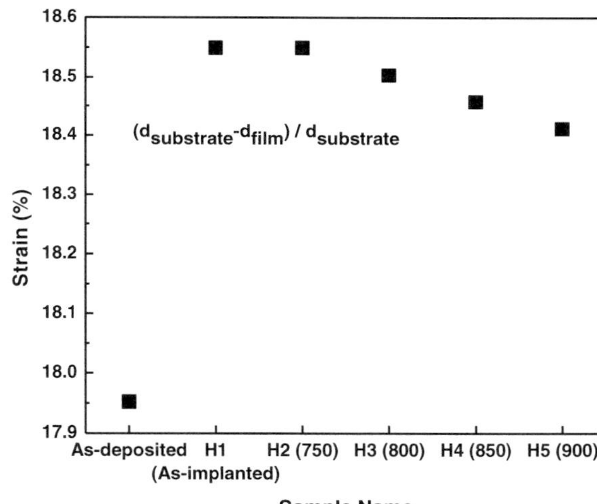

Fig. 2.19 Strain on the ZnO films due to implantation

implantation may have reduced the intrinsic defects in the sample, leading to lower concentration. However, the increased number of atoms in the films leads to higher scattering, thus reducing the Hall mobility. Upon annealing the samples, at higher temperatures, the carrier concentration and Hall mobility start to increase.

Hall measurements were obtained for Samples B to E to check whether hydrogen ions have any effect on the electrical properties of the thin films. Interestingly, hydrogen ions was found to have no effect on the electrical properties of the films, as the carrier concentration and Hall mobility values of Samples H2–H5 are similar to those of Samples B–E, respectively. The increase in the carrier concentration and Hall mobility of the annealed samples are only due to the

Table 2.4 Carrier concentration, Hall mobility and conductivity of different sample at 300 K

Sample name	Carrier concentration (cm^{-3})		Hall mobility (cm^2/V s)	
	Unimplanted	Implanted	Unimplanted	Implanted
As-deposited	1.01×10^{17}		16.1	
As-implanted	NA	4.5×10^{16}	NA	8.86
Annealed at 750 °C	1.13×10^{17}	1.24×10^{17}	18.3	33.9
Annealed at 800 °C	3.35×10^{17}	2.37×10^{17}	23.2	21.9
Annealed at 850 °C	5.75×10^{17}	8.85×10^{17}	60.6	54.4
Annealed at 900 °C	1.07×10^{18}	1.14×10^{18}	67.5	61.3

Reprinted from S. Nagar et al. "Increased photoluminescence of hydrogen-implanted ZnO thin films deposited using pulsed laser deposition technique", *Journal of Luminescence*, Vol. 15, pp. 307–311, 2014; with permission from Elsevier

reduction of the intrinsic defects of the films due to heat treatment. However, in all cases, the films demonstrated n-type behaviour which was obvious as hydrogen acts as donor in ZnO thin films [110–113].

2.4.1.3 Optical Properties

Low-temperature PL measurements of the obtained samples were executed in order to determine the optical properties of the implanted ZnO thin films (Fig. 2.20). A dominant donor-bound exciton (D°X) peak around 3.36 eV and a shoulder around 3.37 eV corresponding to the FX peak were observed for all the samples, which further confirms the n-type behaviour of the samples. The peaks corresponding to the extended defects due to implantation and the second LO-phonon replica of the D°X peak around 3.33 and 3.22 eV, respectively, were also observed in Samples H2–H6 [72, 104, 105]. Deep-level defect peaks around 2.5 eV, corresponding to defects such as Zn_i, V_O and implantation-related defects, were also observed for all the samples. However, the intensity of this peak is substantially weak when compared with the NBE peak intensity. This suggests that the ZnO films are of very high quality.

Temperature-dependent PL spectrum of different samples was performed to calculate the thermal activation energy of the samples using Eq. 2.3 (Table 2.5). Figure 2.21 shows the integrated PL peak intensity of the D°X peak for various samples with respect to temperature.

$$I = I_0 * (1 + \exp(-E_A/kT)) \tag{2.3}$$

where I and I_0 are the integrated PL peak intensity at temperature T K and 8 K, E_A is the activation energy and k is the Boltzmann constant.

The activation energy was found to decrease for Sample H1 due to the increased number of defects caused by implantation. On annealing the samples, the activation energy increases marginally with temperature. However, the activation energy is

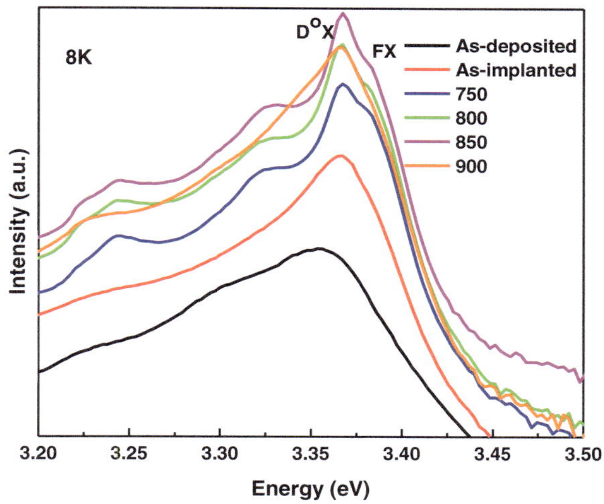

Fig. 2.20 PL spectra of different samples taken at 8 K (Reprinted from S. Nagar et al. "Increased photoluminescence of hydrogen-implanted ZnO thin films deposited using pulsed laser deposition technique", *Journal of Luminescence*, Vol. 15, pp. 307–311, 2014; with permission from Elsevier)

Table 2.5 Thermal activation energy for different samples

Sample name	Thermal activation energy (meV)
As-deposited	66.7
As-implanted	26.5
Annealed at 750 °C	36.98
Annealed at 800 °C	38.6
Annealed at 850 °C	40.5
Annealed at 900 °C	41

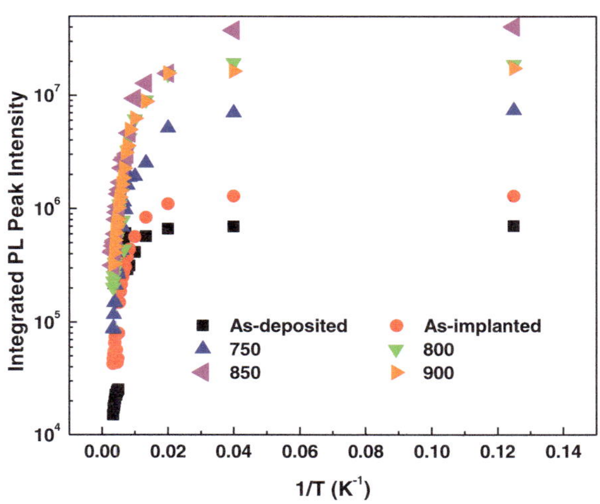

Fig. 2.21 Integrated PL peak intensity with respect to temperature for different samples

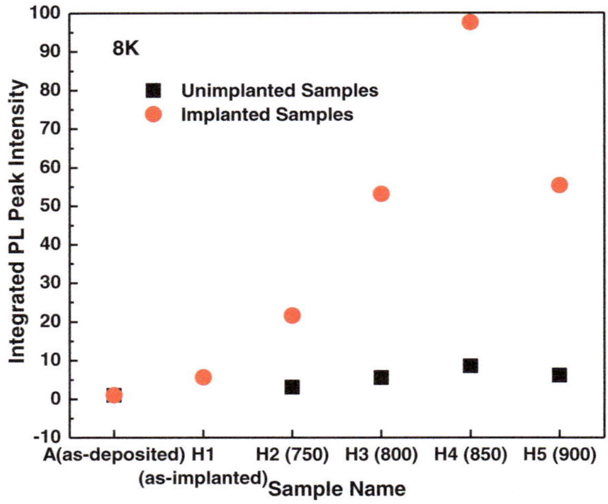

Fig. 2.22 Photoluminescence (PL) peak intensity at 8 K for unimplanted and implanted samples for the D°X peak (Reprinted from S. Nagar et al. "Increased photoluminescence of hydrogen-implanted ZnO thin films deposited using pulsed laser deposition technique", *Journal of Luminescence*, Vol. 15, pp. 307–311, 2014; with permission from Elsevier)

still lower than that of Sample A. The formation of shallow donor levels owing to hydrogen implantation leads to lower activation energy in Samples H2−H6 [110–113].

Figure 2.22 illustrates the NBE PL peak intensity for the implanted and unimplanted samples. Notably, the figure shows an obvious increase in the NBE PL peak intensity for the unimplanted sample, with increase in annealing temperature, due to the reduction of defects. A sample annealed at 850 °C demonstrated the highest enhancement of up to nine times that of Sample A. On the other hand, for the implanted sample (Sample H1), the NBE PL peak intensity improved by a factor of four. When the implanted samples were annealed at higher temperatures, the intensity further increased up to 850 °C. When the annealing temperature further increased, the peak intensity reduced, though remaining quite high. The intensity of Sample H4 is as high as 100 times that of Sample A. This result shows that hydrogen implantation and subsequent annealing had some effect on the optical properties of the thin films.

While implantation did not affect the electrical properties of the thin films, their optical properties revealed much improvement in terms of optical output. To understand the reason behind such a behaviour, thermally stimulated current (TSC) was undertaken to understand about the effect of implantation on the defect traps in the ZnO thin films (Fig. 2.23). In TSC measurements, the electron and hole traps are filled by illumination at low temperatures and by subsequent warming the sample in dark while recording the current due to the thermal emission of carriers

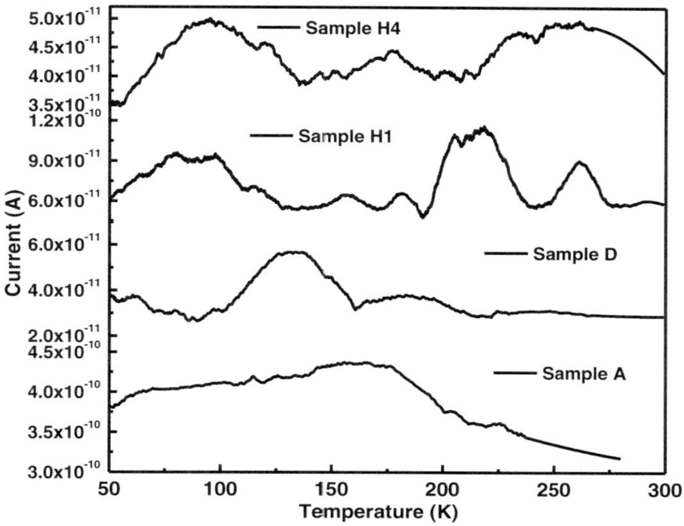

Fig. 2.23 Thermally stimulated current spectra of Samples A, D, H1 and H4 (Reprinted from S. Nagar et al. "Increased photoluminescence of hydrogen-implanted ZnO thin films deposited using pulsed laser deposition technique", *Journal of Luminescence*, Vol. 15, pp. 307–311, 2014; with permission from Elsevier)

from the traps [114]. All the samples were first cooled down from room temperature to 8 K, during which the dark current was measured with respect to temperature.

Illumination, for trap filling at 8 K, was performed with a xenon lamp for 30 min. The TSC current was then subsequently measured while warming up at a rate of 5 K/min under a bias of 2 V. A TSC peak around 162 K is observed for the as-deposited sample, which is resolved into two peaks upon annealing at 132 and 185 K. Although TSC measurements cannot reveal the exact nature of the trap, it is believed that these peaks are due to V_O, as they have activation energy in the range of 0.25–0.33 eV calculated from Eq. 2.4 [114–117].

$$E_T = kT_m \ln(T_m^4/\beta) \tag{2.4}$$

where E_T is the activation energy of a related trap, T_m is the peak temperature for the particular trap and β is the heating rate. Upon implantation and subsequent annealing, three other peaks at 87, 215 and 261 K are observed along with relatively small peaks around 160 and 185 K. The exact origins of these peaks are still unknown, but the hydrogen implantation provides clues to the origins of these traps. As the electrical properties of the films do not change even after annealing, it may be possible that these traps are electrically inactive. However, during PL measurements, the trapped electrons are released due to laser illumination, giving rise to increased PL intensity in these peaks. Such an enhanced optical luminescence in ZnO films can be utilised to fabricate devices with very high optical efficiency.

2.4.2 Conclusion

The effects of hydrogen implantation at a low energy of 50 keV and of subsequent annealing on the PLD-deposited ZnO thin films were investigated. A strong c-axis-oriented ⟨002⟩ ZnO films have been deposited in each case. However, the strain developed in the films due to implantation caused the peaks to shift to higher 2θ angles. Van der Pauw Hall measurements did not show any change in the carrier concentration and Hall mobility of the implanted and annealed samples, compared to as-annealed samples. While the PL results showed a dominant D°X for all the samples, a significant increase in the PL emission (×4 and ×100 times) was observed for the implanted sample and sample annealed at 850 °C. The formation of hydrogen-related traps due to implantation has caused an increased PL emission from the sample. To the best of our knowledge, this report is one of the first in which an improvement in the luminescence intensity has been observed. Such an enhancement in the optical luminescence of the ZnO thin films may be helpful in fabricating highly efficient ZnO-based devices.

Chapter 3
Implantation Studies

Abstract Ion implantation is a key tool that has developed in recent years for the fabrication of devices. It has the added advantage of providing lateral selectivity, appropriate doping area and fluence control along with localised doping. Ion implantation studies have been performed with the goal of doping ZnO with group I and group V elements to make p-type films. The Low-Energy Accelerator Facility at BARC, Mumbai, was used to implant lithium and phosphorus ions. Lithium ions were found to occupy deep acceptor states in ZnO and thus acting as donors in the films. Hence, no acceptor peaks were observed in the films implanted with lithium. On the other hand, when the films were implanted with phosphorus ions, an increase in the acceptor peaks was observed for the implanted and annealed films. However, the films were still n-type in nature. Plasma immersion ion implantation technique was used to implant the sputter-deposited ZnO thin films with phosphorus and nitrogen ions followed by subsequent annealing to remove any implantation-related defects. In both cases, a strong acceptor-bound-exciton (A°X) peak was observed around 3.35 eV, from PL measurements, in the thin films annealed at temperatures of 900–1000 °C confirming that the films have converted into p-type. The acceptor activation energy was calculated to be 125 and 118 eV for phosphorus- and nitrogen-implanted samples, respectively. This proves that phosphorus ion and nitrogen ion act as shallow acceptor levels in ZnO giving rise to p-type behaviour. PL measurements for the p-type samples were performed over a period of time to check the reliability of the p-type films. For the phosphorus-implanted samples, the p-type was found to exist up to a period of 6 months, although the PL intensity was found to reduce drastically. For the

Part of the chapter have been reprinted from the following:[S. Nagar et al. "Structural, electrical and optical characteristics of lithium-implanted ZnO thin films", Superlattices and Microstructures, Vol. 53, Pg 164–172, 2013][S. Nagar et al. "Effect of phosphorus irradiation in the structural, electrical and optical characteristics of ZnO thin films", Journal of Luminescence, Vol. 132, Pg 1089–1094, 2012][S. Nagar et al. "Evidence of strong acceptor peaks in ZnO thin films doped with phosphorus by plasma immersion ion implantation technique", Journal of Luminescence, Vol. 137, Pg 55–58, 2013][S. Nagar et al. "Realization of reliable p-type ZnO thin films by nitrogen implantation using plasma immersion ion implantation", Superlattices and Microstructures, Vol. 75, Pg 9–16, 2014]

S. Nagar and S. Chakrabarti, *Optimisation of ZnO Thin Films*,
DOI 10.1007/978-981-10-0809-2_3

nitrogen-implanted samples, the p-type was seen even after a period of 9 months and even the PL peak intensity was similar to the freshly made sample.

Keywords Low-Energy Accelerator Facility · Plasma immersion ion implantation · Annealing · Reliability

3.1 Introduction

Ion implantation is one of the key tools in the field of device fabrication. It has the added advantage of providing lateral selectivity, appropriate doping area and fluence control along with localised doping. Ion implantation technique was used to dope elements in ZnO thin films with group I and group V elements.

3.2 Conventional Ion Implantation Studies

CII was performed on ZnO film, deposited by the PLD technique. The Low-Energy Accelerator Facility (LEAF) at BARC, Mumbai, was used for the purpose. We doped lithium (group I) and phosphorus (group V) ions with the intention of achieving p-type ZnO films.

3.2.1 Deposition of ZnO

ZnO thin films have been deposited using PLD system over ⟨001⟩ sapphire substrates. A 99.999% pure ZnO target (1 inch in diameter) was used for ablation via a KrF excimer laser (248 nm, 20 ns pulse). The energy density used for the ablation was fixed at 1.8 J/cm^2. The substrate was first degreased properly using trichloroethylene (TCE), acetone and isopropyl alcohol (IPA) for 2 min each prior to deposition at 400 °C. The target-to-substrate distance was kept at 5 cm. The deposition was performed in a high-vacuum chamber under a background oxygen pressure of 75 mTorr for 40 min. The thickness of the films thus obtained was measured to be around 500 nm using α-profiler. Prior to deposition, the chamber was kept in a high vacuum of 3×10^{-5} mTorr. Thus, Sample A1 was obtained.

3.2.2 Lithium Implantation Studies

3.2.2.1 Experimental Details

Li ion implantation was performed over the deposited films at low energies of 40 and 50 keV and a constant dose of 5×10^{13} ions/cm^2 at room temperature, in order to obtain samples B1 and C1, respectively, using LEAF at BARC, Mumbai. The projected range of 165 and 207 nm, respectively, was estimated using TRIM calculations. Samples B1 and C1 were subjected to rapid thermal annealing (AS ONE 150, Annealsys) at 650–750 °C, in Ar environment for 30 s to yield Samples B2, B3 (implanted at 40 keV) and C2, C3 (implanted at 50 keV), respectively.

3.2.2.2 Results and Discussion

Structural Properties

Figures 3.1 and 3.2 depict the XRD pattern of the obtained samples. The presence of ⟨002⟩ peak in all the samples confirms growth of highly c-axis-oriented films. The drastically diminished peak intensity for Samples B1 and C1 (compared to A1) implies deterioration of film crystallinity due to inclusion of Li ions, deterioration which is subsequently regained on annealing. This phenomenon can be further verified by looking at the FWHM values of the samples (Table 3.1): Samples B2, B3 and C2, C3 show lower values, thus confirming the reduced defects and greater crystallinity.

AFM study was performed to study the surface morphology of the obtained samples (Figs. 3.3 and 3.4). Figures 3.3b and 3.4b show better grain formation in Samples B1 and C1 as compared to that in A1 (as shown in Figs. 3.3a, 3.4a).

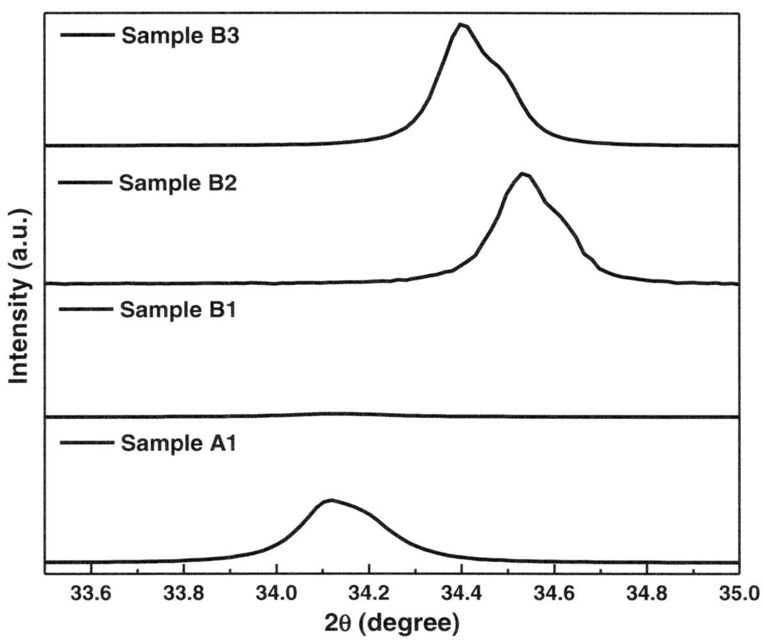

Fig. 3.1 XRD pattern for films obtained after implantation at 40 keV showing the ⟨002⟩ ZnO peaks

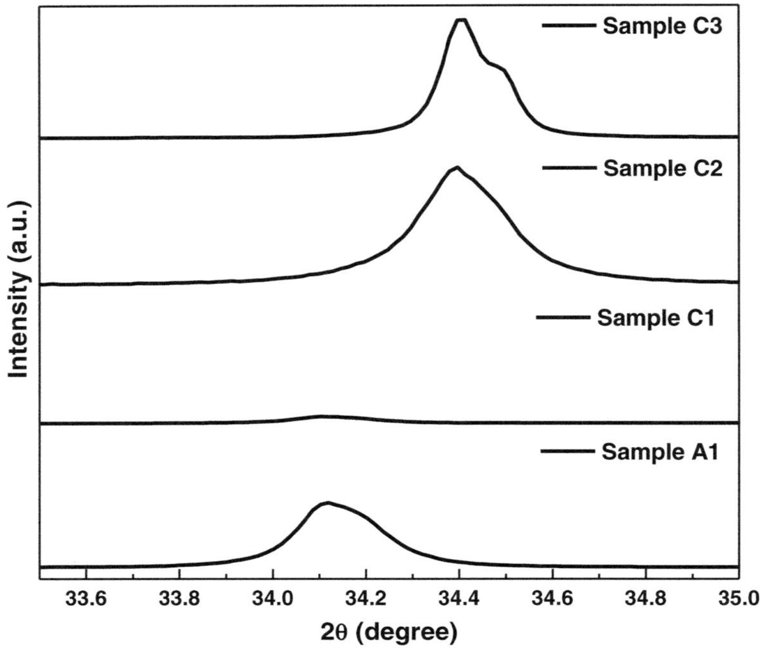

Fig. 3.2 XRD pattern for films obtained after implantation at 50 keV showing the ⟨002⟩ ZnO peaks

Table 3.1 FWHM values of the various films

Sample name	FWHM value (°)
A1	0.217
B1	0.217
B2	0.178
B3	0.171
C1	0.191
C2	0.163
C3	0.102

Reprinted from S. Nagar et al. "Structural, electrical and optical characteristics of lithium-implanted ZnO thin films", *Superlattices and Microstructures*, Vol. 53, pp. 164–172, 2013; with permission from Elsevier

A possible reason might be the generation of heat in the sample due to implantation, which causes an increase in the root mean square (RMS) roughness value, measured over an area of 1 μm × 1 μm (Table 3.2). As the implanted samples are subjected to annealing at 650 °C, some of the smaller grains merge to form larger ones, thus raising the roughness values in Samples B2 and C2. A probable reason of higher roughness value for Samples B3 and C3 may be the formation of micro-voids, resulting from the merging of smaller grains into larger ones due to high-temperature annealing.

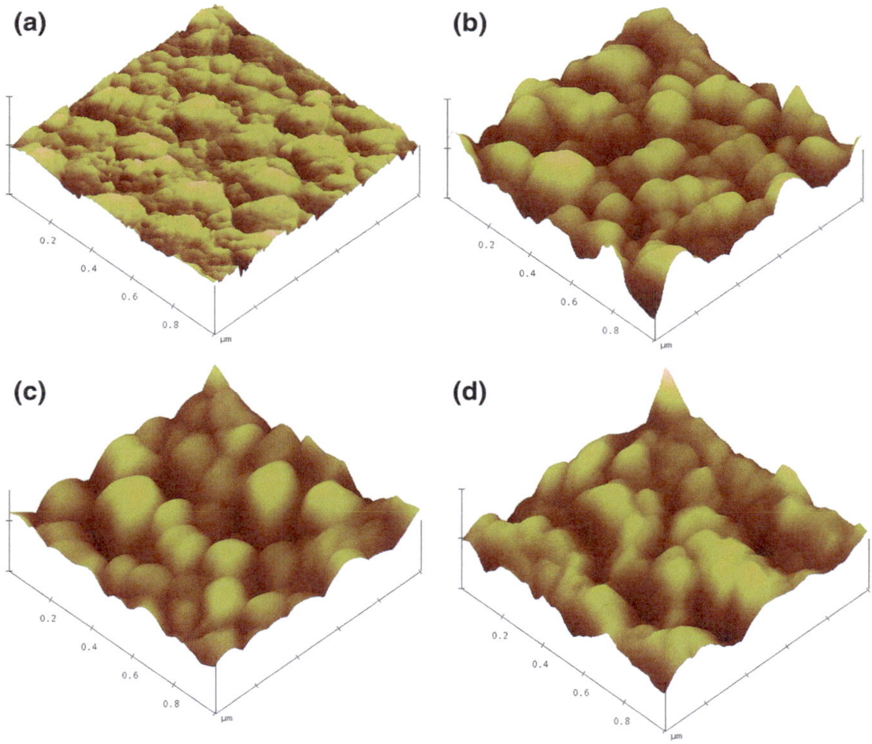

Fig. 3.3 AFM figures of the obtained samples. **a** Sample A1, **b** Sample B1, **c** Sample B2 and **d** Sample B3

Surface morphology of the obtained samples was assessed from SEM images, as shown in Figs. 3.5 and 3.6. Better grain formation was observed in Samples B1 and C1 (Figs. 3.5b and 3.6b), as compared to the Sample A1 (Figs. 3.5a and 3.6a). A possible cause of better grain formation might be related to the generation of heat in those samples during implantation. Formation of microvoids can also be observed in these samples, which may be due to the increased defects in those samples.

Electrical Properties

The effects of implantation on the film's electrical properties were surveyed by carrying out temperature-dependent Van der Pauw Hall measurements of the samples in the range of 80–300 K (Figs. 3.7 and 3.8). Carrier concentration, Hall mobility and resistivity of various samples at room temperature are shown in Table 3.3. The implanted samples exhibited the expected n-type characteristics over the entire temperature range due to the presence of implantation-induced defects, and they showed an increase in carrier concentration in B1 and a reduced carrier

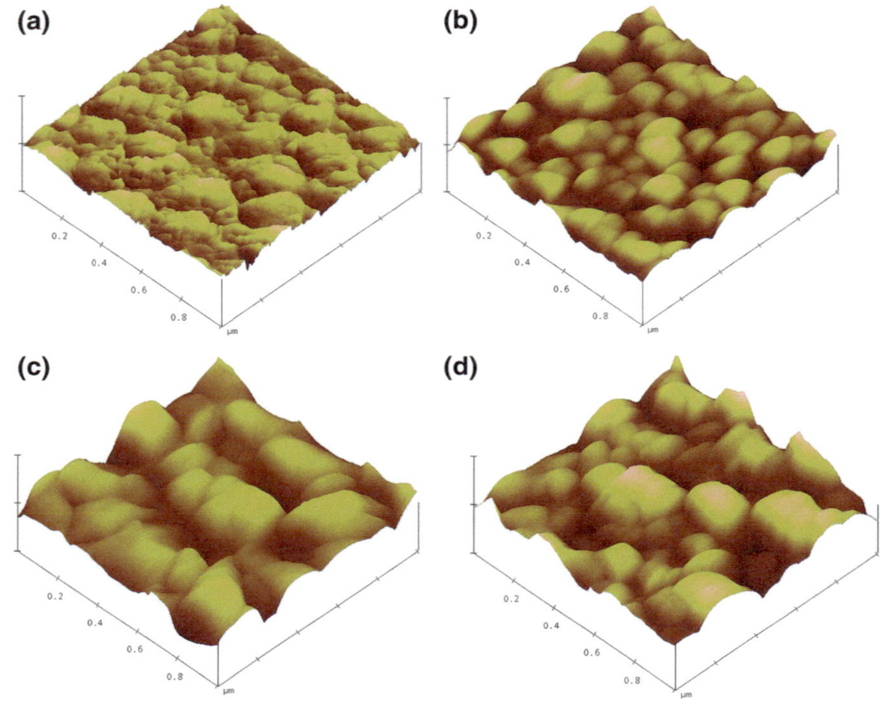

Fig. 3.4 AFM figures of the obtained samples. **a** Sample A1, **b** Sample C1, **c** Sample C2 and **d** Sample C3

Table 3.2 Root mean square (RMS) roughness values of the samples

Sample name	RMS roughness (nm)
A1	7.09
B1	8.12
B2	12.37
B3	13.47
C1	8.11
C2	12.87
C3	13.47

concentration in C1 as compared to A1. The reduction in concentration in C1 may be due to fewer defects and denser grains as seen from AFM and SEM images. The implanted samples were subjected to rapid thermal process at 650–750 °C, not only to reduce the defects but also to activate the Li ions to occupy Zn interstitial sites and lead to p-type films. However, the samples continued to show n-type characteristics. At the same time, significant changes in the carrier concentration, resistivity and Hall mobility were noticed in these films. For the samples annealed at 650 °C (Samples B2 and C2), the carrier concentration and resistivity are found to reduce. However,

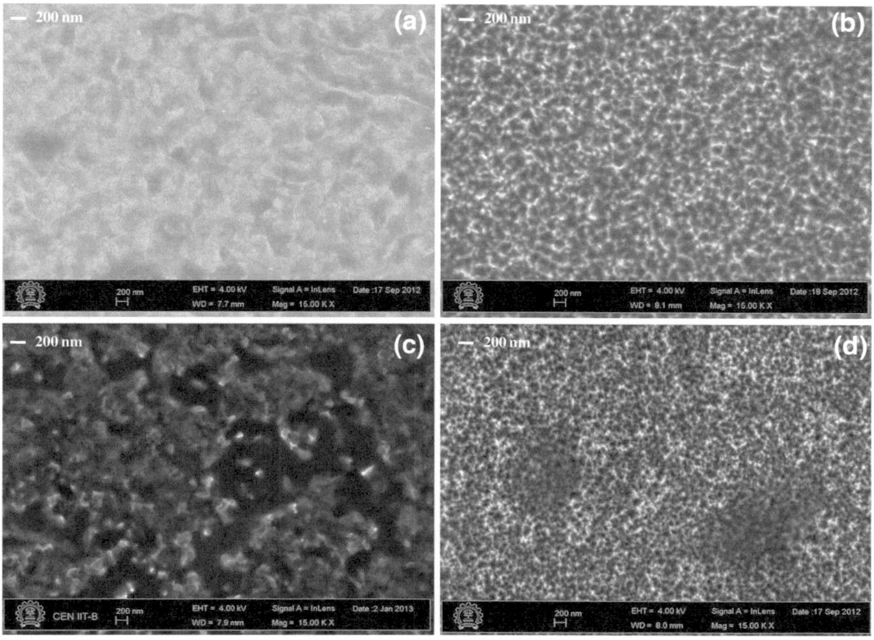

Fig. 3.5 SEM images. **a** Sample A1, **b** Sample B1, **c** Sample B2 and **d** Sample B3

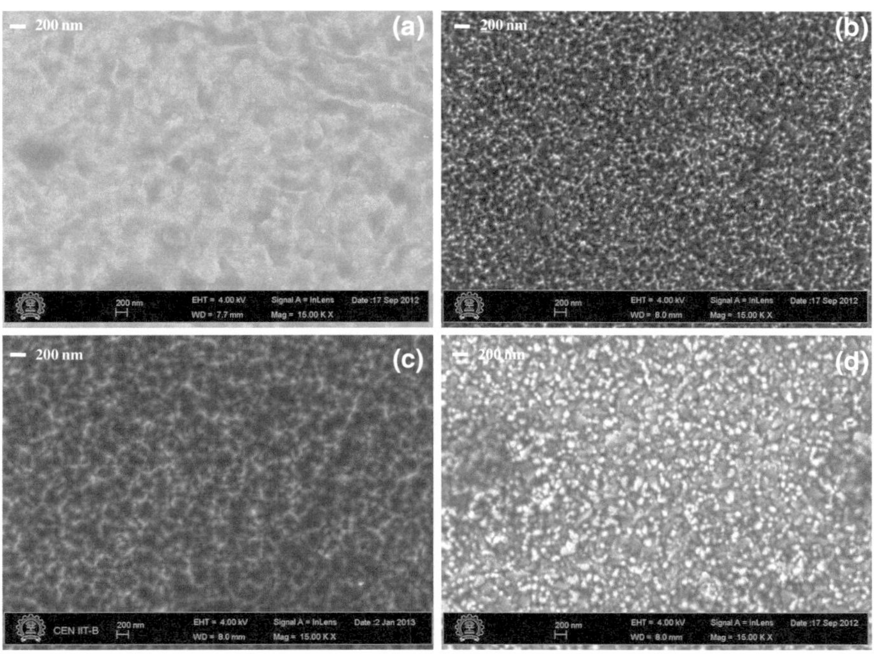

Fig. 3.6 SEM images. **a** Sample A1, **b** Sample C1, **c** Sample C2 and **d** Sample C3

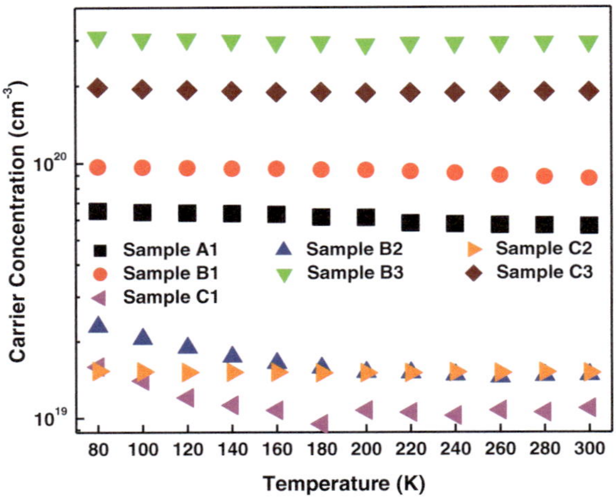

Fig. 3.7 Temperature-dependent carrier concentration for the obtained samples (Reprinted from S. Nagar et al. "Structural, electrical and optical characteristics of lithium-implanted ZnO thin films", *Superlattices and Microstructures*, Vol. 53, pp. 164–172, 2013; with permission from Elsevier)

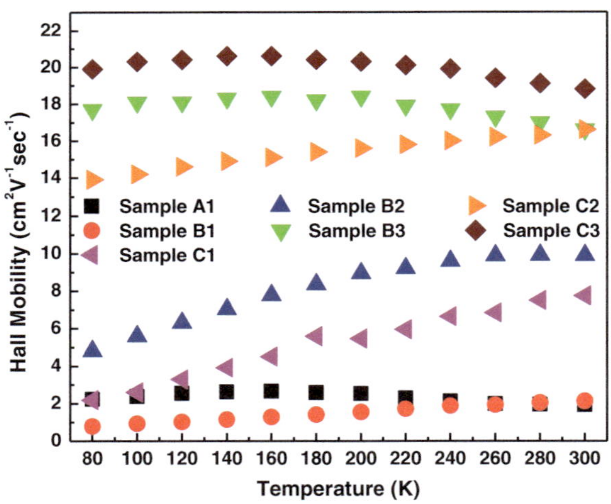

Fig. 3.8 Temperature-dependent Hall mobility for the obtained samples (Reprinted from S. Nagar et al. "Structural, electrical and optical characteristics of lithium-implanted ZnO thin films", *Superlattices and Microstructures*, Vol. 53, pp. 164–172, 2013; with permission from Elsevier)

Table 3.3 Carrier concentration, Hall mobility and resistivity values of the obtained samples taken at room temperature

Sample name	Carrier concentration (cm^{-3})	Hall mobility (cm^2/V s)	Resistivity (Ω cm)
A1	5.64×10^{19}	1.94	5.35×10^{-2}
B1	8.68×10^{19}	2.14	3.4×10^{-2}
B2	1.13×10^{19}	35.2	1.57×10^{-2}
B3	2.9×10^{20}	16.9	1.27×10^{-2}
C1	2.1×10^{19}	7.16	4.15×10^{-2}
C2	1.51×10^{19}	21	1.96×10^{-2}
C3	1.95×10^{20}	20.2	1.59×10^{-3}

for Samples B3 and C3, the carrier concentration increases, while resistivity decreases. The aggravation of vacancy clusters due to implantation, which grows into microvoids, might be a probable reason for the increase in concentration. These microvoids are easier to recover at lower temperatures, thus explaining lower concentration for Samples A2 and B2 [68]. Moreover, Lopatiuk et al. have also reported that the introduction of lithium ions in ZnO films tends to introduce deep electron traps [118]. The combination of deep electron traps and microvoids may have led to such an observation. Moreover, for all the annealed samples, the Hall mobility increases, probably due to minimised implantation-related defects.

Optical Properties

Low-temperature (8 K) PL spectra were analysed to assess the change in optical properties due to implantation (Figs. 3.9 and 3.10). A prominent NBE around 3.36 eV, corresponding to the donor-bound-exciton (D°X) peak, was observed in all implanted and annealed samples, confirming the n-type conductivity of the films, as shown by the Hall measurement results [72, 104]. It is interesting to note that no deep-level peaks were observed for any of the samples. This may be due to the small ionic radii of Li ions, which would not markedly affect the crystal structure, although implantation-related defects do occur, as seen from SEM images. Another peak is observed around 3.33 eV, which is attributed to the exciton bound to an extended defect, as reported by Wagner et al. [105]. The intensity of this peak reduces for Samples B1, B3, C1 and C3 compared with A1, perhaps due to the better grain formation in these samples. But for Sample B2, this peak increases, while the peak was not observed in Sample C2. The intensity of this peak seems to increase for Samples B3 and C3 when compared with B1 and C1. A possible reason might be the increased microvoid formation in the samples as observed by SEM

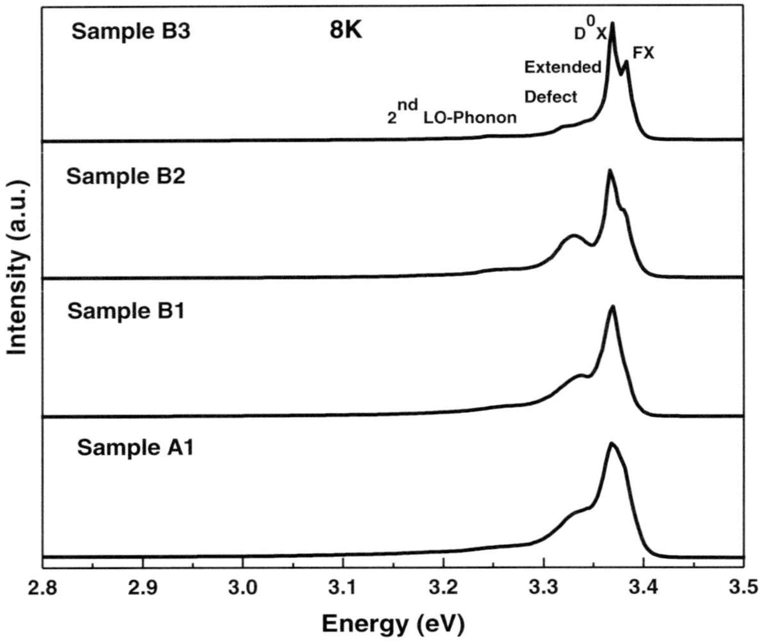

Fig. 3.9 PL spectra of the samples, obtained after implantation at 40 keV, taken at 8 K. No deep-level peaks in the samples are observed

images. A peak is observed around 3.22 eV, which is attributed to the second LO-phonon replica because:

$$3.365 - 0.072 - 0.072 = 3.221 \tag{3.1}$$

where 3.365 eV is the energy corresponding to the D°X peak and 0.072 eV is the energy of the LO phonon. The absence of the first LO-phonon replica may be because it is hidden in the background of the exciton-bound defect peak around 3.33 eV. A high-intensity LO-phonon peak was observed in Sample C2 and may be a reason for the absence of the extended defect peak around 3.33 eV. For Samples B3 and C3, FX peak around 3.38 eV was also present. Due to the increased carrier concentration (as determined by Hall measurements) in these samples, some excitonic transitions might have occurred, which would explain the observed FX peak. However, no acceptor peak was visible in any of the samples.

The temperature-dependent PL spectra of all samples are shown in Figs. 3.11 and 3.12. The prominent D°X peak at lower temperatures started to decrease with temperature, while the FX peak started to dominate at higher temperatures. The enhanced thermal dissociation of bound excitons into free excitons causes this kind

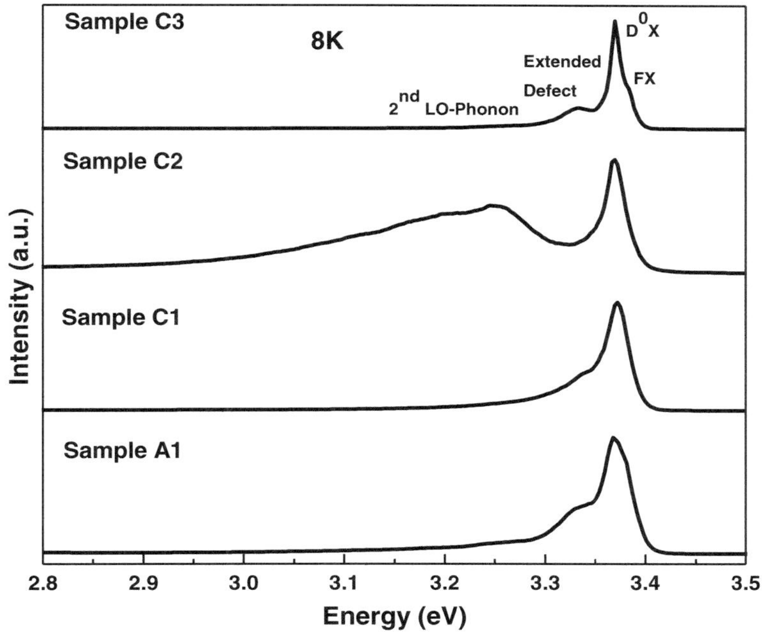

Fig. 3.10 PL spectra of the samples, obtained after implantation at 50 keV, taken at 8 K. No deep-level peaks in the samples are observed

of observation [108]. To depict the optical quality of the films, the integrated PL intensity of the obtained samples was plotted against the inverse of the temperature (Figs. 3.13 and 3.14). The results indicate that both implanted samples have better optical behaviour than do the as-deposited samples, which may be due to the denser grain formation in the implanted samples (Figs. 3.3b, 3.4b, 3.5b and 3.6b). As shown in Fig. 3.13, Sample B2 provides the best luminescence among all the samples. Figure 3.14 depicts samples implanted with 50 keV of energy. In this case, Sample C2 shows the least luminescence, while Sample C3 has the highest. The presence of microvoids in C2 may have caused the reduction in its optical quality, whereas the presence of denser grains in C3 led to its higher optical quality.

Quantitative fitting of different samples was done, using Figs. 3.13 and 3.14, to calculate the thermal activation energy using Eq. 2.3. The results have been tabulated in Table 3.4. The increase of defects and electron traps leads to a reduction in activation energy for B1 and C1. Upon annealing of the implanted samples, the activation energy increased to a high value of 147.28, 176.54, 223.04 and 236.59 meV for Samples B2, B3, C2 and C3, respectively. The reduced strain and defects in the films due to annealing lead to this increase in activation energy. Moreover, it has been shown by Wardle et al. [119] and Lopatiuk et al. [118] that

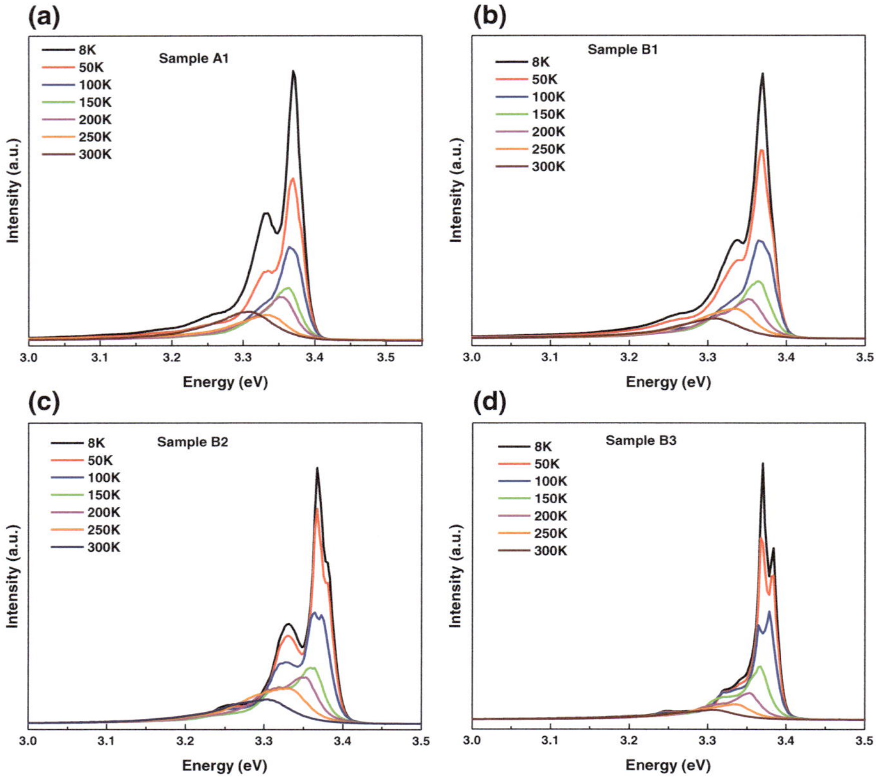

Fig. 3.11 Temperature-dependent PL spectra for Samples A1, B1, B2 and B3

the high values in these samples are due to the deep Li acceptors, which cause trapping of non-equilibrium electrons.

3.2.2.3 Conclusion

Li ion implantation was performed on ZnO films at low energies (40 and 50 keV) with the intention to make p-type films, and a detailed study on the structural, electrical and optical properties was carried out. Subsequent annealing of the samples was performed at 650–750 °C. XRD results confirmed the deposition of highly c-axis-oriented ⟨002⟩ ZnO films. Hall measurement results revealed increased electron carrier concentration for samples annealed at 750 °C. Although no acceptor peaks were visible in the PL spectra of the implanted samples, significant changes with respect to the defect have been observed. The implantation of Li ions has some significant changes in the electrical and optical quality of the ZnO

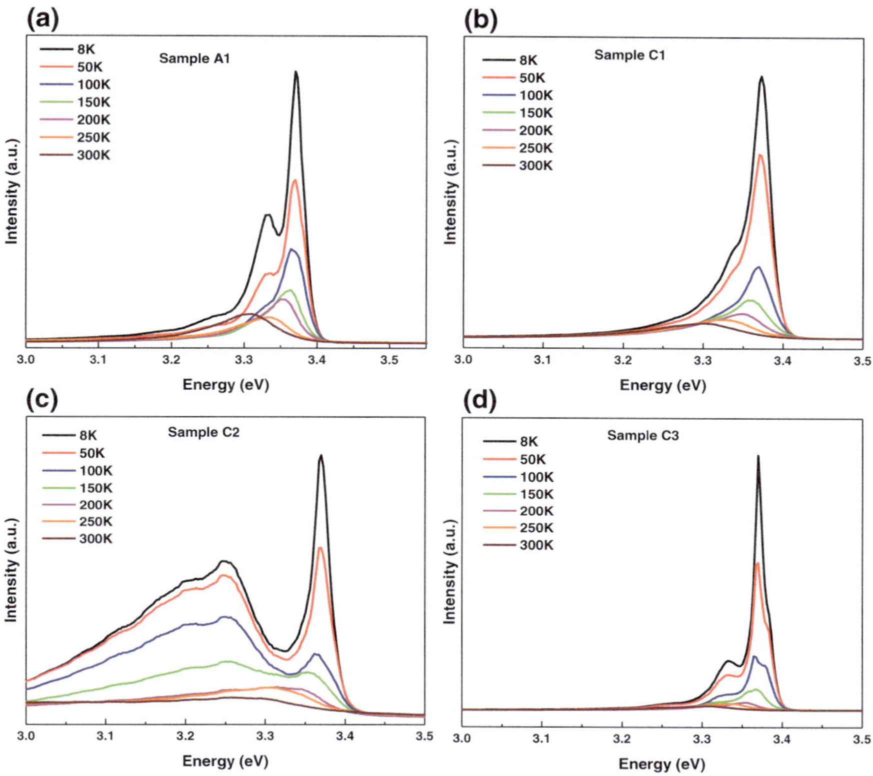

Fig. 3.12 Temperature-dependent PL spectra for Samples A1, C1, C2 and C3

Fig. 3.13 Comparison of the integrated PL intensity at 8 K for Samples A1, B1, B2 and B3 (Reprinted from S. Nagar et al. "Structural, electrical and optical characteristics of lithium-implanted ZnO thin films", *Superlattices and Microstructures*, Vol. 53, pp. 164–172, 2013; with permission from Elsevier)

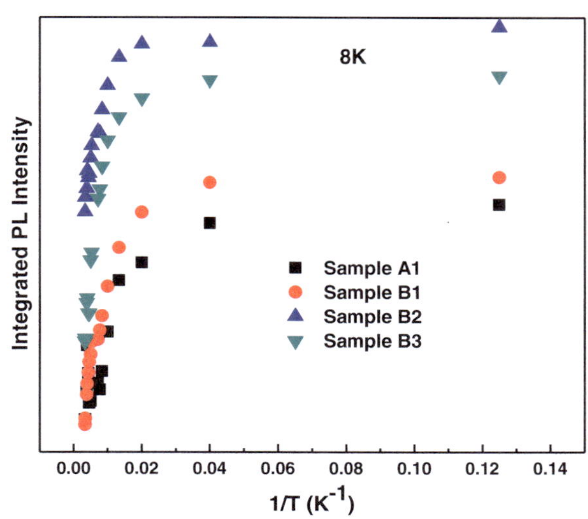

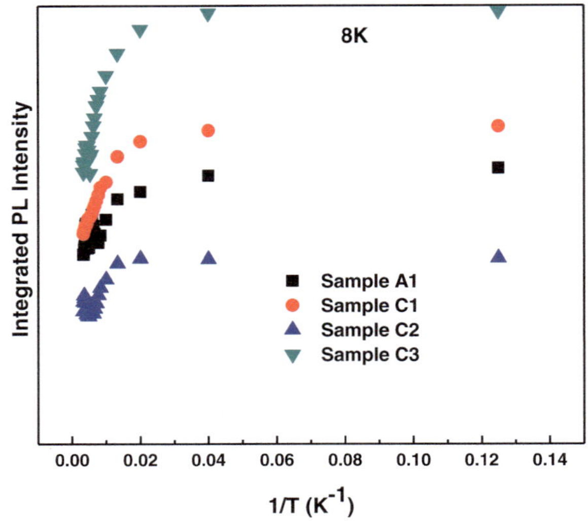

Fig. 3.14 Comparison of the integrated PL intensity at 8 K for Samples A1, C1, C2 and C3 (Reprinted from S. Nagar et al. "Structural, electrical and optical characteristics of lithium-implanted ZnO thin films", *Superlattices and Microstructures*, Vol. 53, pp. 164–172, 2013; with permission from Elsevier)

Table 3.4 Thermal activation energy for the various samples

Sample name	Thermal activation energy (meV)
A1	89.84
B1	68.3
B2	147.28
B3	236.59
C1	72.07
C2	176.54
C3	223.04

Reprinted from S. Nagar et al. "Structural, electrical and optical characteristics of lithium-implanted ZnO thin films", *Superlattices and Microstructures*, Vol. 53, pp. 164–172, 2013; with permission from Elsevier

thin films caused when Li forms deep acceptors in the ZnO films, thus leading to trapping of non-equilibrium electrons.

3.2.3 Phosphorus Implantation Studies

3.2.3.1 Experimental Details

Implantation of phosphorus ions was carried out using a beam accelerating energy of 50 keV and dosage of 8×10^{14} ions/cm^2 (Sample D1). LEAF at BARC, Mumbai, was used for this purpose. TRIM calculations measured the projected range of 917 Å. After implantation, rapid thermal annealing process was carried out in Ar ambient at temperatures of 650–750 °C to obtain Samples D2 and D3, respectively. One of the samples was also annealed at 750 °C in oxygen environment to visualise the effect of various background gases on the implanted films (Sample D4).

3.2.3.2 Results and Discussion

Structural Properties

XRD studies reveal deposition of highly c-axis-oriented ⟨002⟩ films (Fig. 3.15). The presence of only (001) family peaks certifies preferential growth of ZnO in the ⟨001⟩ direction due to its lowest surface free energy. The FWHM of the Sample D1 was higher than in A1, which is to be expected, as implantation causes defects in the film. While Sample D2 did show slight improvement in the FWHM as compared to Sample D1, the FWHM value was considerably lower in Samples D3 and D4 indicating that the defects caused by implantation have reduced when annealed at higher temperatures. It is also interesting to note that for Samples D1, D2 and D3, only the (001) family of peaks is visible, while Sample D4 also showed a small peak at 31.5° corresponding to ⟨100⟩ direction clearly representing the

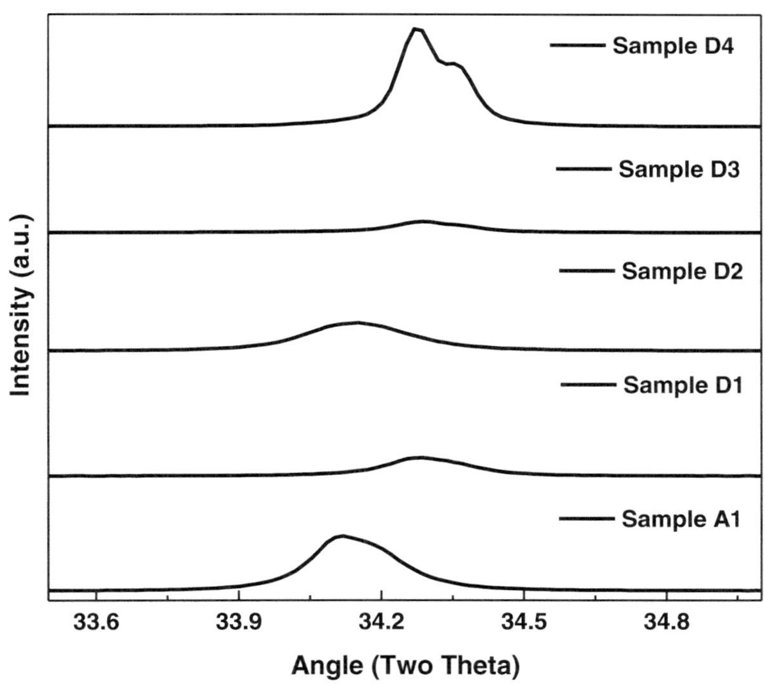

Fig. 3.15 XRD patterns for the obtained films showing the ⟨002⟩ and ⟨004⟩ ZnO peaks

Table 3.5 FWHM values of different films

Sample name	FWHM value (°)
A1	0.217
D1	0.257
D2	0.224
D3	0.183
D4	0.165

Reprinted from S. Nagar et al. "Effect of phosphorus irradiation in the structural, electrical and optical characteristics of ZnO thin films", *Journal of Luminescence*, Vol. 132, pp. 1089–1094, 2012; with permission from Elsevier

polycrystalline nature of the film. Thus, the effect of background gas environment during annealing can be easily identified. Table 3.5 shows the FWHM values of different samples.

Atomic force microscopy was performed to understand the morphological changes observed in the samples with implantation and annealing in different environments (Fig. 3.16). Very little grain formation can be detected for Sample A1 when compared to Samples D1, D2 and D3. The internal heating of the samples as a result of implantation leads to substantial grain formation. This tends to increase the RMS roughness for Sample D1 when compared to A1, measured over an area of 1 μm × 1 μm (Table 3.6). The RMS roughness values for Samples D2 and D3 were reduced. Better formation of grains was observed in Sample D2 when compared with Sample D1, leading to reduced roughness. When the sample is further heated at higher temperatures, then some small grains merge together to form larger grains, resulting in a slight increase in roughness. However, in Sample D4, the same grains diffused, causing the roughness to continue to decrease. The diffusion of some grains might be a probable reason for the polycrystallinity of the film, as has been discussed above.

SEM imaging performed on the samples further validates the above claim (Fig. 3.17). The formation of better grains in D1 as compared to A1 can be clearly observed. Moreover, many implanted-related defects are also observed in D1, which may have contributed to increase in the roughness of the film. In Sample D2, grains merge, leading to increased roughness of the films. In Sample D3, the formation of spherical grains can be clearly observed. Moreover, the defects in Samples D3 and D4 are also reduced when compared to D1. As shown in Fig. 3.16e, the SEM image of Sample D4 also proves that annealing in oxygen environment has caused the grains to diffuse, leading to polycrystalline films.

Electrical Properties

All the samples were subjected to room temperature Hall measurement by employing Van der Pauw geometry to study the effect of the implantation. The results, as tabulated in Table 3.7, clearly exhibit n-type behaviour for all the samples. A slight increase in the carrier concentration and consequent decrease in

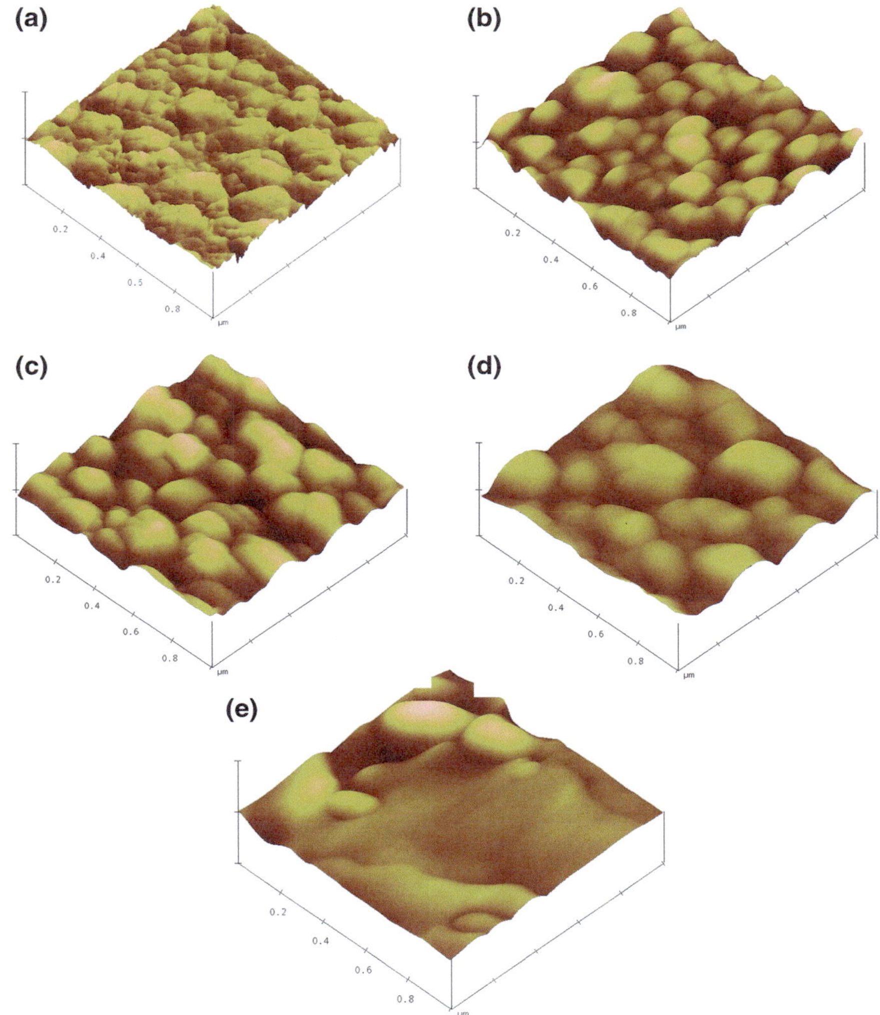

Fig. 3.16 AFM images of the obtained samples: **a** Sample A1, **b** Sample D1, **c** Sample D2, **d** Sample D3 and **e** Sample D4 (Figures (**a–d**) reprinted from S. Nagar et al. "Effect of phosphorus irradiation in the structural, electrical and optical characteristics of ZnO thin films", *Journal of Luminescence*, Vol. 132, pp. 1089–1094, 2012; with permission from Elsevier)

Hall mobility appear in Sample D1, which is to be expected due to the increase in the number of ions as a result of implantation. A marked reduction in the carrier concentration and subsequent increase in Hall mobility were observed for Sample D2, while in D3 the carrier concentration and Hall mobility increased. The improvement in mobility might be due to the reduction of defects in heat treatment. It can be clearly seen from SEM images that the grains in D2 are small and very

Table 3.6 Root mean square (RMS) roughness of samples

Sample name	RMS roughness (nm)
A1	7.09
D1	10.07
D2	8.66
D3	9.31
D4	4.9

Reprinted from S. Nagar et al. "Effect of phosphorus irradiation in the structural, electrical and optical characteristics of ZnO thin films", *Journal of Luminescence*, Vol. 132, pp. 1089–1094, 2012; with permission from Elsevier

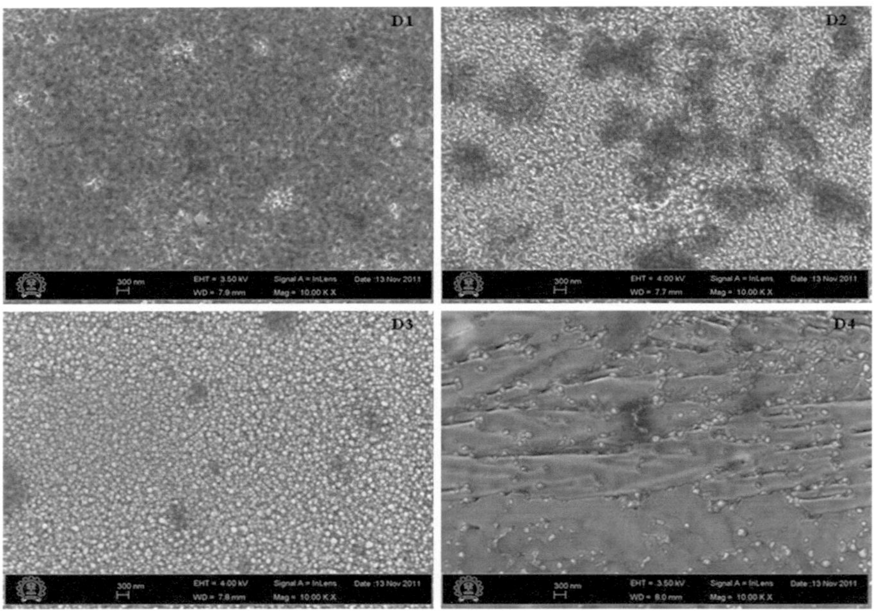

Fig. 3.17 SEM images of the different samples

closely packed, unlike in D3. As a result, the grain boundary scattering in D3 is much larger compared to that of D2, leading to higher carrier concentration values and lower Hall mobility values. The comparative smooth surface of Sample D4 with respect to other samples in combination with annealing effects has caused the reduction in carrier concentration and increase in the Hall mobility for the sample. The reduction in concentration and increase of mobility for most of the annealed samples prove that compensation of n-type character has taken place due to P-doping. Temperature-dependent Hall measurements were performed in all the samples to check whether lowering of temperature caused any type conversion in the samples (Figs. 3.18 and 3.19). However, no such observation was found, and samples continuously depicted n-type carriers in the whole temperature range.

Table 3.7 Carrier concentration and Hall mobility of various samples at room temperature

Sample name	Type of conductivity	Carrier concentration (cm^{-3})	Mobility ($cm^2\ V^{-1}\ s^{-1}$)
A1	n-type	4.5×10^{19}	2.1
D1	n-type	9.69×10^{19}	0.727
D2	n-type	5.6×10^{18}	31.4
D3	n-type	1.36×10^{20}	12.44
D4	n-type	4×10^{18}	54.3

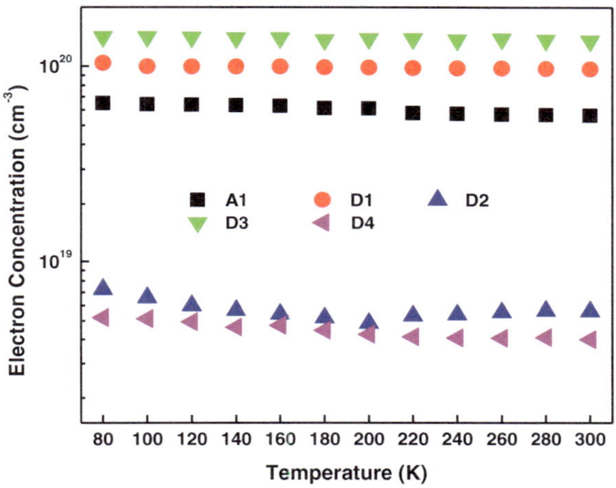

Fig. 3.18 Temperature-dependent electron carrier concentration for the various samples

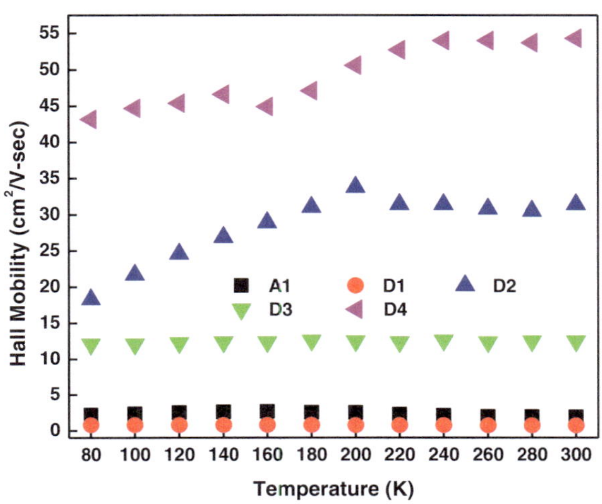

Fig. 3.19 Temperature-dependent Hall mobility of the obtained samples

Optical Properties

The optical characteristics of the samples were accomplished by low-temperature (8 K) PL study (Fig. 3.20). A prominent NBE at around 3.38 eV with no deep-level emission was noticed for Sample A1, verifying the growth of high-quality ZnO film. For Sample D1, a decrease in the NBE peak intensity is detected. In addition, a broad deep-level emission centred at 2.55 eV is observed. The large FWHM value of this peak indicates that this emission derives from the origin of different point defects occurring due to P-implantation, along with the Zn_i and V_O. An increase in the intensity of the NBE and deep-level emission is observed for Sample D2 along with a lower FWHM value (1.4 eV) as compared to Sample D1 (3.9 eV). When annealing at lower temperature, the point defects, occurring due to implantation, might have been converted into particular type of defect (Zn_i or V_O), explaining such an observation. An increase of the NBE peak intensity along with the subsidised deep-level peak is witnessed in Sample D3, which was annealed at 750 °C. This indicates that due to annealing at higher temperatures, the defects due to implantation are completely removed. This also explains the increase in intensity of the NBE. Although Sample D4 shows an improved NBE, the occurrence of deep-level peak for the sample clearly demonstrates the role of background gas environment in reducing the defects. According to Lin et al., this role is correlated with the formation of defects and some glassy phase (MPO_4^-) [10]. It is interesting to note a slight redshift in the peak position of the NBE for Samples D2, D3 and D4. The development and relaxation of lattice strain in the films, due to the incorporation of the P-ions and subsequent annealing in the ZnO lattice, might be a possible reason for such a redshift [120].

Inset of Fig. 3.20 shows the PL spectra near the NBE region for the samples. A prominent donor-bound-exciton (D°X) peak at approximately 3.36 eV is seen for the implanted samples, while the FX peak at 3.38 eV is dominant in Sample A1, confirming the n-type behaviour of all the samples as proved from the Hall measurements [72, 104]. The FX peak is absent from the P-implanted samples. The free-electron–acceptor (FA) peak around 3.31 eV is seen for all the samples, but its intensity is found to increase for Samples D1, D2, D3 and D4, clearly indicating that incorporation of phosphorus ions in the ZnO films does have some effect in increasing the acceptor concentration. Moreover, for the implanted sample, we also see a donor-bound-acceptor pair (DAP) peak at 3.27 eV, which further clarifies the role of P-implantation in increasing the acceptor concentration [104].

Temperature-dependent PL spectra of the various samples were also measured (Fig. 3.21). A decrease in the dominant PL peak intensity is realised for all the samples with respect to increase in temperature, which is expected due to increase of defects at higher temperatures. However, for the FA peak around 3.31 eV, a slight increase in the intensity has been detected up to 150 K, followed by the quenching of the peak at higher temperatures for Sample D1. For the remaining samples, the decay was consistent with thermal characteristics of the FA transition [35]. The optical binding energy due to the acceptors can be predicted from the FA transition using Eq. 3.2:

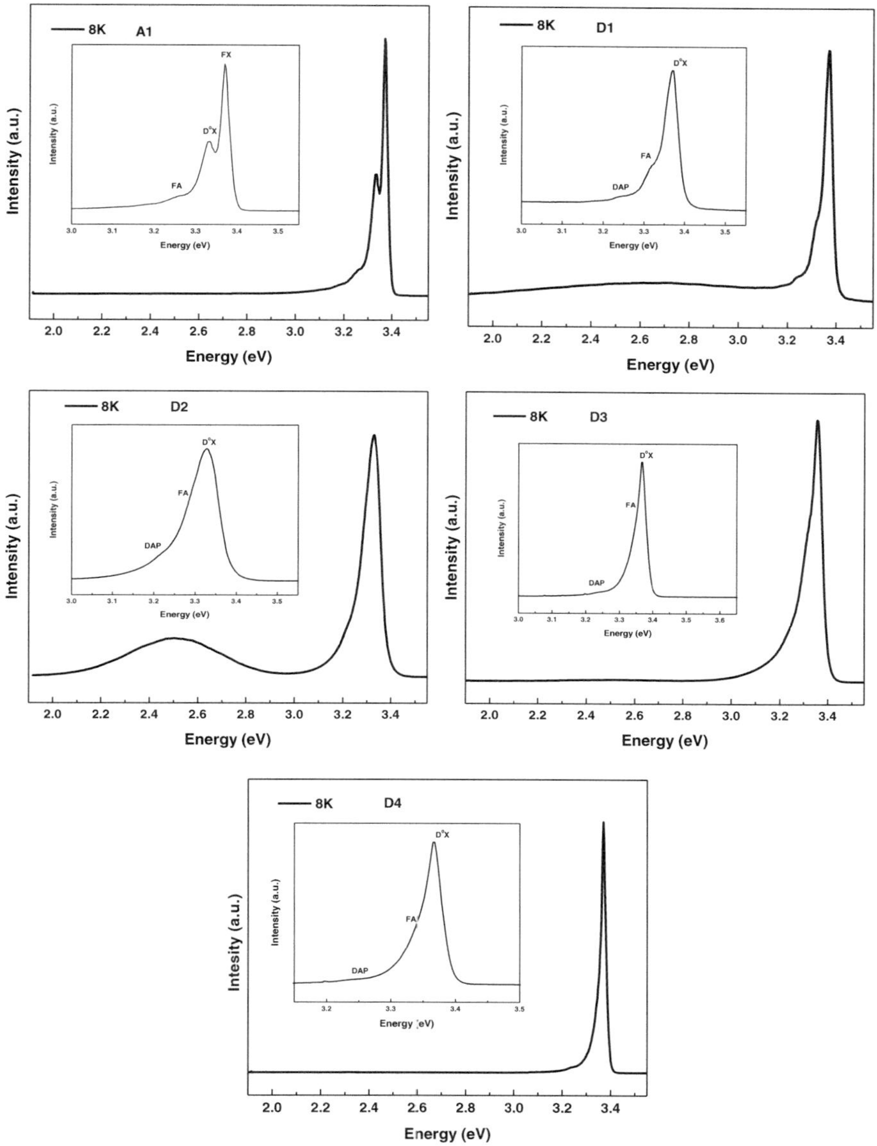

Fig. 3.20 PL spectra of different samples taken at 8 K

$$E_A = E_g - E_{FA} + k_B T/2 \tag{3.2}$$

where E_A, E_g and E_{FA} are the acceptor, bandgap and FA energies, respectively. Neglecting the thermal energy term at temperature of 8 K and using the standard

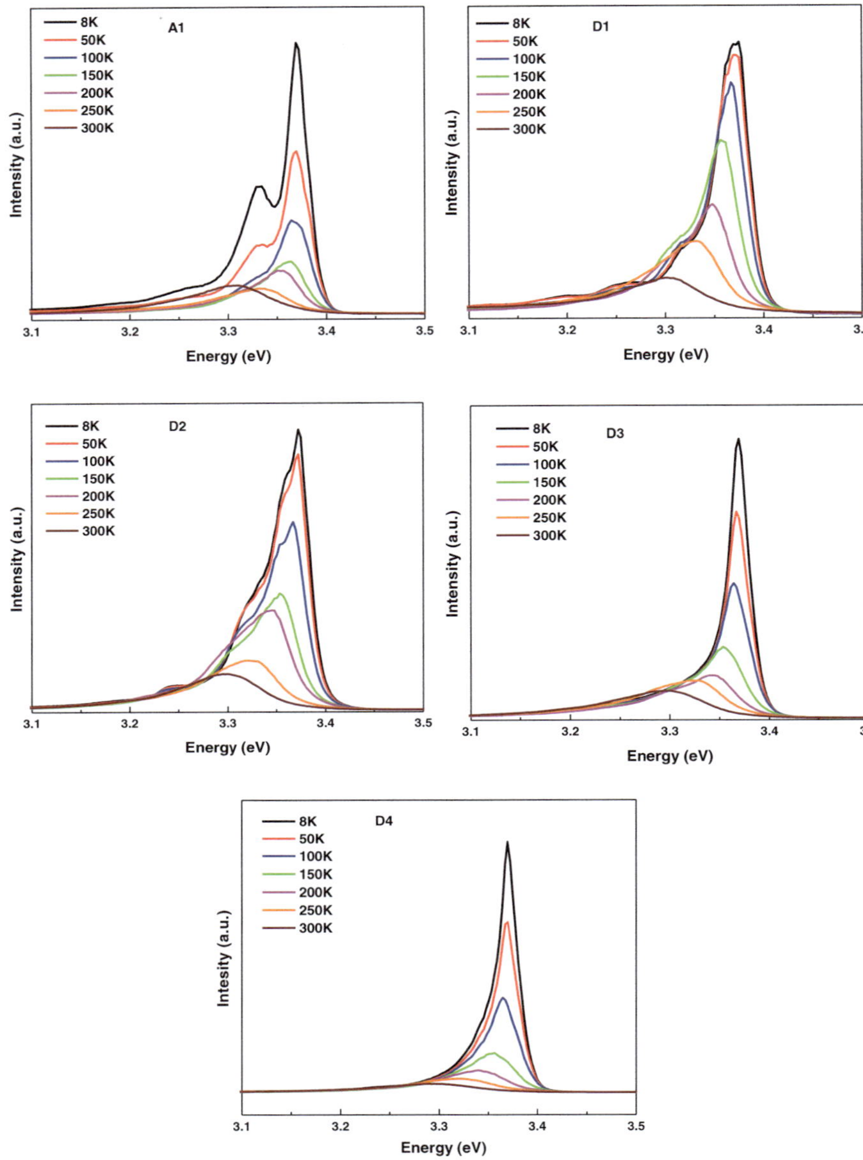

Fig. 3.21 Temperature-dependent PL spectra of different samples (Figures A1, D1, D2 and D3 reprinted from S. Nagar et al. "Effect of phosphorus irradiation in the structural, electrical and optical characteristics of ZnO thin films", *Journal of Luminescence*, Vol. 132, pp. 1089–1094, 2012; with permission from Elsevier)

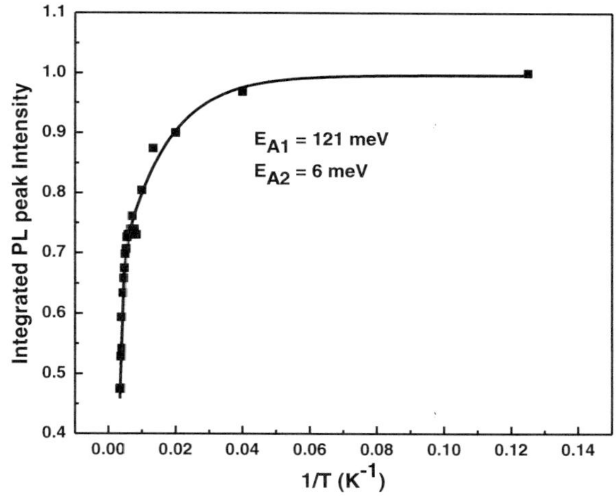

Fig. 3.22 Normalised PL peak intensity of the FA peak for Sample D3 plotted against the inverse temperature (Reprinted from S. Nagar et al. "Effect of phosphorus irradiation in the structural, electrical and optical characteristics of ZnO thin films", *Journal of Luminescence*, Vol. 132, pp. 1089–1094, 2012; with permission from Elsevier)

value of bandgap energy (E_g = 3.437 eV), the acceptor binding energy was calculated to be around 120 meV. The temperature dependence of the integrated PL peak intensity for the FA peak for Sample D3 is shown in Fig. 3.22, which was analysed using Eq. 3.3:

$$I = I_0/\{1 + a_1 \exp(-E_{a1}/k_B T) + a_2 \exp(-E_{a2}/k_B T)\} \tag{3.3}$$

where I_0 is the integrated PL peak intensity at 8 K, E_{ai} (i = 1, 2) are the activation energies of the thermal quenching processes, and a_1 and a_2 are constants. The energies of E_{a1} and E_{a2} were calculated to be 121 and 6 meV, respectively. In Eq. 3.3, E_{a1} corresponds to the activation energy of the FA peak and E_{a2} is associated with the temperature-dependent carrier capture cross-section of the recombination centres [41]. Similar curves were also obtained for other samples. Thus, phosphorus can be used as an acceptor to obtain p-type ZnO films. However, implantation parameters and the post-implantation annealing temperatures need further optimisation to obtain p-type ZnO films.

3.2.3.3 Conclusion

An attempt to make p-type ZnO by using phosphorus ion implantation was carried out at a low energy of 50 keV with fluence 8×10^{14} ions/cm^2. Highly c-axis-oriented ⟨002⟩ ZnO films were obtained. The results of PL measurements showed an increase in the defects due to implantation, which then reduced when the samples were heated at a high temperature of 750 °C. The increase in the FA and DAP peak intensities for the implanted samples indicated that the acceptor concentration in the ZnO film had increased. Therefore, the approach used in this study can be employed to achieve p-type ZnO. The activation energy of the FA peak was calculated from the temperature-dependent PL spectra and was found to be around 120 meV, which is comparable to previously reported results of the acceptor activation energy.

3.3 Plasma Immersion Ion Implantation Studies

3.3.1 Deposition of ZnO

Undoped ZnO thin films were deposited using radio frequency (RF) magnetron sputtering on highly resistive ⟨100⟩ n-type silicon substrates. A high-purity ZnO target (99.999%) with a 5 inch diameter was used. The target-to-substrate distance was kept at 70 mm. The deposition was performed for 40 min in an Ar ambient of 7×10^{-3} mbar at room temperature. A base vacuum of 2×10^{-5} mbar was achieved prior to the deposition. A resultant thickness of 350 nm, measured through ellipsometry, was achieved.

3.3.2 Phosphorus Implantation Studies

3.3.2.1 Experimental Details

The samples were subsequently subjected to phosphorus implantation using the plasma immersion ion implantation (PIII) technique to obtain Sample P1. A high-voltage negative pulse of 2 kV was applied to the target for 30 s. The negative pulse had an ON time of 10 μs and a RF of 5 kHz. The chamber pressure of 1×10^{-1} mbar was achieved from phosphine (PH_3) gas during implantation, which was carried out using RF plasma power of 900 W. After implantation, the samples were rapid thermal annealed at 700, 800, 900 and 1000 °C in oxygen environment for 10 s to eradicate implantation-related defects from the sample to obtain Samples P2, P3, P4 and P5 respectively.

3.3.2.2 Results and Discussion

Structural Properties

Figure 3.23 shows the SEM images of the different samples. The presence of defects due to phosphorus implantation in Sample A can be clearly observed. With an increase in annealing temperature, grains grow, and large grains in the films are clearly visible for Sample E, implying the removal of any implantation-related defects.

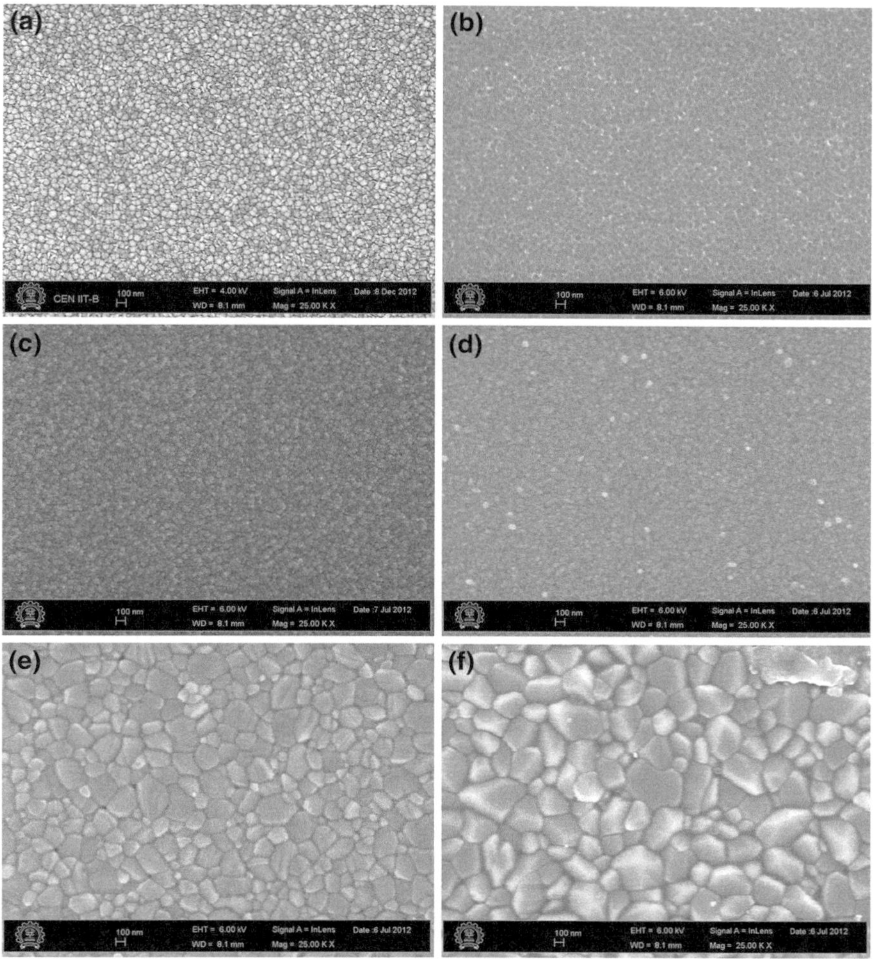

Fig. 3.23 SEM images of the obtained samples **a** as-deposited, **b** Sample P1, **c** Sample P2, **d** Sample P3, **e** Sample P4 and **f** Sample P5 (Figures (**b–e**) reprinted from S. Nagar et al. "Evidence of strong acceptor peaks in ZnO thin films doped with phosphorus by plasma immersion ion implantation technique", *Journal of Luminescence*, Vol. 137, pp. 55–58, 2013; with permission from Elsevier)

Optical Properties

Low-temperature PL (8 K) spectra of various samples are shown in Fig. 3.24. An expected donor-bound-exciton (D°X) peak around 3.36 eV is observed for Sample P1 along with deep-level defect peaks centred at 2.5 eV corresponding to the Zn_i, V_O and implantation-related defects [72, 121]. For Sample P2, the NBE almost

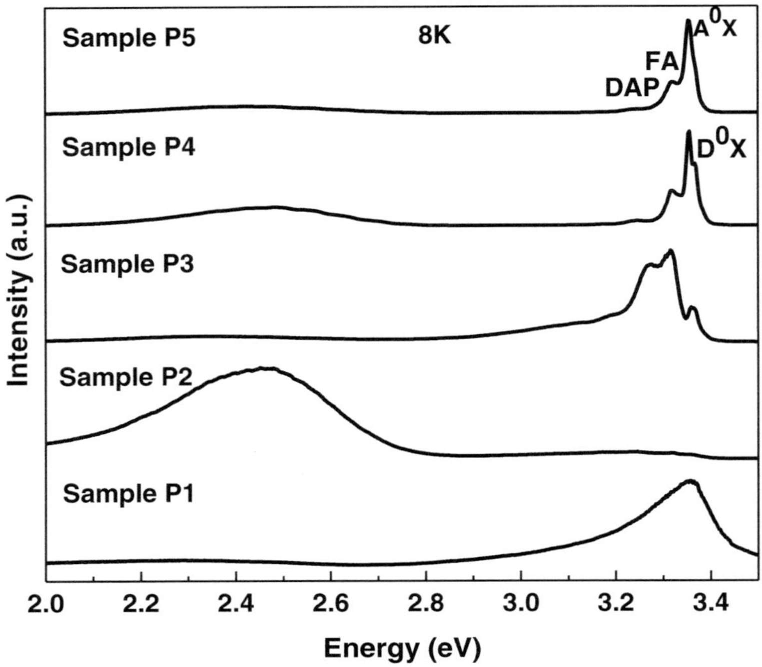

Fig. 3.24 PL spectra of different samples measured at 8 K showing the evolution of A°X peak with increase in annealing temperature (Reprinted from S. Nagar et al. "Evidence of strong acceptor peaks in ZnO thin films doped with phosphorus by plasma immersion ion implantation technique", *Journal of Luminescence*, Vol. 137, pp. 55–58, 2013; with permission from Elsevier)

disappears, while the deep-level defect peak becomes dominant, signifying the increased number of defects in the sample. Upon annealing temperature increase, the NBE again starts to dominate the PL spectra as seen in Samples P3, P4 and P5. However, a noteworthy change in the emissions is visible for the different samples. Whereas a FA peak around 3.32 eV is dominant in Sample P3, the A°X peak around 3.35 eV becomes dominant for Samples P4 and P5. This result clearly depicts a change in carrier type from n-type for Samples P1 and P2 to p-type for Samples P3, P4 and P5 due to P-implantation [49, 72, 121]. Since the implanted samples are annealed at higher temperatures, the P-ions receive sufficient thermal energy to occupy the V_O positions in the ZnO lattice and form shallow acceptors, thus increasing the acceptor concentration and giving rise to p-type films. To further validate the importance of phosphorus implantation and subsequent annealing, PL measurements were performed on the as-deposited and annealed samples without implantation (Fig. 3.25). The absence of any acceptor peaks in these samples proves that implantation of P-ions leads to an increase in acceptors and thus p-type

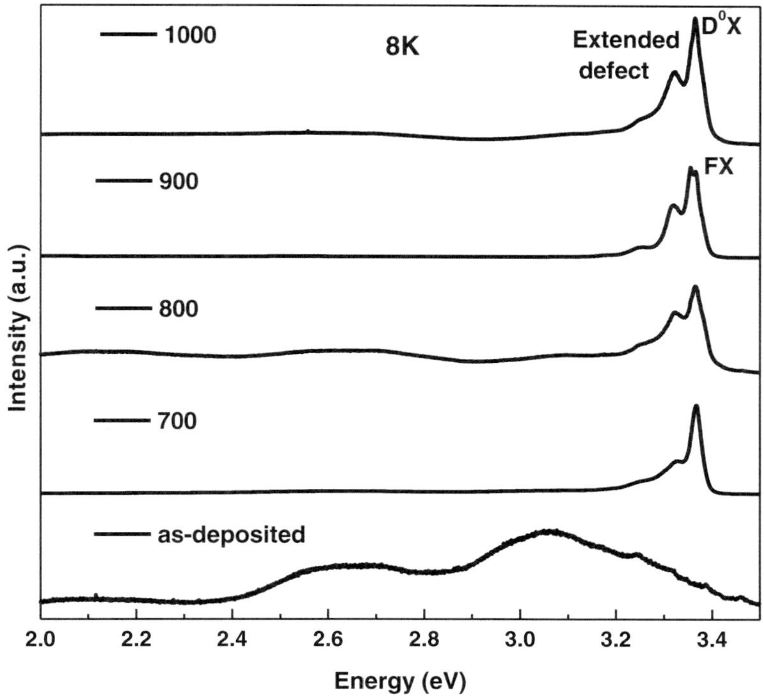

Fig. 3.25 PL spectra of unimplanted and annealed samples measured at 8 K. No A°X peak is visible in the samples (Reprinted from S. Nagar et al. "Evidence of strong acceptor peaks in ZnO thin films doped with phosphorus by plasma immersion ion implantation technique", *Journal of Luminescence*, Vol. 137, pp. 55–58, 2013; with permission from Elsevier)

film formation. The presence of the FA peak around 3.32 eV in Samples P4 and P5 and the DAP peak around 3.25 eV in Samples P3, P4 and P5 further confirms the increase in acceptors. Moreover, with regard to annealing the samples at higher temperatures, the defect peaks are also minimised, revealing reduced numbers of acceptor-, donor-, and implantation-related defects. This clearly illustrates that annealing the samples at higher temperatures improves film quality and changes carrier type.

To clearly visualise the effect of annealing on the P-ions, a secondary ion mass spectroscopy (SIMS) study was performed on the samples (Fig. 3.26). Increased P counts along the depth of the ZnO film can be clearly observed at higher temperatures. This finding further supports the PL and SEM results discussed above. In Sample P5, it is observed that some probable intermixing between the ZnO and Si occurs. Since the n-type Si was doped with phosphorus atoms, it may be possible that the P atoms from Si diffuse into the ZnO films and increase its count. However,

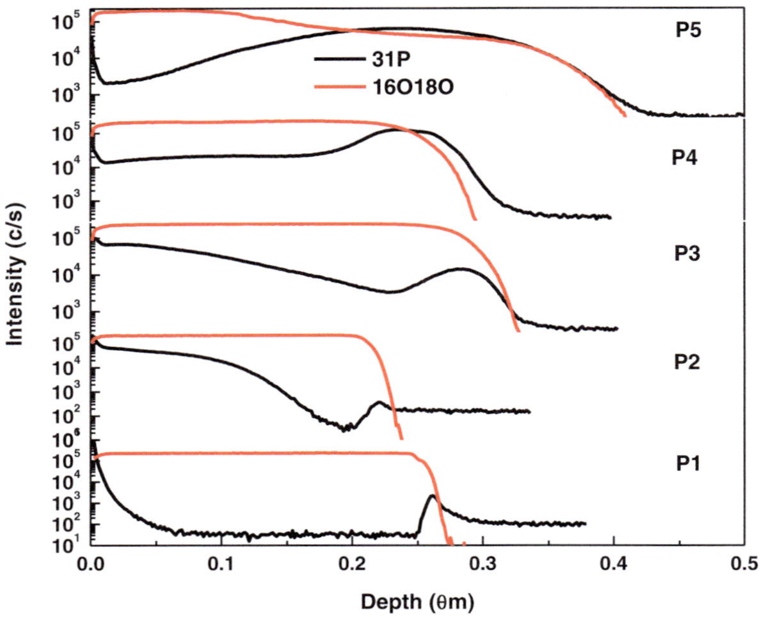

Fig. 3.26 SIMS data for the various samples depicting an increase in phosphorus counts with annealing (Reprinted from S. Nagar et al. "Evidence of strong acceptor peaks in ZnO thin films doped with phosphorus by plasma immersion ion implantation technique", *Journal of Luminescence*, Vol. 137, pp. 55–58, 2013; with permission from Elsevier)

it is not contributing towards p-doping, i.e. acceptor concentration, because PL of unimplanted annealed samples did not exhibit any acceptor peak. To further confirm the p-type behaviour of the samples, Van der Pauw Hall measurements were attempted, but the high resistivity of the samples made such measurements impossible.

Temperature-dependent PL measurements for Sample P5 are shown in Fig. 3.27. While the dominant A°X peak diminishes exponentially with temperature, the FX peak dominates at higher temperatures. The increasing number of FXs at higher temperatures leads to the following observation. The exponential decay of the acceptor peak with temperature is shown in the inset of Fig. 3.27. Quantitative fitting of this peak was performed using Eq. 3.4:

$$I = I_0/[1 + A * \exp(-E_A/k_B T)] \tag{3.4}$$

where I_0 is the integrated PL peak intensity at T = 8 K, E_A is the acceptor activation energy, and A is the peak fitting constant. The acceptor activation energy was thus determined to be 125 meV. This finding was similar to that obtained using spectroscopic observation where Eq. 3.2 was applied. The acceptor activation energy

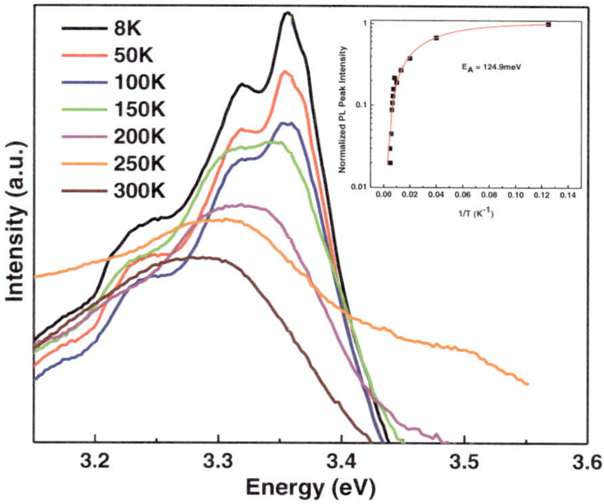

Fig. 3.27 Temperature-dependent PL spectra of Sample P5. *Inset* variation of acceptor peak intensity with temperature for Sample P5. The acceptor activation energy was calculated to be 125 meV (Reprinted from S. Nagar et al. "Evidence of strong acceptor peaks in ZnO thin films doped with phosphorus by plasma immersion ion implantation technique", *Journal of Luminescence*, Vol. 137, pp. 55–58, 2013; with permission from Elsevier)

was measured to be 120 meV, which is similar to the value calculated above. The shallow acceptor activation energy proves that P acts as a good dopant for producing p-type ZnO thin films.

Reliability Studies

Low-temperature PL (8 K) has been performed on the p-type samples over a period of 8 months to check the stability of the attained p-type films with time (Fig. 3.28). In the case of Sample P5, a dominant FA peak is observed after 4 and 6 months, while for Sample P4, the FA peak is visible even after a period of 8 months. However, for Sample P5, another peak corresponding to A°X peak is observed after 4 months, while a D°X peak is seen after 6 months. In P4, another peak corresponding to D°X peak is visible even after 4 months, and no A°X could be observed. This finding clearly indicates that the Sample P5 was still p-type after 4 months, but after 6 months, it starts converting back to n-type due to self-compensation, while Sample P4 starts to convert to n-type even after 4 months. However, after a period of 8 months, Sample P5 has deteriorated and thus no significant PL emission is observed. In the case of Sample P3, a strong D°X peak is observed even after a period of 4 months, which indicates that the ZnO film has completely converted to n-type after the given period.

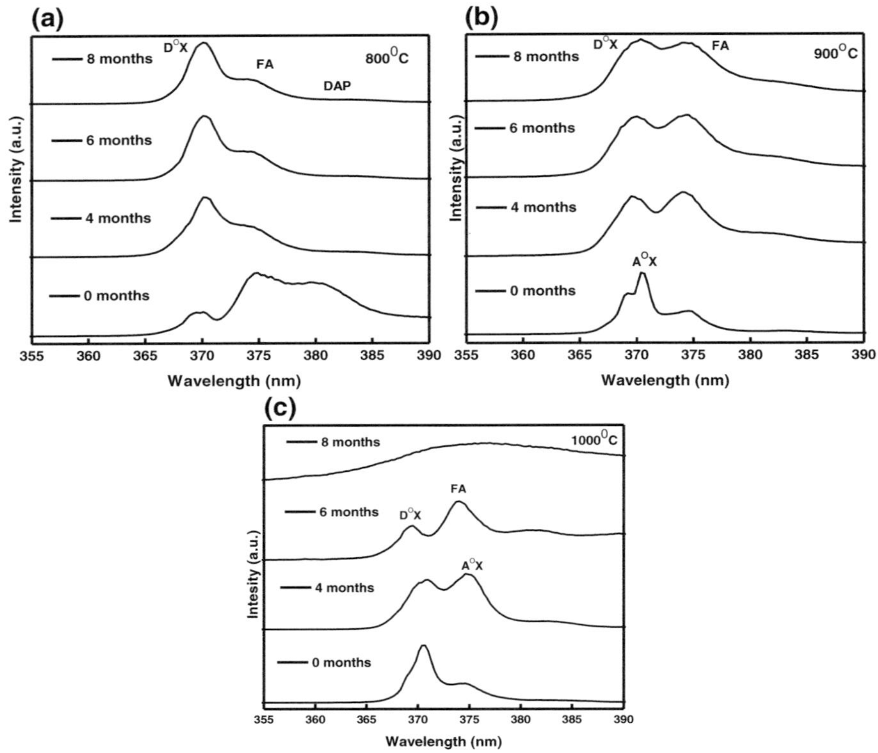

Fig. 3.28 PL spectra of **a** P3, **b** P4 and **c** P5, taken over a period of 8 months

3.3.2.3 Conclusion

PIII technique was used to implant P-ions on 350-nm ZnO thin films to create p-type ZnO films. The implanted samples are subsequently annealed at 700–1000 °C. Reduced numbers of defects and proper grain formation with increasing annealing temperature were visible in the SEM images. The incorporation of P-ions in the film was visualised in the SIMS study. The low-temperature PL studies revealed a gradual transition from n-type to p-type characteristics, with increasing annealing temperature. A strong acceptor peak for the sample annealed at 1000 °C with shallow acceptor activation energy of 125 meV confirmed the formation of p-type ZnO. The p-type behaviour of the thin film was maintained up to a period of 6 months, although the intensity reduced drastically. However, with better optimisation of deposition and implantation parameters, it may be possible to increase the reliability of the obtained p-type films. These results can help with the successful fabrication of future ZnO-based optoelectronic devices, such as LEDs and LDs.

3.3.3 *Nitrogen Implantation Studies*

3.3.3.1 Experimental Details

Nitrogen ion implantation was carried out on the ZnO films, deposited by RF sputtering, using PIII to obtain Sample N1. An RF of 5 kHz was applied on a high-voltage negative pulse of 2 kV with a pulse width of 10 μs. The ion implantation was carried out for 30 s in nitrogen plasma under a power of 900 W. A 2×10^{-5} mbar vacuum was achieved in a high-vacuum chamber prior to implantation. During implantation, the vacuum pressure was increased to 1×10^{-1} mbar. It is known that ion implantation induces defects in films. To reduce or remove such defects, the ion-implanted film samples were subjected to rapid thermal annealing in an oxygen atmosphere at 700, 800, 900 or 1000 °C for 10 s. As a result, Samples N2, N3, N4 and N5, respectively, were prepared.

3.3.3.2 Results and Discussion

Structural Properties

SEM images of Samples N1–N5 are shown in Fig. 3.29. A high number of defects were observed in Samples N1 and N2. Grain formation occurs upon ion implantation and annealing, and grain size increased with annealing temperature. Large grains are visible in Sample N5. These results indicate the removal of implantation-induced defects induced via annealing.

Optical Properties

Low-temperature (8 K) PL spectra for the samples are shown in Fig. 3.30. While a NBE is visible for as-deposited unimplanted sample, it is not visible in Samples N1 and N2. However, deep-level defect peaks around 1.9 and 2.5 eV, corresponding to V_O, Zn_i and implant-related defects, can be seen in the spectra of these samples [72, 121]. The occurrence of defect peaks in Samples N1 and N2 supports the observation of defects in the SEM images (Fig. 3.29a, b). In annealed Samples N3–N5, NBEs are clearly observed along with reduced deep-level defect peaks, which support the reduction of defects and increase in grain formation observed in these samples (Fig. 3.29c–e). However, there were significant changes in the PL spectra of some samples. A dominant FA peak at ~3.32 eV is present in Sample N3 along with peaks at 3.25–3.36 eV, which correspond to the DAP peak and D°X peak, respectively. This suggests that nitrogen implantation leads to an increase in acceptors in ZnO film. Upon further increasing the annealing temperature (i.e. Samples N4 and N5), A°X peaks, around 3.35 eV, dominate the spectra. In the PL spectra for the as-deposited and annealed samples without any implantation, no

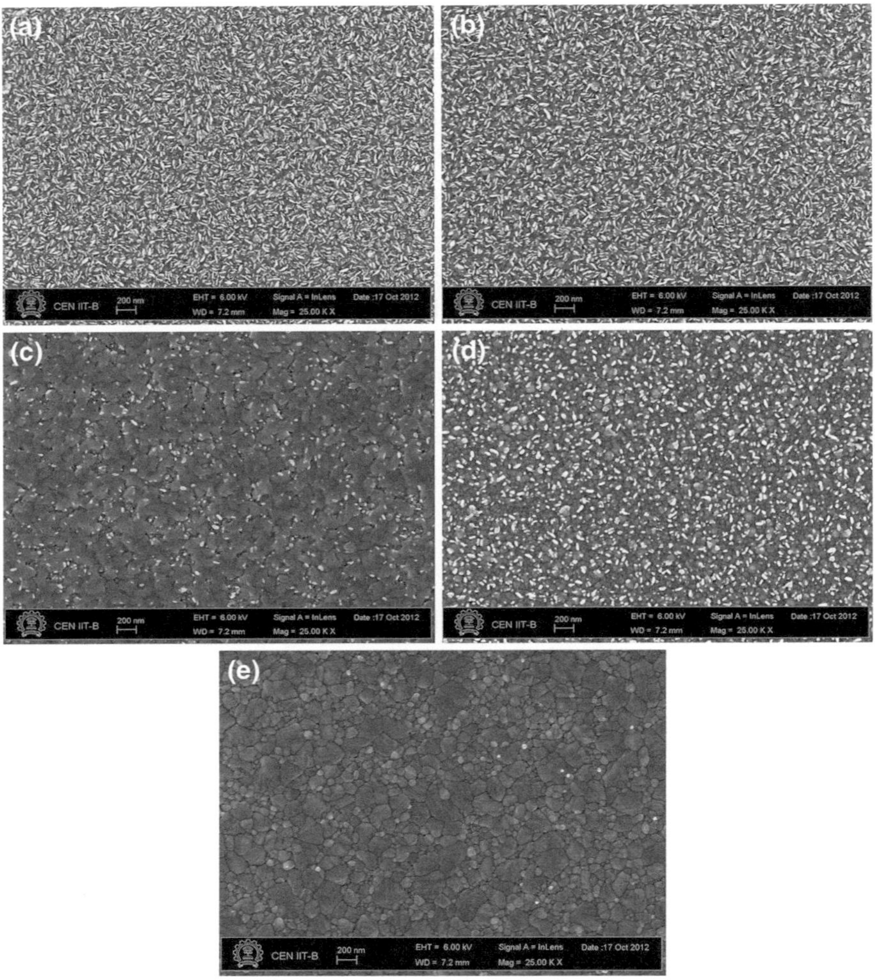

Fig. 3.29 SEM images of the different samples: **a** Sample N1, **b** Sample N2, **c** Sample N3, **d** Sample N4 and **e** Sample N5 (Reprinted from S. Nagar et al. "Realization of reliable p-type ZnO thin films by nitrogen implantation using plasma immersion ion implantation", *Superlattices and Microstructures*, Vol. 75, pp. 9–16, 2014; with permission from Elsevier)

dominant acceptor peaks were visible (Fig. 3.25). These spectra show the importance of nitrogen implantation in achieving p-type ZnO films. In addition, Fig. 3.30 shows that FA and DAP peaks are also visible in the implanted and annealed samples. While a D°X peak appears as a shoulder peak in Sample N4, no such peak was observed in Sample N5. Thus, we infer that Samples N4 and N5 have converted into p-type. This conversion takes place because at higher temperatures, the

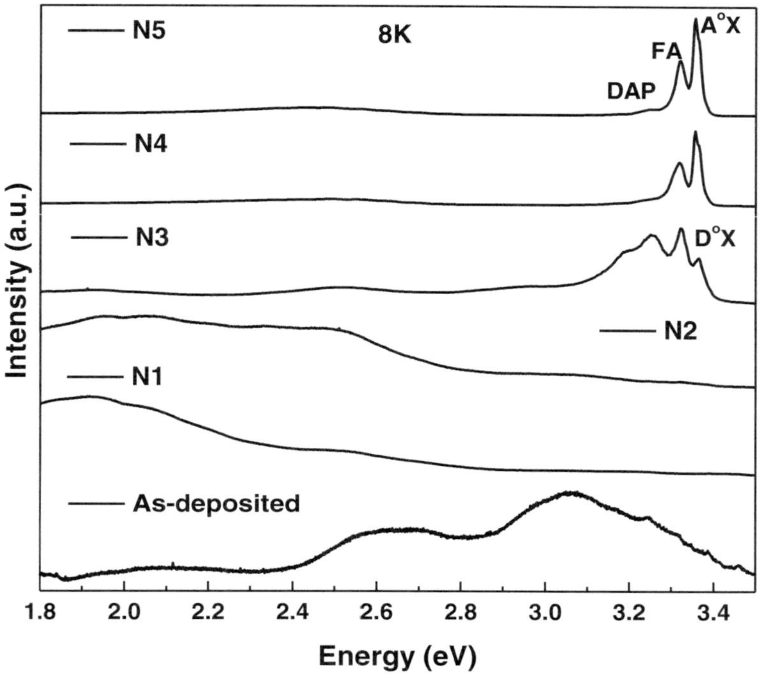

Fig. 3.30 PL spectra of Samples N1–N5 taken at 8 K. Marked A°X peaks can be observed at ~3.35 eV in the spectra for Samples N4 and N5

nitrogen atoms in the film are activated and occupy lattice sites, thus contributing to an increase in acceptors in the films and subsequently forming a p-type film.

A SIMS assessment was undertaken to determine the effect of annealing on the implanted nitrogen ions and to determine the nitrogen concentration in each of the samples (Fig. 3.31). Sample nitrogen concentration was determined after calibration by using a standard N/ZnO sample to acquire quantitative information. The results showed an increase in nitrogen concentration from 1×10^{18} cm^{-3} in Sample N1 to 3×10^{18} cm^{-3} in Sample N5 near the surface. Moreover, at higher annealing temperatures, nitrogen diffusion to greater depths is evident. Although SIMS cannot specify the lattice sites that are occupied by the implanted atoms, the PL results hint that nitrogen atoms in the film are activated and occupy lattice sites, thus contributing to an increase in acceptors in the films and subsequently forming a p-type film for higher annealing temperatures.

The PL spectra recorded at various temperatures between 8 K and 300 K are shown in Fig. 3.32. The dominant A°X peak detected at low temperatures decreases exponentially with increasing temperature to give rise to an FX peak at higher temperatures. The presence of large number of free excitons at high temperatures leads to the dominance of this peak at those high temperatures. However, the FA peak remains visible throughout the temperature range tested. Figure 3.32 inset

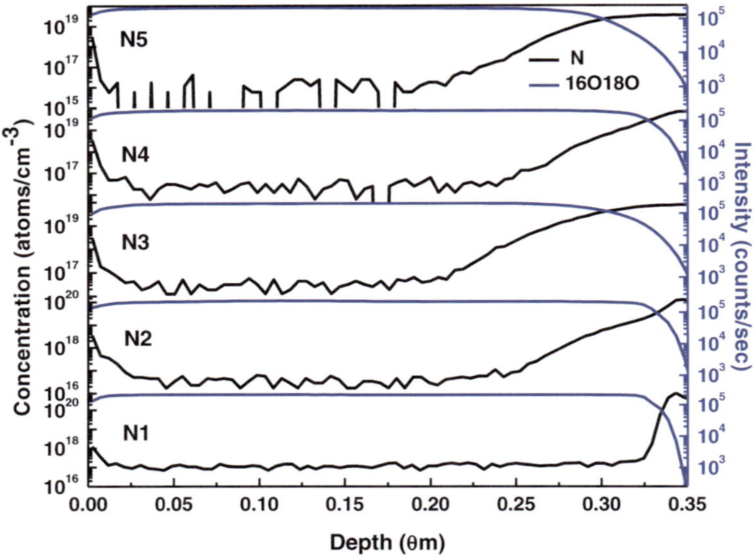

Fig. 3.31 SIMS data for the various samples, depicting an increase in nitrogen concentration with annealing (Reprinted from S. Nagar et al. "Realization of reliable p-type ZnO thin films by nitrogen implantation using plasma immersion ion implantation", *Superlattices and Microstructures*, Vol. 75, pp. 9–16, 2014; with permission from Elsevier)

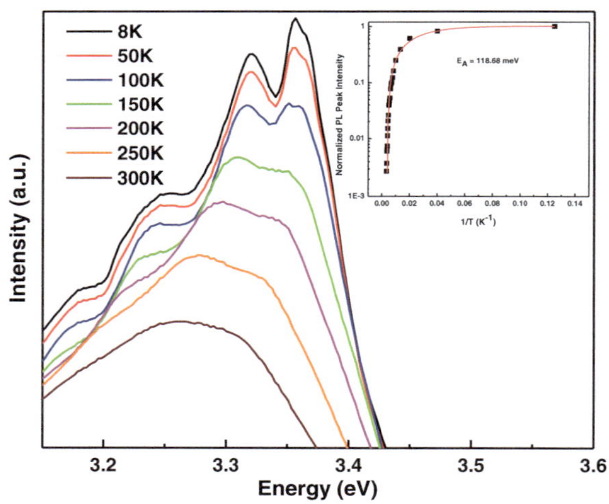

Fig. 3.32 Temperature-dependent PL spectra for Sample P5. *Inset* shows a decrease in acceptor peak intensity with increasing temperature. Acceptor activation energy was 118 meV (Reprinted from S. Nagar et al. "Realization of reliable p-type ZnO thin films by nitrogen implantation using plasma immersion ion implantation", *Superlattices and Microstructures*, Vol. 75, pp. 9–16, 2014; with permission from Elsevier)

shows the normalised intensity of the A°X peak with respect to the inverse temperature. The curve was fitted using Eq. 3.4. The acceptor activation energy (E_A) was thus calculated to be around 118 meV. This shallow acceptor activation energy further indicates that the annealed implanted samples are p-type in nature.

Reliability Studies

The stability of the obtained p-type ZnO thin films was checked over a period of 9 months by performing low-temperature PL (8 K) measurements (Fig. 3.33). There was not much change in the PL spectra of any of the p-type samples. Samples N4 and N5 continue to show a dominant A°X peak along with the FA peak, while the dominant peak in Sample N3 is the FA peak. These are one of the few results

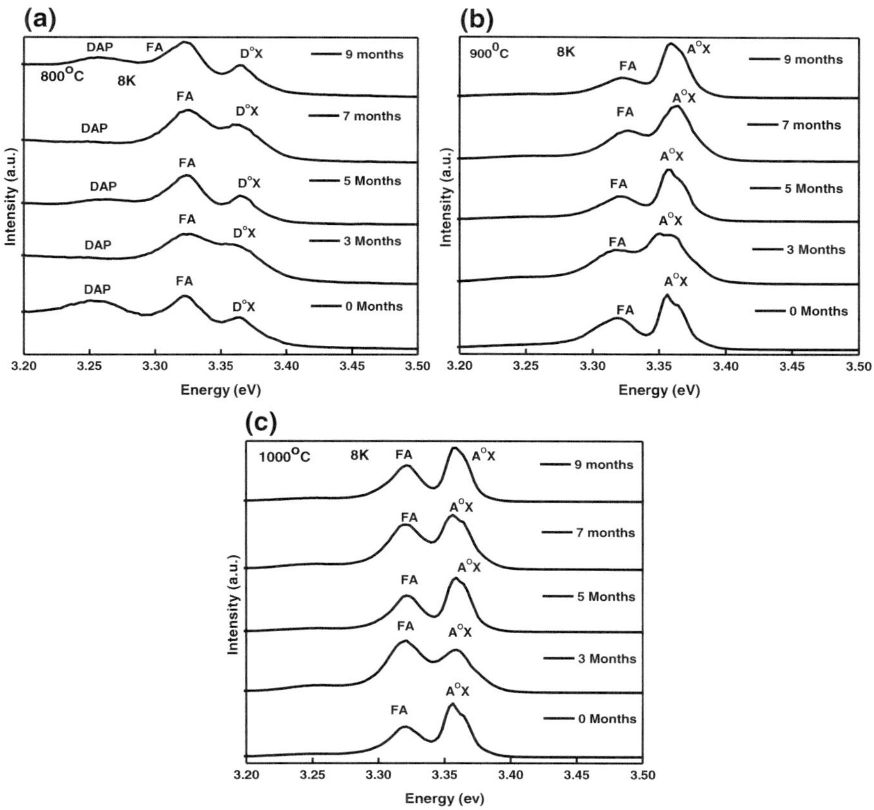

Fig. 3.33 PL spectra of **a** N3, **b** N4 and **c** N5, taken over a period of 9 months (Reprinted from S. Nagar et al. "Realization of reliable p-type ZnO thin films by nitrogen implantation using plasma immersion ion implantation", *Superlattices and Microstructures*, Vol. 75, pp. 9–16, 2014; with permission from Elsevier)

Table 3.8 A comparison of the reliable p-type ZnO obtained by the authors with the published reports

Authors	p-type dopant	Characterisation technique	p-type stability duration
Nagar et al.	P	PL	4–6 months
	N	PL	9 months
Barnes et al. [122]	N	Hall	1–2 days
Lu et al. [123]	Li–N	Hall	3–4 months
Kim et al. [42]	P	Hall, PL	8 months
Lin et al. [19]	Na	Hall, PL	11 months
Allenic et al. [124]	P	Hall	18 months

which demonstrate the reliability of p-type ZnO over a period of time. However, most of the reliability results are demonstrated using Hall measurement which is not a very reliable technique. A much more reliable technique to demonstrate p-type behaviour is PL measurements wherein the peak positions can easily determine the presence of acceptors in the films. Table 3.8 tabulates the reliability of the p-type ZnO over a period of time for the results obtained along with some other reported results.

3.3.3.3 Conclusion

Nitrogen implantation was carried out using PIII on ZnO thin films deposited by RF magnetron sputtering. The samples were subjected to rapid thermal annealing at temperatures between 700 and 1000 °C in ambient oxygen to remove implantation-related defects that were visible in SEM images. PL spectra taken at 8 K clearly showed the presence of strong acceptor peaks for samples annealed at 900–1000 °C with weak deep-level defect peaks. The acceptor activation energy calculated from temperature-dependent PL data was $\sim$118 meV, which confirms that nitrogen incorporation produces shallow acceptor levels and results in p-type ZnO films. The PL spectra done after a period of 9 months still showed a dominant $A^{\circ}X$ peak at low temperature, clearly proving that the p-type behaviour was maintained even after 9 months. The method described in this study would help in the successful fabrication of ZnO-based devices such as LEDs and LDs. As mentioned in Sect. 1.2, among all the p-type dopants, N is best suited because of its similar atomic size to oxygen which makes it easier to substitute without leading to any defect in the crystal. Also, nitrogen tends to form the shallowest acceptor levels in ZnO which makes it suitable for obtaining p-type ZnO. Moreover, nitrogen was implanted using PIII which causes lesser defects in the films. These lesser defects increase the probability of obtaining high-quality p-type ZnO films. Thus, an improved p-type behaviour is observed in N-implanted films which are much more stable.

Chapter 4
Fabrication of Optoelectronics Devices

Abstract Once reliable and reproducible p-type ZnO was achieved, different heterojunction and homojunction devices were fabricated. The heterojunction p–n junction diode was fabricated by depositing p-type ZnO films over low resistivity n-Si substrates. The p-type ZnO was achieved by phosphorus as well as nitrogen implantation. The current–voltage characteristics of the fabricated p–n heterojunction diode showed a clear rectifying behaviour with a threshold voltage of 3.3 V was observed for the phosphorus-implanted device. For the nitrogen-implanted device, a threshold voltage of 1.7 V was attained. This low threshold voltage may help to increase the lifetime of the devices. Homojunction LED was fabricated over high resistivity n-Si substrates, such that the effect of substrate conduction is nullified. The p-type ZnO was deposited by the phosphorus and nitrogen implantation as described above. The n-type ZnO was deposited over the p-ZnO by PLD technique using the optimised temperature and oxygen parameters of 650 °C and 40 mTorr, respectively. Room temperature electroluminescence (RTEL) of the fabricated device (phosphorus implantation) clearly depicted the emission of UV light around 3.18 eV. However, EL emission is dominated by a broad emission around 1.8 eV. This observation is based on the presence of deep-level defects in ZnO films. RTEL for the device fabricated by nitrogen-implanted p-ZnO showed a broad emission around 1.8 eV, corresponding to the red emission, is observed from the device. However, no UV emission was observed from the fabricated device.

Keywords Device fabrication · Heterojunction diode · Homojunction diode · Electroluminescence

---

Part of the chapter has been reprinted from[S. Nagar et al. "Realization of reliable p-type ZnO thin films by nitrogen implantation using plasma immersion ion implantation", Superlattices and Microstructures, Vol. 75, Pg 9-16, 2014]

S. Nagar and S. Chakrabarti, *Optimisation of ZnO Thin Films*,
DOI 10.1007/978-981-10-0809-2_4

4.1 Introduction

As mentioned in Chap. 1, the main aim of our work is to fabricate ZnO-based optoelectronics devices once the high quality and reliable p-type ZnO are achieved. In this chapter, we look into the fabrication of these devices. Fabrication of a semiconductor device requires many essential processes such as device fabrication, mask preparation, lithography, etching, lift-off and metallisation, among others.

4.2 Fabrication Steps

Flow chart of the fabrication process is shown in Fig. 4.1.

- **Cleaning of substrate**: The silicon wafer was first subjected to the common RCA cleaning for removal of organic contamination, thin oxide layer and ionic contamination.
- **ZnO film growth**: The p-type ZnO was deposited over the RCA-cleaned silicon substrate by the processes, described in Sects. 3.3.2 and 3.3.3. The n-type ZnO thin films were deposited over p-ZnO by PLD using the optimised values of temperature and oxygen pressure described in Sects. 2.2 and 2.3.
- **Cleaning of devices**: The device thus prepared was degreased using acetone, IPA and DI water for 3 min each and dried using a nitrogen gas jet.
- **Mesa formation**: Optical lithography technique was used to form mesa patterns with the help of the mesa mask. The lithography parameters used for the purpose are shown in Table 4.1.

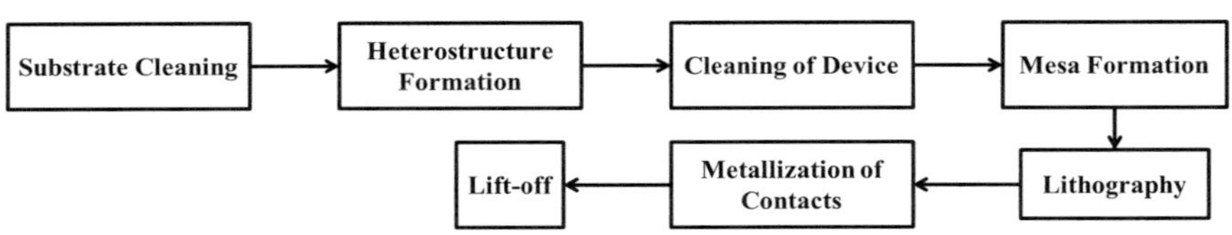

Fig. 4.1 Flow chart of processes performed during fabrication of ZnO-based devices

Table 4.1 Lithography parameters for mesa formation

Serial No.	Process	Optimised parameter
1	Photoresist	S1813
2	Spinning	3000 rpm for 30 s
3	Prebaking	90 °C for 3 min
4	Exposure	4.5 s
5	Developer	MF-319
6	Developed time	45 s

Mesa defined by lithography was then etched away using a dilute HCl (HCl: H_2O::1:250). The samples were kept in the solution for 25 s to etch away 350 nm of ZnO thin film.

- **Contact formation**: Once the mesa formation takes place, it is required to make ohmic contacts for the top and bottom contact for the proper functioning of the p–n junction diode. Once the metallisation was complete, lift-off process was carried out, for which the sample was kept in acetone for 5 min, followed by sonication.

4.3 Heterojunction Devices

4.3.1 p-ZnO/n-Si

4.3.1.1 Phosphorus-Doped p-Type ZnO

The p-type ZnO was prepared by the technique described in Sect. 3.3.2. A sample similar to Sample P5 was prepared over low-resistive n-type Si substrate and fabricated as described in Sect. 4.2. A Ni (20 nm)/Au (200 nm) was used to make contact for the p-type ZnO film, while Al was used as the contact for n-type Si [87]. Current–voltage characteristics of the fabricated p–n heterojunction diode are shown in Fig. 4.2. A clear rectifying behaviour with a threshold voltage of 3.3 V was observed.

4.3.1.2 Nitrogen-Doped p-Type ZnO

The p-type ZnO was prepared by the technique described in Sect. 3.3.3. A sample similar to Sample N5 was prepared over low-resistive n-type Si substrate and fabricated as described in Sect. 4.2. The contact used was similar to the one described in Sect. 4.3.1.1. Current–voltage characteristics of the fabricated p–n heterojunction diode are shown in Fig. 4.3. The threshold voltage of the junction was determined to

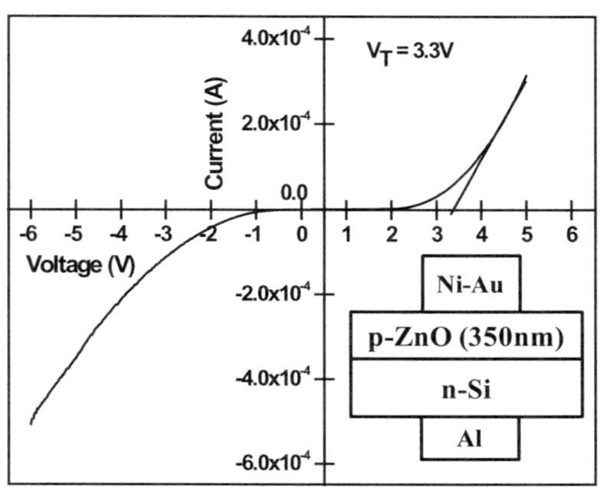

Fig. 4.2 Current–voltage (*I–V*) characteristics of a p-ZnO/n-Si heterojunction diode with a threshold voltage of 1.7 V. *Inset* shows a schematic of the fabricated heterojunction device

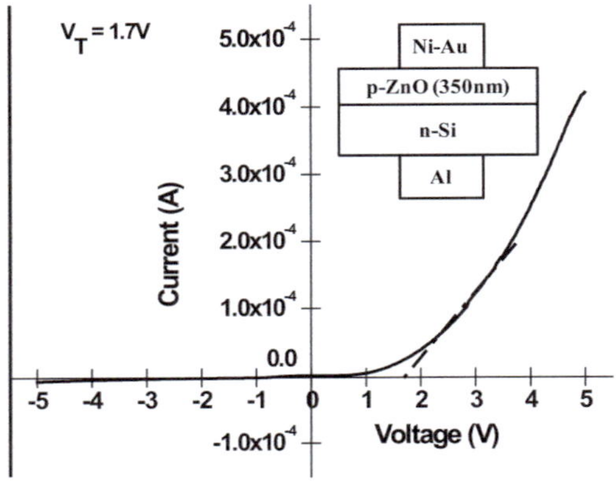

Fig. 4.3 Current–voltage (*I–V*) characteristics of a p-ZnO/n-Si heterojunction diode with a threshold voltage of 1.7 V. *Inset* shows a schematic of the fabricated heterojunction device (Reprinted from S. Nagar et al. "Realization of reliable p-type ZnO thin films by nitrogen implantation using plasma immersion ion implantation", *Superlattices and Microstructures*, Vol. 75, pp. 9–16, 2014; with permission from Elsevier)

be ~1.7 V, which is similar to previously obtained values [125, 126]. Such a low threshold voltage would increase the lifetime of such ZnO-based devices.

4.3.2 p-ZnO/p-Si Detector

The fabrication of the device was carried out as mentioned in Sect. 4.2. The p-type ZnO film was prepared through nitrogen implantation, as explained in Sect. 3.3.3. Al was used as the bottom contact for p-Si, while a Ni/Au stack was used as the contact for the p-ZnO layer. Figure 4.4 shows the spectral response of the detector thus fabricated. White light was used as the excitation source for measuring the response. Peaks at 1.03 μm, 515 nm and 344 nm were observed.

Fig. 4.4 Spectral response for the fabricated device. *Inset* the fabricated device

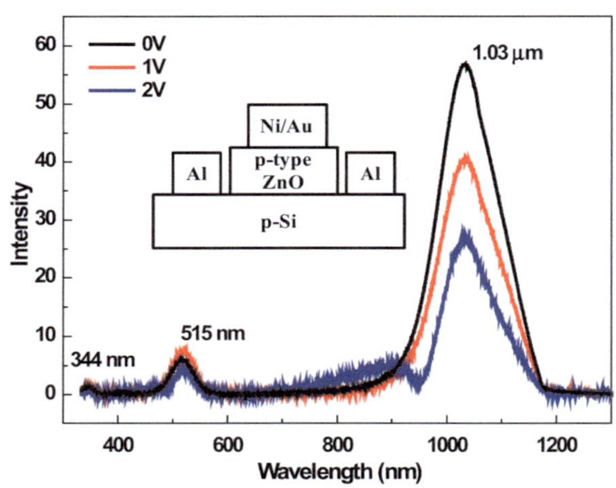

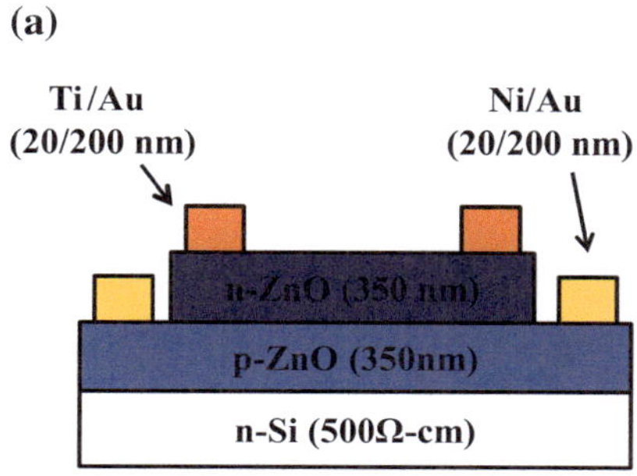

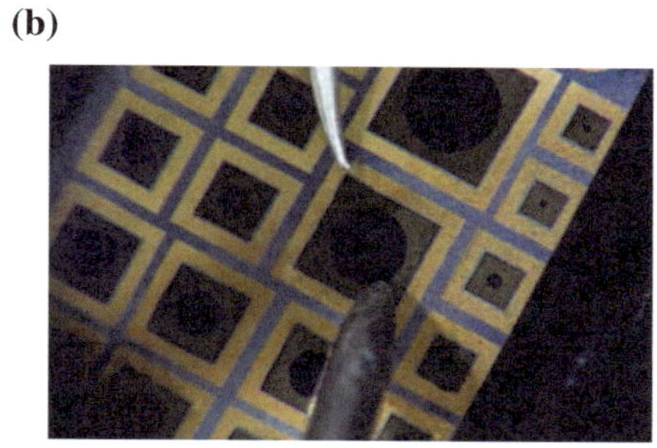

Fig. 4.5 **a** Cross section; **b** top-view of the fabricated device along with probing. The p-type ZnO is made by both P-doping as well as N-doping

4.4 Homojunction Devices

4.4.1 p-ZnO/n-ZnO Homojunction LED

The p-type ZnO was prepared using the technique described in Sects. 3.3.2 and 3.3.3. The n-type ZnO layer was deposited using the PLD technique with the optimised parameters, described in Sects. 2.2 and 2.3. The device was fabricated as described in Sect. 4.2. A Ni/Au (20/200 nm) stack was used for the p-type contacts, while a stack of Ti/Au (20/200 nm) was used as the n-type contact [87]. The cross section and top-view of the device thus fabricated is shown in Fig. 4.5.

4.4.1.1 Phosphorus-Doped p-Type ZnO

The room temperature electroluminescence (RTEL) spectrum of the fabricated device is as shown in Fig. 4.6. The snapshot of the RTEL emission is as depicted in the inset of Fig. 4.6. The RTEL spectrum was obtained by applying a forward bias current of 50 mA. Although the spectrum was dominated by the peak around 1.8 eV, corresponding to deep-level defects, a UV emission around 3.18 eV was also observed. While no emission was observed in the reverse bias condition, confirming the emission from the ZnO p–n homojunction, the red emission in the forward bias was so obvious that it was visible even with the naked eye in darkness. The dominance of the deep-level defect peak around 1.8 eV is attributed to the fact that most of the UV emission was absorbed by the thick n-type layer and also because the device structure was not optimised [19, 77, 127, 128].

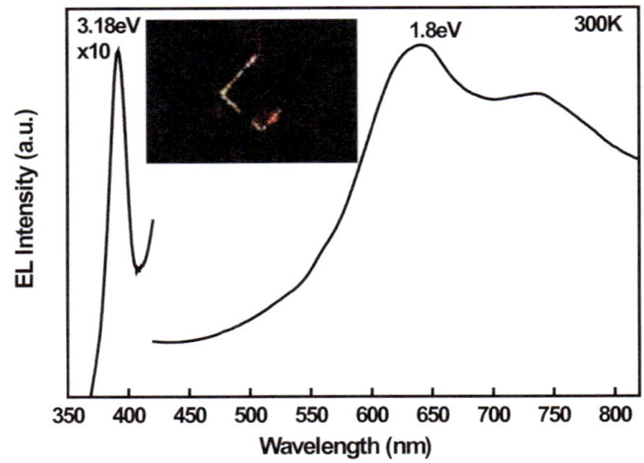

Fig. 4.6 RTEL spectra of the fabricated p-ZnO:P/n-ZnO homojunction diode. *Inset* shows the image of the emitted light from the device

4.4.1.2 Nitrogen-Doped p-Type ZnO

The RTEL spectrum shows a broad emission around 1.8 eV (Fig. 4.7). However, no UV emission was observed from the EL spectra. A forward bias current of 50 mA was applied to the device for taking the EL spectra. The fact that no EL emission was observed from the n-Si/p-ZnO heterojunction diode proves that the emission is from the p–n homojunction device. The emission around 1.8 eV may be attributed to the deep-level defects in the ZnO, to the absorption of the NBE by the thick n-layer and to the fact that the device structure was not optimised [19, 77, 127, 128].

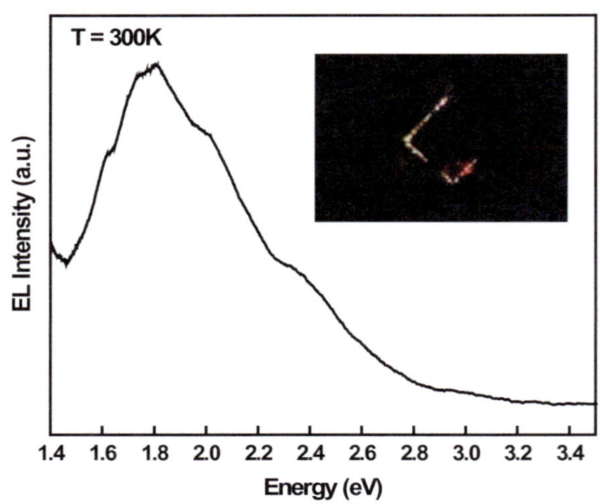

Fig. 4.7 RTEL spectra of the fabricated p-ZnO:N/n-ZnO homojunction diode. *Inset* shows the image of emitted light from the device

4.5 Conclusion

Successful fabrication of p-ZnO/n-Si heterojunction diode has been demonstrated having clear rectification behaviour. A p-ZnO/p-Si heterojunction detector with spectral response peaks at 1.03 μm, 515 nm and 344 nm has been realised. Finally, p-ZnO/n-ZnO homojunction LED has been fabricated. RTEL demonstrated dominant peak around 1.8 eV for both the homojunction devices. However, a small peak around 3.18 eV was also observed for the P-doped device. The devices fabricated and characterised above are not among the best reported in the literature [48, 76, 77, 88, 96, 97, 99, 100]. Nevertheless, attainment of highly stable p-type ZnO is one of the major steps in realising successful optoelectronics devices, and with proper optimisation of the device structure and fabrication steps, it will be possible to obtain desired results which will be at par with reported data.

Chapter 5
Summary and Future Works

Abstract The summary of the work and future work has been discussed in this chapter.

Keywords ZnMgO · Quantum wells · High-electron-mobility transistors

The wide application of ZnO in the field of optoelectronic application, due to its wide bandgap and large exciton-binding energy, has made it a very promising material for researchers across the globe. However, the difficulty of obtaining good quality, reliable and reproducible p-type ZnO has restricted the ZnO-based devices to research only, and commercial availability remains limited. The present research is focused on achieving good quality, stable p-type ZnO films by the implantation technique, which would facilitate selective area doping of the material.

PLD-deposited materials are important in depositing high-quality thin films at lower temperatures, with exact stoichiometry as the target material. Moreover, by varying the various PLD parameters, the various properties of the thin films can be changed. As the basic aim of this research was to obtain good quality p-type ZnO films required to fabricate optoelectronic devices, the PLD parameters of deposition temperature and oxygen pressure have been optimised so as to achieve very low carrier concentration, a reasonable value of Hall mobility and very high optical luminescence. Improvement in the properties of the optimised ZnO film was furthered by hydrogen implantation. A two-order increase in the optical quality of the films was observed as a result of this process.

In order to achieve p-type ZnO films, CII was carried out on the PLD-deposited ZnO films followed by annealing. Lithium and phosphorus ions were implanted for the purpose. However, no type conversion could be observed in any of the samples. While the Li-implanted samples did not demonstrate an increase in the acceptor concentration, the same was observed in the phosphorus-implanted sample. Because the conventional implantation technique did not result in the required p-type any films, we tried implanting ions using PIII technique. To do so, the ZnO films were deposited using the RF sputtering method. Nitrogen and phosphorus ions were implanted using this method, which was followed by subsequent rapid

S. Nagar and S. Chakrabarti, *Optimisation of ZnO Thin Films*,
DOI 10.1007/978-981-10-0809-2_5

thermal annealing to remove the defects. A dominant acceptor peak in the PL measurement was observed in these samples, proving the type conversion of the ZnO films. The obtained p-type ZnO films were studied over a period of 9 months. The phosphorus-implanted samples started to degrade over a period of 8 months, but the nitrogen-implanted samples continued to demonstrate acceptor peaks even after 9 months, showing that the obtained sample was quite stable.

Once the stable p-type ZnO was achieved, various heterojunction and homojunction optoelectronic devices were fabricated. A p-Si/p-ZnO heterojunction device revealed detector characteristics, with the spectral response resulting in peaks at various positions. p-ZnO/n-ZnO homojunction LED was fabricated. The p-type films were obtained by both nitrogen- and phosphorus-implanted samples, and the n-type films were deposited using the optimised PLD parameters. RTEL was observed in both these devices with dominant deep-level peaks and very little peak in the NBE region.

During the course of this research, very encouraging results have been reported towards achieving p-type ZnO films which has helped in fabricating successful homojunction LEDs. We have also reported a way to increase the luminescence properties of the ZnO thin films. However, this research work is only a small part of the wide spectrum towards making ZnO as a potential optoelectronics material. Hence, further studies need to be performed in the future to visualise the dream. Based on the experiments performed, the future work in this field can be broadly divided into material and device perspectives.

From the material perspective, the various implantation parameters of the CII can be optimised so as to obtain p-type ZnO using lithium and phosphorus ions. Other group I and group V elements can also be studied using conventional ion implantation. Moreover, PIII can be used over the PLD-deposited samples to obtain p-type ZnO films and study its reliability over a period of time. Further, co-doping methods can also use boron and nitrogen or phosphorus as group III and group V elements so as to obtain p-type films.

From the device perspective, the top n-type layer should be made thinner so as to reduce light absorption. Further, the device fabrication parameters must be optimised in order to obtain RTEL in the NBE region of ZnO. Different materials like ZnMgO can be used to further improve device characteristics, increasing efficiency and lowering dark current. ZnMgO can also be used along with ZnO films to form ZnO/ZnMgO-based quantum well structures. The heterostructures based on these quantum wells can be used to fabricate optoelectronic devices such as LEDs, lasers and some electronic devices such as thin film transistors and high-electron-mobility transistors.

ZnO, as a material, has a lot of potential in the field of emerging field of UV emitters and detectors. The realisation of stable p-type ZnO and ZnO-based devices encourages further research towards achieving commercial success.

References

1. Ozgur, U., Alivov, Y.I., Liu, C., Teke, A., Reshchikov, M., Dogan, S., Avrutin, V., Cho, S.J., Morkoc, H.: A comprehensive review of ZnO materials and devices. J. Appl. Phys. **98**, 041301–041301-103 (2005)
2. Look, D.: Recent advances in ZnO materials and devices. Mater. Sci. Eng. B **80**, 383–387 (2001)
3. Phillips, J., Bowen, W., Cagin, E., Wang, W.: Comprehensive Semiconductor Science and Technology, vol. 6.03. Elsevier Science (2011)
4. Wellenius, P.: Nitrogen Doping and Ion Beam Processing of Zinc Oxide Thin Film. North Carolina State University (2006)
5. Bian, J., Li, X., Zhang, C., Chen, L., Yao, Q.: Synthesis and characterization of two-layer-structured ZnO pn homojunctions by ultrasonic spray pyrolysis. Appl. Phys. Lett. **84**, 3783–3785 (2004)
6. Yan, Y., Zhang, S., Pantelides, S.: Control of doping by impurity chemical potentials: predictions for p-type ZnO. Phys. Rev. Lett. **86**, 5723–5726 (2001)
7. Van De Walle, C.G.: Strategies for controlling the conductivity of wide band gap semiconductors. Phys. Status Solidi B. **229**:221–228 (2002)
8. Gandhi, S.K.: VLSI Fabrication Principles, Silicon and Gallium Arsenide, Second edn. Wiley, New York (2008)
9. Lee, W., Hwang, D.K., Jeong, M.C., Lee, M., Oh, M.S., Choi, W.K., Myoung, J.M.: Fabrication and properties of As-doped ZnO films grown on GaAs (0 0 1) substrates by radio frequency (rf) magnetron sputtering. Appl. Surf. Sci. **221**, 32–37 (2004)
10. Lin, C.C., Chen, S.Y., Cheng, S.Y.: Physical characteristics and photoluminescence properties of phosphorous-implanted ZnO thin films. Appl. Surf. Sci. **238**, 405–409 (2004)
11. Walukiewicz, W.: Defect formation and diffusion in heavily doped semiconductors. Phys. Rev. B **50**, 5221 (1994)
12. Van de Walle, C.G., Laks, D., Neumark, G., Pantelides, S.: First-principles calculations of solubilities and doping limits: Li, Na, and N in ZnSe. Phys. Rev. B **47**, 9425 (1993)
13. Park, C., Zhang, S., Wei, S.-H.: Origin of p-type doping difficulty in ZnO: the impurity perspective. Phys. Rev. B **66**, 073202 (2002)
14. Look, D.C., Jones, R., Sizelove, J., Garces, N.Y., Giles, N.C., Halliburton, L.E.: The path to ZnO devices: donor and acceptor dynamics. Phys. Status Solidi A. **195**:171–177 (2003)
15. Zeng, Y., Ye, Z., Xu, W., Li, D., Lu, J., Zhu, L., Zhao, B.: Dopant source choice for formation of p-type ZnO: Li acceptor. Appl. Phys. Lett. **88**:062107–062107-3 (2006)
16. Zeng, Y.-J., Ye, Z.-Z., Xu, W.-Z., Chen, L.-L., Li, D.-Y., Zhu, L.-P., Zhao, B.-H., Hu, Y.-L.: Realization of p-type ZnO films via monodoping of Li acceptor. J. Cryst. Growth **283**, 180–184 (2005)
17. Lu, J., Zhang, Y., Ye, Z., Zeng, Y., He, H., Zhu, L., Huang, J., Wang, L., Yuan, J., Zhao, B.: Control of p-and n-type conductivities in Li-doped ZnO thin films. Appl. Phys. Lett. **89**:112113–112113-3 (2006)

S. Nagar and S. Chakrabarti, *Optimisation of ZnO Thin Films*,
DOI 10.1007/978-981-10-0809-2

18. Yang, L., Ye, Z., Zhu, L., Zeng, Y., Lu, Y., Zhao, B.: fabrication of p-type zno thin films via DC reactive magnetron sputtering by using Na as the dopant source. J. electr. Mater. **36**, 498–501 (2007)
19. Lin, S., Lu, J., Ye, Z., He, H., Gu, X., Chen, L., Huang, J., Zhao, B.: p-type behavior in Na-doped ZnO films and ZnO homojunction light-emitting diodes. Solid State Commun. **148**, 25–28 (2008)
20. Lin, S., He, H., Lu, Y., Ye, Z.: Mechanism of Na-doped p-type ZnO films: suppressing Na interstitials by codoping with H and Na of appropriate concentrations. J. Appl. Phys. **106**:093508–093508-5 (2009)
21. Gupta, M.K., Sinha, N., Singh, B., Kumar, B.: Synthesis of K-doped p-type ZnO nanorods along (100) for ferroelectric and dielectric applications. Mater. Lett. **64**, 1825–1828 (2010)
22. Jun, W., Yintang, Y.: Deposition of K-doped p type ZnO thin films on (0001) Al_2O_3 substrates. Mater. Lett. **62**, 1899–1901 (2008)
23. Li, X., Keyes, B., Asher, S., Zhang, S., Wei, S.-H., Coutts, T.J., Limpijumnong, S., Van de Walle, C.G.: Hydrogen passivation effect in nitrogen-doped ZnO thin films. Appl. Phys. Lett. **86**:122107–122107-3 (2005)
24. Look, D., Reynolds, D., Litton, C., Jones, R., Eason, D., Cantwell, G.: Characterization of homoepitaxial p-type ZnO grown by molecular beam epitaxy. Appl. Phys. Lett. **81**, 1830–1832 (2002)
25. Ashrafi, A., Suemune, I., Kumano, H., Tanaka, S.: Nitrogen-doped p-type ZnO layers prepared with H_2O vapor-assisted metalorganic molecular-beam epitaxy. Jpn. J. Appl. Phys. **41**, L1281–L1284 (2002)
26. Ye, Z.Z., Lu, J.G., Chen, H.H., Zhang, Y.Z., Wang, L., Zhao, B.H., Huang, J.Y.: Preparation and characteristics of p-type ZnO films by DC reactive magnetron sputtering. J. Crys. Growth **253**, 258–264 (2003)
27. Wang, C., Ji, Z., Liu, K., Xiang, Y., Ye, Z.: p-Type ZnO thin films prepared by oxidation of Zn_3N_2 thin films deposited by DC magnetron sputtering. J. Cryst. Growth **259**, 279–281 (2003)
28. Minegishi, K., Koiwai, Y., Kikuchi, Y., Yano, K., Kasuga, M., Shimizu, A.: Growth of p-type zinc oxide films by chemical vapor deposition. Jpn. J. Appl. Phys. **36**, L1453–L1455 (1997)
29. Li, X., Yan, Y., Gessert, T., DeHart, C., Perkins, C., Young, D., Coutts, T.: p-type ZnO thin films formed by CVD reaction of diethylzinc and NO gas. Electrochem. Solid-state Lett. **6**, C56–C58 (2003)
30. Rommeluere, J., Svob, L., Jomard, F., Mimila-Arroyo, J., Lusson, A., Sallet, V., Marfaing, Y.: Electrical activity of nitrogen acceptors in ZnO films grown by metalorganic vapor phase epitaxy. Appl. Phys. Lett. **83**, 287–289 (2003)
31. Suemune, I., Ashrafi, A., Ebihara, M., Kurimoto, M., Kumano, H., Seong, T.Y., Kim, B.J., Ok, Y.W.: Epitaxial ZnO growth and p-type doping with MOMBE. Phys. Status Solidi B. **241**:640–647 (2004)
32. Xu, W., Ye, Z., Zhou, T., Zhao, B., Zhu, L., Huang, J.: Low-pressure MOCVD growth of p-type ZnO thin films by using NO as the dopant source. J. Cryst. Growth **265**, 133–136 (2004)
33. Murphy, T., Chen, D., Cagin, E., Phillips, J.: Electronic properties of ZnO epilayers grown on c-plane sapphire by plasma-assisted molecular beam epitaxy. J. Vac. Sci. Technol. B Microelectr. Nanometer Struct. **23**, 1277–1280 (2005)
34. Dadgar, A., Oleynik, N., Bläsing, J., Deiter, S., Forster, D., Bertram, F., Diez, A., Seip, M., Greiling, A., Christen, J.: Heteroepitaxy and nitrogen doping of high-quality ZnO. J. Cryst. Growth **272**, 800–804 (2004)
35. Hwang, D.K., Kim, H.S., Lim, J.H., Oh, J.Y., Yang, J.H., Park, S.J., Kim, K.K., Look, D., Park, Y.: Study of the photoluminescence of phosphorus-doped p-type ZnO thin films grown by radio-frequency magnetron sputtering. Appl. Phys. Lett. **86**:151917–151917-3 (2005)

36. Vaithianathan, V., Lee, B.T., Kim, S.S.: Pulsed-laser-deposited p-type ZnO films with phosphorus doping. J. Appl. Phys. **98**:043519–043519-4 (2005)
37. Bang, K.-H., Hwang, D.-K., Park, M.-C., Ko, Y.-D., Yun, I., Myoung, J.-M.: Formation of p-type ZnO film on InP substrate by phosphor doping. Appl. Surf. Sci. **210**, 177–182 (2003)
38. Kang, S.-H., Hwang, D.-K., Park, S.-J.: Low-resistance and highly transparent Ni/indium-tin oxide ohmic contacts to phosphorous-doped p-type ZnO. Appl. Phys. Lett. **86**:211902–211902-3 (2005)
39. Lee, J.-M., Kim, K., Tampo, H., Yamada, A., Niki, S.: Ohmic contact to phosphorous-doped ZnO using Pt/Ni/Au for p-n homojunction diode. J. Electrochem. Soc. **153**, G1047–G1050 (2006)
40. Lee, W.-J., Kang, J., Chang, K.: Defect properties and p-type doping efficiency in phosphorus-doped ZnO. Phys. Rev. B **73**, 024117 (2006)
41. Shih, Y., Chien, J., Chen, M., Yang, J., Shiojiri, M.: P-type ZnO: P films fabricated by atomic layer deposition and thermal processing. J. Electrochem. Soc. **158**, H516–H520 (2011)
42. Kim, K.K., Kim, H.S., Hwang, D.K., Lim, J.H., Park, S.J.: Realization of p-type ZnO thin films via phosphorus doping and thermal activation of the dopant. Appl. Phys. Lett. **83**, 63–65 (2003)
43. Ryu, Y., Lee, T., Leem, J., White, H.: Fabrication of homostructural ZnO p–n junctions and ohmic contacts to arsenic-doped p-type ZnO. Appl. Phys. Lett. **83**, 4032–4034 (2003)
44. Vaithianathan, V., Lee, B.T., Kim, S.S.: Preparation of As-doped p-type ZnO films using a Zn_3As_2/ZnO target with pulsed laser deposition. Appl. Phys. Lett. **86**, 62101 (2005)
45. Kang, H.S., Kim, G.H., Kim, D.L., Chang, H.W., Ahn, B.D., Lee, S.Y.: Investigation on the p-type formation mechanism of arsenic doped p-type ZnO thin film. Appl. Phys. Lett. **89**:181103–181103-3 (2006)
46. Limpijumnong, S., Zhang, S., Wei, S.H., Park, C.: Doping by large-size-mismatched impurities: the microscopic origin of arsenic-or antimony-doped p-type zinc oxide. Phys Rev Lett **92**, 155504 (2004)
47. Sun, J., Zhao, J., Liang, H., Bian, J., Hu, L., Zhang, H., Liang, X., Liu, W., Du, G.: Realization of ultraviolet electroluminescence from ZnO homojunction with n-ZnO/p-ZnO: As/GaAs structure. Appl. Phys. Lett. **90**:121128–121128-3 (2007)
48. Liu, W., Bian, J., Hu, L., Liang, H., Zang, H., Sun, J., Zhao, Z., Liu, A., Du, G.: Electroluminescence from a ZnO homojunction device grown by pulsed laser deposition. Solid state Commun. **142**, 655–658 (2007)
49. Look, D., Renlund, G., Burgener, R., Sizelove, J.: As-doped p-type ZnO produced by an evaporation/sputtering process. Appl. Phys. Lett. **85**, 5269–5271 (2004)
50. Nagar, S., Chakrabarti, S.: Evidence of p-doping in ZnO films deposited on GaAs. Thin Solid Films **518**, 4542–4545 (2010)
51. Xiu, F., Yang, Z., Mandalapu, L., Zhao, D., Liu, J., Beyermann, W.: High-mobility Sb-doped< equation> p</equation>-type ZnO by molecular-beam epitaxy. Appl. Phys. Lett. **87**:152101–152101-3 (2005)
52. Pan, X., Ye, Z., Li, J., Gu, X., Zeng, Y., He, H., Zhu, L., Che, Y.: Fabrication of Sb-doped p-type ZnO thin films by pulsed laser deposition. Appl. Surf. Sci. **253**, 5067–5069 (2007)
53. Aoki, T., Shimizu, Y., Miyake, A., Nakamura, A., Nakanishi, Y., Hatanaka, Y.: p-Type ZnO layer formation by excimer laser doping. Phys. Status Solidi B. **229**:911–914 (2002)
54. Lopatiuk-Tirpak, O., Chernyak, L., Xiu, F., Liu, J., Jang, S., Ren, F., Pearton, S., Gartsman, K., Feldman, Y., Osinsky, A.: Studies of minority carrier diffusion length increase in p-type ZnO: Sb. J. Appl. Phys. **100**:086101–086101-3 (2006)
55. Lopatiuk-Tirpak, O., Schoenfeld, W., Chernyak, L., Xiu, F., Liu, J., Jang, S., Ren, F., Pearton, S., Osinsky, A., Chow, P.: Carrier concentration dependence of acceptor activation energy in p-type ZnO. Appl. Phys. Lett. **88**:202110–202110-3 (2006)

56. Ohara, K., Seino, T., Nakamura, A., Aoki, T., Kominami, H., Nakanishi, Y., Hatanaka, Y.: Sb excimer-laser doping in ZnO films prepared by oxidation of sulfide on Si. Appl. Surf. Sci. **244**, 369–372 (2005)
57. Wang, P., Chen, N., Yin, Z., Dai, R., Bai, Y.: p-type $Zn_{1-x}Mg_xO$ films with Sb doping by radio-frequency magnetron sputtering. Appl. Phys. Lett. **89**:202102–202102-3 (2006)
58. Przeździecka, E., Kamińska, E., Pasternak, I., Piotrowska, A., Kossut, J.: Photoluminescence study of p-type ZnO: Sb prepared by thermal oxidation of the Zn-Sb starting material. Phys. Rev. B **76**, 193303 (2007)
59. Guo, W., Allenic, A., Chen, Y., Pan, X., Che, Y., Hu, Z., Liu, B.: Microstructure and properties of epitaxial antimony-doped p-type ZnO films fabricated by pulsed laser deposition. Appl. Phys. Lett. **90**:242108–242108-3 (2007)
60. Chen, L., Lu, J., Ye, Z., Lin, Y., Zhao, B., Ye, Y., Li, J., Zhu, L.: p-type behavior in In–N codoped ZnO thin films. Appl. Phys. Lett. **87**:252106–252106-3 (2005)
61. Bin, W., Yue, Z., Jiahua, M., Wenbin, S.: Ag–N dual-accept doping for the fabrication of p-type ZnO. Appl. Phys. A **94**, 715–718 (2009)
62. Nakahara, K., Takasu, H., Fons, P., Yamada, A., Iwata, K., Matsubara, K., Hunger, R., Niki, S.: Interactions between gallium and nitrogen dopants in ZnO films grown by radical-source molecular-beam epitaxy. Appl. Phys. Lett. **79**, 4139–4141 (2001)
63. Ye, J., Gu, S., Li, F., Zhu, S., Zhang, R., Shi, Y., Zheng, Y., Sun, X., Lo, G., Kwong, D.: Correlation between carrier recombination and p-type doping in P monodoped and In–P codoped ZnO epilayers. Appl. Phys. Lett. **90**:152108–152108-3 (2007)
64. Kumar, M., Kim, S.-K., Choi, S.-Y.: Formation of Al–N co-doped p-ZnO/n-Si (100) heterojunction structure by RF co-sputtering technique. Appl. Surf. Sci. **256**, 1329–1332 (2009)
65. Kumar, M., Kim, T.-H., Kim, S.-S., Lee, B.-T.: Growth of epitaxial p-type ZnO thin films by codoping of Ga and N. Appl. Phys. Lett. **89**:112103–112103-3 (2006)
66. Yuan, G., Ye, Z., Zhu, L., Qian, Q., Zhao, B., Fan, R., Perkins, C.L., Zhang, S.: Control of conduction type in Al-and N-codoped ZnO thin films. Appl. Phys. Lett. **86**:202106–202106-3 (2005)
67. Lu, J., Ye, Z., Zhuge, F., Zeng, Y., Zhao, B., Zhu, L.: p-type conduction in N-Al co-doped ZnO thin films. Appl. Phys. Lett. **85**, 3134–3135 (2004)
68. Chen, Z., Kawasuso, A., Xu, Y., Naramoto, H., Yuan, X., Sekiguchi, T., Suzuki, R., Ohdaira, T.: Production and recovery of defects in phosphorus-implanted ZnO. J. Appl. Phys. **97**:013528–013528-6 (2005)
69. Lin, C.C., Chen, S.Y., Cheng, S.Y., Lee, H.Y.: Properties of nitrogen-implanted p-type ZnO films grown on SiN/Si by radio-frequency magnetron sputtering. Appl. Phys. Lett. **84**, 5040 (2004)
70. Braunstein, G., Muraviev, A., Saxena, H., Dhere, N., Richter, V., Kalish, R.: p type doping of zinc oxide by arsenic ion implantation. Appl. Phys. Lett. **87**:192103–192103-3 (2005)
71. Vaithianathan, V., Hishita, S., Park, J.Y., Kim, S.S.: Photoluminescence in phosphorous-implanted ZnO films. J. Appl. Phys. **102**:086107–086107-3 (2007)
72. Teke, A., Özgür, Ü., Doğan, S., Gu, X., Morkoç, H., Nemeth, B., Nause, J., Everitt, H.: Excitonic fine structure and recombination dynamics in single-crystalline ZnO. Phys. Rev. B **70**, 195207 (2004)
73. Alivov, Y.I., Johnstone, D., Özgür, Ü., Avrutin, V., Fan, Q., Akarca-Biyikli, S., Morkoç, H.: Electrical and optical properties of n-ZnO/p-SiC heterojunctions. Jpn. J. Appl. Phys. **44**, 7281 (2005)
74. Ye, J., Gu, S., Zhu, S., Liu, W., Liu, S., Zhang, R., Shi, Y., Zheng, Y.: Electroluminescent and transport mechanisms of n-ZnO/p-Si heterojunctions. Appl. Phys. Lett. **88**, 182112 (2006)
75. Chen, P., Ma, X., Yang, D.: Ultraviolet electroluminescence from ZnO/p-Si heterojunctions. J. Appl. Phys. **101**:053103–053103-4 (2007)

76. Tsukazaki, A., Ohtomo, A., Onuma, T., Ohtani, M., Makino, T., Sumiya, M., Ohtani, K., Chichibu, S.F., Fuke, S., Segawa, Y.: Repeated temperature modulation epitaxy for p-type doping and light-emitting diode based on ZnO. Nat. Mater. **4**, 42–46 (2004)
77. Lim, J.H., Kang, C.K., Kim, K.K., Park, I.K., Hwang, D.K., Park, S.J.: UV electroluminescence emission from ZnO light emitting diodes grown by high temperature radiofrequency sputtering. Adv. Mater. **18**, 2720–2724 (2006)
78. Alivov, Y.I., Van Nostrand, J., Look, D.C., Chukichev, M., Ataev, B.: Observation of 430 nm electroluminescence from ZnO/GaN heterojunction light-emitting diodes. Appl. Phys. Lett. **83**, 2943–2945 (2003)
79. Alivov, Y.I., Kalinina, E., Cherenkov, A., Look, D.C., Ataev, B., Omaev, A., Chukichev, M., Bagnall, D.: Fabrication and characterization of n-ZnO/p-AlGaN heterojunction light-emitting diodes on 6H-SiC substrates. Appl. Phys. Lett. **83**, 4719 (2003)
80. Osinsky, A., Dong, J., Kauser, M., Hertog, B., Dabiran, A., Chow, P., Pearton, S., Lopatiuk, O., Chernyak, L.: MgZnO/AlGaN heterostructure light-emitting diodes. Appl. Phys. Lett. **85**, 4272 (2004)
81. Chuang, R.W., Wu, R.-X., Lai, L.-W., Lee, C.-T.: ZnO-on-GaN heterojunction light-emitting diode grown by vapor cooling condensation technique. Appl. Phys. Lett. **91**:231113–231113-3 (2007)
82. Xu, H.Y., Liu, Y., Liu, Y., Xu, C., Shao, C., Mu, R.: Ultraviolet electroluminescence from p-GaN/i-ZnO/n-ZnO heterojunction light-emitting diodes. Appl. Phys. B **80**, 871–874 (2005)
83. Kim, D.C., Han, W.S., Cho, H.K., Kong, B.H., Kim, H.S.: Multidimensional ZnO light-emitting diode structures grown by metal organic chemical vapor deposition on p-Si. Appl. Phys. Lett. **91**:231901–231901-3 (2007)
84. Nakamura, A., Ohashi, T., Yamamoto, K., Ishihara, J., Aoki, T., Temmyo, J., Gotoh, H.: Full-color electroluminescence from ZnO-based heterojunction diodes. Appl. Phys. Lett. **90**:093512–093512-3 (2007)
85. Xi, Y., Hsu, Y., Djurišić, A., Ng, A., Chan, W., Tam, H., Cheah, K.: NiO/ZnO light emitting diodes by solution-based growth. Appl. Phys. Lett. **92**, 113505 (2008)
86. Ohta, H., Kawamura, K.-I., Orita, M., Hirano, M., Sarukura, N., Hosono, H.: Current injection emission from a transparent p–n junction composed of p-$SrCu_2O_2$/n-ZnO. Appl. Phys. Lett. **77**, 475–477 (2000)
87. Tsukazaki, A., Kubota, M., Ohtomo, A., Onuma, T., Ohtani, K., Ohno, H., Chichibu, S.F., Kawasaki, M.: Blue light-emitting diode based on ZnO. arXiv preprint cond-mat/0504587 (2005)
88. Liu, W., Gu, S., Ye, J., Zhu, S., Liu, S., Zhou, X., Zhang, R., Shi, Y., Zheng, Y., Hang, Y.: Blue-yellow ZnO homostructural light-emitting diode realized by metalorganic chemical vapor deposition technique. Appl. Phys. Lett. **88**:092101–092101-3 (2006)
89. Neamen, D.A.: Semiconductor Physics and Devices. McGraw Hill, Boston (2003)
90. Ievtushenko, A., Lashkarev, G., Lazorenko, V., Karpyna, V., Sichkovskyi, V., Kosyachenko, L., Rchuk, V., Klyarchuk, O., Bosy, V., Korzhinski, F.: Ultraviolet detectors based on ZnO:N thin films with different contact structures. Acta Phys. Polonica A **114**, 1123–1129 (2008)
91. Fabricius, H., Skettrup, T., Bisgaard, P.: Ultraviolet detectors in thin sputtered ZnO films. Appl. Opt. **25**, 2764–2767 (1986)
92. Zheng, X., Li, Q.S., Zhao, J., Chen, D., Zhao, B., Yang, Y., Zhang, L.C.: Photoconductive ultraviolet detectors based on ZnO films. Appl. Surf. Sci. **253**, 2264–2267 (2006)
93. Zhang, D., Brodie, D.: Photoresponse of polycrystalline ZnO films deposited by rf bias sputtering. Thin Solid Films **261**, 334–339 (1995)
94. Pillai, P., Pillai, C., Mendiratta, R.: Space-charge polarisation in ZnO photoconductors. J. Phys. D Appl. Phys. **12**, 961 (1979)

95. Mandalapu, L., Xiu, F., Yang, Z., Liu, J.: Ultraviolet photoconductive detectors based on Ga-doped ZnO films grown by molecular-beam epitaxy. Solid-state Electr. **51**, 1014–1017 (2007)
96. Ryu, Y., Lee, T., Lubguban, J., White, H., Park, Y., Youn, C.: ZnO devices: Photodiodes and p-type field-effect transistors. Appl. Phys. Lett. **87**:153504–153504-3 (2005)
97. Suhaila, A., Salmana, S., Naouma, F., Thjeela, H.: ZnO/Porous-silicon photovoltaic UV detector. J. Electr. Devices **13**, 900–909 (2012)
98. Jeong, I.-S., Kim, J.H., Im, S.: Ultraviolet-enhanced photodiode employing n-ZnO/p-Si structure. Appl. Phys. Lett. **83**, 2946–2948 (2003)
99. Wang, K., Vygranenko, Y., Nathan, A.: Optically transparent ZnO-based n–i–p ultraviolet photodetectors. Thin Solid Films **515**, 6981–6985 (2007)
100. Wang, K., Vygranenko, Y., Nathan, A.: ZnO-based pin and nip heterostructure ultraviolet sensors: a comparative study. J. Appl. Phys. **101**:114508–114508-5 (2007)
101. Ohta, H., Kamiya, M., Kamiya, T., Hirano, M., Hosono, H.: UV-detector based on pn-heterojunction diode composed of transparent oxide semiconductors, p-NiO/n-ZnO. Thin Solid Films **445**, 317–321 (2003)
102. Tapily, K., Gu, D., Baumgart, H.: Growth Mechanism of ALD ZnO Films Investigated by Physical Characterization. ECS Transactions **33**, 355–363 (2010)
103. Paraguay, D.F., Estrada, L.W., Acosta, N.D., Andrade, E., Miki-Yoshida, M.: Growth, structure and optical characterization of high quality ZnO thin films obtained by spray pyrolysis. Thin Solid Films. **350**:192–202 (1999)
104. Meyer, B., Alves, H., Hofmann, D., Kriegseis, W., Forster, D., Bertram, F., Christen, J., Hoffmann, A., Straßburg, M., Dworzak, M.: Bound exciton and donor–acceptor pair recombinations in ZnO. Phys. Status Solidi B. **241**:231–260 (2004)
105. Wagner, M., Callsen, G., Reparaz, J., Schulze, J.H., Kirste, R., Cobet, M., Ostapenko, I., Rodt, S., Nenstiel, C., Kaiser, M.: Bound excitons in ZnO: Structural defect complexes versus shallow impurity centers. Phys. Rev. B **84**, 035313 (2011)
106. Hsieh, P.T., Chen, Y.C., Wang, C.M., Tsai, Y.Z., Hu, C.C.: Structural and photoluminescence characteristics of ZnO films by room temperature sputtering and rapid thermal annealing process. Appl. Phys. A. Mater. Sci. Process. **84**, 345–349 (2006)
107. Wang, X., Buyanova, I., Chen, W., Pan, C., Tu, C.: Effects of stoichiometry on defect formation in ZnO epilayers grown by molecular-beam epitaxy: An optically detected magnetic resonance study. J. Appl. Phys. **103**:023712–023712-4 (2008)
108. Misra, P., Sharma, T., Kukreja, L.: Temperature dependent photoluminescence processes in ZnO thin films grown on sapphire by pulsed laser deposition. Curr. Appl. Phys. **9**, 179–183 (2009)
109. Jung, S., Park, W., Cheong, H., Yi, G.C., Jang, H.M., Hong, S., Joo, T.: Time-resolved and time-integrated photoluminescence in ZnO epilayers grown on Al_2O_3 (00.1) by metalorganic vapor phase epitaxy. Appl. Phys. Lett **80**, 1924 (2002)
110. Thomas, D., Lander, J.: Hydrogen as a donor in zinc oxide. J. Chem. Phys. **25**, 1136 (1956)
111. Van de Walle, C.G.: Hydrogen as a cause of doping in zinc oxide. Physical review letters **85**, 1012 (2000)
112. Cox, S., Davis, E., Cottrell, S., King, P., Lord, J., Gil, J., Alberto, H., Vilao, R., Duarte, J. P., de Campos, N.A.: Experimental confirmation of the predicted shallow donor hydrogen state in zinc oxide. Phys. Rev. Lett. **86**, 2601 (2001)
113. Lee, J.-K., Nastasi, M., Hamby, D., Lucca, D.: Optical observation of donor-bound excitons in hydrogen-implanted ZnO. Appl. Phys. Lett. **86**:171102–171102-3 (2005)
114. Fang, Z.-Q., Claflin, B., Look, D.C., Farlow, G.C.: Electron irradiation induced deep centers in hydrothermally grown ZnO. J. Appl. Phys. **101**:086106–086106-3 (2007)
115. Simpson, J., Cordaro, J.F.: Characterization of deep levels in zinc oxide. J. Appl. Phys. **63**, 1781–1783 (1988)

116. Kuriyama, K., Ooi, M., Matsumoto, K., Kushida, K.: Thermally stimulated current studies on deep levels in hydrothermally grown single crystal ZnO bulk. Appl. Phys. Lett. **89**:242113–242113-3 (2006)
117. Fang, Z.-Q., Claflin, B., Look, D.C.: Effects of annealing in N_2 ambient on traps and persistent conduction in hydrothermally grown ZnO. J. Appl. Phys. **103**:073714–073714-5 (2008)
118. Lopatiuk, O., Chernyak, L., Osinsky, A., Xie, J.: Lithium-related states as deep electron traps in ZnO. Appl. Phys. Lett. **87**:214110–214110-3 (2005)
119. Wardle, M., Goss, J., Briddon, P.: Theory of Li in ZnO: A limitation for Li-based p-type doping. Phys. Rev. B **71**, 155205 (2005)
120. Zhao, D., Xu, S., Xie, M., Tong, S., Yang, H.: Stress and its effect on optical properties of GaN epilayers grown on Si (111), 6H-SiC (0001), and c-plane sapphire. Appl. Phys. Lett. **83**, 677–679 (2003)
121. Sun, J., Lu, Y., Liu, Y., Shen, D., Zhang, Z., Li, B., Zhang, J., Yao, B., Zhao, D., Fan, X.: The activation energy of the nitrogen acceptor in p-type ZnO film grown by plasma-assisted molecular beam epitaxy. Solid State Commun. **140**, 345–348 (2006)
122. Barnes, T.M., Olson, K., Wolden, C.A.: On the formation and stability of p-type conductivity in nitrogen-doped zinc oxide. Appl. Phys. Lett. **86**:112112–112112-3 (2005)
123. Lu, J., Zhang, Y., Ye, Z., Zhu, L., Wang, L., Zhao, B., Liang, Q.: Low-resistivity, stable p-type ZnO thin films realized using a Li–N dual-acceptor doping method. Appl. Phys. Lett. **88**:222114–222114-3 (2006)
124. Allenic, A., Guo, W., Chen, Y., Katz, M.B., Zhao, G., Che, Y., Hu, Z., Liu, B., Zhang, S. B., Pan, X.: Amphoteric phosphorus doping for stable p-type ZnO. Adv. Mater. **19**, 3333–3337 (2007)
125. Ryu, Y., Kim, W., White, H.: Fabrication of homostructural ZnO p–n junctions. J. Cryst. Growth **219**, 419–422 (2000)
126. Xiong, G., Wilkinson, J., Mischuck, B., Tuzemen, S., Ucer, K., Williams, R.: Control of p-and n-type conductivity in sputter deposition of undoped ZnO. Appl. Phys. Lett. **80**, 1195–1197 (2002)
127. Liang, H., Feng, Q., Sun, J., Zhao, J., Bian, J., Hu, L., Zhang, H., Luo, Y., Du, G.: Room temperature electroluminescence from the ZnO homojunction grown on an n+-Si substrate by metal–organic chemical vapor deposition. Semicond. Sci. Technol. **23**, 025014 (2008)
128. Du, G., Liu, W., Bian, J., Hu, L., Liang, H., Wang, X., Liu, A., Yang, T.: Room temperature defect related electroluminescence from ZnO homojunctions grown by ultrasonic spray pyrolysis. Appl. Phys. Lett. **89**:052113–052113-3 (2006)

MIX
Papier aus verantwortungsvollen Quellen
Paper from responsible sources
FSC® C105338

If you have any concerns about our products,
you can contact us on
ProductSafety@springernature.com

In case Publisher is established outside the EU,
the EU authorized representative is:
Springer Nature Customer Service Center GmbH
Europaplatz 3, 69115 Heidelberg, Germany

Printed by Libri Plureos GmbH
in Hamburg, Germany